THE PRESTIGE LABEL

DISCOGRAPHIES
SERIES EDITOR: Brian Rust

Atlantic Records: A Discography
Compiled by Michel Ruppli

The Savoy Label: A Discography
Compiled by Michel Ruppli

The Prestige Label: A Discography
Compiled by Michel Ruppli

THE PRESTIGE LABEL
A Discography

Compiled by Michel Ruppli
with assistance from Bob Porter

Discographies, Number 3

GREENWOOD PRESS
Westport, Connecticut • London, England

HOUSTON PUBLIC LIBRARY

Library of Congress Cataloging in Publication Data

Ruppli, Michel.
  The Prestige label.

  (Discographies ; no. 3 ISSN 0192-334X)
  Includes index of artists.
  1. Jazz music—United States—Discography.
2. Blues (Songs, etc.)—United States—Discography.
3. Gospel music—United States—Discography.
I. Porter, Bob. II. Prestige Records (Firm)
III. Title. IV. Series.
ML156.2.R786   016.7899'12   79-8294
ISBN 0-313-22019-0

Library of Congress Catalog Card Number: 79-8294
ISBN: 0-313-22019-0
ISSN: 0192-334X

First published in 1980

Greenwood Press
A division of Congressional Information Service, Inc.
51 Riverside Avenue, Westport, Connecticut 06880

Printed in the United States of America

10 9 8 7 6 5 4 3 2 1

Contents

Acknowledgments

This book could not have been made without the invaluable help and collaboration provided by Bob Porter as a member of the Prestige staff when the first edition was compiled (1969-1970). Bob put all Prestige files at my disposal and conducted much of the research himself, answering all queries and checking all details. My deepest thanks go to him for his strong support.

The completeness of this work has been greatly enhanced by help from Erik Raben (Denmark) and from past members of the Prestige staff: Chris Albertson, Ira Gitler, and Don Schlitten.

Particular mention goes to Bob Rhodes (England) whose collaboration brought me to the label discography concept and gave birth to this book.

I would like to acknowledge all the people who provided additional details, including: Josh Berg (Norway), Patsy Booker (U.S.A.), Bert Bradfield (France), Reg Cooper (England), Charles Delaunay (France), Michel Delorme (France), Bob Harrison (England), Gordon Inglis (England), Karl Emil Knudsen (Denmark), Harry Nicolausson (Sweden), Francois Postif (France), Alexandre Rado (France), Jeanne Rausch (U.S.A.), Wim Van Eyle (The Netherlands), and Niels Winther (Denmark).

I made large use of the following publications: *Jazz Records, 1942-1968*, by J. G. Jepsen, *Jazz Directory*, by A. McCarthy, *Hot Discographie Encyclopedique* by Charles Delaunay, and of the magazines and periodicals: *Jazz Catalogues, Jazz Statistics, Discographical Forum, Jazz Hot, Jazz Monthly, Jazz Journal, Down Beat*, and *Soul Bag*.

Finally, this book is a tribute to Bob Weinstock, founder of Prestige Records, whose name remains closely associated with so many essential sessions of the era covered in following pages.

MICHEL RUPPLI
April 1979

Foreword

This book is an updated version of the previous "Prestige Jazz Sessions (1949-1971)," which was published in 1973 in Copenhagen by Karl-Emil Knudsen. It contains a detailed listing of all recordings made or issued by Prestige Records between 1949 and 1979.

All known details on jazz, blues, and gospel sessions are included in this discography. Other releases (mostly folk music) are not detailed but are mentioned in record numerical lists.

Part 1 of this book is devoted to Prestige sessions listed in chronological order. It includes details on personnel, recording dates, and titles. The individual matrix number is shown in front of each title for sessions up to October 1963 but no matrix number was allocated after this date. All known U.S. issue numbers are mentioned including releases on Prestige subsidiaries: Par, New Jazz, Swingville, Bluesville, Moodsville, and Tru-Sound labels.

Part 2 is composed of all sessions leased or purchased from other labels or independent producers and then reissued by Prestige Records. This includes many Fantasy sessions reissued after Prestige was purchased by Fantasy.

The book is completed by record numerical listings: singles in Part 3 and albums in Part 4. Part 4 also includes a table of foreign equivalents. An index by artists allows the reader easy access.

Information given in this book is based on Prestige files, which are not absolutely complete as one early part was destroyed. Some anomalies (duplication of matrix numbers, titles without matrix number, matrix numbers not used) have been carefully checked with files. They often resulted from production split between various people and matrix numbers being allocated prior to recording.

Recording locations and dates are given when known. The New York City location is given for all sessions made in Rudy Van Gelder's nearby New Jersey studios, located in Hackensack from 1954 to the June 20, 1959 session, and in Englewood Cliffs later on. Most sessions recorded between 1954 and 1974 were made in these studios.

Although all efforts have been made during the years to make this book as complete as possible, there is still much room for corrections and additions which would be welcomed by the author.

Introduction

From its very beginnings, the Prestige label was one of the most famous independent labels devoted to new trends in jazz.

Founded in 1949 by Bob Weistock, the label was first established in New York City (446 West 50th Street) and used various studios in the city (Nola Studios, Beltone Studios, and so on). In the 1950s, most sessions were made in Rudy Van Gelder's studios in Hackensack, New Jersey, which were used also in the 1960s after their transfer to Englewood Cliffs, New Jersey in July 1959. In 1967, Prestige itself moved to Bergenfield, New Jersey (203 South Washington Avenue), close to Van Gelder's studios. It remained there until May 1971 when it was sold to Fantasy, a San Francisco label, which progressively transferred all activity to Fantasy's new Berkeley studios. New sessions were recorded in Berkeley in the 1970s, but the number of sessions decreased almost completely in the 1976-1978 period; most issues in this time span were part of a reissue program made of 2LP sets.

Prestige label was made famous by recordings from the 1949-1969 period when many great jazz names made "classic" sessions: the "cool" school, with early sessions involving Lennie Tristano and Lee Konitz; Stan Getz's confirmation as leader; sessions by Gene Ammons, Miles Davis, Art Farmer, Red Garland, Wardell Gray, Modern Jazz Quartet, Thelonious Monk, Jackie McLean, Sonny Rollins; John Coltrane's debut as leader; resurgence of blues and mainstream sessions with the Bluesville, Swingville, and Moodsville labels begun in 1960; Booker Ervin's famous "book" album series; organ/tenor combos of the late 1950s and early 1960s with artists Shirley Scott/Eddie Davis, followed by groups with Jack McDuff, Richard "Groove" Holmes, and Johnny "Hammond" Smith; and the confirmation of some individuals such as Barry Harris and Pat Martino as great performers.

Many classic sessions leased from other labels were reissued on the Prestige label, and recent years saw reissues taken from the Fantasy conglomerate (Riverside, Milestone, and Fantasy labels). As a result, the index of artists appearing on Prestige records is a real who's who of jazz with, however, some noticeable exceptions like Louis Armstrong, Count Basie, and Ornette Coleman.

The quality of original Prestige sessions was enhanced by the work of involved producers including Bob Weinstock, Chris Albertson, Ozzie Cadena, Esmond Edwards, Ira Gitler, Cal Lampley, Bob Porter, and Don Schlitten, and by Rudy Van Gelder the sound engineer in the majority of sessions.

List of
Abbreviations Used

Part 1
Original Prestige Recordings

LENNIE TRISTANO QUINTET:
Lee Konitz(as)Lennie Tristano(p)Billy Bauer(g)Arnold Fishkin(b)Shelly
Manne(dm).
Supervision:Bob Weinstock   NYC,January 11,1949

JRC3A	Progression	NJ832;Pr.832,PREP1308,PRLP101, PR24046
JRC3	Tautology-1	PRLP7004,PRLP7250,P-24081
JRC4A	Retrospection-2	NJ832;Pr.832,PREP1308,PRLP101, PRLP7004,PRLP7250,P-24081
JRC8J	Subconscious Lee	NJ808,80-001;Pr.808,PREP1308, PRLP7004,PRLP7250,P-24052,P-24081
JRC11B	Judy-2	NJ808,80-001;Pr.808,PREP1308, PRLP7004,PRLP7250,P-24081

-1:as "Progression" on PRLP7004,PRLP7250.
-2:Manne out.

TERRY GIBBS NEW JAZZ PIRATES:
Shorty Rogers(tp)Earl Swope(tb)Stan Getz(ts)Terry Gibbs(vb)George
Wallington(p)Curley Russell(b)Shadow Wilson(dm).
Supervision:Bob Weinstock   NYC,March 14,1949

JRC12A1	Michelle,pt.1	NJ804;PRLP7255
JRC12A2	Michelle,pt.2	-
JRC12E	Michelle	Pr.729,PREP1312,PRLP104
JRC13B	T and S	NJ800;Pr.800,PREP1312,PRLP104, PRLP7255
JRC14C	Terry's tune	NJ800;Pr.800,PREP1312,PRLP104, PRLP7255
JRC15D	Cuddles-1	NJ803,NJ811;Pr.811,PREP1312,PRLP 104,PRLP7255

-1:as "Speedway" on NJ811,Pr.811,PRLP104.
PRLP7255=PR7434.

STAN GETZ FIVE BROTHERS:
Stan Getz(ts,bs-1)Zoot Sims,Al Cohn,Allen Eager,Brew Moore(ts)Walter
Bishop Jr.(p)Gene Ramey(b)Charlie Perry(dm)Gerry Mulligan(arr).
Supervision:Bob Weinstock   NYC,April 8,1949

JRC16	Battleground	NJLP102;Pr.724,PREP1309,PRLP7022
JRC16E	Battleground	NJ818*;Pr.818;Esq(E)10-407
JRC17	Four and one Moore-2	PREP1309,PRLP7022,PR24046
JRC17E	Four and one Moore-2,3	NJ802*,NJ802**,NJLP102;Pr.802
JRC18C	Five brothers-1,4	NJ802**,NJLP102;PREP1309,PRLP7022 PR24019,PR24046,Pr.802
JRC18D	Five brothers-1,4	NJ802*
JRC19B	Battle of the saxes	NJ1401,NJLP102;Pr724,PREP1309, PRLP7022,PR24019

*:yellow label;**:red label.
-2:based on 'Indiana'.
-3:as "Five brothers" on NJ802*.
-4:based on "Rose of the Rio Grande".As "Four and one Moore" on NJ802*.

NJLP102=PRLP102;PRLP7022=PRLP7252.

JAY JAY JOHNSON'S BOPPERS:
Kenny Dorham(tp)Jay Jay Johnson(tb)Sonny Rollins(ts)John Lewis(p)
Leonard Gaskin(b)Max Roach(dm).
Supervision:Bob Weinstock   NYC,May 26,1949

JRC20B	Elysees	NJ803,NJ810;Pr.810
JRC21C	Opus V	NJ806;Pr.806
JRC22C	Hi-Lo	- -
JRC23D	Fox hunt	Pr.810

All titles also issued on PREP1330,PRLP109,PRLP7023,PRLP7253,LP16-4,
P-24067.

STAN GETZ QUARTET:
Stan Getz(ts)Al Haig(p)Gene Ramey(b)Stan Levey(dm).
Supervision:Bob Weinstock   NYC,June 21,1949

JRC24E	Indian Summer	Pr.740,PREP1310,PRLP108,PRLP7002, PR24019
JRC25E	Long Island sound	NJ805;Pr.710,PREP1310,PRLP102, PRLP7002,PR24019
JRC26D	Mar-cia	NJ805;Pr.710,PREP1310,PRLP102, PRLP7002
JRC27B	Prezervation(JRC60)	NJ818;Pr.818,PREP1342,PRLP7013, PR7516,PR24019
JRC27C	Crazy chords	NJ811;Pr.811,PREP1310,PRLP108, PRLP7002,PR24019

PRLP7002=NJLP8214,PRLP7337,PRLP7256.

LEE KONITZ QUINTET:
Lee Konitz(as)Warne Marsh(ts)Sal Mosca(p)Arnold Fishkin(b)Denzil Best
(dm).
Supervision:Bob Weinstock   NYC,June 28,1949

JRC28	untitled	rejected
JRC29	untitled	-
JRC30G	Marshmallow	NJ807;Pr.807,PREP1314,PRLP101, PRLP7004,P-24081
JRC31D	Fishin' around	NJ807;Pr.807,PREP1314,PRLP101, PRLP7004,P-24081

PRLP7004=PR7250.
Note:Some copies of NJ807 show matrix numbers as JRC29:Marshmallow and
JRC30:Fishin' around.

DON LANPHERE QUARTET:
Don Lanphere(ts)Duke Jordan(p)Tubby Phillips(b)Roy Hall(dm).
                                          NYC,July 2,1949

JRC32A	Spider's webb	NJ810;PR7849,P-24081
JRC33A	Strike up the band	- -

KAI WINDING SEXTETTE:
Kai Winding(tb)Brew Moore(ts)Gerry Mulligan(bs)George Wallington(p)
Curley Russell(b)Roy Haynes(dm).
Supervision:Bob Weinstock   NYC,August 23,1949

JRC34	Sid's bounce	NJ809;Pr.809,PREP1331,PRLP109, PRLP7023,LP16-4,P-24067;ST8306
JRC35	Broadway(JRC904)	NJ816;Pr.816,P-24081
JRC35	Broadway(alt.take)	PREP1331,PRLP109,PRLP7023,P-24067 LP16-4;ST8306
JRC36	Waterworks(JRC905)	NJ816;Pr.816,P-24081
JRC36	Waterworks(alt.take)	PREP1331,PRLP109,PRLP7023,LP16-4, P-24067;ST8306
JRC37A	A night on bop mountain	PREP1331,PRLP109,PRLP7023,LP16-4, P-24067;ST8306
JRC37B	A night on bop mountain	NJ809;Pr.809,PR24046

DON LANPHERE QUINTET:
Fats Navarro(tp)Don Lanphere(ts)Al Haig(p)Tommy Potter(b)Max Roach(dm).
Supervision:Bob Weinstock   NYC,September 20,1949

JRC35   Wailing wall(3:42)   unissued
JRC35   Wailing wall(2:27)*   -
JRC35   Wailing wall(2:21)*   -
JRC35D   Wailing wall(3:41)   NJ819;Pr.819,PRLP113;NJLP8296;
                                         P-24081
JRC35   Wailing wall(3:50)   PREP1321,PR24046
JRC36   Go(1:43)*   unissued
JRC36B   Go(3:11)   -
JRC36BC   Go(3:22)   NJ812;Pr.812
JRC36C   Go(3:22)   PREP1321,PRLP113;NJLP8296;P-24081
JRC36   Go(1:45)*   unissued
JRC36   Go(3:04)   -
JRC37   Infatuation(1:15)*   unissued
JRC37B   Infatuation(3:33)   NJ819;Pr.819,PREP1321;NJLP8296;
                                         P-24081
JRC37   Infatuation(1:15)*   unissued
JRC37   Infatuation(3:28)   -
JRC38   Stop(1:00)*   -
JRC38B   Stop(3:57)   NJ812;Pr.812,PREP1321,PRLP113;
                                         NJLP8296;P-24081
JRC38   Stop(4:16)   unissued

*:incomplete take.
Note:JRC36BC is a spliced master:the first two choruses are from master
JRC36B and the remaining part is from master JRC36C.

LEE KONITZ QUINTET:
Lee Konitz(as)Warne Marsh(ts)Sal Mosca(p)Arnold Fishkin(b)Jeff Morton
(dm).
Supervision:Bob Weinstock   NYC,September 27,1949

JRC39F   Tautology   NJ813;Pr.813,PREP1314,PRLP101,
                                         PRLP7004,P-24081
JRC40B   Sound Lee   NJ813;Pr.813,PREP1314,PRLP101,
                                         PRLP7004,P-24081

PRLP7004=PRLP7250

JAY JAY JOHNSON'S BOPPERS:
Jay Jay Johnson(tb)Sonny Stitt(ts)John Lewis(p)Nelson Boyd(b)Max Roach
(dm).
Supervision:Bob Weinstock   NYC,October 17,1949

JRC600A Afternoon in Paris   Melodisc(E)1122
JRC600C Afternoon in Paris   NJ820;Pr.820,PREP1332,PRLP123,
                                         PRLP7024,P-24044,P-24081
JRC601A Elora   NJ814
JRC601B Elora   NJ814;Pr.814,PREP1332,PRLP123,
                                         PRLP7024,P-24044,P-24081
JRC602A Teapot   Melodisc(E)1121
JRC602B Teapot   NJ820;Pr.820,PREP1332,PRLP123,
                                         PRLP7024,P-24044,P-24081
JRC603B Blue mode   NJ814
JRC603C Blue mode   NJ814;Pr.814,PREP1332,PRLP123,
                                         PRLP7024,P-24044,P-24081

PRLP7024=PR7248.
All titles and takes shown have been issued on PR7839.
Note:JRC601A appears as JRC601B in the wax of NJ814.Two versions of
NJ814 have been issued,one with JRC601A/JRC603B and one with JRC601B/
JRC603C.

WARDELL GRAY QUARTET:
Wardell Gray(ts)Al Haig(p)Tommy Potter(b)Roy Haynes(dm).
Supervision:Bob Weinstock   NYC,November 11,1949

JRC46	Twisted(3:26)	P-24062
JRC46	Twisted(3:16)	unissued
JRC46	Twisted(2:41)*	-
JRC46D	Twisted(3:06)	NJ817;Pr.707,PR24046
JRC46	Twisted(2:53)	PRLP115,PRLP7008,PR7343,P-24062
JRC47	Southside(2:41)	unissued
JRC47	Southside(2:38)	-
JRC47	Southside(3:07)	-
JRC47	Southside(2:43)*	-
JRC47E	Southside(3:11)	NJ828;Pr.711,PRLP115,PRLP7008, PR7343,P-24062
JRC47	Southside(2:09)*	unissued
JRC47	Southside(2:50)	P-24062
JRC48	Easy living(4:35)	-
JRC48B	Easy living(4:10)(ed?)	NJ817;Pr.707,PRLP115,PRLP7008, PR7343,P-24081
JRC49A	Sweet Lorraine(3:52)	NJ828;Pr.711,PRLP115,PRLP7008, PR7343,P-24062;MV37;ST8319

*:incomplete take.
Note:NJ817 issued as by AL HAIG QUARTET,featuring Wardell Gray.Intro
and coda of JRC48B are edited out on this record.

SONNY STITT QUARTET:
Sonny Stitt(ts)Bud Powell(p)Curley Russell(b)Max Roach(dm).
Supervision:Bob Weinstock   NYC,December 11,1949

JRC1000A	All God's chillun got rhythm	Pr.705
JRC1001	Sonny side	Pr.722
JRC1002B	Bud's blues	Pr.706
JRC1003A	Sunset	Pr.705

All titles also issued on PRLP103,PRLP7024,PRLP7248,PR7839,P-24044.

STAN GETZ QUARTET:
Stan Getz(ts)Al Haig(p)Tommy Potter(b)Roy Haynes(dm).
                                        NYC,January 6,1950

BL1200C	Stardust-1	Birdland 6002;PR7516
BL1201B	Goodnight my love-1	
BL1202C	There's a small hotel	Birdland 6001;Pr.708,PREP1311, Pr.45-250,PRLP104,PRLP7002,MV35, PR24019
BL1203A	Too marvellous for words	Pr.729,45-283,PREP1311,PRLP104, PRLP7002,PR24019
BL1204A	I've got you under my skin	PRLP104
BL1204B	I've got you under my skin	Birdland 6001;Pr.708,PREP1311, Pr.45-250,PRLP7002,MV34
BL1205	What's new	Pr.740,45-283,PREP1311,PRLP104, PRLP7002
JRC1210	Intoit	NJ867;Pr.867,PREP1342,PRLP7013, PR7516,PR24019

-1:Junior Parker(vo)added.Birdland 6002 issued as by JUNIOR PARKER acc.
by Stan Getz Quartet.

PRLP7002=NJLP8214,PRLP7256,PR7337.

SONNY STITT QUARTET:
Sonny Stitt(ts)Bud Powell(p)Curley Russell(b)Max Roach(dm).
Supervision:Bob Weinstock   NYC,January 26,1950

JRC1004D Strike up the band	PR.758,PRLP103,P-24044	
JRC1005B I want to be happy	- - -	
JRC1006D Taking a chance on love	Pr.722 - -	
JRC1007A Fine and dandy	Pr.706 - -	
JRC1007B Fine and dandy	P-24081	

All titles and takes shown issued on PRLP7024,PRLP7248,PR7839.

EDDIE DAVIS AND HIS ORCHESTRA:
Eddie "Lockjaw" Davis(ts)Wynton Kelly(p)Frank Skeete(b)Al Casey(g)
Lee Abrams(dm)Carl Davis(vo).
                                             NYC,February 7,1950

BL1206	I'm gonna eat you with a spoon voCD	Birdland 6003
BL1207	Little Rock-1	Birdland 6004;Pr.866,P-24081
BL1208	If the motif is right voCD	Birdland 6003
BL1209	The Lock-2	Birdland 6004;Pr.866,P-24081

-1:as "Sweet and lovely" on Prestige issues.
-2:as "Squattin' " on Prestige issues.

SONNY STITT QUARTET:
Sonny Stitt(ts)Kenny Drew(p)Tommy Potter(b)Art Blakey(dm).
Supervision:Bob Weinstock   NYC,February 17,1950

JRC1008 Avalon	PRLP7133
JRC1009A Later	Pr.704,PRLP126,PRLP7077
JRC1010A Ain't misbehavin'	- - -
JRC1011 Mean to me	Pr.752,PRLP111,PRLP7133
JRC1012 Stairway to the stars	Pr.824,886,LP126 -

All titles also issued on PR7585.

AL HAIG TRIO:
Al Haig(p)Tommy Potter(b)Roy Haynes(dm).
Supervision:Bob Weinstock   NYC,February 27,1950

JRC1100C Liza	NJ822;PREP1328,PRLP175,PR7516
JRC1101C Stars fell on Alabama	- - - -
JRC1102C Stairway to the stars	NJ823;Pr.823,EP1328,LP175,PR7516
JRC1103A Opus caprice	- - - - -
	P-24052

All titles also issued on P-24081.

GENE AMMONS-SONNY STITT BAND:
Bill Massey-1(tp)Eph Greenlea-1(tb)Gene Ammons(ts)Sonny Stitt(ts,bs)
Duke Jordan(p)Tommy Potter(b)Jo Jones(dm).
Supervision:Bob Weinstock   NYC,March 5,1950

BL1220 Bye bye-1	Pr.713,845,LP112,PR7823,P-24058
BL1221 Let it be-1	- -
BL1222-1 Blues up and down	PRLP7050,PR7823
BL1222-2 Blues up and down	Birdland 6005;Pr.709,PREP1316, LP107,LP7050,PR7823
BL1222-3 Blues up and down	PRLP7050,PR7823
BL1223-1 You can depend on me	Birdland 6005;Pr.709,PREP1316, LP107,LP7050,PR7823
BL1223-2 You can depend on me	PRLP7050,PR7823

TEDDY WILLIAMS:
Teddy Williams(vo)with Gene Ammons(ts)Sonny Stitt(ts,bs)Duke Jordan(p)
Tommy Potter(b)Jo Jones(dm).
Supervision:Bob Weinstock   NYC,March 5,1950

BL1224   Touch of the blues voTW   Pr.715,PR7823
BL1225   Dumb woman blues voTW   -

CHUBBY JACKSON AND HIS ORCHESTRA:
Howard McGhee,Al Porcino,Don Ferrara(tp)Kai Winding,Jay Jay Johnson(tb)
Charlie Kennedy(as)Zoot Sims,Georgie Auld(ts)Gerry Mulligan(bs)Tony
Aless(p)Chubby Jackson(b)Don Lamond(dm).
Supervision:Bob Weinstock   NYC,March 15,1950

JRC63   Flying the Coop(JRC1104)   NJ825,LP8280;Pr.825,EP1323
JRC64   I may be wrong(JRC1105)   -   -   -   EP1318,LP7013
JRC65   New York(JRC1106)   NJ836;Pr.836,EP1323
JRC66   Sax appeal(JRC1107)   NJ830;Pr.830
JRC67   Hot dog(JRC1108)   NJLP8280;Pr.745,EP1323
JRC68   Why not?(JRC1109)   NJ836;Pr.836,EP1323
JRC69   Leavin' town(JRC1110)   NJ830;Pr.830
JRC70   So what-1(JRC1111)   NJLP8280;Pr.745,842,EP1318,LP7013

-1:McGhee,Porcino,Ferrara and Auld out.

All titles also issued on PRLP105,PR7641

LEE KONITZ QUINTET:
Lee Konitz(as)Sal Mosca(p)Billy Bauer(g)Arnold Fishkin(b)Jeff Morton
(dm).
Supervision:Bob Weinstock   NYC,April 7,1950

JRC71   Rebecca-1   NJ834;Pr.834
JRC72C   You go to my head-2   NJ827;Pr.827
JRC73   Ice cream Konitz   NJ834;Pr.834
JRC74B   Palo alto   NJ827;Pr.827

-1:as and g only.
-2:p out.

All titles issued on PREP1315,PRLP108,PRLP7004,PRLP7250.

STAN GETZ QUARTET:
Stan Getz(ts)Tony Aless(p)Percy Heath(b)Don Lamond(dm).
Supervision:Bob Weinstock   NYC,April 14,1950

JRC75C   You stepped out of a dream   NJ867;Pr.867,EP1313,LP108,LP7002
JRC76A   My old flame   PRLP7002,PR24019
JRC76B   My old flame   NJ829;Pr.712,45-240,EP1313,LP102
JRC77A   The lady in red   PRLP7002,PR24019
JRC77B   The lady in red   NJ829;Pr.712,45-240,EP1313,LP102
JRC78B   Wrap your troubles in dreams NJ1401;Pr.724,EP1313,LP108,LP7002
                                       PR24019

PRLP7002=PR7256,PR7337,NJLP8214.

WARDELL GRAY QUARTET:
Wardell Gray(ts)Phil Hill(p)John Richardson(b)Art Mardigan(dm).
Supervision:Bob Weinstock   Detroit,April 25,1950

JRC79A   A sinner kissed an angel(3:05)Pr.723,LP115,LP7008,P-24062.
JRC80   Blue Gray(2:44)   unissued
JRC80B   Blue Gray(2:39)   Pr.714,LP115,LP7008,P-24062
JRC80   Blue Gray(2:37)   unissued
JRC81   Grayhound(3:25)   -
JRC81B   Grayhound(2:58)   Pr.723,LP115,LP7008,P-24062
JRC81   Grayhound(3:12)   unissued
JRC82   Treadin'(2:32)   -
JRC82   Treadin'(0:57)   -
JRC82C   Treadin'(3:43)   Pr.714,LP115,LP7008,P-24062

All titles from LP7008 also issued on PR7343.

GENE AMMONS-SONNY STITT BAND:
Bill Massey(tp)Benny Green(tb)Gene Ammons(ts)Sonny Stitt(bs)Duke
Jordan(p)Tommy Potter(b)Art Blakey(dm).
Supervision:Bob Weinstock   NYC,April 26,1950

85	Chabootie	Pr.741,LP107,P-24058
86	Who put the sleeping pills in Rip Van Winkle's coffee	Pr.721
87	Gravy(Walkin'*)	Pr.717,LP112,P-24058*
88	Easy glide	- -

All titles also issued on PR7823.

GENE AMMONS/SONNY STITT QUARTET:
Gene Ammons-1 or Sonny Stitt-2(ts)Duke Jordan(p)Gene Wright(b)Wesley
Landers(dm).
Supervision:Bob Weinstock   NYC,June 28,1950

89	I wanna be loved-1	Pr.717,LP107,PR7823,P-24058
90A	Count every star-2	Pr.718 - LP7133,PR7585
91	I can't give you anything but love-1	Pr.731,845,LP112,PR7823,P-24058
92A	Nice work if you can get it-2	Pr.718,LP126,LP7133,PR7585,P-24044
93A	There'll never be another you-2	PRLP126,LP7133,PR7585
94A	Blazin'-2	- - - P-24044

LEO PARKER QUARTET:
Leo Parker(as,bs)Al Haig(p)Oscar Pettiford(b)Max Roach(dm).
-1:Jack "The Bear" Parker(dm)replaces Roach.
Supervision:Bob Weinstock   NYC,July 20,1950

JRC95	Mona Lisa(2:45)*	unissued
JRC95	Mona Lisa(3:03)	P-24081
JRC96A	Who's mad-1(2:55)	-
JRC97	Darn that dream(1:23)*	unissued
JRC97	Darn that dream(2:52)	P-24081
JRC98B	I'll cross my fingers(2:27)	Pr.720,P-24081
JRC99A	Mad lad returns-1(2:38)	- PR24046
JRC99	Mad lad returns-1(3:15)	unissued
JRC99	Mad lad returns-1(2:48)	-
JRC99	Mad lad returns-1(2:20)*	-

*:incomplete take.

GENE AMMONS BAND:
Bill Massey(tp)Matthew Gee(tb)Gene Ammons(ts,vo)Sonny Stitt(bs)
Charlie Bateman(p)Gene Wright(b)Wesley Landers(dm).
Supervision:Bob Weinstock   NYC,July 27,1950

100	Back in your own backyard	Pr.725,LP112,P-24058
101	Sweet Jennie Lou voGA	Pr.731 -
102	La vie en rose	Pr.721,844,LP112
103	Seven eleven	Pr.725,LP107,P-24058

WARDELL GRAY ALL STARS:
Clark Terry(tp)Sonny Criss(as)Wardell Gray,Dexter Gordon(ts)Jimmy Bunn
(p)Billy Hadnott(b)Chuck Thompson(dm).
                          Hula Hut Club,LA,August 27,1950

(1231)	Jazz on sunset,pts.1 & 2	Pr.778,LP128
(1232)	Jazz on sunset,pts.3 & 4	Pr.779 -
(1233)	Kiddo,pts.1 & 2 -1	Pr.759 -
(1234)	Kiddo,pts.3 & 4 -1	Pr.760 -

-1:Gordon out.
All titles also issued on PRLP7008,PR7343,P-24062.
Note:Jazz on sunset=Move;Kiddo=Scrapple from the apple.

ZOOT SIMS QUARTET:
Zoot Sims(ts)John Lewis(p)Curley Russell(b)Don Lamond(dm).
Supervision:Bob Weinstock   NYC,September 16,1950

104   My silent love   Pr.726,LP118
105   Jane-O   Pr.732   -
106   Dancing in the dark   Pr.726   -
107   Memories of you   Pr.732   -

All titles also issued on PRLP7026,PR16009,P-24061.

DIZZY GILLESPIE SEXTET:
Dizzy Gillespie(tp)Jimmy Heath(as)Jimmy Oliver(ts)Milt Jackson(p)
Percy Heath(b)Joe Harris(dm).
Supervision:Bob Weinstock   NYC,September 16,1950

108   She's gone again voDG   Pr.736,PR24030
109A   Nice work if you can get it   - LP113,PR24030
110A   Thinking of you   Pr.728   -
111   Too much weight (unknown,vo)

All titles issued on NJLP8296=PR16002.

SONNY STITT BAND:
Bill Massey(tp)Matthew Gee(tb)Sonny Stitt(ts)Gene Ammons(bs)Junior
Mance(p)Gene Wright(b)Wesley Landers(dm)Larry Townsend(vo).
Supervision:Bob Weinstock   NYC,October 8,1950

112   To think you've chosen me voLT Pr.728
113   After you've gone   Pr.727,LP126,LP7133,P-24044
114   Our very own   -   -   -   -
115   'S wonderful   Pr.746,843,LP148,LP7133,P-24044

All titles also issued on PR7585.

GENE AMMONS-SONNY STITT BAND:
Gene Ammons,Sonny Stitt-1(ts)Junior Mance(p)Gene Wright(b)Wesley
Landers(dm).
Supervision:Bob Weinstock   NYC,October 28,1950

116   Stringin' the Jug,pt.1 -1   Pr.748,EP1316,LP107,LP7050
117   Stringin' the Jug,pt.2 -1   -   -   -   -
118   When I dream of you   Pr.805,LP112,P-24058
119   A lover is blue   -   -

All titles also scheduled on PR7871(not issued).

SONNY STITT QUARTET:
Sonny Stitt(ts)Junior Mance(p)Gene Wright(b)Art Blakey(dm).
Supervision:Bob Weinstock   NYC,December 15,1950

120   Nevertheless   Pr.826,LP111,LP7133
121   Jeepers creepers   - LP148 -
122   Imagination   Pr.733,LP111,LP7077,EP1346;MVLP2
123   Cherokee   -   -   -   -

All titles also issued on PR7612,P-24044.

JIMMY McPARTLAND ALL STARS:
Jimmy McPartland(c)Vic Dickenson(tb)Gene Sedric(cl,ts)Marian McPartland
(p)Max Wayne(b)Bob Varney(dm).
                                   Chicago,December 21,1950

MCP600 Use your imagination   Pr.304
MCP602 Come back sweet Papa   Pr.303
MCP603 Manhattan   -
MCP605 Davenport blues   Pr.304

GENE AMMONS BAND:
Bill Massey(tp)Matthew Gee(tb)Gene Ammons(ts,vo)Sonny Stitt(ts,bs)
Junior Mance(p)Gene Wright(b)Teddy Stewart(dm).
Supervision:Bob Weinstock   NYC,January 16,1951

124A Around about one A.M.   Pr.735
125   Jug   -   844,LP127
126B Wow   Pr.805   -
127B Blue and sentimental   Pr.741   -

All titles also issued on P-24058

MILES DAVIS SEXTET:
Miles Davis(tp)Benny Green(tb)Sonny Rollins(ts)John Lewis(p)Percy
Heath(b)Roy Haynes(dm).
Supervision:Bob Weinstock   NYC,January 17,1951

128A Morpheus   Pr.734,EP1320,LP113,LP7025
129B Down   Pr.742   -   -   -
130B Blue room-1   PRLP140,PR24046
130BB Blue room-1   Pr.734,EP1320,LP7025;MV32
131A Whispering   Pr.742,EP1320,LP113,LP7025

-1:Green and Rollins out.
All titles also issued on PR7674,P-24054.
PRLP7025=PRLP7168.MV32=PR7322.

SONNY ROLLINS QUARTET:
Sonny Rollins(ts)Miles Davis(p)Percy Heath(b)Roy Haynes(dm).
Supervision:Bob Weinstock   NYC,January 17,1951

132   I know   PRLP137,LP7029,LP7269,PR7856

SONNY STITT QUARTET:
Sonny Stitt(ts)Charles Bateman(p)Gene Wright(b)Art Blakey(dm).
Supervision:Bob Weinstock   NYC,January 31,1951

133   Liza   Pr.757,EP1346,LP111,LP7077,PR7585
134   Can't we be friends   Pr.739   -   -   -   -
135   This can't be love   Pr.831*

*:some pressings only(see 147)

GENE AMMONS BAND:
Bill Massey(tp)Al Outcalt(tb)Sonny Stitt(ts)Gene Ammons(bs)Charles
Bateman(p)Gene Wright(b)Art Blakey(dm)Larry Townsend(vo).
Supervision:Bob Weinstock   NYC,January 31,1951

136A New blues up and down,pt.1   Pr.877,LP127,LP7050,PR7871*
137A New blues up and down,pt.2   -   -   -   -

*:scheduled,but not issued.

Teddy Stewart(dm)replaces Blakey.Same date.

138   The thrill of your kiss voLT Pr.746,PR7612
139   If the moon turns green boLT Pr.739   -

SONNY STITT QUARTET:
Sonny Stitt(ts,bs)Charles Bateman(p)Gene Wright(b)Teddy Stewart(dm).
Supervision:Bob Weinstock   NYC,February 1,1951

146   P.S.I love you   Pr.757,LP111,LP7077,PR7612,P-24044
147   This can't be love   Pr.831   -   -   -   -

140/145:see next page.

LEE KONITZ SEXTET:
Miles Davis(tp)Lee Konitz(as)Sal Mosca(p)Billy Bauer(g)Arnold Fishkin
(b)Max Roach(dm).
Supervision:Bob Weinstock   NYC,March 8,1951

140B	Odjenar	Pr.753;NJ853
141B	Ezz-thetic	Pr.743;NJ843
142B	Hi-Beck	- -
143B	Yesterdays-1	NJ855
143	Yesterdays-1,2	Pr.755

-1:dm out.
-2:tp out.
First four titles also issued on PREP1319,LP116,LP7013,PR16011,PR7827,
NJ8295

LEE KONITZ DUO:
Lee Konitz(as)Billy Bauer(g).
Supervision:Bob Weinstock   NYC,March 13,1951

144B	Indian Summer	Pr.753;NJ853;PRLP116
145A	Duet for saxophone and guitar	Pr.755;NJ855 -

Both titles also issued on PRLP7013,PR16011,NJ8295.

GENE AMMONS BAND:
Bill Massey(tp)Eli Dabney(tb)Gene Ammons(ts)Rudy Williams(bs)Clarence
Anderson(p)Earl May(b)Teddy Stewart(dm)Sally Early(vo).
Supervision:Bob Weinstock   NYC,June 29,1951

148	Ammons boogie	Pr.901,LP127,P-24058
149	Echo chamber blues	- - -
150	Sirocco	Pr.903 -
151	Fine and foxy voSE	- -

THE CABINEERS:
The Cabineers(vocal quartet)with MERCER ELLINGTON QUARTET:Billy Taylor
(p)Sal Salvador(g)Sam Bell(b)Mercer Ellington(dm).
                                    NYC,July 2,1951

152A	Each time	Pr.904
153A	My,my,my	Pr.902
154A	Lost	Pr.904
155A	Baby,where'd you go	Pr.902

SONNY STITT QUARTET:
Sonny Stitt(ts)Clarence Anderson(p)Earl May(b)Teddy Stewart(dm).
Supervision:Bob Weinstock   NYC,August 14,1951

156	Down with it	Pr.752
157	For the fat man	Pr.831
158	Splinter	
159	Confessin'	Pr.787

All titles issued on PRLP148,PR7612,P-24044.

GENE AMMONS QUARTET:
Gene Ammons(ts)Clarence Anderson(p)Earl May(b)Teddy Stewart(dm).
Supervision:Bob Weinstock   NYC,August 14,1951

160C	Hot stuff	Pr.754
161A	Them there eyes	
162B	When the Saints go marching in	Pr.754
163A	Archie	

All titles issued on PRLP149,P-24058.

ZOOT SIMS QUARTET:
Zoot Sims(ts)Harry Biss(p)Clyde Lombardi(b)Art Blakey(dm).
Supervision:Bob Weinstock   NYC,August 14,1951

164	Trotting(3:19)	unissued
164	Trotting(1:58)	-
164	Trotting(3:46)*	-
164	Trotting(3:45)	Pr.751,LP118,LP7026,P-24061
165	It had to be you	Pr.781 - - -
166A	Swingin' -1	Pr.751 - - -
166	Zoot swings the blues-1	LP117 - -
167	Coolin' the blues	unissued
168	East of the sun	PRLP117,LP7026,P-24061
169	I wonder who	Pr.781,LP118,LP7026,P-24061

*:incomplete take.
-1:166A & 166 issued on P-24061 as "Zoot swings the blues,takes 1 & 2".

GERRY MULLIGAN NEW STARS:
Jerry Lloyd(Hurwitz),Nick Travis(tp)Ollie Wilson(tb)Allen Eager(ts)
Gerry Mulligan,Max McElroy(bs)George Wallington(p)Phil Leshin(b)Walter
Bolden(dm)Gail Madden-1(maracas).
Supervision:Bob Weinstock.   NYC,August 27,1951

170	Kaper	rejected
171D	Roundhouse	NJ861;Pr.761,EP1317,LP120,LP7006
172C	Ide's side	- - EP1318 - -
173C	Bweebida bwobbida-1	Pr.762,EP1317 - -
174A	Kaper-1	- - - -
175A	Funhouse-2	Pr.763 - - -
176A	Mullenium-2	- EP1318 - -
177A	Mulligan too-3	PRLP141 -

-2:Lloyd,Travis & Wilson out.
-3:Lloyd,Travis,Wilson & McElroy out.
All titles from LP7006 also issued on PR7251,PR24016.

JOHNNY GREEN:
Johnny Green(vo)with unknown acc.
                                   NYC,September 3,1951

178	Pepsi bounce	Par 909
179	Low boat	-
180	Stranger in town	unissued
181	Low blues	-

GENE SMITH:
Gene Smith(p,vo).
                                   NYC,September 24,1951

182	Flying home	unissued
183	Make believe	Pr.914
184	That old black magic	unissued
185	Dancing in the dark	-
186	Over the rainbow	-
187	When your lover has gone	-
188	Perdido boogie	-
189	Serenade in blue	-
190	Where or when	-
191	Country boogie	-
192	Jumpin' with Symphony Sid	-
193	Stuffy	-
194	Again	-
195	I must have my baby back	-
196	Late hour boogie	Pr.914
197	Dedication to Albert Ammons	unissued

RED RODNEY QUINTET:
Red Rodney(tp)Jimmy Ford(ts,vo)Phil Raphael(p)Phil Leshin(b)Phil
Brown(dm).
Supervision:Bob Weinstock   NYC,September 27,1951

198	The baron		PRLP122;ST8306
199	Mark		– –
200	Smoke gets in your eyes	NJ865;Pr.765	– –
201	If you are but a dream		– –
202	Coogan's bluff	NJ865;Pr.765	– –
203	Red wig		– –
204	This time the dream's on me		– –
205	Don't take your love from me voJF unissued		

RALPH WILLIS:
Ralph Willis(vo,g).

                                             NYC,October 3,1951

206	Seven years blues	unissued
207	Dan girl blues	–
208	Old home blues	Pr.919
209	It's bad	unissued
210	Salty dog	Pr.919
211	I've been a fool	unissued
212	Wishing boogie	–
213	Krooked woman blues	–
214	Walkin' guitar blues	–

BENNY GREEN AND HIS BAND:
Benny Green(tb)Big Nick Nicholas(ts)Rudy Williams(bs)Eddie "Lockjaw"
Davis(ts)Teddy Brannon(p)Tommy Potter(b)Art Blakey(dm).
Supervision:Bob Weinstock   NYC,October 5,1951

221	Green junction	Pr.773,EP1343
222	Flowing river	– –
223	Whirl-a-licks	Pr.908;Par 908,PREP1343
224	Bennie's pennies-1	– – –
225	Jumpin' journey	unissued
226	Tenor sax shuffle	Pr.920
227	Sugar syrup	–

-1:based on "Pennies from heaven".
All titles issued on PREP1343 also issued on PRLP123,PRLP7023,LP16-4,
P-24067.

MILES DAVIS SEXTET:
Miles Davis(tp)Jackie McLean-1(as)Sonny Rollins(ts)Walter Bishop(p)
Tommy Potter(b)Art Blakey(dm).
Supervision:Bob Weinstock   NYC,October 5,1951

228	Conception-1	Pr.868,EP1349,LP124,LP7013,PR7457, PR24022;NJ8296
229	Out of the blue-1	Pr.876,EP1361,LP140,LP7012
230	Denial-1	–
231	Bluing,pts.1 & 2 -1	Pr.846,EP1355,LP140,LP7012
231	Bluing,pt.3 -1	Pr.868 – – –
232	Dig -1	Pr.777,45-321,EP1339,LP124,LP7012, PR7298
233	My old flame	Pr.766,EP1339,LP124,LP7013, PR24022;NJ8296
234	It's only a paper moon	Pr.817,EP1349,LP124,LP7012,45-321

LP7012=PR7281;LP7013=NJ8296,PR16002.
All titles from this session also issued on PR7744,P-24054.

LEM DAVIS QUARTET:
Lem Davis(as)Teacho Wiltshire(p)Leonard Gaskin(b)Teddy Lee(dm).
                                      NYC,October 16,1951

215   The glory of love   Pr.911
216   Sin   -
217   This is always   Pr.915
218   Knock hop   -
219   Problem child   Pr.912
220   She's a wine-o   -

AL VEGA TRIO:
Al Vega(p)John Lawler(b)Sonny Tacaloff(dm,bongo).
                                      Boston,October   ,1951

235   Cheek to cheek   NJ864
236   Bye bye blues   unissued
237   I love you   -
238   Beans   -
239   There's no you   -
240   I only have eyes for you   Pr.771
241   Makin' whoopee   NJ864
242   Try a little tenderness   unissued
243   Jeepers creepers   -
244   Fantastic   Pr.771

TEDDY COHEN TRIO:
Teddy Cohen(Teddy Charles)(vb)Don Roberts(g)Kenny O'Brien(b).
                                      NYC,November 10,1951

245   I got it bad   unissued
246   O'Brien's flying   PRLP132
247   This is new   -
248   Old man river
249   Liza   unissued
250   Tenderly   PRLP132
251   Basin Street blues   -
252   I'll remember April   NJ838;PRLP132
253   The lady is a tramp   -   -
254   Blue moon   -

GENE AMMONS BAND:
Bill Massey(tp)Eli Dabney(tb)Gene Ammons(ts)Sonny Stitt(ts,bs)Clarence
Anderson(p)Ernie Shepard(b)Ted Stewart(dm).
Supervision:Bob Weinstock   NYC,November 14,1951

255   Undecided   Pr.916,LP149,P-24058
256   Until the real thing comes along Pr.921 -   -
257   Because of rain   -   -
258   Charmaine   Pr.916 -

JOE HOLIDAY QUINTET:
Joe Holiday(ts)Jordin Fordin(org)Clarence Johnson(b)Milton Hayes(dm)
Nick De Luca(bongo).
                                      NYC,December 13,1951

259   Hello to you   Pr.848,LP131
260   Nice and easy   -
261   Blue Holiday   Pr.815 -
262   This is happiness   Pr.767 -   PR24046
263   Mambo Holiday   Pr.772 -
264   Mighty like a rose   Pr.767 -
265   I hadn't anyone till you   Pr.815 -
266   Like someone in love   Pr.848 -

SONNY ROLLINS QUARTET:
Sonny Rollins(ts)Kenny Drew(p)Percy Heath(b)Art Blakey(dm).
Supervision:Bob Weinstock   NYC,December 17,1951

267	Time on my hands	PRLP137
268	Mambo bounce	Pr.769,LP135,PR24004
269	This love of mine	- LP137
270	Shadrack	Pr.780 -
271	Slow boat to China	-
272	With a song in my heart	Pr.780 - PR24004;MV35
273	Scoops	-
274	Newk's fadeaway	- PR24004

All titles also issued on PRLP7029,PR7269,PR7856

Dr.ALVIN A.CHILDS:
Dr. Alvin A.Childs(preaching)with congregation,acc.by unknown p,org.
                                    NYC,December 17 or 18,1951

| 275 | Healing prayer,pt.1 | Pr.2002 |
| 276 | Healing prayer,pt.2 | - |

H-BOMB FERGUSON:
H-Bomb Ferguson(vo)with JACK "THE BEAR" PARKER'S BAND:unknown ts,p,b,
Jack "The Bear" Parker(dm).
                                    NYC,December   ,1951

275	I'll get you baby	unissued
276	Feel like I do	Pr.918
277	Money mad woman	unissued
278	My love	Pr.918
279	Whiskey head gal	unissued
280	Little girl blue	-
281	My number's up	-
282	I'm wise baby	-
283	Paradiddle Joe	-
284	Jumpin' at Jack's	-

285/286:see next page.

THE CABINEERS:
The Cabineers(vocal quartet)with TEACHO WILTSHIRE'S BAND:Lem Davis(as)
unknown ts,p,b,dm.
                                    NYC,December 20,1951

| 287 | What's the matter with you | Pr.917 |
| 288 | Baby mine | - |

JOHN BENNINGS:
John Bennings(vo)with TEACHO WILTSHIRE'S BAND:unknown ts,org,p,g,b,dm.

                                    NYC,December 20,1951

| 289 | Goofin' the roofin' | Pr.922 |
| 290 | Come on home | - |

LEM DAVIS:
Lem Davis(as)others unknown.

                                    NYC,December 20,1951

| 291 | Pretty | Pr.776 |
| 292 | Hoppy's hop | - |

THE DIXIEAIRES:
J.C.Ginyard,Joe Floyd,Johnny Hines,Jimmy Smith(vo)Abe Green(g).
NYC,December 20,1951

293	In the land where I'm bound	unissued
294	King Jesus will fit your battles	-
295	Step right on board	-
296	The governor	Pr.2001
297	Bloodstained banner	-
298	I'm going through	unissued

CHARLIE MARIANO BOSTON ALL STARS:
Joe Gordon(tp)Sonny Truitt(tb)Charlie Mariano(as)Jim Clark(ts)George
Meyers(bs)Ray Frazee,Dick Twardzick(p)Jack Lawler(b)Carl Goodman,
Gene Hlenncannon(dm).
Boston,December   ,1951

299A	Boston uncommon		PRLP130
299B	Boston uncommon		-
300A	The wizard	NJ842;Pr.785	-
300B	The wizard		-
301	Mariners		-
302	Aviary		-
303	Tzoris		-
304	Autumn in New York	NJ842;Pr.785	-

BROWNIE McGHEE:
Brownie McGhee(vo,g)Ralph Willis(p,vo).
NYC,December   ,1951

305	It's too late	Par 1306
306	Put in the sand	unissued
307	I'll never love again	Par 1306
308	Cold chills	Pr.923
309	Remember last night	unissued
310	Amen	Pr.923
311	Country jail blues	unissued

BROWNIE McGHEE:
Brownie McGhee(vo,g).
NYC,January 3,1952

285	Heart in sorrow	Par 1301
286	Operator long distance	-

WARDELL GRAY SEXTET:
Art Farmer(tp)Wardell Gray(ts)Hampton Hawes(p)Harper Crosby(b)Larry
Marable(dm)Robert Collier(conga).
Supervision:Jack Andrews
LA,January 21,1952

312	April skies	Pr.840
313	Bright boy	-
314	Jackie	Pr.853
315	Farmer's market	Pr.770
316	Sweet and lovely-1	Pr.853
317	Lover man-2	Pr.770

-1:Farmer & Collier out;-2:Collier out.
All titles also issued on PRLP147,LP7009,PR7343,P-24062.

DOROTHY McLEOD SINGERS:

                                        NYC,January 23,1952
318   My record will be there   unissued
319   Never turn back   -
320   Rock of ages   -
321   Stop now   -
322   Our father   -
323   Wait up on the Lord   -

THE GOSPEL ECHOES:

324   I heard of a city called heaven   unissued
325   Will you be there?   -
326   I believe   -
327   He'll never let go my hand   -
328   I'm getting nearer   -
329   Just when I need Him most   -

KING PLEASURE:
Merrill Stepter(tp)Lem Davis(as)Ray Abrams(ts)Cecil Payne(bs)Teacho
Wiltshire(p)Leonard Gaskin(b)Teddy Lee(dm)King Pleasure,Blossom Dearie
(vo).
                                        NYC,February 19,1952
330   Moody mood for love voKP,BD   Pr.924,PR7586,PR24017
332   Exclamation blues voKP   -   -   -

BOBBY HARRIS:
Bobby Harris(vo)with same band.Same date.

331   I do believe voBH   Pr.925
333   Rub a little boogie voBH   -

SONNY STITT BAND:
Bill Massey,Joe Newman,John Hunt(tp-1)Sonny Stitt(ts)John Houston(p)
Ernie Shepard(b)Shadow Wilson(dm)Humberto Morales(conga,timbales).
Supervision:Bob Weinstock   NYC,February 25,1952
335   Cool mambo-1   Pr.775,LP135
336   Sonny sounds   Pr.824,886,LP148
337   Blue mambo-1   Pr.775,LP135
338   Stitt's it   Pr.787,LP148

All titles also issued on PRLP7077,PR7612.

JOHN BENNINGS:
John Bennings(vo)with unknown ts,p,g,b,dm. -1:band vocal.

                                        NYC,April   ,1952
339   Walking all night-1   Par 1302
340   Timber   Pr.929
341   I want you baby   Par 1302
342   Third degree blues   Pr.929

BENNIE GREEN with STRINGS:
Bennie Green(tb)John Malachi(p)Tommy Potter(b)Osie Johnson(dm)Alan Lane,
Harold Sonn,Autrey McKissack,Max Waxler,Adam Micevich,Donald White
(strings).
                                   Chicago,May 13,1952
343   Serenade to love   Pr.790,EP1304
344   Embraceable you   Pr.847   -
345   Stardust   -   -
346   There's a small hotel   ` Pr.790   -

All titles also issued on PRLP7030,LP16-4.

JOE HOLIDAY:
Joe Holiday(ts)Jordin Fordin(org)Clarence Johnson(b)Sam Woodyard(dm)
Ulysses Hampton(bongo,conga).
                                   NYC,July 31,1952
347   Donde   Pr.791,LP135
348   Joe black mambo   -   -
349   Serenata   Pr.786   -
350   Cuban nightingale   -   -

GEORGE WALLINGTON TRIO:
George Wallington(p)Charlie Mingus(b)Max Roach(dm)Chuck Wayne-1(mandole)
Supervision:Bob Weinstock   NYC,September 4,1952
351   Love beat-1   Pr.788,LP136,PR7587
352   Summer rain   Pr.803   -   -
353   Escalating   -   -
354   Laura   -   -

George Wallington(p)Oscar Pettiford(b)Max Roach(dm).
Supervision:Bob Weinstock   NYC,September 4,1952
355   Tenderly   Pr.   LP136,PR7587
356   When your old wedding ring was new
                                   Pr.803   -   -
357   Red,white and blue   Pr.788   -   -
358   Arrivederci   -   -

ZOOT SIMS SEXTET:
Kai Winding(tb)Zoot Sims,Al Cohn(ts)George Wallington(p)Percy Heath(b)
Art Blakey(dm).
Supervision:Bob Weinstock   NYC,September 8,1952
359   Tangerine   PREP1348,LP138
360   Zootcase   -   -
361   The red door   -
362   Morning fun-1   -

-1:Winding out.
All titles also issued on PRLP7022,PR7252,P-24061.

ANNIE ROSS:
Annie Ross(vo)with Teacho Wiltshire(p)Ram Ramirez(org)Percy Heath(b)Art
Blakey(dm).
                                   NYC,October 9,1952
363   Twisted   Pr·794,PREP1301
364   Farmer's market   Pr.839   -

George Wallington(p)replaces Wiltshire.Same date.
365   The time was right   Pr.839,PREP1301
366   Annie's lament   Pr.794   -

All four titles also issued on PRLP7128,PR7828.

THELONIOUS MONK TRIO:
Thelonious Monk(p)Gary Mapp(b)Art Blakey(dm).
Supervision:Bob Weinstock   NYC,October 15,1952

367   Little rootie tootie   Pr.850,EP1329,P-24052
368   Sweet and lovely   Pr.795   -
369   Bye-ya   Pr.795,45-162,EP1329
370   Monk's dream   Pr.850   -

All titles also issued on PRLP7027,PRLP7159,PR7508,PR7751,PR24006,LP142.

PAULA GRIMES:
Paula Grimes(vo)with TEACHO WILTSHIRE'S BAND:unknown ts,org,p,b,dm.

                                        NYC,November 6,1952
375   Own darn fault this time   Pr.857
376   Miss my Daddy   Pr.801
377   Sighin' and cryin'   -
378   Makin' a fool of myself   Pr.857

RUDY FERGUSON:
Rudy Ferguson(vo?)with TEACHO WILTSHIRE'S BAND:details unknown.

                                        NYC,November 6,1952

379   Cool goofin'   Pr.798
380   Baby I need you so   -
381   Goofin' and jivin'   unissued
382   Goofin' in a goofball way   -

THE MELLO MOODS:
The Mello Moods(vocal quartet)with TEACHO WILTSHIRE'S BAND:unknown p,
g,b,dm.
                                        NYC,November 6,1952

383   Call on me   Pr.799
384   I tried and tried and tried   -
385   I'm lost   Pr.856
386   When I woke up this morning   -

BILLY TAYLOR TRIO:
Billy Taylor(p)Earl May(b)Charlie Smith(dm).
Supervision:Ira Gitler   NYC,November 18,1952

371   They can't take that away from me Pr.796,LP139
372   All too soon   -   -
373   Accent on youth   Pr.797 -
374   Give me the simple life   -   -

All titles also issued on PRLP7015,LP16-2.

HAMPTON HAWES QUARTET:
Hampton Hawes(p)Larry Bunker(vb)Clarence Jones(b)Lawrence Marable(dm).
                                        LA,December   ,1952
      Terrible T   PRLP212,LP7067,ST8307
      Fanfare   -   -   -
      Just squeeze me   -   -   -
      I'll remember April   -   -   -
      Hamp's paws   -   -   -   PR24052
      Move   -   -   -
      Once in a while   -   -   -
      Buzzy   -   -   -

[18]

BILLY TAYLOR TRIO:
Billy Taylor(p)Earl May(b)Charlie Smith(dm).
Supervision:Ira Gitler   NYC,December 10,1952

387   Little girl blue   PRLP139,PRLP7015
388   The man with a horn   Pr.822,EP1336,LP165,LP7015
389   Let's get away from it all   -   -   -   -
390   Lover   Pr.849,LP139,LP7071;MV35

All titles also issued on LP16-2.

CHARLIE FERGUSON ORCHESTRA/KING PLEASURE:
Ed "Tiger" Lewis(tp)Charlie Ferguson(ts)Ed Swanston(p)Peck Morrison(b)
Herb Lovelle(dm)King Pleasure,Betty Carter(vo).
                                          NYC,December 12,1952

391   When day is done   Pr.855
392   Stop talkin',start walkin'   -
393   Because   unissued
394   Red top voKP,BC   Pr.821,EP1338,LP208,45-124,PR24017
395   Jumpin' with Symphony Sid voKP   -   -   -   45-182   -
396   Life alone   unissued
397   Stop walkin',wtart talkin'   -
398   Christmas song-1   -

-1:vocal by The Mello Moods.

394/395 also issued on PRLP7128,PR7586.These two titles were issued as
by KING PLEASURE.

THELONIOUS MONK TRIO:
Thelonious Monk(p)Gary Mapp(b)Max Roach(dm).
Supervision:Ira Gitler   NYC,December 18,1952

399   Trinkle tinkle   Pr.838,LP142
400   These foolish things   -   -
401   Bemsha swing   -
402   Reflections   -

All titles also issued on PRLP7027,LP7159,PR7508,PR7751,PR24006.

MODERN JAZZ QUARTET:
Milt Jackson(vb)John Lewis(p)Percy Heath(b)Kenny Clarke(dm).
Supervision:Ira Gitler   NYC,December 22,1952

403   All the things you are   Pr.828,EP1303,PR7421
404   La ronde   -   -   PR7425
405   Vendome   Pr.851 -   -
406   Rose of the Rio Grande   -   -   PR7421

All titles also issued on PRLP160,LP7059,PR7749,PR24005.

TEDDY CHARLES QUARTET:
Teddy Charles(vb)Jimmy Raney(g)Dick Nivison(b)Ed Shaughnessy(dm).
Supervision:Ira Gitler   NYC,December 23,1952

407   Edging out   PREP1350,LP143
408   Nocturne   -
409   Composition for four pieces   -
410   Night in Tunisia   PREP1350 -

All titles also issued on NJ8295.

JOE CARROLL:
Joe Carroll(vo)with Bill Graham(bs)Ed Swanston(p)Peck Morrison(b)Al
Jones(dm).
                                    NYC,December 30,1952

411   I was in the mood   Pr.829
412   Pennies from heaven   Pr.861
413   Got a penny,Benny   Pr.829
414   Two wrongs won't make it right Pr.861

All titles also issued on PR7828.

TEDDY CHARLES TRIO:
Teddy Charles(vb)Hall Overton(p)Ed Shaughnessy(dm).
Supervision:Ira Gitler   NYC,January 19,1953

415   Decibels   PRLP150
416   Mobiles   -
417   Antiphony   -
418   Metalizing   -

SAM MOST SEXTET:
Doug Mettome(tp)Sam Most(fl,cl)Dick Hyman(p)Chuck Wayne(g)Clyde
Lombardi(b)Jack Moffet(dm).
                                    NYC,January 20,1953

419   Undercurrent blues   PREP1322
420   First with the Most   -
421   Sometimes I'm happy   -
422   Takin' a chance on love   -

423/430:see next page.

ZOOT SIMS QUINTET:
Zoot Sims(ts)Chester Slater(org)Lord Westbrook(g)Peck Morrison(b)Tim
Kennedy(dm).
                                    NYC,January 23,1953

431   There I've said it again   Pr.852,PREP1306
432   Jaguar   -   -
433   Dream   -
434   Baby please come home   -

AL VEGA TRIO:
Al Vega(p)Jack Lawler(b)Jimmy Zitano(dm,bongo).
Supervision:Ira Gitler   Boston,January 26,1953

435   Two sleepy people   PRLP152
436   Speak low   -
437   Autumn serenade   -
438   Sentimental moods   -
439   Carioca   -
440   Mirage in blue   -
441   When Johnny comes marching home -
442   Very Vega   -
443   Lullaby of Birdland   -

CHARLIE MARIANO QUINTET:
Herb Pomeroy(tp)Charlie Mariano(as)Dick Twardzick(p)Bernie Griggs(b)
Jimmy Wisner(dm).
Supervision:Ira Gitler   Boston,January 27,1953

444   Bye bye blues   PRLP153
445   Bess you is my woman   -
446   Barsac   -
447   Stella by starlight   -
448   I'm old fashioned   -
449   Erosong   -

MILES DAVIS:
Miles Davis(tp)Sonny Rollins,Charlie Parker(as "Charlie Chan")(ts)Walter
Bishop(p)Percy Heath(b)Philly Joe Jones(dm).
Supervision:Ira Gitler   NYC,January 30,1953

450	Compulsion	PRLP7044,PR7822,PR24022		
451-1	The serpent's tooth	-	-	-
451-2	The serpent's tooth	-	-	-
452	Round about midnight-1	-	-	-

-1:Rollins & Parker out.

BILLY VALENTINE:
Billy Valentine(vo,p)Mickey Baker(g).
                                          NYC,February 6,1953

453	I wanta love you	Par 1308
454	Sweetheart is you	unissued
455	Let's do the thing	-
456	Gamblin' man	Par 1308

MILES DAVIS ALL STARS PLAY AL COHN:
Miles Davis(tp)Sonny Truitt-1(tb)Al Cohn,Zoot Sims(ts)John Lewis(p)
Leonard Gaskin(b)Kenny Clarke(dm).
Supervision:Ira Gitler   NYC,February 19,1953

423	Tasty pudding	Pr.884,LP154
424	Willie the wailer	-
425	Floppy-1	-
426	For adults only	-

All titles also issued on PRLP7025,LP7168,PR7674,P-24054.

EDDIE JEFFERSON & IRV TAYLOR:
Eddie Jefferson,Irv Taylor(vo)with Seldon Powell(ts)Ed Swanston(p)Peck
Morrison(b)Herbie Lovelle(dm).
                                          NYC,February 20,1953

427	Strictly instrumental	Pr.858,PR7828
428	Old shoes	-
429	Stop talkin',start walkin'	Pr.858 -
430	Be kind to me	-

TEDDY CHARLES WEST COASTERS:
Frank Morgan(as)Wardell Gray(ts)Sonny Clark(p)Teddy Charles(vb)Dick
Nivison(b)Lawrence Marable(dm).
Supervision:Teddy Charles   LA,February 20,1953

467	The man I love	PREP1307
468	Lavonne	-
469	So long Broadway	Pr.889,PREP1307
470	Paul's cause	-

All titles also issued on PRLP7008,PR7343,P-24062.

JOE HOLIDAY BAND:
Idriss Sulieman(tp)Eddie Bert(tb)Earl Warren(as)Joe Holiday(ts)Cecil
Payne(bs)John Acea(p)Franklin Skeete(b)Max Roach(dm).
Supervision:Ira Gitler   NYC,March 4,1953

457	Cotton candy	Pr.871,EP1305,LP191	
458	And now it is love	-	-
459	My funny Valentine	Pr.883	-
460	Martha's harp	Pr.887	-

CHARLIE FERGUSON SEXTET:
Seldon Powell(ts)Charlie Ferguson(bs)Eddie Swanston(p,org)Lord West-
brook(g)John "Peck" Morrison(b)Tim Kennedy(dm).
                                       NYC,March 9,1953
461   Jay walker   unissued
462   Lids for mids   -
463   Hand in hand   -
464   Small talk   -
465   Me and you   -
466   Close out   -

JIMMY RANEY QUINTET:
Stan Getz(as "Sven Coolson")(ts)Hall Overton(p)Jimmy Raney(g)Red
Mitchell(b)Frank Isola(dm).
Supervision:Ira Gitler   NYC,April 23,1953
471   Signal   PRLP156
472   Lee   -
473   Round midnight   -
474   Motion   -

All titles also issued on PRLP7255,PR7434.

BILLY TAYLOR:
Billy Taylor(p)Earl May(b)Charlie Smith(dm)Jose Mangual,Ubaldo Nieto,
Chico Guerrero(bongos,conga).
Supervision:Ira Gitler   NYC,May 7,1953
475   I love the mambo   Pr.869,EP1327
476   Candido   Pr.870   -
477   Early morning mambo   Pr.869   -
478   Mambo azul   Pr.870   -

All titles also issued on PRLP7071.

MILES DAVIS QUARTET:
Miles Davis(tp)John Lewis(p)Percy Heath(b)Max Roach(dm).
Supervision:Ira Gitler   NYC,May 19,1953
479   When lights are low   Pr.902,PR7457,P-24077
480   Tune up   Pr.884   -
481   Miles ahead   Pr.902,PR24012
482   Smooch-1   Pr.884,45-353,PR7352,PR24012

-1:Charlie Mingus(p)replaces Lewis.

All titles also issued on PREP1326,LP161,LP7054,PR7822.

GEORGE WALLINGTON TRIO:
George Wallington(p)Curley Russell(b)Max Roach(dm).
Supervision:Ira Gitler   NYC,May 25,1953
483   Among friends   PRLP158,PR7587
484   My nephew and I   -   -
485   Variations   -   -
486   Squeezers breezers   -   -
487   Cuckoo around the clock   -   -
488   I married an angel   -   -
489   Ours   -   -

TADD DAMERON-A STUDY IN DAMERONIA:
Clifford Brown,Idriss Sulieman(tp)Herb Mullins(tb)Gigi Gryce(as)Benny
Golson(ts)Oscar Estelle(bs)Tadd Dameron(p,arr)Percy Heath(b)Philly Joe
Jones(dm).
Supervision:Ira Gitler   NYC,June 11,1953

490	Philly Joe Jones	PREP1353,LP159,LP7055	
491-1	Choose now		-
491-2	Choose now	PRLP159	-
492	Dial B for beauty	PREP1353,LP159	-
493	Theme of no repeat	-	-

All titles also issued on PR16008,PR7662,ST8301,PR24049.

THE CONTEMPORARY JAZZ ENSEMBLE:
Bob Norden(tp)Bob Silberstein(as)Ed Summerlin(ts)Jim Straney(p)Neil
Courtney(b)Bill Porter(dm).
                                      Rochester,N.Y.,June   ,1953

494	Variation	PRLP163
495	Preluda and jazz	-
496	Prelude:Go forth	-
497	Fantasia and fugue:Poinciana	-
498	All the things you are	-

MODERN JAZZ QUARTET:
Milt Jackson(vb)John Lewis(p)Percy Heath(b)Kenny Clarke(dm).
Supervision:Ira Gitler   NYC,June 25,1953

499	The Queen's fancy	Pr.873,45-174,PR7425	
500	Delaunay's dilemma	Pr.882	-
501	Autumn in New York	-	45-174,PR7421
502	But not for me	Pr.873	-

All titles also issued on PREP1325,LP160,LP7057,PR7749,PR24005.

ART FARMER SEPTET:
Art Farmer(tp)Jimmy Cleveland(tb)Oscar Estelle(as,bs)Clifford Solomon
(ts)Quincy Jones(p,arr)Bill Montgomery(b)Sonny Johnson(dm).
Supervision:Ira Gitler   NYC,July 2,1953

503	Work of Art	PREP1354,LP162,PR24032	
504	The little bandmaster	-	
505	Mau Mau	Pr.875,EP1354,LP162,PR24032	
506	Up in Quincy's room	-	

All titles also issued on PRLP7031,NJLP8278

JAMES "DEACON" WARE:
James "Deacon" Ware(vo)with Gerry Wiggins(p)Red Callender(b)Bill
Douglas(dm).
                                      LA,   1953

507	Poinciana
508	The clon-six-song

TEDDY CHARLES QUARTET:
Shorty Rogers(tp)Teddy Charles(vb,p)Curtis Counce(b)Shelly Manne(dm).
Supervision:Teddy Charles   LA,August 21,1953

515	Wailing dervish	PRLP164,LP7028	
516	Variations on a theme by Bud	-	-
517	Further out	-	-
518	Etudiez le cahier	-	-

TEDDY CHARLES QUINTET-COLLABORATION:
Shorty Rogers(tp)Jimmy Giuffre(cl,ts,bs)Teddy Charles(vb,p)Curtis
Counce(b)Shelly Manne(dm).
Supervision:Teddy Charles   LA,August 31,1953

519	Free	PRLP169,LP7078	
520	Evolution	-	-
521	Margo	-	LP7028
522	Bobalob	-	-

KING PLEASURE:
King Pleasure(vo)with John Lewis(p)Percy Heath(b)Kenny Clarke(dm)Dave
Lambert Singers(vo).
Supervision:Ira Gitler   NYC,September 29,1953

513	Sometimes I'm happy	Pr.860,EP1338	
514	This is always	-	-

Both titles also issued on PRLP208,LP7128,PR7586,PR24017.

SONNY ROLLINS with THE MODERN JAZZ QUARTET:
Sonny Rollins(ts)Milt Jackson(vb)John Lewis(p)Percy Heath(b)Kenny
Clarke(dm).
Supervision:Ira Gitler   NYC,October 7,1953

509	In a sentimental mood	Pr.874,45-284,EP1337		
510	The stopper	-	45-173	-
511	Almost like being in love	Pr.45-284	-	
512	No Moe	PR24004	-	

All titles also issued on PRLP7029,LP7269,PR7856.

BILLY TAYLOR TRIO:
Billy Taylor(p)Earl May(b)Charlie Smith(dm).
Supervision:Ira Gitler   NYC,November 2,1953

523	Cool and caressing	Pr.895,EP1333,LP168,LP7016			
524	Who can I turn to?	Pr.900,EP1336,LP165	-		
525	My one and only love	-	-	-	-
526	Tenderly	PREP1333,LP168	-		
527	I've got the world on a string	Pr.888	-	-	-
528	Bird watcher	Pr.895	-		
529	B.T.'s D.T.'s	PREP1335,LP165	-		
530	Hey lock	-	-	LP7015	

All titles also issued on PRLP16-2.

THELONIOUS MONK QUINTET:
Julius Watkins(frh)Sonny Rollins(ts)Thelonious Monk(p)Percy Heath(b)
Willie Jones(dm).
Supervision:Ira Gitler   NYC,November 13,1953

531	Let's call this	PREP1352,LP166,LP7053,PR24006	
532-1	Think of one	-	PR24046
532-2	Think of one	PREP1352,LP166	-	PR24006
533	Friday the 13th	-	LP7075	-

All titles also issued on PR7751.
PRLP7053=PR7245,PR7363;PRLP7075=LP7169,PR7656.

JOE HOLIDAY:
Joe Holiday(ts)Billy Taylor(p,org)Earl May(b)Charlie Smith(dm,conga)
Ubaldo Nieto(timbales)Jose Mangual(bongo)Machito(maracas).
Supervision:Ira Gitler   NYC,December 9,1953

534	Sleep	Pr.883,LP171	
535	Besame mucho	Pr.878	-
536	I don't want to walk without you	Pr.887	-
537	Fiesta	Pr.878	-

KING PLEASURE:
King Pleasure(vo)with John Lewis(p)Percy Heath(b)Kenny Clarke(dm).
Supervision:Ira Gitler   NYC,December 24,1953

538 Parker's mood   Pr.880,45-182
539 What can I say dear   -   PR24046

Both titles also issued on PRLP208,LP7128,PR7586,PR24017.

BILLY TAYLOR TRIO:
Billy Taylor(p)Earl May(b)Charlie Smith(dm).
Supervision:Ira Gitler   NYC,December 29,1953

540 That's all   Pr.888,EP1351,LP168
541 The little things   Pr.892
542 Nice work if you can get it   -   -   MV33
543 The surrey with the fringe on top   PRLP168

All titles also issued on PREP1334,LP7016,LP16-2.

TEDDY CHARLES/BOB BROOKMEYER QUARTET:
Bob Brookmeyer(vtb)Teddy Charles(vb,p)Teddy Kotick(b)Ed Shaughnessy(dm)
Nancy Overton(vo).
Supervision:Ira Gitler   NYC,January 6,1954

544 Star eyes   Pr.   LP178
545 Nobody's heart voNO   Pr.889 -
546 Revelation   -
547 Loup-garou   -

All titles also issued on PRLP7066,NJ8294.

JAMES MOODY & HIS BAND:
Dave Burns(tp)William Shepherd(tb)James Moody(as,ts-1)Numa "Pee Wee"
Moore(bs)Sadik Hakim(p)John Latham(b)Joe Harris(dm)Eddie Jefferson(vo).
Supervision:Bob Weinstock   NYC,January 8,1954

548 N.J.R.(I'm gone)-1   Pr.881,EP1324,PR24015
549 A hundred years from today   -   -
550 Keepin' up with Jonesy-1   Pr.885 -
551 Workshop voEJ   -   -   PR24015

All titles also issued on PRLP192,LP7072,LP7179,PR7663.

ART FARMER QUINTET:
Art Farmer(tp)Sonny Rollins(ts)Horace Silver(p)Percy Heath(b)Kenny
Clarke(dm).
Supervision:Bob Weinstock   NYC,January 20,1954

552 Wisteria-1   PRLP177
553 Soft shoe   -
554 Confab in tempo   -
555 I'll take romance   -

All titles also issued on NJLP8258,PR7665,PR24032.-1:Rollins out.

MILES DAVIS QUARTET:
Miles Davis(tp)Horace Silver(p)Percy Heath(b)Art Blakey(dm).
Supervision:Bob Weinstock   NYC,March 15,1954

556 Four   Pr.898,P-24052,P-24077
557 That old devilcalled love   -   PR7352   -
558 Blue haze   .   Pr.893,PR24012.

All titles also issued on PREP1360,LP161,LP7054,PR7822

MILES DAVIS QUINTET:
Miles Davis(tp)Dave Schildkraut(as)Horace Silver(p)Percy Heath(b)Kenny
Clarke(dm).
Supervision:Bob Weinstock   NYC,April 3,1954

```
559   Solar                         PRLP185,LP7076,PR7457
560   You don't know what love is-1     -          -      PR7352,45-376
561   Love me or leave me               -          -
562   I'll remember April           PRLP185,LP7054
```

-1:Schildkraut out.

All titles also issued on P-24077.
PRLP7076=PR7608.

JAMES MOODY & HIS BAND:
Dave Burns(tp)William Shepherd(tb)James Moody(as-1,ts-2)Numa "Pee Wee"
Moore(bs)Jimmy Boyd(p)John Latham(b)Joe Harris(dm)Iona Wade(vo).
Supervision:Bob Weinstock   NYC,April 12,1954

```
564   That man o' mine voIW         Pr.890
565   Over the rainbow-1            Pr.896,LP7179
566   Jack raggs-2                      -          -
567   Mambo with Moody-1            Pr.890      -      PR24015
```

All titles also issued on PRLP192,LP7072,PR7663,PREP1369.

Note:Matrix number 563 was not used.

MILES DAVIS ALL STAR SEXTET:
Miles Davis(tp)Jay Jay Johnson(tb)Lucky Thompson(ts)Horace Silver(p)
Percy Heath(b)Kenny Clarke(dm).
Supervision:Bob Weinstock   NYC,April 29,1954

```
568   Blue 'n 'boogie               PREP1358,LP7076
569   Walkin'                       Pr.45-157,EP1357,LP7076,PR7457
```

Both titles also issued on PRLP182,PR7608,P-24077.

THELONIOUS MONK QUINTET:
Ray Copeland(tp)Frank Foster(ts)Thelonious Monk(p)Curley Russell(b)
Art Blakey(dm).
Supervision:Bob Weinstock   NYC,May 11,1954

```
570   Wee see                       PRLP180
571   Smoke gets in your eyes           -
572   Locomotive                        -
573   Hackensack                        -
```

All titles also issued on PRLP7053,PR7245,PR7363,PR7848,PR24006.

ART FARMER QUINTET:
Art Farmer(tp)Gigi Gryce(as)Horace Silver(p)Percy Heath(b)Kenny Clarke
(dm).
Supervision:Bob Weinstock   NYC,May 19,1954

```
574   A night at Toni's             PRLP181,LP7085,PR24032
575   Blue concept                      -          -         -
576   Deltitnu                          -          -
577   Stupendous Lee                    -          -
```

JIMMY RANEY QUARTET:
Hall Overton(p)Jimmy Raney(g)Teddy Kotick(b)Art Mardigan(dm).
Supervision:Bob Weinstock   NYC,May 28,1954

```
578   Minor                         NJEP1701,LP1101
579   Some other Spring                 -          -
580   Double image                  NJEP1702    -
581   On the square                     -          -
```

All titles also issued on PRLP201,LP7089.

ART FARMER SEPTET:
Art Farmer(tp)Jimmy Cleveland(tb)Charlie Rouse(ts)Danny Bank(bs)Horace
Silver(p)Percy Heath(b)Kenny Clarke(dm).
Supervision:Bob Weinstock   NYC,June 7,1954

582	Evening in Paris	Pr.894,LP7031,PR24032	
583	Wildwood	Pr.891	-	-
584	Elephant walk	Pr.894	-	-
585	Tia Juana	Pr.891	-	

PRLP7031=NJLP8278.

MILT JACKSON QUINTET:
Henry Boozier(tp)Milt Jackson(vb)Horace Silver(p)Percy Heath(b)Kenny
Clarke(dm).
Supervision:Bob Weinstock   NYC,June 16,1954

586	Opus de funk	PREP1356,LP183	
587	I've lost your love	PREP1365	-
588	Buhaina	-	-
589	Soma	PREP1356	-

All titles also issued on PRLP7059,PR7655,PR24048.

MILES DAVIS QUINTET:
Miles Davis(tp)Sonny Rollins(ts)Horace Silver(p)Percy Heath(b)Kenny
Clarke(dm).
Supervision:Bob Weinstock   NYC,June 29,1954

590	Airegin	PRLP187,LP7109,PR24012	
591	Oleo	-	-	-
592-1	But not for me	Pr.915,LP187,LP7109,PR24012	
592-2	But not for me	-	P-24077
593	Doxy	PRLP187,LP7109,PR24012	

All titles and takes shown also issued on PR7847,LP16-3.

ZOOT SIMS QUINTET:
Stu Williamson(tp,vtb)Zoot Sims(ts)Kenny Drew(p)Ralph Pena(b)Jimmy
Pratt(dm).
                                         LA,July 16,1954

639	Howdy podner	NJLP1102
640	Toot No.2	-
641	Indian Summer	-
642	What's new?	-

All titles also issued on NJLP8280,PRLP202,P-24061.

BILLY TAYLOR TRIO:
Billy Taylor(p)Earl May(b)Charlie Smith(dm).
Supervision:Bob Weinstock   NYC,July 30,1954

594	Time for Tex	Pr.	LP184,LP7071
595	Moonlight in Vermont		-	-
596	I'll be around		-	-
597	Biddy's beat		-	-
598	Eddie's tune	Pr.904	-	-
599	Mood for Mendes		-	-
600	Goodbye	Pr.904	-	-
601	Lullaby of Birdland		-	-

JIMMY RANEY QUINTET:
John Wilson(tp)Phil Woods(as)Jimmy Raney(g)Bill Crow(b)Joe Morello(dm).
Supervision:Bob Weinstock   NYC,August 11,1954
602   Stella by starlight   NJLP1103
603   Jo-Anne   -
604   Back and blow   -
605   Five   -

All titles also issued on PRLP203,PR7673.

SONNY ROLLINS QUINTET:
Kenny Dorham(tp)Sonny Rollins(ts)Elmo Hope(p)Percy Heath(b)Art Blakey
(dm).
Supervision:Bob Weinstock   NYC,August 18,1954
606   Movin' out   PRLP186
607   Swingin' for Bumsy   -
608   Silk 'n' satin   -
609   Solid   -   PR24004

All titles also issued on PRLP7058,PR7433.

JOE HOLIDAY:
Joe Holiday(ts)Billy Taylor(p)Earl May(b)Charlie Smith(dm).
Supervision:Bob Weinstock   NYC,August 25,1954
610   I love you much   Pr.897,PRLP171
611   Chasin' the bongo   -   -
612   It might as well be Spring   Pr.901   -

BILLY TAYLOR TRIO:
Billy Taylor(p)Earl May(b)Charlie Smith(dm)Candido Camero(conga).
Supervision:Bob Weinstock   NYC,September 7,1954
613   Dectivity   PRLP7051
614   A live one   PREP1344,LP188   -
615   Mambo inn   -   -   -
616   Bit of Bedlam   -
617   Hearing bells   -
618   Love for sale   PRLP188;MV34   -

THELONIOUS MONK TRIO:
Thelonious Monk(p)Percy Heath(b)Art Blakey(dm).
Supervision:Bob Weinstock   NYC,September 22,1954
619   Work   PRLP189,LP7075
620   Nutty   -   -
621   Blue Monk   Pr.45-162,LP189,LP7027
622   Just a gigolo-1   -   -

-1:p solo.

All titles also issued on PR7848,PR24006.
PRLP7075=LP7169,PR7656;PRLP7027=LP7159,PR7508.

JAMES MOODY AND HIS BAND:
Dave Burns(tp)William Shepherd(tb)James Moody(as-1,ts-2)Numa "Pee Wee"
Moore(bs)Jimmy Boyd(p)John Latham(b)Clarence Johnson(dm).
Supervision:Bob Weinstock   NYC,September 29,1954
623-1 It might as well be Spring-2   Pr.903,LP7056
623-2 It might as well be Spring-1   -   -   MV35
624   Blues in the closet-2   PREP1363,LP7072
625   Moody's mood for love-1,2   Pr.899,EP1363,LP7072,PR24015

All titles also issued on PRLP198,LP7179,PR7663.
PRLP7056=PR7554.

PHIL WOODS NEW JAZZ QUINTET:
Jon Eardley(tp)Phil Woods(as)George Syran(p)Teddy Kotick(b)Nick
Stabulas(dm).
Supervision:Bob Weinstock   NYC,October 12,1954

626   Pot pie   PREP1364;NJLP1104
627   Open door   -
628   Robins' bobbin'   -
629   Mad about the girl   PREP1364   -

All titles also issued on PRLP204,NJLP8291.

SONNY ROLLINS QUARTET:
Sonny Rollins(ts)Thelonious Monk(p)Tommy Potter(b)Art Taylor(dm).
Supervision:Bob Weinstock ÷   NYC,October 25,1954

630   I want to be happy   PRLP190,LP7075
631   The way you look tonight   -   -   PR24004
632   More than you know   -   LP7058

PRLP7058=PR7433;PRLP7075=PRLP7169,PR7656.

ART FARMER QUARTET:
Art Farmer(tp)Wynton Kelly(p)Addison Farmer(b)Herbie Lovelle(dm).
Supervision:Bob Weinstock   NYC,November 9,1954

633   I've never been in love before Pr.   LP193,PR24032
634   I'll walk alone   Pr.906   -
635   Gone with the wind   -
636   Alone together   -   PR24032
637   Preamp   -
638   Autumn nocturne   Pr.906   -

All titles also issued on NJLP8258,PR7665.

639/642:see page 27.

GENE AMMONS BAND:
Nat Howard(tp)Henderson Chambers(tb)Gene Ammons(ts)Gene Easton(bs)John
Houston(p)Ben Stuberville(b)George Brown(dm).
Supervision:Bob Weinstock   NYC,November 26,1954

643   Sock   Pr.911,45-403,P-24058
644   What I say   Pr.916   -
645   Count your blessings   Pr.907
646   Cara mia   -

All titles also issued on PR7400.

JUAN TIRADO MAMBO BAND:
Don Elliot(vb)Hector Romero(p)John Drernak(b)Juan Tirado(timbales)
Frank Conlon(bongo)Eleuterio Frasquera(conga).
                                   NYC,December 2,1954

647   Farmer's market mambo   unissued
648   Shake it easy   Pr.909
649   Cha cheando   -
650   All for you   unissued

JAY AND KAI:
Jay Jay Johnson,Kai Winding(tb)Dick Katz(p)Peck Morrison(b)Al Harewood
(dm).
Supervision:Bob Weinstock   NYC,December 3,1954

651   Riviera   PREP1362
652   Dinner for one please James   -
653   Hip bones   -
654   Wind bag   -
655   We'll be together again   PREP1368
656   Don't argue   Pr.919,EP1368
657   How long has this been going on   -   MV33
658   Bags' groove   Pr.919   -

All titles from previous session also issued on PRLP195,LP7030,PR7253,
P-24067,LP16-4.

KING PLEASURE:
King Pleasure(vo)with QUINCY JONES' BAND:Jay Jay Johnson,Kai Winding
(tb)Lucky Thompson(ts)Danny Bank(bs)Jimmy Jones(p)Paul Chambers(b)
Joe Harris(dm)Jon Hendricks,Eddie Jefferson,The Three Riffs(vo)Quincy
Jones(arr,dir).
Supervision:Bob Weinstock   NYC,December 7,1954

659	Don't get scared voKP,JH,EJ	Pr.913,45-124,LP208,LP7128
660	I'm gone voKP,EJ,TR	Pr.908 - -
661	You're crying	-
662	Funk junction	Pr.913

All titles also issued on PR7586,PR24017.

BILLY TAYLOR AT TOWN HALL:
Billy Taylor(p)Earl May(b)Percy Brice(dm).
Supervision:Bob Weinstock   NYC,December 17,1954

663	A foggy day	PRLP194,LP7093
664	I'll remember April	- -
665	Sweet Georgia Brown	- -
666	Theodora	- -
667	How high the moon	- -

All titles also issued on Status ST8313.

MODERN JAZZ QUARTET:
Milt Jackson(vb)John Lewis(p)Percy Heath(b)Kenny Clarke(dm).
Supervision:Bob Weinstock   NYC,December 23,1954

672	I'll remember April	rejected
673	Django	Pr.45-417,EP1370,PR7425
674	One bass hit	-
675	Milano	- PR7425

Last three titles also issued on PRLP170,LP7057,PR7749,PR24005.

MILES DAVIS ALL STARS:
Miles Davis(tp)Milt Jackson(vb)Thelonious Monk(p)Percy Heath(b)Kenny
Clarke(dm).
Supervision:Bob Weinstock   NYC,December 24,1954

676-1	Bags' groove	PRLP196,LP7109,PR7457,PR24012
676-2	Bags' groove	- P-24077
677	Bemsha swing	PRLP200,LP7150 PR24012
678	Swing Spring	PRLP196 - -
679-1	The man I love	PRLP200 - -
679-2	The man I love	- P-24077

All titles also issued on PR7650,LP16-3.

JON EARDLEY QUARTET:
Jon Eardley(tp)Pete Jolly(as "Pete Cera")(p)Red Mitchell(b)Larry Bunker
(dm).
                                        LA,December 25,1954

668	Late leader	NJLP1105;PRLP205
669	Indian Spring	- -
670	Black	- -
671	Cross	- -

TEDDY CHARLES QUARTET:
Teddy Charles(vb,p)J.R.Monterose(ts)Charlie Mingus(b)Jerry Segal(dm).
Supervision:Bob Weinstock   NYC,January 6,1955
680   Violetta   NJLP1106
681   Relaxo abstracto   -
682   Speak low   -
683   Jay walkin'   -
684   The night we called it a day -
685   I can't get started   -

All titles also issued on PRLP206,LP7078.

MODERN JAZZ QUARTET:
Milt Jackson(vb)John Lewis(p)Percy Heath(b)Kenny Clarke(dm).
Supervision:Bob Weinstock   NYC,January 9,1955
686   La ronde(4 part suite)   PRLP170,LP7057,PR7425,PR7749,
                                   PR24005

JAMES MOODY AND HIS BAND:
Dave Burns(tp)William Shepherd(tb)James Moody(as-1,ts-2)Numa "Pee Wee"
Moore(bs)Jimmy Boyd(p)John Latham(b)Clarence Johnson(dm)Eddie Jefferson
(vo).
Supervision:Bob Weinstock   NYC,January 28,1955
687   Nobody knows the trouble-1 Pr.914,LP198,LP7179
688   I got the blues voEJ -2   Pr.917   -   EP1363,PR 4015
689   Blue walk-2   -   -   -
690   Faster James-   Pr.914   -

All titles also issued on PRLP7056,PR7554,PR7663.

PHIL WOODS QUINTET:
Jon Eardley(tp)Phil Woods(as)George Syran(p)Teddy Kotick(b)Nick
Stabulas(dm).
Supervision:Bob Weinstock   NYC,February 4,1955
691   Horse shoe curve   PRLP191
692   Cobblestones   -
693   Sea beach   -
694   Toos bloos   -

All titles also issued on NJLP8291.

GENE AMMONS BAND:
Nat Howard(tp)Henderson Chambers(tb)Gene Ammons(ts)Gene Easton(bs)John
Houston(p)Ben Stuberville(b)George Brown(dm)Earl Coleman(vo).
Supervision:Bob Weinstock   NYC,February 8,1955
694   This is always voEC   Pr.910,P-24058
695   Blues roller   Pr.911   -
696   My last affair voEC   Pr.910
697   Our love is here to stay   Pr.916,P-24058

JIMMY RANEY QUINTET:
John Wilson(tp)Hall Overton(p)Jimmy Raney(g)Teddy Kotick(b)Nick
Stabulas(dm).
Supervision:Bob Weinstock   NYC,February 18,1955
698   Spring is here   PRLP199,LP7089
699   Tomorrow fairly cloudy   -   -
700   What's new?   -   -
701   One more for the mode   -   -

FREDDIE REDD TRIO:
Freddie Redd(p)John Ore(b)Ron Jefferson(dm).
Supervision:Bob Weinstock   NYC,February 28,1955
702   Debut   PRLP197
703   Lady J.Blues   -
704   The things we did last Summer   -
705   Ready Freddie   -

All titles also issued on PRLP7067,Status ST8307.

706:not used.

JIMMY RANEY QUINTET:
John Wilson(tp)Hall Overton(p)Jimmy Raney(g)Teddy Kotick(b)Nick
Stabulas(dm).
Supervision:Bob Weinstock   NYC,March 8,1955
707   A foggy day   PRLP199,LP7089
708   Someone to watch over me   -   -
709   Cross your heart   -   -
710   You don't know what love is   -   -

TONY LUIS TRIO:
Tony Luis(p)Ron Andrews(b)Hank Nanni(dm).
Supervision:Bob Weinstock   NYC,March 10,1955
711   Harvey's house   PREP1373
712   Tunerville Tommy   -
713   What is there to say   -
714   Gone with the wind   -

TERRY MOREL:
Terry Morel(vo)with TONY LUIS TRIO:Tony Luis(p)Ron Andrews(b)Hank Nanni
(dm).
Supervision:Bob Weinstock   NYC,March 10,1955
715   But not for me   PREP1374
716   I remember you   -
717   I can't get started   -
718   Love for sale   -

JON EARDLEY QUINTET:
Jon Eardley(tp)J.R.Monterose(ts)George Syran(p)Teddy Kotick(b)Nick
Stabulas(dm).
Supervision:Bob Weinstock   NYC,March 14,1955
719   Sid's delight   PRLP207
720   Demanton   -
721   If you could see me now   -
722   Hey there   -

BILLY TAYLOR-A TOUCH OF TAYLOR:
Billy Taylor(p)Earl May(b)Percy Brice(dm).
Supervision:Bob Weinstock   NYC,April 10,1955
723   Early bird   PRLP7001
724   A bientôt   -
725   Memories of Spring   -
726   Ever so easy   -
727   Day dreaming   -
728   Radioactivity   -
729   Purple mood   -
730   Long Tom   -
731   A grand night for swingin'   -
732   Blue clouds   -
733   Live it up   -
734   Daddy-O   -

PRLP7001=PR7664.

MILT JACKSON QUARTET:
Milt Jackson(vb)Horace Silver(p)Percy Heath(b)Connie Kay(dm).
Supervision:Bob Weinstock   NYC,May 20,1955

735   Wonder why   Pr.   LP7003
736   I should care   -
737   My funny Valentine   -
738   Stonewall   Pr.45-102   -
739   Moonray   -
740   The nearness of you   -

All titles also issued on PRLP7224,PR7655,PR24048,LP16-1.

ART FARMER QUINTET:
Art Farmer(tp)Gigi Gryce(as)Freddie Redd(p)Addison Farmer(b)Art Taylor
(dm).
Supervision:Bob Weinstock   NYC,May 26,1955

741   Blue lights   PRLP209,LP7085
742   Capri   -   -
743   Infant's song   -   -
744   Social call   -   -

MILES DAVIS-THE MUSINGS OF MILES:
Miles Davis(tp)Red Garland(p)Oscar Pettiford(b)Philly Joe Jones(dm).
Supervision:Bob Weinstock   NYC,June 7,1955

745   I didn't   Pr.   LP7007
746   Will you still be mine?   -   PR7352
747   Green haze   Pr.45-103   -
748   I see your face before me   -   PR7352,MVLP2
749   A night in Tunisia   Pr.45-114   -
750   A gal in calico   -

All titles also issued on PRLP7221,P-24064.

BENNY GREEN SEXTET:
Benny Green(tb)Charlie Rouse(ts)Cliff Smalls(p)Paul Chambers(b)Osie
Johnson(dm)Candido Camero(conga).
Supervision:Bob Weinstock   NYC,June 10,1955

751   Sometimes I'm happy   Pr.918,LP210
752   Laura   -
753   Body and soul   Pr.918   -
754   Say,Jack!   -   PR7776

All titles also issued on PRLP7052,LP7160,P-24067.

GENE AMMONS ALL STARS:
Art Farmer(tp)Lou Donaldson(as)Gene Ammons(ts)Freddie Redd(p)Addison
Farmer(b)Kenny Clarke(dm).
Supervision:Bob Weinstock   NYC,June 16,1955

755   Juggernaut   PRLP211,LP7050,P-24036
756   Woofin' and tweetin'   Pr.45-166,LP211,LP7050

BOB BROOKMEYER QUARTET:
Bob Brookmeyer(vtb,p-1)Jimmy Raney(g)Teddy Kotick(b)Mel Lewis(dm).
Supervision:Bob Weinstock   NYC,June 30,1955

757   Under the lilacs-1   PRLP214
758   Rocky scotch   -
759   Potrezebrie   -
760-1 They say it's wonderful-1   -

All titles also issued on PRLP7066,NJLP8294.

MODERN JAZZ QUARTET-CONCORDE:
Milt Jackson(vb)John Lewis(p)Percy Heath(b)Connie Kay(dm).
Supervision:Bob Weinstock   NYC,July 2,1955

760-2	Ralph's new blues	PR24005		
761	All of you	PR7421;MVLP2,MV34;PR24005		
762	I'll remember April	-		-
763	Gershwin ballad medley:			
	Soon/	PR7421;MV33;PR24005		
	Love walked in/	-		
	Our love is here to stay/	-	PR24005	
	For you,for me,for evermore	-	-	MV33
764	Concorde	PR7425,P-24052		
765	Softly as in a morning sunrise	Pr.45-115,PR7421		

All titles also issued on PRLP7005,LP16-1.

JIM CHAPIN SEXTET:
Don Stratton(tp)Billy Byers(tb)Phil Woods(as)Sonny Truitt(p)Charles
Andrus(b)Jimmy Chapin(dm).
                                  NYC,July   ,1955

766	Sonny's tune	PRLP213
767	In a little Spanish town	-
768	The goof and I	-
769	Cherokee	-

Note:These titles have been purchased.More titles from this session
have been issued on Classic Editions CJ6,but do not belong to Prestige
catalogue.

ELMO HOPE TRIO-MEDITATIONS:
Elmo Hope(p)John Ore(b)Willie Jones(dm).
Supervision:Bob Weinstock   NYC,July 28,1955

770	All the things you are	PRLP7010
771	Ghost of a chance	-
772	Falling in love with love	-
773	Quit it	-
774	Huh	-
775	My heart stood still	-
776	It's a lovely day	-
777	I'm in the mood for love	-
778	Lucky strike	-
779	Blue Moe	-
780	Elmo's fire	-

PRLP7010=PR7675.

MILES DAVIS-MILT & MILES:
Miles Davis(tp)Jackie McLean-1(as)Milt Jackson(vb)Ray Bryant(p)Percy
Heath(b)Art Taylor(dm).
Supervision:Bob Weinstock   NYC,August 5,1955

781	Dr.Jackie-1	PRLP7034
782	Bitty Ditty	-
783	Minor march-1	-
784	Blues changes	-

PRLP7034=PR7540.

JAMES MOODY & HIS BAND:
Dave Burns(tp)William Shepherd(tb)James Moody(as,ts)Numa "Pee Wee" Moore
(bs)Jimmy Boyd(p)John Latham(b)Clarence Johnson(dm)Eddie Jefferson(vo).
Supervision:Bob Weinstock   NYC,August 23,1955

785	There'll never be another you	Pr.	LP7011	
786	Disappointed voEJ	Pr.45-141	-	PR24015
787	Hard to get		-	
788	Little Rocky		-	

All titles also issued on PR7740.

Same.
                                    NYC,August 24,1955

789	Big Ben	PRLP7011
790	Little John	-
791	Show eyes	-
792	And you called my name	-
793	Jammin' with James	PRLP7056,PR24015

All titles also issued on PR7740.

BENNIE GREEN BLOWS HIS HORN:
Bennie Green(tb)Charlie Rouse(ts)Clifton Smalls(p)Paul Chambers(b)
Osie Johnson(dm).
Supervision:Bob Weinstock   NYC,September 22,1955

794-1	Groovin' the blues	Pr.920,LP7052,PR7776		
794-2	Groovin' the blues	-		
795	Travelin' light	-		
796	Hi yo Silver-1	Pr.920	-	PR7776
797	One track	-		

-1:Bennie Green also vocal on this title.
All titles also issued on PRLP7160.

ELMO HOPE/FRANK FOSTER-WAIL,FRANK,WAIL:
Freeman Lee-1(tp)Frank Foster(ts)Elmo Hope(p)John Ore(b)Art Taylor(dm).
Supervision:Bob Weinstock   NYC,October 4,1955

798	Zarou-1	PRLP7021
799	Fosterity-1	-
800	Shout out-1	-
801	Wail,Frank,wail	-
802	Yaho	-
803	Georgia on my mind	-

ART FARMER QUINTET-EVENING IN CASABLANCA:
Art Farmer(tp)Gigi Gryce(as)Duke Jordan(p)Addison Farmer(b)Philly Joe
Jones(dm).
Supervision:Bob Weinstock   NYC,October 21,1955

804	Forecast	PRLP7017,PR24032	
805	Sans souci	-	
806	Evening in Casablanca	-	PR24032
807	Satellite	-	
808	Nica's tempo	-	
809	Shabozz	-	

PRLP7017=NJLP8289.

GENE AMMONS BAND:
Nat Woodyard(tp)Edwin Moore(tb)Gene Ammons(ts)Cecil Payne(bs)Lawrence
Wheatley(p)Ernie Shepard(b)George Brown(dm)Earl Coleman(vo).
Supervision:Bob Weinstock   NYC,November 4,1955

810	Blues for turfers	Pr. PR7400,P-24058
811	Rock-roll	Pr.921,45-403,PR7400,P-24058
812	Ghost of a chance voEC	
813	Haven't changed a thing voEC	Pr.921

MILES DAVIS QUINTET-MILES:
Miles Davis(tp)John Coltrane(ts)Red Garland(p)Paul Chambers(b)Philly
Joe Jones(dm).
Supervision:Bob Weinstock   NYC,November 16,1955

814	Stablemates	Pr.	LP7014	
815	How am I to know?		-	
816	Just squeeze me	Pr.45-268	-	
817	There is no greater love-1		-	PR7352
818	Miles theme(The theme*)		-	PMS100
819	S' posin'	Pr.45-268	-	

-1:Coltrane out.

All titles also issued on PR7254,P-24064*.

PHIL WOODS QUARTET-WOODLORE:
Phil Woods(as)John Williams(p)Teddy Kotick(b)Nick Stabulas(dm).
Supervision:Bob Weinstock   NYC,November 25,1955

820	Be my love	PRLP7018
821	Woodlore	-
822	Falling in love all over again	-
823	Get happy	-
824	Strollin' with Pam	-
825	On a slow boat to China	-

SONNY ROLLINS QUARTET-WORK TIME:
Sonny Rollins(ts)Ray Bryant(p)George Morrow(b)Max Roach(dm).
Supervision:Bob Weinstock   NYC,December 2,1955

826	There's no business like			
	show business	PRLP7020,P-24082		
827	Paradox	-	PR24004	
828	Raincheck	-	P-24082	
829	There are such things	-	-	MVLP2
830	It's alright with me	-	-	

All titles also issued on PRLP7246,PR7750.

JAMES MOODY & HIS BAND:
Dave Burns(tp)William Shepherd(tb)James Moody(as,ts)Numa "Pee Wee" Moore
(bs)Jimmy Boyd(p)John Latham(b)Clarence Johnson(dm).
Supervision:Bob Weinstock   NYC,December 12,1955

831	The golden touch	PRLP7036	
832	The nearness of you	-	
833	The donkey serenade	-	PR24015
834	Moody's blue again	-	
835	The strut	PRLP7056	
836	A sinner kissed an angel	-	
837	Wail Moody wail	PRLP7036,PR24015	

All titles also issued on PR7853.
PRLP7056=PR7554.

THE JON EARDLEY SEVEN:
Jon Eardley(tp)Milt Gold(tb)Phil Woods(as)Zoot Sims(ts)George Syran(p)
Teddy Kotick(b)Nick Stabulas(dm).
Supervision:Bob Weinstock   NYC,January 13,1956

838	Eard's word	PRLP7033
839	Koo Koo	-
840	Ladders	-
841	Leap year	-
842	There's no you	-
843	On the minute	-

PRLP7033=Status ST8309.

GEORGE WALLINGTON-JAZZ FOR THE CARRIAGE TRADE:
Donald Byrd(tp)Phil Woods(as)George Wallington(p)Teddy Kotick(b)Bill
Bradley(dm).
Supervision:Bob Weinstock   NYC,January 20,1956

844   Our delight   PRLP7032
845   Foster Dulles   -
846   Our love is here to stay   -
847   But George   -
848   Together we wail   -
849   What's new   -

JACKIE McLEAN QUINTET-LIGHTS OUT:
Donald Byrd(tp)Jackie McLean(as)Elmo Hope(p)Doug Watkins(b)Art Taylor
(dm).
Supervision:Bob Weinstock   NYC,January 27,1956

850   A foggy day   PRLP7035
851   Kerplunk   -
852   Up   -
853   Lorraine   -
854   Inding   -
855   Lights out   Pr.45-104,LP7035;BVLP1009

All titles also issued on NJLP8263,PR7757,P-24076.

EARL COLEMAN:
Earl Coleman(vo)with Art Farmer(tp)Gigi Gryce(as)hank Jones(p)Oscar
Pettiford( )Shadow Wilson(dm).
Supervision:Bob Weinstock   NYC,March 2,1956

856   No love,no nothing   PRLP7045
857   It's you or no one   -
858   Come rain or come shine   -

TADD DAMERON OCTET-FONTAINEBLEAU:
Kenny Dorham(tp)Henry Coker(tb)Sahib Shihab(as)Joe Alexander(ts)Cecil
Payne(bs)Tadd Dameron(p,arr)John Simmons(b)Shadow Wilson(dm).
Supervision:Bob Weinstock   NYC,March 9,1956

859   Fontainebleau   PRLP7037,PR24049
860   Delirium   -   -
861   Clean is the scene   -   -
862   Flossie Lou   -   -
863   Bullabeige   -

All titles also issued on PR7842,PR16007 and alsoplanned on Status
ST8300(not issued).

MILES DAVIS-COLLECTOR'S ITEMS:
Miles Davis(tp)Sonny Rollins(ts)Tommy Flanagan(p)Paul Chambers(b)Art
Taylor(dm).
Supervision:Bob Weinstock   NYC,March 16,1956

864   In your own sweet way   PRLP7044
865   No line   -
866   Weird blues   -

All titles also issued on PR7847,PR24022.

SONNY ROLLINS PLUS FOUR:
Clifford Brown(tp)Sonny Rollins(ts)Richie Powell(p)George Morrow(b)
Max Roach(dm).
Supervision:Bob Weinstock   NYC,March 22,1956

867   I feel a song comin' on   PRLP7038,P-24050
868   Pent-up house   -   -
869   Valse hot   -   PR24004
870   Kiss and run   -   P-24050
871   Count your blessings-1   -   PR24004

-1:Brown out.

All titles from previous session also issued on PR7291,PR7821.

 BENNIE GREEN & ART FARMER:
Art Farmer(tp)Bennie Green(tb)Clifton Smalls(p)Addison Farmer(b)Philly
Joe Jones(dm).
Supervision:Bob Weinstock   NYC,April 13,1956

872   My blue heaven   PRLP7041
873   Sky coach   -
874   Cliff dweller   -   PR7776
875   Let's stretch   -   -
876   Gone with the wind   -

GIL MELLE QUARTET:
Gil Melle(as,bs)Joe Cinderella(g)Bill Phipps(b)Ed Thigpen(dm).
Supervision:Bob Weinstock   NYC,April 20,1956

877   Adventory swing   PRLP7040
878   Mark one   -
879   Dedicatory blues   -

GENE AMMONS-THE HAPPY BLUES:
Art Farmer(tp)Jackie McLean(as)Gene Ammons(ts)Duke Jordan(p)Addison
Farmer(b)Art Taylor(dm)Candido Camero(conga).
Supervision:Bob Weinstock   NYC,April 23,1956

880   The happy blues   PRLP7039,45-112,P-24036
881   The great lie   -
882   Can't we be friends   -
883   Madhouse   -   P-24036

All titles also issued on PR7654.

ELMO HOPE-INFORMAL JAZZ:
Donald Byrd(tp)John Coltrane,Hank Mobley(ts)Elmo Hope(p)Paul Chambers
(b)Philly Joe Jones(dm).
Supervision:Bob Weinstock   NYC,May 7,1956

884   Weejah   PRLP7043
885   Polka dots and moonbeams   -
886   On it   -
887   Avalon   -

All titles also issued on PR7670,Milestone M47037.

MILES DAVIS NEW QUINTET:
Miles Davis(tp)John Coltrane(ts)Red Garland(p)Paul Chambers(b)Philly
Joe Jones(dm).
Supervision:Bob Weinstock   NYC,May 11,1956

888   In your own sweet way   PRLP7166,PR24034
889   Diane   Pr.45-248,LP7200,PR24034;MV37;
                                  ST8319
890   Trane's blues   PRLP7166,PR24034
891   A dream I had last night-1 PRLP7200,PR7352,PR24034
892   It could happen to you   PRLP7129,PR24001
893   Woody'n you   -   PR7373,PR24001
894   Ahmad's blues-2   PRLP7166,PR7752,PR24034
895   The surrey with the fringe
                        on top   Pr.45-248,LP7200,PR7322,PR24034;
                                  MV32
896   It never entered my mind   Pr.45-165,LP7166,PR7322,PR24034;
                                  MV32
897   When I fall in love-1   Pr.45-195,LP7200,PR7352,PR24034
898   Salt peanuts   -   PR7373   -
899   Four   PRLP7166
900   The theme,I   -   -
901   The theme,II   -   -

[38]

-1:Coltrane out.Issued as "Something I dreamed last night" on PR7352.
-2:Davis & Coltrane out.

PRLP7200=PR7580.

SONNY ROLLINS-TENOR MADNESS:
Sonny Rollins(ts)Red Garland(p)Paul Chambers(b)Philly Joe Jones(dm).
Supervision:Bob Weinstock   NYC,May 24,1956

902   My reverie   PRLP7047
903   The most beautiful girl in
                      the world   -
904   Paul's pal   -
905   When your lover has gone   -   PR24004
906   Tenor madness-1   -   -

-1:John Coltrane(ts)added.

PRLP7047=PR7657.All titles also issued on P-24082.

907:not used.

GIL MELLE QUARTET:
Gil Melle(as,bs)Joe Cinderella(g)Bill Phipps(b)Ed Thigpen(dm).
Supervision:Bob Weinstock   NYC,June 1,1956

908   Dominica   PRLP7040
909   Ballet time   -
910   Iron works   -

EARL COLEMAN:
Earl Coleman(vo)with Art Farmer(tp)Hank Jones(p)Wendell Marshall(b)
Wilbert Hogan(dm).
Supervision:Bob Weinstock   NYC,June 8,1956

911   Social call   PRLP7045
912   Reminiscing   -
913   Say it isn't so   -

PHIL WOODS SEPTET-PAIRING OFF:
Donald Byrd,Kenny Dorham(tp)Phil Woods,Gene Quill(as)Tommy Flanagan(p)
Doug Watkins(b)Philly Joe Jones(dm).
Supervision:Bob Weinstock   NYC,June 15,1956

914   The Stanley stomper   PRLP7046
915   Cool aid   -
916   Pairing off   -
917   Suddenly it's Spring   -

All titles also issued on P-24065.

SONNY ROLLINS QUARTET-SAXOPHONE COLOSSUS:
Sonny Rollins(ts)Tommy Flanagan(p)Doug Watkins(b)Max Roach(dm).
Supervision:Bob Weinstock   NYC,June 22,1956

918   You don't know what love is   Pr.   LP7079
919   St.Thomas   Pr.45-108   -   PR24004
920   Strode rode   -   -
921   Blue seven   -
922   Moritat   Pr.45-173   -

All titles also issued on PR7326,P-24050.

BENNIE GREEN QUINTET:
Bennie Green(tb)Eric Dixon(ts)Lloyd Mayers(p)Sonny Wellesley(b)Bill
English(dm).
Supervision:Bob Weinstock   NYC,June 29,1956

923   East of the little big horn   PRLP7049
924   It's you or no one   -
925   But not for me   -
926   The things we did last Summer   -
927   Walkin' (down)   -   PR7776

JACKIE McLEAN QUINTET:
Donald Byrd(tp)Jackie McLean(as)Mal Waldron(p)Doug Watkins(b)Art
Taylor(dm).
Supervision:Bob Weinstock   NYC,July 13,1956

928   Sentimental journey-1   PRLP7048
929   Why was I born-1   -
930   Contour   -

-1:Byrd out.

All titles also issued on NJLP8279,P-24076.

GENE AMMONS ALL STARS-JAMMIN' WITH GENE:
Donald Byrd,Art Farmer(tp)Jackie McLean(as)Gene Ammons(ts)Mal Waldron
(p)Doug Watkins(b)Art Taylor(dm).
Supervision:Bob Weinstock   NYC,July 13,1956

940   Jammin' with Gene   PRLP7060,PR7306
941   We'll be together again   -
942   Not really the blues   -   P-24036

PRLP7060=PR7781.

JACKIE McLEAN SEXTET:
Donald Byrd-1(tp)Jackie McLean(as)Hank Mobley-1(ts)Mal Waldron(p)Doug
Watkins(b)Art Taylor(dm).
Supervision:Bob Weinstock   NYC,July 20,1956

931   When I fall in love   PRLP7048
932   Abstractions   -
933   Confirmation-1   -

All titles also issued on NJLP8279,P-24076.

HANK MOBLEY-MOBLEY'S MESSAGE:
Donald Byrd(tp)Jackie McLean-1(as)Hank Mobley(ts)Barry Harris(p)Doug
Watkins(b)Art Taylor(dm).
Supervision:Bob Weinstock   NYC,July 20,1956

934   Bouncing with Bud   PRLP7061
935   52nd Street scene   -
936   Au privave-1   -
937   Minor disturbance   -
938   Little girl blue-2   -
939   Alternating current   -

-2:Byrd out.

All titles also issued on PR7661,ST8311,P-24063.

943:not used.

HANK MOBLEY'S SECOND MESSAGE:
Kenny Dorham(tp)Hank Mobley(ts)Walter Bishop(p)Doug Watkins(b)Art
Taylor(dm).
Supervision:Bob Weinstock   NYC,July 27,1956

944   These are the things I love-1   PRLP7082
945   Message from the border   -
946   The latest   -
947   Xlento   -
948   I should care   -
949   Crazeology   -

-1:Dorham out.

All titles also issued on PR7667,P-24063.

TWO TRUMPETS:
Art Farmer,Donald Byrd(tp)Jackie McLean(as)Barry Harris(p)Doug Watkins
(b)Art Taylor(dm).
Supervision:Bob Weinstock   NYC,August 3,1956

950   The third   PRLP7062
951   Contour   -
952   When your lover has gone-1   -   MVLP2
953   Round about midnight-2   -
954   Dig   -

-1:Byrd & McLean out;-2:Farmer & McLean out.

All titles also issued on PR7344,P-24066.

GIL MELLE-GIL'S GUESTS:
Art Farmer(tp)Hal McKusick(as,fl)Gil Melle(bs)Julius Watkins(frh)Joe
Cinderella(g)Vinnie Burke(b)Ed Thigpen(dm).
Supervision:Bob Weinstock   NYC,August 10,1956

955   Black Island   PRLP7063
956   Tomorrow   -
957   Soudan   -

RED GARLAND-A GARLAND OF RED:
Red Garland(p)Paul Chambers(b)Art Taylor(dm).
Supervision:Bob Weinstock   NYC,August 17,1956

958   A foggy day   PRLP7064;MV33
959   My romance   -
960   What is this thing called love   -   MV34
961   Makin' whoopee   -   45-143
962   September in the rain   -
963   Little girl blue   -
964   Blue Red   -   45-105
965   Constellation   -

GIL MELLE-GIL'S GUESTS:
Kenny Dorham(tp)Hal McKusick(as,fl)Gil Melle(bs)Don Butterfield(tu)Joe
Cinderella(g)Vinnie Burke(b)Ed Thigpen(dm).
Supervision:Bob Weinstock   NYC,August 24,1956

966   Still life   PRLP7063
967   Sixpence   -
968   Ghengis   -

ALL NIGHT LONG:
Donald Byrd(tp)Hank Mobley(ts)Jerome Richardson(ts,fl)Mal Waldron(p)
Kenny Burrell(g)Doug Watkins(b)Art Taylor(dm).
Supervision:Bob Weinstock   NYC,December 28,1956

1044	Flickers	PRLP7073,PR24025
1045	Boo-Lu	- -
1046	Li'l Hankie	- -
1047	Medley:Body and soul/	ST8317;PR7448
	Tune up	-
1048	All night long	PRLP7073,PR7313,PR24025

PRLP7073=LP7289.

Note:Medley(1047) was later divided and the two tracks issued as
separate entities.

ALL DAY LONG:
Donald Byrd(tp)Frank Foster(ts,fl)Tommy Flanagan(p)Kenny Burrell(g)
Doug Watkins(b)Art Taylor(dm).
Supervision:Bob Weinstock   NYC,January 4,1957

1049	C.P.W.	PR7448;ST8317	
1050	Slim Jim	PRLP7081,PR24025	
1051	Say listen	- -	
1052	A.T.	- -	
1053	All day long	- -	PR7298;BVLP1009

PRLP7081=PR7277.

GENE AMMONS ALL STARS-FUNKY:
Art Farmer(tp)Jackie McLean(as)Gene Ammons(ts)Mal Waldron(p)Kenny
Burrell(g)Doug Watkins(b)Art Taylor(dm).
Supervision:Bob Weinstock   NYC,January 11,1957

1054	Pint size	PRLP7083	
1055	King size	-	
1056	Funky	-	PR7306,P-24036
1057	Stella by starlight	-	-

GIL MELLE:
Donald Byrd(tp)Phil Woods(as)Gil Melle(bs)Joe Cinderella(g)Vinnie Burke
(b)Ed Thigpen(dm).
Supervision:Bob Weinstock   NYC,January 18,1957

1058	Funk for star people	unissued
1059	Golden age	-
1060	Herbie	-

EARTHY:
Art Farmer(tp)Hal McKusick(as)Al Cohn(ts)Mal Waldron(p)Kenny Burrell(g)
Teddy Kotick(b)Ed Thigpen(dm).
Supervision:Bob Weinstock   NYC,January 25,1957

1061	Earthy	PRLP7102
1062	What's not	-
1063	I wouldn't	-
1064	The front line	-
1065	Dayee	-

THREE TRUMPETS:
Donald Byrd,Idriss Sulieman,Art Farmer(tp)Hod O'Brien(p)Addison Farmer
(b)Ed Thigpen(dm).
Supervision:Bob Weinstock   NYC,January 26,1957

1066	Palm Court Alley	PRLP7092
1067	Who's who?	-
1068	Diffusion of beauty	-
1069	Forty quarters	-
1070	You gotta dig it	-

All titles also issued on PR7344.

JACKIE McLEAN-JACKIE'S PAL:
Bill Hardman(tp)Jackie McLean(as)Mal Waldron(p)Paul Chambers(b)Philly
Joe Jones(dm).
Supervision:Bob Weinstock   NYC,August 31,1956

969   Sweet doll   PRLP7068
970   Just for Marty   -
971   Dee's dilemma   -
972   It could happen to you-1   -
973   Su-blues   -
974   Steeplechase   -

-1:McLean out.

PRLP7068=NJLP8290.

TENOR CONCLAVE:
Hank Mobley,Al Cohn,Zoot Sims,John Coltrane(ts)Red Garland(p)Paul
Chambers(b)Art Taylor(dm).
Supervision:Bob Weinstock   NYC,September 7,1956

975   Just you,just me   PRLP7074,P-24084
976   Tenor conclave   -   -
977   How deep is the ocean   -   -
978   Bob's boys   -

PRLP7074=PR7249.

BLIND WILLIE McTELL LAST SESSION:
Blind Willie McTell(vo,g).
                                         Atlanta,September   ,1956

      Baby it must be love   BVLP1040
      Dying crapshooters blues   -
      Pal of mine   -
      Don't forget it   -
      Kill it Kid   -
      That will never happen no more   -
      My blue heaven   unissued
      Beedle Um bum   BVLP1040,BV1055
      A married man's a fool   -
      A to Z blues   -
      Goodbye blues   unissued
      Basin Street blues   -
      Salty dog   BVLP1040
      Wabash cannonball   -
      St.James infirmary   unissued
      If I had wings   -
      untitled instrumental blues   -
      Easy life   BVLP1040

BVLP1040=PR7809.

SONNY ROLLINS PLAYS FOR BIRD:
Kenny Dorham(tp)Sonny Rollins(ts)Wade Legge(p)George Morrow(b)Max Roach
(dm).
Supervision:Bob Weinstock   NYC,October 5,1956

979   I've grown accustomed to her
                          face-1   PRLP7095,ST8315,P-24050
980   Kids know   -   -
981   The house I live in   PRLP7207   -
982   Bird medley:
         I remember you-1/   PRLP7095
         Star eyes/   -   P-24050
         My melancholy baby/   -
         They can't take that away
                          from me-1/   -   45-128;MV33
         Old folks-2/   -
(continued on next page)

```
        Just friends-2/                    PRLP7095
        My little Suede shoes-2            -
-1:Dorham out;-2:Rollins out.

All titles also issued on PR7553.

BARBARA LEA:
Barbara Lea(vo)with Johnny Windhurst(tp)Dick Cary (alto horn)Richard
Lowman(p)Al Hall(b)Osie Johnson(dm).
Supervision:Bob Weinstock            NYC,October 18,1956

983    Baltimore oriole               PRLP7065
984    I had myself a true love       -
985    Nobody else but me             -
986    Thursday's child               -

BARBARA LEA:
Barbara Lea(vo)with Johnny Windhurst(tp)Dick Cary (alto horn-1,p)Al
Casamenti(g)Al Hall(b)Osie Johnson(dm).
Supervision:Bob Weinstock            NYC,October 19,1956

987    My honey's lovin' arms-1       PRLP7065
988    I've got a pocket full         -
989    Where have you been?           -
990    I'm comin' Virginia            -
991    Honey in the honeycomb         -
992    Gee baby ain't I good to you-2 -
993    I feel at home with you        -
994    Blue skies-1                   -

-2:Windhurst out.

MILES DAVIS QUINTET:
Miles Davis(tp)John Coltrane(ts)Red Garland(p)Paul Chambers(b)Philly
Joe Jones(dm).
Supervision:Bob Weinstock            NYC,October 26,1956

995    If I were a bell               PRLP7129,45-123,PR24001,PR7457
996    Well,you needn't               PRLP7200,PR7373,PR24034
997    Round about midnight           Pr.45-413,LP7150,PR7373,PR24012
998    Half Nelson                    PRLP7166,PR24034
999    You're my everything           PRLP7129,PR7373,PR24001
1000   I could write a book           Pr.45-413,LP7129,PR7322,PR24001;
                                       MV32
1001   Oleo                           Pr.45-395,LP7129,PR7373,PR24001
1002   Airegin                        PRLP7094,PR7373,PR24001
1003   Tune up                        Pr.45-395,LP7094,PR7373,PR24001
1004   When lights are low            PRLP7094,PR24001
1005   Blues by five                  -         -
1006   My funny Valentine-1           Pr.45-353,LP7094,PR7322,PR24001;
                                       MV32

PRLP7200=PR7580.

THE YOUNG BLOODS:
Donald Byrd(tp)Phil Woods(as)Al Haig(p)Teddy Kotick(b)Charlie Persip(dm)
Supervision:Bob Weinstock            NYC,November 2,1956

1007   Once more                      PRLP7080
1008   House of Chan                  -
1009   In walked George               -
1010   Lover man                      -
1011   Dewey Square                   -
1012   Dupeltook                      -

All titles also issued on P-24066.
```

MAL WALDRON QUINTET-MAL 1:
Idriss Sulieman(tp)Gigi Gryce(as)Mal Waldron(p)Julian Euell(b)Arthur
Edgehill(dm).
Supervision:Bob Weinstock   NYC,November 9,1956

1013   Shome   PRLP7090
1014   Transfiguration   -
1015   Dee's dilemma   -
1016   Stablemates   -
1017   Bud study   -
1018   Yesterdays   -

All titles also issued on P-24068.

ART FARMER-FARMER'S MARKET:
Art Farmer(tp)Hank Mobley(ts)Kenny Drew(p)Addison Farmer(b)Elvin Jones
(dm).
Supervision:Bob Weinstock   NYC,November 23,1956

1019   Reminiscing-1   NJLP8203
1020   By myself-1   -
1021   Wailin' with Hank   -
1022   Ad-dis-un   -
1023   Farmer's market   -   PR24032
1024   With Prestige   -   -

TADD DAMERON QUARTET-MATING CALL:
John Coltrane(ts)Tadd Dameron(p)John Simmons(b)Philly Joe Jones(dm).
Supervision:Bob Weinstock   NYC,November 30,1956

1025   Mating call   PRLP7070
1026   Soultrane   -
1027   Gnid   -
1028   Super jet   -
1029   On a misty night   -   PR7426
1030   Romas   -

PRLP7070=LP7247,PR7745.All titles also issued on P-24084.

SONNY ROLLINS-TOUR DE FORCE:
Sonny Rollins(ts)Kenny Drew(p)George Morrow(b)Max Roach(dm)Earl Coleman
(vo).
Supervision:Bob Weinstock   NYC,December 7,1956

1031   B.Swift   PRLP7126,LP7207,P-24082
1032   My ideal voEC   -   PR24046
1033   Sonny boy   PRLP7207,P-24082
1034   Two different worlds voEC   PRLP7126
1035   Ee-ah   Pr.45-128,LP7126,LP7207,P-24082
1036   B.Quick   -   -   -   -

JACKIE McLEAN-McLEAN'S SCENE:
Bill Hardman(tp)Jackie McLean(as)Red Garland(p)Paul Chambers(b)Art
Taylor(dm).
Supervision:Bob Weinstock   NYC,December 14,1956

1037   Gone with the wind   NJLP8212
1038   McLean's scene   -
1039   Mean to me   -

RED GARLAND TRIO:
Red Garland(p)Paul Chambers(b)Art Taylor(dm).
Supervision:Bob Weinstock   NYC,December 14,1956

1040   Willow weep for me   PRLP7113
1041   If I were a bell   PRLP7086
1042   I know why   -
1043   What can I say dear   PRLP7113

KENNY BURRELL-BLUE MOODS:
Cecil Payne(bs)Tommy Flanagan(p)Kenny Burrell(g)Doug Watkins(b)Elvin
Jones(dm).
Supervision:Bob Weinstock   NYC,February 1,1957

1071	Perceptions	PRLP7088
1072	Carol-1	unissued
1073	Drum boogie	Pr.45-308,LP7088
1074	Kenny's sound	unissued
1075	All of you-1	PRLP7088
1076	Strictly confidential	-
1077	Don't cry baby	Pr.45-110,45-308,LP7088

PRLP7088=PR7308.   -1:Payne out.

JACKIE McLEAN SEXTET:
Bill Hardman(tp)Ray Draper(tu)Jackie McLean(as)Mal Waldron(p)Doug
Watkins(b)Art Taylor(dm).
Supervision:Bob Weinstock   NYC,February 8,1957

1078	Flickers	PRLP7087
1079	Help	-
1080	Minor dream	-
1081	Beau Jack-1	-
1082	Mirega-1	-

-1:Draper out.

PRLP7087=Status ST8323.

FOUR ALTOS:
Phil Woods,Sahib Shihab,Gene Quill,Hal Stein(as)Mal Waldron(p)Tommy
Potter(b)Louis Hayes(dm).
Supervision:Bob Weinstock   NYC,February 9,1957

1083	Pedal eyes	PRLP7116
1084	Kokochee	-
1085	No more nights	-
1086	Kinda kanonic	-
1087	Staggers	-
1088	Don't blame me	-

JACKIE McLEAN QUARTET:
Jackie McLean(as)Mal Waldron(p)Arthur Phipps(b)Art Taylor(dm).
Supervision:Bob Weinstock   NYC,February 15,1957

1089	I hear a rhapsody	NJLP8231
1090	Embraceable you	NJLP8253
1091	I never knew	NJLP8231
1092	These foolish things	NJLP8253
1093	Our love is here to stay	NJLP8212
1094	I cover the waterfront	NJLP8253
1095	What's new	NJLP8231
1096	Old folks	NJLP8212
1097	Bean and the boys	NJLP8231
1098	Strange blues	PR7500
1099	Outburst	NJLP8212

OLIO:
Thad Jones(tp)Frank Wess(ts,fl)Teddy Charles(vb)Mal Waldron(p)Doug
Watkins(b)Elvin Jones(dm).
Supervision:Teddy Charles   NYC,February 16,1957

1100	Touché	PRLP7084
1101	Pot pourri	-
1102	Blues without Woe	-
1103	Hello Frisco	-
1104	Dakar	-
1105	Embraceable you	-

PRLP7084=Status ST8310.

[46]

ART TAYLOR-TAYLOR'S WAILERS:
Donald Byrd(tp)Jackie McLean(as)Charlie Rouse(ts)Ray Bryant(p)Wendell
Marshall(b)Art Taylor(dm).
Supervision:Bob Weinstock   NYC,February 25,1957

1106	Exhibit A	PRLP7117,PR7342
1107	Cubano chant	- -
1108	Well you needn't	- -
1109	Batland	- -
1110	Off minor	- -
1111	Drum solo	unissued

GEORGE WALLINGTON QUINTET-THE NEW YORK SCENE:
Donald Byrd(tp)Phil Woods(as)George Wallington(p)Teddy Kotick(b)Nick
Stabulas(dm).
Supervision:Bob Weinstock   NYC,March 1,1957

1112	In Salah	PRLP16-5
1113	Up children reel	-
1114	Graduation day-1	-
1115	Indian Summer	-
1116	Dis mornin'	-
1117	Sol's Ollie	-

-1:Byrd & Woods out.

All titles also issued on NJLP8207.

TWO GUITARS:
Donald Byrd(tp)Jackie McLean(as)Mal Waldron(p)Jimmy Raney,Kenny Burrell
(g)Doug Watkins(b)Art Taylor(dm).
Supervision:Bob Weinstock   NYC,March 5,1957

1118	Dead heat	PRLP7119
1119	Blue Duke	-
1120	Pivot	-
1121	This way	-
1122	Little Melonae	-
1123	Close your eyes-1	-
1124	Out of nowhere-2	-

-1:Kenny Burrell(g)with p,b,dm only;-2:Jimmy Raney(g)with p,b,dm only.

MOSE ALLISON-BACK COUNTRY SUITE:
Mose Allison(p,vo)Taylor LaFargue(b)Frank Isola(dm).
Supervision:Bob Weinstock   NYC,March 7,1957

1125	New ground	Pr.45-111,LP7091	
1126	Train	-	
1127	Warm night	Pr.45-111 -	
1128	Blues(A young man)	-	PR7279,PR10052
1129	Saturday	-	
1130	Scamper	-	
1131	January	-	
1132	Promised land	-	
1133	Spring song	-	
1134	Highway 49	-	
1135	I thought about you	-	PR7446
1136	In Salah	-	
1137	You won't let me go	-	
1138	One room country shack	Pr.45-111 -	PR7279,PR10052
1139	Blueberry hill	-	

All titles also issued on PR24002.

Note:Back country suite is made of masters 1125/1134 inclusively.

BOBBY JASPAR-FLUTE FLIGHT:
Bobby Jaspar(fl)Tommy Flanagan(p)Doug Watkins(b)Bobby Donaldson(dm).
Supervision:Ozzie Cadena   NYC,March 12,1957

1140   Solacium   PRLP7124
1141   Flute bass blues   -
1142   Flute Bob   -

RAY DRAPER QUINTET:
Webster Young(tp)Jackie McLean(as)Ray Draper(tu)Mal Waldron(p)Spanky
DeBrest(b)Ben Dixon(dm).
Supervision:Bob Weinstock   NYC,March 15,1957

1143   House of Davis   PRLP7096
1144   Terry Ann   -
1145   You're my thrill   -
1146   Pivot   -
1147   Jackie's dolly   -
1148   Mimi's interlude   -

HERBIE MANN/BOBBY JASPAR:
Herbie Mann,Bobby Jaspar(ts,fl)Tommy Flanagan(p)Joe Puma(g)Wendell
Marshall(b)Bobby Donaldson(dm).
Supervision:Ozzie Cadena   NYC,March 21,1957

1149   Chasin' the bird   PRLP7101,PR7432
1150   Budo   PRLP7124   -
1151   Somewhere else   PRLP7101
1152   Let's march   Pr.45-113,PRLP7101
1153   Tel Aviv   -   PR7432
1154   Tuttie fluttie   Pr.45-416,PRLP7124   -

RED GARLAND'S PIANO:
Red Garland(p)Paul Chambers(b)Art Taylor(dm).
Supervision:Bob Weinstock   NYC,March 22,1957

1155   Please send me someone to love Pr.45-109,LP7086
1156   The very thought of you   -
1157   Stomping at the Savoy   Pr.45-151   -
1158   Almost like being in love   -
1159   Strike up the band   rejected
1160   I can't give you anything
                       but love   PRLP7086
1161   Why was I born   PR7752
1162   But not for me   PRLP7086

INTERPLAY:
Idriss Sulieman,Webster Young(tp)John Coltrane,Bobby Jaspar(ts)Mal
Waldron(p)Kenny Burrell(g)Paul Chambers(b)Art Taylor(dm).
Supervision:Bob Weinstock   NYC,March 22,1957

1163   Anatomy   PRLP7112,PR7341
1164   Interplay   -   -
1165   Light blue   -   -
1166   Soul eyes   -   -
1167   C.T.A.-1   PRLP7117,LP7229,PR7342

-1:John Coltrane(ts) with p,b,dm only.

PHIL & QUILL:
Phil Woods,Gene Quill(as)George Syran(p)Teddy Kotick(b)Nick Stabulas(dm).
Supervision:Bob Weinstock   NYC,March 29,1957

1168	Creme de funk	PRLP7115,P-24065	
1169	Lazy like	-	-
1170	Nothing but soul	-	-
1171	A night at St.Nicks	-	-
1172	Black cherry fritters	-	-
1173	Altology	-	-
1174	Airegin	NJLP8204	-
1175	Solar	-	

RAY BRYANT TRIO:
Ray Bryant(p)Ike Isaacs(b)Specs Wright(dm).
Supervision:Bob Weinstock   NYC,April 5,1957

1176	Django	PRLP7098
1177	Splittin'	-
1178	Daahoud	-
1179	Sonar	-
1180	The thrill is gone	-
1181	Golden earrings	-
1182	Angel eyes	-
1183	Blues changes	-

All titles also issued on NJLP8227,P-24038.

JAMMIN' IN HI-FI WITH GENE AMMONS:
Idriss Sulieman(tp)Jackie McLean(as)Gene Ammons(ts)Mal Waldron(p)Kenny
Burrell(g)Paul Chambers(b)Art Taylor(dm).
Supervision:Bob Weinstock   NYC,April 12,1957

1184	The twister	PRLP7110,PR7306	
1185	Cattin'	-	
1186	Pennies from heaven	-	P-24036
1187	Four	-	-

PRLP7110=PRLP7176.

COOLIN':
Idriss Sulieman(tp)John Jenkins(as)Teddy Charles(vb)Mal Waldron(p)
Addison Farmer(b)Jerry Segal(dm).
Supervision:Teddy Charles   NYC,April 14,1957

1188	The eagle flies	NJLP8216
1189	Bunin	-
1190	Reiteration	-
1191	Song of a star	-
1192	Staggers	-
1193	Everything happens to me-1	-

-1:Jenkins out.

THE CATS:
Idriss Sulieman(tp)John Coltrane(ts)Tommy Flanagan(p)Kenny Burrell(g)
Doug Watkins(b)Louis Hayes(dm).
Supervision:Bob Weinstock   NYC,April 18,1957

1194	Eclypso	NJLP8217
1195	Solacium	-
1196	Minor mishap	-
1197	How long has this been going on-1	-
1198	Tommy's time	-

-1:p,b,dm only.

All titles also issued on P-24059.

MAL WALDRON-MAL 2:
Bill Hardman(tp)Jackie McLean(as)John Coltrane(ts)Mal Waldron(p)Julian
Euell(b)Art Taylor(dm).
Supervision:Bob Weinstock   NYC,April 19,1957

1199	Pot pourri	PRLP7111,PR7341,P-24068
1200	J.M.'s dream doll	- - -
1201	Don't explain	- - -
1202	Blue calypso	ST8316;PR24046,P-24069
1203	Falling in love with love	- -

BARBARA LEA:
Barbara Lea(vo)with Dick Cary (p)Al Casamenti(g)Al Hall(b).
                                          NYC,April 19,1957

1204	Will I find my love today	PRLP7100
1205	Aren't you glad you're you	unissued
1206	Autumn leaves	PRLP7100
1207	Ain't misbehavin'	-

DAKAR:
John Coltrane(ts)Cecil Payne(bs)Pepper Adams(bs)Mal Waldron(p)Doug
Watkins(b)Art Taylor(dm).
Supervision:Teddy Charles   NYC,April 20,1957

1208	Dakar	PRLP16-6,PR7313,45-315
1209	Mary's blues	-
1210	Route 4	-
1211	Velvet scene	-
1212	Witches pit	-
1213	Cat walk	-

All titles also issued on PR7280.

BARBARA LEA:
Barbara Lea(vo)with Dick Cary (alto horn)Ernie Caceres(bs)Garvin
Bushell(bassoon)Jimmy Lyon(p,celeste)Jimmy Raney(g)Beverly Peer(b)
Osie Johnson(dm).
Supervision:Bob Mantler   NYC,April 24,1957

1214	Sleep peaceful,Mr.Used-to-be	PRLP7100
1215	I'm old fashioned	unissued
1216	The very thought of you	PRLP7100
1217	I've got my eyes on you	-

GIL MELLE QUARTET:
Gil Melle(bs)Joe Cinderella(g)George Duvivier(b)Shadow Wilson(dm).
Supervision:Bob Weinstock   NYC,April 26,1957

1218	Walter ego	PRLP7097
1219	Jacqueline	-
1220	It don't mean a thing	-
1221	Full house	-
1222	Quadrama	-
1223	In a sentimental mood	-
1224	Rush hour in Hong Kong	-

BARBARA LEA:
Barbara Lea(vo)with Johnny Windhurst(tp)Dick Cary (p,alto horn)Ernie
Caceres(bs,cl)Al Casamenti(g)Al Hall(b)Osie Johnson(dm).
Supervision:Bob Mantler   NYC,April 26,1957

We could make such beautiful things	PRLP7100	
Am I in love?	-	
Mountain greenery	-	45-101
More than you know	-	

Note:Matrix numbers for above titles are 1225/1228,but order remains
unknown.

TEO MACERO with THE PRESTIGE JAZZ QUARTET:
Teo Macero(ts)Teddy Charles(vb)Mal Waldron(p)Addison Farmer(b)Jerry
Segal(dm).
Supervision:Teddy Charles   NYC,April 27,1957

1229	Ghost story	PRLP7104
1230	Please don't go	–
1231	Just Spring	–
1232	Star eyes	–
1233	Polody	–
1234	What's not	–

BARBARA LEA:
Barbara Lea(vo)with Johnny Windhurst(tp)Dick Cary (alto horn)Jimmy
Lyon(p)Jimmy Raney(g)Beverly Peer(b).
Supervision:Bob Mantler   NYC,May 1,1957

You'd be so nice	PRLP7100
True love	–
A straw hat full of lilacs	Pr.45-101
unknown title	unissued
unknown title	–

Note:Matrix numbers for above titles are 1235/1239,but order remains
unknown.

ALTO MADNESS:
Jackie McLean,John Jenkins(as)Wade Legge(p)Doug Watkins(b)Art Taylor
(dm).
Supervision:Bob Weinstock   NYC,May 3,1957

1240	Bird feathers	NJLP8204
1241	Easy living	PRLP7114
1242	Windy city	–
1243	Pondering	–
1244	The lady is a tramp	–
1245	Alto madness	–

PRLP7114=NJLP8312.

KENNY BURRELL-BARRY GALBRAITH:
Kenny Burrell,Barry Galbraith(g)Leonard Gaskin(b)Bobby Donaldson(dm).
Supervision:Ozzie Cadena   NYC,May 10,1957

1246	Billie's bounce	ST8318;PR7448	
1247	Prelude to a kiss	–	–
1248	It don't mean a thing	–	–
1249	unknown title	rejected	

PAUL QUINICHETTE'S NEW STARS:
Curtis Fuller(tb)Sonny Red,John Jenkins(as)Paul Quinichette(ts)Mal
Waldron(p)Doug Watkins(b)Ed Thigpen(dm).
Supervision:Bob Weinstock   NYC,May 10,1957

1250	Circles-1	PRLP7103
1251	Blue dots	Pr.45-106,LP7103
1252	Sunny side of the street-2	–
1253	My funny Valentine	unissued
1254	Cool-lypso	PRLP7103

-1:Jenkins out;-2:Red & Fuller out.

CURTIS FULLER QUINTET:
Curtis Fuller(tb)Sonny Red(as)Hank Jones(p)Doug Watkins(b)Louis Hayes
(dm).
Supervision:Bob Weinstock   NYC,May 11,1957

1255	Transportation blues	PRLP7107
1256	Young number five	–
1257	Blue Lawson	–
1258	Alicia	ST8317
1259	What is this thing called love	PRLP7107
1260	Namely you	–

CURTIS FULLER with RED GARLAND:
Curtis Fuller(tb)Sonny Red(as)Red Garland(p)Paul Chambers(b)Louis Hayes
(dm).
Supervision:Bob Weinstock   NYC,May 14,1957

1261   Cinderella   NJLP8277
1262   Cashmere   -
1263   Moonlight becomes you   -
1264   Stormy weather   -
1265   Seeing Red   -
1266   Roc and Troll   -

MAL WALDRON-MAL 2:
Idriss Sulieman(tp)Sahib Shihab(as,bs)John Coltrane(ts)Mal Waldron(p)
Julian Euell(b)Ed Thigpen(dm).
Supervision:Bob Weinstock   NYC,May 17,1957

1267   The way you look tonight   PRLP7111,PMS100
1268   From this moment on   -
1269   One by one   -

All titles also issued on PR7341,P-24068.

CATTIN' WITH JOHN COLTRANE AND PAUL QUINICHETTE:
John Coltrane,Paul Quinichette(ts)Mal Waldron(p)Julian Euell(b)Ed
Thigpen(dm).
Supervision:Bob Weinstock   NYC,May 17,1957

1270   Cattin'   PRLP7158
1271   Anatomy   -
1272   Vodka   -
1273   Sunday   -
1274   Tea for two-1   ST8317
1275   Exactly like you   PRLP7158

-1:Coltrane out.

CURTIS FULLER AND HAMPTON HAWES with FRENCH HORNS:
Julius Watkins,Dave Amram(frh)Curtis Fuller(tb)Sahib Shihab(as)Hampton
Hawes(p)Addison Farmer(b)Jerry Segal(dm).
Supervision:Teddy Charles   NYC,May 18,1957

1276   Ronnie's tune   PRLP16-5
1277   Roc and Troll   -
1278   A-drift   -
1279   Lyriste-1   -
1280   Five Spot   -
1281   No crooks   -

-1:Teddy Charles(p)replaces Hawes.

All titles also issued on Status ST8305.

1282/1283:not used.

RED GARLAND TRIO:
Red Garland(p)Kenny Burrell-1(g)Paul Chambers(b)Art Taylor(dm).
Supervision:Bob Weinstock   NYC,May 24,1957

1284   Billy boy   Pr.45-125,PR7658,P-24052
1285   It could happen to you   -
1286   Four-1   -
1287   Walkin' -1   -
1288   You keep comin' back like a song   -
1289   Everybody's somebody's fool   -
1290   The masquerade is over   -
1291   Hey now   Pr.45-125,LP7113,PR7658

JOHN COLTRANE:
Johnny Splawn(tp)John Coltrane(ts)Sahib Shihab(bs)Mal Waldron(p)Paul
Chambers(b)Albert Heath(dm).
Supervision:Bob Weinstock   NYC,May 31,1957

1292   Straight street   PRLP7105
1293   While my lady sleeps-1   -   MVLP2
1294   Chronic blues   -

-1:Shihab out.

Red Garland(p)replaces Maldron.Same date.

1295   Bakai   PRLP7105;NJLP8292
1296   Violets for your fur-1   -   PR7426
1297   Time was-1   -   45-107
1298   I hear a rhapsody-1   PRLP7188,PR7581

-1:Splawn & Shihab out.

All titles from this date issued also on PR24014.
PRLP7105=PR7609.

WEBSTER YOUNG-FOR LADY:
Webster Young(c,tp)Paul Quinichette(ts)Mal Waldron(p)Joe Puma(g)Earl
May(b)Ed Thigpen(dm).
Supervision:Bob Weinstock   NYC,June 14,1957

1299   The lady   PRLP7106
1300   God bless the child   -
1301   Moanin' low   -
1302   Don't explain   -
1303   Good morning heartache   -
1304   Strange fruit   -

AFTER HOURS:
Thad Jones(tp)Frank Wess(fl)Mal Waldron(p)Kenny Burrell(g)Paul
Chambers(b)Art Taylor(dm).
Supervision:Bob Weinstock   NYC,June 21,1957

1305   Count one   PRLP7118
1306   Empty street   -
1307   Blue jelly   -
1308   Steamin'   -

PRLP7118=PR7278.

PRESTIGE JAZZ QUARTET:
Teddy Charles(vb)Mal Waldron(p)Addison Farmer(b)Jerry Segal(dm).
Supervision:Teddy Charles   NYC,June 22,1957

1309   Friday the thirteenth   PRLP7108
1310   Dear Elaine   -
1311   Take three part jazz   -

Same.
                                         NYC,June 28,1957
1312   Melba waltz   PRLP7108

RAY DRAPER/JACKIE McLEAN:
Webster Young(tp)Ray Draper(tu)Jackie McLean(as)John Meyers(p)Bill
Salter(b)Larry Ritchie(dm).
Supervision:Bob Weinstock   NYC,July 12,1957

1313   Disciples love affair   PR7500
1314   Millie's pad   -
1315   Not so strange-1   -

-1:Young & Draper out.

Note:This session was recorded under Ray Draper's name,but issued
under McLean's name.

PHIL WOODS with RED GARLAND-SUGAN:
Ray Copeland(tp)Phil Woods(as)Red Garland(p)Teddy Kotick(b)Nick
Stabulas(dm).
Supervision:Bob Weinstock   NYC,July 19,1957

1316   Au privave   PRLP16-5
1317   Steeplechase   -
1318   Last fling   -
1319   Sugan   -
1320   Green pines   -
1321   Scrapple from the apple   -

All titles also issued on Status ST8304.

JENKINS,JORDAN & TIMMONS:
John Jenkins(as)Clifford Jordan(ts)Bobby Timmons(p)Wilbur Ware(b)
Dannie Richmond(dm).
Supervision:Bob Weinstock   NYC,July 26,1957

1322   Cliff's edge   NJLP8232
1323   Princess   -
1324   Soft talk   -
1325   Tenderly   -
1326   Blue Jay   -
1327   Diggin' for Diz   unissued

RED GARLAND TRIO:
Red Garland(p)Paul Chambers(b)Art Taylor(dm).
Supervision:Bob Weinstock   NYC,August 9,1957

1328   Will you still be mine   PRLP7113
1329   Lost April   PR7752
1330   C jam blues   PRLP7113
1331   Gone again   -
1332   Tweedle dee dee   PR7752
1333   The P.C.Blues   -

JOHN COLTRANE:
John Coltrane(ts)Earl May(b)Art Taylor(dm).
Supervision:Bob Weinstock   NYC,August 16,1957

1334-1 Trane's slow blues   PRLP7188,PR24014
1334-2 Slowtrane   PR7378
1335   Like someone in love   PRLP7188,PR7426,PR24014
1336   I love you   Pr.45-249,45-415,LP7188,PR7426,
                                             PR24014

PRLP7188=PR7581

JOHN COLTRANE with THE RED GARLAND TRIO-TRANE-ING IN:
John Coltrane(ts)Red Garland(p)Paul Chambers(b)Art Taylor(dm).
Supervision:Bob Weinstock   NYC,August 23,1957

1337   You leave me breathless   Pr.45-415,LP7123,PR7426
1338   Bass blues   -
1339   Soft lights and sweet music   -
1340   Trane-ing in   Pr.45-119 -
1341   Slow dance   -

All titles also issued on PR7651,PR24003.

JACKIE McLEAN SEXTET:
Webster Young(tp)Curtis Fuller(tb)Jackie McLean(as,ts)Gil Coggins(p)
Paul Chambers(b)Louis Hayes(dm).
Supervision:Bob Weinstock   NYC,August 30,1957

1342   Jackie's ghost   NJLP8231
1343   What's new-1   PR7500
1344   Chasing the Bird   NJLP8231
1345   A long drink of the blues   NJLP8253
1345-2 A long drink of the blues   -

-1:Young & Fuller out.

GIL EVANS PLUS TEN:
Johnny Carisi,Jake Koven(tp)Jimmy Cleveland(tb)Bart Varsalona(bass tb)
Willie Ruff(frh)Zeke Tolin(Lee Konitz)(as)Steve Lacy(ss)Dave Kurtzer
(bassoon)Gil Evans(p,arr,cond)Paul Chambers(b)Jo Jones(dm).
Supervision:Bob Weinstock   NYC,September 6,1957

1346   Remember   PRLP7120;NJLP8215;PR7756,PR24049
1347   Ella speed   rejected

WHEELIN' AND DEALIN':
Frank Wess(fl,ts)John Coltrane,Paul Quinichette(ts)Mal Waldron(p)Doug
Watkins(b)Art Taylor(dm).
Supervision:Bob Weinstock   NYC,September 20,1957

1348   Dealin'   PRLP7131;ST8327
1348   Dealin'(alt.take)   ST8316
1349   Wheelin'   PRLP7131;ST8327
1349   Wheelin'(alt.take)   ST8316
1350   Robbins' nest   PRLP7131;ST8327
1351   Things ain't what they used
                          to be   Pr.45-122,LP7131;ST8327

All titles and takes shown also issued on P-24069.

GIL EVANS AND TEN:
Louis Mucci,Jake Koven(tp)Jimmy Cleveland,Bart Varsalona(tb)Willie
Ruff(frh)Lee Konitz(as "Zeke Tolin")(as)Steve Lacy(ss)Dave Kurtzer
(bassoon)Gil Evans(p,arr,cond)Paul Chambers(b)Nick Stabulas(dm).
Supervision:Bob Weinstock   NYC,September 27,1957

1347   Ella speed   PRLP7120
1352   Nobody's heart   -
1353   If you can see me now   -

All titles also issued on NJLP8215,PR7756,PR24049

Same.
                                       NYC,October 10,1957

1354   Big stuff   PRLP7120
1355   Just one of those things   -   MV34
1356   Jambangle   -

All titles also issued on NJLP8215,PR7756,PR24049.

YUSEF LATEEF:
Wilbur Harden(flh)Yusef Lateef(fl,ts,argol)Hugh Lawson(p,bells)Ernie
Farrow(b)Oliver Jackson(dm).
Supervision:Bob Weinstock   NYC,October 11,1957

1357   Playful flute   PRLP7122,P-24035
1358   Taboo   NJLP8218,NJLP8292,PR24007
1359   Ecaps   NJLP8234;PR7748,PR24007
1360   All alone   NJLP8218,PR7447   -
1361   Anastasia   -   ST8319,MV37,PR24007
1362   Love and humour   Pr.45-127,LP7122,P-24035
1363   Buckingham   -   -
1364   Lambert's joint   NJLP8218
1365   Meditation   Pr.45-127,LP7122,PR7447,P-24035
1366   Mahaba   NJLP8218;PR24007
1367   Minor mood   -   -
1368   Take the A train   PRLP7122,P-24035

PRLP7122=NJLP8261,PR7398;NJLP8218=PR7653

PAUL QUINICHETTE-FOR BASIE:
Shad Collins(tp)Paul Quinichette(ts)Nat Pierce(p)Freddie Green(g)
Walter Page(b)Jo Jones(dm).
Supervision:Bob Weinstock   NYC,October 18,1957

1369	Rock-a-bye Basie	PRLP7127
1370	Texas shuffle	-
1371	Out the window	-
1372	Diggin' for Dex	-
1373	Jive at five	-

PRLP7127=SV2036.

ROOTS:
Idriss Sulieman(tp)Jimmy Cleveland(tb)Cecil Payne(bs)Tommy Flanagan(p)
Doug Watkins(b)Elvin Jones(dm).
Supervision:Bob Weinstock   NYC,October 25,1957

| 1374 | Motherless child | NJLP8202 |
| 1375 | Down by the riverside | - |

STEVE LACY-SOPRANO TODAY:
Steve Lacy(ss)Wynton Kelly(p)Buell Neidlinger(b)Dennis Charles(dm).
Supervision:Bob Weinstock   NYC,November 1,1957

1376	Daydream	PRLP7125
1377	Alone together	-
1378	Work	-
1379	Rockin' in rhythm	-
1380	Easy to love	-
1381	Little girl,your Daddy is calling you	-

PRLP7125=ST8308.

MOSE ALLISON-LOCAL COLOR:
Mose Allison(tp,p,vo)Addison Farmer(b)Nick Stabulas(dm).
Supervision:Bob Weinstock   NYC,November 8,1957

1382	Town	PRLP7121,PR7423
1383	Mojo woman	- -
1384	Crepuscular air	-
1385	Carnival	- PR7423
1386	I'll never be free	-
1387	Don't ever say goodbye	-
1388	Ain't you a mess	-
1389	Trouble in mind	-
1390	Lost mind	- PR7279,PR10052
1391	Parchman farm	Pr.45-130,45-295,LP7121,PR7279, PR7313,PR10052

All titles also issued on PR24002.

RED GARLAND QUINTET:
Donald Byrd(tp)John Coltrane(ts)Red Garland(p)George Joyner(b)Art
Taylor(dm).
Supervision:Bob Weinstock   NYC,November 15,1957

1392	Our delight	PRLP7130
1393	They can't take that away from me	-
1394	Woody'n you	PRLP7181
1395	I got it bad and that ain't good	-
1396	Undecided	PRLP7209
1397	Soul junction	PRLP7181
1398	What is there to say	PRLP7209
1399	Birks' works	PRLP7181
1400	Hallelujah	-
1401	All morning long	PRLP7130;BVLP1009

PRLP7209=ST8325;PRLP7130 + PRLP7181 = PR24023.

ROOTS:
Idriss Sulieman(tp)Frank Rehak(tb)Pepper Adams(bs)Bill Evans(·p)Doug
Watkins(b)Louis Hayes(dm).
Supervision:Bob Weinstock   NYC,December 6,1957

1402   Roots   NJLP8202
1403   Sometimes I feel like a
                    motherless child unissued
1404-1 Down by the riverside   -
1404-2 Down by the riverside   -

RED GARLAND QUINTET:
Donald Byrd(tp)John Coltrane(ts)Red Garland(p)George Joyner(b)Art
Taylor(dm).
Supervision:Bob Weinstock   NYC,December 13,1957

1405   Billie's bounce   PRLP7229
1406   Solitude   PRLP7209
1407   Two bass hit   -
1408   Soft winds   -
1409   Lazy Mae   PRLP7229

PRLP7229=ST8325.

RAY DRAPER QUINTET:
Ray Draper(tu)John Coltrane(ts)Gil Coggins(p)Spanky DeBrest(b)Larry
Ritchie(dm).
Supervision:Bob Weinstock   NYC,December 20,1957

1410   Under Paris skies   NJLP8228
1411   Clifford's kappa   -
1412   Filide   -
1413   Two sons   -
1414   Paul's pal   -
1415   I hadn't anyone till you   -
1416   This is no laughing matter   unissued

HAL McKUSICK-TRIPLE EXPOSURE:
Billy Byers(tb)Hal McKusick(cl,as,ts)Eddie Costa(p)Paul Chambers(b)
Charlie Persip(dm).
Supervision:Bob Weinstock   NYC,December 27,1957

1417   Interim   NJLP8204
1418   Saturday night   PRLP7135
1419   Don't worry 'bout me   NJLP8204
1420   Con alma   -
1421   Something new   PRLP7135
1422   Blues half-smiling   -
1423   A touch of Spring   -
1424   The settlers and the Indians   -
1425   I'm glad there is you   -

GENE AMMONS ALL STARS:
Jerome Richardson(fl)John Coltrane(as-1,ts-2)Gene Ammons,Paul Quinich-
ette-3(ts)Pepper Adams-4(bs)Mal Waldron(p)George Joyner(b)Art Taylor(dm).
Supervision:Bob Weinstock   NYC,January 3,1958

1426   Ammons joy-2,3   PRLP7201
1427   Groove blues-2,3   -
1428   The real McCoy-1,3,4   PRLP7132
1429   That's all   -
1430   It might as well be Spring-2,3PRLP7201
1431   Cheek to cheek-2   PRLP7132
1432   Jug handle   PRLP7201,PR7306
1433   Blue hymn-2   Pr.45-121,LP7132;BVLP1010

JOHN COLTRANE QUINTET:
Donald Byrd(tp)John Coltrane(ts)Red Garland(p)Paul Chambers(b)Louis
Hayes(dm).
Supervision:Bob Weinstock   NYC,January 10,1958

1434	Lush life	Pr.45-249,LP7188,PR24014
1435	The believer	Pr.45-315,LP7292,P-24037
1436	Nakatini serenade	- -
1437	Come rain or come shine	PR7378
1438	Lover	-

PRLP7188=PR7581.

MOSE ALLISON-YOUNG MAN MOSE:
Mose Allison(tp-1,p,vo)Addison Farmer(b)Nick Stabulas(dm).
Supervision:Bob Weinstock   NYC,January 24,1958

1439	Somebody else is taking my place	PRLP7137,PR7446
1440	Bye bye blues	-
1441	How long has this been going on?	- PR7446
1442	Don't get around much anymore	Pr.45-130,LP7137,PR7279,PR10052
1443	I hadn't anyone till you	- - -
1444	My kinda love	- PR7446
1445	Sleepy time gal	-
1446	I told ya I loved ya,now get out	- PR7446
1447	Baby let me hold your hand	- PR7279,PR10052
1448	Stroll-1	-

All titles also issued on P-24055.

MAL WALDRON-MAL3/SOUNDS:
Art Farmer(tp)Eric Dixon(fl)Calo Scott(cello)Mal Waldron(p)Julian Euell
(b)Elvin Jones(dm)Elaine Waldron(vo).
Supervision:Bob Weinstock   NYC,January 31,1958

1449	Tensions	NJLP8201
1450	Ollie's caravan	-
1451	The cattin' toddler	-
1452	Portrait of a young mother voEW	-
1453	For every man there's a woman voEW	-

RED GARLAND TRIO:
Red Garland(p)Paul Chambers(b)Art Taylor(dm).
Supervision:Bob Weinstock   NYC,February 7,1958

1454	Since I fell for you	PR7838
1455	It's a blue world	-
1456	Teach me tonight	-
1457	Crazy rhythm	PRLP7229,PR7838
1458	This can't be love	PR7838
1459	September song	rejected

JOHN COLTRANE with THE RED GARLAND TRIO-SOULTRANE:
John Coltrane(ts)Red Garland(p)Paul Chambers(b)Art Taylor(dm).
Supervision:Bob Weinstock   NYC,February 7,1958

1460	Russian lullaby	PRLP7142
1461	Theme for Ernie	-
1462	You say you care	-
1463	Good bait	Pr.45-139,LP7142
1464	I want to talk about you	Pr.45-177 -

All titles also issued on PR7531,PR24003.

HERBIE MANN-JUST WAILIN':
Herbie Mann(fl)Charlie Rouse(ts)Mal Waldron(p)Kenny Burrell(g)George
Joyner(b)Art Taylor(dm).
Supervision:Bob Weinstock   NYC,February 14,1958

```
1465    Minor groove              NJLP8211
1466    Gospel truth              -
1467    Blue echoes               -
1468    Trinidad                  -
1469    Jumpin' with Symphony Sid -
1470    Blue dip                  -
```

TINY GRIMES & COLEMAN HAWKINS-BLUES GROOVE:
Musa Kaleem(fl)Coleman Hawkins(ts)Ray Bryant(p)Tiny Grimes(g)Earl
Wormack(b)Teagle Fleming Jr.(dm).
Supervision:Bob Weinstock   NYC,February 28,1958

```
1470    Soul station              PRLP7138;PR7753
1471    Blues wail                -         -      45-116
1472    A smooth one              -         -
1473    April in Paris            -         -
1474    Marchin' along-1          -         -
1475    Tiny Bean                 -
```

-1:Kaleem out.

PRLP7138=SV2035.

KENNY BURRELL & JOHN COLTRANE:
John Coltrane(ts)Tommy Flanagan(p)Kenny Burrell(g)Paul Chambers(b)
Jimmy Cobb(dm).
Supervision:Bob Weinstock   NYC,March 7,1958

```
1476    Lyresto                   NJLP8276
1477    Why was I born-1          -
1478    Freight Trane             -         Pr.45-281
1479    I never knew              -
1480    Big Paul                  -
```

All titles also issued on PR7532,P-24059.

DOROTHY ASHBY-HIP HARP:
Dorothy Ashby(harp)Frank Wess(fl)Gene Wright(b)Art Taylor(dm).
Supervision:Bob Weinstock   NYC,March 21,1958

```
1481    Small hotel               PRLP7140
1482    Charmaine                 -         MV37;ST8319
1483    Jollity                   -
1484    Moonlight in Vermont      -
1485    Dancing in the dark       -
1486    Back talk                 -
1487    Pawky                     -
```

PRLP7140=PR7638.

JOHN COLTRANE-SETTIN' THE PACE:
John Coltrane(ts)Red Garland(p)Paul Chambers(b)Art Taylor(dm).
Supervision:Bob Weinstock   NYC,March 26,1958

```
1488    Rise and shine            PRLP7213
1489    I see your face before me -
1490    If there is someone lovelier  -
1491    Little Melonae            -
1492    By the numbers            Pr.45-394,PR7378
```

PRLP7213=PR7746.

RED GARLAND TRIO PLUS RAY BARRETTO-MANTECA:
Red Garland(p)Paul Chambers(b)Art Taylor(dm)Ray Barretto(conga).
Supervision:Bob Weinstock   NYC,April 11,1958

1493	Exactly like you	PRLP7139
1494	Mort's report	-
1495	Lady be good	-
1496	A portrait of Jenny	PR24046
1497	'S wonderful	PRLP7139
1498	Manteca	Pr.45-120,LP7139

MOSE ALLISON-RAMBLIN' WITH MOSE:
Mose Allison(tp,p,vo)Addison Farmer(b)Nick Stabulas(dm)or Ronnie Free
(dm).
Supervision:Bob Weinstock   NYC,April 18,1958

1499	Saritha	PRLP7215	
1500	Stranger in paradise	-	
1501	Ingenue	-	
1502	You belong to me	-	PR7446
1503	Old man John	-	
1504	Ramble	-	
1505	The minstrels	-	PR7423
1506	I got a right to cry	-	PR7279,PR10052
1507	Ol' devil moon	-	
1508	Kissin' bug	-	PR7446

GENE AMMONS-BLUE GENE:
Idriss Sulieman(tp)Gene Ammons(ts)Pepper Adams(bs)Mal Waldron(p)Doug
Watkins(b)Art Taylor(dm)Ray Barretto(conga).
Supervision:Bob Weinstock   NYC,May 2,1958

1509	Blue greens and beans	Pr.45-140,LP7146	
1510	Hip tip	-	
1511	Scamperin'	-	
1512	Blue Gene	-	PR7306

JOHN COLTRANE-BLACK PEARLS:
Donald Byrd(tp)John Coltrane(ts)Red Garland(p)Paul Chambers(b)Art
Taylor(dm).
Supervision:Bob Weinstock   NYC,May 23,1958

1513	Black pearls	Pr.45-373,PR7316
1514	Lover come back to me	-
1515	Sweet sapphire blues	-

All titles also issued on P-24037.

SHIRLEY SCOTT TRIO:
Shirley Scott(org)George Duvivier(b)Arthur Edgehill(dm).
Supervision:Bob Weinstock   NYC,May 27,1958

1516	It could happen to you	Pr	LP7195
1517	There'll never be another you		-
1518	Summertime	Pr.45-147	-
1519	Brazil	Pr.	LP7143
1520	The Scott	Pr.45-117	-
1521	Baby won't you please come home		
		Pr.45-156,LP7195	
1522	Indiana	-	-
1523	Cherokee	Pr.	LP7143
1524	Nothing ever changes		-
1525	Trees		-
1526	All of you	Pr.45-117	-
1527	Goodbye	Pr.45-118	-
1528	Four	-	-
1529	S' posin'	Pr.	LP7195
1530	Ebb tide	Pr.45-167,PR7440	
1531	Slaughter on 10th Avenue	Pr.	PR7424
1532	Miles theme		-

THE EDDIE "LOCKJAW" DAVIS COOKBOOK:
Eddie "Lockjaw" Davis(ts)Jerome Richardson(ts,fl)Shirley Scott(org)
George Duvivier(b)Arthur Edgehill(dm).
Supervision:Bob Weinstock   NYC,June 20,1958

1524	The chef	Pr.45-126,LP7141		
1525	Have horn will blow	-		
1526	In the kitchen	Pr.45-129	-	45-296
1527	But beautiful	Pr.45-144	-	
1528	Three deuces	Pr.45-126	-	

All titles also issued on PR7660,P-24039.

RED GARLAND TRIO:
Red Garland(p)Paul Chambers(b)Art Taylor(dm)Ray Barretto-1(conga).
Supervision:Esmond Edwards   NYC,June 27,1958

1529	East of the sun-1	P-24078
1530	Blues in mambo-1	-
1531	Lover-1	-
1532	Estrellita-1	-
1533	Five o'clock whistle-1	-
1534	I've got you under my skin	unissued
1535	I can't see for looking	PR7276
1536	Soon	-
1537	It might as well be Spring-1	P-24078
1538	A tisket a tasket-1	-
1539	Black out	PR7276
1540	Castle rock	-

JOHN COLTRANE QUINTET:
Wilbur Harden(tp)John Coltrane(ts)Red Garland(p)Paul Chambers(b)Jimmy
Cobb(dm).
Supervision:Bob Weinstock   NYC,July 11,1958

1541	Spring is here	PR7243,PR7322,MV32
1542	Invitation	-
1543	I'm a dreamer,aren't we all	PR7353
1544	Love Thy neighbor	Pr.45-267,PR7268
1545	Don't take your love from me	PR7243
1546	Stardust	Pr.45-267,PR7268,PR7298
1547	My ideal	PR7353
1548	I'll get by	PR7243

All titles also issued on P-24056.
PR7243=PR7825.

TINY GRIMES-CALLIN' THE BLUES:
J.C.Higginbotham(tb)Eddie "Lockjaw" Davis(ts)Ray Bryant(p)Tiny Grimes(g)
Wendell Marshall(b)Osie Johnson(dm).
Supervision:Bob Weinstock   NYC,July 18,1958

1549	Dood I did	ST8318
1550	Lost weekend	-
1551	Grimes times	PRLP7144
1552	Air mail special	-
1553	Callin' the blues	-
1554	Blue Tiny	-

PRLP7144=SVLP2004.All titles from this session also planned on PR7863
(never issued).

MOSE ALLISON-CREEK BANK:
Mose Allison(p,vo)Addison Farmer(b)Ronnie Free(dm).
Supervision:Bob Weinstock   NYC,August 15,1958

1555	Creek bank	PRLP7152,PR7423
1556	Moon and cypresses	- -
1557	Mule	- -
1558	Dinner on the ground	- -
1559	Prelude to a kiss	-
1560	If I didn't care	- PR7446
1561	Cabin in the sky	-
1562	If you live	- PR7279,PR10052
1563	The seventh son	Pr.45-150,45-295,LP7152,PR7279, PR7298,PR10052
1564	Yardbird suite	PRLP7152

All titles also issued on P-24055.

RED GARLAND TRIO PLUS RAY BARRETTO-ROJO:
Red Garland(p)George Joyner(b)Charlie Persip(dm)Ray Barretto(conga).
Supervision:Bob Weinstock   NYC,August 22,1958

1565	Mr.Wonderful	PRLP7193
1566	We kiss in a shadow-1	-
1567	Darling je vous aime beaucoup	-
1568	Ralph J.Gleason blues	-
1569	You better go now-1	-
1570	Rojo	-

-1:Barretto out.

PRESTIGE BLUES SWINGERS-OUTSKIRTS OF TOWN:
Art Farmer,Idriss Sulieman(tp)George "Buster" Cooper(tb)Jerome Richard-
son-fl,as)Jimmy Forrest(ts)Pepper Adams(bs)Ray Bryant(p)Tiny Grimes(g)
Wendell Marshall(b)Osie Johnson(dm)Jerry Valentine(arr).
Supervision:Esmond Edwards   NYC,August 29,1958

1571	Sent for you yesterday	Pr. LP7145
1572	Blue flute	Pr.45-132 -
1573	I'm gonna move to the outskirts of town	- -
1574	I wanna blow,blow,blow	-
1575	Jelly jelly	-
1576	Blues a-swingin'	-

PRLP7145=PR7787.

BASIE REUNION:
Buck Clayton,Shad Collins(tp)Paul Quinichette(ts)Jack Washington(bs)
Nat Pierce(p)Freddie Green(g)Eddie Jones(b)Jo Jones(dm).
Supervision:Esmond Edwards   NYC,September 5,1958

1577	Blues I like to hear	PRLP7147
1578	Roseland shuffle	-
1579	John's idea	-
1580	Love jumped out	-
1581	Baby don't tell on me	-

PRLP7147=SV2037.

EDDIE "LOCKJAW" DAVIS QUARTET:
Eddie "Lockjaw" Davis(ts)Shirley Scott(org)George Duvivier(b)Arthur
Edgehill(dm).
Supervision:Esmond Edwards   NYC,September 12,1958

1582	Tangerine	Pr.45-148,LP7154
1583	Pots ' n'pans	PR7301
1584	Old devil moon	Pr.45-137,LP7154
1585	I'll never be the same	Pr.45-148 -
1586	I let a song go out of my heart	Pr.45-138 -
1587	You stepped out of a dream	- -
1588	It's a blue world	PR7301
1589	Blue Lou	-
1590	Avalon	PR7791
1591	Too close for comfort	PRLP7154
1592	Willow weep for me	Pr.45-155,PR7791
1593	But not for me	PRLP7154
1594	Strike up the band	PRLP7219
1595	Just a lucky so and so	- PR7710
1596	Body and soul	Pr.45-137,LP7154
1597	Pennies from heaven	PR7301,PR7313

DOROTHY ASHBY-IN A MINOR GROOVE:
Frank Wess(fl)Dorothy Ashby(harp)Gene Wright(b)Roy Haynes(dm).
Supervision:Esmond Edwards   NYC,September 19,1958

1598	Bohemia after dark	NJLP8209
1599	Yesterdays	-
1600	Rascality	-
1601	Autumn in Rome	-
1602	It's a minor thing	-
1603	Taboo	-
1604	Alone together	-
1605	You'd be so nice to come home to	- MV34

NJLP8209=PR7639.

MAL WALDRON TRIO-MAL 4:
Mal Waldron(p)Addison Farmer(b)Kenny Dennis(dm).
Supervision:Esmond Edwards   NYC,September 26,1958

1606	By myself	NJLP8208
1607	Like someone in love	-
1608	Get happy	-
1609	J.M.'s dream doll	-
1610	Splidium dow	-
1611	Love Spann	-
1612	Too close for comfort	-

JEROME RICHARDSON SEXTET:
Jimmy Cleveland(tb)Jerome Richardson(fl,ts)Hank Jones(p)Kenny Burrell
(g)Joe Benjamin(b)Charlie Persip(dm).
Supervision:Esmond Edwards   NYC,October 10,1958

1613	Delicious trimmings	NJLP8205
1614	Way in blues	-
1615	Minorally	-
1616	Caravan	-
1617	Lyric-1	-

-1:Cleveland out.

[63]

STEVE LACY PLAYS THE MUSIC OF THELONIOUS MONK:
Steve Lacy(ss)Mal Waldron(p)Buell Neidlinger(b)Elvin Jones(dm).
Supervision:Esmond Edwards   NYC,October 17,1958

1618	Hornin' in	NJLP8206
1619	Skippy	-
1620	Reflections	-
1621	Four in one	-
1622	Bye-ya	-
1623	Ask me now	-
1624	Let's call this	-

SHIRLEY SCOTT TRIO:
Shirley Scott(org)George Duvivier(b)Arthur Edgehill(dm).
Supervision:Esmond Edwards   NYC,October 23,1958

1625	Mr.Wonderful	PRLP7155
1626	How deep is the ocean	-
1627	Time on my hands	Pr.45-145,LP7155
1628	Sweet Lorraine	MVLP5
1629	Out of this world	PR7440
1630	Hong Pong	Pr.45-145;LP7155
1631	Can't see for looking	PRLP7195
1632	Takin' care of business	Pr.45-147,LP7155
1633	Gee baby ain't I good to you	Pr.45-179;MVLP5
1634	That's where it's at	PR7440
1635	Cafe style	-
1636	Cherry	Pr.45-136,LP7155
1637	Diane	- -
1638	I should care-1	MVLP5
1639	Send me someone to love	Pr.45-135,LP7155
1640	Until the real thing comes along-1	
		MVLP5

-1:Shirley Scott plays piano on these titles.

COLEMAN HAWKINS-SOUL:
Coleman Hawkins(ts)Ray Bryant(p)Kenny Burrell(g)Wendell Marshall(b)
Osie Johnson(dm).
Supervision:Esmond Edwards   NYC,November 7,1958

1641	I hadn't anyone till you	Pr.45-131,LP7149,P-24083
1642	Greensleeves	- - -
1643	Groovin'	-
1644	Sunday mornin'	-
1645	Until the real thing comes along	- P-24083
1646	Sweetnin'	-
1647	Soul blues	Pr.45-161 - P-24083

PRLP7149=SV2038.

ROY HAYNES-WE THREE:
Phineas Newborn(p)Paul Chambers(b)Roy Haynes(dm).
Supervision:Esmond Edwards   NYC,November 14,1958

1648	Sneakin' around	NJLP8210
1649	Reflections	-
1650	Sugar Ray	-
1651	Our delight	- PR24052
1652	Solitaire	-
1653	After hours	-

1654/1663:not used.

THE RED GARLAND TRIO:
Red Garland(p)Paul Chambers(b)Art Taylor(dm).
Supervision:Esmond Edwards   NYC,November 21,1958

```
1664    And the angels sing             MVLP6
1665    I'll never stop loving you      -
1666    Blues for Ann                   -
1667    I love you yes I do             -
1668    Bassment blues                  -
1669    T'ain't nobody's business       -
```

RED GARLAND-ALL KINDS OF WEATHER:
Red Garland(p)Paul Chambers(b)Art Taylor(dm).
Supervision:Esmond Edwards   NYC,November 27,1958

```
1670    'Tis Autumn                     PRLP7148
1671    Summertime                      -
1672    Spring will be a little late
                        this year       -
1673    Stormy weather                  -
1674    Winter wonderland               -
1675    Rain                            -
```

EDDIE "LOCKJAW" DAVIS COOKBOOK:
Jerome Richardson(fl,ts)Eddie "Lockjaw" Davis(ts)Shirley Scott(org)
George Duvivier(b)Arthur Edgehill(dm).
Supervision:Esmond Edwards   NYC,December 5,1958

```
1676    The broilers                    PRLP7161,P-24039
1677    The goose hangs high            PRLP7219
1678    Simmerin'
1679    Heat' n'serve                   -
1680    My old flame
1681    Stardust                        Pr.45-155,LP7161,P-24039
1682    High fry                        PR7301,PR7710
1683    Skillet                         PRLP7161,P-24039,PR7710
1684    Smoke this                      PR7301
1685    I surrender dear                Pr.45-146,LP7161,P-24039
1686    Jaws                            PR7301
1687    The rev                         Pr.45-146,LP7161,P-24039;
                                        BVLP1010
```

PRLP7161=PR7782.

RAY BRYANT-ALONE WITH THE BLUES:
Ray Bryant(p).
Supervision:Esmond Edwards   NYC,December 19,1958

```
1688    Me and the blues(Blues No.1)    NJLP8213
1689    Rockin' chair                   -
1690    Just a lucky so and so          rejected
1691    Lover man                       NJLP8213
1692    Joy(Blues No.2)                 NJ45-505,LP8213
1693    Blues No.3                      -
1694    Stocking feet(Blues No.4)       NJ45-505  -
1695    My blues(Blues No.5)            -
```

All titles from NJLP8213 also issued on PR7837,P-24038.

JOHN COLTRANE:
Freddie Hubbard-1(tp)John Coltrane(ts)Red Garland(p)Paul Chambers(b)
Art Taylor(dm).

Supervision:Esmond Edwards   NYC,December 26,1958

```
1696    Do I love you because you're beautiful-1 PR7292,P-24037
1697    Then I'll be tired of you-1     PR7268
1698    Something I dreamed last night  PR7353
1699    Bahia                           -
1700    Goldsboro express-2             -
1701    Time after time                 PR7268,PR7426
```

-2:Garland out.

ARNETT COBB-BLOW,ARNETT,BLOW:
Arnett Cobb,Eddie "Lockjaw" Davis(ts)Wild Bill Davis(org)George
Duvivier(b)Arthur Edgehill(dm).
Supervision:Esmond Edwards   NYC,January 9,1959

1702	Dutch kitchen bounce	Pr.	LP7151
1703	Go,Red,go		-
1704	When I grow too old to dream	Pr.45-133	-
1705	The Eely one		-
1706	Go power	Pr.45-133	-
1707	The fluke		-

PRLP7151=PR7835.

PRESTIGE BLUES SWINGERS-STASCH:
Idriss Sulieman(tp)Jerome Richardson(fl,as)Coleman Hawkins(ts)Pepper
Adams(bs)Ray Bryant(p)Wendell Marshall(b)Walter Bolden(dm)Jerry
Valentine(arr).
Supervision:Esmond Edwards   NYC,February 5,1959

1708	Stasch	SVLP2013
1709	Since I fell for you	-
1710	Roll 'em	-
1711	Trust in me	-
1712	Skrouk	-
1713	My babe	-

MOSE ALLISON-AUTUMN SONG:
Mose Allison(p,vo)Addison Farmer(b)Ronnie Free(dm).
Supervision:Esmond Edwards   NYC,February 13,1959

1714	Spires	Pr.	LP7189	
1715	Promenade		-	
1716	It's crazy		-	PR7446
1717	Autumn song		-	
1718	The devil in the canefield		-	PR7423
1719	Strange		-	PR7446
1720	That's all right	Pr.45-190	-	PR7279,PR10052
1721	Do nothin' till you hear from me	Pr.45-150	-	- -
1722	Eyesight to the blind	Pr.45-190	-	
1723	Groovin' high		-	

HAL SINGER-BLUE STOMPIN':
Charlie Shavers(tp)Hal Singer(ts)Ray Bryant(p)Wendell Marshall(b)Osie
Johnson(dm).
Supervision:Esmond Edwards   NYC,February 20,1959

1724	The blast off	PRLP7153
1725	Windy	-
1726	Midnight	-
1727	With a song in my heart	-
1728	Fancy pants	-
1729	Blue stompin'	Pr.45-134,LF7153

PRLP7153=SVLP2023.

ARNETT COBB-SMOOTH SAILING:
Buster Cooper(tb)Arnett Cobb(ts)Austin Mitchell(org)George Duvivier(b)
Osie Johnson(dm).
Supervision:Esmond Edwards   NYC,February 27,1959

1730	Blues in my heart	PRLP7184	
1731	Ghost of a chance	-	
1732	Let's split	-	
1733	Smooth sailing	-	PR7711,45-185
1734	Charmaine	-	
1735	Cobb's mob	-	
1736	Blues around dusk	-	

MAL WALDRON TRIO-IMPRESSIONS:
Mal Waldron(p)Addison Farmer(b)Albert Heath(dm).
Supervision:Esmond Edwards   NYC,March 20,1959

1737	Champs Elysees	NJLP8242
1738	C'est formidable	−
1739	Ciso	−
1740	You stepped out of a dream	−
1741	All the way	−
1742	All about us	−
1743	With a song in my heart	−

COLEMAN HAWKINS-HAWK EYES:
Charlie Shavers(tp)Coleman Hawkins(ts)Ray Bryant(p)Tiny Grimes(g)George
Duvivier(b)Osie Johnson(dm).
Supervision:Esmond Edwards   NYC,April 3,1959

1744	Stealin' the Bean	PRLP7156
1745	Through for the night	−
1746	La Rosita-1	−
1747	Hawk eyes	−
1748	C'mon in	−
1749	I never knew	unissued

PRLP7156=SVLP2039,PR7857.

RED GARLAND-RED IN BLUESVILLE:
Red Garland(p)Sam Jones(b)Art Taylor(dm).
Supervision:Esmond Edwards   NYC,April 17,1959

1750	Trouble in mind	Pr.45-160,LP7157
1751	He's a real gone guy	Pr.45-151 −
1752	See see rider	−
1753	St.Louis blues	−
1754	M-Squad	Pr.45-143 −
1755	That's your red wagon	Pr.45-160 −

SHIRLEY SCOTT-SCOTTIE PLAYS THE DUKE:
Shirley Scott(org)George Duvivier(b)Arthur Edgehill(dm).
Supervision:Esmond Edwards   NYC,April 24,1959

1756	Just squeeze me	Pr.45-149,LP7163
1757	Just a-sittin' and a-rockin'	Pr.45-154 −
1758	In a mellotone	Pr.45-149 −
1759	Prelude to a kiss	Pr.45-154 −
1760	C jam blues	−
1761	I've got it bad and that ain't good	−
1762	Caravan	−
1763	In a sentimental mood	−

VERY SAXY:
Coleman Hawkins,Eddie "Lockjaw" Davis,Buddy Tate,Arnett Cobb(ts)Shirley
Scott(org)George Duvivier(b)Arthur Edgehill(dm).
Supervision:Esmond Edwards   NYC,April 29,1959

1764	Light and lovely	PRLP7167
1765	Very saxy	− PR7710
1766	Foot pattin'	−
1767	Fourmost	−
1768	Lester leaps in	−

EDDIE "LOCKJAW" DAVIS-JAWS IN ORBIT:
Steve Pulliam(tb)Eddie "Lockjaw" Davis(ts)Shirley Scott(org)George
Duvivier(b)Arthur Edgehill(dm).
Supervision:Esmond Edwards   NYC,May 1,1959

1769	Intermission riff	PRLP7171
1770	Our delight	–
1771	Bingo domingo	–	PR7710
1772	Bahia	–
1773	Can't get out of this mood	–
1774	Foxy	–

ARNETT COBB-PARTY TIME:
Arnett Cobb(ts)Ray Bryant(p)Wendell Marshall(b)Art Taylor(dm)Ray
Barretto(conga).
Supervision:Esmond Edwards   NYC,May 14,1959

1780	Cocktails for two	Pr.	LP7165
1781	Flying home	–	PR7711
1782	When my dreamboat comes home	Pr.45-153	–	–
1783	Lonesome road	–	–
1784	Blues in the closet	–
1785	Party time	–
1786	Slow poke	–

WILLIS JACKSON:
Willis Jackson(ts)Jack McDuff(org)Bill Jennings(g)Tommy Potter(b)Alvin
Johnson(dm).
Supervision:Esmond Edwards   NYC,May 25,1959

1775	Gator's tail	PRLP7183,PR7702
1776	Gil's pills	PR7428	–
1777	Memories of you	PRLP7162
1778	A smooth one	PRLP7172
1779	The man I love	–
1787	Please Mr.Jackson	Pr.45-142,LP7162,PR7702
1788	Dinky's mood	–	–
1789	How deep is the ocean	PRLP7172
1790	Come back to Sorrento	Pr.45-170,LP7162
1791	Cool grits	Pr.45-159,LP7162;BVLP1010
1792	Angel eyes	PR7428
1793	Three little words	PR7364
1794	She's funny that way	PRLP7183
1795	633 Knock	PRLP7162

PRLP7162=PR7783;PRLP7172=PR7830;PRLP7183=PR7850.

ART TAYLOR-TAYLOR'S TENORS:
Frank Foster,Charlie Rouse(ts)Walter Davis(p)Sam Jones(b)Art Taylor(dm).
Supervision:Esmond Edwards   NYC,June 3,1959

1796	Cape Millie	NJLP8219
1797	Little Chico	–
1798	Fidel	–
1799	Rhythm-a-ning	–
1800	Straight no chaser	–
1801	Dacor	–

All titles also issued on PR7342.

BENNY GOLSON-GONE WITH GOLSON:
Curtis Fuller(tb)Benny Golson(ts)Ray Bryant(p)Tom Bryant(b)Al Harewood
(dm).
Supervision:Esmond Edwards   NYC,June 20,1959

1802	Staccato swing	NJLP8235
1803	Autumn leaves	-
1804	Blues after dark	-
1805	Soul me	-
1806	A bit of heaven	PR24046
1807	Jam for Bobbie	NJLP8235

COLEMAN HAWKINS PLUS THE RED GARLAND TRIO:
Coleman Hawkins(ts)Red Garland(p)Doug Watkins(b)Charles "Specs" Wright
(dm).
Supervision:Esmond Edwards   NYC,August 12,1959

1808	Bean's blues	SVLP2001	
1809	I want to be loved	-	Pr.P-24083
1810	It's a blue world	-	-
1811	Red beans	-	-
1812	Blues for Ron	-	

RED GARLAND TRIO:
Red Garland(p)Doug Watkins(b)Specs Wright(dm).
Supervision:Esmond Edwards   NYC,August 12,1959

1813	Satin doll	unissued
1814	The man I love	-
1815	Mr.Wonderful	P-24078
1816	A little bit of Basie	unissued
1817	Blue velvet	P-24078
1818	Blues in the closet	-

TINY GRIMES-TINY IN SWINGVILLE:
Jerome Richardson(fl-1,ts-2,bs-3)Ray Bryant(p)Tiny Grimes(g)Wendell
Marshall(b)Art Taylor(dm).
Supervision:Esmond Edwards   NYC,August 13,1959

1819	Ain't misbehavin' -2	SVLP2002	
1820	Down with it-1,2	-	
1821	Durn tootin' -2	-	Pr.45-158
1822	Annie Laurie-3	-	-
1823	Home sick-3	-	
1824	Frankie and Johnnie-2	-	

BILL JENNINGS-ENOUGH SAID:
Jack McDuff(org)Bill Jennings(g)Wendell Marshall(b)Alvin Johnson(dm).
Supervision:Esmond Edwards   NYC,August 21,1959

1825	Dark eyes	PRLP7164
1826	Tough gain	-
1827	Dig Uncle Will	-
1828	It's Alvin again	ST8318
1829	Volare	PRLP7164
1830	It could happen to you	-
1831	Enough said	Pr.45-152,LP7164;BVLP1010
1832	Blue jams	-

PRLP7164=PR7788.

BENNY GOLSON-GROOVIN' WITH GOLSON:
Curtis Fuller(tb)Benny Golson(ts)Ray Bryant(p)Paul Chambers(b)Art
Blakey(dm).
Supervision:Esmond Edwards   NYC,August 28,1959

1833'	My blue house	NJ	LP8220
1834	I didn't know what time it was	-	
1835	The stroller	-	
1836	Yesterdays	NJ45-503	-
1837	Drum boogie	-	-

MODERN JAZZ DISCIPLES:
Mike Kelley(tb)Curtis Peagler(as,ts)Bill Brown(p)Lee Tucker(b)Roy
McCurdy(dm).
Supervision:Esmond Edwards   NYC,September 8,1959

1838	A'little taste	NJLP8222
1839	Slippin' and glidin'	-
1840	Hapnin'	NJLP8240
1841	Disciples blues	NJLP8222
1842	Hike's delight	-
1843	Perhaps	-
1844	After you've gone	-
1845	Dottie	unissued

JOHNNY "HAMMOND" SMITH-ALL SOUL:
Johnny "Hammond" Smith(org)Thornel Schwartz(g)George Tucker(b)Leo
Stevens(dm).
Supervision:Esmond Edwards   NYC,September 11,1959

1846	The masquerade is over	NJ45-502,LP8221;Pr.45-164	
1847	Pennies from heaven	-	
1848	All soul	NJ45-502	- Pr.45-164,PR7777
1849	Goin' places	-	
1850	Sweet cookies	NJ45-501	-
1851	Easy like	-	
1852	Secret love	NJ45-501	-

AL SMITH-HEAR MY BLUES:
Al Smith(vo)with Eddie "Lockjaw" Davis(ts)Shirley Scott(p)Wendell
Marshall(b)Arthur Edgehill(dm).
Supervision:Esmond Edwards   NYC,September 20,1959

1853	Night time is the right time	BV45-805,LP1001	
1854	I'll be alright	-	
1855	I've got the right kind of lovin'	-	
1856	Never let me go	-	
1857	I've got a girl	-	
1858	Tears in my eyes	BV45-801	-
1859	Come on pretty baby-1	-	-
1860	Pledging my love-1	. BV45-805	-

-1:Davis out.

BVLP1001=BV1069.

LEM WINCHESTER-WINCHESTER SPECIAL:
Benny Golson(ts)Lem Winchester(vb)Ray Bryant(p)Wendell Marshall(b)Art
Taylor(dm).
Supervision:Esmond Edwards   NYC,September 25,1959

1861	Mysticism	NJ	LP8223
1862	The Dude	-	
1863	How are things in Glocca Morra	-	
1864	Will you still be mine	-	
1865	Down Fuzz	NJ45-504	-
1866	If I were a bell-1	-	-

-1:Golson out.

RED GARLAND AT THE PRELUDE:
Red Garland(p)Jimmy Rowser(b)Charles "Specs" Wright(dm).
Supervision:Esm.Edwards   Prelude Club,NYC,October 2,1959

1867	There'll never be another you	PRLP7170
1868	Let me see	-
1869	We kiss in the shadow	ST8314
1870	Blues in the closet	-
1871	Li'l darling	
1872	One o'clock jump	PRLP7170,ST8326
1873	Perdido	Pr.45-168,LP7170
1874	Bye bye blackbird	-
1875	Like someone in love	ST8314
1876	Marie	ST8326
1877	A foggy day	-
1878	Satin doll	PRLP7170
1879	Mr.Wonderful	ST8326
1880	Just squeeze me	Pr.45-168,LP7170
1881	Bohemian blues	ST8326
1882	Prelude blues	PRLP7170
1883	It's a blue world	unissued

YUSEF LATEEF-CRY!TENDER:
Lonnie Hillyer(tp)Yusef Lateef(fl,ts,oboe)Hugh Lawson(p)Herman Wright
(b)Frank Gant(dm).
Supervision:Esmond Edwards   NYC,October 16,1959

1884	Cry!Tender	NJ		LP8234;PR24007
1885	The snow is green		-	
1886	If you could see me now		-	PR7447
1887	Dolopous	NJ45-506	-	PR24007
1888	Yesterdays	-	-	PR7447,PR24007
1889	Sea breeze	Pr.45-419	-	-
1890	Butter's blues		-	

NJLP8234=PR7748.

ROAMIN' WITH JEROME RICHARDSON:
Jerome Richardson(fl,ts,bs)Richard Wyands(p)George Tucker(b)Charlie
Persip(dm).
Supervision:Esmond Edwards   NYC,October 21,1959

1891	Poinciana	NJLP8226
1892	Friar tuck	-
1893	Up at Teddy's hill	-
1894	Warm valley	-
1895	Candied sweets	-
1896	I never knew	-

OLIVER NELSON-MEET OLIVER NELSON:
Kenny Dorham(tp)Oliver Nelson(ts)Ray Bryant(p)Wendell Marshall(b)Art
Taylor(dm).
Supervision:Esmond Edwards   NYC,October 30,1959

1897	Jams and jellies	NJLP8224
1898	Ostinato	-
1899	Passion flower	-
1900	Booze baby blues	-
1901	Don't stand up	-
1902	Waht's new	-

JOHNNY "HAMMOND" SMITH-THAT GOOD FEELING:
Johnny "Hammond" Smith(org)Thornel Schwartz(g)George Tucker(b)Leo
Stevens(dm).
Supervision:Esmond Edwards   NYC,November 4,1959

1903	Autumn leaves	NJLP8229	
1904	My funny Valentine	-	
1905	Bye bye blackbird	-	PR7777
1906	I'll remember April	NJ45-509,LP8229	
1907	Puddlin'	-	
1908	Billie's bounce	-	
1909	That good feeling	NJ45-509	-

WILLIS JACKSON:
Willis Jackson(ts)Bill Jennings(g)Jack McDuff(org)Wendell Marshall(b)
Alvin Johnson(dm).
Supervision:Esmond Edwards   NYC,November 9,1959

1910	Glad a see ya	PR7364
1911	On the sunny side of the street	
		Pr.45-170,LP7172
1912	When I fall in love	PRLP7211
1913	East breeze	PRLP7183
1914	Blue strollin'	PRLP7172
1915	Medley:September song/	PR7428
	Easy living/Deep purple	-

PRLP7172=PR7830;PRLP7183=PR7850.

KENNY DORHAM-QUIET KENNY:
Kenny Dorham(tp)Tommy Flanagan(p)Paul Chambers(b)Art Taylor(dm).
Supervision:Esmond Edwards   NYC,November 13,1959

1916	Old folks	NJLP8225;PR7754	
1917	My ideal	-	-
1918	Blue spin shuffle	-	-
1919	Mack the knife	-	-
1920	Lotus blossom	NJLP8225	-
1921	I had the craziest dream	-	-
1922	Alone together	-	-
1923-1	Blue Friday	-	-

WILLIE DIXON-WILLIE'S BLUES:
Harold Ashby-1(ts)Memphis Slim(p)Wally Richardson-2(g)Willie Dixon(b,vo)
Gus Johnson(dm).
Supervision:Esmond Edwards   NYC,December 3,1959

1923-2	Move me-1	unissued	
1924	That's all I want baby-1	BV	LP1003
1925	Don't you tell nobody		-
1926	Good understanding-1		-
1927	I got a razor-3		-
1928	That's my baby-2		-
1929	Nervous-2	BV45-803	-
1930	Sittin' and cryin' the blues-1,2	-	-
1931	Built for comfort-1,2		-
1932	Youth to you		-
1933	Slim's thing		-
1934	Go easy		-

-3:Johnson out.

[72]

SHIRLEY SCOTT-SOUL SEARCHING:
Shirley Scott(org)Wendell Marshall(b)Arthur Edgehill(dm).
Supervision:Esmond Edwards   NYC,December 4,1959

1935	Duck and rock	Pr.45-167,PRLP7173
1936	Boss	-
1937	You won't let me go	-
1938	Plunk,plunk,plunk	-
1939	Soul searching	-
1940	Moanin'	Pr.45-179	-
1941	Gee baby ain't I good to you	-
1942	Oh-oh	Pr.45-163;MV30
1943	Misty	-	45-296;MV30

RED GARLAND TRIO PLUS EDDIE "LOCKJAW" DAVIS:
Eddie "Lockjaw" Davis-1(ts)Red Garland(p)Sam Jones(b)Art Taylor(dm).
Supervision:Esmond Edwards   NYC,December 11,1959

1944	When your lover has gone-1	MVLP1
1945	We'll be together again-1	-
1946	I heard you cry last night	-
1947	The Red blues	-
1948	Untitled blues-1	PR24046
1949	Softly baby-1	MVLP1
1950	Blue room	-
1951	Wonder why	-
1952	Stella by starlight	-

BUDDY TATE-TATE'S DATE:
Pat Jenkins(tp)Eli Robinson(tb)Ben Richardson(cl,as,bs)Buddy Tate(ts)
Sadik Hakim(p)Wendell Marshall(b)Osie Johnson(dm).
Supervision:Esmond Edwards   NYC,December 18,1959

1953	Moon dog	SVLP2003
1954	You 'n 'me	-
1955	Blow low	-
1956	Miss Ruby Jones	-
1957	Idling	-
1958	No kiddin'	-

EDDIE "LOCKJAW" DAVIS-BACALAO:
Eddie "Lockjaw" Davis(ts)Shirley Scott(org)George Duvivier(b)Arthur
Edgehill(dm)Ray Barretto(bongo)Luis Perez(conga).
Supervision:Esmond Edwards   NYC,December 20,1959

1959	Come rain or come shine	Pr.	LP7178
1960	Last train from Overbrook	Pr.45-171	-
1961	Dobbin' with Redd Foxx	-	-
1962	That old black magic	-
1963	Sometimes I'm happy	-
1964	Dancero	-
1965	Fast spiral	-
1966	When your lover has gone	-
1967	Yes indeed-1	PRLP7173

-1:org,b,dm only.

BENNY GOLSON-GETTIN' WITH IT:
Curtis Fuller(tb)Benny Golson(ts)Tommy Flanagan(p)Doug Watkins(b)Art
Taylor(dm).
Supervision:Esmond Edwards   NYC,December 23,1959

1968	April in Paris	NJLP8248
1969	Tippin' on through	-
1970	Blue streak	-
1971	Baubles,bangles and beads	-
1972	Bob Hurd's blues	-

COLEMAN HAWKINS ALL STARS:
Joe Thomas(tp)Vic Dickenson(tb)Coleman Hawkins(ts)Tommy Flanagan(p)
Wendell Marshall(b)Osie Johnson(dm,tambourine-1).
Supervision:Esmond Edwards   NYC,January 8,1960

1973   You blew out the flame   SVLP2005
1974   I'm beginning to see the light -
1975   More bounce to the Vonce-1   -
1976   Cool blue   -
1977   Some stretching   -

BILL JENNINGS-GLIDE ON:
Al Jennings(vb,g)Jack McDuff(org,p)Bill Jennings(g)Wendell Marshall(b)
Alvin Johnson(dm).
Supervision:Esmond Edwards   NYC,January 12,1960

1978   Alexandria,Virginia   Pr.   LP7177
1979   There will never be another you   -
1980   Fiddlin'   -
1981   Azur te   -
1982   Billin' and bluin'   Pr.45-175 -
1983   Glide on   -
1984   Miss Jones   -
1985   Cole slaw   Pr.45-175 -

MILDRED ANDERSON-PERSON TO PERSON:
Mildred Anderson(vo)with Eddie "Lockjaw" Davis(ts)Shirley Scott(org)
George Duvivier(b)Arthur Edgehill(dm).
Supervision:Esmond Edwards   NYC,January 22,1960

1986   Good king Daddy   BV   LP1004
1987   Person to person   BV45-804 -
1988   Kidney stew   -
1989   Connections   BV45-804 -
1990   I'm free   -
1991   Please don't go   -
1992   Hello little boy   -
1993   I didn't have a chance   -
1994   Ebb tide   -

JACK McDUFF-BROTHER JACK:
Jack McDuff(org)Bill Jennings(g)Wendell Marshall(b)Alvin Johnson(dm).
Supervision:Esmond Edwards   NYC,January 25,1960

1995   Organ grinder's swing   Pr.45-169,LP7174
1996   Drowsy   -
1997   Noon train   -
1998   Mr.Wonderful   -
1999   Mack 'n 'Duff   -
2000   You're driving me crazy   -   PR7596
2001   Brother Jack   Pr.45-169 -   PR7481,PR24013
2002   Light blues   -

All titles also issued on PR7785,PR7836.

COLEMAN HAWKINS-AT EASE WITH COLEMAN HAWKINS:
Coleman Hawkins(ts)Tommy Flanagan(p)Wendell Marshall(b)Osie Johnson(dm)
Supervision:Esmond Edwards   NYC,January 29,1960

2003   Trouble is a man   MVLP7
2004   While we're young   -
2005   Then I'll be tired of you   -
2006   Poor butterfly   -
2007   For you,for me,for evermore   -
2008   At dawning   -
2009   I'll get by   -
2010   Mighty lak a rose   -

All titles also issued on P-24083.

EDDIE "LOCKJAW" DAVIS-AT EASE:
Eddie "Lockjaw" Davis(ts)Shirley Scott(org)George Duvivier(b)Arthur
Edgehill(dm).
Supervision:Esmond Edwards   NYC,January 31,1960

2011	It could happen to you	MVLP4
2012	What's new	-
2013	The very thought of you	-
2014	Serenade in blue	-
2015	Man with horn	-
2016	The man I love	- MV33
2017	Smoke gets in your eyes	-
2018	I cover the waterfront	-
2019	The Christmas song	Pr.45-186
2020	Santa Claus is coming to town	-

ARNETT COBB-MORE PARTY TIME:
Arnett Cobb(ts)Tommy Flanagan(p)Sam Jones(b)Art Taylor(dm)Danny Barra-
janos(conga).
Supervision:Esmond Edwards   NYC,February 16,1960

2021	Swanee river	PRLP7175
2022	Blue Lou	-
2023	Blue me	-
2024	Sometimes I'm happy	-
2025	Fast ride	PRLP7216,PR7711
2026	Lover come back to me	Pr.45-172,LP7175

ARNETT COBB-MOVIN' RIGHT ALONG:
Arnett Cobb(ts)Bobby Timmons(p)Sam Jones(b)Art Taylor(dm)Buck Clarke
(conga).
Supervision:Esmond Edwards   NYC,February 17,1960

2027	Exactly like you	PRLP7216
2028	Down by the riverside	PRLP7175,PR7711
2029	Softly as in a morning sunrise	PRLP7216
2030	The nitty gritty	- PR7711
2031	Walkin'	-
2032	All I do is dream of you	-
2033	Ghost of a chance	Pr.45-185,LP7216
2034	The shy one	-

WILLIS JACKSON:
Willis Jackson(ts)Jack McDuff(org)Bill Jennings(g)Milton Hinton(b)
Alvin Johnson(dm)Buck Clarke(conga).
Supervision:Esmond Edwards   NYC,February 26,1960

2035	Where are you	PRLP7211
2036	This nearly was mine	PRLP7183
2037	Sportin'	PRLP7211
2038	Dancing on the ceiling	PR7428
2039	Keep on a blowin'	Pr.45-178,LP7172,PR7702
2040	It might as well be Spring	PR7364
2041	This 'll get to ya	Pr.45-393,45-724,PR7364,PR7702

PRLP7183=PR7850;PRLP7172=PR7830.

THE RETURN OF ROOSEVELT SYKES:
Clarence Perry Jr.(ts)Roosevelt Sykes(p,vo)Frank Ingalls,Floyd Ball(g)
Armand "Jump" Jackson(dm).
Supervision:Esmond Edwards   NYC,March 1,1960

2042	Swanee river	unissued
2043	47 St.Live	-
2044	Number nine	BVLP1006
2045	Runnin' the boogie	-
2046	Calcutta	-
2047	Hangover	-
2048	Comin' home	-
2049	Long,lonesome night	-

Same.
Supervision:Esmond Edwards   NYC,March 2,1960

2050	Drivin' wheel	BVLP1006
2051	Night time is the right time	-
2052	Set the meat outdoors	-
2053	Selfish woman-1	-
2054	Hey big Mama	-
2055	Stompin' the boogie	-

-1:Roosevelt Sykes(p,vo)alone.

All titles from BVLP1006 also issued on Fantasy F-24717.

AL CASEY-BUCK JUMPIN':
Rudy Powell(cl,as)Herman Foster(p)Al Casey(g)Jimmy Lewis(b)Belton Evans
(dm).
Supervision:Esmond Edwards   NYC,March 7,1960

2068	Rosetta	SVLP2007
2069	Ain't misbehavin'	-
2070	Buck jumpin' -1	-
2071	Casey's blues	-
2072	Honeysuckle rose	-
2073	Body and soul-2	-
2074	Don't blame me	-
2075	Fast blues	unissued
2076	I'm gonna sit right down	-

-1:Powell & Foster out;-2:Powell out.

LONNIE JOHNSON-BLUES BY LONNIE:
Hal Singer(ts)Claude Hopkins(p)Lonnie Johnson(vo,g)Wendell Marshall(b)
Bobby Donaldson(dm).
Supervision:Chris Albertson   NYC,March 8,1960

2056	You will need me	BV	LP1007
2057	I don't hurt anymore		-
2058	You don't move me	BV45-806	-
2059	Big leg woman		-
2060	One sided love affair		-
2061	There must be a way		-
2062	She's drunk again		-
2063	There is no love		-
2064	Blues round my door		-
2065	She devil		-
2066	Don't ever love	BV45-806	-
2067	No love for sale-1		-

-1:Singer out.

GIGI GRYCE-SAYIN' SOMETHING:
Richard Williams(tp)Gigi Gryce(as)Richard Wyands(p)Reggie Workman(b)
Granville "Mickey" Roker(dm).
Supervision:Esmond Edwards   NYC,March 11,1960

2077	Leila's blues	NJLP8230
2078	Blues in the jungle-1	-
2079	Down home	-
2080	Back breaker	-
2081	Let me know	-
2082	Jones bones-1	-

-1:Williams out.

REX STEWART-THE HAPPY JAZZ:
Rex Stewart(c,kazoo,vo)John Dengler(bass sax,kazoo,wbd)Wilbert Kirk
(hca,tambourine)Jerome Darr,Chauncey Westbrook(g)Benny Moten(b)Charles
"Chuck" Lampkin(dm).
Supervision:Esmond Edwards   NYC,March 18,1960

2079A   Four or five times   SVLP2006
2080A   Please don't talk about me   -
2081A   If I could be with you   -
2082A   I would do most anything for you -
2083   San   -
2084   Red ribbon   -
2084A   Nagasaki   -
2085   You can depend on me   -
2086   Tell me   -
2087   Rasputin   -

SVLP2006=PR7728.

OLIVER NELSON-TAKIN' CARE OF BUSINESS:
Oliver Nelson(as,ts)Lem Winchester(vb)Johnny "Hammond" Smith(org)
George Tucker(b)Roy Haynes(dm).
Supervision:Esmond Edwards   NYC,March 22,1960

2088   Doxy   NJ   LP8233
2089   Groove   -
2090   All the way   -
2091   Lou's good blues   -
2092   In time   -
2093   Trane whistle   NJ45-507 -

CLAUDE HOPKINS-YES INDEED!:
Emmett Berry(tp)Buddy Tate(ts)Claude Hopkins(ts)Wendell Marshall(b)
J.C.Heard(dm).
Supervision:Esmond Edwards   NYC,March 25,1960

2088   What is this thing called loveSVLP2009
2089   Empty bed blues   -
2090   Willow weep for me   -
2091   Yes indeed!   -
2092   It don't mean a thing   -
2093   Morning glory   -
2094   Is it so?   -

PEE WEE RUSSELL-SWINGIN' WITH PEE WEE:
Buck Clayton(tp)Pee Wee Russell(cl)Tommy Flanagan(p)Wendell Marshall(b)
Osie Johnson(dm).
Supervision:Esmond Edwards   NYC,March 29,1960

2094   Wrap your troubles in dreams SVLP2008
2095   What can I say dear   -
2096   Midnight blue   -
2097   I would do most anything for you -
2098   Englewood   -
2099   Lulu's back in town   -
2100   The very thought of you   -

SVLP2008=PR7672.

THE SWINGVILLE ALL STARS:
Taft Jordan(tp)Hilton Jefferson(as)Al Sears(ts)Don Abney(p)Wendell
Marshall(b)Gus Johnson(dm).
Supervision:Esmond Edwards   NYC,March 31,1960

2124   New Carnegie blues   SVLP2010
2125   Rockin' in rhythm   -
2126   Willow weep for me   -
2127   Things ain't what they used to be-
2128   Tenderly   -
2129   Li'l darling   -

ERIC DOLPHY-OUTWARD BOUND:
Freddie Hubbard(tp)Eric Dolphy(as-1,bass cl-2,fl-3)Jaki Byard(p)
George Tucker(b)Roy Haynes(dm).
Supervision:Esmond Edwards   NYC,April 1,1960

```
2101   G.W.-1                       NJLP8236
2102   245 -1                         -
2103   On green Dolphin Street-2      -
2104   Glad to be unhappy-3,4         -
2105   Les-1                          -
2106   Miss Toni-1                    -
2107   April fool                   PR7382,P-24070
```

-4:Hubbard out.

All titles from NJLP8236 also issued on PR7311,PR24008.

RED GARLAND ALONE:
Red Garland(p).
Supervision:Esmond Edwards   NYC,April 2,1960

```
2108   In the evening               MVLP10
2109   These foolish things         MVLP3
2110   Chains of love               MVLP10
2111   The nearness of you          MVLP3
2112   Wee baby blues               MVLP10
2113   When your lover has gone     MVLP3
2114   Blues in the closet          MVLP10
2115   You are too beautiful        MVLP3,MV35
2116   Trane's blues                MVLP10
2117   When I fall in love          MVLP3
2118   Cloudy                       MVLP10
2119   Tired                          -
2120   I got it bad                 MVLP3
2121   My last affair                 -
2122   Sent for you yesterday       MVLP10
2123   Nancy with the laughing face MVLP3
```

LONNIE JOHNSON-BLUES AND BALLADS:
Lonnie Johnson(vo,g)Elmer Snowden(g)Wendell Marshall(b).
Supervision:Chris Albertson   NYC,April 5,1960

```
2130   Savoy blues                  BVLP1011
2131   Lester leaps in              unissued
2132   Blue and hill alone            -
2133   On the sunny side of the street -
2134   C jam blues                    -
2135   New Orleans blues              -
2136   Careless love                  -
2137   Saint Louis blues            BVLP1011
2138   Elmer's blues                  -
2139   Stormy weather               unissued
2140   Jelly roll baker             BVLP1011;Pr.45-310
2141   Ain't gonna give             unissued
2142   Haunted house                BVLP1011
2143   Blues for Chris                -
2144   Birth of the blues           unissued
2145   Farewell blues                 -
2146   There's no love                -
2147   Backwater blues              BVLP1011,BV1055
2148   I ain't got nobody           unissued
2149   Memories of you              BV45-812,LP1011
2150   I'll get along somehow         -        -   Pr.45-310
2151   I found a dream
```

Note:Chris Albertson claimed titles issued on BVLP1011 were the only
material recorded and gave recording date as May 16,1960.Above details
are listed as found in Prestige files.

SHIRLEY SCOTT TRIO:
Shirley Scott(org)George Tucker(b)Arthur Edgehill(dm)Earl Coleman(vo).
Supervision:Esmond Edwards   NYC,April 8,1960

2152	I thought I'd let you know	MVLP5
2153	Spring is here	-
2154	I didn't know what time it was	- MV35
2155	Lover man	-
2156	Crazy rhythm voEC	unissued
2157	The things you are voEC	-
2158	Autumn leaves	PR7424
2159	Bridge blue	-
2160	Bye bye blackbird	MVLP5

EDDIE "LOCKJAW" DAVIS/SHIRLEY SCOTT:
Eddie "Lockjaw" Davis(ts)Shirley Scott(org)Wendell Marshall(b)Arthur
Edgehill(dm)Ray Barretto(conga).
Supervision:Esmond Edwards   NYC,April 12,1960

2161	I wished on the moon	MVLP30
2162	From this moment on	PR7456
2163	Give me a kiss goodnight	MVLP30
2164	Moon of Manakoora	-
2165	Just friends	-
2166	Speak low	-

LEM WINCHESTER-LEM'S BEAT:
Oliver Nelson,Curtis Peagler(as,ts)Lem Winchester(vb)Billy Brown(p)
Wendell Marshall(b)Art Taylor(dm).
Supervision:Esmond Edwards   NYC,April 19,1960

2167	Your last chance	NJLP8239
2168	Friendly persuasion-1	-
2169	Lady Day-2	-
2170	Just friends-2	-
2171	Lem and aide-2	-
2172	Eddy's dilemma	-

-1:Brown out;-2:Roy Johnson(p)replaces Brown.

THE NEW SCENE OF KING CURTIS:
Nat Adderley(as "Little Brother")(tp)King Curtis(ts)Wynton Kelly(p)
Paul Chambers(b)Oliver Jackson(dm).
Supervision:Ozzie Cadena   NYC,April 21,1960

2181	Have you heard?	NJLP8237
2182	Da du dah	-
2183	Little Brother soul	-
2184	Willow weep for me-1	-
2185	Shout up	unissued
2186	In a funky groove	NJLP8237

-1:Adderley out.

All titles from NJLP8237 also issued on PR7789,PR24033.

JOHNNY "HAMMOND" SMITH-TALK THAT TALK:
Oliver Nelson-1(ts)Johnny "Hammond" Smith(org)George Tucker(b)Art
Taylor(dm)Ray Barretto(conga).
Supervision:Esmond Edwards   NYC,April 22,1960

2173	Minors allowed-1	NJLP8241	
2174	Portrait of Jenny	-	MV37;ST8319;PR7777
2175	Rip tide-1	-	
2176	Bennie's diggin' -1	-	
2177	An affair to remember	-	PR7777
2178	The end of a love affair	-	Pr.45-193
2179	Talk that talk	-	
2180	Misty	-	

MEMPHIS SLIM:
Memphis Slim(vo,p)Lafayette Thomas(g)Wendell Marshall(b).
Supervision:Esmond Edwards   NYC,April 26,1960

2187   Raining the blues   BVLP1031;Fantasy F-24705
2188   Baby doll   BVLP1018   —
2189   Rack 'em back Jack   —   —
2190   Blue Brew   —
2191   Lucille   BVLP1031;Fantasy F-24705
2192   Teasing the blues   BVLP1018   —
2193   Darling I miss you so   rejected
2194   Don't you think you're so smartBVLP1031;Fantasy F-24705
2195   Brenda   BVLP1018   —
2196   No strain   BVLP1031
2197   Nice stuff

JOHN LEE HOOKER:
John Lee Hooker(vo,g).
Supervision:Esmond Edwards   NYC,April 29,1960

2198   Sally Mae   unissued
2199   I like to see you walk   Vee Jay VJLP1033
2200   Take me as I am   Vee Jay VJ397,LP1033
2201   You're looking good again tonight   —
2202   Moanin' blues   unissued
2203   Wednesday evening blues   Vee Jay VJLP1033,LP8502
2204   You're gonna miss me when I'm gone   unissued
2205   Dirty ground hog   —
2206   untitled instrumental   —
2207   Five long years   Vee Jay VJLP1033
2208   When my first wife left me   —   LP8502
2209   She loves my best friend   unissued
2210   Come and ride with me   —
2211   My heart in misery   —

Note:Material from this session was sold to Vee Jay.

GIGI GRYCE-THE HAP'NIN'S:
Richard Williams(tp)Gigi Gryce(as)Richard Wyands(p)Julian Euell(b)
Granville "Mickey" Roker(dm).
Supervision:Esmond Edwards   NYC,May 3,1960

2212   Summertime   NJLP8246
2213   Lover man   —
2214   Minorally   —
2215   Don't worry about me   —
2216   Frankie and Johnnie   —
2217   Nica's tempo   —

JOE NEWMAN-JIVE AT FIVE:
Joe Newman(tp)Frank Wess(fl,ts)Tommy Flanagan(p)Eddie Jones(b)Oliver
Jackson(dm).
Supervision:Esmond Edwards   NYC,May 4,1960

2218   Taps Miller   SVLP2011
2219   Jive at five   —
2220   Wednesday's blues   —
2221   More than you know   —
2222   Don't worry 'bout me   —
2223   Cuein' the blues   —

FRANK WESS QUARTET:
Frank Wess(fl,ts)Tommy Flanagan(p)Eddie Jones(b)Bobby Donaldson(dm).
Supervision:Esmond Edwards   NYC,May 9,1960

2224	It's so peaceful	MVLP8
2225	But beautiful	-
2226	Stella by starlight	-
2227	Gone with the wind	-
2228	I see your face before me	-
2229	Star eyes	-
2230	Rainy afternoon	- Pr.45-271

SHAKEY JAKE-GOOD TIMES:
Shakey Jake(vo,hca)Jack McDuff(org)Bill Jennings(g).
Supervision:Esmond Edwards   NYC,May 11,1960

2231	Good times	BVLP1008
2232	Tear drops	
2233	Worried blues	-
2234	My foolish heart	BV45-807,LP1008
2235	Jake's blues-1	- -
2236	Still your fool	-
2237	Call me when you need me	-
2238	Keep-a loving me baby	-
2239	Sunset blues-1	-
2240	Huffin' and puffin'-1	-
2241	You spoiled my baby-2	-
2242	Just Shakey	-

-1:no vocal on these titles;-2:McDuff out.

BUD FREEMAN ALL STARS:
Harold "Shorty" Baker(tp)Bud Freeman(ts)Claude Hopkins(p)George
Duvivier(b)J.C.Heard(dm).
Supervision:Esmond Edwards   NYC,May 13,1960

2243	Shorty's blues	SVLP2012
2244	March on,march on	-
2245	Hector's dance	-
2246	'S posin'	-
2247	But not for me	-
2248	Something sweet to remember you by	-
2249	Love me or leave me	-
2250	I let a song go out of my heart	-

DOUG WATKINS-SOULNIK:
Yusef Lateef(fl,ts,oboe)Hugh Lawson(p)Doug Watkins(b,cello)Herman
Wright(b)Lex Humphries(dm).
Supervision:Esmond Edwards   NYC,May 17,1960

2251	I remember you	NJLP8238
2252	Confessin'	-
2253	One guy	-
2254	Imagination	-
2255	Andre's bag	-
2256	Soulnik	-

All titles also issued on PR7832 as by YUSEF LATEEF.

THE TOMMY FLANAGAN TRIO:
Tommy Flanagan(p)Tommy Potter(b)Roy Haynes(dm).
Supervision:Esmond Edwards   NYC,May 18,1960

2257	You go to my head	MVLP9
2258	In the blue of the evening	-
2259	Velvet moon	-
2260	Come Sunday	-
2261	Jes' fine	-
2262	Born to be blue	-
2263	In a sentimental mood	-

MODERN JAZZ DISCIPLES-RIGHT DOWN FRONT:
Curtis Peagler(as,ts)William Kelley(normaphone)Bill Brown(p)Lee
Tucker(b)Wilbur "Slim" Jackson(dm).
Supervision:Esmond Edwards   NYC,May 24,1960

2264	Kelley's line	NJLP8240
2265	Along came Cheryl	-
2266	Right down front	-
2267	Ros-Al	-
2268	The happy blues	-
2269	Autumn serenade	-
2270	My funny Valentine	-

OLIVER NELSON-SCREAMIN' THE BLUES:
Richard Williams(tp)Eric Dolphy(fl,as-3,bass cl-4)Oliver Nelson(as-1,
ts-2)Richard Wyands(p)George Duvivier(b)Roy Haynes(dm).
Supervision:Esmond Edwards   NYC,May 27,1960

2271	Three seconds-2,3	NJ	LP8243
2272	Altoitis-1,3		-
2273	The meetin'-2,3		-
2274	The drive-1,3		-
2275	March on,march on-2,3		-
2276	Screamin' the blues-2,4	NJ45-508	-

All titles also issued on ST8324,P-24060.

KEN McINTYRE-STONE BLUES:
John Mancebo Lewis(tb)Ken McIntyre(fl,as)Dizzy Sal(p)Paul Morrison(b)
Bobby Ward(dm).
Supervision:Esmond Edwards   NYC,May 31,1960

2277	Smax	NJLP8259
2278	Charshee	-
2279	I'll close my eyes	-
2280	Blanche	-
2281	Melliflous	-
2282	Cornballs	-
2283	Stone blues	-

BETTY ROCHE-SINGIN' AND SWINGIN':
Betty Roche(vo)with Jimmy Forrest(ts)Jack McDuff(org)Bill Jennings(g)
Wendell Marshall(b)Roy Haynes(dm).
Supervision:Esmond Edwards   NYC,June 3,1960

2284	When I fall in love	Pr.	LP7187
2285	September song		-
2286	A foggy day	Pr.45-181	-
2287	Day by day		-
2288	Come rain or come shine	Pr.45-181	-
2289	Blue moon		-
2290	Where or when		-
2291	Until the real thing comes along		-
2292	Billie's bounce		-

LEM WINCHESTER-ANOTHER OPUS:
Frank Wess(ts,fl)Lem Winchester(vb)Hank Jones(p)Eddie Jones(b)Gus
Johnson(dm).
Supervision:Esmond Edwards   NYC,June 4,1960

2298	Another opus	NJLP8244
2299	Both barrels	-
2300	Blues prayer	-
2301	The meetin'	-
2302	Like someone in love	-

GIGI GRYCE-THE RAT RACE BLUES:
Richard Williams(tp)Gigi Gryce(as)Richard Wyands(p)Julian Euell(b)
Granville "Mickey" Roker(dm).
Supervision:Esmond Edwards   NYC,June 7,1960

2293	Blues in bloom	NJLP8262
2294	Boxer's blues	-
2295	Strange feelin'	-
2296	The rat race blues	-
2297	Monday through Sunday	-

GENE AMMONS-BOSS TENOR:
Gene Ammons(ts)Tommy Flanagan(p)Doug Watkins(b)Art Taylor(dm)Ray
Barretto(conga).
Supervision:Esmond Edwards   NYC,June 16,1960

2303	Close your eyes	Pr.	LP7180
2304	Savoy		-
2305	Blue Ammons		- PR7306
2306	Confirmation		-
2307	Hittin' the Jug	Pr.45-176	-
2308	Canadian sunset		- 45-390,LP7180,PR7708, P-10084*
2309	My romance	PRLP7180	

*2308 is edited on P-10084.

All titles also issued on PR7534.

GENE AMMONS-ANGEL EYES:
Gene Ammons(ts)Frank Wess(ts,fl)Johnny "Hammond" Smith(org)Doug
Watkins(b)Art Taylor(dm).
Supervision:Esmond Edwards   NYC,June 17,1960

2310	Gettin' around	Pr.	PR7369
2311	Blue room		-
2312	Water Jug		
2313	Angel eyes		Pr.45-371,45-721,PR7369,PR7708, P-10084
2314	Velvet soul		Pr.45-336,PR7320
2315	In Sid's thing		-

All titles also issued on P-24071.

ETTA JONES-DON'T GO TO STRANGERS:
Etta Jones(vo)with Frank Wess(ts,fl)Richard Wyands(p)Skeeter Best(g)
George Duvivier(b)Roy Haynes(dm).
Supervision:Esmond Edwards   NYC,June 21,1960

2316	On the street where you live	Pr.	LP7186,ST8315
2317	Something to remember you by		-
2318	Bye bye blackbird		-
2319	Where or when		
2320	All the way	Pr.45-198	-
2321	Yes,Sir,that's my baby		-
2322	Don't go to strangers		Pr.45-180,45-389,LP7186,PR7443
2323	I love Paris		-
2324	Fine and mellow		- PR7443
2325	If I had you	Pr.45-180	-

SHIRLEY SCOTT-SOUL SISTER:
Shirley Scott(org)Lem Winchester(vb)George Duvivier(b)Arthur Edgehill
(dm).
Supervision:Esmond Edwards   NYC,June 23,1960

2326	Like young	Pr.	PR7392
2327	Sonnymoon for two	-	
2328	On green Dolphin Street	Pr.45-437	-
2329	Blues for Tyrone	-	-
2330	The more I see you	-	
2331	Get me to the church on time	-	ST8315
2332	Now's the time	PR7440	

KEN McINTYRE-LOOKING AHEAD:
Ken McIntyre(fl-1,as-2)Eric Dolphy(fl-3,bass cl-4,as-5)Walter Bishop Jr.
(p)Sam Jones(b)Art Taylor(dm).
Supervision:Esmond Edwards   NYC,June 28,1960

2333	George's tune-2,5	NJLP8247;P-24085	
2334	They all laughed-2,5	-	-
2335	Dianna-1,4	-	-
2336	Curtsy-2,5	-	-
2337	Lautir-2,5	-	-
2338	Head shakin'-1,3	-	-

LITTLE BROTHER MONTGOMERY-TASTY BLUES:
Little Brother Montgomery(p;vo)Lafayette Thomas(g)Julian Euell(b).
Supervision:Esmond Edwards   NYC,July 1,1960

2339	Satellite blues	BVLP1012
2340	No special rider	-
2341	Cry,cry baby	-
2342	Brother's boogie	-
2343	Vicksburg blues-1	-
2344	Tasty blues	-
2345	Pleading blues	-
2346	Santa Fe	-
2347	Sneaky Pete blues	-
2348	Something keeps worrying me	-
2349	How long brother	-
2350	Deep fried	-

-1:piano solo.

All titles also issued on PR7807,Fantasy F-24717.

ROY HAYNES-JUST US:
Richard Wyands(p)Eddie De Haas(b)Roy Haynes(dm).
Supervision:Esmond Edwards   NYC,July 5,1960

2351	As long as there's music	NJLP8245
2352	Con alma	-
2353	Speak low	-
2354	Down home	-
2355	Sweet and lovely	-
2356	Cymbalism	-
2357	Well now	-

SHIRLEY SCOTT-MUCHO MUCHO:
Shirley Scott(org)Gene Casey(p)Bill Ellington(b)Manny Ramos(timbales)
Phil Diaz(bongos)Juan Amalbert(conga).
Supervision:Esmond Edwards   NYC,July 8,1960

2358	The lady is a tramp	PRLP7182
2359	Muy azul	-
2360	I get a kick out of you	-
2361	Walkin'	-
2362	Tell me	-
2363	Mucho mucho	-

JACK McDUFF-TOUGH DUFF:
Jimmy Forrest(ts)Lem Winchester(vb)Jack McDuff(org)Bill Elliot(dm).
Supervision:Esmond Edwards   NYC,July 12,1960

2361A	Smooth sailing	Pr.	LP7185
2362A	Autumn leaves		-
2363A	Yeah baby	Pr.45-184	-
2364	Tippin' in		-
2365	Mean to me		- PR7596
2366	Tough Duff		- PR7481,PR24013

PRLP7185=PR7814.

RED GARLAND TRIO:
Red Garland(p,org-1)Sam Jones(b)Art Taylor(dm).
Supervision:Esmond Edwards   NYC,July 15,1960

2367	Back sliding	PR7288
2368	Revelation blues	-
2369	Everytime I feel the spirit-1	-
2370	Hallelo-Y'all	-
2371	Blues in the night	PR7307
2371B	Rocks in my bed	-
2372	Soul burnin'	-
2373	You'll never be free	PR7288

LARRY YOUNG-TESTIFYING:
Joe Holiday(ts)Larry Young(org)Thornel Schwartz(g)Jimmy Smith(dm).
Supervision:Esmond Edwards   NYC,August 2,1960

2374	Wee dot	NJLP8249
2375	Exercise for Chihuahuas	-
2376	Testifying	-
2377	When I grow too old to dream	-
2378	Some thorny blues	-
2379	Flamingo	-
2380	Falling in love with love	-

JIMMY FORREST-FORREST FIRE!:
Jimmy Forrest(ts)Larry Young(org)Thornel Schwartz(g)Jimmy Smith(dm).
Supervision:Esmond Edwards   NYC,August 9,1960

2381	When your lover has gone	NJ	LP8250
2382	Dexter's deck		-
2383	Bags' groove		-
2384	Help		-
2385	Jim jams		-
2386	Remember	Pr45-197	-

AL SMITH-MIDNIGHT SPECIAL:
Al Smith(vo)with King Curtis(ts)Robert Banks(p,org)Jimmy Lee(g)Leonard
Gaskin(b)Bobby Donaldson(dm).
Supervision:Ozzie Cadena   NYC,August 11,1960

2387	I've been mistreated	BV	LP1013
2388	You're a sweetheart	BV45-808	-
2389	Don't worry about me		-
2390	Ride on midnight special	BV45-808	-
2391	The bells		-
2392	Goin' to Alabama		-
2393	I'll never let you go		-
2394	I can't make it myself		-

ERIC DOLPHY-OUT THERE:
Eric Dolphy(as-1,bass cl-2,cl-3,fl-4)Ron Carter(cello)George Duvivier
(b)Roy Haynes(dm).
Supervision:Esmond Edwards   NYC,August 15,1960
2395   Out there-1   NJLP8252
2396   Feathers-1   -
2397   The baron-2   -
2398   Serene-2   -
2399   Sketch of Melba-4   -
2400   17 West-4   -
2401   Eclipse-3   -

All titles also issued on PR7652,PR24007.

WILLIS JACKSON:
Willis Jackson(ts)Bill Jennings(g)Jack McDuff(org)Wendell Marshall(b)
Bill Elliot(dm).
Supervision:Esmond Edwards   NYC,August 16,1960
2402   Contrasts   PRLP7211
2403   Cookin' sherry   Pr.45-207,LP7211,PR7702
2404   Blue gator   Pr.45-187,LP7183
2405   Try a little tenderness   -
2406   T'gether(Tu'gether*)   Pr.45-411*,PR7364
2407   Mellow blues   PRLP7211

PRLP7183=PR7850.

THE LATIN JAZZ QUINTET with ERIC DOLPHY-CARIBE:
Eric Dolphy(as-1,bass cl-2,fl-3)Charlie Simons(vb)Gene Casey(p)Bill
Ellington(b)Manny Ramos(dm,timbales)Juan Amalbert(conga).
Supervision:Esmond Edwards   NYC,August 19,1960
2408   Sunday go meetin'-3   NJLP8251
2409   First bass line-2   -
2410   Mambo Ricci-1   -
2411   Blues in 6/8 -1   -
2412   Spring is here-3   -
2413   Caribe-1   -

BROWNIE McGHEE and SONNY TERRY:
Brownie McGhee(vo,g)Sonny Terry(hca,vo).
                                    NYC,August 22,1960
        Pawn shop   BV45-809,LP1002
        Let me be your little dog   BV45-802   -
        You don't know   -   PR14023
        Betty and Dupree's blues   -
        Back to New Orleans   -
        Stranger here   BV45-802   -
        Fox hunt   -
        I'm prison bound   -
        Louise Louise   -
        Baby how long   -
        Freight train   BV45-818   -
        Blues all around my head   BV   LP1020;PR7715
        East coast blues   -   -
        Muddy water   -   -
        Beggin' and cryin'   BV45-818   -
        My plan   -
        Trying to destroy me   -
        Everything I had is gone   -
        Jealous man   -
        Understand me   -
        Blues of happiness   -

All titles from BVLP1002 also issued on PR14013,Fantasy F-24708.
All titles from BVLP1020 also issued on Fantasy F-24721.

Same.

NYC,possibly same date

Too nicey Mama voMcG,ST	BV45-809,LP1005
Sonny's squall voBMcG	-
Red river blues voBMcG,ST	-
Black gal voMcG	-
Blues before sunrise voMcG	-
Sweet lovin' kid voMcG,ST	-
Midnight special voMcG,ST	-
Take this hammer voMcG,ST	-
Meet me down at the bottom voMcG	-
Tryin'to win voMcG,ST	-

All titles also issued on Fantasy F-24721.

Same. -1:Roy Haynes(dm)added.

NYC,August 22,1960

I got a woman	BVLP1033;PR7715
Hold me in your arms	-
The C.C. and O.blues	-
That's why I'm walkin'-1	-
Wrong track-1	-
Blue feeling-1	-
House lady-1	-
I know better-1	-
The devil's gonna get you	-
Don't you lie to me	- PR7715

All titles also issued on Fantasy F-24708.

OLIVER NELSON-NOCTURNE:
Oliver Nelson(as,ts)Lem Winchester(vb)Richard Wyands(p)George Duvivier
(b)Roy Haynes(dm).
Supervision:Esmond Edwards   NYC,August 23,1960

2414	Bob's blues	MVLP13
2415	Azure te	- Pr.45-269
2416	Time after time	-
2417	Early morning	-
2418	Nocturne	-
2419	In a sentimental mood	-
2420	Man with the horn	-

2421:not used.
2422/2434:see next page.

BLIND GARY DAVIS-HARLEM STREET SINGER:
Blind Gary Davis(vo,g).
Supervision:Kenneth Goldstein   NYC,August 24,1960

2435	I belong to the band	BVLP1015
2436	I'm the light of the world	Fantasy F-24704
2437	Let us get together right down there	BVLP1015
2438	Samson and Delilah	-
2439	The sun going down	unissued
2440	Lo,I be with you always	BVLP1015
2441	Keep your...	unissued
2442	You got to go down	-
2443	Goin' to sit down on the banks of the river	BVLP1015
2444	Twelve gates to the city	-
2445	Tryin' to get home	-
2446	Lord,I feel just like goin' on	-

(session continued on next page)

```
2447    Pure religion                        BVLP1015
2448    Great chance since I been born       -
2449    Death don't have no mercy            -
2450    By and by I'm going to see the King      unissued
2451    I know I have another building           -
2452    Earth have no sorrow-1               -
2453    Joy to know Him                      -
2454    Don't move my bed till Holy Ghost comes  -
```

All titles from BVLP1015 also issued on PR14028,PR7805,Fantasy F-24704.

JOHN   WRIGHT-SOUTH SIDE SOUL:
John Wright(p)Wendell Roberts(b)Walter McCants(dm).
Supervision:Esmond Edwards   NYC,August 30,1960

```
2422    Sin corner                           Pr.45-188,LP7190
2423    La Salle Street after hours          -
2424    63rd and Cottage groove              -
2425    45th and Calmet                      -
2426    35th Street blues                    -
2427    Amen corner                          Pr.45-188    -
2428    South side soul                      -
```

EDDIE "LOCKJAW" DAVIS/JOHNNY GRIFFIN-BATTLE STATIONS:
Eddie "Lockjaw" Davis,Johnny Griffin(ts)Norman Simmons(p)Victor Sproles
(b)Ben Riley(dm).
Supervision:Esmond Edwards   NYC,September 2,1960

```
2429    Pull my coat                         Pr.45-183,LP7282
2430    What's happening?                    -
2431    Abundance                            -
2432    63rd Street theme                    -
2433    Hey Jim                              -
2434    If I had you                         -
```

OLIVER NELSON-SOUL BATTLE:
Oliver Nelson,King Curtis,Jimmy Forrest(ts)Gene Casey(p)George Duvivier
(b)Roy Haynes(dm).
Supervision:Esmond Edwards   NYC,September 9,1960

```
2455    Blues at the Five Spot               PRLP7223
2456    Blues for M.F.(Mort Fega)            -
2457    Anacrisis                            -
2458    Soul street                          NJLP8293
2459    In passing                           PRLP7223
2460    Perdido                              -      PR7712
```

ROOSEVELT SYKES-THE HONEYDRIPPER:
King Curtis(ts)Robert Banks(org)Roosevelt Sykes(p,vo)Leonard Gaskin(b)
Belton Evans(dm).
Supervision:Esmond Edwards   NYC,September 14,1960

```
        Miss Ida B-1                         BV45-810,LP1014
        Satellite baby                       -
        Mislead mother                       -
        Yes Lawd                             -
        I hate to be alone                   -
        Jail bait-1                          -
        Lonely day-1,2                       -
        Pocketful of money                   -
        She ain't for nobody-2               -
```

-1:Banks out;-2:Curtis out.
All titles also issued on PR7722

Note:Matrix numbers for above titles are 2477/2485 but right order
remains unknown.

SUNNYLAND SLIM-SLIM'S SHOUT:
King Curtis(ts)Robert Banks(org)Sunnyland Slim(p,vo)Leonard Gaskin(b)
Belton Evans(dm).
Supervision:Ozzie Cadena   NYC,September 15,1960

I'm prison bound-1	BV45-816,LP1016	
Slim's shout	-	
The devil is a busy man	-	
Brownskin woman	-	
Shake it	BV45-816	-
Decoration day	-	
Baby how long	BV45-811	-
Sunnyland special	-	
Harlem can't be heaven-1	-	
It's you baby	BV45-811	-
Everytime I get to drinking	unissued	
Tired of you clowning	-	

Note:Matrix numbers for above titles are 2486/2497,but order remains
unknown.
BVLP1016=PR7723.   -1:Curtis out.

ETTA JONES:
Etta Jones(vo)with Oliver Nelson(ts)Lem Winchester(vb)Richard Wyands(p)
George Duvivier(b)Roy Haynes(dm).
Supervision:Esmond Edwards   NYC,September 16,1960

2461	The more I see you	PR7284
2462	They can't take that away from me	-
2463	Our love is here to stay	unissued
2464	That's all there is to that-1	Pr.45-191,LP7194
2465	Easy living-2	-
2466	Canadian sunset-2	Pr.45-191,45-389,LP7194,PR7443
2467	I've got it bad	PR7284
2468	Give me the simple life	rejected
2469	I only have eyes for you-1	PRLP7194
2470	Almost like being in love-1	-

-1:Nelson & Winchester out;-2:Nelson out.

PRLP7194=PR7784.

KING CURTIS-SOUL MEETING:
Nat Adderley(tp)King Curtis(ts)Wynton Kelly(p)Sam Jones(b)Belton Evans
(dm).
Supervision:Ozzie Cadena   NYC,September 18,1960

2471	Do you have soul now?	PRLP7222	
2472	Jeep's blues	-	
2473	Soul meeting	-	NJ45-510
2474	What is this thing called love	-	
2475	Lazy soul	-	
2476	All the way	-	NJ45-510

All titles also issued on PR7833,PR24033.

EDDIE "LOCKJAW" DAVIS BIG BAND-TRANE WHISTLE:
Clark Terry,Richard Williams,Bob Bryant(tp)Jimmy Cleveland,Melba Liston
(tb)Oliver Nelson(as,arr)Eric Dolphy(as)Eddie "Lockjaw" Davis(ts)Jerome
Richardson,George Barrow (ts,fl)Bob Ashton(bs)Richard Wyands(p)Wendell
Marshall(b)Roy Haynes(dm)Ernie Wilkins-1(arr).
Supervision:Esmond Edwards   NYC,September 20,1960

2498	Walk away	PRLP7206
2499	Trane whistle	-
2500	Whole Nelson	-

(session continued on next page)

```
2501   The stolen moment            PRLP7206
2502   Jaws-1                       -
2503   You are too beautiful-1      -

PRLP7206=PR7834.

MILDRED ANDERSON-NO MORE IN LIFE:
Mildred Anderson(vo)with Al Sears(ts)Robert Banks(org)Lord Westbrook(g)
Leonard Gaskin(b)Bobby Donaldson(dm).
Supervision:Ozzie Cadena          NYC,September 26,1960

2504   Roll 'em Pete                BVLP1017
2505   What more can a woman do     -
2506   I'm lost                     -
2507   Everybody's got somebody but me  -
2508   I ain't mad at you           -
2509   Hard times                   -
2510   That old devil called love   -
2511   Mistreater                   -
2512   No more in life              -

SHIRLEY SCOTT-LIKE COZY:
Shirley Scott(org)George Duvivier(b)Arthur Edgehill(dm).
Supervision:Esmond Edwards         NYC,September 27,1960

2513   You do something to me       MVLP19,MV34
2514   More than you know           -
2515   Once in a while              -
2516   Little girl blue             -
2517   Laura                        -    MV37;ST8319
2518   Like Cozy                    -
2519   My heart stood still         -
2520   'Deed I do                   -

LARRY YOUNG-YOUNG BLUES:
Larry Young(org)Thornel Schwartz(g)Wendell Marshall(b)Jimmie Smith(dm).
Supervision:Esmond Edwards         NYC,September 30,1960

2521   African blues                NJLP8264
2522   Little white lies            -
2523   Nica's dream                 -
2524   Minor dream                  -
2525   Something new                -
2526   Young blues                  -
2527   A midnight angel             -

BROWNIE McGHEE-BROWNIE'S BLUES:
Brownie McGhee(vo,g)Sonny Terry(hca)Bennie Foster(g).
Supervision:Ozzie Cadena           NYC,October 6,1960

2584   Little black engine          BVLP1042;PR7715
2585   I don't know the reason      -
2586   Trouble in mind              -
2587   Everyday I have the blues    -
2588   Goin' back to the country    unissued
2589   Door to success              BVLP1042
2590   Jump little children         -    PR7715
2591   Lonesome play                -
2592   One thing for sure           -
2593   The killin' floor            -
```

LEM WINCHESTER-WITH FEELING:
Lem Winchester(vb)Richard Wyands(p)George Duvivier(b)Roy Haynes(dm).
Supervision:Esmond Edwards   NYC,October 7,1960

2528   With a song in my heart   MVLP11
2529   But beautiful   -
2530   The kids   -
2531   The love and beloved   -
2532   Butterfly   -
2533   Why don't they understand   -
2534   My romance   -   MV35
2535   Skylark   -

2536/2560:JEAN RITCHIE-October 8,1960(not jazz)
2537/2583:ED McCURDY-October 9,1960(not jazz)

SONNY TERRY-SONNY'S STORY:
Sonny Terry(vo,hca)Sticks McGhee(g)J.C.Burris,Belton Evans(dm).
Supervision:Ozzie Cadena   NYC,October 13,1960

2594   Telephone blues   BVLP1025
2595   Great tall engine   -
2596   Get on my feet after while   -
2597   Four o'clock blues   -
2598   Sonny's story   -
2599   I ain't gonna be your dog no more -
2600   My baby done gone   -
2601   Worried blues   -
2602   High powered woman   -
2603   Pepper headed woman   -
2604   Hoo wee baby   -
2605   California blues   -

JOHNNY "HAMMOND" SMITH-GETTIN' THE MESSAGE:
Lem Winchester(vb)Johnny "Hammond" Smith(org)Eddie McFadden(g)Wendell
Marshall(b)Bill Erskine(dm).
Supervision:Esmond Edwards   NYC,October 14,1960

2606   Dementia   Pr.   LP7217
2607   Princess   -
2608   Gettin' the message   -
2609   Swanee river   Pr.45-209   -
2610   Just say so long   -
2611   Lid flippin'   -

BUDDY TATE-TATE-A-TATE:
Clark Terry(tp,flh)Buddy Tate(ts)Tommy Flanagan(p)Larry Gales(b)Art
Taylor(dm).
Supervision:Esmond Edwards   NYC,October 18,1960

2612   Groun' hog   SVLP2014
2613   Buddy's tate-a-tate   -
2614   Snatchin' it back   -
2615   All too soon   -
2616   Take the A train   -
2617   No.20 Ladbroke Square   -

SONNY TERRY-SONNY IS KING:
Sonny Terry(vo,hca)Lightnin' Hopkins(g)Leonard Gaskin(b)Belton Evans
(dm).
Supervision:Ozzie Cadena   NYC,October 26,1960

2618   One monkey don't stop the show BVLP1059
2619   Changed the lock on my door   -
2620   Tater pie   -
2621   Diggin' my potatoes   -
2622   So sweet

BVLP1059=PR7802.

LIGHTNIN' HOPKINS:
Lightnin' Hopkins(vo,g)Sonny Terry(hca)Leonard Gaskin(b)Belton Evans
(dm).
Supervision:Ozzie Cadena   NYC,October 26,1960

2623	Rocky mountain blues	BV	LP1029		
2624	Got to move your baby	BV45-813	–	BV1084;Pr.45-391,	
		PR7592			
2625	So sorry to leave you	BV	LP1029		
2626	Take a trip with me	–			
2627	Last night blues	BV45-821	–	BV1084	
2628	Lightnin's stroke	–			
2629	Hard to love a woman	BV45-817	–	BV1084	
2630	Conversation blues	–			

BVLP1029=BV1081,PR7831.

ARNETT COBB-SIZZLIN':
Arnett Cobb(ts)Red Garland(p)George Tucker(b)J.C.Heard(dm).
Supervision:Esmond Edwards   NYC,October 31,1960

2631	The way you look tonight	PRLP7227	
2632	Sizzlin'	–	
2633	Black velvet	–	PR7711
2634	Sweet Georgia Brown	–	
2635	Blue sermon	–	
2636	Georgia on my mind	–	

ARNETT COBB-BALLADS BY COBB:
Same.Red Garland(p,celeste-1).
Supervision:Esmond Edwards   NYC,November 1,1960

2637	Hurry home	MVLP14
2638	Blue and sentimental	–
2639	Willow weep for me	–
2640	Darn that dream	–
2641	Why try to change me now-1	–
2642	P.S.I love you	–
2643	Your wonderful love	–

ARBEE STIDHAM-TIRED OF WANDERING:
King Curtis(ts)John Wright(p)Arbee Stidham(vo,g)Leonard Gaskin(b)
Armand "Jump" Jackson(dm).
Supervision:Ozzie Cadena   NYC,November 7,1960

2662	Last goodbye blues	BVLP1021
2663	You can't live in this world	–
2664	Pawnshop	–
2665	I'm tired of wandering	–
2666	I want to belong to you	–
2667	Wee baby blues	–
2668	You keep me yearning	–
2669	My heart will always belong to you	–
2670	People what would you do	–
2671	Teenage kiss	–

JOHN WRIGHT-NICE 'N 'TASTY:
John Wright(p)Wendell Marshall(b)J.C.Heard(dm).
Supervision:Esmond Edwards   NYC,November 8,1960

2644	Things are getting better	Pr.	LP7197
2645	Witchcraft	–	
2646	The very thought of you	–	
2647	The Wright way	–	
2648	Pie face	–	
2649	You do it	Pr.45-203	–
2650	Yes I know	–	–
2651	Darn that dream	–	

LIGHTNIN' HOPKINS-LIGHTNIN':
Lightnin' Hopkins(vo,g)Leonard Gaskin(b)Belton Evans(dm).
Supervision:Ozzie Cadena   NYC,November 9,1960

2652	Automobile blues	BV	LP1019;Pr.45-343
2653	You better watch yourself	-	
2654	Thinkin' about an old friend	-	
2655	The walkin' blues	BV45-821 -	BV1084;PR7592
2656	Back to New Orleans	BV45-817 -	- -
2657	Katie Mae	BV45-825 -	
2658	Down there baby	-	
2659	Mean old Frisco	-	
2660	Shinin' moon	-	
2661	Come back baby	-	

BVLP1019=PR7811.

CURTIS JONES-TROUBLE BLUES:
Curtis Jones(vo,p)Robert Banks(org)Johnny "Moose John" Walker-1(g)
Leonard Gaskin(b)Belton Evans(dm).
Supervision:Ozzie Cadena   NYC,November 9,1960

2672	Weekend blues-1	BVLP1022
2673	Good woman blues-1	-
2674	A whole lot of talk for you-1	-
2675	Suicide blues-1	-
2676	Please say yes-2	-
2677	Lonesome bedroom blues	-
2678	Fool blues-1	-
2679	Good time special	-
2680	Love season	-
2681	Low down worried blues	-
2682	Pinetop's boogie woogie	unissued
2683	Trouble blues	BVLP1022

-2:Banks out.

AL CASEY QUARTET:
Lee Anderson(p)Al Casey(g)Jimmy Lewis(b)Belton Evans(dm).
Supervision:Esmond Edwards   NYC,November 10,1960

2684	I'm beginning to see the light	MVLP12
2685	Dancing in the dark	-
2686	A case of blues	-
2687	Don't worry about me	-
2688	Blue moon	-
2689	These foolish things	-
2690	All alone	-

ROBERT PETE WILLIAMS-FREE AGAIN:
Robert Pete Williams(vo,g).

Baton Rouge,La.,November 14,1960

Free again	BVLP1026
Almost dead blues	-
Rolling stone	-
Two wings	-
A thousand miles from nowhere	-
Thumbing a ride	-
I've grown so ugly	-
Death blues	-
Hobo worried blues	-
Hay cutting song	-

All titles also issued on PR7808,Fantasy F-24716.

MEMPHIS SLIM:
Memphis Slim(p,vo)Buster "Harpie" Brown-1(hca).
Supervision:Esmond Edwards   NYC,November 15,1960

2691	When your dough roller is gone	BVLP1018
2692	You're gonna need my help one day	BVLP1031
2693	My baby left me	-
2694	Angel child-1	-
2695	The I.C.Blues-1	BVLP1018
2696	Motherless child	-
2697	Lonesome traveller-1	BVLP1031
2698	Blues & disgusted	BVLP1018
2699	Darling I miss you so	BVLP1031
2700	Hey Slim	BVLP1018
2701	Just blues	-
2702	Beer drinkin' woman	-
2703	Fast and free	BVLP1031

All titles also issued on Fantasy F-24705.

SHAKEY JAKE-MOUTH HARP BLUES:
Shakey Jake(vo,hca)Robert Banks(p)Jimmy Lee(g)Leonard Gaskin(b)Junior
Blackmon(dm).
Supervision:Ozzie Cadena   NYC,November 17,1960

2704	Angry lover	BVLP1027
2705	Things is all right	-
2706	My broken heart	-
2707	It won't happen again	-
2708	Gimme a smile	-
2709	Easy baby	-
2710	Love you baby	-
2711	Jake's cha cha	-
2712	Mouth harp blues	-
2713	Things are different baby	-

ST.LOUIS JIMMY-GOIN' DOWN SLOW:
St.Louis Jimmy(vo)with Robert Banks(p)Jimmy Lee-1(g)Leonard Gaskin(b)
Belton Evans(dm).
Supervision:Ozzie Cadena   NYC,November 19,1960

2714	Some sweet day-1	BVLP1028
2715	Dog house blues-1	-
2716	Poor boy	-
2717	Mother's day	-
2718	My heart is loaded with trouble	-
2719	I'm Saint Louis bound	-
2720	Goin' down slow	-
2721	Sweet as she can be	-
2722	Monkey faced woman	-
2723	Nothin' but the blues	-

2724/2734:no information.

AL SEARS SWINGS THE THING:
Al Sears(ts)Don Abney(p)Wally Richardson(g)Wendell Marshall(b)Joe
Marshall(dm).
Supervision:Esmond Edwards   NYC,November 29,1960

2735	Already all right	SVLP2018	
2736	Take-off road	-	Pr.45-192
2737	Moving out	-	
2738	Record hop	-	Pr.45-192
2739	The thrill is gone	-	
2740	Ain't no use	-	
2741	Out of nowhere	-	
2742	In a mellow tone	-	

BUDD JOHNSON-LET'S SWING:
Keg Johnson(tb)Budd Johnson(ts)Tommy Flanagan(p)George Duvivier(b)
Charlie Persip(dm).
Supervision:Esmond Edwards   NYC,December 2,1960

2743   Someone to watch over me   SVLP2015
2744   Uptown Manhattan   -
2745   Downtown Manhattan   -
2746   Falling in love with love   -
2747   I only have eyes for you   -
2748   Blues by Budd   -
2749   Serenade in blue   -

LATIN JAZZ QUINTET:
Bobby Capers(as)Will Coleman(vb)Jose Ricci(p)Bill Ellington(b)Ernest
Phil Newsom(dm,timbales)Juan Amalbert(conga,leader).
Supervision:Esmond Edwards   NYC,December 6,1960

2750   Red top   ST8321
2751   Uno lament-1   unissued
2752   Dilly Dali   ST8321
2753   Polly's delight   TRU15003
2754   Summertime   -
2755   Blue moon   -
2756   'Round midnight   -

-1:Artie Jenkins(p)replaces Ricci.

JIMMY NEELEY TRIO-MISIRLOU:
Jimmy Neeley(p)Michel Mulia(b)Rudy Lawless(dm).
Supervision:Esmond Edwards   NYC,December 16,1960

2757   Gettin' a taste   TRU15002
2758   Witchcraft   -
2759   Misirlou   -
2760   Time after time   -
2761   My one and only love   -
2762   Oh(The chase)   -
2763   Lament of the lonely   -
2764   Gone with the wind   -
2765   Love is a many splendoured thing   -

BUCK CLAYTON-BUCK AND BUDDY:
Buck Clayton(tp)Buddy Tate(ts)Sir Charles Thompson(p)Gene Ramey(b)
Mousie Alexander(dm).
Supervision:Esmond Edwards   NYC,December 20,1960

2766   High life   SVLP2017
2767   Can't we be friends   -
2768   Birdland Betty   -
2769   Kansas City nights   -
2770   When a woman loves a man   -
2771   Thou swell   -

All titles also issued on PR24040.

ERIC DOLPHY-FAR CRY!:
Booker Little(tp)Eric Dolphy(as-1,bass cl-2,fl-3)Jaki Byard(p)Ron Carter
(b)Roy Haynes(dm).
Supervision:Esmond Edwards   NYC,December 21,1960

2772   Ode to Charlie Parker-3   NJLP8270
2773   Mrs.Parker of K.C.-2   -
2774   It's magic-2,4   -
2775   Serene   PR24046
2776   Miss Ann-1   NJLP8270
2777   Far cry-1   -
2778   Left alone-3,4   -
2779   Tenderly-5   -

-4:Little out.
-5:Eric Dolphy(as)unaccompanied.

All titles from NJLP8270 also issued on PR7747,P-24053.
2773 issued on P-24053 as "Bird's mother".

LONNIE JOHNSON-LOSING GAME:
Lonnie Johnson(vo,g,p-1).
Supervision:Esmond Edwards   NYC,December 28,1960

2780	My little kitten Susie	BVLP1024
2781	New Year's blues	-
2782	Losing game	-
2783	Moanin' blues	-
2784	New Orleans blues	-
2785	Slow and easy	-
2786	Evil woman-1	-
2787	Lines on my face	-
2788	Four walls and me	-
2789	What a difference a day makes	-
2790	Summertime	-
2791	You won't let me go	-

BVLP1024=PR7724.

COLEMAN HAWKINS-NIGHT HAWK:
Coleman Hawkins,Eddie "Lockjaw" Davis(ts)Tommy Flanagan(p)Ron Carter
(b)Gus Johnson(dm).
Supervision:Esmond Edwards   NYC,December 30,1960

2792	Pedalin'	SVLP2016;PR7671	
2793	There is no greater love	-	-
2794	Don't take your love from me	-	-
2795	In a mellotone	-	-
2796	Night Hawk	-	-
2797	Lover		-

2798/2809:DOMENICO ALVARADO-December 30,1960(not jazz).

BILLY TAYLOR-INTERLUDE:
Billy Taylor(p)Doug Watkins(b)Ray Mosca(dm).
Supervision:Esmond Edwards   NYC,January 3,1961

2810	You tempt me	MVLP16
2811	Do you dream too	-
2812	You're all that matters	-
2813	Interlude	-
2814	You're mine	-
2815	My heart sings	-
2816	I sigh	-
2817	Here today,gone tomorrow love	-
2818	All alone	-

EDDIE "LOCKJAW" DAVIS/JOHNNY GRIFFIN QUINTET:
Eddie "Lockjaw" Davis,Johnny Griffin(ts)Junior Mance(p)Larry Gales(b)
Ben Riley(dm).
Supervision:Esmond Edwards
                    Minton's Playhouse,NYC,January 6,1961

Light and lovely	PRLP7191,PR7357,PR7407		
Straight no chaser	-		-
Woody'n you	-		-
Ringo Domingo	-	PR7309	-
I'll remember April		PR7309	
Billie's bounce	PR7309		
Epistrophy			
Well you needn't	-		

(session continued on next page)

```
In walked Bud              PR7330
Land of dreams             -
Bean-O                     -
Robbin's nest              -
Our delight                -
Theme                      -
Dee Dee's dance            PR7357
Billie's bounce            -
Epistrophy                 -
```

WILLIS JACKSON-REALLY GROOVIN':
Willis Jackson(ts)Jimmy Neeley(p)Wendell Marshall(b)Gus Johnson(dm)
Juan Amalbert(conga).
Supervision:Esmond Edwards   <u>NYC,January 10,1961</u>

```
2819  I remember Clifford      PRLP7196
2820  Cat meal                 -         PR7770
2821  Sweet Peter Charleston   -         -
2822  Estrellita               MVLP17
2823  A twist of the blues     PRLP7196
2824  Careless love            Pr.45-194,LP7196
2825  Again                              -
2826  He said,she said,I said  Pr.45-194  -
```

SHORTY & DOC:
Shorty Baker,Doc Cheatham(tp)Walter Bishop(p)Wendell Marshall(b)J.C.
Heard(dm).
Supervision:Esmond Edw rds   <u>NYC,January 17,1961</u>

```
2827  Baker's dozen            SVLP2021
2828  Night train              -
2829  Lullaby in rhythm        -
2830  I didn't know what time it was  -
2831  Chitlin's                -
2832  Good Queen Bess          -
```

BETTY ROCHE-LIGHTLY AND POLITELY:
Betty Roche(vo)with Jimmy Neeley(p)Wally Richardson(g)Michel Mulia(b)
Rudy Lawless(dm).
Supervision:Esmond Edwards   <u>NYC,January 24,1961</u>

```
2833  Just squeeze me          PRLP7198
2834  For all we know          -
2835  Rocks in my bed          -
2836  Maybe you'll be there    -
2837  I had the craziest dream -
2838  Polka dots and moonbeams -
2839  Jim                      -
2840  Why shouldn't I?         -
2841  I got it bad             -
2842  Someone to watch over me -
```

GENE AMMONS-NICE 'N 'COOL:
Gene Ammons(ts)Richard Wyands(p)Doug Watkins(b)J.C.Heard(dm).
Supervision:Esmond Edwards   <u>NYC,January 26,1961</u>

```
2843  I remember you           MVLP18
2844  Willow weep for me       -
2845  Someone to watch over me -    MV33
2846  Something wonderful      -    MV35
2847  Till there was you       -    MV38
2848  Something I dreamed last night  -
2849  Answer me my love        -
2850  Little girl blue         -
```

All titles also issued on P-24079.

GENE AMMONS-JUG:
Gene Ammons(ts)Richard Wyands(p)Doug Watkins(b)J.C.Heard(dm).
Supervision:Esmond Edwards   NYC,January 27,1961

2851	Miss Lucy	Pr.45-201,LP7192
2852	Exactly like you	Pr.45-189 - PR7708,P-10084
2853	Ol' man river	- -
2854	Easy to love	- MV34
2855	Namely you-1	Pr.45-201 -
2856	Let it be you-1	Pr.45-276 -
2857	Seed shack	- - PR7298,PR7306,
		P-10084* ,45-390
2858	Tangerine	PRLP7192

-1:Clarence Anderson(p,org)replaces Wyands.

*:2857 is edited on P-10084.

JACK McDUFF-THE HONEYDRIPPER:
Jimmy Forrest(ts)Jack McDuff(org)Grant Green(g)Ben Dixon(dm).
Supervision:Esmond Edwards   NYC,February 3,1961

2859	Blues and tonic	PRLP7199
2860	Whap!	-
2861	The honeydripper	Pr.45-199,LP7199,PR7481,PR24013
2862	I want a little girl	- PR7596
2863	Mr.Lucky	- -
2864	Dink's blues	-

JOHNNY "HAMMOND" SMITH:
Freddie McCoy(vb)Johnny "Hammond" Smith(org)Eddie McFadden(g)Wendell
Marshall(b)Leo Stevens(dm).
Supervision:Esmond Edwards   NYC,February 14,1961

2865	Spring is here	PRLP7203
2866	Autumn leaves	PR7420
2867	Opus de funk	Pr.45-407,PR7420
2868	Almost like being in love	-
2869	Ribs and chips	PRLP7203
2870	Cry me a river	-
2871	Invitation	-

PRLP7203=PR7786.

BUDDY TATE-GROOVIN' WITH TATE:
Buddy Tate(cl,ts)Ronnell Bright(p)Wally Richardson(g)George Tucker(b)
Roy Brooks(dm).
Supervision:Esmond Edwards   NYC,February 17,1961

2872	A lucky so and so	SVLP2029
2873	The salt mines	-
2874	Blues for Trix	-
2875	Makin' whoopee	-
2876	East of the sun	-
2877	Overdrive	-
2878	Boardwalk	-

CLAUDE HOPKINS-LET'S JAM:
Joe Thomas(tp)Buddy Tate(ts,cl-1)Claude Hopkins(p)Wendell Marshall(b)
J.C.Heard(dm).
Supervision:Esmond Edwards   NYC,February 21,1961

2879	Safari stomp	SVLP2020
2880	Late evening	-
2881	The way you look tonight	-
2882	I surrender dear	-
2883	I would do most anything for you	-
2884	Offbeat blues	-
2885	I apologize	-

WALT DICKERSON:
Walt Dickerson(vb)Austin Crowe(p)Bob Lewis(b)Andrew Cyrille(dm).
Supervision:Esmond Edwards   NYC,February 24,1961

2886	Infinite you	rejected
2887	Evelyn	-
2888	Death and taxes	-
2889	Elizabeth	-
2890	Time	-
2891	The cry	-

COLEMAN HAWKINS-THE HAWK RELAXES:
Coleman Hawkins(ts)Ronnell Bright(p)Kenny Burrell(g)Ron Carter(b)Andrew
Cyrille(dm).
Supervision:Esmond Edwards   NYC,February 28,1961

2892	Just a gigolo	MVLP15
2893	Under a blanket of blue	-
2894	More than you know	-
2895	Speak low	-
2896	When day is done	-
2897	I'll never be the same	-
2898	Moonglow	-

OLIVER NELSON-STRAIGHT AHEAD:
Oliver Nelson(cl-1,as-2,ts-3)Eric Dolphy(as-4,bass cl-5,fl-6)Richard
Wyands(p)George Duvivier(b)Roy Haynes(dm).
Supervision:Esmond Edwards   NYC,March 1,1961

2899	Six and four-2,4	NJLP8255
2900	Mama Lou-2,5,6	-
2901	Images-2,5	-
2902	Ralph's new blues-1,3,5	-
2903	111-44 -2,5	-
2904	Straight ahead-2,4	-

All titles also issued on P-24060.

SHIRLEY SCOTT-SATIN DOLL:
Shirley Scott(org)George Tucker(b)Mack Simpkins(dm).
Supervision:Esmond Edwards   NYC,March 7,1961

2905	It don't mean a thing	Pr.		PR7283
2906	Satin doll	Pr.45-292	-	PR7298
2907	C jam blues	-	-	
2908	Perdido	-		
2909	Mood indigo	-		
2910	Solitude	-		
2911	Things ain't what they used to be	-		

WALT DICKERSON-THIS IS WALT DICKERSON:
Walt Dickerson(vb)Austin Crowe(p)Bob Lewis(b)Andrew Cyrille(dm).
Supervision:Esmond Edwards   NYC,March 7,1961

2912	Infinite you	NJLP8254
2913	Evelyn	-
2914	Death and taxes	-
2915	The cry	-
2916	Elizabeth	-
2917	Time	-

JAKI BYARD-HERE'S JAKI:
Jaki Byard(as-1,p)Ron Carter(b)Roy Haynes(dm).
Supervision:Esmond Edwards   NYC,March 14,1961

2918   Mellow septet   NJLP8256   P-24086
2919   D.D.L.J.   -   -
2920   Medley:Bess you is my woman/   -   MV33   -
        It ain't necessarily so   -   -   -
2921   Cinco y quatro   -   -
2922   Giant steps   -   -
2923   To my wife   -   -
2924   Garnerin' a bit   -   -
2925   When sunny gets blue-1   PR7397   -

RED GARLAND:
Richard Williams(tp)Oliver Nelson(as,ts)Red Garland(p)Peck Morrison(b)
Charlie Persip(dm).
Supervision:Esmond Edwards   NYC,March 16,1961

2926   Soft winds   P-24078
2927   Avalon   -
2928   On green Dolphin Street   PR7307
2929   Skinny's blues   P-24078
2930   If you could see me now   PR7307

JOE NEWMAN-GOOD 'N ' GROOVY:
Joe Newman(tp)Frank Foster(ts)Tommy Flanagan(p)Eddie Jones(b)Bill
English(dm).
Supervision:Esmond Edwards   NYC,March 17,1961

2931   A.M.Romp   SVLP2019
2932   Loop-D-loop   -
2933   Li'l darlin'   -
2934   To Rigmor   -
2935   Mo-lasses   -   Pr.45-196
2936   Just squeeze me   -

JIMMY HAMILTON-IT'S ABOUT TIME:
Clark Terry(tp,flh)Britt Woodman(tb)Jimmy Hamilton(cl-1,ts-2)Tommy
Flanagan(p)Wendell Marshall(b)Mel Lewis(dm).
Supervision:Esmond Edwards   NYC,March 21,1961

2937   Nits and wits-1   SVLP2022
2938   Gone with the blues-2   -
2939   Mr.Good blues-1,2   -
2940   Peanut head-1   -
2941   Stupid but not crazy-1   -
2942   Two for one-1   -

SHIRLEY SCOTT:
Shirley Scott(org)Ronnell Bright(p)Wally Richardson(g)Peck Morrison(b)
Roy Haynes(dm).
Supervision:Esmond Edwards   NYC,March 24,1961

2943   Travelin' light   PR7456
2944   You're my everything   -
2945   Savoy   -
2946   Worksong   PR7424
2947   Down by the riverside   PR7456
2948   Chapped chops   PR7424

ETTA JONES:
Etta Jones(vo)with Jimmy Neeley(p)Wally Richardson(g)Michel Mulia(b)
Rudy Lawless(dm).
Supervision:Esmond Edwards   NYC,March 30,1961

2949	Give me the simple life	PR7284;PR7443
2950	And maybe you'll be there	PRLP7194
2951	My heart tells me	-
2952	Looking back	PR7284
2953	Till there was you	PRLP7194,45-198
2954	And the angels sing	PR7284
2955	Love is the thing	PRLP7194;PR7443
2956	Fools rush in	-
2957	Through a long and sleepless night-	
2958	Answer me my love	PR7284
2959	Reverse the charges	- PR7443
2960	And this is my beloved	unissued

FURRY LEWIS-BACK ON MY FEET AGAIN:
Furry Lewis(vo,g).

                            April 3,1961

John Henry	BVLP1036
When my baby left me	-
Shake 'em on down	-
Big chief blues	-
Old blue	-
I'm going back to Brownsville	-
Back on my feet again	-
White lightnin'	-
Roberta	-
St.Louis blues	-

All titles also issued on PR7810,Fantasy F-24703.

FURRY LEWIS-DONE CHANGED MY MIND:
Furry Lewis(vo,g).

                            April 4,1961

Baby you don't want me	BVLP1037
Done changed my mind	-
Goin' to Kansas City	-
Judge Boushay blues	-
Casey Jones	-
This time tomorrow	-
I will turn your money green	-
Frankie and Johnny	-
Longing blues	-
Long tall gal blues	-

All titles also issued on Fantasy F-24703.

JIMMY HAMILTON-CAN'T HELP SWINGIN':
Jimmy Hamilton(cl-1,ts-2)Tommy Flanagan(p)Wendell Marshall(b)Earl
Williams(dm).
Supervision:Esmond Edwards   NYC,April 4,1961

2961	Baby won't you please come home-2	SVLP2028
2962	Town tavern rag-2	-
2963	Pan fried-1,2	-
2964	Definite difference-2	-
2965	Route 9W-2	-
2966	Lullaby of the leaves-2	-
2967	There is no greater love-2	-
2968	Dancing on the ceiling-1	

WILLIS JACKSON-IN MY SOLITUDE:
Willis Jackson(ts)Richard Wyands(p)Peck Morrison(b)Mickey Roker(dm).
Supervision:Esmond Edwards   NYC,April 11,1961

2969   Home   MVLP17
2970   Nancy   -   MV37;ST8319
2971   They didn't believe me   -
2972   Nobody knows the trouble I've seen-
2973   Motherless child   -
2974   It never entered my mind   -
2975   Girl of my dreams   PRLP7196
2976   Solitude   MVLP17

PINK ANDERSON-CAROLINA BLUES MAN:
Pink Anderson(vo,g).
Supervision:Sam Charters   Spartanburg,N.C.,April 12,1961

        Baby please don't go   BVLP1038
        My baby left me this morning   -
        Mama where did you stay last night-
        Big house blues   -
        Meet me in the bottom   -
        Weeping willow blues   -
        Baby I'm going away   -
        Thousand women blues   -
        I had my fun   -
        Everyday in the week   -
        Try some of that   BV1055

THE SWINGVILLE ALL STARS:
Joe Newman(tp)J.C.Higginbotham(tb)Jimmy Hamilton(cl)Hilton Jefferson(as)
Coleman Hawkins(ts)Claude Hopkins(p)Tiny Grimes(g)Wendell Marshall(b)
Billy English(dm).
Supervision:Esmond Edwards   NYC,April 14,1961

2977   Jammin' in Swingville   SV2025
2978   Spring's swing   SV2024
2979   Love me or leave me   -
2980   Cool sunrise   SV2025

All titles also issued on SV4001,PR24051.

SIDNEY MAIDEN-TROUBLE AN' BLUES:
Sidney Maiden(vo,hca)K.C.Douglas(g).
Supervision:Chris Strachwitz   Berkeley,April 16,1961

        Buy me an airplane   BVLP1035
        Sweet little woman   -
        My black name   -
        Sidney's fox chase   -
        San Quentin blues   -
        Tell me somebody   -
        Blues an' trouble   -
        Hand-me-down baby   -
        Sidney's worried life blues   -
        Me and my chauffeur   -
        Coal black mare   -
        I'm going back home   -
        Sweet little woman   unissued
        Sugar Mama   -
        Bottle up and go   -
        Bottle up and go   -
        Sidney's shuffle   -
        Me and my chauffeur   -

MERCY DEE WALTON-PITY AND A SHAME:
Mercy Dee Walton(vo,p)Sidney Maiden(hca)Otis Cherry(dm)Marcellus
Thomas(vo).
Supervision:Chris Strachwitz   Berkeley,April 16,1961
            Call the asylum   unissued
            Mad blues voMT   –
            Pity and a shame   BVLP1039
            Shady lane   –
            After the fight   –
            Your friend and woman   –
            One room country shack   –
            The drunkard   –
            Five card hand   –
            Have you ever been out in the
                            country   –
            My little angel   –
            Sidney's and Mercy's shuffle –

Note:Further titles from this session have been issued on Arhoolie.

JIMMY FORREST-OUT OF THE FORREST:
Jimmy Forrest(ts)Joe Zawinul(p)Tommy Potter(b)Clarence Johnston(dm).
Supervision:Esmond Edwards   NYC,April 18,1961
2981   This can't be love   PRLP7202
2982   Yesterdays   –
2983   I cried for you   –
2984   I've got a right to cry   –
2985   By the river St.Marie   –
2986   Bolo blues   Pr.45-197,LP7202,PR7712
2987   That's all   PRLP7202
2988   Crash program   –

KING CURTIS-TROUBLE IN MIND:
King Curtis(as,ts,g,vo)Paul Griffin(p)Al Casey,Mae Pierce(g)Jimmy Lewis
(b)Belton Evans(dm)The Cookies(vo).
Supervision:Esmond Edwards   NYC,April 25,1961
2989   Trouble in mind   TRU45-401,TRU15001
2990   Bad bad whiskey   –
2991   Don't deceive me voTC   –
2992   But that's all right   TRU45-401   –
2993   I have to worry voTC   TRU45-406   –
2994   Nobody wants you when you're
                   down and out   –
2995   Woke up this morning   –
2996   Ain't nobody's business   –
2997   Deep fry   –
2998   Jivin' time   TRU45-406   –   PR7709

GENE CASEY:
Gene Casey(p)George Tucker(b)Granville "Mickey" Roker(dm)Ray Barretto
(conga).
Supervision:Esmond Edwards   NYC,April 28,1961
2999   untitled original   unissued
3000   untitled ballad   –
3001   untitled original   –
3002   Close your eyes   –
3003   Blue Lou   –
3004   untitled blues   –

WALT DICKERSON-SENSE OF DIRECTION:
Walt Dickerson(vb)Austin Crowe(p)Edgar Bateman(b)Eustis Guillemet Jr.
(dm).
Supervision:Esmond Edwards   NYC,May 5,1961

3005   If I should loose you   NJLP8268
3006   Ode to a boy   -
3007   Sense of direction   -
3008   Why?   -
3009   Togetherness   -
3010   You go to my head   -
3011   What's new?   -
3012   The good earth   -

JOE NEWMAN-JOE HAPNIN'S:
Joe Newman(tp)Tommy Flanagan(p)Wendell Marshall(b)Billy English(dm).
Supervision:Esmond Edwards   NYC,May 9,1961

3013   Oh,Gee   SVLP2027
3014   Dacquiri   -
3015   The very thought of you   -
3016   Strike up the band   -
3017   The continental   -
3018   Blues for Slim   -
3019   For you   -

DON ELLIS-NEW IDEAS:
Don Ellis(tp,p-1)Jaki Byard(as,p)Al Francis(vb)Ron Carter(b)Charlie
Persip(dm).
Supervision:Esmond Edwards   NYC,May 11,1961

3020   Despair to hope-3   NJLP8257
3021   Solo-2   -
3022   Cock and bull   -
3023   Imitation   -
3024   Tragedy-1   -
3025   Uh-huh   -
3026   Prelude & fugue   unissued
3027   Natural H   NJLP8257
3028   Four and three-4   -

-2:Francis out;-3:Carter out;-4:Persip out.

NJLP8257=PR7607

JOHNNY "HAMMOND" SMITH:
Johnny "Hammond" Smith(org)Freddie McCoy(vb)Eddie McFadden(g)Wendell
Marshall(b)Leo Stevens(dm).
Supervision:Esmond Edwards   NYC,May 12,1961

3029   Sad eyes   Pr.45-407,PR7420,PR7777
3030   Shirley's theme   -
3031   If someone had told me   -
3032   Que pasa   PRLP7203
3033   Gone with the wind   PR7420
3034   Stimulation   PRLP7203,PR7705
3035   Sticks and stones   Pr.45-193,LP7203
3036   Because you left me   -   PR7777

PRLP7203=PR7786

[104]

HENRY TOWNSEND-TIRED BEIN' MISTREATED:
Henry Townsend(vo,p-1,g)Tommy Bankhead(g).
Supervision:Sam Charters   St.Louis,May 17,1961

        Cairo's my baby's home   BVLP1041
        Tired of being mistreated   -
        Rocks have been my pillow   -
        The train is coming   -
        She just walked away   -
        I asked her if she loved me   -
        I got tired   -
        My home ain't there   -
        All my money gone-1   -
        She drove me to drinking   -
        My baby have come back   -

THE SWINGVILLE ALL STARS:
Joe Thomas(tp)Vic Dickenson(tb)Pee Wee Russell(cl)Al Sears,Buddy Tate
(ts)Cliff Jackson(p)Danny Barker(g)Joe Benjamin(b)J.C.Heard(dm).
Supervision:Esmond Edwards   NYC,May 19,1961

3037   Things ain't what they used to be SV2024
3038   So glad   SV2025
3039   I want to be happy-1   -
3040   I may be wrong   SV2024
3041   Phoenix   -
3042   Years ago   SV2025
3043   Vic's spot   SV2024

-1:p,b,dm only.

All titles also issued on SV4001,PR24051.

AHMED ABDUL-MALIK-THE MUSIC OF AHMED ABDUL-MALIK:
Tommy Turrentine(tp)Bilal Abdurrahman(cl,perc)Eric Dixon(ts)Calo Scott
(cello)Ahmed Abdul-Malik(b)Andrew Cyrille(dm).
Supervision:Esmond Edwards   NYC,May 23,1961

3044   La Ibkey   NJ45-512,LP8266,LP8292
3045   The hustlers   -   -
3046   Hannibal's carnivals   -
3047   Out of nowhere   NJLP8282
3048   Nights on Saturn   NJLP8266
3049   Don't blame me   -
3050   Oud blues   -

LATIN JAZZ QUINTET:
Bobby Capers(as)Willie Coleman(vb)Artie Jenkins(p)Bill Ellington(b)
Phil Newsom(dm,timbales)Juan Amalbert(conga,dir).
Supervision:Esmond Edwards   NYC,May 23,1961

3051   Sunday go to meetin'   ST8321
3052   Ain't dat right   TRU15003
3053   Milestones   ST8321
3054   April afternoon   TRU15003
3055   Mambo Bobbie   ST8321
3056   Rip a dip   -
3057   Monk's bread   -
3058   Out of this world   Tru.45-413,TRU15003
3059   Blues waltz   ST8321

ERNESTINE ALLEN-LET IT ROLL:
Ernestine Allen(vo)with King Curtis(ts)Paul Griffin(p)Al Casey,
Chauncey Westbrook(g)Jimmy Lewis(b)Belton Evans(dm).
Supervision:Esmond Edwards   NYC,May 30,1961

3060	Baubles,bangles and beads	TRU15004	
3061	Miss Allen's blues	-	
3062	I want a little boy	-	
3063	Love for sale	-	
3064	Lullaby of Broadway	-	
3065	Mean o' evil	-	
3066	The man I love	-	
3067	Tea for two	-	
3068	Let it roll	-	45-405

SHIRLEY SCOTT-HIP SOUL:
Stanley Turrentine(as "Stan Turner")(ts)Shirley Scott(org)Herb Lewis
(b)Roy Brooks(dm).
Supervision:Esmond Edwards   NYC,June 2,1961

3069	411 West	Pr.	LP7205	
3070	Out of this world		-	PR7773
3071	Stanley's time		-	
3072	Be myself		-	
3073	Trane's blues		-	
3074	Hip soul	Pr.45-200	-	PR7707

ETTA JONES AND STRINGS-SO WARM:
Etta Jones(vo)with Joe Singer,Richard Berg(frh)Mal Waldron(p)George
Duvivier(b)Bill English(dm)& strings,Oliver Nelson(arr,cond).
Supervision:Esmond Edwards   NYC,June 9,1961

3075	All my life	PRLP7204	
3076	If you were mine	-	PR7443
3077	You don't know what love is	-	
3078	I wish I didn't love you so	-	

GENE AMMONS:
Clark Terry,Hobart Dotson(tp)Oliver Nelson(as)Gene Ammons,Red Holloway,
George Barrow(ts)Bob Ashton(bs)Richard Wyands(p)Wendell Marshall(b)Bill
English(dm)Ray Barretto(conga).
Supervision:Esmond Edwards   NYC,June 13,1961

3079	Things ain't what they used to be		PR7287	
3080	Makin' whoopee		-	
3081	I want to be loved	Pr.45-319	-	
3082	Lullaby of the leaves		-	
3083	Too marvellous for words		PR7275	
3084	Love,I've found you	Pr.45-294	-	PR7313
3085	The song is you		PR7320	

ROLAND ALEXANDER-PLEASURE BENT:
Marcus Belgrave(tp)Roland Alexander(ts)Ronnie Mathews(p)Gene Taylor
(b)Clarence Stroman(dm).
Supervision:Esmond Edwards   NYC,June 17,1961

	Pleasure bent	NJLP8267
	I'll be around	-
	Dorman Road	-
	Lil's blues	-
	Orders to take out	-
	My melancholy baby	-

RON CARTER-WHERE?:
Eric Dolphy(as-1,bass cl-2,fl-3)Mal Waldron(p)Ron Carter(b-4,cello)
George Duvivier(b-4)Charlie Persip(dm).
Supervision:Esmond Edwards   NYC,June 20,1961

3086   Rally-2,4   NJLP8265
3087   Where?   -
3088   Yes indeed-3,4   -
3089   Bass duet-4   -
3090   Saucer eyes-3   -
3091   Softly as in a morning sunrise-1 -

All titles also issued on PR7843,P-24053.

CLEA BRADFORD-THESE DUES:
Clea Bradford(vo)with Clark Terry(tp)Oliver Nelson(ts)Patti Bown(p)
Chauncey Westbrook(g)George Duvivier(b)Bill English(dm).
Supervision:Esmond Edwards   NYC,June 21,1961

3092   This can't be love   TRU15005
3093   It you but knew   -
3094   They can't take that away from me-
3095   This love of mine   -
3096   Somebody loves me   -
3097   Willow weep for me   -
3098   Skylark   -
3099   These dues   -
3100   I'll never stop loving you   -
3101   I cried for you   -

All titles also issued on ST8320.

JOHN WRIGHT-MAKIN' OUT:
Eddie Williams(ts)John Wright(p)Wendell Marshall(b)Roy Brooks(dm).
Supervision:Esmond Edwards   NYC,June 23,1961

3102   Street   Pr.   LP7212
3103   Kitty   -
3104   Back in Jersey   -
3105   Soul search   -
3106   Sparkie   -
3107   Like someone in love   -
3108   It could happen to you   -
3109   Makin' out   Pr.45-212 -

MAL WALDRON-THE QUEST:
Eric Dolphy(as-1,cl-2)Booker Ervin(ts)Mal Waldron(p)Ron Carter(cello)
Joe Benjamin(b)Charlie Persip(dm).
Supervision:Esmond Edwards   NYC,June 27,1961

3110   Thirteen-1   NJLP8269
3111   Dequilty-1   -
3112   Status seeking-1   -
3113   Warp and woof-1   -
3114   Warm canto-2   -
3115   Fire waltz-1   -
3116   We did it-1   -

NJLP8269=PR7579.All titles also issued on P-24085.

[107]

TAFT JORDAN PLAYS ELLINGTON-MOOD INDIGO:
Taft Jordan(tp)Richard Wyands(p)Kenny Burrell(g)Joe Benjamin(b)Charlie
Persip(dm).
Supervision:Esmond Edwards   NYC,June 30,1961

3117	I didn't know about you	MVLP21
3118	In a sentimental mood	-
3119	Do nothin' till you hear from me	-
3120	Sophisticated lady	-
3121	Mood indigo	-
3122	Warm valley	-
3123	Lost in meditation	-

GENE CASEY:
Gene Casey(p)Bill Ellington(b)Ray Barretto(conga)John Pacheco,Manny
Oquendo(perc).
Supervision:Esmond Edwards   NYC,July 7,1961

3124	Azur te	unissued
3125	Old devil moon	-
3126	Lover come back to me	-
3127	The Pachanea twist	-

LIGHTNIN' HOPKINS:
Lightnin' Hopkins(vo,g).
                                             Houston,Texas,July 7,1961

Black gal	BV1057
Baby don't you tear my clothes	-
Good morning little school girl	-
Coffee blues	-

ROLAND KIRK-KIRK'S WORK:
Roland Kirk(ts,strich,manzello,fl,siren)Jack McDuff(org)Joe Benjamin(b)
Art Taylor(dm).
Supervision:Esmond Edwards   NYC,July 11,1961

3128	Kirk's work	Pr.45-255,LP7210
3129	Makin' whoopee	-
3130	Funk underneath	Pr.45-280,45-420,LP7210
3131	Doin' the sixty-eight	Pr.45-255,LP7210
3132	Too late now	-
3133	Skater's waltz	-
3134	Three for Dizzy	Pr.45-311 -

All titles also issued on PR7450,P-24080.

KING CURTIS-IT'S PARTY TIME:
King Curtis,Sam Taylor(ts)Ernie Hayes(org)Paul Griffin(p)Billy Butler
(g)Jimmy Lewis(b)Ray Lucas(dm).
Supervision:Esmond Edwards   NYC,July 11,1961

3135	Slow motion-1	TRU15008	
3136	Firefly	-	PR7709
3137	Something frantic	-	PR7775
3138	Keep movin'	-	-

-1:tp,bongo added.

PETE FRANKLIN-GUITAR PETE'S BLUES:
Pete Franklin(p-1,g,vo).
Supervision:Arthur Rosenbaum   Indianapolis,July 12,1961

        I got to find my baby   BV1068
        Lonesome bedroom blues-1   -
        Prison bound   -
        Black gal-1   -
        Grievin' me   -
        Rocky mountains   -
        Six white horses-1   -
        Sail on   -
        My old lonesome blues-1   -
        Guitar Pete's blues   -

SCRAPPER BLACKWELL-Mr.SCRAPPER'S BLUES:
Scrapper Blackwell(p-1,g,vo).
Supervision:Arthur Rosenbaum   Indianapolis,July   ,1961

        "A" blues   BVLP1047
        Going where the moon crosses
                        the yellow dog-
        Nobody knows you when you're
                        down & out   -
        Little girl blues   -
        George Street blues   -
        Blues before sunrise   -
        Little boy blues   -
        "E" blues   -
        Shady lane-1   -
        Penal farm blues   -

LONNIE JOHNSON with VICTORIA SPIVEY-IDLE HOURS:
Cliff Jackson(p)Victoria Spivey(p-1,vo)Lonnie Johnson(vo,g).
Supervision:Chris Albertson   NYC,July 13,1961

270   Long time blues   voVS   BVLP1044
271   Idle hours   voVS   -
272   Leave me or love me   voLJ   -
273   Darling I miss you so   voLJ   -
274   Please baby   voLJ   -
275   End it all   voLJ   -
276   Good luck darling   voLJ   -
277   You are my life   voLJ   -
278   Oh yes,baby   voLJ   -
279   No more cryin'   voLJ   -
280   You have no love in your heart
                              voLJ   -
281   I got the blues so bad-1   voVS   -

Note:Matrix numbers for above titles belong to series used by Chris
Albertson Productions.

JACK McDUFF-GOODNIGHT IT'S TIME TO GO:
Harold Vick(ts)Jack McDuff(org)Grant Green(g)Joe Dukes(dm).
Supervision:Esmond Edwards   NYC,July 14,1961

3139   Godiva Brown   PR7666
3140   Our Miss Brooks   rejected
3141   Sanctified waltz   Pr.45-211,LP7220,PR7481
3142   Goodnight it's time to go   -   -
3143   McDuff speaking   -
3144   I'll be seeing you   -
3145   A smooth one   -

ERIC DOLPHY AT THE FIVE SPOT:
Booker Little(tp)Eric Dolphy(as-1,bass cl-2,fl-ᴠ)Mal Waldron(p)Richard
Davis(b)Ed Blackwell(dm).
Supervision:Esmond Edwards
Five Spot Cafe,NYC,July 16,1961

3146	(Warming up and tuning)	rejected
3147	Status seeking-1	PR7382,P-24070
3148	God bless the child-2	- -
3149	Agression-2	PR7294,P-34002
3150	Like someone in love-3	- -
3151	Fire waltz-1	NJLP8260 -
3152	Bee vamp-2	- -
3153	The prophet-1	- -
3154	Number eight(Potsa lotsa)-1	PR7334 -
3155	Booker's waltz-2	- -

3156:not used.

PR7294=PR7826;NJLP8260=PR7611.

CLIFF JACKSON-UPTOWN AND LOWDOWN:
Ed Allen(tp)Rudy Powell(cl)Elmer Snowden(bjo)Cliff Jackson(p)Abe Bolar
(b)Floyd Casey(wbd,kazoo).
Supervision:Chris Albertson
NYC,July 20,1961

282	Wolverine blues	SVLP2026
283	Sheik of Araby	-
284	I found a new baby	-
285	Blues in Englewood	-

Note:Matrix numbers are from Chris Albertson series.

CLARK TERRY-EVERYTHING'S MELLOW:
Clark Terry(tp)Junior Mance(p)Joe Benjamin(b)Charlie Persip(dm).
Supervision:Esmond Edwards
NYC,July 21,1961

3157	Among my souvenirs	MVLP20
3158	In the alley	-
3159	Michelle	-
3160	As you desire me	-
3161	Out in the cold again	-
3162	This is always	-
3163	Lullaby	-
3164	You'd be so nice	unissued
3165	The simple waltz	MVLP20

ETTA JONES AND STRINGS-SO WARM:
Etta Jones(vo)with Ray Alonge(frh)Arthur Clarke,Jerome Richardson,Phil
Bodner,Eric Dixon(reeds)George Duvivier(b)Charlie Persip(dm)& strings,
Oliver Nelson(arr,dir).
Supervision:Esmond Edwards
NYC,July 25,1961

3166	You better go now	PRLP7204
3167	I laughed at love	-
3168	Can you look me in the eyes	-
3169	This is my beloved	-

LIGHTNIN' HOPKINS-BLUES IN THE BOTTLE:
Lightnin' Hopkins(vo,g).

Houston,Texas,July 26,1961

Buddy Brown's blues	BV	LP1045
Wine spodee-o-dee		-
Sail on little girl,sail on	BV45-814	-
Death bells	-	-
DC 7		-
Going to Dallas to see my pony run		-
Jailhouse blues		-
Blues in the bottle		-
Beans,beans,beans		-
Catfish blues		-
My Grandpa is old too		-

DICK WELLSTOOD-UPTOWN AND LOWDOWN:
Herman Autrey(tp)Gene Sedric(cl,ts)Dick Wellstood(p)Milt Hinton(b)
Zutty Singleton(dm).
Supervision:Chris Albertson   NYC,July 27,1961

297	Yachtclub swing	SVLP2026
298	Brush lightly	-
299	Blook's blues	-

Note:Matrix numbers are from Chris Albertson series.

3170/3172:no information.These numbers could have been assigned to previous session.

ETTA JONES AND STRINGS-SO WARM:
Etta Jones(vo)with Ray Alonge(frh)Arthur Clarke,Jerome Richardson,Phil
Bodner,Eric Dixon(reeds)George Duvivier(b)Charlie Persip(dm)& strings,
Oliver Nelson(arr,dir).
Supervision:Esmond Edwards   NYC,July 28,1961

3173	I'm through with love	Pr.	LP7204
3174	Hurry home	Pr.45-205	-
3175	Unchained melody	-	-
3176	How deep is the ocean		-

Rev.GARY DAVIS-HAVE A LITTLE FAITH:
Rev.Gary Davis(vo,g).

August 10,1961

You got to move	BVLP1032,45-819
I'm glad I'm that number	- -
There's a table sittin' in heaven	-
Motherless children	-
There's a bright side somewhere	-
Crucifixion	-
I'll be alright some day	-
You better mind	-
A little more faith	-
I'll fly away	-
God's gonna separate	-
When I die I'll live again	-

All titles also issued on Fantasy F-24704.

INTRODUCING MEMPHIS WILLIE B.:
Memphis Willie Borum(g,hca-1,vo).
Supervision:Sam Charters   Memphis,August 12,1961

    Brownsville blues   BVLP1034
    Country girl blues-1   —
    Highway 61   —
    Bad girl blues   —
    The stuff is here-1   —
    Overseas blues   —
    Stop crying blues   —
    Worried man blues   —
    Mailman blues-1   —
    Everyday I have the blues   —
    Mattie Mae-1   —
    Grief will kill you   —

MEMPHIS WILLIE B.-HARD WORKING MAN BLUES:
Same.Same session.

    Car machine blues   BVLP1048,BV1055
    Lonesome home blues   —
    L & N blues   —
    Hard working man blues   —
    Dying mother blues   —
    Honey maker blues   —
    P 38 blues   —
    Funny cape~ blues   —
    Good potatoes
    I have found somebody new   —
    Uncle Sam blues   —
    Wine drinking woman   —

PINK ANDERSON-BALLAD & FOLK SINGER:
Pink Anderson(vo,g).
                             Spartanburg,S.C.,August 14,1961

    The Titanic   BV1071
    Bo weevil   —
    John Henry   —
    Betty and Dupree   —
    Sugar baby   —
    The wreck of the old 97   —
    I will fly away   —
    The Kaiser   —
    In the evening   —

BABY TATE-SEE WHAT YOU HAVE DONE:
Baby Tate(vo,g).
                             Spartanburg,S.C.,August 14,1961

    Dupree blues   BV1072
    See what you have done   —
    What I have done to you   —
    Baby I'm going   —
    Hey Mama,hey pretty girl   —
    When your woman don't want you around
                           —
    Trucking them blues away   —
    Baby you just don't know   —
    Lonesome over there   —
    I ain't got no loving baby now   —

LUCILLE HEGAMIN with WILLIE THE LION AND HIS CUBS:
Lucille Hegamin(vo)with Henry Goodwin(tp)Cecil Scott(cl,ts)Willie "The
Lion" Smith(p)Gene Brooks(dm).
Supervision:Chris Albertson   NYC,August 16,1961

300	Arkansas blues	BVLP1052
301	Has anybody seen Corine?	-
302	You'll want my love	-
303	St.Louis blues	-

VICTORIA SPIVEY with BUSTER BAILEY BLUES BUSTERS:
Victoria Spivey(vo,p-1)with Sidney De Paris(tp,tu)J.C.Higginbotham(tb)
Buster Bailey(cl)Cliff Jackson-2(p)Zutty Singleton(dm).
Supervision:Chris Albertson   NYC,August 16,1961

304	Black snake blues-1	BVLP1052
305	Goin' back home-1	-
306	I got the blues so bad-2	-
307	Let him beat me	-

ALBERTA HUNTER with BUSTER BAILEY BLUES BUSTERS:
Alberta Hunter(vo)with Sidney De Paris(tp,tu)J.C.Higginbotham(tb)Buster
Bailey(cl)Cliff Jackson(p)Zutty Singleton(dm).
Supervision:Chris Albertson   NYC,August 16,1961

308	I got a mind to ramble	BVLP1052
309	I've got myself a working man	-
310	Chirpin' the blues	-
311	You gotta reap just what you sow	-

SHIRLEY SCOTT-BLUE SEVEN:
Joe Newman(tp)Oliver Nelson(ts)Shirley Scott(org)George Tucker(b)Roy
Brooks(dm).
Supervision:Esmond Edwards   NYC,August 22,1961

3177	Blue seven	Pr.45-421,PR7376
3178	How sweet	PR7440
3179	Give me the simple life	PR7376
3180	Wagon wheels	-
3181	Don't worry about it	-
3182	Nancy	-

OLIVER NELSON-MAIN STEM:
Joe Newman(tp)Oliver Nelson(as,ts)Hank Jones(p)George Duvivier(b)
Charlie Persip(dm)Ray Barretto(conga).
Supervision:Esmond Edwards   NYC,August 25,1961

3183	Latino	Pr. LP7236
3184	J and B	-
3185	Ho!	-
3186	Tipsy	-
3187	Tangerine	-
3188	Main stem	Pr.45-202 -

JIMMY FORREST-SIT DOWN AND RELAX:
Jimmy Forrest(ts)Hugh Lawson(p)Calvin Newborn(g)Tommy Potter(b)
Clarence Johnston(dm).
Supervision:Esmond Edwards   NYC,September 1,1961

3189	Tin tin deo	PRLP7235	
3190	Rocks in my bed	-	PR7712
3191	Tuxedo junction	-	
3192	The moon was yellow	-	
3193	Moonglow	-	
3194	Organ grinder's swing	-	
3195	That's all	NJLP8293	

YUSEF LATEEF-EASTERN SOUNDS:
Yusef Lateef(ts,fl,oboe)Barry Harris(p)Ernie Farrow(b)Lex Humphries(dm).
Supervision:Esmond Edwards   NYC,September 5,1961

3196	Love theme from "The Robe"	MVLP22;PR7447
3197	Three faces of Balal	-
3198	Plum blossom	-
3199	Love theme from "Spartacus"	- Pr.45-254,45-419,PR7447
3200	Snafu	- -
3201	Purple flower	-
3202	Ching Miau	-
3203	Don't blame me	-
3204	Blues for the Orient	- Pr.45-332

All titles also issued on PR7319,PR24035.

JESSIE POWELL-IT'S PARTY TIME:
Jessie Powell(ts)Adriano Acea(p)Albert Winston(org)Billy Pyles(g)
William Curtis(b)Ray Barretto(conga).
Supervision:Esmond Edwards   NYC,September 12,1961

3205	Jumpin' salty	Tru.45-404,TRU15007
3206	Malaguena	- -
3207	Feelin' no pain	-
3208	When you're smiling	Tru.45-414 -

BUCK AND BUDDY BLOW THE BLUES:
Buck Clayton(tp)Buddy Tate(ts,cl-1)Sir Charles Thompson(p)Gene Ramey
(b)Gus Johnson(dm).
Supervision:Esmond Edwards   NYC,September 15,1961

3209	Dallas delight	SVLP2030
3210	Blue ebony	-
3211	A swinging doll	-
3212	Don't mind if I do	-
3213	Rompin' at Red Bank	-
3214	Blue creek-1	-
3215	Blue breeze	-

All titles also issued on PR24040.

KING CURTIS-OLD GOLD:
King Curtis(as,ts)Jack McDuff(org)Billy Butler,Eric Gale(g)Bob Bushnell
(b)Ray Lucas(dm)Willie Rodriguez(conga,bongo).
Supervision:Esmond Edwards   NYC,September 19,1961

3216	Night train	TRU15006;PR7775
3217	You came a long way from St.Louis	- PR7709
3218	Honky tonk	- -
3219	Fever	- PR7775
3220	Tuxedo junction	- -
3221	Lean baby	- -
3222	The hucklebuck	- 45-412;PR7775

VICTORIA SPIVEY with LONNIE JOHNSON-WOMAN BLUES:
Victoria Spivey(vo,p)Lonnie Johnson(g,vo).
Supervision:Leonard Kunstadt   NYC,September 21,1961

	Grow old together	BVLP1054
	I'm a red hot Mama	- BV1055
	Thursday girl	-
	Christmas without Santa Claus	-
	Let's ride together	-
	Wake up Daddy	-

Lonnie Johnson(vo,g).Same date.

	There'll be some changes made	unissued
	She is something	-

KING CURTIS-OLD GOLD:
King Curtis(as,ts)Jack McDuff(org)Billy Butler,Eric Gale(g)Bob Bushnell
(b)Ray Lucas(dm)Willie Rodriguez(conga,bongo).
Supervision:Esmond Edwards   NYC,September 22,1961

3223	Soft	TRU15006;PR7775
3224	Tippin' in	-
3225	So rare	Tru.45-412,TRU15006
3226	Harlem nocturne	TRU15006;PR7709

VICTORIA SPIVEY:
Victoria Spivey(p,vo).
Supervision:Leonard Kunstadt   NYC,September 26,1961

That man   BVLP1054,BV1055
A big one   -
What is this thing they're
                talking about   -
Beautiful world   -

LONNIE JOHNSON:
Lonnie Johnson(vo,g).
Supervision:Leonard Kunstadt   NYC,September 26,1961

Baby I love it   unissued
Make love to me baby   -

Note:Confirmation of Lonnie Johnson titles from September 21 & 26 has
not been found in Prestige files.

OLIVER NELSON-AFRO-AMERICAN SKETCHES:
Ernie Royal,Joe Newman,Jerry Kail,Joe Wilder(tp)Urbie Green,Britt
Woodman,Paul Faulise(tb)Julius Watkins,Ray Alonge,Jim Buffington(frh)
Oliver Nelson(as,ts,arr)Jerry Dodgion(as,fl)Bob Ashton(fl,ts,cl)Don
Butterfield(tu)Charles McCracken,Peter Makis(cello)Art Davis(b)Ed
Shaughnessy(dm)Ray Barretto(bongo,conga).
Supervision:Esmond Edwards   NYC,September 29,1961

3227	Message	PRLP7225
3228	There's a yearnin'	-
3229	Jungleaire	rejected

Ernie Royal,Joe Newman,Jerry Kail,Joe Wilder(tp)Urbie Green,Britt
Woodman,Paul Faulise(tb)Oliver Nelson(as,ts,arr)Jerry Dodgion(as,fl)
Eric Dixon(ts,fl)Bob Ashton(fl,ts,cl)Arthur Clarke(bs)Don Butterfield
(tu)Patti Bown(p)Charles McCracken,Peter Makis(cello)Art Davis(b)Ed
Shaughnessy(dm)Ray Barretto(bongo,conga).Same date.

3230	Desillusioned	PRLP7225
3231	Freedom dance	-
3232	Emancipation	Pr.45-213,LP7225

BIG JOE WILLIAMS-BLUES FOR 9 STRINGS:
Big Joe Williams(vo,g)Larry Johnson(hca)Willie Dixon(b).
                                          NYC,October 7,1961

38 pistol blues   BVLP1056
I'm a fool about my baby   -
Pearly Mae   -
Walking blues   -
Highway 45   -
Meet me in the bottom   -
Skinny Mama   -
Jockey ride blues   -
Coal and iceman blues   -
Army man blues   -
Black gal   -
Pallet on the floor   -
(session continued on next page)

BIG JOE WILLIAMS-STUDIO BLUES:
Big Joe Williams(vo,g)Larry Johnson-1(hca)Willie Dixon(b).
NYC,October 7,1961

Levee camp blues	BV1083	
Low down dirty shame-1	-	
Gambling man	-	
Ain't gonna rain no more-1	-	
Feel so good	-	
Prowling ground hog	-	
Back home again-2	-	
Sugar babe-1	-	
Tell me Mama	-	
Studio blues	-	

-2:Dixon out.

GENE AMMONS:
Gene Ammons(ts)Walter Bishop(p)Art Davis(b)Art Taylor(dm)Ray Barretto
(conga).
Supervision:Esmond Edwards   NYC,October 17,1961

3233	The breeze and I	Pr.45-206,LP7208
3234	Carbow	Pr.45-441,PR7445
3235	Moonglow	Pr.45-226,LP7208
3236	The masquerade is over	PR7445
3237	I'm beginning to see the light	-
3238	Jug's blue blues	PRLP7208
3239	Lester leaps in	-

GENE AMMONS:
Gene Ammons(ts)Patti Bown(p)George Duvivier(b)Art Taylor(dm)Ray
Barretto(conga).
Supervision:Esmond Edwards   NYC,October 18,1961

3240	The five o'clock whistle	PRLP7208
3241	I sold my heart to the junkman	Pr.45-226,LP7208
3242	Song of the islands	PR7445
3243	Up tight	Pr.45-206,LP7208
3244	Travellin'	PR7445
3245	Soft Summer breeze	- PR7708
3246	Don't go to strangers	Pr.45-441,PR7445

JIMMY FORREST-MOST MUCH!:
Jimmy Forrest(ts)Hugh Lawson(p)Tommy Potter(b)Clarence Johnston(dm)
Ray Barretto(conga).
Supervision:Esmond Edwards   NYC,October 19,1961

3247	I love you	NJLP8293
3248	Sonny boy	-
3249	Soft winds	PRLP7218
3250	My buddy	-
3251	Robbin's nest	- PR7712
3252	Most much	-
3253	Mathilda	-
3254	Annie Laurie	Pr.45-208,LP7218,PR7712
3255	Autumn leaves	PRLP7218

JESSIE POWELL-IT'S PARTY TIME:
Jessie Powell(ts)Steve Gordon(p)Bill Pyles(g)Jimmy Lewis(b)Belton
Evans(dm).
Supervision:Esmond Edwards   NYC,November 3,1961

3256	Tonight	Tru.45-407,TRU15007
3257	Cool	- -
3258	Hot stuff	Tru.45-414 -
3259	Bobbie's twist	-

OLIVER NELSON-AFRO-AMERICAN SKETCHES:
Clyde Raesinger,Ernie Royal,Joe Newman(tp)Melba Liston,Billy Byers,Paul
Faulise(tb)Don Butterfield(tu)Oliver Nelson(as,ts,arr)Eric Dixon(ts,fl)
Art Davis(b)Ed Shaughnessy(dm)Ray Barretto(conga,bongos).
Supervision:Esmond Edwards   NYC,November 10,1961

3260   Goin' up North   Pr.45-269,LP7225
3261   Jungleaire   -

STEVE LACY-EVIDENCE:
Don Cherry(tp)Steve Lacy(ss)Carl Brown(b)Billy Higgins(dm).
Supervision:Esmond Edwards   NYC,November 14,1961

3262   Who knows   NJLP8271
3263   The mystery song   -
3264   San Francisco holiday   -
3265   Evidence   -
3266   Something to live for   -
3267   Black beauty   unissued
3268   Let's cool one   NJLP8271

SHIRLEY SCOTT PLAYS HORACE SILVER:
Shirley Scott(org)Henry Grimes(b)Otis Finch(dm).
Supervision:Esmond Edwards   NYC,November 17,1961

3269   Moon Ray   PRLP7240
3270   Doodlin'   -
3271   The preacher   -
3272   Senor blues   -
3273   Sister Sadie   Pr.45-230,LP7240
3274   Strollin'   PRLP7240

SHIRLEY SCOTT-HIP TWIST:
Stanley Turrentine(ts)Shirley Scott(org)George Tucker(b)Otis Finch(dm).
Supervision:Esmond Edwards   NYC,November 17,1961

3275   Ridin' and runnin'   PRLP7226
3276   At last   -
3277   Violent blues   -   PR7707
3278   The very thought of you   -   PR7773
3279   All tore down   -
3280   Hip twist   -   45-210
3281   That's all   -

JIMMY NEELEY TRIO:
Jimmy Neeley(p)Michel Mulia(b)Les Jenkins(dm).
Supervision:Esmond Edwards   NYC,November 24,1961

3282   See who   unissued
3283   Joy blues   -
3284   Grits & greens   -
3285   Someone like you   -
3286   Pub crawlin'   -
3287   What's cookin'   -

DOUG QUATTLEBAUM-SOFTEE MAN BLUES:
Doug Quattlebaum(vo,g).
Supervision:Pete Welding   Philadelphia,November 27,1961

        Sweet little woman   BVLP1065
        Whiskey headed woman   -
        Trouble in mind   -
        You is one black rat   -
        On my way to school   -
        You ain't no good   -
        Come back blues   -
(session continued on next page)

[117]

```
                Mama don't allow me to stay
                        out all night long      BVLP1065
                Big leg woman                   -
                Love my baby                    -
                Black night is falling          -
                Baby,take a chance with me      -
                So sweet                        -
                Worried life blues              -
```

GENE AMMONS-TWISTING THE JUG:
Joe Newman(tp)Gene Ammons(ts)Jack McDuff(org)Wendell Marshall(b)Walter
Perkins(dm)Ray Barretto(conga).
Supervision:Esmond Edwards   NYC,November 28,1961

```
3288    Stormy Monday blues             PRLP7238,PR7774
3289    Satin doll                      -        PR7708
3290    Twisting the Jug                Pr.45-214,LP7238,PR7774
3291    Born to be blue                 PRLP7238
3292    Down the line                   -
3293    Moten swing                     -
```

All titles also issued on P-24071.

A DIXIELAND SOUND SPECTACULAR-AT THE JAZZ BAND BALL:
Dick Wellstood(p)Leonard Gaskin(b)Herb Lovelle(dm)with:
-1:Yank Lawson(tp)Cutty Cutshall(tb)Edmond Hall(cl) and/or:
-2:Doc Cheatham(tp)Vic Dickenson(tb)Buster Bailey(cl).
Supervision:Esmond Edwards   NYC,November 30,1961

```
                Tin roof blues-1                SVLP2031
                Muskrat ramble                  -
                At the jazz band ball-1,2       -
                Mack the knife-2                -
                Hindustan-2                     -
                Keepin' out of mischief now     -
```

BROTHER JACK McDUFF-ON WITH IT:
Harold Vick(ts)Jack McDuff(org)Eddie Diehl(g)Joe Dukes(dm).
Supervision:Esmond Edwards   NYC,December 1,1961

```
3294    Your nose is open               PR7851
3295    The last goodun                 -
3296    Scram                           PR7275
3297    Dink's dream                    PR7851
3298    Groanin'                        -
3299    Hey lawdy Mama                  -
3300    Drown in my own tears           -
```

EDDIE "BLUESMAN" KIRKLAND-THAT'S THE BLUES MAN:
Eddie Kirkland(vo,hca,g)with King Curtis' band:King Curtis,Oliver
Nelson(ts)Herman Foster(p)Billy Butler(g)Jimmy Lewis(b)Frank Shea(dm).
Supervision:Esmond Edwards   NYC,December 8,1961

```
3301    I tried                         TRU15010
3302    Man of stone                    -
3303    Chill me baby                   Pr.45-316
3304    Train gone done                 Tru.45-409,TRU15010
3305    I'm going to keep lovin' you                        -
3306    Something's gone wrong in my life
                                        Tru.45-409          -
3307    Baby you know it's true                             -
```

WILLIS JACKSON & JACK McDUFF-TOGETHER AGAIN,AGAIN:
Willis Jackson(ts)Jack McDuff(org)Bill Jennings(g)Jimmy Lewis(b)Frank
Shea(dm).
Supervision:Esmond Edwards   NYC,December 13,1961

3308   Jambalaya   Pr.45-221,PR7428
3309   Backtrack(That twistin' train)   Tru.45-410;PR7428
3310   Without a song   -   -
3311   Shake crawl   -

JESSIE POWELL-IT'S PARTY TIME:
Jessie Powell(ts)Adriano Acea(p)Bill Pyles(g)Jimmy Lewis(b)Wilbert
Hogan(dm).
Supervision:Esmond Edwards   NYC,December 15,1961

3312   Trees   TRU15007
3313   The Texas twister   -
3314   Blues on the rocks   -
3315   From the soul   -

JOHN WRIGHT-THE LAST AMEN:
John Wright(p)Eugene Taylor(b)Walter McCants(dm).
Supervision:Esmond Edwards   NYC,December 19,1961

3316   Les I can't   ST8322
3317   Be my love   -
3318   Stella by starlight   -
3319   The last amen   -
3320   But beautiful   -
3321   Do I love you   -
3322   Sheba   -
3323   More than you know   -

YUSEF LATEEF-INTO SOMETHING:
Yusef Lateef(ts,fl,oboe)Barry Harris(p)Herman Wright(b)Elvin Jones(dm).
Supervision:Esmond Edwards   NYC,December 29,1961

3324   When you're smiling-1   NJLP8272;PR7447
3325   Koko's tune-1   -   PR24007
3326   Water pistol-1   -
3327   I'll remember April   -   Pr.45-332,PR24007
3328   Rasheed   -   -
3329   P.Bouk   -
3330   You've changed   -   PR7447 ·

-1:Harris out.

NJLP8272=PR7637.

COLEMAN HAWKINS-GOOD OLD BROADWAY:
Coleman Hawkins(ts)Tommy Flanagan(p)Major Holley(b)Eddie Locke(dm).
Supervision:Esmond Edwards   NYC,January 2,1962

3331   Here I'll stay   MVLP23
3332   Smoke gets in your eyes   -
3333   Wanting you   -
3334   Get out of town   -   MV34
3335   The lan that got away   -
3336   A fellow needs a girl   -
3337   I talk to the trees   -
3338   Strange music   -

KING CURTIS-IT'S PARTY TIME:
King Curtis(as,ts)Sam Taylor-1(ts)Ernie Hayes(org)Paul Griffin(p)Billy
Butler(g)Jimmy Lewis(b)Ray Lucas(dm).
Supervision:Esmond Edwards   NYC,January 5,1962

3339	Low down-1	Tru.45-422,TRU15008;PR7775		
3340	The hully gully twist		-	PR7709
3341	The party time twist-1		-	-
3342	Free for all-1	Tru.45-415	-	PR7775
3343	Easy like-1		-	
3344	I'll wait for you	Tru.45-422	-	
3345	Hot saxes-1		-	PR7709

LIGHTNIN' HOPKINS-SMOKES LIKE LIGHTNIN':
Lightnin' Hopkins(vo,g).

Houston,Texas,January   ,1962

T model blues	BV1070;Pr.45-374	
Jackstropper blues	-	
You cook all right	-	Pr.45-374
You never miss the water	-	
Let's do the Susie Q	-	
Smokes like Lightnin'	-	

WALT DICKERSON-RELATIVITY:
Walt Dickerson(vb)Austin Crowe(p)Ahmed Abdul-Malik(b)Andrew Cyrille(dm).
Supervision:Esmond Edwards   NYC,January 16,1962

3346	It ain't necessarily so	NJLP8275
3347	Relativity	-
3348	The unknown	-
3349	Sugar lump	-
3350	Autumn in New York	-
3351	Stepping out	-
3352	I can't get started	-

JOHNNY "HAMMOND" SMITH-LOOK OUT:
Seldon Powell(ts)Johnny "Hammond" Smith(org)Clement Wells(vb)Wally
Richardson(g)Leo Stevens(dm).
Supervision:Esmond Edwards   NYC,January 22,1962

3353	Upset	NJLP8288
3354	Soul grits	-
3355	Let's everybody say amen	-
3356	There'll never be a love	-
3357	Que sera baby	-
3358	Clemente	-
3359	I'm glad there is you	-

JACK McDUFF with GENE AMMONS-MELLOW GRAVY:
Gene Ammons,Harold Vick(ts)Jack McDuff(org)Eddie Diehl(g)Joe Dukes(dm).
Supervision:Esmond Edwards   NYC,January 23,1962

3360	Watch out	PRLP7228,PR7774
3361	Mellow gravy	Pr.45-219,LP7228,PR7774,PR24013
3362	Ballad for baby	PR7275
3363	Strollin'	PRLP7228
3364	Mr.Clean	-
3365	Christopher Columbus	-
3366	Buzzin' around	- PR24013

JAKI BYARD-HI-FLY:
Jaki Byard(p)Ron Carter(b)Pete La Roca(dm).
Supervision:Esmond Edwards   NYC,January 30,1962

3367   Hi-fly   NJLP8273;P-24086
3368   'Round midnight   -   -
3369   Tillie Butterball   -   -
3370   Blues in the closet   -   -
3371   Hear to hear   -   -
3372   Lullaby of Birdland   -   -
3373   There are many worlds   -   -
3374   Excerpts from Yamakraw   -   -

ETTA JONES-FROM THE HEART:
Etta Jones(vo)with Lloyd Mayers(p)Wally Richardson(g)Bob Bushnell(b)
Ed Shaughnessy(dm)& strings,Oliver Nelson(arr,dir).
Supervision:Esmond Edwards   NYC,February 8,1962

3375   Just friends   Pr.45-215,LP7214
3376   I'll never be free   -
3377   There goes my heart   -
3378   Funny   -   PR7443

Etta Jones(vo)with Joe Wilder(tp)Jerry Dodgion,Oliver Nelson(as)George
Barrow,Bob Ashton(ts)Lloyd Mayers(p)Wally Richardson(g)Bob Bushnell(b)
Ed Shaughnessy(dm).
Supervision:Esmond Edwards   NYC,February 9,1962

3379   Makin' whoopee   Pr.   LP7214
3380   You came a long way from St.Louis Pr.45-215 -
3381   Look for the silver lining   -
3382   The masquerade is over   -
3383   By the bend of the river   -
3384   Good morning heartache   -
3385   They can't take that away from me   -

KING CURTIS-DOIN' THE DIXIE TWIST:
Britt Woodman(tb)King Curtis(ts)Paul Griffin(p)Billy Butler,Carl Lynch
(g)Jimmy Lewis(b)Ray Lucas(dm).
Supervision:Esmond Edwards   NYC,February 15,1962

3386   Alexander's ragtime band   TRU15009
3387   A shanty in old shanty town   -
3388   Basin Street blues
3389   When the Saints go marching in Tru.45-415,TRU15009;PR7709
3390   St.Louis blues   TRU15009
3391   Royal garden blues   -   PR7775
3392   Up a lazy river
3393   Sweet Georgia Brown   -   PR7709
3394   Muskrat ramble
3395   St.James infirmary   -   PR7775

SONNY STITT & JACK McDUFF-STITT MEETS BROTHER JACK:
Sonny Stitt(ts)Jack McDuff(org)Eddie Diehl(g)Art Taylor(dm)Ray Barretto
(conga).
Supervision:Esmond Edwards   NYC,February 16,1962

3396   Thirty three ninety six   Pr.45-282,PR7244,PR7701
3397   All of me   -   PR7769
3398   Pam ain't blue   Pr.45-263   -   PR7701
3399   When sunny gets blue   -   PR7769
3400   'nother fu'ther   Pr.45-239   -   PR7313,PR7701
3401   Ringin' in   Pr.45-263   -   -
3402   Time after time   -   PR7769

PR7244=PR7452.

LIGHTNIN' HOPKINS:
Lightnin' Hopkins(vo,g)Billy Bizor(hca-1,vo-2)Spider Kilpatrick(dm).
Supervision:Mack McCormick   Houston,Texas,February 17,1962

         How many more years I got   BVLP1057
         Black Cadillac ,   -
         Walking this road by myself-1   -   PR7714
         The devil jumped the black man-1   -   -
         My baby don't stand no cheatingBV45-825,LP1061
         You is one black rat   -
         The fox chase-1,2   -
         Mojo hand   BV1084   -   Pr.45-343
         Mama blues-1,2   -   Pr.45-452
         My black name   BVLP1070
         Ida Mae   .   -   PR7714

GENE AMMONS & SONNY STITT-SOUL SUMMIT:
Gene Ammons,Sonny Stitt(ts)Jack McDuff(org)Charlie Persip(dm).
Supervision:Esmond Edwards   NYC,February 19,1962

3403   Dumplin'   PRLP7234
3404   Tubby   Pr.45-294,LP7234
3405   Shuffle twist   PRLP7234,PR7774
3406   Sleeping Susan   -
3407   Out in the cold again   -
3408   When you wish upon a star   -   PR7774

PRLP7234=PR7454.

LIGHTNIN' HOPKINS:
Buster Pickens(p)Lightnin' Hopkins(vo,g)Donald Cooks(b)Spider
Kilpatrick(dm).
Supervision:Mack McCormick   Houston,Texas,February 20,1962

         Prison farm blues   BVLP1070;PR7714
         Worried life blues   BVLP1057   -
         Happy blues for John Glenn   BV45-820,LP1057;PR7714
         Sinner's prayer   BV45-822,LP1061,BV1084;
                                          Pr.45-391,PR7592
         Angel child   BV45-822,LP1061
         I got a leak in this old building   -   PR7714
         Pneumonia blues   BVLP1061;Pr.45-452,PR7714
         Have you ever been mistreated   -

SAM "THE MAN" TAYLOR-THE BAD AND THE BEAUTIFUL:
Sam Taylor(ts)Lloyd Mayers(p)Wally Richardson(g)Art Davis(b)Ed
Shaughnessy(dm).
Supervision:Esmond Edwards   NYC,February 20,1962

3409   Ruby   MVLP24,MV37;ST8319
3410   Love song from Suzie Wong   -   Pr.45-256
3411   Laura
3412   Anastasia   -   Pr.45-256
3413   Barefoot Contessa   -
3414   Gloria   -
3415   The bad and the beautiful   -   45-601
3416   Anna   -

BIG JOE WILLIAMS AT FOLK CITY:
Big Joe Williams(vo,g,kazoo).
                        Gerde's Folk City,NYC,February 26,1962

        Mink coat blues   BV1067
        Burned child is seared of fire -
        Baby,I ain't gonna let you go   -
        Trouble gonna take me to my grave-
        Bugle blues   -
        Just want to be your man   -
        I'm gonna do it this time   -
        She's doggin' me   -
        How do you want your rollin' done-
        I can't sign my name   -
        Bottle up and go   -
        I'm tired woman   -

LARRY YOUNG-GROOVE STREET:
Bill Leslie(ts)Larry Young(org)Thornel Schwartz(g)Jimmie Smith(dm).
Supervision:Esmond Edwards   NYC,February 27,1962

3417   Talkin' 'bout J.C.   PRLP7237
3418   Here's Bill   unissued
3419   Gettin' into it   PRLP7237
3420   I found a new baby   -
3421   Sweet Lorraine
3422   Groove Street   Pr.45-216,LP7237

EDDIE "BLUESMAN" KIRKLAND-THAT'S THE BLUES MAN:
Eddie Kirkland(vo,hca,g)with KING CURTIS' BAND:King Curtis,Oliver Nelson
(ts)George Stubbs(p)Billy Butler(g)Jimmy Lewis(el b)Ray Lucas(dm).
Supervision:Esmond Edwards   NYC,March 9,1962

3423   Saturday night stomp   TRU15010
3424   I'm gonna forget you   -
3425   Down on my knees   -
3426   Don't take my heart   -
3427   Daddy please don't cry   -
3428   Have mercy on me   Pr.45-316

DIZZY REECE-ASIA MINOR:
Dizzy Reece(tp)Joe Farrell(fl-1,ts)Cecil Payne(bs)Hank Jones(p)Ron Carter
(b)Charlie Persip(dm).
Supervision:Esmond Edwards   NYC,March 13,1962

3429   The shadow of Kahn   NJLP8274
3430   The story of love-1   -
3431   Yamask   -
3432   Spiritus Parkus   -
3433   Summertime   -
3434   Ackmet   -   NJLP8292

FRANK WESS-SOUTHERN COMFORT:
Al Aarons(tp)Frank Wess(fl,ts)George Barrow(bs)Tommy Flanagan(p)George
Duvivier(b)Osie Johnson(dm)Ray Barretto(conga)Oliver Nelson(arr).
Supervision:Esmond Edwards   NYC,March 22,1962

3435   Blue skies   PRLP7231
3436   Blues for Butterball   -
3437   Dancing in the dark   -
3438   Shufflin'   -
3439   Summer frost   -
3440   Gin's beguine   -
3441   Southern comfort   Pr.45-217,LP7231

HONI GORDON SINGS-HONI:
Honi Gordon(vo)with Ken McIntyre(fl,as)Jaki Byard(p)Wally Richardson(g)
George Duvivier(b)Ed Shaughnessy(dm).
Supervision:Esmond Edwards   NYC,March 23,1962

```
3442   Ill wind                    PRLP7230
3443   Love affair                  -
3444   Strollin'                    -
3445   Lament of the lonely         -
3446   Walkin' out the door         -
3447   Why                          -
3448   My Kokomo                    -
3449   Why try to change me now     -
3450   Cupid                        -
```

COLEMAN HAWKINS-THE JAZZ VERSION OF NO STRINGS:
Coleman Hawkins(ts)Tommy Flanagan(p)Major Holley(b)Eddie Locke(dm).
Supervision:Esmond Edwards   NYC,March 30,1962

```
3451   Look no further              MV25
3452   No strings                   -
3453   The sweetest sounds          -  MV35
3454   Nobody told me               -
3455   Maine                        rejected
```

WILLIS JACKSON-THUNDERBIRD:
Willis Jackson(ts)Freddie Roach(org)Bill Jennings(g)Wendell Marshall(b)
Frank Shea(dm)Ray Barretto(conga).
Supervision:Esmond Edwards   NYC,March 31,1962

```
3456   Thunderbird                  Pr.45-221,LP7232
3457   California sun               PRLP7232,PR7770
3458   Back and forth               -     -
3459   Body and soul                -
3460   A penny serenade             -
3461   Lady be good                 -
```

BUDDY LUCAS:
Buddy Lucas(ts,hca,tambourine)Al Williams(p)Wally Richardson,Carl
Lynch(g)Bob Bushnell(b)Herb Lovelle(dm).
Supervision:Ozzie Cadena   NYC,March 31,1962

```
SA100  The rattle                   TRU15011
SA101  Papa Dee Dee                 -
SA102  Fall out                     -
SA103  Crash party                  -
SA104  Show down                    Tru.45-416,TRU15011
```

Note:Matrix numbers in SA series were used by Ozzie Cadena for his
Sound of America production company.

COLEMAN HAWKINS-THE JAZZ VERSION OF NO STRINGS:
Coleman Hawkins(ts)Tommy Flanagan(p)Major Holley(b)Eddie Locke(dm).
Supervision:Esmond Edwards   NYC,April 3,1962

```
3462   Maine                        MV25
3463   The man who has everything   -
3464   Loads of love                -
3465   Be my host                   -  MV38
3466   La la la                     -
```

THE SOLID TRUMPET OF COOTIE WILLIAMS:
Cootie Williams(tp)Nat Jones(p)Harold Dodson(b)Bill Peeples(dm).
Supervision:Sid Wayman   Miami,April 4,1962

             Concerto for Cootie   MV27
             Sugar blues   -
             You're nobody 'till somebody
                             loves you   -
             Some of these days   -
             Night train   -
             Around the world in 80 days   -
             Liza   -
             Birmingham blues   -

ETTA JONES-LONELY AND BLUE:
Etta Jones(vo)with Patti Bown(p)Wally Richardson(g)George Duvivier(b)
Ed Shaughnessy(dm).
Supervision:Esmond Edwards   NYC,April 6,1962

3467   Good for nothing else   PR7241
3468   You don't know my mind   -
3469   And I'll be there   Pr.45-233,PR7241
3470   I miss you so   -   PR7443
3471   In the dark   Pr.45-233 -
3472   I wonder   -
3473   I'm pulling through   -

LONNIE JOHNSON-ANOTHER NIGHT TO CRY:
Lonnie Johnson(vo,g).
                                          April 6,1962

             Another night to cry   BVLP1062
             I got news for you baby   -
             Blues after hours   -
             You didn't mean what you said -
             Fine booze and heavy dues   -
             I've got to get rid of you   -
             Bow legged baby   -
             Make love to me baby   -
             Lots of loving   -
             A story about Barbara   -
             Goodbye Kitten   -

THE GATE CITY SINGERS:
Vocal group,including Leroy Gilligan,Richard Henderson,Joseph Davison,
Bernard Patton,with Robert Banks(org)Nathaniel Sanford(g)Benjamin Milas
(b)Herbie Lovelle(dm).
Supervision:Ozzie Cadena   NYC,April 7,1962

SA105 The day is past and gone-LG,RH unissued
SA106 No time to lose-JD   Tru.45-7,TRU60002
SA107 Something with me-LG,RH   -   -
SA108 Good news-BP   unissued
SA109 Beams of heaven-LG,BP,RH   TRU60002
SA110 Every now and then-LG,RH   -

JOHN WRIGHT-Mr.SOUL:
John Wright(p)Wendell Marshall(b)Walter Perkins(dm).
Supervision:Esmond Edwards   NYC,April 10,1962

3474   Our waltz   Pr.   LP7233
3475   Blue prelude   Pr.45-218 -
3476   What's new   -
3477   Strut   Pr.45-218 -
3478   Now hang in there   -
3479   Shake   -
3480   Everything's gonna work out fine -
3481   Mr.Soul   -

[125]

B.B.B. & Co.:
Shorty Sherock(tp)Barney Bigard(cl)Benny Carter(as)Ben Webster(ts)Jimmy
Rowles(p)Dave Barbour(g)Leroy Vinnegar(b)Mel Lewis(dm).
Supervision:Leonard Feather   LA,April 10,1962

L2032-1	Opening blues	SVLP2032
L2032-2	Lula	-
L2032-3	When lights are low	-
L2032-4	You can't tell the difference	-

SA111/120:ALFREDITO VALDES-April 11,1962(not jazz).

GENE AMMONS:
Gene Ammons(ts)Patti Bown(p)George Duvivier(b)Walter Perkins(dm)Etta
Jones(vo).
Supervision:Esmond Edwards   NYC,April 13,1962

3482	But not for me voEJ	PR7275
3483	If you are but a dream voEJ	- PR7443
3484	The party's over	Pr.45-319,PR7287
3485	Cool cool Daddy voEJ	PR7275,PR7313
3486	Lascivious	PR7287
3487	Soft winds	-
3488	Scam	PR7400

THE SOULFUL MOODS OF GENE AMMONS:
Gene Ammons(ts)Patti Bown(p)George Duvivier(b)Ed Shaughnessy(dm).
Supervision:Esmond Edwards   NYC,April 14,1962

3489	Two different worlds	MV28
3490	But beautiful	-
3491	Skylark	-
3492	On the street of dreams	- Pr.45-253
3493	You'd be so nice to come home to	-
3494	Under a blanket of blue	-
3495	I'm glad there's you	-
3496	Three little worlds	-

All titles also issued on P-24079.

LATIN JAZZ QUINTET-THE CHANT:
Bobby Capers(as)Willie Gardner(p)William Bivens(vb)Bill Ellington(b)
Victor Allende(bongo)Manny Ramos(timbales)Juan Amalbert(conga,dir).
Supervision:Esmond Edwards   NYC,April 20,1962

3497	Jackie's mambo	TRU15012
3498	Dorian	-
3499	A lot of livin' to do	unissued
3500	Yesterdays child	TRU15012
3501	Star eyes	-
3502	G.T.'s theme	-
3503	There's no you	-
3504	The chant	-
3505	Invitation	-

BUDDY LUCAS-DOWN HOME TURNAROUND:
Buddy Lucas(ts,hca,tambourine)Bobby Banks(p,org)Wally Richardson(g)Carl
Lynch(bass g)Bob Bushnell(b,el b)Herbie Lovelle(dm)The Shouters(Dionne
Warwick,Dee Dee Warwick,Sylvia Shemwell)(vo).
Supervision:Ozzie Cadena   NYC,April 22,1962

SA121	Long boy	Tru.	TRU15011
SA122	Hokus pocus	Tru.45-416	-
SA123	Down home turnaround	Tru.45-420	-
SA124	April showers	-	-
SA125	Moonglow	-	-

SA126:not used.

BROWNIE McGHEE & SONNY TERRY AT THE 2nd FRET:
Brownie McGhee(vo,g)Sonny Terry(vo,hca).
Supervision:Kenneth Goldstein
The 2nd Fret,Philadelphia,April   ,1962

Evil hearted me	BVLP1058	
Sick man	-	
Barking bull dog	-	
Spread the news around	-	
Backwater blues	-	PR7715
Custard pie	-	
Wholesale dealing Papa	-	
Motorcycle blues	-	
Hand in hand	-	
I woke up one morning and I could hardly see	-	

All titles also issued on PR7803.

EDDIE "LOCKJAW" DAVIS-GOIN' TO THE MEETING:
Eddie "Lockjaw" Davis(ts)Horace Parlan(p)Buddy Catlett(b)Art Taylor(dm)
Willie Bobo(William Correa)(conga).
Supervision:Esmond Edwards   NYC,May 1,1962

3506	Yes yes	Pr.	LP7242
3507	Please send me someone to love	Pr.45-220	-
3508	Our love is here to stay		-
3509	Goin' to the meetin'	Pr.45-220	-
3510	Oh Babee		-
3511	Night and day		-
3512	Pass the hat		-
3513	Little cougar		-
3514	People will say we're in love	-	MV35

THE CAPITOL CITY STARS:
Walter Mikell,John Nobel,Edwin Hall,Elliot McIlwain,William Jeter(vo)with
Amos Bell(p)Robert Banks(org).
Supervision:Ozzie Cadena   NYC,May 3,1962

SA127	It's all right	Tru.	TRU60003
SA128	Friends talk about me	Tru.45-3	-
SA129	There'll be no rest for the weary	-	
SA130	Jesus I love to call your name	-	

ETTA JONES-LONELY AND BLUE:
Etta Jones(vo)with Budd Johnson(ts)Patti Bown(p)Art Davis(b)Ed Shaughnessy
(dm).
Supervision:Esmond Edwards   NYC,May 4,1962

3515	Out in the cold again	PRLP7241	
3516	My gentleman friend	-	PR7443
3517	Gee baby ain't I good to you	-	
3518	Trav'lin' light	-	

CLARK TERRY-THE NIGHT LIFE:
Clark Terry(tp,flh)Lester Robinson(tb)Budd Johnson(ts)George Barrow(bs)
Eddie Costa(p,vb)Art Davis(b)Ed Shaughnessy(dm).
Supervision:Esmond Edwards   NYC,May 11,1962

3519	Night life	MV26
3520	Once upon a time	-
3521	It's fun to think	-
3522	I've just seen her	-

Same.
Supervision:Esmond Edwards   NYC,May 15,1962

3523   If I were you   MV26
3524   Fight song   -
3525   Same language   -
3526   What a country   -

LIGHTNIN' HOPKINS-HOOTIN' THE BLUES:
Lightnin' Hopkins(vo,g).
Supervision:Shel Kagan
                   The Second Fret,Philadelphia,May 17,1962

        Blues is a feeling   PR14021
        Me and Ray Charles   -
        In the evening   -
        Ain't it crazy   -
        Last night I lost the best friend
                            I ever had -
        Everything   -
        I work down on the chain gang   -
        Meet me in the bottom   -

PR14021=PR7806.

THE CLEFS OF CALVARY:
James Phelps,Calvin April,Ezell Wilkins,Willie Harris,Lester Earl(vo)
with Richard Franklin(g)Leo Farley(b).
Supervision:Ozzie Cadena   NYC,May 17,1962

SA131   Save me   Tru.45-1,TRU60001
SA132   God's love   -   -
SA133   Goin' down to the river   -
SA134   Wait a little longer   -
SA135   Trouble of this world   Tru.45-9   -
SA136   Oh Lord remember me   -

Same.
Supervision:Ozzie Cadena   NYC,May 18,1962

SA137   Baptized   Tru.45-5,TRU60001
SA138   A stranger in any land   -   -
SA139   Where the blood's running warm Tru.45-9   -
SA140   God knows the reason why   -
SA141   Jesus is a friend of mine   -
SA142   Father forgive me   -

THE BACK HOME CHOIR-COME OUT OF THE WILDERNESS:
incl.Janie Ross,Ophelia Little,Mildred Lane,Minnie Sirmans,Bill Thomas,
Rev.Banks,Joe DeLoatch,Robert Ross(vo)
Supervision:Ozzie Cadena   May   ,1962

        He's so mighty-JR   TRU60004,45-4
        I trust Him-OL,ML   -   45-8
        Ride on King Jesus-MS   -
        Without God I can do nothing-BT   -
        He knows how much we can bear-RB   -
        Climbing high mountains-RB   -   45-4
        Come out of the wilderness-JdL   -   45-8
        Yes I found Him-RR   -
        Jesus-OL,RB   -
        Jordan river-RB   -

THE PENTECOSTAL CHOIR OF DETROIT-SAVED:

Supervision:Ozzie Cadena   May   ,1962
        Save me if you will   TRU60005
        In the shelter of the rock   -
        Prayer wheel turning   -
        God's creation   -
        It's wonderful to know the Lord -
        How glad I am   -
THE PSALMS OF GRACE-TIME IS WINDING UP:
Vocal group,including Ethel Miller,James Stamp,Juanita Lynch,Ruth
Torrance,J.W.Stevenson
Supervision:Ozzie Cadena   May   ,1962
        Till the day is done   TRU60006
        There's not a friend like Him -
        Jesus loves me   -
        Move up a little higher   -
        I've been in the storm   -
        I'll overcome   -
        He will provide   -
        I know you're going to miss me -
        He's alright   -
        Time is winding up   -
THE GATE CITY SINGERS:

Supervision:Ozzie Cadena   NYC,May 29,1962
SA143 Peace in the valley   Tru.45-2,TRU60002
SA144 Delivrance will come   -
SA145 I'll fly away   -
SA146 Out on the ocean sailing   -
SA147 I'm here in Jesus' name   -
SA148 I thank you Jesus   Tru.45-2 -
JIMMY FORREST:
Ernie Royal(tp)Jimmy Cleveland(tb)George Barrow,Seldon Powell,Jimmy
Forrest(ts)Chris Woods(p)Mundell Lowe(g)Richard Davis(b)Ed Shaughnessy
(dm)Oliver Nelson(arr,dir).
Supervision:Esmond Edwards   NYC,June 1,1962
3527   Soft Summer breeze   NJLP8293;Pr.45-223
3528   Just a-sittin' and a-rockin'   -   PR7712
3529   Experiments in terror   -   Pr.45-223
SA148/157:ANDRES HERNANDEZ & HIS SEXTET CARIBE-June 4,1962(not jazz).
HENRY "RED" ALLEN-Mr.ALLEN:
Henry "Red" Allen(tp,vo)Lannie Scott(p)Frank Skeete(b)Jerry Potter(dm).
Supervision:Esmond Edwards   NYC,June 5,1962
3530   Cherry   SVLP2034
3531   Sleepy time gal   -
3532   I ain't got nobody   -
3533   There's a house in Harlem   -
3534   Just in time   -
3535   Nice work if you can get it   -
3536   Biffly blues   -
3537   St.Louis blues   -
SVLP2034=PR7755.

JOHNNY "HAMMOND" SMITH-COOKS WITH WILLIS JACKSON:
Willis Jackson(ts)Johnny "Hammond" Smith(org)Eddie McFadden(g)Leo
Stevens(dm).
Supervision:Esmond Edwards   NYC,June 12,1962

3538   Sonja dreamland   PRLP7239
3539   Delicious   -
3540   Besame mucho   -
3541   Neckbones   -
3542   Good 'nuff   -   PR7705
3543   Y'all   -
3544   Nobody knows the trouble I've seen-

PRLP7239=PR7846.

THE CAPITOL CITY STARS:

Supervision:Ozzie Cadena   NYC,June   ,1962

SA158 We've come this far by faith   TRU60003
SA159 It's gonna rain   -
SA160 Lord guide my mind   -
SA161 Another day   -
SA162 Gonna walk right out   -
SA163 I love the Lord   Tru.45-6,TRU60003
SA164 I'm so glad   -   -
SA165 My God called me this morning TRU60003

FAYE ADAMS:
Faye Adams(vo)with orchestra dir.by Oliver Nelson.
Supervision:Esmond Edwards   NYC,June 26,1962

3545   Goodnight my love   Pr.45-224
3546   You can trust in me   -
3547   Come on to me   unissued
3548   Blue raindrops   -

RHODA SCOTT TRIO:
Joe Thomas(ts)Rhoda Scott(org)Carl Lynch(g)Bill Elliot (dm)The Shouters
(vo).
Supervision:Ozzie Cadena   NYC,June 29,1962

SA166 I only have eyes for you   TRU15013

Herb Lovelle(dm)replaces Elliot.Same date.

SA167 Stand by me   TRU15013
SA168 If you're lonely   Tru.45-417
SA169 Hey-hey-hey   -

Note:Matrix numbers for this session are shown in Prestige session book
as SA172/175.As sequence SA170/175 is used for August 23,1962 session,
it is believed that SA166/169 are the correct numbers for session
above.

JIMMY GRISSOM:
Jimmy Grissom(vo)with Oliver Nelson(as,ts)Dick Hyman(org)Hank Jones(p)
Wendell Marshall(b)Ed Shaughnessy(dm)& strings.
Supervision:Esmond Edwards   NYC,July 3,1962

3549   I've got you on my mind   Pr.45-225
3550   Lover's reverie   -
3551   Love has a thousand eyes   unissued
3552   Get yourself another fool   -

WADE WALTON-SHAKE 'EM ON DOWN:
Wade Walton(vo,hca,g)Memphis Mango-1(g).
                                    Clarksdale,c.Summer 1962

        Big fat Mama   BVLP1060
        Choo choo de shoo shoo-1   -
        Short hair woman   -
        Forty-four   -
        Kansas City blues   -
        Rock me Mama   -
        Blues stay away from me   -
        Parchman farm   -
        Big six   -
        Shake 'em down   -

ROBERT CURTIS SMITH-CLARKSDALE BLUES:
Robert Curtis Smith(vo,g).
                                    Clarksdale,c.Summer 1962

        Catfish   BVLP1064
        Put your arms around me   -
        Rock me Mama   -
        Council spur blues   -
        I feel so good   -
        I'm going away   -
        Ain't that loving you baby   -
        Get a real young woman   -
        See my chauffeur   -
        Sunflower river blues   -
        Katy Mae   -
        Goody goody   -
        Can you remember me   -
        I hate to leave you with tears
                        in my eyes   -

3553/3558:DUKE OF IRON CALYPSO BAND-NYC,August 14,1962(not jazz).

COLEMAN HAWKINS-MAKE SOMEONE HAPPY:
Coleman Hawkins(ts)Tommy Flanagan(p)Major Holley(b)Eddie Locke(dm).
Supervision:Esmond Edwards   NYC,August 16,1962

3559   Cry like the wind   MV31
3560   Have I told you   -
3561   Make someone happy   -
3562   Out of my dreams   -
3563   Climb every mountain   -   MV38
3564   I believe in you   -   -
3565   Wouldn't it be lovely   -   ST8315

AHMED ABDUL-MALIK-SOUNDS OF AFRICA:
Richard Williams(tp)Bilal Abdurrahman(cl,darubeka)Edwin Steede(as)Taft
Chandler(ts)Rupert Alleyne(fl)Calo Scott(cello,v)Ahmed Abdul-Malik(b,
oud)Rudy Collins(dm)Montego Joe(conga,bongo)Chief Bay(African dm).
Supervision:Esmond Edwards   NYC,August 22,1962

3566   Wakida Hena   NJLP8282
3567   Listen to my friends   unissued
3568   African bossa nova   NJLP8282
3569   Suffering   -
3570   Communication   -
3571   untitled oud solo   unissued
3572   Nadusilma   NJLP8282

LEONARD GASKIN-DARKTOWN STRUTTER'S BALL:
Red Richards(p)Leonard Gaskin(b)Herb Lovelle(dm)with:
-1:Herman Autrey(tp)Dickie Wells(tb)Herb Hall(cl) and/or:
-2:Pee Wee Erwin(tp)"Big Chief" Russell Moore(tb)Bud Freeman(ts).
Supervision:Ozzie Cadena   NYC,August 23,1962

SA170 Ballin' the Jack-1   SVLP2033
SA171 Memphis blues-1   -
SA172 I guess I'll have to change
                           my mind   -
SA173 Darktown strutter's ball-1,2   -
SA174 It had to be you-2   -
SA175 Farewell blues-2   -

LEONARD GASKIN-DIXIELAND HITS:
Sidney De Paris(tp)Benny Morton(tb)Kenny Davern(cl)Charlie Queener(p)
Lee Blair(bjo)Leonard Gaskin(b)Herb Lovelle(dm).
Supervision:Ozzie Cadena   NYC,August 28,1962

SA176 Pistol packin' Mama   SV2040
SA177 You call everyone darling   -
SA178 You always hurt the one you love -
SA179 Yellow rose of Texas   -
SA180 It is no secret   -
SA181 Just because of you   unissued
SA182 Someday   SV2040
SA183 Riders in the sky   -

GENE AMMONS:
Gene Ammons(ts)Mal Waldron(p)Wendell Marshall(b)Ed Thigpen(dm)
Supervision:Esmond Edwards   NYC,September 5,1962

3573   Light 'n up   PR7320
3574   Shortstop   PR7400
3575   They say you're laughing at me   -   PR7708
3576   It's the talk of the town   PR7369   -
3577   Salome's tune   PR7320
3578   Blue coolade   PR7400
3579   A stranger in town   PR7320,45-336
3580   You go to my head   PR7369

3581/3604:not used.

DAVE PIKE-BOSSA NOVA CARNIVAL:
Clark Terry(flh)Dave Pike(vb,marimba)Kenny Burrell(g)Chris White(b)
Rudy Collins(dm)Jose Paulo(cabassa,bandero).
Supervision:Elliot Mazur   NYC,September 6,1962

3605   Samba lero   rejected
3606   Philumba   NJLP8281
3607   Sono   -
3608   Serenidade   rejected
3609   Carnival samba   NJLP8281
3610   Ginha   -

Terry out.
Supervision:Elliot Mazur   NYC,September 7,1962

3611   Sausalito   NJLP8281
3612   Mel valita   -   Pr.45-228
3608   Serenidade   -
3605   Samba lero   -
3605A Samba lero(short version)   Pr.45-228
3605B Samba lero(version with vocal) unissued
3613   Minha saudade   -

Rev.GARY DAVIS:
Rev.Gary Davis(vo,g).

                                    Philadelphia,September 8,1962
          If I had my way   PR13072
          Sally where you get your
                    liquor from   -
          You got to move   -

GENE AMMONS-BAD!BOSSA NOVA:
Gene Ammons(ts)Hank Jones(p)John "Bucky" Pizzarelli(g)Kenny Burrell(g)
Norman Edge(b)Oliver Jackson(dm)Al Hayes(bongos).
Supervision:Ozzie Cadena   NYC,September 9,1962
3614   Pagan love song   Pr.45-227,LP7257
3615   Anna   -   -   MV37;ST8319;MV34
3616   Ca' purange(Jungle soul*)(?) Pr.45-229 - P-10084*,45-707*
3617   Yellow bird   -
3618   Cae cae   -
3619   Moito Mato Grosso   Pr.45-245   -
*3616 is edited on P-10084.
All titles also issued on PR7552.

KENNY BURRELL/COLEMAN HAWKINS-BLUESY BURRELL:
Coleman Hawkins(ts)Tommy Flanagan(p)Kenny Burrell(g)Major Holley(b)
Eddie Locke(dm)Ray Barretto(conga).
Supervision:Ozzie Cadena   NYC,September 14,1962
3620   Out of this world-1   MV29;Pr.45-238
3621   Guilty-1,2   -
3622   No more-2   -
3623   Montana blues   - Pr.45-238
3624   I thought about you-2   - Pr.45-260
3625   Tres talbras   -
3626   It's getting dark   - Pr.45-260

-1:Hawkins out;-2:Barretto out.

MV29=PR7578.

3627/3630:DUKE OF IRON CALYPSO BAND-September 19,1962(not jazz).

WALT DICKERSON-TO MY QUEEN:
Walt Dickerson(vb)Andrew Hill(p)George Tucker(b)Andrew Cyrille(dm).
Supervision:Ozzie Cadena   NYC,September 21,1962
3631   To my queen   NJLP8283
3632   How deep is the ocean   -
3633   God bless the child   -

RED GARLAND-WHEN THERE ARE GREY SKIES:
Red Garland(p)Wendell Marshall(b)Charlie Persip(dm).
Supervision:Ozzie Cadena   NYC,October 9,1962
3634   I ain't got nobody   PR7258
3635   Nobody knows the trouble I've seen -
3636   St.James infirmary   -
3637   Baby won't you please come homePr.45-231,PR7258
3638   My honey's lovin' arms   -
3639   Sonny boy   Pr.45-231   -
3640   My blue heaven   unissued

BROTHER JACK McDUFF-SCREAMIN':
Leo Wright(as)Jack McDuff(org)Kenny Burrell(g)Joe Dukes(dm).
Supervision:Ozzie Cadena   NYC,October 23,1962

3641	He's a real gone guy	Pr.45-232,PR7259		
3642	Soulful drums		-	PR24013
3643	After hours		-	
3644	Screamin'	Pr.45-246	-	PR7481,PR24013
3645	I cover the waterfront		-	PR7596
3646	One o'clock jump		-	

RHODA SCOTT:
Joe Thomas(ts)Rhoda Scott(org)Leonard Gaskin(b)Bill Elliot(dm).
Supervision:Ozzie Cadena   NYC,October 24,1962

SA184-6	In my little corner of the world	Tru.45-418	
SA185-7	Endlessly	TRU15013	
SA186-10	Sha-bazz	Tru.45-419,TRU15013	
SA187-4	If this isn't love		-
SA188-2	Ebb tide		-
SA189-3	Splanky		-
SA190-3	Fly me to the moon	Tru.45-418	-

WILLIS JACKSON-SHUCKIN':
Willis Jackson(ts)Tommy Flanagan(p)Kenny Burrell(g)Eddie Calhoun(b)Roy
Haynes(dm)Juan Amalbert(conga)Montego Joe,Jose Paulo(perc).
Supervision:Ozzie Cadena   NYC,October 30,1962

3647	Cachita	Pr.	PR7260	
3648	I left my heart in San Francisco	Pr.45-234	-	
3649	Amor		-	
3650	Mama Inez		-	
3651	What kind of fool am I	Pr.45-234,	-	;MV38
3652	Shuckin'		-	PR7770

EDDIE "LOCKJAW" DAVIS:
Eddie "Lockjaw" Davis(ts)Don Patterson(org)Paul Weeden(g)George
Duvivier(b)Billy James(dm).
Supervision:Ozzie Cadena   NYC,November 15,1962

3653	Day by day	Pr.	PR7271
3654	Robbin's nest	Pr.45-257	-
3655	Beano	unissued	
3656	Street lights	Pr.	PR7261
3657	Sweet and lovely	Pr.45-236	-
3658	I only have eyes for you	-	-
3659	The way you look tonight		-
3660	It's a pity to say goodnight		-
3661	Time on my hands		-
3662	There'll never be another you	Pr.	PR7271
3663	Beano	Pr.45-279	-
3664	What's new		-
3665	Too marvellous for words		-
3666	A foggy day	Pr.45-257	-

ETTA JONES:
Etta Jones(vo)with Jerome Richardson(fl,ts)Ernie Hayes(org)Kenny Burrell
John "Bucky" Pizzarelli(g)Sam Bruno(b)Bobby Donaldson(dm).
Supervision:Ozzie Cadena   NYC,November 28,1962

3667	If I loved you	Pr.	PR7272
3668	Hilili hi lo	Pr.45-237	-
3669	Nature boy	-	PR7284
3670	A gal from Joe's	Pr.45-278,PR7272	

SHIRLEY SCOTT-HAPPY TALK:
Shirley Scott(org)Earl May(b)Roy Brooks(dm).
Supervision:Ozzie Cadena   NYC,December 5,1962

3671	Happy talk	Pr.45-235,PR7262,PR7360		
3672	Jitterbug waltz	-	-	-
3673	Sweet slumber		-	-
3674	Where or when	Pr.45-408	-	-
3675	I hear a rhapsody		-	-
3676	My romance	Pr.45-408	-	-

TED CURSON-FIRE DOWN BELOW:
Ted Curson(tp)Gildo Mahones(p)George Tucker(b)Roy Haynes(dm)Montego Joe
(conga).
Supervision:Ozzie Cadena   NYC,December 10,1962

3677	Fire down below	Pr.45-241,PR7263	
3678	The very young	-	-
3679	Baby has gone bye bye		-
3680	Show me	-	MV38;ST8315
3681	Falling in love with love		-
3682	Only forever		-

Note:Matrix numbers for this session are shown as 3647/3652 in Prestige
session book,but according to numerical sequence and recording date,
numbers shown above likely are the correct ones.

3683/3689:not used.

DAVE PIKE-LIMBO CARNIVAL:
Leo Wright(as,fl)Dave Pike(vb,marimba)Jimmy Raney(g)George Duvivier(b)
William Correa(dm)Ray Barretto(conga).
Supervision:Elliot Mazur   NYC,December 12,1962

3690	Limbo rock	NJ8284;Pr.45-242
3691	La bamba	- Pr.45-252
3692	Sly mongoose	unissued
3693	Matilda	NJ8284
3694	Jamaica farewell	- Pr.45-242

Dave Pike(vb,marimba)Tommy Flanagan(p)Ahmed Abdul-Malik(b)William
Correa(dm)Ray Barretto(conga).
                             Same date.

3695	My little Suede shoes	NJ8284;Pr.45-252
3696	Mambo bounce	-
3697	St.Thomas	-
3698	Out of the blue	unissued
3699	Catin latin	NJ8284
3700	Calypso blues	

WILLIS JACKSON-NEAPOLITAN NIGHTS:
Willis Jackson(ts)Gildo Mahones(p)John "Bucky" Pizzarelli(g)George
Tucker(b)Bobby Donaldson(dm)Montego Joe(conga).
Supervision:Ozzie Cadena   NYC,December 19,1962

3701	Arrivederci Roma	Pr.45-277,PR7264	
3702	Neapolitan nights	Pr.45-243	-
3703	Volare		-
3704	Al di la		-
3705	Mama	Pr.45-243	-
3706	Verdi's vonce		- PR7770

DAVE PIKE PLAYS THE JAZZ VERSION OF OLIVER!:
Dave Pike(vb)Tommy Flanagan(p)Jimmy Raney(g)George Tucker(b)Walter
Perkins(dm).
Supervision:Don Schlitten   NYC,December 28,1962
3707   It's a fine life   MV36
3708   Who will buy   -
3709   I'd do anything   -
3710   Food,glorious food   -
3711   Boy for sale   -
3712   Where is love   - Pr.45-244
3713   As long as he needs me   - MV38;Pr.45-244
JACK McDUFF:
Blue Mitchell(tp)Buster Cooper(tb)Danny Turner(as)Harold Vick(ts)
Charles Davis(bs)Jack McDuff(org)Eddie Diehl(g)Joe Dukes(dm).
Supervision:Ozzie Cadena   NYC,January 2,1963
3714   Midnight sun   unissued
3715   9.20 special   PR7791
JACK McDUFF-SOMETHING SLICK:
Eric Dixon(fl,ts)Harold Vick(ts)Jack McDuff(org)Kenny Burrell(g)Joe
Dukes(dm)Ray Barretto(conga).
Supervision:Ozzie Cadena   NYC,January 8,1963
3716   Something slick   Pr.45-246,PR7265,PR7481
3717   How high the moon   -
3718   Shaky   PR7666
3719   Love walked in   PR7347
3720   Easy livin'   unissued
3721   It's a wonderful world   PR7265,PR7596
3722   Smut   -
3723   Our Miss Brooks   -
SHIRLEY SCOTT-THE SOUL IS WILLING:
Stanley Turrentine(ts)Shirley Scott(org)Major Holley(b)Grassella
Oliphant(dm).
Supervision:Ozzie Cadena   NYC,January 10,1963
3724   I feel alright   Pr.45-275,PR7267,PR7313
3725   Secret love   - PR7773
3726   Remember   -
3727   Stolen sweets   -
3728   The soul is willing   Pr.45-259 -
3729   Yes indeed   - PR7707
PR7267=PR7845.

FRANK WESS-YO HO!:
Thad Jones(tp)Frank Wess(fl,ts)Gildo Mahones(p)Buddy Catlett(b)Roy
Haynes(dm).
Supervision:Ozzie Cadena   NYC,January 24,1963
3730   Everything I love   unissued
3731   Little me   Pr.45-247,PR7266;MV38
3732   Cold miner   Pr.45-271 -
3733   Poor you   -
3734   The long road   -
3735   Yo ho   -
3736   The lizard   Pr.45-247 -

PONY POINDEXTER PLAYS THE BIG ONES:
Pony Poindexter(ss,as)Gildo Mahones(p)George Tucker(b)Jimmie Smith(dm).
Supervision:Ozzie Cadena   NYC,January 31,1963

3800   Love me tender   NJ8285;Pr.45-251
3801   Sack o'woe   unissued
3802   Moody's mood for love   -
3803   Twistin' U.S.A.   NJ8285
3804   Moon river   -
3805   Poinciana   -
3806   San Antonio Rose   -
3807   Midnight in Moscow   -   Pr.45-251
3808   Green eyes   -
3809   Blue and sentimental   unissued
3810   Wade in the water   -
3811   Fly me to the moon   NJ8285

ETTA JONES:
Etta Jones(vo)with Larry Young(org)Kenny Cox(p)Kenny Burrell(g)George
Tucker(b)Jimmie Smith(dm).
Supervision:Ozzie Cadena   NYC,February 4,1963

3737   There are such things   Pr.   PR7272
3738   Someday my prince will come Pr.45-278   -
3739   Some enchanted evening   -
3740   Old folks-1   Pr.45-262   -   PR7443
-1:Young & Cox out.

GILDO MAHONES:
Larry Young(org)Gildo Mahones(p)Peck Morrison(b)Oliver Jackson(dm).
Supervision:Ozzie Cadena   NYC,February 4,1963

3741   I'm shooting high   PR16004
3742   I never knew   unissued
3743   Bali Ha'i   PR16004,PR7339,45-285

ETTA JONES:
Etta Jones(vo)with Larry Young(org)Kenny Cox(p)Kenny Burrell(g)Peck
Morrison(b)Oliver Jackson(dm).
Supervision:Ozzie Cadena   NYC,February 12,1963

3744   It's magic   PR7272
3745   Like someone in love   -
3746   I heard a rich man sing the blues unissued
3747:not used
3748   Love walked in   Pr.45-262,PR7272

JACK McDUFF/KENNY BURRELL-CRASH!:
Harold Vick(ts)Jack McDuff(org)Kenny Burrell(g)Joe Dukes(dm)Ray
Barretto(conga).
Supervision:Ozzie Cadena   NYC,February 26,1963

3749-1 Grease monkey   PR7347,PR24013
3750-2 The breeze and I   -   PR7596,PR24013,45-367
3751   Moody McDuff   PR7666
3752-4 Call it stormy Monday   PR7347
3753-1 Nica's dream   -   45-367
3754-6 We'll be together again   -   PR7596

LARRY YOUNG TRIO:
Booker Ervin(ts)Larry Young(org)Jerry Thomas(dm).
Supervision:Ozzie Cadena   NYC,February 28,1963

3755   Absotively posalutely   unissued
3756   You don't know what love is -
3757   Autumn leaves   -
3758   Old folks   -

LUCKY THOMPSON PLAYS JEROME KERN AND NO MORE:
Lucky Thompson(as,ts)Hank Jones(p)Wendell Marshall(b)Dave Bailey(dm).
Supervision:Don Schlitten   NYC,March 8,1963

3759	They didn't believe me	MV39	
3760	Long ago and far away	-	
3761	Who	-	Pr.45-261
3762	Why do I love you	-	
3763	Lovely to look at	-	Pr.45-261
3764	Dearly beloved	-	
3765	Look for the silver lining	-	
3766	Why was I born	-	
3767	No more	-	

RHODA SCOTT-LIVE AT THE KEY CLUB:
Joe Thomas(ts)Rhoda Scott(org)Bill Elliot(dm).
Supervision:Ozzie Cadena The Key Club,Newark,N.J.,March 23,1963

Hey-hey-hey	TRU15014	
Sha-bozz	-	
Work song		
I-yi-yi-yi	-	45-421
Watermelon man	-	
Midnight sun	-	
Little darlin'	-	
Danny boy	-	

WILLIS JACKSON-LOOSE:
Frank Robinson(tp)Willis Jackson(ts)Carl Wilson(org)Bill Jones(g)Joe
Hadrick(dm).
Supervision:Ozzie Cadena   NYC,March 26,1963

3768	She's my love	PR7273	
3769	Secret love	Pr.45-258,PR7273	
3770	When my dreamboat comes home	-	
3771	Y'all	Pr.45-277	-
3772	Now you know it	unissued	
3773	After hours	PR7273	
3774	What will I tell my heart	-	

ROY HAYNES-CRACKLIN':
Booker Ervin(ts)Ronnie Mathews(p)Larry Ridley(b)Roy Haynes(dm).
Supervision:Ozzie Cadena   NYC,April 10,1963

3775	Scoochie	NJ8286	
3776	Dorian	-	Pr.45-264
3777	Sketch of Melba	-	
3778	Honey dew	-	Pr.45-264
3779	Under Paris skies	-	
3780	Bad news blues	-	

JIMMY WITHERSPOON-BABY,BABY,BABY:
Jimmy Witherspoon(vo)with Leo Wright(as,tambourine)Gildo Mahones(p)
Kenny Burrell(g)George Tucker(b)Jimmie Smith(dm).
Supervision:Ozzie Cadena   NYC,May 6,1963

3781	Bad bad whiskey	Pr.	PR7290,PR7713	
3782	Baby,baby,baby	Pr.45-266	-	-
3783	One scotch,one bourbon,one beer	-	-	
3784	Blues and trouble		-	
3785	Mean old Frisco	Pr.45-274	-	PR7298,PR7713
3786	Sail on little girl	-	-	
3787	Lonely boy		-	
3788	Rocks in my bed		-	

PR7290=PR7855.

3789/3793:see page 140.

JESSE FULLER:
Jesse Fuller(vo,g,hca,kazoo,fotdella,cymbals).
                                    May 13,1963
        San Francisco bay blues   PR14006,PR14023
        Everybody works at home but
                    my old man   -
        Beale Street blues   -
        Let me hold you in my arms tonight
                                      -
        Where could I go but to the Lord -
        You're no good   -
        I want a little girl just like
          the girl that married dear
                        old Dad   -
        Old man Mose   -
        Crazy waltz   -
        Brother lowdown   -
        Pretty little girl walkin' down
                        the street   -
        The dozens   -
        Animal fair   -
        Key to the Highway   PR7368
        Tickling the strings   -
        Stranger blues   -
        Cincinnati blues   -
        Trouble if I don't use my head -

Same.
                                    May 14,1963
        I've been so doggone lonesome PR14006
        Red river blues   PR7368
        How long,how long blues   -
        You can't keep a good man down -
        Midnight special   -
        Fables aren't nothing but
                    doggone lies   -
        Brownskin gal,I got my eyes on
                        you   -
        Hump on your back   -
PR14006=PR7718
All titles from both sessions also issued on Fantasy F-24707.

CLAUDE HOPKINS-SWING TIME!:
Bobby Johnson(tp)Vic Dickenson(tb)Claude Hopkins(p)Wendell Marshall(b)
Ferdinand Everett(dm).
Supervision:Don Schlitten   NYC,May 22,1963
3794   I cried for you   SV2041
3795   Somebody loves me   -
3796   Stormy weather   -
3797   Cryin' my heart   -
3798   Love me or leave me   -
3799   Mitzi   -
3800A   On the sunny side of the street -

3800/3811:see page 137.

WILLIS JACKSON:
Frank Robinson(tp)Willis Jackson(ts)Carl Wilson(org)Pat Azzara(Pat
Martino)(g)Joe Hadrick(dm).
Supervision:Ozzie Cadena   NYC,May 23,1963

3812	Brother Elijah	Pr.45-293,PR7285,PR7313
3813	Fly me to the moon	PR7296
3814	The good life	-
3914	Days of wine and roses	-
3915	Angel eyes	-
3916	As long as she needs me	Pr.45-303,PR7296
3917	Doot dat	PR7285

Note:Matrix numbers 3815/3913 have not been used.

Same,with Leonard Gaskin(b)added.
Supervision:Ozzie Cadena   NYC,May 24,1963

3918	Troubled times	Pr.45-303,PR7296
3919	Walk right in	-
3920	Gra-a-vy	Pr.45-293,PR7285,PR7298
3921	Grease	-
3922	Stompin' at the Savoy	-

SHIRLEY SCOTT-DRAG 'EM OUT:
Shirley Scott(org)Major Holley(b)Roy Brooks(dm).
Supervision:Ozzie Cadena   NYC,May 27,1963

3789	Johnny one note	unissued	
3790	Drag 'em out	PR7305	
3791	The song is ended	-	
3792	The second time around	Pr.45-305,PR7305	
3793	Out of it	-	-

LIGHTNIN' HOPKINS-GOIN' AWAY:
Lightnin' Hopkins(vo,g)Leonard Gaskin(b)Herbie Lovelle(dm).
                                          NYC,June 4,1963

Business you're doin'	BV45-823,BV1073,BV1084;PR7592			
Wake up old lady	-	-	-	-
Stranger blues	-			
Don't embarass me lady	-			
Little sister's boogie	-			
Goin' away	BV45-824	-		
You better stop here	-	-		
I'm wit it	-			

JACK McDUFF-LIVE!:
Red Holloway(ts)Jack McDuff(org)George Benson(g)Joe Dukes(dm).
                           The Front Room,Newark,N.J.,June 5,1963

3923	Rock candy	Pr.45-273,45-722,PR7274,PR7298,
		PR7481,PR24013
3924	It ain't necessarily so	PR7274
3925	Sanctified samba	Pr.45-265,PR7274,PR7703
3926	Whistle while you work	- -
3927	A real good'un	Pr.45-273 - PR7703
3928	Undecided	-
	Undecided(alt.take)	PR7492
	Love walked in	PR7529
	Midnight sun	-

[140]

AHMED ABDUL-MALIK-EASTERN MOODS:
Bilal Abdurrahman(as,cl,fl,perc)Ahmed Abdul-Malik(b,oud)William Henry
Allen(b,perc).
Supervision:Ozzie Cadena   NYC,June 13,1963

3929   Sa-ra-ga-ya-hindi   PR16003
3930   Sho-habebe   -
3931   Summertime   -
3932   Magrebi   -
3933   Ancient scene   -

BOOKER ERVIN-EXULTATION!:
Frank Strozier(as)Booker Ervin(ts)Horace Parlan(p)Butch Warren(b)
Walter Perkins(dm).
Supervision:Don Schlitten   NYC,June 19,1963

3942   Mooche mooche   PR7293
3943   Tune in   -
3944   Mour   -
3945   Black and blue   -
3946   Just in time   -
3946   Just in time(short take)   Pr.45-270
3947   No man's land   PR7293
3947   No man's land(short take) Pr.45-270,PR7298

All titles and takes shown also issued on PR7844.

PONY POINDEXTER-GUMBO:
Pony Poindexter(ss,as)Booker Ervin(ts)Gildo Mahones(p)George Tucker(b)
Jimmie Smith(dm).
Supervision:Ozzie Cadena   NYC,June 27,1963

3934   Creole girl   PR16001
3935   French market   -
3936   Gumbo filet   -
3937   4-11-44   -   45-272

Same,with Al Grey(tb)added.Same date.

3938   Happy strut   Pr.45-272,PR16001
3939   Front o'town   -
3940   Back o'town   -
3941   Moody dust   -

JIMMY WITHERSPOON:
Jimmy Witherspoon(vo)with Bobby Bryant(tp,flh)Jimmy Allen(ts)Arthur
Wright(hca)Ernie Freeman(as "Ernst Von Funkestein")(p)Herman Mitchell
(g)Jimmy Bond(b)Jimmy Miller(dm).
Supervision:Dave Axelrod   LA,July 8,1963

3948   Endless sleep   PR7290
3949   I can't hardly see   -
3950   I'll go on living   -
3951   It's a lonesome world   -

All titles also issued on PR7855.

GILDO MAHONES:
Leo Wright(as)Gildo Mahones(p)Kenny Burrell(g)George Tucker(b)Jimmie
Smith(dm).
Supervision:Ozzie Cadena   NYC,August 15,1963

3952   Love nest   unissued
3953   Tales of Brooklyn   PR16004,PR7339
3954   Hey girl-1   Pr.45-285,PR16004
3955   I never knew   unissued

-1:Ozzie Beck(vo)added.

JIMMY WITHERSPOON-EVENIN' BLUES:
Jimmy Witherspoon(vo)with Clifford Scott(as-1,fl-2,ts)Bert Kendrix(p-3,
org)T-Bone Walker(g)Clarence Jones(b)Wayne Robertson(dm).
Supervision:Dave Axelrod   LA,August 15,1963

Crab me a freight-1	Pr.	PR7300
Money's gettin' cheaper	Pr.45-307	-
Don't let go-4		-
I've been treated wrong		-
Cane River		-	PR7713
Baby how long-3		-
Good rocking tonight		-	PR7713
Kansas City		-	-
Drinking beer-4		-	-
Evenin' blues-2	Pr.45-307	-

-4:Band vocal on these titles.

RED HOLLOWAY:
Hobart Dotson(tp)Red Holloway(ts)George Butcher(org)Charles Lindsay(g)
Thomas Palmer(b)Bobby Durham(dm).
Supervision:Ozzie Cadena   NYC,August 27,1963

3956	Miss Judy Mae	rejected
3957	Moonlight in Vermont	PR7299

GILDO MAHONES:
Gildo Mahones(p)George Tucker(b)Jimmie Smith(dm).
Supervision:Ozzie Cadena   NYC,September 3,1963

3958	Water blues fall	PR16004,PR7339
3959	Good morning heartache	- -
3960	The sweetest sounds	- -
3961	Stormy Monday blues	-

ROY HAYNES-CYMBALISM:
Frank Strozier(as)Ronnie Mathews(p)Larry Ridley(b)Roy Haynes(dm).
Supervision:Ozzie Cadena   NYC,September 10,1963

3962	Modette	NJ8287
3963	La Palomeinding	-
3964	I'm getting sentimental	-
3965	Go' n' git it	-
3966	Medley:Hag/Cymbalism/Oleo	-

SONNY STITT & JACK McDUFF-SOUL SHACK:
Sonny Stitt(as,ts)Jack McDuff(org)Leonard Gaskin(b)Herbie Lovelle(dm).
Supervision:Ozzie Cadena   NYC,September 17,1963

3967	Sunday	PR7297,PR7769
3968	Hairy	
3969	Love nest	- PR7769
3970	untitled blues	unissued
3971	Soul shack	Pr.45-304,PR7297,PR7298,PR7701
3972	For you	- PR7769
3973	untitled blues	unissued
3974	Shadows	PR7297

JACK McDUFF-BROTHER JACK ALIVE!AT THE JAZZ WORKSHOP:
Red Holloway,Harold Vick(ts,fl)Jack McDuff(org)George Benson(g)Joe
Dukes(dm).
                Jazz Workshop,San Francisco,October 3,1963

Blues 1 & 8	PR7286,PR7703
Passing through	Pr.45-286,PR7286
Dink's blues	Pr.45-299 -
Grease monkey	- 45-722,PR7286,PR7313,
	PR7481
Vas dis	PR7286
Somewhere in the night	Pr.45-286,PR7286
Jive samba	- PR7703,PR24013

[142]

RED HOLLOWAY-THE BURNER:
Paul Serrano(tp)Red Holloway(ts)John Patton(org)Eric Gale(g)Leonard
Gaskin(b)Herbie Lovelle(dm).
Supervision:Ozzie Cadena   NYC,October 10,1963

3975   The burner   Pr.   PR7299,PR7778
3976   Miss Judie Mae   -   -
3977   Brethren   -
3978   Monkey sho' can talk   Pr.45-287   -   PR7298
3979   Crib theme   -   -   PR7313

Note:Matrix numbers shown above are the last ones which were ever
allocated to Prestige recordings.

SHIRLEY SCOTT-SOUL SHOUTING:
Stanley Turrentine(ts)Shirley Scott(org)Earl May(b)Grassella Oliphant
(dm).
Supervision:Ozzie Cadena   NYC,October 15,1963

       Gravy waltz   Pr.   PR7312
       In the still of the night   -   PR7773
       Deep down soul   Pr.45-328   -   PR7707
       Serenata   -
       Soul shoutin'   Pr.45-328   -   PR7707

WILLIS JACKSON-MORE GRAVY:
Frank Robinson(tp)Willis Jackson(ts)Carl Wilson(org)Pat Azzara(Pat
Martino)(g)Sam Jones(b)Joe Hadrick(dm).
Supervision:Ozzie Cadena   NYC,October 24,1963

       Fiddlin'   Pr.   PR7317
       More gravy   Pr.45-339   -
       Somewhere along the way   -
       Stuffin'   -
       Nother'n like T'other'n   -
       Pool shark   Pr.45-339   -

THE CLEFS OF CALVARY:
Vocal group with Richard Franklin(org)Ezell Wilkins(p)Leonard Gaskin(b)
Herb Lovelle(dm).
                                  NYC,November 5,1963

       Miracle temple   TRU60007
       You don't know what I've been
                         through -
       Judgement bar   -
       Standing where Jesus is   -
       Walk with me   -
       It's religion   -
       Don't drive me away   -
       On the battlefield   -
       Let it run on me   -
       God's light   -

JIMMY WITHERSPOON-BLUES AROUND THE CLOCK:
Jimmy Witherspoon(vo)with Paul Griffin(org)Lord Westbrook(g)Leonard
Gaskin(b)Herbie Lovelle(dm).
Supervision:Ozzie Cadena   NYC,November 5,1963

       I had a dream   Pr.45-298,PR7314
       Goin' to Chicago   Pr.45-291   -   PR7313
       No rollin'   -   PR7713
       You made me love you   Pr.45-291   -
       My babe   -
       S.K.Blues   Pr.45-298   -
       Whose hat is that   -   PR7713
       Around the clock   -   -
       He gave me everything   -
       I'm going down slow   -

[143]

BOOKER ERVIN-THE FREEDOM BOOK:
Booker Ervin(ts)Jaki Byard(p)Richard Davis(b)Alan Dawson(dm).
Supervision:Don Schlitten   NYC,December 3,1963
          A lunar tune   PR7295
          Cry me not   -
          Grant's stand   -
          A day to mourn   -
          Al's in   -
          Stella by starlight   PR7417

RONNIE MATHEWS-DOIN' THE THANG:
Freddie Hubbard(tp)Charles Davis(bs)Ronnie Mathews(p)Eddie Khan(b)
Albert "Tootie" Heath(dm).
Supervision:Ozzie Cadena   NYC,December 17,1963
          The thang   PR7303
          Ihci Ban   -
          The Orient   -
          Let's get down   -
          Prelude to a kiss-1   -
          1239A   -

-1:p,b,dm only.

BROTHER JACK McDUFF BIG BAND-PRELUDE:
Red Holloway(ts)Jack McDuff(org)George Benson(g)Joe Dukes(dm)with
Danny Stiles,Jerome Kail(tp)Billy Byers,Burt Collins(tb)Don Ashworth,
Robert Northern(frh)Tom McIntosh(tb)George Marge,Marvin Holladay(saxes)
Al Stewart(   )Richard Davis(b)Mel Lewis(dm)Willie Rodriguez(perc)Benny
Golson(arr,dir).
                                  NYC,December 24,1963
          A kettle of fish   Pr.45-344,PR7333
          Candlelight   -
          Put a happy face on   -
          Prelude   Pr.45-320   -
          Mean to me   -
          Carry me home   Pr.45-344   -
          Easy living   -
          Oh!Look at me now   Pr.45-320   -
          Dig Cousin Will   -

BILLY BOY ARNOLD-MORE BLUES ON THE SOUTH SIDE:
Billy Boy Arnold(vo,hca)with Lafayette Leake(p)Mighty Joe Young(g)
Jerome Arnold(el b)Junior Blackman(dm).
                                  Chicago,December 30,1963
          I love only you   PR7389
          Evalena   -
          You're my girl   -   BV45-827
          You don't love me no more -
          Oh,baby   -
          School time   -   BV45-827
          You better cut that out -
          Get out of here   -
          Goin' by the river   -
          Two drinks of wine   -
          I'll forget about you -
          Billy Boy's blues   -
          Playin' with the blues unissued

[144]

SONNY STITT-PRIMITIVO SOUL!:
Sonny Stitt(as)Ronnie Mathews(p)Leonard Gaskin(b)Herbie Lovelle(dm)
Osvaldo Martinez(bongos)Marcelino Valdez(conga).
Supervision:Ozzie Cadena   NYC,December 31,1963
        Slave maidens   PR7302
        Blue blood ritual   -
        Bacon baby   -
        Barefoot ball   -
        Estrellita   -
        Island shout   -

HOMESICK JAMES-BLUES ON THE SOUTH SIDE:
Homesick James Williamson(vo,g)with Lafayette Leake(p)Eddie Taylor(el
b)Clifton James(dm).
                                    Chicago,January 7,1964
        Gotta move   PR7388
        The cloud is crying   -
        Homesick's shuffle   -
        Crossroads   unissued
        Lonesome road   PR7388
        Homesick blues   -
        Stones in my pathway   -
        If I be lucky   unissued
        Workin' with Homesick   PR7388
        Crawlin'   -   BV45-826
        Goin' down swingin'   -
        Johnny Mae   -
        The woman I'm lovin'   -   BV45-826
        She may be your woman   -

WILLIS JACKSON-BOSS SHOUTIN':
Frank Robinson(tp)Willis Jackson(ts)Carl Wilson(org)Pat Azzara(Pat
Martino)(g)George Tucker(b)Joe Hadrick(dm).
Supervision:Ozzie Cadena   NYC,January 9,1964
        Boss St.Louis blues   PR7329
        Que sera,sweetie   -
        Nice and easy   -
        Your wonderful love   -
        Shoutin'   -

RED HOLLOWAY with JACK McDUFF QUARTET-COOKIN' TOGETHER:
Red Holloway(ts)Jack McDuff(org)George Benson(g)Wilfred Middlebrooks
(b)Joe Dukes(dm).
                                    LA,February 6,1964
        Wives and lovers   Pr.45-300,PR7325
        This can't be love   -
        Something funny   -   PR7778
        Brother Red   -
        Denise   Pr.45-300 -
        No tears   Pr.45-325 -
        Shout brother   -   - PR7778
JACK McDUFF:
Red Holloway(ts)Jack McDuff(org)George Benson(g)Joe Dukes(dm).
                                    LA,February 6/7,1964
        Rail head   Pr.45-330,PR7323
        What's new   -
        Bossa nova West   -

THE NOMOS:
Red Holloway(ts)Red Tyler(bs)Jack McDuff(org)George Benson(g)Tommy
Shelvin(el b)Joe Dukes(dm).

LA,February 6/7,1964

Redwood City	PR7791
Redwood City(short take)	Pr.45-301
Step out and get it	-
Long distance-1	unissued

-1:McDuff plays piano on this title.

SHIRLEY SCOTT-TRAVELIN' LIGHT:
Shirley Scott(org)Kenny Burrell(g)Eddie Khan(b)Otis Finch(dm).
Supervision:Ozzie Cadena   NYC,February 17,1964

Travelin' light	Pr.45-337,PR7328
Solar	-
Nice and easy	-
They call it Stormy Monday	-
Baby it's cold outside	-
Kerry dance	Pr.45-337 -

JIMMY WITHERSPOON-BLUE SPOON:
Jimmy Witherspoon(vo)with Gildo Mahones(p)Kenny Burrell(g)Eddie Khan(b)
Roy Haynes(dm).
Supervision:Ozzie Cadena   NYC,February 20,1964

I wonder	PR7327,PR7713
It's a low down dirty shame	-
Nobody knows you when you're down and out	- PR7713
Back to New Orleans	-
It's all in the game	-
Blues in the morning	-
I'll never be free	-
Once there lived a fool	-
For old time's sake	-
This time has come	-

EDDIE CHAMBLEE-ROCKIN' TENOR SAX:
Eddie Chamblee(ts)Dayton Selby(org)Al Griffin(dm).
Supervision:Ozzie Cadena   NYC,February 27,1964

The honeydripper	Pr.45-302,PR7321
You never walk alone	- -
Champin'	Pr.45-329 -
Skang	- -
Softly as I leave you	-
Bye bye blackbird	-
Little things mean a lot	-

BOOKER ERVIN-THE SONG BOOK:
Booker Ervin(ts)Tommy Flanagan(p)Richard Davis(b)Alan Dawson(dm).
Supervision:Don Schlitten   NYC,February 27,1964

The lamp is low	PR7318
Come Sunday	-
All the things you are	-
Just friends	-
Yesterdays	-
Our love is here to stay	-

Rev.GARY DAVIS-GUITAR AND BANJO:
Rev.Gary Davis(vo,g,bjo,hca).

NYC,March 2,1964

Maple leaf rag	PR14033,PR7725
Slow drag	- -
The boy was kissing the girl	- -
Candy man	- -
United States march	- -
Devil's dream	- -
The coon hunt	- -
Mister Jim	- -
Please baby	- -
Fast fox trot	- -
Can't be satisfied	- -

AHMED ABDUL-MALIK-SPELLBOUND:
Ray Nance(c,v)Seldon Powell(ts,fl)Paul Neves(p)Ahmed Abdul-Malik(b)
Walter Perkins(dm)Hamza Aldeen(oud).
Supervision:Don Schlitten   NYC,March 12,1964

Love theme from "Spartacus"	unissued
Spellbound	ST8303
Never on Sunday	-
Body and soul	-
Song of Delilah	-
Cinema blues	-

SONNY STITT-SHANGRI-LA:
Sonny Stitt(as,ts)Don Patterson(org)Billy James(dm).
Supervision:Ozzie Cadena   NYC,March 19,1964

Shangri-La	Pr.45-304,PR7332
Mama don't allow	-
Soul food	-
My new baby	Pr.45-338 -
The eternal one	-
Misty	Pr.45-338 -
Please don't talk about me	
when I'm gone	PR7381,PR7772
42639	- PR7704

WILLIS JACKSON LIVE:
Frank Robinson(tp)Willis Jackson(ts)Carl Wilson(org)Pat Azzara(Pat
Martino)(g)Joe Hadrick(dm).
Supervision:Ozzie Cadena The Allegro,NYC,March 21,1964

Jackson's action	PR7348	
A lot of livin' to do	-	
I wish you love	-	
Monkey hips	-	
A'w right-Do it!	-	
Jive samba	-	45-372
Hello Dolly	PR7380	
Annie Laurie	-	
Blowin' like hell	-	
Blue gator	-	
I'm a fool to want you	-	
Gator tail	-	
Satin doll	-	
The man I love	PR7396	
Perdido	-	
Thunderbird	-	
Polka dots and moonbeams	-	
All soul	-	
Flamingo	-	

(session continued on next page)

```
I can't stop loving you          PR7412
One mint julep                   -
Up a lazy river                  -
Jumpin' with Symphony Sid        -
Tangerine                        -
Ebb tide                         -
Blue gator                       -
Secret love                      -
```

SHIRLEY SCOTT-BLUE FLAMES:
Stanley Turrentine(ts)Shirley Scott(org)Bob Cranshaw(b)Otis Finch(dm).
Supervision:Ozzie Cadena   NYC,March 31,1964

```
As it was                        PR7440
The funky box                    Pr.45-365,PR7338
Hip knees an' legs               -          -      PR7707
Grand Street                     Pr.45-381  -
Flamingo                         -          -      PR7773
Five Spot after dark             Pr.45-381  -
```

KENNY BURRELL-SOUL CALL:
Will Davis(p)Kenny Burrell(g)Martin Rivera(b)Bill English(dm)Ray
Barretto(conga).
Supervision:Ozzie Cadena   NYC,April 7,1964

```
Kenny's theme                    Pr.45-342,PR7315
Mark 1                           -
I'm just a lucky so and so       -
A sleepin' bee                   -
Soul call                        Pr.45-342  -
Here's that rainy day            -
Oh Henry                         PR24046
```

THE DYNAMIC JACK McDUFF:
Red Holloway(ts)Jack McDuff(org)George Benson(g)Joe Dukes(dm)with
big band,Benny Golson(arr,dir).
                                  NYC,April 23,1964

```
Main theme from "The Carpetbaggers"
                                 Pr.45-309,PR7323
Theme from "The Pink Panther"    -          -
You better love me
Once in a lifetime               Pr.45-330  -
```

GEORGE BENSON with JACK McDUFF QUARTET-NEW BOSS GUITAR:
Red Holloway(ts)Jack McDuff(org,p)George Benson(g)Ronnie Boykins(b)
Montego Joe(dm).
                                  NYC,May 1,1964

```
Shadow dancers-1                 Pr.45-317,PR7310
The sweet Alice blues-1          -
I don't know
Just another Sunday              Pr.45-317  -
Will you still be mine           -
Easy living                      -
Rock-a-bye                       -
```

-1:McDuff out.

All titles also issued on P-24072.

LIGHTNIN' HOPKINS-DOWN HOME BLUES:
Lightnin' Hopkins(vo,g)Leonard Gaskin(b)Herbie Lovelle(dm).
                                   NYC,May 4,1964

    Let's go sit on the lawn   Pr.45-326,PR1086;Fantasy F-24702
    I woke up this morning-1   -   -
    I got tired   -   -
    I like to boogie   Pr.45-326   -
    I asked the bossman   -   Fantasy F-24702
    I'm taking the devil of a chance -   -
    Just a wrist watch on my arm   -   -
    I was standing on 75 Highway-1   -   -
    Get it straight   -   -

-1:Lightnin' Hopkins(vo,g)alone.

LIGHTNIN' HOPKINS-SOUL BLUES:
Same.
Supervision:Ozzie Cadena   NYC,May 4/5,1964

    I'm going to build a heaven of
                         my ownPr.45-405,PR7377
    My babe   -
    Too many drivers   -
    I'm a crawling blacksnake   -
    Rocky mountain blues   -
    I mean goodbye   -
    The howling wolf   -
    Black ghost blues   -
    Darling do you remember me   -
    Lonesome graveyard   -

All titles also issued on Fantasy F-24702.

THE EXCITING NEW ORGAN OF DON PATTERSON:
Booker Ervin(ts)Don Patterson(org)Billy James(dm).
Supervision:Ozzie Cadena   NYC,May 12,1964

    'S about time   Pr.   PR7331
    Up in Betty's room   Pr.45-333   -   PR7704
    Oleo   -
    When Johnny comes marching home -
    The good life   -
    Hip cake walk-1   PR7349
    Love me with all your heart   Pr.45-323,PR7381
    People   -

-1:Leonard Houston(as)added.

JOE DUKES with JACK McDUFF QUARTET-THE SOULFUL DRUMS:
Red Holloway(ts)Jack McDuff(org)George Benson(g)Joe Dukes(dm).
                                   NYC,May 14,1964

    Soulful drums   Pr.   PR7324
    Two bass hit   -
    Greasy drums   Pr.45-322   -
    Moanin' bench   -
    My three sons   -
    Moohah the D.J.   Pr.45-322   -

ARRIBA CON MONTEGO JOE:
Leonard Goines(tp)Al Gibbons(ts,fl)Chick Corea(p)Eddie Gomez(b)Milford
Graves(dm,timbales)Robert Crowder(perc)Montego Joe(Roger Sanders)(perc)
Rudy Stevenson(cond).

NYC,May 15,1964

Fat man	Pr.45-324,PR7336
The jinx	-
Too much said	-
Maracatu	-
Dakar	Pr.45-324 -
Calling for the angels in the water	-

JAKI BYARD TRIO:
Jaki Byard(p)Bob Cranshaw(b)Walter Perkins(dm).
Supervision:Ozzie Cadena   NYC,May 21,1964

The track	unissued
Piano forte	-
Jadpuhra	-
Lush life	PR7397

JAKI BYARD-OUT FRONT:
Richard Williams(tp)Booker Ervin(ts)Jaki Byard(p)Bob Cranshaw(b)Walter
Perkins(dm).
Supervision:Ozzie Cadena   NYC,May 28,1964

Out front	PR7397
Two different worlds	-
Searchlight	-
European episode	-
I like to lead when I dance	unissued
After the lights go down	-

Note:Last two titles of this session appeared on some pressings of
album PR7337(Stan Getz Greatest Hits)which were withdrawn.

THE SOULFUL PIANO OF GILDO MAHONES:
Gildo Mahones(p)George Tucker(b)Sonny Brown(dm).
Supervision:Ozzie Cadena   NYC,June 4,1964

Something missing	PR7339
If dreams come true	unissued
Blues for Yna Yna	PR7339
Blue	-
I should care	-
I wish you love	-
I wonder what's become of your love	-
Mambesi	-
Oye ami piano	-
Walkin'	-
Alone together	-
Rainy day love	-

BOBBY TIMMONS-LITTLE BAREFOOT SOUL:
Bobby Timmons(p)Sam Jones(b)Ray Lucas(dm).
Supervision:Joel Dorn   NYC,June 18,1964

Little barefoot soul	Pr.45-334,PR7335,PR7780	
People	PR7387	
Little one	Pr.	PR7335
Nobody knows the trouble I've seen	-	
Cut me loose,Charlie	-	
Ain't thinkin' 'bout it	-	
Walkin',wadin',sittin',ridin'	Pr.45-366	-

WILLIS JACKSON:
Willis Jackson(ts)Ernie Hayes(org)Wally Richardson(g)George Tucker(b)
Calvin Shields(dm)Candido Camero(conga).
Supervision:Cal Lampley   NYC,June 18,1964

    Something private   PR7791
    People   Pr.45-327
    Nightingale   -

BOOKER ERVIN-THE BLUES BOOK:
Carmell Jones(tp)Booker Ervin(ts)Gildo Mahones(p)Richard Davis(b)
Alan Dawson(dm).
Supervision:Don Schlitten   NYC,June 30,1964

    Eerie Dearie   PR7340
    One for Mort   -
    No booze blooze   -
    True blue   -
    Groovin' high   PR7417

DON PATTERSON/BOOKER ERVIN:
Booker Ervin(ts)Don Patterson(org)Billy James(dm).
Supervision:Ozzie Cadena   NYC,July 10,1964

    Donald Duck   Pr.45-364,PR7349
    Sister Ruth   -   -   PR7704
    Rosetta   -
    Under the boardwalk   Pr.45-333   -
    Theme for Dee   PR7381
    Sentimental journey   -
    Just friends   PR7852

JACK McDUFF:
Red Holloway(ts)Jack McDuff(org)George Benson(g)Joe Dukes(dm).
                                           NYC,July   1964

    Scufflin'   PR7404
    Au privave   PR7492
    Hallelujah time   -
    Misconstrued   PR7529
    Lew's piece   PR7567
    Opus de funk   -   PR24013
    Our Miss Brooks   PR7666

Holloway out:

    East of the sun   PR7492
    I got a woman   PR7642

BENNY GOLSON-STOCKHOLM SOJOURN:
Benny Bailey,Bengt-Arne Wallin,Bo Broberg,Bertil Lövgren(tp)Georg
Vernon,Jörgen Johansson(tb)Bengt Olsson,Karl Nyström,Elis Karvall,
Willem Fock(frh)Runo Eriksson(euphonium)Alf Nilsson,Ingvar Holst,Lars
Skoglund,Erik Björkhagen(English h,oboe)Bengt Christiansson,Niels
Wharby,Börje Morelius,Yngve Sandstöm,Gösta Ströberg,Ulf Bergström(fl)
Rune Falk(cl,bs)Torsten Wennberg,Claes Rosendahl(cl,saxes)Bjarne Nerem
(ts)Roman Dylag(b)Egil Johansen(dm)Benny Golson(arr,cond).
Supervision:Lew Futterman   Stockholm,July 14,1964
Overdubbed on:Ake Persson,Eje Thelin(tb)Arne Domnerus(cl,as).
                                Stockholm,August   ,1964
Grachan Moncur III(tb)Cecil Payne(bs).
                                NYC,Autumn   1964

    Stockholm sojourn   PR7361
    Are you real   -
    Waltz for Debby   -
    My foolish heart   -
(continued on next page)

```
           A Swedish villa              PR7361
           I remember Clifford          -
           Tryst                        -
           The call                     -

JIMMY WITHERSPOON-SOME OF MY BEST FRIENDS ARE THE BLUES:
Jimmy Witherspoon(vo)with same band and Jan Johansson(p)Rune Gustafsson
(g).
Supervision:Lew Futterman          Stockholm,July 15/20,1964

           Some of my best friends are the
                            blues Pr.45-341,PR7356
           Everytime I think about you        -
           I never will marry          Pr.45-340  -
           I wanna be around                 -
           Tear drops from my eyes           -
           And the angels sing               -
           Who's sorry now                   -
           I'm comin' down with the blues    -
           You're next               Pr.45-341  -
           Happy blues               Pr.45-340  -
           That's why I'm leaving            -
           One last chance           Pr.45-355  -

CAROL VENTURA-CAROL!:
Similar or same band,Benny Golson(arr,dir).
Supervision:Lew Futterman          Stockholm,July    ,1964
Overdubbed on:Carol Ventura(vo).

                                   NYC,c.Autumn  1964

           Night song                Pr.45-350,PR7358
           Lonesome road                     -
           Bye bye                           -
           Waltz for Debbie                  -
           Lazy Johnnie                      -
           If ever I would leave you         -
           Meditation                        -
           Everybody says don't              -
           When the world was young          -
           Think of me                       -
           Say no more               Pr.45-350  -
           He lied                           -

BROTHER JACK McDUFF:
Red Holloway(ts,fl)Jack McDuff(org)George Benson(g)Joe Dukes(dm)with
same band.String section-1 and female group-2(vo)added.
                                   Stockholm,July    1964

           If ever I would leave you-1,2  PR7404,PR7771
           Hey,lawdy Mama               -      -
           From the bottom up           -      -
           Lexington line-1             -      -

BROTHER JACK McDUFF QUARTET-THE CONCERT McDUFF:
Red Holloway(ts)Jack McDuff(org)George Benson(g)Joe Dukes(dm).
                    Gyllene Cirkeln,Stockholm,July    ,1964

           Swedenin'                 Pr.        PR7362,PR7703
           The girl from Ipanema     Pr.45-351  -
           Another goodun            Pr.        -
           'S okay                   Pr.45-354  -      PR7703
           Save your love from me              -
           Four brothers             Pr.45-354  -
           Lew's piece               Pr.45-351  -
```

GARY McFARLAND/CARLOS JOBIM:
Gary McFarland(vb,vo)Spencer Sinatra(fl)Antonio Carlos Jobim(p,g)Don
Payne(g)Arnie Wise(dm)Willie Rodriguez(perc).
NYC,July 27,1964

The dreamer   Pr.45-331
River girl   -
There by the sea   unissued

RED HOLLOWAY-SAX,STRINGS & SOUL:
Red Holloway(ts)with big band & strings,Benny Golson(arr,cond).
Stockholm,August   ,1964

When Irish eyes are smiling   PR7390
Bossa in blue   -
Where have all the flowers gone -
Nights with Lora   -
If I had a hammer   -   45-346
I wish you love   -   -
Star of David   -
The girls in the park   -

BOBBY TIMMONS-CHUNG KING:
Bobby Timmons(p)Keeter Betts(b)Albert Heath(dm).
Supervision:Ozzie Cadena   NYC,August 12,1964

O grand amor   Pr.   PR7351
Gettin' it togetha'   Pr.45-366 -
Walkin' death   -
Chungking   Pr.45-334 -   PR7780
Someone to watch over me   -
I could have danced all night   -   ST8315

THE MORRIS NANTON TRIO-PREFACE:
Morris Nanton(p)Norman Edge(b)Oliver Jackson(dm).
Supervision:Cal Lampley   NYC,August 14,1964

Ja-da   Pr.45-345
Black Orpheus   Pr.45-368,PR7345
Lawrence of Arabia   -
Things ain't what they used to be -
Gone with the wind   unissued
The sweetest sounds   Pr.45-368,PR7345
Invitation   -

ANDY & THE BEY SISTERS:
Jerome Richardson(fl,ts)Andy Bey(p,vo)Barry Galbraith(g)Milt Hinton(b)
Jo Jones(dm)The Bey Sisters(vo).
Supervision:Cal Lampley   NYC,August 17,1964

Corcovado(Quiet nights)   Pr.45-335,PR7346
Besame mucho   Pr.45-370 -
Since I fell for you   -
September in the rain   -
Smiles   -

Jerome Richardson(fl,ts)Andy Bey(p,vo)Kenny Burrell(g)Richard Davis(b)
Osie Johnson(dm)The Bey Sisters(vo).
Supervision:Cal Lampley   NYC,August 20,1964

A taste of honey   Pr.45-370,PR7346
Night song   -
The swinging preacher   -
Willow weep for me   Pr.45-335 -
Sister Sadie   -

SONNY STITT-SOUL PEOPLE:
Sonny Stitt(as,ts)Booker Ervin(ts)Don Patterson(org)Billy James(dm).
Supervision:Ozzie Cadena   NYC,August 25,1964

       Soul people   Pr.   PR7372
       C jam blues   Pr.45-375   -
       Sonny's book   -
       Medley:I can't get started/   -
              The masquerade is over
       Flyin' home   PR7852
       Groovin' high   unissued

THE MORRIS NANTON TRIO-PREFACE:
Morris Nanton(p)Norman Edge(b)Oliver Jackson(dm).
Supervision:Cal Lampley   NYC,September 3,1964

       This love of mine   Pr.   PR7345
       The pretty time   -
       Theme from "A boy ten feet tall" Pr.45-345 -
       I'll know   -
       Gone with the wind   -

EDDIE BONNEMERE-JAZZ ORIENT-ED:
Eddie Bonnemere(p)Kenny Burrell(g)Joe Scott(b)George Brown(dm)Jimmy
Colloway(timbales)Moncel(conga,bongos).
Supervision:Cal Lampley   NYC,September 10,1964

       Oriental mambo   Pr.   PR7354
       Why run away   -
       East of the sun
       Ankle bells   Pr.45-349   -
       Night song   -
       Man in the raincoat   Pr.45-349   -

LUCKY THOMPSON-LUCKY STRIKES:
Lucky Thompson(ss,ts)Hank Jones(p)Richard Davis(b)Connie Kay(dm).
Supervision:Don Schlitten   NYC,September 15,1964

       In a sentimental mood   PR7365
       Mumba-Neua   -
       Prey-loot   -
       Invitation   -
       Reminiscent   -
       I forgot to remember   -
       Fly with the winds   -
       Mid-nite oil   -

EDDIE BONNEMERE-JAZZ ORIENT-ED:
Eddie Bonnemere(p)Kenny Burrell(g)Joe Scott(b)George Brown(dm)Jimmy
Colloway(timbales)Moncel(conga,bongos).
Supervision:Cal Lampley   NYC,September 21,1964

       Mr.Lucky   PR7354
       When I fall in love
       Mountain high,valley low   -
       Theme from "A boy tenfeet tall"   -
       Lotus land
       Calm beauty   -

BOOKER ERVIN-THE SPACE BOOK:
Booker Ervin(ts)Jaki Byard(p)Richard Davis(b)Alan Dawson(dm).
Supervision:Don Schlitten   NYC,October 2,1964

       Number two   PR7386
       I can't get started   -
       Mojo   -
       There is no greater love   -
       Bass IX   PR7417
       The second number two   -

[154]

A.K.SALIM-AFRO-SOUL DRUM ORGY:
Johnny Coles(tp)Pat Patrick(fl,as,bs)Yusef Lateef(ts,fl,argol)Philemon
Hon(African xylophone,tambor dm)Osvaldo Martinez(bongo,conga,cowbell)
Juan Cadaviejo(conga)William Correa(timbales)A.K.Salim(comp,arr,cond).
Supervision:Ozzie Cadena   NYC,October 8,1964

    Afrika(Africa)   PR7379
    Ngomba ya tempo(Elephant dance) -
    Kumuamkia Mzulu(Salute to a Zulu)-
    Pepo Za Sarari(Trade winds)   -

BOBBY TIMMONS-WORKIN' OUT:
Johnny Lytle(vb)Bobby Timmons(p)Keeter Betts(b)William Hinnant(dm).
Supervision:Ozzie Cadena   NYC,October 21,1964

    Trick hips   PR7387
    This is all I ask   -
    Bags' groove   -   PR7780
    Lela   -

PAT BOWIE-OUT OF SIGHT:
Pat Bowie(vo)with Seldon Powell(ts,fl)Ray Bryant(p)Kenny Burrell(g)
Milt Hinton(b)Osie Johnson(dm).
Supervision:Cal Lampley   NYC,October 23,1964

    The sounds of the night   Pr.   PR7385
    The masquerade is over   -
    What is this thing called love   -
    Get out of town   Pr.45-369 -
Same.
Supervision:Cal Lampley   NYC,October 26,1964

    Don't cha go away mad   Pr.   PR7385
    The music that makes me dance   -
    Joey,joey,joey   Pr.45-347 -
    Will I find my love today   -
Same.
Supervision:Cal Lampley   NYC,October 27,1964

    Moon and sand   Pr.45-347,PR7385
    Lilac wine   -
    I've got your number   Pr.45-369 -
    A new world   -

CHARLES McPHERSON-BEBOP REVISITED:
Carmell Jones(tp)Charles McPherson(as)Barry Harris(p)Nelson Boyd(b)
Albert Heath(dm).
Supervision:Don Schlitten   NYC,November 20,1964

    Passport(Variations on a theme
                 by Bird) PR7359
    Nostalgia   -
    Hot house   -
    Wail   -
    Embraceable you-1   -
    Si si   -
    If I loved you   unissued
-1:Jones out.

OTIS SPANN-THE BLUES WILL NEVER DIE:
Otis Spann(vo,p)James Cotton(vo,hca)James Madison,Muddy Waters(g)Milton
Rector(el b)S.P.Leary(dm).
Supervision:Sam Charters   Chicago,November 21,1964

          The blues will never die   Pr.   PR7391
          I got a feeling   Pr.45-348   -
          One more smile to go voJC   -
          Feelin' good voJC   -
          After awhile   -
          Dust my broom voJC   -
          Straighten up baby voJC   Pr.45-348   -
          Come on   -
          Must have been the devil   -
          Lightnin'   -
          I'm ready   -

PR7391=PR7719.

BOBBY TIMMONS-HOLIDAY SOUL:
Bobby Timmons(p)Butch Warren(b)Walter Perkins(dm).
Supervision:Ozzie Cadena   NYC,November 24,1964

          Winter wonderland   PR7414
          We three kings.   -
          Santa Claus is coming to town   -
          You're all I want for Christmas -
          White Xmas   -
          Xmas song   -
          Deck the halls   -
          Auld lang syne   -

DON PATTERSON-HOLIDAY SOUL:
Don Patterson(org)Pat Martino(g)Billy James(dm).
Supervision:Ozzie Cadena   NYC,November 25,1964

          Jingle bells   PR7415
          Xmas song   -
          Santa Claus is coming to town   -
          Merry Xmas baby   -
          What are you doing New Year's Eve-
          Rudolph the red nosed reindeer   -
          You're all I want for Christmas -
          Silent night   -
          O Holy night   -

CHUCK WAYNE TRIO:
Chuck Wayne(g,bjo)Joe Williams(b)Ronnie Bedford(dm).
Supervision:Cal Lampley   NYC,December 1,1964

          See saw   rejected
          I'll get along   -
          Someone to watch over me   -

LIGHTNIN' HOPKINS-MY LIFE IN BLUES:
Lightnin' Hopkins(vo,g).
Supervision:Sam Charters   NYC,December 2,1964

          I don't want to do nothing with you PR7370
          You is one black rat   -
          Got nowhere to lay my head   -
          Just boogyin'   -
          Take me back   -
          I was down on Dowling Street   -
(session continued on next page)

[156]

Lightnin' Hopkins,talking to Sam Charters.Same date.
```
     I growed up with the blues      PR7370
     My family                       -
     I learn  about the blues        -
     I first came into Houston       -
     I meet Texas Alexander          -
     There were hard times           -
     I make my first record and get my
                            name -   Fantasy F-24702
     My thoughts on the blues        -
```
CHUCK WAYNE-MORNING MIST:
Chuck Wayne(g,bjo)Joe Williams(b)Ronnie Bedford(dm).
Supervision:Cal Lampley   NYC,December 8,1964
```
     I'll get along                  PR7367
     Lil' darlin'                    -
     Alone at last                   -
     Goodbye                         -
     See saw                         -
     Someone to watch over me        -
     Lovely                          -
     The song is you                 -
     Shalimar                        -
     Things ain't what they used to be-
```
JACK McDUFF:
Red Holloway(ts)Jack McDuff(org)George Benson(g)Joe Dukes(dm)with big
band,Benny Golson(arr,cond).
                                     NYC,early   1965
```
     Rockabye                        PR7529,PR7771
     English country gardens         PR7642    -
     Shortnin' bread                 PR7666
```
ANDY & THE BEY SISTERS:
Andy Bey(p,vo)Wally Richardson(g)Lawrence Wormack(b)Earl McKinney(dm)
Salome,Geraldine Bey(vo).
Supervision:Cal Lampley   NYC,January 21,1965
```
     Feeling good                    rejected
     Hallelujah I love her so        -
     Squeeze me                      -
     Solitude                        -
```
FREDDIE McCOY-LONELY AVENUE:
Gil Askey(tp)Tate Houston(bs)Freddie McCoy(vb)James Thomas(org)Napoleon
Allen(g)Martin Rivera(b)Ray Lucas(dm).
Supervision:Cal Lampley   NYC,January 25,1965
```
     Lonely avenue                   Pr.45-356,PR7395,PR7706
     Collard greens                  -       -
     Roell                           -
     When sunny gets blue            -
```
Gil Askey(tp)Dickie Harris(tb)Tate Houston(bs)Freddie McCoy(vb)James
Thomas(org)Martin Rivera(b)Ray Lucas(dm).
Supervision:Cal Lampley   NYC,February 16,1965
```
     Belly full of greens            Pr.45-382,PR7395
     Harlem nocturne                          -      PR7706
     Willow weep for me              Pr.45-382 -
     Feeling good                    -
```

LUCKY THOMPSON-HAPPY DAYS ARE HERE AGAIN:
Lucky Thompson(ss-1,ts-2)Jack Melady-3(harp)Tommy Flanagan(p)George
Tucker(b)Walter Perkins(dm).
Supervision:Don Schlitten   NYC,February 16,1965

    As time goes by-1   Pr.   PR7394
    Safari-1,3   -
    You don't know what love is-3
    Cry me a river-2   Pr.45-361   -
    People-2   -
    Happy days are here again-2   Pr.45-361   -

ANDY AND THE BEY SISTERS:
Andy Bey(p,vo)Kenny Burrell(g)Milt Hinton(b)Osie Johnson(dm)Salome
Bey,Geraldine Bey(vo).
Supervision:Cal Lampley   NYC,February 26,1965

    Feeling good   PR7411
    Tammy   -
    Around midnight   unissued
    Everybody loves my baby   PR7411
    Hallelujah I love her so   -

RONNIE UNDERWOOD:
Dayton Selby(org)Ronnie Underwood,Walter Longley(g)Russell Annaken(b)
Alvin Rogers(dm)& 3 female singers(vo).
                                         NYC,March 10,1965

    Long walk home   Pr.45-352
    Night jet   -

THE JAKI BYARD QUARTET-LIVE AT LENNIE'S:
Joe Farrell(fl,ss,ts,dm)Jaki Byard(p)George Tucker(b)Alan Dawson(dm).
Supervision:Don Schlitten
    Lennie's-on-the-Turnpike,West Peabody,Mass.,April 15,1965

    Twelve   unissued
    Cathy   PR7477
    Dolphy   unissued
    Alan's got rhythm   PR7477
    Ballad medley:Tea for two/Lover/   -
      Strolling along theme/   -
      Cherokee/Shiny stockings   -
    St.Marks pace   unissued
    Bass-ment blues   PR7477
    Broadway   PR7419
    Shiny stockings   -
    Thing what is
    Go to my head   unissued
    Twelve   PR7419
    Dolphy   unissued
    After you've gone   -
    Just strolling along   -
    King David   -
    Denise   PR7419
    Sewers   unissued
    Outside   -
    Spanish tinge   PR7524
    From this moment on   unissued
    The song is you

Same.

<u>Lennie's-on-the-Turnpike</u>,West Peabody,Mass.,April 16,1965

A ballade	unissued
Sewers	-
Denise	-
Dolphy	-
The song is you	-

JOHNNY "HAMMOND" SMITH-THE STINGER:
Houston Person-1,Earl Edwards(ts)Johnny "Hammond" Smith(org)Floyd
Smith(g)John Harris(dm).
Supervision:Cal Lampley   NYC,May 7,1965

Cleopatra and the African knight-1			
	Pr.45-386,PR7408		
Benny's diggin'-1		-	
The stinger-1,2	Pr.45-363	-	PR7705
There is no greater love-2		-	PR7777
Brother John-2	Pr.45-386	-	
You don't know what love is-2		-	

CARMELL JONES-JAY HAWK TALK:
Carmell Jones(tp)Jimmy Heath(ts)Barry Harris(p)George Tucker(b)Roger
Humphries(dm).
Supervision:Don Schlitten   NYC,May 8,1965

Just in time	Pr.	PR7401
Dance of the night child		-
Willow weep for me-1		-
What is this thing called love?		-
Jay hawk talk	Pr.45-362	-
Beep durple		-

-1:Heath out.

THE ROGER KELLAWAY TRIO:
Roger Kellaway(p)Russell George(b)Dave Bailey(dm).
         NYC,May 11,1965

One night stand	PR7399
Organ Morgan	-
I'll follow the sun	-

Same.

         NYC,May 12,1965

Brats	PR7399
Can't you see it	-
Sweet and lovely	-

Same.

         NYC,May 13,1965

Sigma O.N.	PR7399
Ballad of the sad young men	-
The fall of love	-
No more	-

THE MORRIS NANTON TRIO:
Morris Nanton(p)Norman Edge(b)Al Beldini(dm).
Supervision:Cal Lampley   NYC,May 13,1965

Taboo	PR7409
Mood indigo	-
I'll never forget	unissued
Fly me to the moon	-

MONTEGO JOE-WILD AND WARM:
Leonard Goines(tp)Al Gibbons(ts)Arthur Jenkins(p)Ed Thompson(b)Milford
Graves(dm,timbales)Sonny Morgan(perc)Montego Joe(conga).
                                        NYC,May 21,1965

Same old,same old	Pr.	PR7413
Haitian lady		-
Capricious		-
Happy Joe		-
No tears		-
Ouch	Pr.45-400	-
Give it up	-	-
Ewe		-
Bata blues		-
Concumba		-
Lexington Avenue line		-

ANDY AND THE BEY SISTERS:
Andy Bey(p,vo)Milt Hinton(b)Osie Johnson(dm)Salome Bey,Geraldine Bey
(vo).
Supervision:Cal Lampley   NYC,May 27,1965

Squeeze me	PR7411
God bless the child	-
Everytime we say goodbye	-
Solitude	-
Medley:Love is just around the	-
corner/I love you/Love you	-
madly	

THE MORRIS NANTON TRIO:
Morris Nanton(p)Norman Edge(b)Al Beldini(dm).
Supervision:Cal Lampley   NYC,June 16,1965

Something we've got	Pr.45-384,PR7409
Any number can win	-
The masquerade is over	-
My man's gone now	-

CAROL VENTURA-I LOVE TO SING!:
Carol Ventura(vo)with orchestra,Benny Golson(arr,dir).
                                        London,June   ,1965

Please somebody help me	Pr.45-383,PR7405	
No man	-	-
I want to be with you		
Since you looked at me	Pr.45-410?	-
Alone in another town	Pr.45-410	-
Anything goes		-
Thunder and lightning		-
Quiet room		-
Born		-
I won't ever forget you again		-
The old lady of Thread Needle Street		-
Wait till you see her		-

JIMMY WITHERSPOON-SPOON IN LONDON:
Jimmy Witherspoon(vo)with orchestra,Benny Golson(dir)The Lady Birds(vo).
                                        London,June   ,1965

Love me right	Pr.45-378,PR7418	
Make this heart of mine		
smile again	-	-
Oh how I love you	Pr.45-355	-
Free spirits		-

(session continued on next page)

```
I never thought I'd see the day Pr.45-402,PR7418
Man don't cry                       -
Darlin' I thank you                 -
A million more tomorrows            -
Don't come back to me for sympathy  -
Come on and walk with me        Pr.45-358  -
Room for everybody                  -
Two hearts are better than one  Pr.45-358  -
If there wasn't any you         Pr.45-402
```

BOBBY TIMMONS-CHICKEN & DUMPLIN'S:
Bobby Timmons(p-1,vb-2)Lee Otis Bass III(b)Billy Saunders(dm).
Supervision:Cal Lampley   NYC,July 12,1965

```
    Chicken and dumplin's-1      Pr.45-414,PR7429,PR7780
    The telephone song-1              -    -
    Ray's idea                        -
    A Sunday kind of love-2           -
    The return of Gengis Khan-1,2     -
```

DON PATTERSON-SATISFACTION:
Don Patterson(org)Jerry Byrd(g)Billy James(dm).
Supervision:Cal Lampley   NYC,July 19,1965

```
    Satisfaction                 Pr.45-379,PR7430,PR7704
    Walkin'                           -
    Goin' to meetin'             Pr.45-379  -
    Bowl of Yok                       -
    John Brown's body            Pr.45-406  -
```

RICHARD "GROOVE" HOLMES-SOUL MESSAGE:
Richard "Groove" Holmes(org)Gene Edwards(g)Jimmie Smith(dm).
Supervision:Cal Lampley   NYC,August 3,1965

```
    Soul message                 Pr.45-380,PR7435
    Song for my father                -    -
    Misty                        Pr.45-401*,45-723,PR7435,PR7485*,
                                 PR7700

    Groove's groove              Pr.45-401,PR7435
    Dahoud                            -
    The things we did last Summer     -
    Gemini                       unissued
```
*:"Misty" is edited on 45-401 and on PR7485.

CHARLES McPHERSON-CON ALMA!:
Charles McPherson(as)Clifford Jordan(ts)Barry Harris(p)George Tucker(b)
Alan Dawson(dm).
Supervision:Don Schlitten   NYC,August 6,1965

```
    Eronel                       PR7427
    In a sentimental mood             -
    Chasing the Bird                  -
    Con alma                          -
    I don't know                      -
    Dexter rides again                -
```

SYLVIA SYMS-SYLVIA IS:
Sylvia Syms(vo)with Kenny Burrell(g)Milt Hinton(b)Osie Johnson(dm).
Supervision:Cal Lampley   NYC,August 11,1965

```
    As long as I live            PR7439
    God bless the child               -
    Smile                             -
    More than you ever know           -
    If you could see me now           -
    The masquerade is over            -
```

Sylvia Syms(vo)with Kenny Burrell,John "Bucky" Pizzarelli(g)Milt Hinton
(b)Osie Johnson(dm)William Rodriguez(perc).
Supervision:Cal Lampley   NYC,August 13,1965
    How insensitive   PR7439
    Meditation   -
    You are always in my heart   -
    Brazil   -
    Cuande te twiste de   -
    Wild to the wind   -

CHET BAKER QUINTET:
Chet Baker(flh)George Coleman(ts)Kirk Lightsey(p)Herman Wright(b)Roy
Brooks(dm).
Supervision:Richard Carpenter   NYC,August 23/25,1965
    Grade a gravy   Pr.   PR7449
    Serenity   -
    Fine and dandy   -
    Have you met Miss Jones?   -
    Rearin' back   Pr.45-409 -   PR24016
    So easy   -   -   PR24016
    Madison Avenue   PR7460
    Lonely star   -
    Wee too   -
    Tan Gaugin   -
    Cherokee   -
    Bevan beeps   -   PR24016
    Comin' on   PR7478
    Stairway to the stars   -
    No fair lady   -
    When you're gone   -
    Choose now   -
    Chabootie   -
    Carpsie's groove   -
    Hurry   PR7496
    I waited for you   -
    The 490   -
    Cut plug   -
    Boudoir   -
    Etude in three   -
    Sleeping Susan   -
    Go-go   PR7512,PR24016
    Lament for the living   -
    Pot luck   -
    Bud's blues   -
    Romas   -
    On a misty night   -

INTRODUCING ERIC KLOSS:
Eric Kloss(as,ts)Don Patterson(org)Pat Martino(g)Billy James(dm).
Supervision:Cal Lampley   NYC,September 1,1965
    Round midnight   rejected
    Work song   unissued
    Embraceable you   Pr.   PR7442
    All blues   Pr.45-412 -
    That's the way it is   Pr.45-387 -
    Hi-fly   unissued
    Close your eyes   Pr.45-387,PR7442
    S' bout time   -
    Old folks   -

PAT BOWIE-FEELIN' GOOD:
Pat Bowie(vo)with Charles McPherson(as)Tommy Flanagan(p)Al Hall(b)
Osie Johnson(dm).
Supervision:Don Schlitten   NYC,September 7,1965

    Since I fell for you   PR7437
    They can't take that away from me -
    You don't know what love is   -
    Baby won't you please come home -
    Feelin' good   -

Same.
Supervision:Don Schlitten   NYC,September 9,1965

    Wonder why   PR7437
    I wanna be loved   -
    Look down that lonesome road   -
    Why don't you do right   -
    Summertime   -

SONNY STITT-POW!:
Bennie Green(tb)Sonny Stitt(as)Kirk Lightsey(p)Herman Wright(b)Roy
Brooks(dm).
Supervision:Richard Carpenter   NYC,September 10,1965

    I want to be happy   Pr.   PR7459
    Love on the rocks   -
    Blue lights   Pr.45-438 -
    Scramble   -
    Up and over   Pr.45-438 -
    Pride and passion   -
    'Nuff Guff   -

SONNY STITT with DON PATTERSON-NIGHT CRAWLER:
Sonny Stitt(as)Don Patterson(org)Billy James(dm).
Supervision:Cal Lampley   NYC,September 21,1965

    All God's chillun got rhythm   Pr.   PR7436
    Answering service   Pr.45-392 -
    Tangerine   -
    Night crawler   Pr.45-392 -
    Who can I turn to?   Pr.45-404 -
    Star eyes   -   -

FREDDIE McCOY-SPIDER MAN:
Freddie McCoy(vb)Charlie L.Wilson(p)Steve Davis(b)Rudy Lawless(dm).
Supervision:Cal Lampley   NYC,October 6,1965

    You stepped out of a dream   Pr.   PR7487
    That's all   Pr.   PR7444
    Hav' mercy   Pr.45-398 -
    Speak out,Deagan!   -
    Yesterdays   -
    The girl from Ipanema   -
    Spider man   Pr.45-398 -   PR7706

BROTHER JACK McDUFF-HOT BARBECUE:
Red Holloway(ts)Jack McDuff(org)George Benson(g)Joe Dukes(dm).
                                         NYC,October 19,1965

    Hot barbecue   Pr.45-388,PR7422
    The party's over   -
    Brian Patch   -
    Hippy dip   -
    601 1/2 North Poplar   -
    Cry me a river   -
    The three day thang   Pr.45-388 -

All titles also issued on P-24072.

BOOKER ERVIN-THE TRANCE:
Dexter Gordon-1,Booker Ervin(ts)Jaki Byard(p)Reggie Workman(b)Alan
Dawson(dm).
Supervision:Don Schlitten   Munich(Germany),October 27,1965
        Groovin' at the jamboree   PR7462
        Speak low   -
        The trance   -
        Settin' the pace-1   PR7455
        Dexter's deck-1   -

STAN HUNTER & SONNY FORTUNE-TRIP ON THE STRIP:
Sonny Fortune(as,ts)Stan Hunter(org)Sherman Suber(g)John Royal(dm).
Supervision:Cal Lampley   NYC,October 28,1965
        HFR   PR7458
        Once I loved   unissued
        Invitation   PR7458
        Trip on the strip   Pr.45-396,PR7458
        This is all I ask   -
        Sonny's mood   -
        Corn flakes   Pr.45-396 -
        Yesterdays   -
        Serenade in blue   unissued

LARRY & HANK-THE BLUES,A NEW GENERATION:
Larry Johnson(vo,g)Hank Adkins(g).
Supervision:Sam Charters   NYC,November 25,1965
        Four women blues   PR7472
        The captain don't 'low me here -
        Tell your woman 'bout me   -
        Watch dog blues   -
        Death call   -
        Two gun green   -
        When I'm drinking   -
        Whiskey store blues   -
        If you don't want me baby   -
        My gal ain't fat   -
        Country road blues   -
        Take these blues off my mind -

FEARLESS FRANK FOSTER:
Virgil Jones(tp)Frank Foster(ts)Al Dailey(p)Bob Cunningham(b)Alan
Dawson(dm).
Supervision:Cal Lampley   NYC,December 2,1965
        Janie Huk   Pr.   PR7461
        Disapproachment   -
        Raunchy Rita   Pr.45-397 -
        Jitterbug waltz   -
        Baby Ann   Pr.45-397 -
        Thingaroo   -

RED HOLLOWAY-RED SOUL:
Red Holloway(ts)Lonnie Smith(org)George Benson(g)Charles "Chuck" Rainey
(b)Ray Lucas(dm).
                                     NYC,December   ,1965
        Making tracks   PR7473,PR7778
        Movin' on   -
        Good and groovy   -   PR7778
        Get it together   -
        Big fat lady   -

[164]

RED HOLLOWAY-RED SOUL:
Red Holloway(ts)Norman Simmons(p)George Benson(g)Paul Breslin(b)Frank
Severino(dm).

                               NYC,December   ,1965

```
        A tear in my heart              PR7473
        Eagle jaws                         -
        I'm all packed                     -
        The regulars                       -
```

DON PATTERSON with SONNY STITT-THE BOSS MEN:
Sonny Stitt(as)Don Patterson(org)Billy James(dm).
Supervision:Cal Lampley   NYC,December 28,1965

```
        Someday my prince will come     Pr.        PR7466
        Diane                           Pr.45-433   -
        Big C's rock                       -        -      PR7704
        What's new?                        -
        Easy to love                       -
        They say that falling in love
                    is wonderful           -
```

JOHNNY "HAMMOND" SMITH-THE STINGER MEETS THE GOLDEN THRUSH:
Otis Sutton(as)Houston Person(ts)Johnny "Hammond" Smith(org)Eddie
McFadden(g)Leo Stevens(dm)Byrdie Green(vo).
Supervision:Cal Lampley   NYC,January 4,1966

```
        The golden thrush               Pr.45-422,PR7464,PR7705
        Oriole                             -
        How I lost my love                 -
        Broadway                           -
        If I ruled the world voBG          -
        Stormy Monday blues voBG        Pr.45-422   -
        The days of wine and roses voBG voBG unissued
        Make someone happy voBG            -
        Time after time voBG               -
        On a clear day                  PR7464,PR7777
        Blue Jay                           -
```

JAKI BYARD-FREEDOM TOGETHER:
Jaki Byard(ts-1,p,el p,celeste,vb,dm)Richard Davis(b,cello)Alan Dawson
(vb,dm,tympani)Junior Parker(vo,lagerphone).
Supervision:Don Schlitten   NYC,January 11,1966

```
        Nocturne for contrabass         PR7463
        Just you,just me-1                 -
        Getting to know you voJP           -
        Night leaves voJP                  -
        Freedom together                   -
        Ode to Prez-1                      -
        Young at heart                     -
```

BOBBY TIMMONS-SOUL MAN:
Wayne Shorter(ts)Bobby Timmons(p)Ron Carter(b)Jimmy Cobb(dm).
Supervision:Cal Lampley   NYC,January 20,1966

```
        Little waltz                    PR7465
        Einbahnstrasse(One way street)     -
        Damn if I know                     -
        Cut me loose Charlie               -
        Tom Thumb                          -
        Tenaj                              -
        Remembrance                     unissued
```

JACK McDUFF:
Red Holloway(ts)Jack McDuff(org)George Benson(g)Joe Dukes(dm)with big
band,Benny Golson(arr,cond).

NYC,February   ,1966

Walk on by	Pr.45-399,PR7476,PR7771
Talking 'bout my woman	Pr.45-423 - -
Jersey bounce	- -
Too many fish in the sea	Pr.45-399 - -

Red Holloway(ts)Harold Ousley(ts)Jack McDuff(org)Pat Martino(g)Joe
Dukes(dm).

NYC,February   ,1966

Haitian lady	Pr. PR7476
For those who choose	Pr.45-423 -
Song of the soul-1	-
The live people	PR7492
Stop it	PR7529
More-1	PR7567
That's when we thought of love	-
How high the moon	PR7642
Chicken feet	PR7666

-1:Holloway out.

PUCHO & THE LATIN SOUL BROS.:
Vincent McEwan(tp)Claude Bartee(ts)William Bivens(vb)John Spruill(p)
John Hart(b)Richard Landrum(conga)Norberto Apellaniz(bongo)Henry "Pucho'
Brown(timbales,leader).
Supervision:Cal Lampley   NYC,February 15,1966

Cantelope Island	Pr.45-426,PR7471
The shadow of your smile	-
Yesterdays	-
Goldfinger	-
Strange things	-
Walk on by	-
Just for kicks	-
Vietnam mambo	Pr.45-426 -
And I love her	-

DON FRIEDMAN-METAMORPHOSIS:
Don Friedman(p)Attila Zoller(g)Richard Davis(b)Joe Chambers(dm).
Supervision:Cal Lampley   NYC,February 22,1966

Extensions	PR7488
Wakin' up	-
Spring sign	-
Dream bells	-
Troubadours groovedour	-
Drive	-

GEORGE BRAITH-LAUGHING SOUL:
George Braith(ss,ts,C melody sax)John Patton(org)Grant Green(g)Eddie
Diehl(rhythm g)Victor Sproles(b)Ben Dixon(dm)Richard Landrum(conga).
Supervision:Cal Lampley   NYC,March 1,1966

Creenshaw West	Pr. PR7474
Chop sticks	-
Coolodge(Collage)	Pr.45-430 -
Cantelope woman	- -
Little flame	-
Hot sauce	-
With malice towards none	-
Chunky checks	-
Please let me do it	-
Love song	unissued

ERIC KLOSS:
Eric Kloss(as,ts)Richard "Groove" Holmes(org)Gene Edwards(g)Grady Tate
(dm).
Supervision:Cal Lampley   NYC,March 14,1966

    The shadow of your smile   Pr.45-412,PR7469
    I'm glad there's you   unissued
    Sonnymoon for two   -
    The days of wine and roses   -
    When I fall in love   -
    Secret love   -
    Gemini   PR7469
    I wish you love   unissued
    Got you on my mind   -

RICHARD "GROOVE" HOLMES:
Richard "Groove" Holmes(org)Gene Edwards(g)Freddie Waits(dm).
Supervision:Cal Lampley   NYC,March 15,1966

    Groove 3/4   unissued
    Denise   PR7741
    Oriental blues   unissued
    Up jumped Spring   PR7741
    Later   PR7791
    Blues for Yna Yna   unissued
    The girl from Ipanema   -
    The more I see you   -
    Dis here   -

ERIC KLOSS-LOVE AND ALL THAT JAZZ:
Eric Kloss(as,ts)Don Patterson(org)Vinnie Corrao(g)Billy James(dm).
Supervision:Cal Lampley   NYC,April 11,1966

    You'd be so nice to come home to PR7469
    Love for sale   -
    I'll remember April   unissued
    Just for fun-k   PR7469
    No blues   -
    I'm glad there's you   -

RICHARD "GROOVE" HOLMES-LIVING SOUL:
Richard "Groove" Holmes(org)Gene Edwards(g)George Randall(dm).
Supervision:Cal Lampley   NYC,April 22,1966

    Blues   unissued
    Moanin'   -
    Blues for Yna Yna   PR7468
    Back home again in Indiana   unissued
    The girl from Ipanema   PR7468
    Jeri   unissued
    This here   -
    Living soul   Pr.45-427,PR7468,PR7700
    Misty   unissued
    Over the rainbow   PR7468
    Nica's dream   unissued
    Night Trane   -
    Softly as in a morning sunrise -
    Straight no chaser   -
    Gemini   PR7468
    Genene   unissued
    When I grow too old to dream   -
    Lady be good   -
    Up jumped Spring   -

FREDDIE ROACH:
Freddie Roach(org)Clifton "Skeeter" Best(g)Ray Lucas(dm)King Errison (conga).
Supervision:Cal Lampley   NYC,June 13,1966
        Written on the wind   unissued
        You'd better hold on   -
        Moody's mood for love   -
        You've got your troubles,I've
                    got mine Pr.45-429,PR7490
HOUSTON PERSON-UNDERGROUND SOUL:
Mark Levine(tb)Houston Person(ts)Charles Boston(org)Frank Jones(dm).
Supervision:Cal Lampley   NYC,June 16,1966
        Alleluia   PR7491
        What the world needs now is love -
        Tears   -
        Ballin'   -
        The pimp   -   PR7779
        If you could see me now   -
        Strike up the band   -
        Underground soul   -
FREDDIE McCOY-FUNK DROPS:
James Robinson(tp)Laurdine Patrick(bs)Freddie McCoy(vb)Alfred Williams (org)John Blair(el v)Napoleon Allen(g)Albert Winston(el b)Bernard Purdie(dm).
Supervision:Cal Lampley   NYC,June 21,1966
        Funk drops   Pr.45-425,PR7470
        My babe   -   -
        The sleepy lagoon   -
        Somewhere   unissued
Freddie McCoy(vb)JoAnne Brackeen(p)Augustus Turner(b)George Scott(dm).
Supervision:Cal Lampley   NYC,June 22,1966
        And I love her   PR7470
        Moye   -
        Tough talk   -
        Theodora   -
        High heel sneakers   -
FRANK FOSTER:
Virgil Jones(tp)Frank Foster(ts)Pat Rebillot(p)Billy Butler(g)Bob Cunningham,Richard Davis(b)Alan Dawson(dm). -1:Cunningham out.
Supervision:Cal Lampley   NYC,June 27,1966
        Show the good side-1   Pr.45-439,PR7479
        Night song   -
        Green grass   unissued
THE FREDDIE ROACH SOUL BOOK:
Edlin "Buddy" Terry(ts)Freddie Roach(org)Vinnie Corrao(g)Jackie Mills (dm)King Errison-1(conga).
Supervision:Cal Lampley   NYC,June 28,1966
        One track mind   Pr.45-429,PR7490
        Tenderly   Pr.45-432 -
        The bees   -
        The spirit   unissued
        Avatara   PR7490
        The thing   unissued
        The more I see you   -
        Spacious   Pr.45-432,PR7490
-1:King Errison is present on two titles only.

BYRDIE GREEN-THE GOLDEN THRUSH STRIKES AT MIDNIGHT:
Byrdie Green(vo)with Virgil Jones(tp)Gene Walker(as)Johnny "Hammond"
Smith(org,arr,cond)Eddie Diehl(g)Jimmy Lewis(b)John Harris(dm).
Supervision:Cal Lampley   NYC,July 6,1966

      In the dark   Pr.45-440,PR7503
      Goin' out of my head   -   -
      It hurts so bad   -
      Gin house blues   -
      How long blues   -
      Falling in love   -
      The shadow of your smile   -
      Somebody groovy   -
      Hurt   -

RICHARD "GROOVE" HOLMES:
Blue Mitchell-1(tp)Harold Vick-1(ts)Richard "Groove" Holmes(org)Gene
Edwards(g)George Randall(dm).
Supervision:Cal Lampley   NYC,July 7,1966

      Autumn leaves   PR7741
      Things ain't what they used
                         to be-1   -
      There is no greater love-1   -
      What now my love   Pr.45-427,45-723,PR7485,PR7700
      The more I see you   Pr.45-428   -
      The shadow of your smile   PR7485,PR7768

FRANK FOSTER:
Virgil Jones(tp)Frank Foster(ts)Pat Rebillot(p)Billy Butler(g)Richard
Davis(b)Bob Cunningham(dm).
Supervision:Cal Lampley   NYC,July 11,1966

      While the city sleeps   Pr.   PR7479
      Skanarooney(Skankaroony*)   Pr.45-439   -*
      Chiquita loco   -
      Strangers in the night   unissued

MORRIS NANTON TRIO:
Morris Nanton(p)Norman Edge(b)Al Beldini(dm).
Supervision:Cal Lampley   NYC,July 13,1966

      Soul fingers   unissued
      I gotta go   -
      The lamp is low   -
      Call me   -
      Georgia   -
      What's they name   -
      What now my love   -
      People   -

DON PATTERSON-SOUL HAPPENING:
Don Patterson(org)Vinnie Corrao(g)Billy James(dm).
Supervision:Cal Lampley   NYC,August 5,1966

      Strangers in the night   Pr.   PR7484
      La bamba   Pr.45-424   -
      Wade in the water   -
      Love letters   -
      Wee dot   -
      Up tight   Pr.45-424   -   PR7704
      There will never be another you unissued

[169]

RICHARD "GROOVE" HOLMES:
Richard "Groove" Holmes(org)Gene Edwards(g)George Randall(dm).
Supervision:Cal Lampley   NYC,August 12,1966

        On the street where you live   Pr.45-428,PR7485
        Summertime   -   PR7768
        Strangers in the night   -
        There will never be another you   -
        The shadow of your smile   rejected

EDDIE DANIELS:
Eddie Daniels(ts,cl)Roland Hanna(p)Richard Davis(b)Mel Lewis(dm).
Supervision:Cal Lampley   NYC,September 8,1966

        Felicidad   PR7506
        How deep is the ocean   -
        The Spanish flee   -
        That waltz   -

BOOKER ERVIN-HEAVY!!:
Jimmy Owens(tp,flh)Garnett Brown(tb)Booker Ervin(ts)Jaki Byard(p)
Richard Davis(b)Alan Dawson(dm). -1:tp,tb out.
Supervision:Don Schlitten   NYC,September 9,1966

        Bachafillen   PR7499
        You don't know what love is-1   -
        Aluminum baby   -
        Not quite that   -
        Bei mir bist du schoen   -

EDDIE DANIELS:
Eddie Daniels(ts,cl)Roland Hanna(p)Richard Davis(b)Mel Lewis(dm).
Supervision:Cal Lampley   NYC,September 12,1966

        Falling in love with love   PR7506
        Love's long journey   -
        Time marches on   -
        The rocker   -

JOHNNY "HAMMOND" SMITH-LOVE POTION No.9:
Virgil Jones(tp)Gene Walker(ts)Johnny "Hammond" Smith(org)Eddie Diehl
(g)John Harris(dm).
Supervision:Cal Lampley   NYC,September 28,1966

        A taste of honey   PR7482
        Blues on Sunday   -
        The impossible dream   -
        The shadow of your smile   -
        Kimberley's delight   -
        Love potion No.9   -   PR7705
        Sunny   -
        Up comes Monday   -

BOBBY TIMMONS:
Bobby Timmons(p)Lee Otis Bass(b)Billy Higgins(dm).
Supervision:Cal Lampley   NYC,September 30,1966

        Giblets   PR7483
        Turkey wings   -
        Angel eyes   -
        Cracklin' bread   -   PR7780

[170]

CHARLES McPHERSON:THE QUINTET-LIVE!:
Lonnie Hillyer(tp)Charles McPherson(as)Barry Harris(p)Ray McKinney(b)
Billy Higgins(dm).
Supervision:Don Schlitten   Five Spot,NYC,October 13,1966

Cheryl	unissued
Here's that rainy day	PR7480
On the moon	unissued
I believe in you	-
Suddenly it's Spring	-
Shaw nuff	PR7480
Never let me go	-
I concentrate on you	unissued
Equinox	
The viper	PR7480
Blues for Alice	unissued
I can't get started	PR7480
Epistrophy	unissued
Cheryl	-
Suddenly	PR7480
The viper	unissued
You're my thrill	-
Lover	-

BOBBY TIMMONS:
Bobby Timmons(p)Lee Otis Bass(b)Billy Higgins(dm).
Supervision:Cal Lampley   NYC,October 14,1966

Stolen sweets	PR7483	
Make someone happy	-	
Sauce meat	-	PR7780

SONNY CRISS-THIS IS CRISS:
Sonny Criss(as)Walter Davis(p)Paul Chambers(b)Alan Dawson(dm).
Supervision:Don Schlitten   NYC,October 21,1966

When sunny gets blue	Pr.	PR7511
Days of wine and roses		-
Black coffee		-
Greasy	Pr.45-435	-
Sunrise sunset	-	-
Love for sale	unissued	
Skylark	PR7511	
Steve's blues	-	

PUCHO & HIS LATIN SOUL BROS.:
Vincent McEwan(tp)Claude Bartee(ts)Harold Alexander(ts,fl)William
Bivens(vb)John Spruill(p)James Phillips(b)William Curtis(dm)Richard
Landrum(conga)Norberto Apellaniz(bongo)Henry "Pucho" Brown(timbales,
leader).
Supervision:Cal Lampley   NYC,November 8/10,1966

What a piece	Pr.45-436,PR7502
The groover	-
Reach out,I'll be there	-
Soul Yamie	-
Alfie	-
Early Autumn	-
Aye Mama	Pr.45-436 -
Something black	-
Caravin	-
Don't do it	-

BILLY HAWKS-NEW GENIUS OF THE BLUES:
Billy Hawks(org,hca,vo)Joe Jones(g)Henry Terrell(dm).
Supervision:Cal Lampley   NYC,November 15,1966

    Got my mojo working   PR7501
    I wish you love   -
    I'll wait for you baby   -
    Why do these happen to me   -
    Let me love you before you go   -
    Mean woman blues   -
    I got a woman   -
    I just wanna make love to you   -
    Hawks blues   -
    untitled blues   unissued
    Everytime it rains   PR7501

GEORGE BRAITH:
George Braith(ss,C melody sax)Jane Getz(p)Jay Carter(g)Victor Davis(el
b,org)Victor Allende(conga)Ben Dixon(dm)Ellen Shashoyan,Bunnie Foy,
Adrienne Barbeau(vo).
Supervision:Cal Lampley   NYC,November 21,1966

    Our blessings-1   PR7515
    Find your soul   unissued
    Shadowy pines   -
    Lovers never say goodbye   -
    You keep me hanging on   -
    Evelyn Anita   PR7515

-1:Cal Lampley(dm)added.

RICHARD "GROOVE" HOLMES-SPICY:
Richard "Groove" Holmes(org)Gene Edwards,Joe Jones(g)George Randall
(dm)Richard Landrum(conga).
Supervision:Cal Lampley   NYC,November 28,1966

    Never on Sunday   Pr.45-431,PR7493
    Boo-d-doo   -   -   PR7700
    If I had a hammer   Pr.45-442   -
    1-2-3   -   -
    A day in the life of a fool   -
    Work song   -
    When lights are low   -
    Old folks   -
    Teach me tonight   unissued

MORRIS NANTON-SOUL FINGERS:
Morris Nanton(p)Norman Edge(b)Al Beldini(dm)Johnny Murray Jr.(conga)
Pucho & The Latin Soul Brothers(vo-1).
Supervision:Cal Lampley   NYC,December 5,1966

    Troubles of the world-1   Pr.45-434,PR7467
    The shadow of your smile   -   -
    Georgia   -
    Fly me to the moon   -
    I'll remember April   -
    Whistle stop   -
    The Summer wind   -
    L-O-V-E   -
    The lamp is low   -
    Soul fingers   -

TEDDY EDWARDS-NOTHIN' BUT THE TRUTH:
Teddy Edwards(ts)Walter Davis Jr.(p)Phil Orlando(g)Paul Chambers(b)
Billy Higgins(dm)Montego Joe(conga,bongos).
Supervision:Don Schlitten   NYC,December 13,1966

        Brazilian skies   PR7518
        Raunchy raunchy man   unissued
        On the street where you live   PR7518
        The amen corner   unissued
        But beautiful   PR7518
        Lovin' it,lovin' it   Pr.45-443,PR7518
        Games that lovers play   -
        Nothin' but the truth   Pr.45-443   -

ERIC KLOSS-GRITS AND GRAVY:
Eric Kloss(ts)Danny Bank(ss,fl,perc)Teddy Charles(vb)Alfred Williams
(p)Billy Butler(g)Ronald Boykins(b)Robert J.Gregg(dm)Ed Bland(arr).
Supervision:Cal Lampley   NYC,December 21,1966

        A day in the life of a fool   Pr.45-444,PR7486
        A slow hot wind   -   -
        Comin' home baby   unissued
        If I had a hammer   -
        Grits and gravy   PR7486

Eric Kloss(ts)Jaki Byard(p)Richard Davis(b)Alan Dawson(dm).
Supervision:Cal Lampley   NYC,December 22,1966

        Milestones   PR7486
        Softly as in a morning sunrise -
        You don't know what love is   -
        When I fall in love   unissued
        Repeat   .   PR7486
        Gentle one   -
        Psychodelicates in rag   unissued

GEORGE BRAITH:
George Braith(as,ts,C melody sax)Jane Getz(p)Eddie Diehl(g)Bill Salter
(b)Popito Allende(conga)Angel Allende(dm,bongo,tambourine)Freddie
Briggs,Gilbert Braithwaite,Chico Torres(perc)Bunnie Foy,Juanita
Williams,Evelyn Blakey(vo).
Supervision:Cal Lampley   NYC,January 3,1967

        Monkey cha cha   unissued
        Laura   PR7515
        Evelyn Anita   unissued
        Dee Do   -
        Embraceable you   PR7515
        Del's theme   -
        Splashes of love   -
        Musart   -

FREDDIE ROACH-MOCHA MOTION:
Freddie Roach(org)Vinnie Corrao(g)Eddie Gladden(dm)Ralph Dorsey(conga).
Supervision:Don Schlitten   NYC,January 5,1967

        Here comes the Mocha man   PR7507
        Samba de Orpheo   -
        Stinky fingers   -
        Warning shot   -
        Money   -
        Good morning time   -
        Straighten up and fly right   unissued
        Johnny's comin' home no more   Pr.45-454,PR7507
        Please don't talk about me   unissued
        Tenderly   -

TRUDY PITTS-INTRODUCING TRUDY PITTS:
Trudy Pitts(org)Pat Martino(g)Bill Carney(dm)Garnell Johnson(conga).
Supervision:Cal Lampley   NYC,February 15,1967

    It was a very good year   Pr.   PR7523
    Siete   -
    Fidlin'   -
    Steppin' in minor   Pr.45-448 -
    Something wonderful   -
    Matchmaker   -
    Music for girl watchers   -

JAKI BYARD-ON THE SPOT!:
Jimmy Owens(tp,flh)Jaki Byard(as,p)Paul Chambers(b)Billy Higgins(dm).
Supervision:Don Schlitten   NYC,February 16,1967

    Snow flakes   unissued
    Clean visit   Pr.   PR7524
    Alexander's ragtime band   Pr.45-445 -
    Second balcony jump   -
    GEB piano roll   -
    J.B.'s medley   unissued
    P.C.Blues   Pr.   PR7524
    A toodle-oo,toodle-oo   Pr.45-445 -
    I fall in love too easily   -
    On the spot   -

TRUDY PITTS:
Trudy Pitts(org)Pat Martino(g)Bill Carney(dm)Garnell Johnson(conga).·
Supervision:Cal Lampley   NYC,February 21,1967

    Spanish flea   Pr.   PR7523
    Night song   -
    Take five   Pr.45-448 -

EDLIN "BUDDY" TERRY-ELECTRIC SOUL!:
Jimmy Owens(tp,flh)Edlin "Buddy" Terry(ts,el sax)Harold Mabern(el p)
Ron Carter(b)Freddie Waits(dm).
Supervision:Cal Lampley   NYC,February 23,1967

    Everything is everything   Pr.   PR7525
    Hey,Nellie   -
    Jimmy   Pr.45-447 -
    Alfie   -
    Electric soul   Pr.45-447 -
    The Ubangi that got away   -
    Band bandit   -

JOHNNY "HAMMOND" SMITH-EBB TIDE:
Virgil Jones(tp)Houston Person(ts)Johnny "Hammond" Smith(org)Thornel
Schwartz(g)Jimmy Lewis(b)John Harris(dm).
Supervision:Cal Lampley   NYC,March 3,1967

    Sin in   Pr.   PR7494
    Ebb tide   Pr.45-449 -   PR7705
    Knock on wood   -
    The in crowd   -
    Summertime   -
    Stand by me   Pr.45-449 -
    Gettin' up   -
    The soulful blues   -

SYLVIA SYMS:
Sylvia Syms(vo)with Jerome Richardson(fl,alto fl)John "Bucky" Pizzarel-
li,Gene Bertoncini(g)Sam Bruno(b)Bobby Rosengarden(dm).
Supervision:Cal Lampley   NYC,March 9,1967

    I will wait for you   Pr.   PR7489
    The games that lovers play   -
    Vaya con Dios   Pr.45-446   -
    Solitaire   unissued

JOE JONES:
Limerick Knowles Jr.(org)Joe Jones(g)Alexander Witherspoon(el b)
Jos.R.Brancato(Bud Kelly)(dm).
Supervision:Cal Lampley   NYC,March 15,1967

    Games   PR7557
    When she walks by   unissued
    Cherokee   -
    Right now   PR7557
    Time after time   unissued
    Call me   PR7557
    Blues for Bruce   -
    Always   unissued

SONNY CRISS-PORTRAIT OF SONNY CRISS:
Sonny Criss(as)Walter Davis(p)Paul Chambers(b)Alan Dawson(dm).
Supervision:Don Schlitten   NYC,March 23,1967

    Blues in the closet   PR7526
    On a clear day   -   PR7742
    Smile   -
    A million or more times   -
    Wee(Allen's alley)   -
    God bless the child   -
    All the things you are   unissued

FREDDIE McCOY:
Edward David Williams,Wilbur "Dud" Bascomb(tp)Freddie McCoy(vb)JoAnne
Brackeen(p,org)Wally Richardson(g)Eustis Guillemet(el b)Ray Lucas(dm).
Supervision:Cal Lampley   NYC,April 10,1967

    Summer in the City   Pr.45-450,PR7487
    Lightning strikes   -
    Call me   -
    One cylinder   -
    Huh!   -

SYLVIA SYMS-FOR ONCE IN MY LIFE:
Sylvia Syms(vo)with Johnny "Hammond" Smith(org)Thornel Schwartz(g)
Charles Wellesley(b)John Harris(dm)Richard Landrum(conga).
Supervision:Cal Lampley   NYC,April 18,1967

    For once in my life   Pr.   PR7489
    Yesterdays   -
    Solitaire   Pr.45-446   -
    You don't know what love is   -
    Who(will take his place)   -
    You don't have to say you love me -
    Don't take your love from me   -
    I will wait for you   unissued

BYRDIE GREEN-I GOT IT BAD:
Byrdie Green(vo)with Houston Person(ts)Johnny "Hammond" Smith(org)
Thornel Schwartz(g)Jimmy Lewis(b)John Harris(dm)Ralph Jones(arr).
Supervision:Cal Lampley   NYC,April 20,1967

     See see rider   PR7509
     I got it bad   -
     Yesterdays kisses   -
     The poor side of town   -
     I've been lonely too long   -
     I had a man   -
     Hold on to him   -
     This bitter earth   -
     People   -

BARRY HARRIS-LUMINESCENCE!:
Slide Hampton(tb)Junior Cook(ts)Pepper Adams(bs)Barry Harris(p)Bob
Cranshaw(b)Lennie McBrowne(dm).
Supervision:Don Schlitten   NYC,April 20,1967

     Luminescence   PR7498
     Like this!   -
     Webb City   -
     Dance of the infidels   -
     Even Steven   -
     My ideal   -
     Nicaragua   -

RICHARD "GROOVE" HOLMES-SUPER SOUL:
Richard "Groove" Holmes(org)with The Super Big Soul Band,Richard Evans
(dir).
Supervision:Cal Lampley   Chicago,April 26,1967

     Ain't that peculiar   Pr.45-451,PR7497
     Why don't you do right   -
     In between heartaches   -
     Function at the junction   -
     Tennessee waltz   -

Same.
Supervision:Cal Lampley   Chicago,April 27,1967

     Super soul   Pr.45-451,PR7497,PR7700
     On green Dolphin Street   -   PR7768
     I'll wait for you   -
     Back home in Indiana   -
     Bluesette   -

PAT MARTINO-EL HOMBRE:
Danny Turner(fl)Trudy Pitts(org)Pat Martino(g)Mitch Fine(dm)Vance
Anderson,Abdu Johnson(perc).
Supervision:Cal Lampley   NYC,May 1,1967

     El hombre   PR7513
     One for Rose   -
     Cisco   -
     Song for my mother   unissued
     Waltz for Geri   PR7513
     G major blues   unissued
     Just friends   PR7513
     Once I loved   -

FREDDIE McCOY:
Freddie McCoy(vb)JoAnne Brackeen(p)Eustis Guillemet(b)Kalil Madhi(dm)
Dave Blum(arr,cond).
Supervision:Cal Lampley   NYC,May 4,1967

    My funny Valentine   PR7487
    1-2-3   -
    Peas ' n' rice   -   PR7706,45-450

DON PATTERSON with FATHEAD NEWMAN-MELLOW SOUL:
David "Fathead" Newman(fl,as,ts)Don Patterson(org)Billy James(dm).
Supervision:Cal Lampley   NYC,May 10,1967

    Dubbin' with Red Fox   PR7510
    Music to think by   -
    Humppa snappa blues   -   PR7704
    These foolish things   -
    Head   -
    Mellow soul   -   PR7772

TEDDY EDWARDS-IT'S ALRIGHT:
Jimmy Owens(tp,flh)Garnett Brown(tb)Teddy Edwards(ts)Cedar Walton(p)
Ben Tucker(b)Lennie McBrowne(dm).
Supervision:Don Schlitten   NYC,May 24 & 27,1967

    Going home   PR7522
    Back alley blues   -
    Mamacita Lisa   -
    Wheelin' and dealin'   -
    It's all right   -
    The cellar dweller   -
    Afraid of love   -
    Moving in   -

RICHARD "GROOVE" HOLMES-GET UP AND GET IT:
Teddy Edwards(ts)Richard "Groove" Holmes(org)Pat Martino(g)Paul
Chambers(b)Billy Higgins(dm).
Supervision:Don Schlitten   NYC,May 29,1967

    Get up and get it   PR7514
    Lee-Ann   -
    Body and soul   -
    Broadway   -
    Groove's Blues Groove   -   PR7700
    Pennies from heaven   -

HOUSTON PERSON-CHOCOMOTIVE:
Frankie Jones(tp)Houston Person(ts)Cedar Walton(p)Bob Cranshaw(b)
Alan Dawson(dm).
Supervision:Don Schlitten   NYC,June 14,1967

    Since I fell for you   PR7517
    Chocomotive   -   PR7779
    Up,up and away   -
    More   -
    You are going to hear from me   -
    Girl talk   -
    Close quarters   -

FREDDIE ROACH-MY PEOPLE(SOUL PEOPLE):
Kiane Zawadi(tb,euphonium-1)James Anderson(ss)Roland Alexander,Conrad
Lester(ts)Henry White(flh)Freddie Roach(org,fl-2,p-3,vo)Eddie Wright(g)
Eddie Gladden(dm).
Supervision:Jerry Field   NYC,June 22 & 29,1967

          Prince Street   Pr.   PR7521
          Straight ahead-2   -
          Mas que nada-1   -
          Drunk-3   -
          My people(Soul people) voFR Pr.45-454   -
          I'm on my way   -
          Respectfully yours   -
          Freddie   -

CEDAR WALTON-CEDAR!:
Kenny Dorham(tp)Junior Cook(ts)Cedar Walton(p)Leroy Vinnegar(b)Billy
Higgins(dm).
Supervision:Don Schlitten   NYC,July 10,1967

          Short stuff-1   PR7519
          Twilight waltz-1   -
          My ship-2   -
          Take the A train   unissued
          Heads and shoulders   PR7519
          Come Sunday   -
          Turquoise twice   -

-1:Cook out;-2:Dorham & Cook out.

ERIC KLOSS-FIRST CLASS KLOSS:
Jimmy Owens(tp,flh)Eric Kloss(as,ts)Cedar Walton(p)Leroy Vinnegar(b)
Alan Dawson(dm).
Supervision:Don Schlitten   NYC,July 14,1967

          The chasin' game   Pr.   PR7520
          African cookbook   -
          Chitlins con carne   -
          Comin' home baby   Pr.45-704   -
          Walkin'   -
          One for Marianne   -
          When I fall in love   unissued
          Night train   -
          Take the A train   -

PUCHO & THE LATIN SOUL BROS.-SHUCKIN' AND JIVIN':
Vincent McEwan(tp)Claude Bartee(ts)William Bivens(vb)Neal Creque(p)
Jimmy Phillips(b)Norberto Apellaniz(bongo)Cecil Jackson(conga)Henry
"Pucho" Brown(timbales,leader)Jackie Soul,The Soul Sisters(vo).
Supervision:Don Schlitten   NYC,August 9,1967

          Maiden voyage   Pr.   PR7528
          Swing thing   -
          Return to me
          Shuckin' and jivin' voJS,SS Pr.45-458   -   PR7679
          Dearly beloved   -
          You are my sunshine voJS   Pr.45-458   -   PR7679
          See see rider voJS   -   -
          How insensitive   -

[178]

SONNY CRISS-UP,UP AND AWAY:
Sonny Criss(as)Cedar Walton(p)Tal Farlow(g)Bob Cranshaw(b)Lenny McBrowne
(dm).
Supervision:Don Schlitten   NYC,August 18,1967

  Up,up and away   PR7530,PR7742
  This is for Benny   -
  Sunny   - PR7742
  Paris blues   -
  Willow weep for me   -
  Scrapple from the apple   -
DON PATTERSON with HOUSTON PERSON-FOUR DIMENSIONS:
Houston Person(ts)Don Patterson(org)Pat Martino(g)Billy James(dm).
Supervision:Don Schlitten   NYC,August 25,1967

  Sandu   PR7533
  Freddie Tooks Jr.   -
  Can't help loving that man unissued
  Embraceable you   PR7533
  Red top   -
  Last train from Overbrook - PR7704
ERIC KLOSS-LIFE FORCE:
Jimmy Owens(tp,flh)Eric Kloss(ts)Pat Martino(g)Ben Tucker(b)Alan Dawson
(dm).

             NYC,September 18,1967

  My heart is in the Highlands PR7535
  You're turning my greens around -
  Life force   -
  Soul Daddy   -
  St.Thomas   -
  Nocturno   -

TRUDY PITTS-THESE BLUES ARE MINE:
Trudy Pitts(org)Pat Martino(g)Bill Carney(dm).
Supervision:Cal Lampley   NYC,September 21,1967

  The house of the rising sun Pr. PR7538
  Eleanor Rigby   -
  Count nine
  Man and woman   -
  A whiter shade of pale Pr.45-461 -
  These blues of mine   -
Same.
Supervision:Cal Lampley   NYC,September 25,1967

  9/4   unissued
  Up,up and away   -
  What the world needs now PR7538
  Teddy makes three   -
  Organology   -
  Just us two   -

JOHNNY "HAMMOND" SMITH-SOUL FLOWERS:
Earl Edwards,Houston Person(ts)Johnny "Hammond" Smith(org)Wally Richard-
son(g)Jimmy Lewis(el b)John Harris(dm)Richard Landrum(conga).
Supervision:Cal Lampley   NYC,September 27,1967

  Days of wine and roses Pr. PR7549
  Ode to Billie Joe   -
  Tara's theme   -
  Alfie   -
  You'll never walk alone   -
  N.Y.P.D.   Pr.45-455 -
  I got a woman   -
  Dirty apple   Pr.45-455 -
  Here comes that rainy day   - PR7705

FREDDIE McCOY:
Edward Williams,Wilbur "Dud" Bascomb(tp)Freddie McCoy(vb)JoAnne
Brackeen(p)Dave Blum(org)Wally Richardson(g)Joseph Macho(el b)Ray
Lucas(dm).
Supervision:Cal Lampley   NYC,October 2,1967

    I was made to love her   Pr.   PR7542
    You keep me hanging on   -
    A whiter shade of pale   Pr.45-456   -
    Tony's pony   -
    Take my love(and shove it up your heart) -

PAT MARTINO-STRINGS!:
Joe Farrell(fl-1,ts-2)Pat Martino(g)Cedar Walton(p)Ben Tucker(b)Walter
Perkins(dm)Dave Levin,Ray Appleton(perc-3).
Supervision:Don Schlitten   NYC,October 2,1967

    Querido-1   PR7547
    Lean years-2   -
    Mom-1   -
    Minority-2   -
    Strings-1,3   -

FREDDIE McCOY:
Freddie McCoy(vb)JoAnne Brackeen(p)Dave Blum(org)Don Payne(el b)Ray
Lucas(dm).
Supervision:Cal Lampley   NYC,October 4,1967

    Beans & greens   Pr.45-456,PR7542,PR7706
    Making whoopee   -
    Doxie   -
    6th Avenue strole   -

GEORGE BRAITH:
George Braith(saxes)John Hicks(p)Herbert Lewis(b)Roy Haynes(dm).
Supervision:Cal Lampley   NYC,October   ,1967

    Tara's theme   unissued
    Fat man   -
    Too beautiful   -
    untitled original   -

HOUSTON PERSON-TRUST IN ME:
Houston Person(ts)Cedar Walton(p)Paul Chambers(b)Lenny McBrowne(dm)
Ralph Dorsey(conga).
Supervision:Don Schlitten   NYC,October 13,1967

    Trust in me   PR7548
    Sometimes I feel like a
         motherless child   -
    Hey there   -
    My little Suede shoes   -
    One mint julep   -   PR7779
    Airegin   unissued
    That old black magic   PR7548
    The second time around   -

WILLIS JACKSON-SOUL GRABBER:
Wilbur "Dud" Bascomb,Sammy Lowe(tp)Willis Jackson(ts)Haywood Henry(bs)
Carl Wilson(org)Wally Richardson,Lloyd Davis(g)Bob Bushnell(el b)
Lawrence Wright(dm).
Supervision:Cal Lampley   NYC,October 20,1967

    Ode to Billie Joe   Pr.   PR7551
    I dig rock and roll   -
    The song of Ossanha   Pr.45-457 -
    These blues are made for walking   -

WILLIS JACKSON-SOUL GRABBER:
Wilbur "Dud" Bascomb,Sammy Lowe(tp)Willis Jackson(ts)Carl Wilson(org)
Lloyd Davis(g)Bob Bushnell(el b)Lawrence Wright(dm).
Supervision:Cal Lampley   NYC,October 25,1967
        Rhode Island red   PR7551
        Just squeeze me   PR7791
        Alfie-1   PR7551
        Sunny   -
        Girl talk   -
        Sometimes I'm happy   -
        Soul grabber   Pr.45-457,PR7551
-1:Willis Jackson plays "gator" horn.

JAKI BYARD with ELVIN JONES-THE SUNSHINE OF MY SOUL:
Jaki Byard(p,g-1)David Izenzon(b)Elvin Jones(dm,tympani).
Supervision:Don Schlitten   NYC,October 31,1967
        Cast away-1   PR7550
        Chandra   -
        Diane's melody   -
        Sunshine   -
        St.Louis blues   -
        Trendsition Zildjian   -
        Valhalla express   unissued
        Medley   -

BUDDY TERRY-NATURAL SOUL:
Woody Shaw(tp,flh)Edlin "Buddy" Terry(ts)Joe Thomas(ts,fl)Robbie Porter
(bs)Larry Young(p,org)Jiggs Chase(org)Wally Richardson(g)Jimmy Lewis
(el b)Edward Gladden(dm).
Supervision:Cal Lampley   NYC,November 15,1967
        A natural woman   Pr.45-459,PR7541
        Sunday go-to-meeting blues -*   -
        (Natural soul*)
        Quiet days and lonely nights   -
        Pedro,the one arm bandit -
        Don't be so mean   -
        The revealing time   -

PUCHO AND THE LATIN SOUL BROS.-BIG STICK:
Neal Creque(p,org,clavinet)William Bivens(vb,p,clavinet,perc)Norberto
Apellaniz(bongo)Cecil Jackson(conga)Henry "Pucho" Brown(timbales,conga,
leader)Jackie Soul & The Soul Sisters(vo).
Supervision:Don Schlitten   NYC,December 5,1967
        Sunny   PR7555,PR7679
        No one knows   -   -
        Here's that rainy day   -
        Cold shoulder   -
        Medley:Yesterday/Goin' out -
            of my head   -
        Big stick   -   PR7679
        Up,up and away   unissued
        Left in the cold·   PR7555,PR7679
        Swamp people   -

BILLY HAWKS-MORE HEAVY SOUL!:
Edlin "Buddy" Terry-1(ts)Billy Hawks(org,vo)Maynard Parker(g)Henry
Terrell(dm).
Supervision:Cal Lampley   NYC,December 6,1967
        O baby(I believe I'm losing you) PR7556
        Drown in my own tears-1   -
        Whip it on me   -
        What more can I do?   -
        Heavy soul   -
        You've been a bad girl   -
        I'll be back-1   -
        I can make it   -
        That's your bag   -

JOE JONES:
Joe Jones(g)Ron Carter(b)Ben Dixon(dm)Richard Landrum(conga,bongo).
Supervision:Cal Lampley   NYC,December 12,1967
        The beat goes on   PR7557
        There is a mountain   -
        Sticks and stones   -
        The mindbender   -
        untitled blues   unissued

RICHARD "GROOVE" HOLMES-SOUL POWER:
Richard "Groove" Holmes(org)Wally Richardson,Steve Wolfe(g)Jimmy Lewis
(b)Ben Dixon(dm)Dave Blum(conga).
Supervision:Cal Lampley   NYC,December 19,1967
        Gimme a little sign   Pr.45-460,PR7543
        How can I be sure   -
        Girl talk   -   PR7768
        Soul power   Pr.45-460 -   PR7700
        Since I fell for you   -
        The preacher   -
        Sunny   -
        Corcovado   unissued

TRUDY PITTS-BUCKETFUL OF SOUL:
Trudy Pitts(org)Wilbert Longmire(g)Bill Carney(dm).
Supervision:Cal Lampley   NYC,December 20,1967
        Bucket full of soul   Pr.45-461,PR7560
        W.T.Blues   unissued
        Renaissance   PR7560
        Cabaret   unissued

ERIC KLOSS-WE'RE GOING UP:
Jimmy Owens(tp,flh)Eric Kloss(ts)Kenny Barron(p)Bob Cranshaw(b)Alan
Dawson(dm).
Supervision:Don Schlitten   NYC,December 22,1967
        I long to belong to you   Pr.   PR7565
        Get the money blues   Pr.45-704   -
        Gentle is my lover   -
        Blues up tight
        Bluze-jay-oh style   unissued
        We're going up   PR7565
        Of wine and you   -

[182]

PAT MARTINO-EAST:
Eddie Green(p)Pat Martino(g)Ben Tucker,Tyrone Brown-1(b)Lenny McBrowne
(dm).
Supervision:Don Schlitten   NYC,January 8,1968
          Close your eyes   PR7562
          Mr.P.C.   -
          Trick   -
          Lazy bird   -
          Dark Avenue petite   -
          East-1   -

SONNY CRISS-THE BEAT GOES ON:
Sonny Criss(as)Cedar Walton(p)Bob Cranshaw(b)Alan Dawson(dm).
Supervision:Don Schlitten   NYC,January 12,1968
          Somewhere my love   PR7558
          The beat goes on   -   PR7742
          Georgia rose   -
          Ode to Billie Joe   -   PR7742
          Calidad   -
          Yesterdays   -

FREDDIE McCOY:
Freddie McCoy(vb)JoAnne Brackeen(p,org)Wally Richardson(g)Lawrence
Evans(el b)Ray Appleton(dm)Steve Wolfe(sitar)Dave Blum(arr).
Supervision:Cal Lampley   NYC,January 24,1968
          Ride on   PR7561
          Pet sounds   -
          I am a walrus   -
          Salem soul song   -   45-462
          Sorry 'bout that   -

JOHNNY "HAMMOND" SMITH-DIRTY GRAPE:
Houston Person,Earl Edwards(ts)Johnny "Hammond" Smith(org)Wally
Richardson(g)Jimmy Lewis(el b)John Harris(dm)Richard Landrum(conga).
Supervision:Cal Lampley   NYC,January 31,1968
          Dirty grape   Pr.45-463,PR7564,PR7705
          She's gone again   -
          High heel sneakers   -
          Black strap molasses   -
          Please send me someone to love -
          To Sir with love   -
          Love is a hurting thing   -
          Animal farm   Pr.45-463   -

CHARLES McPHERSON-FROM THIS MOMENT ON:
Charles McPherson(as)Cedar Walton(p)Pat Martino(g)Peck Morrison(b)
Lenny McBrowne(dm).
Supervision:Don Schlitten   NYC,January 31,1968
          Without you   PR7559
          From this moment on   -
          Little sugar baby   -
          I like the way you shake
                            that thing -
          Once in a lifetime   -
          The good life   -
          You've changed   -

[183]

FREDDIE McCOY-SOUL YOGI:
Freddie McCoy(vb)JoAnne Brackeen(p)Lawrence Evans(b)Ray Appleton(dm)
Emanuel Green,Peter Dimitriades,Joseph Malignaggi(v).
Supervision:Cal Lampley   NYC,February 5,1968

    Soul yogi   Pr.45-462,PR7561,PR7706
    What now my love   -
    Mysterioso   -
    Autumn leaves   -

WALLY RICHARDSON-SOUL GURU:
Zane Zacharoff(bass cl)Wally Richardson,Everett Barksdale(g)Richard
Davis(b)Orville Mason(el b)Robert "Bobby" Donaldson(dm)Montego Joe
(conga,Indian dm).
Supervision:Cal Lampley   NYC,February 5,1968

    Monday,Monday   PR7569
    Lonely river   -
    Soul guru   -
    Senor boogaloo   -
    Khyber Pass boogaloo   -

Ernie Hayes(p)Wally Richardson(g)Jimmy Lewis(b)Bobby Donaldson(dm).
Supervision:Cal Lampley   NYC,February 7,1968

    Willow weep for me   unissued
    Surf side shuffle   PR7569
    Elbow blues   -
    Square heels,white stockings   -
    Ja-vi-gin boogaloo   unissued
    Church is out   -

TRUDY PITTS:
Trudy Pitts(org,vo)Wilbert Longmire(g)Bill Carney(dm).
Supervision:Cal Lampley   NYC,February 8,1968

    My waltz   PR7560
    Come dawn   -
    Trees   unissued
    Love for sale   PR7560
    Satin doll   -
    Please keep my dreams   -
    The shadow of your smile   -
    Lil' darlin'   -

RICHARD "GROOVE" HOLMES-THE GROOVER:
Richard "Groove" Holmes(org)Earl Maddox,George Freeman(g)Billy Jackson
(dm).
Supervision:Cal Lampley   NYC,February 14,1968

    Speak low   PR7570,PR7768
    Blue moon   -
    Walrus   -
    I'll remember April   -
    My scenery   -
    Just friends   -
    Hold on brother   unissued

DON PATTERSON-BOPPIN' AND BURNIN':
Howard McGhee(tp)Charles McPherson(as)Don Patterson(org)Pat Martino(g)
Billy James(dm).
Supervision:Don Schlitten   NYC,February 22,1968

    Pisces soul   PR7563
    Island fantasy   -
    Epistrophy   -
    Donna Lee   -   PR7772
    Now's the time   -

HAROLD MABERN-A FEW MILES FROM MEMPHIS:
George Coleman,Buddy Terry(ts)Harold Mabern(p)William Lee(b)Walter
Perkins(dm).
Supervision:Cal Lampley   NYC,March 11,1968

    A treat for Bea   Pr.   PR7568
    A few miles from Memphis   Pr.45-714   -
    B and B   -
    Syden blue   -
    To wane   -
    A kind of a hush   -
    Walkin' back   -

HOUSTON PERSON-BLUE ODYSSEY:
Curtis Fuller(tb)Houston Person(ts)Pepper Adams(bs)Cedar Walton(p,arr)
Bob Cranshaw(b)Frankie Jones(dm).
Supervision:Don Schlitten   NYC,March 12,1968

    Blue odyssey   PR7566,PR7779
    Holy land   -
    I love you yes I do   -
    Funky London   -
    Please send me someone to love   -
    Starr burst   -

WILLIS JACKSON-STAR BAG:
Willis Jackson(ts)Trudy Pitts(org)Bill Jennings(g)Jimmy Lewis(el b)
Bobby Donaldson(dm)Victor Allende(conga).
Supervision:Cal Lampley   NYC,March 22,1968

    More   PR7571
    Yellow days   -
    The girl from Ipanema   -
    Smoke rings   -
    Star bag   -
    Good to the damn bone   -

BYRDIE GREEN- SISTER BYRDIE:
Byrdie Green(vo)with Johnny "Hammond" Smith(org)Wally Richardson(g)
Jimmy Lewis(b)John Harris(dm)Lynn Daniels,Lucille Burgess,Ann Craig
(vocal ensemble).
Supervision:Cal Lampley   NYC,March 22,1968

    Where there's a will   PR7574
    You'll never walk alone   -
    Since you've been gone   -
    Let them talk   -
    When a woman's in love   -

ILLINOIS JACQUET ON PRESTIGE!-BOTTOMS UP:
Illinois Jacquet(ts)Barry Harris(p)Ben Tucker(b)Alan Dawson(dm).
Supervision:Don Schlitten   NYC,March 26,1968

    Sassy   Pr.   PR7575
    You left me alone   -   P-24057
    Bottoms up   Pr.45-701   -   -
    Jivin' with Jack the bellboy   -
    Port of Rico   Pr.45-701   -   P-24057
    Ghost of a chance   -   -
    Our delight   -   -
    Don't blame me   unissued

BYRDIE GREEN-SISTER BYRDIE:
Byrdie Green(vo)with Johnny "Hammond" Smith(org)Wally Richardson(g)
Jimmy Lewis(b)John Harris(dm)Lynn Daniels,Lucille Burgess,Ann Craig
(vocal ensemble).
Supervision:Cal Lampley   NYC,April 1,1968

        You'd better sit down kids   PR7574
        Return of the prodigal son   -
        Muddy waters   -
        I can't love without you   -
        Doctor Feelgood   -
        Night time is the right time   -

JAKI BYARD with STRINGS!:
Ray Nance(vo,v)Jaki Byard(p,org-1)George Benson(g)Ron Carter(cello)
Richard Davis(b)Alan Dawson(dm,vb-2).
Supervision:Don Schlitten   NYC,April 2,1968

        Music to watch girls by-1   PR7573
        Cat's cradle conference rag-2   -
        Falling rains of life-2   -
        How high the moon   -
        Ray's blues voRN   -

PUCHO AND THE LATIN SOUL BROS.-HEAT!:
Al Pazant(tp)Eddie Pazant(ts,bs,fl)William Bivens(vb)Neal Creque(p,org)
Jimmy Phillips(b)Norberto Apellaniz(bongo)Cecil Jackson(conga)Henry
"Pucho" Brown(timbales,leader)Jackie Soul(vo)& strings.
Supervision:Don Schlitten   NYC,April 23,1968

        Payin' dues   Pr.   PR7572,PR7679
        I can't stop loving you   -   -
        Let love find you   -   -
        The presence of your heart   -
        Candied jam heat   Pr.45-702 -
        Georgia on my mind   -   -   PR7679
        Wanderin' rose   -
        Psychedelic Pucho   -

DUKE EDWARDS and THE YOUNG ONES-IS IT TOO LATE?:
Richard Woodson(tb)Bernard Moore(ts,ss,fl)Doug Richardson(ts)Julian
Brown(org)Wayne Prue(g)Clayton Johnson(dm)Duke Edwards(vo,perc) and
all on vocal ensemble.
Supervision:Cal Lampley   Montreal(Canada),April 29,1968

        Man   Pr.   PR7590
        Is it too late   Pr.45-706   -

Same.
Supervision:Cal Lampley   Montreal(Canada),April 30,1968

        Don't cry baby   PR7590
        Black elephant   -
        Why   -
        Reach for a star   -

SONNY CRISS ORCHESTRA-SONNY'S DREAM:
Conte Candoli(tp)Dick Nash(tb)Ray Draper(tu)Sonny Criss(as,ss)David
Sheer(as)Teddy Edwards(ts)Pete Christlieb(bs)Tommy Flanagan(p)Al
McKibbon(b)Everett Brown(dm)Horace Tapscott(comp,arr).
Supervision:Don Schlitten   LA,May 8,1968

        Sonny's dream   PR7576
        The golden pearl   -
        The black apostles   -
        Ballad for Samuel   -
        Sandy and Niles   -
        Daughter of Cochise   -
        Sonny's dream   -

[186]

THE EXCITEMENT OF TRUDY PITTS:
Trudy Pitts(org)Wilbert Longmire(g)Bill Carney(dm).
Supervision:Cal Lampley
                         Live at Baron's,NYC,May 24,1968

    Untitled original   unissued
    Never my love   Pr.   PR7583
    Autumn leaves   -
    W.T.Blues   -
    Maiden voyage   unissued
    Trudy 'n ' blue   Pr.45-705,PR7583
    The look of love   unissued
    untitled original bossa nova -

CEDAR WALTON-SPECTRUM:
Blue Mitchell(tp)Clifford Jordan(ts)Cedar Walton(p)Richard Davis(b)
Jack De Johnette(dm).
Supervision:Don Schlitten   NYC,May 24,1968

    Lady Charlotte   PR7591
    Higgins holler   -
    Spectrum   -
    Jake's milkshakes   -
    Days of wine and roses-1   -

-1:p,b,dm only.

BARRY HARRIS-BULL'S EYE:
Kenny Dorham(tp)Charles McPherson(ts)Pepper Adams(bs)Barry Harris(p)
Paul Chambers(b)Billy Higgins(dm).
Supervision:Don Schlitten   NYC,June 4,1968

    Bull's eye   PR7600
    Clockwise-1   -
    Off Monk   -
    Barengo   -
    Off minor-1   -
    Oh,so Basal   -

-1:p,b,dm only.

DON PATTERSON-OPUS DE DON:
Blue Mitchell(tp)Junior Cook(ts)Don Patterson(org)Pat Martino(g)Billy
James(dm).
Supervision:Don Schlitten   NYC,June 5,1968

    Dem New York dues   PR7577
    Sir John   -
    Opus de Don   -
    Little Shannon   -   PR7772
    Stairway to the stars   -

FREDDIE McCOY-LISTEN HERE:
Edward Williams,Wilbur "Dud" Bascomb(tp)Melba Liston,Quentin Jackson
(tb)Freddie McCoy(vb)JoAnne Brackeen(el p,org)Wally Richardson(g)Jimmy
Lewis(el b)Bernard Purdie(dm)Gene Walker(as)Montego Joe(conga).
Supervision:Cal Lampley   NYC,June 10,1968

    Don't tell me that   PR7582
    MacArthur Park   -

Freddie McCoy(vb)JoAnne Brackeen(el p)Raymond McKinney(b)Al Dreares(dm)
Supervision:Cal Lampley   NYC,June 10,1968

    Listen here   Pr.45-712,PR7582,PR7706
    Love for sale   -
    Short circuit   -
    Stone wall   -

PAT MARTINO-BAIYINA(THE CLEAR EVIDENCE):
Gregory Herbert(as,fl)Pat Martino,Bobby Rose(g)Richard Davis(b)Charlie
Persip(dm)Reggie Ferguson(tabla)Balakrishna(tamboura).
Supervision:Don Schlitten   NYC,June 11,1968

    Baiyina   PR7589
    Distant land   -
    Where   love's a grown up God   -
    Israfel   -

JOHNNY "HAMMOND" SMITH-NASTY:
Houston Person(ts)Johnny "Hammond" Smith(org)John Abercrombie(g)Grady
Tate(dm).
Supervision:Cal Lampley   NYC,June 18,1968

    If I were a bell   PR7588
    Speak low   -
    Song for my father   -
    Unchained melody   -
    Nasty   -
    Four bowls of soup   -

SONNY CRISS-ROCKIN' IN RHYTHM:
Sonny Criss(as)Eddie Green(p)Bob Cranshaw(b)Alan Dawson(dm).
Supervision:Don Schlitten   NYC,July 2,1968

    Misty roses   Pr.   PR7610
    Eleanor Rigby   Pr.45-703   -   PR7742
    Rockin' in rhythm   -   -
    The masquerade is over   -
    When the sun comes out   -
    Sunnymoon for two   -

CHARLES KYNARD-PROFESSOR SOUL:
Charles Kynard(org)Cal Green(g)Johnny Kirkwood(dm).
Supervision:Bob Porter   LA,August 6,1968

    By the time I get to Phoenix PR7599
    J.C.   -
    Christo redentor   -
    Sister Lovie   -
    Professor soul   -
    Delilah   -

ERIC KLOSS-SKY SHADOWS:
Eric Kloss(as,ts)Jaki Byard(p)Pat Martino(g)Bob Cranshaw(b)Jack De
Johnette(dm).
Supervision:Don Schlitten   NYC,August 13,1968

    The girl with the fall in her hair PR7594
    In a country soul garden   -
    Sky shadows   -
    I'll give you everything   -
    January's child   -

ILLINOIS JACQUET-THE KING!:
Joe Newman(tp)Illinois Jacquet(ts,bassoon-1)Milt Buckner(p,org)Billy
Butler(g)Al Lucas(b,tu)Joe Jones(dm)Montego Joe(conga,bongos).
Supervision:Don Schlitten   NYC,August 20,1968

    A haunting melody   Pr.45-708,PR7597
    I wish I knew how it would feel
                   to be free   -
    The king   Pr.45-708   -   P-24057
    How high the moon   -   -
    Blue and sentimental   -   -
    Caravan-1   -

RICHARD "GROOVE" HOLMES-THAT HEALIN' FEELIN':
Rusty Bryant(as,ts)Richard "Groove" Holmes(org)Billy Butler(g)Herbie
Lovelle(dm).
Supervision:Bob Porter   NYC,August 26,1968

    That healin' feelin'   Pr.   PR7601
    See see rider   Pr.45-718 -
    Irene court   -
    Castle rock   -
    Laura   -
    On a clear day   -   PR7768

CHARLES McPHERSON-HORIZONS:
Charles McPherson(as)Nasir Rashid Hafiz(vb)Cedar Walton(p)Pat Martino
(g)Walter Booker(b)Billy Higgins(dm).
Supervision:Don Schlitten   NYC,August 27,1968

    Horizons   PR7603
    Ain't that somethin'   -
    Night eyes   -
    She loves me   -
    I should care   -
    Lush life   -

WILLIS JACKSON-SWIVEL HIPS:
Willis Jackson(ts)Jackie Ivory(p)Bill Jennings(g)Ben Tucker(b)Jerry
Potter(dm)Ralph Dorsey(conga).
Supervision:Bob Porter   NYC,September 9,1968

    Florence of Arabia   Pr.   PR7602
    Win,lose or draw   -
    By the time I get to Phoenix   -
    Swivel hips   Pr.45-719 -
    You understand me?   -
    Chug-a-mug   unissued
    In a mellotone   PR7602

THE JAKI BYARD EXPERIENCE:
Roland Kirk(cl,ts,manzello,whistle,kirkbam)Jaki Byard(p)Richard Davis
(b)Alan Dawson(dm).
Supervision:Don Schlitten   NYC,September 17,1968

    Evidence   PR7615
    Teach me tonight   -
    Parisian thoroughfare   -
    Shine on me-1   -
    Hazy Eve   -
    Memories of you-1   -

-1:Davis & Dawson out. All titles also issued on P-24080.

SONNY STITT-SOUL ELECTRICITY!:
Sonny Stitt(as,ts,el sax)Don Patterson(org)Billy Butler(g)Billy James
(dm).
Supervision:Bob Porter   NYC,September 23,1968

    Stella by starlight   Pr.   PR7635
    P.S. I love you   -
    Lover man   Pr.45-710 -
    Strike up the band
    Candy   Pr.45-710 -
    All the things you are   -
    Over the rainbow   -
    Bye bye blackbird   -

DON PATTERSON-FUNK YOU:
Charles McPherson(as)Sonny Stitt(as,ts)Don Patterson(org)Pat Martino
(g)Billy James(dm).
Supervision:Don Schlitten   NYC,September 24,1968

    My man string   PR7613
    Airegin   -
    Ratio plus proportion   -   PR7772
    Funk in 3/4   -
    Little angie   -
    It's you or no one   -

EDDIE JEFFERSON-BODY AND SOUL:
Dave Burns(tp)James Moody(ts,fl)Barry Harris(p)Steve Davis(b)Bill
English(dm)Eddie Jefferson(vo)Ed Williams(spoken introduction).
Supervision:Don Schlitten   NYC,September 27,1968

    Filthy McNasty   Pr.45-716,PR7619
    Now's the time   -
    So what   -
    Body and soul   -
    Mercy,mercy,mercy   Pr.45-716   -
    Psychedelic Sally   Pr.45-709   -
    There I go,there I go again
    See if you can get to that Pr.45-709   -
    Oh Gee   -

JOE JONES-MY FIRE:
Harold Mabern(p)Joe Jones(g)Peck Morrison(b)Bill English(dm)Richard
Landrum(conga).
Supervision:Bob Porter   NYC,October 21,1968

    For Big Hal   PR7617
    Take all   -
    Light my fire   -
    Time after time   -
    St.James infirmary   -
    Ivan the Terrible   -

WILLIS JACKSON-GATOR'S GROOVE:
Willis Jackson(ts)Jackie Ivory(p)Bill Jennings(g)Jerry Potter(dm)Richard
Landrum(conga).
Supervision:Bob Porter   NYC,November 11,1968

    Stolen sweets   PR7648
    A day in the life of a fool -
    Blue Jays   -
    Brother Ray   -
    This is the way I feel   -
    Long tall Dexter   -

HOUSTON PERSON-SOUL DANCE:
Houston Person(ts)Billy Gardner(org)Joe Jones(g)Frankie Jones(dm).
Supervision:Bob Porter   NYC,November 18,1968

    Groovin' and groovin'   Pr.   PR7621
    Soul dance   Pr.45-713   -
    Never let me go   -
    Blue seven   -
    What a difference a day made -
    Snake eyes   Pr.45-713   -
    Here's that rainy day   -   PR7779
    Tear drops from my eyes   -

PEPPER ADAMS/ZOOT SIMS-ENCOUNTER!:
Zoot Sims(ts)Pepper Adams(bs)Tommy Flanagan(p)Ron Carter(b)Elvin Jones
(dm).
Supervision:Fred Norsworthy   NYC,December 11 & 12,1968

    In and out   PR7677
    Star-crossed lovers   -
    Cindy's tune   -
    Serenity   -
    I've just seen her   -
    Elusive   -
    Punjab   -
    Verdandi   -

THIS IS BILLY BUTLER!:
Houston Person(ts)Ernie Hayes(p,org)Billy Butler(g,bass g)Bob Bushnell
(el b)Rudy Collins(dm).
Supervision:Bob Porter   NYC,December 16,1968

    The Twang thang   PR7622
    Work song   -
    She is my inspiration   -
    Bass-ic blues   -
    The soul roll   -
    Cherry   -

HAROLD MABERN-RAKIN' AND SCRAPIN':
Blue Mitchell(tp)George Coleman(ts)Harold Mabern(p,el p-1)Bill Lee(b)
Hugh Walker(dm).   NYC,December 23,1968
Supervision:Bob Porter

    Rakin' and scrapin'   Pr.45-720,PR7624
    Such is life   -
    Aon   -
    I heard it through the grapevine-1
                                     Pr.45-714 -
    Valerie   -

ERIC KLOSS-IN THE LAND OF THE GIANTS:
Eric Kloss(as)Booker Ervin(ts)Jaki Byard(p)Richard Davis(b)Alan Dawson
(dm).
Supervision:Don Schlitten   NYC,January 2,1969

    Things ain't what they used to be PR7627
    Sock it to me Socrates   -
    Summertime   -
    So what   -
    Santa Clink   unissued
    When two lovers touch   PR7627

CEDAR WALTON-THE ELECTRIC BOOGALOO SONG:
Blue Mitchell(tp)Clifford Jordan(ts)Cedar Walton(p,el p)Bob Cranshaw(b)
Mickey Roker(dm).
Supervision:Don Schlitten   NYC,January 14,1969

    Electric boogaloo song   PR7618
    Sabbatical   -
    A shorter glimpse   unissued
    Impressions of Scandinavia   PR7618
    You stepped out of a dream   -
    Con alma   unissued
    Ugetsu   PR7618

SONNY CRISS-I'LL CATCH THE SUN:
Sonny Criss(as)Hampton Hawes(p)Monty Budwig(b)Shelly Manne(dm).
Supervision:Don Schlitten   LA,January 20,1969

    I'll catch the sun   PR7628
    I thought about you   -
    California screamin'   -
    Cry me a river   -
    Don't rain on my parade   -
    Blue sunset   -

PUCHO AND THE LATIN SOUL BROS.-DATELINE:
Al Pazant(tp)Kiane Zawadi,Barry Rogers(tb)Eddie Pazant(ts,fl)William
Bivens(vb)Neal Creque(p)William Allen(b)Joe Armstrong(dm)Norberto
Apellaniz(bongos)Richard Landrum(conga)Henry "Pucho" Brown(timbales,
leader).
Supervision:Don Schlitten   NYC,February 11,1969

    Yambo   PR7616
    Used to Louis   -
    Dateline   -
    Ain't nothin' can't happen   -
    Bim   -
    How did it happen   -

JAMES MOODY-DON'T LOOK AWAY NOW!:
James Moody(as,ts)Barry Harris(p)Bob Cranshaw(el b)Alan Dawson(dm)
Eddie Jefferson(vo).
Supervision:Don Schlitten   NYC,February 14,1969

    Don't look away now   PR7625,PR24015
    Hear me   -
    Hey,Herb!Where's Alpert? voEJ   -   PR24015
    Last train from Overbrook   -   -
    Easy living   -
    Hey there   unissued
    Darben the Red Foxx   PR7625
    When I fall in love   -

RUSTY BRYANT RETURNS:
Rusty Bryant(ts)Sonny Phillips(org)Grant Green(g)Bob Bushnell(b)Herb
Lovelle(dm).
Supervision:Bob Porter   NYC,February 17,1969

    Streak-o-lean   Pr.   PR7626
    Night flight   -
    Zoo boogaloo   Pr.45-728 -
    The cat   -
    Ready Rusty?   -
    All day long   -

CHARLES KYNARD-THE SOUL BROTHERHOOD:
Blue Mitchell(tp)David "Fathead" Newman(ts)Charles Kynard(org)Grant
Green(g)Jimmy Lewis(el b)Mickey Roker(dm).
Supervision:Bob Porter   NYC,March 10,1969

    The soul brotherhood   PR7630
    Jealjon   -
    Piece o' pisces   -
    Big City   -
    Blue Farouk   -

ILLINOIS JACQUET BIG BAND-THE SOUL EXPLOSION:
Ernie Royal,Joe Newman,Russell Jacquet(tp)Matthew Gee(tb)Illinois
Jacquet(ts)Frank Foster(ts,arr)Cecil Payne(bs)Milt Buckner(p,org,arr)
Wally Richardson(g)Al Lucas(b)Al Foster(dm)Jimmy Mundy(arr).
Supervision:Don Schlitten   NYC,March 25,1969

        The eighteenth hole   PR7629
        St.Louis blues   -   P-24057
        The soul explosion   -   45-726
        After hours   -   P-24057
        Still king   unissued
        I'm a fool to want you   PR7629,P-24057

DEXTER GORDON QUARTET PLUS GUEST:
Dexter Gordon,James Moody(ts)Barry Harris(p)Buster Williams(b)Albert
"Tootie" Heath(dm).
Supervision:Don Schlitten   NYC,April 2,1969

        Montmartre   PR7623,P-24087
        Lady Bird   PR7680   -
        Sticky wicket   -   -

Moody out.
Supervision:Don Schlitten   NYC,April 4,1969

        Those were the days   PR7623,P-24087
        Stanley the steamer   -   -
        The rainbow people   -   -
        Boston Bernie   PR7680   -
        Meditation   -   -
        Fried bananas   -   -
        Dinner for one please James   unissued

JOHNNY "HAMMOND" SMITH-SOUL TALK:
Rusty Bryant(as,ts,el sax)Johnny "Hammond" Smith(org)Wally Richardson
(g)Bob Bushnell(b)Bernard Purdie(dm).
Supervision:Bob Porter   NYC,May 19,1969

        This guy's in love with you   Pr.   PR7681
        Soul talk   Pr.45-725   -
        Purdie dirty   -
        untitled blues   unissued
        All soul   PR7681
        Danny boy   unissued
        Up to date   PR7681

DON PATTERSON-OH HAPPY DAY!:
Virgil Jones(tp)George Coleman-1,Houston Person(ts)Don Patterson(org)
Frankie Jones(dm).
Supervision:Bob Porter   NYC,June 2,1969

        Oh happy day   Pr.45-717,PR7640
        Blue 'n' boogie-1   -
        Perdido-1   -   PR7772
        Hip trip-1   -
        Good time theme   -
        Blues for Mom-1   PR7852

CEDAR WALTON-SOUL CYCLE:
James Moody(ts-1,fl-2)Cedar Walton(p,el p)Rudy Stevenson(g)Reggie
Workman(b)Albert "Tootie" Heath(dm).
Supervision:Don Schlutten   NYC,June 25,1969

        I should care-2   PR7693
        Quiet dawn-2   -
        My cherie amour-2   -
        Sundown express-1   -
        Easy walker-3   -
        Lil' darlin'   unissued
        Pensativa-3   PR7693

-3:p,b,dm only.

HAROLD MABERN-WORKIN' AND WAILIN':
Virgil Jones(tp,flh-1)George Coleman(ts)Harold Mabern(p,el p-2)Buster
Williams(b)Leo Morris(Idris Muhammad)(dm).
Supervision:Bob Porter   NYC,June 30,1969

    Too busy thinking about my baby-2 PR7687
    A time for love-1   -
    Waltzing westward   -
    I can't understand what I see in you -
    Strozier's mode   -
    Blues for Phineas   -

ERIC KLOSS-TO HEAR IS TO SEE:
Eric Kloss(as,ts,overdubbing unison)Chick Corea(p,el p)Dave Holland(b)
Jack De Johnette(dm).
Supervision:Don Schlitten   NYC,July 22,1969

    Lorastone   PR7689
    Children of the morning   -
    Stone groove   -
    Cynara   -
    The kingdom within   -
    To hear is to see   -
    Free improvisation   unissued

JAKI BYARD-SOLO PIANO:
Jaki Byard(p).
Supervision:Don Schlitten   NYC,July 31,1969

    Seasons   PR7686
    Hello young lovers   -
    New Orleans strut   -
    Spanish tinge No.2   -
    The Hollis stomp   -
    Top of the Gate rag   -
    Basin Street ballad   -
    Medley:I know a place/Let   -
       the good times roll   -
    Do you know what it means to
          miss New Orleans   -

JOE JONES-BOOGALOO JOE:
Rusty Bryant(ts)Sonny Phillips(org,el p)Joe Jones(g)Eddie Mathias(el b)
Bernard Purdie(dm).
Supervision:Bob Porter   NYC,August 4,1969

    Boogaloo Joe   PR7697
    Atlantic City soul   -
    Boardwalk blues   -
    6:30 blues   -
    People are talking   -
    Dream on a little dreamer   -

CHARLES KYNARD-REELIN' WITH THE FEELIN':
Wilton Felder(ts)Charles Kynard(org)Joe Pass(g)Carol Kaye(el b)Paul
Humphrey(dm).
Supervision:Bob Porter   NYC,August 11,1969

    Be my love   PR7688
    Soul reggae   -
    Slowburn   -
    Stomp   -
    Reelin' with the feelin'   -
    Boogalooin'   -

EDDIE JEFFERSON-COME ALONG WITH ME:
Bill Hardman(tp)Charles McPherson(as)Barry Harris(p)Gene Taylor(b)
Bill English(dm)Eddie Jefferson(vo).
Supervision:Don Schlitten   NYC,August 12,1969

            Baby girl-1   PR7698
            Come along with me   -
            When you're smiling   -
            Son of the preacher man   -
            The preacher   -
            Please leave me alone   -
            Yardbird suite   -
            Dexter digs in   -

-1:Hardman & McPherson out.

HOUSTON PERSON-GOODNESS!:
Houston Person(ts)Sonny Phillips(org)Billy Butler(g)Bob Bushnell(el b)
Frankie Jones(dm)Buddy Caldwell(conga).
Supervision:Bob Porter   NYC,August 25,1969

            Hard times   Pr.   PR7678
            Goodness   Pr.45-730 -
            Jamilah   -   -   PR7779
            Brother H.   -
            Close your eyes   -
            Hey driver!   -

PR7678=PR10027.

DON PATTERSON QUARTET:
Sonny Stitt(ts,el sax)Don Patterson(org)Grant Green(g)Billy James(dm).
Supervision:Bob Porter   NYC,September 15,1969

            Alexander's ragtime band   PR7738
            Good bait   PR7816
            Creepin' home   PR7738
            Brothers 4   -
            Starry night   PR7816
            Donnybrook   -
            St.Thomas   -
            Mud turtle   -
            Tune up   PR7852
            Walk on by   PR7738

ILLINOIS JACQUET-THE BLUES:THAT'S ME!:
Illinois Jacquet(ts,bassoon-1)Wynton Kelly(p)Tiny Grimes(g)Buster
Williams(b)Oliver Jackson(dm).
Supervision:Don Schlitten   NYC,September 16,1969

            Still king   PR7731
            For once in my life   -   P-24057
            Everyday I have the blues   -   -
            The blues:that's me !   -
            The galloping latin   -
            'Round midnight-1   -   P-24057

BILLY BUTLER-GUITAR SOUL:
Seldon Powell(fl-1,el sax)Sonny Phillips(org)Billy Butler(g-2,classic
g-3,bass g-4)Bob Bushnell(el b)Specs Powell(dm).
Supervision:Bob Porter   NYC,September 22,1969

            The thumb-1,4   PR7734
            Golden earrings-3,5   -
            B and B calypso-4   -
            Blow for the crossing-4   -
            Medley:Autumn nocturne/You go   -
               to my head-3,5
            Honky tonk-3   -
            Seven come eleven-3   -

[195]

-5:Billy Butler alone.

TAL FARLOW RETURNS:
John Scully(p)Tal Farlow(g)Jack Six(b)Alan Dawson(dm).
Supervision:Don Schlitten   NYC,September 23,1969

       Summertime   PR7732
       My romance   -
       I'll remember April   -
       Sometime ago   -
       Straight no chaser   -
       Crazy he calls me   -
       Darn that dream   -

All titles also issued on P-24042.

RUSTY BRYANT-NIGHT TRAIN NOW!:
Rusty Bryant(as,ts,el sax)Jimmy Carter(org)Joe Jones(g)Eddie Mathias(b)
Bernard Purdie(dm).
Supervision:Bob Porter   NYC,October 6,1969

       Funky Mama-2   PR7735
       With these hands-1   -
       Night train-2   -
       Cootie boogaloo-2,3   -
       Funky rabbits-1,3   -
       Home fries-2,3   -

-1:as;-2:ts;-3:el sax.

SONNY PHILLIPS-SURE 'NUFF:
Virgil Jones-1(tp)Houston Person(ts)Sonny Phillips(org)Joe Jones(g)Bob
Bushnell(el b)Bernard Purdie(dm).
Supervision:Bob Porter   NYC,October 20,1969

       Sure 'nuff,sure 'nuff-1 PR7737
       Mobile to Chicago-1   -
       Be yourself-1   -
       The other blues   -
       Oleo   -
       Two different worlds   rejected

SONNY STITT-NIGHT LETTER:
Sonny Stitt(el sax)Gene Ludwig(org)Pat Martino(g)Randy Gelispie(dm).
Supervision:Bob Porter   NYC,October 27,1969

       Blue string   PR7759
       Sleepy time down South   -
       You'll never know   -
       String and the Jug   -
       Night letter   -
       Pretend   -
       Stitt's tune   -

GENE AMMONS-THE BOSS IS BACK:
Gene Ammons,Prince James-1,Houston Person-2(ts)Junior Mance(p)Buster
Williams(b)Frankie Jones(dm)Candido Camero(conga).
Supervision:Bob Porter   NYC,November 10,1969

       Tastin' the Jug   Pr.   PR7739
       I wonder   -
       Ger-ru-1   PR7792
       Here's that rainy day   PR7739
       Madame Queen   Pr.45-737 -
       The jungle boss-1,2   Pr.45-729 -

PR7739=PR10023;PR7792=PR10021.

GENE AMMONS-BROTHER JUG!:
Gene Ammons(ts)Sonny Phillips(org)Billy Butler-1(g)Bob Bushnell(el b)
Bernard Purdie(dm).
Supervision:Bob Porter   NYC,November 11,1969

        Jungle strut-1   Pr.45-737,PR7792,P-10084,PR10021
        Didn't we   Pr.45-734 -   -   -
        Real gone guy   -   -
        Feelin' good   PR7739,PR10023
        Blue velvet   PR7792,PR10021
        Son of a preacher man-1   Pr.45-734 -   -

BARRY HARRIS TRIO-MAGNIFICENT:
Barry Harris(p)Ron Carter(b)Leroy Williams(dm).
Supervision:Don Schlitten   NYC,November 25,1969

        You sweet and fancy lady   PR7733
        Vonce   -
        Ah-leu-cha   -
        Bean and the boys   -
        Sun dance   -
        Just open your heart   -
        I'll keep loving you   -
        My old flame   -
        Dexterity   -
        These foolish things   -

CHARLIE EARLAND-BLACK TALK:
Virgil Jones(tp)Houston Person(ts)Charlie Earland(org)Melvin Sparks(g)
Leo Morris(Idris Muhammad)(dm)Buddy Caldwell-1(conga).
Supervision:Bob Porter   NYC,December 15,1969

        Here comes Charlie   PR7758
        Black talk   -   45-731
        Aquarius   -
        More today than yesterday-1 -   45-732
        The mighty burner-1   -   -

PR7758=PR10024.

JOHNNY "HAMMOND" SMITH-BLACK FEELING:
Virgil Jones(tp)Rusty Bryant(ts)Johnny "Hammond" Smith(org)Wally
Richardson(g)Jimmy Lewis(b)Bernard Purdie(dm).
Supervision:Bob Porter   NYC,December 22,1969

        J.H.Boogaloo   PR7736
        Black feeling-1   -
        Dig on it-1   -
        When sunny gets blue   -
        Kindra-1,2   -
        Soul talk-1970   -

-1:Leo Johnson(ts)added;-2:Bryant out.

CHARLES McPHERSON-McPHERSON'S MOOD:
Charles McPherson(as)Barry Harris(p)Buster Williams(b)Roy Brooks(dm).
Supervision:Don Schlitten   NYC,December 23,1969

        McPherson's mood   PR7743
        Explorations   -
        Mish-mash-bash   -
        I get a kick out of you   -
        My cherie amour   -
        Opalescence   -

ERIC KLOSS-CONSCIOUSNESS!:
Eric Kloss(as,ts)Chick Corea(el p)Pat Martino(g)Dave Holland(b)Jack
De Johnette(dm).
Supervision:Don Schlitten   NYC,January 6,1970

    Kay   PR7793
    Sunshine superman   -
    Outward wisdom   -
    Consciousness   -
    Song to aging children   -

PUCHO & THE LATIN SOUL BROTHERS-JUNGLE FIRE:
Al Pazant(tp)Eddie Pazant(ts)Seldon Powell(ts,fl,el sax)William Bivens
(vb,perc)Neal Creque(el p)Billy Butler(g)Seborn Westbrook(el b)Bernard
Purdie(dm)Henry "Pucho" Brown(timbales,leader)Joe Armstrong(conga)
Norberto Apellaniz(bongo)Sonny Phillips(arr).
Supervision:Bob Porter   NYC,January 12,1970

    Friendship train   PR7765
    Got myself a good man   -
    Jamilah   -
    The spokerman   -
    Cloud 9   -

HAROLD MABERN-GREASY KID STUFF:
Lee Morgan(tp)Hubert Laws(ts,fl)Harold Mabern(p)Joe Jones-1(g)Buster
Williams(b,el b)Idris Muhammad(Leo Morris)(dm).
Supervision:Bob Porter   NYC,January 26,1970

    I want you back-1   PR7764
    Greasy kid stuff   -
    Alex the great   -
    XKE   -
    John Neely-Beautiful people   -
    I haven't got anything better
            to do   -

GENE AMMONS:
Gene Ammons(ts)Wynton Kelly(p)George Duvivier(b)Rudy Collins(dm)Henry
"Pucho" Brown-1(conga).
Supervision:Bob Porter   NYC,February 2,1970

    Calypso blues-1   unissued
    Night lights   -
    Nature boy   -
    The Christmas song   PR24046
    Sweet Lorraine   unissued
    Lush life   -

BOOGALOO JOE JONES-RIGHT ON BROTHER:
Rusty Bryant(as,ts)Charlie Earland(org)Joe Jones(g)Jimmy Lewis(el b)
Bernard Purdie(dm).
Supervision:Bob Porter   NYC,February 16,1970

    Right on   Pr.45-733,PR7766
    Someday we'll be together   -   -
    Things ain't what they used to be -
    Let it be me   -
    Poppin'   -
    Brown bag   -

PR7766=PR10025.

HOUSTON PERSON-THE TRUTH!:
Houston Person(ts)Sonny Phillips(org)Billy Butler(g)Bob Bushnell(el b)
Frankie Jones(dm)Buddy Caldwell(conga).
Supervision:Bob Porter   NYC,February 23,1970
        Wadin'   Pr.45-735,PR7767
        The pulpit   -
        Cissy strut   -
        On the Avenue   -
        If I ruled the world   -
        For your love   Pr.45-735   -

PR7767=PR10026.

PAT MARTINO-DESPERADO:
Eddie Greene(el p)Pat Martino(12 string g)Tyrone Brown(el b)Sherman
Ferguson(dm).
Supervision:Bob Porter   NYC,March 9,1970
        Express   PR7795
        Desperado   -
        Oleo   -
        Dearborn walk   -
        A portrait of Diana   -
        Blackjack-1   -

-1:Eric Kloss(ss)added.

CHARLES KYNARD-AFRO-DISIAC:
Houston Person(ts)Charles Kynard(org)Grant Green(g)Jimmy Lewis(el b)
Bernard Purdie(dm).
Supervision:Bob Porter   NYC,April 6,1970
        Afro-disiac   PR7796
        Chanson du nuit   -
        Sweetheart   -
        Odds on   -
        Belladonna   -
        Trippin'   -

BILLY BUTLER-YESTERDAY,TODAY & TOMORROW:
Jerome Richardson(ts,fl)Sonny Phillips(org,el p)Billy Butler,Everett
Barksdale,Bill Suyker(g)Chuck Rainey(el b)Jimmy Johnson(dm).
Supervision:Bob Porter   NYC,April 27,1970
        The Butler did it   PR7797
        Evening dreams   -
        C jam blues   rejected

SONNY PHILLIPS-BLACK MAGIC:
Eddie Pazant(ts)Sonny Phillips(org,el p)Melvin Sparks(g)Jimmy Lewis
(el b)Ben Dixon(dm)Buddy Caldwell(conga).
Supervision:Bob Porter   NYC,May 18,1970
        Make it plain   PR7799
        Bean pie   -
        I'm an old cowhand   -
        Wakin' up   -
        The brotherhood   -
        Over the rainbow   -

CHARLIE EARLAND-BLACK DROPS:
Virgil Jones(tp)Clayton Pruden(tb)Jimmy Heath(fl,ss,ts)Charlie Earland
(org)Maynard Parker(g)Jimmy Turner(dm).
Supervision:Bob Porter   NYC,June 1,1970

Lazybird	Pr.	PR7815
Letha		-
Buck green		-
Don't say goodbye		-
Sing a simple song	Pr.45-736	-
Raindrops keep falling on my head	-	-

PR7815=PR10029.

RUSTY BRYANT-SOUL LIBERATION:
Virgil Jones(tp)Rusty Bryant(as,ts)Charlie Earland(org)Melvin Sparks
(g)Idris Muhammad(dm).
Supervision:Bob Porter   NYC,June 15,1970

Cold duck time	Pr.	PR7798
Lou-Lou		-
Freeze dried soul		-
The ballad of Oren Bliss		-
Soul liberation	Pr.45-738	-

PR7798=PR10028.

BILLY BUTLER-YESTERDAY,TODAY AND TOMORROW:
Houston Person(ts)Ernie Hayes(org,el p)Billy Butler(g)Jimmy Lewis(el b)
Jimmy Johnson(dm).
Supervision:Bob Porter   NYC,June 29,1970

Dancing on the ceiling	PR7797
Yesterday,today & tomorrow	-
Girl talk	-
Hold it	-
Sweet Georgia Brown	-
In a mellotone	rejected

DEXTER GORDON-THE PANTHER!:
Dexter Gordon(ts)Tommy Flanagan(p)Larry Ridley(b)Alan Dawson(dm).
Supervision:Don Schlitten   NYC,July 7,1970

The panther	PR7829
Body and soul	-
Valse Robin	-
Mrs.Miniver	-
The Christmas song	-
The blues walk	-

PR7829=PR10030.

GENE AMMONS/DEXTER GORDON-THE CHASE!:
Gene Ammons-1,Dexter Gordon-2(ts)John Young(p)Cleveland Eaton(b)Steve
McCall(dm).
Supervision:Joe Segal
     (Afternoon set)North Park Hotel,Chicago,July 26,1970

Polka dots and moonbeams-2	PR10010
The happy blues-1	-

Gene Ammons,Dexter Gordon(ts)Jodie Christian(p)Rufus Reid(b)Wilbur
Campbell(dm)Vi Redd(vo).
Supervision:Joe Segal
     (Evening set)North Park Hotel,Chicago,July 26,1970

Lonesome lover blues No.1 voVR	PR10010
The chase	-

From previous sets:

```
        Lonesome lover blues No.2 voVR  unissued
        Wee dot-2                        PR24046
        Ballad medley:                   unissued
          My funny Valentine-1/            -
          Lover man-1/I can't get          -
          started-2/Misty-2                -
```

-1:Gordon out;-2:Ammons out.

SONNY PHILLIPS-BLACK ON BLACK:
Rusty Bryant(as,ts)Sonny Phillips(org)Melvin Sparks(g)Jimmy Lewis(el b)
Bernard Purdie(dm).
Supervision:Bob Porter   NYC,July 27,1970

```
        Check it out                    PR10007
        Proud Mary                        -
        The doll house                    -
        Black on black                    -
        Blues in Maude(s flat             -
        When I fall in love             rejected
```

DEXTER GORDON-THE JUMPIN' BLUES:
Dexter Gordon(ts)Wynton Kelly(p)Sam Jones(b)Roy Brooks(dm).
Supervision:Don Schlitten   NYC,August 27,1970

```
        Evergreenish                    PR10020
        Rhythm-a-ning-1                   -
        For sentimental reasons           -
        If you could see me now           -
        Star eyes                         -
        The jumpin' blues                 -
```

-1:issued as "Straight no chaser".

MELVIN SPARKS-SPARKS!:
Virgil Jones(tp)John Manning(ts)Leon Spencer Jr.(org)Melvin Sparks(g)
Idris Muhammad(dm).
Supervision:Bob Porter   NYC,September 14,1970

```
        Thank you                       Pr.45-739,PR10001
        Spill the wine                    -
        Charlie Brown-1                   -
        The stinker-1                     -
        I didn't know what time it was    -
```

-1:Houston Person(ts)added.

CHARLIE EARLAND-LIVING BLACK!:
Gary Chandler(tp)Grover Washington Jr.(ts)Charlie Earland(org)Maynard
Parker(g)Jesse Kilpatrick(dm)Buddy Caldwell(conga).
Supervision:Bob Porter   The Key Club,Newark,N.J.,September 17,1970

```
        Key Club cookout                PR10009
        Milestones                        -
        Killer Joe                        -
        Westbound No.9                    -
        More today than yesterday       unissued
        Message from a black man          -
        Don't let me lose this dream      -
        By the time I get to Phoenix      -
        untitled original                 -
        untitled original                 -
        untitled blues                    -
```

JOHNNY "HAMMOND" SMITH-HERE IT IS:
Houston Person(ts)Johnny "Hammond" Smith(org)James Clark(g)Jimmy Lewis
(el b)Eddie Gee(dm).
Supervision:Bob Porter   NYC,September 21,1970

        You made me so very happy   PR10002
        Stormy   -

Bernard Purdie(dm)replaces Gee.Same date.

        Here it is   PR10002
        Gina D   -
        Danny boy   -
        The Nubs   -

HOUSTON PERSON-PERSON TO PERSON:
Virgil Jones(tp)Houston Person(ts)Sonny Phillips(org,el p)Grant Green
(g)Jimmy Lewis(el b)Idris Muhammad(dm)Buddy Caldwell(conga).
Supervision:Bob Porter   NYC,October 12,1970

        Teardrops   Pr.   PR10003
        The son of my man   Pr.45-740   -
        Close to you   -   -
        Yester-me,yester-you,yesterday   -
        Drown in my own tears   -
        Up at Joes/Down at Jims   -

IDRIS MUHAMMAD-BLACK RHYTHM REVOLUTION:
Virgil Jones(tp)Clarence Thomas(ss,ts)Harold Mabern(el p)Melvin Sparks
(g)Jimmy Lewis(el b)Idris Muhammad(dm)Buddy Caldwell(conga).
Supervision:Bob Porter   NYC,November 2,1970

        By the Red Sea   PR10005
        Super bad   -
        Express yourself   -
        Soulful drums   -
        Wander   -

GENE AMMONS-THE BLACK CAT:
Gene Ammons(ts)Harold Mabern(p,el p-1)George Freeman(g)Ron Carter(b)
Idris Muhammad(dm).
Supervision:Bob Porter   NYC,November 11,1970

        Long long time-1   PR10006
        Something-1   -
        Jug eyes   -
        The black cat   -
        Piece to keep away evil spirits -
        Hi Ruth!   -

-1:9 violins,Bill Fisher(arr)overdubbed on.
                                       NYC,November 18,1970

BOOGALOO JOE JONES-NO WAY!:
Grover Washington Jr.(ts)Sonny Phillips(org,el p)Butch Cornell-1(org)
Joe Jones(g)Jimmy Lewis(el b)Bernard Purdie(dm).
Supervision:Bob Porter   NYC,November 23,1970

        No way   PR10004
        If you were mine   -
        Georgia on my mind   -
        I'll be there   -
        Sunshine alley-1   -
        Holdin' back-1   -

LEON SPENCER Jr.-SNEAK PREVIEW:
Virgil Jones(tp)Grover Washington Jr.(ts)Leon Spencer Jr.(org)Melvin
Sparks(g)Idris Muhammad(dm)Buddy Caldwell(conga).
Supervision:Bob Porter   NYC,December 7,1970

    First gravy   PR10011
    Sneak preview   -
    Message from the meters   -
    5-10-15-20   -
    Someday my prince will come   -
    The slide   -

CHARLES KYNARD-WA-TU-WA-ZUI:
Virgil Jones(tp)Rusty Bryant(ts)Charles Kynard(org,el p)Melvin Sparks
(g)Jimmy Lewis(el b)Idris Muhammad(dm).
Supervision:Bob Porter   NYC,December 14,1970

    Zebra walk   PR10008
    Wa-Tu-Wa-Zui   -
    Something   -
    Winter's child   -
    Change up   -
    Close to you   rejected

BILLY BUTLER-NIGHT LIFE:
Jesse Powell,Houston Person-1(ts)Johnny "Hammond" Smith(org,el p)Billy
Butler(g)Bob Bushnell(el b)Jimmy Johnson(dm).
Supervision:Bob Porter   NYC,December 21,1970

    Wave   PR7854
    Prelude to a kiss   -
    Peacock alley   -
    In a mellotone-1   -
    Watch what happens-1   -
    Night life   -

SONNY STITT-TURN IT ON!:
Virgil Jones(tp)Sonny Stitt(ts)Leon Spencer Jr.(org)Melvin Sparks(g)
Idris Muhammad(dm).
Supervision:Bob Porter   NYC,January 4,1971

    Miss Riverside   PR10012
    The Bar-B-Que man   -
    Turn it on   -
    Cry me a river-1   -
    There are such things-1   -

-1:Jones out.

BERNARD PURDIE-PURDIE GOOD:
Tippy Larkin(tp)Charlie Brown,Warren Daniels(ts)Harold Wheeler(el p)
Bill Nichols,Ted Dunbar(g)Gordon Edwards(el b)Bernard Purdie(dm)Norman
Pride(conga).
Supervision:Bob Porter   NYC,January 11,1971

    Everybody's talkin'   PR10013
    Cold sweat   -
    Montego Bay   -
    Wasteland   -
    You turn me on   -
    Purdie good   -

GENE AMMONS/SONNY STITT-YOU TALK THAT TALK!:
Gene Ammons,Sonny Stitt(ts)Leon Spencer(org)George Freeman(g)Idris
Muhammad(dm).
Supervision:Bob Porter   NYC,February 8,1971

    Katea's dance   PR10019
    Out of it   -
    The people's choice   -
    You talk that talk   -
    The sun died-1   -
    Body and soul-2   -

-1:Stitt out;-2:Ammons out.

RUSTY BRYANT-FIREEATER:
Rusty Bryant(ts)Leon Spencer Jr.(org)Wilbert Longmire(g)Idris Muhammad
(dm).
Supervision:Bob Porter   NYC,February 22,1971

    The Hooker   PR10014
    Mister S   -

Bill Mason(org)replaces Spencer.Same date.

    Free at last   PR10014
    Once I loved   unissued
    Fireeater   PR10014

MELVIN SPARKS-SPARKPLUG:
Virgil Jones(tp)Grover Washington Jr.(ts)Leon Spencer Jr.(org)Melvin
Sparks(g)Idris Muhammad(dm).
Supervision:Bob Porter   NYC,March 1,1971

    Who's goin' to take the weight PR10016
    Sparkplug   rejected

Reggie Roberts(org)replaces Spencer.
Supervision:Bob Porter   NYC,March 8,1971

    Sparkplug   PR10016
    Conjunction Mars   -
    Dig Dis   -
    Alone together   -

HOUSTON PERSON-HOUSTON EXPRESS:
Ernie Royal,Thad Jones,Harold "Money" Johnson(tp)Jack Jeffers,Garnett
Brown(tb)Harold Vick(fl,ts)Houston Person(ts)Babe Clark(bs)Jimmy Watson
(org)Paul Griffin(p,el p)Billy Butler(g)Gerry Jemmott(el b)Bernard
Purdie(dm)Buddy Caldwell(conga)Horace Ott(arr,cond).
Supervision:Bob Porter   NYC,April 8,1971

    Young,gifted and black   PR10017
    The Houston express   -
    Lift every voice   -
    Enjoy   -

Cecil Bridgewater(tp)Houston Person(ts)Babe Clark(bs)Jimmy Watson(org)
Ernie Hayes(org,el p)Billy Butler(g)Gerry Jemmott(el b)Bernard Purdie
(dm)Buddy Caldwell(conga).
Supervision:Bob Porter   NYC,April 9,1971

    Just my imagination   PR10017
    (For God's sake)Give more
       power to the people   -
    Nemo   unissued
    Chains of love   PR10017

JOHNNY "HAMMOND" SMITH-WHAT'S GOIN ON?:
Grover Washington Jr.(ts)Johnny "Hammond" Smith(org)James Clark(g)
Jimmy Lewis(el b)Eddie Gee(dm).
Supervision:Bob Porter   NYC,April 12,1971

    What's goin' on?-2,3   PR10015
    Smokin' Kool   -
    I'll be there-1,2   -
    L & J -3   -
    Between the sheets   -

-1:Ted Dunbar(g)replaces Clark.Same date.
-2:strings overdubbed on in July 1971.
-3:horns overdubbed on in July 1971.

CHARLES EARLAND-SOUL STORY:
Gary Chandler(tp)Jimmy Vass(fl,ss,as)Houston Person(ts)Charles Earland
(org,vo)Maynard Parker(g)Jesse Kilpatrick Jr.(dm)Buddy Caldwell(conga,
tambourine).
Supervision:Bob Porter   NYC,May 3,1971

    Don't let me lose this dream   unissued
    Betty's dilemma   PR10018
    Happy medium voCE   -
    Love story   -
    Never can say goodbye   unissued

Virgil Jones(tp)Clifford Adams Jr.(tb)Arthur Grant(ts,fl)Charles
Earland(org)Maynard Parker(g)Arthur Jenkins(conga).
                                  NYC,   1971

    One for Scotty   PR10018
    My Scorpio lady   -
    I was made to love her   -

FUNK,Inc.:
Gene Barr(ts)Bobby Watley(org,vo)Steve Weakley(g)Jimmy Munford(dm,vo)
Cecil Hunt(conga).
                                             1971

    Kool is back   PR10031
    Bowlegs   -   45-754
    Sister Janie   -
    The thrill is gone   -   45-754
    The whipper   -   45-752

LEON SPENCER Jr.-LOUISIANA SLIM:
Virgil Jones(tp)Grover Washington Jr.(ts,fl)Leon Spencer Jr.(org)
Melvin Sparks(g)Idris Muhammad(dm)Buddy Caldwell(conga).
                                 NYC,July 7,1971

    Louisiana Slim   PR10033
    Mercy mercy me   -
    (They long to be)Close to you -
    Our love will never die   -
    The trouble with love   -

SONNY STITT-BLACK VIBRATIONS:
Virgil Jones(tp)Sonny Stitt(as-1,ts)Leon Spencer Jr(org)Melvin Sparks
(g)Idris Muhammad(dm).
Supervision:Bob Porter   NYC,July 9,1971

    Goin' to D.C. -1   PR10032
    Black vibrations   -
    Where is love? -1   -
    Them funky changes   -

Don Patterson(org)replaces Spencer.Same date.

      Aires   PR10032
      Calling card   -

GENE AMMONS-MY WAY:
Ernie Royal,Robert Prado(tp)Garnett Brown(tb)Gene Ammons,Richard Landry
(ts)Roland Hanna(el p)Ted Dunbar(g)Chuck Rainey(el b)Idris Muhammad(dm)
Omar Clay(perc)Patricia Hall,Linda Wolfe,Yvonne Fletcher,Loretta Ritter
(voices-1)& strings-1,Bill Fisher(arr,cond).
                                 NYC,July   ,1971

      What's goin' on-1   PR10022
      Chicago .breakdown   -

Gene Ammons(ts)Roland Hanna(el p).Same date.

      A house is not a home   PR10022

Ernie Royal,Robert Prado(tp)Garnett Brown(tb)Gene Ammons,Richard Landry
(ts)Billy Butler(g)Ron Carter(b)Idris Muhammad(dm)Omar Clay-1(perc)
Patricia Hall,Linda Wolfe,Yvonne Fletcher,Loretta Ritter(voices-2)&
strings-3,Bill Fisher(arr,cond).
                                 NYC,July 26,1971

      Sack full of dreams-1,2,3 PR10022
      My way-3   -   P-10084
      Back to Merida-1,2   -

BOOGALOO JOE JONES-WHAT IT IS:
Grover Washington Jr.(ts)Butch Cornell(org)Ivan "Boogaloo Joe" Jones(g)
Jimmy Lewis(el b)Bernard Purdie(dm)Buddy Caldwell(conga,bongos).
Supervision:Bob Porter   NYC,August 16,1971

      Ain't no sunshine   PR10035
      I feel the earth move   -
      Fadin'   -
      What it is   -
      Let them talk   -
      Inside Job   -

IDRIS MUHAMMAD-PEACE AND RHYTHM:
Virgil Jones(tp)Clarence Thomas(fl,ss,ts,bells)Melvin Sparks,Alan
Fontaine(g)Jimmy Lewis(el b)Idris Muhammad(dm,autohorn,cabassa,gong,
cowbell)Buddy Caldwell(congas)Sakinah Muhammad(vo).
Supervision:Bob Porter   NYC,September 13,1971

      Brother you know you're doing
                 wrong voSM   PR10036
      Don't knock my love   -
      I'm a believer voSM   -

Virgil Jones(tp)Clarence Thomas(fl,ss,ts,bells)Kenny Barron(el p)
William Bivens(vb)Ron Carter(b)Idris Muhammad(dm,autohorn,cabassa,gong,
cowbell)Buddy Caldwell(congas)Angel Allende(timbales,perc).
Supervision:Bob Porter   NYC,September 20,1971

      Peace and rhythm suite: PR10036
        Peace   -
        Rhythm   -

RUSTY BRYANT-WILDFIRE:
Rusty Bryant(ts)Bill Mason(org)Jimmy Ponder,Ernest Reed-1(g)Idris
Muhammad(dm)Buddy Caldwell(conga).
                                NYC,October 4,1971

      Wildfire   PR10037
      It's impossible   -
      Riders on the storm   -
      The Alobamo kid   -
      If you really love me   -
      All that I've got   -

BERNARD PURDIE-SHAFT:
Gerry Thomas,Danny Moore(tp)Charlie Brown,Willie Bridges(ts)Neal
Creque(el p)Billy Nichols(g)Gordon Edwards(el b)Bernard Purdie(dm)
Norman Pride(conga).

	NYC,	1971
Shaft-1,2	PR10038	
Way back home	-	
Attica	-	
Changes	-	
Summer melody	-	
Butterfingers-2	-	

-1:Houston Person(ts)Lloyd Davis(g)added;-2:Charlie Brown out.

MELVIN SPARKS-AKILAH!:
Ernie Royal-1,Virgil Jones-3(tp)Hubert Laws-4(fl)George Coleman-1,
Sonny Fortune-2(as)Dave Hubbard(ts-4,fl-5)Leon Spencer(org)Melvin
Sparks(g)Idris Muhammad(dm)Buddy Caldwell(conga).

	NYC,	1971
Love the life you live-2,3	PR10039	
On the up-2	-	
All wrapped up-3,4	-	
Akilah-1,2,3	-	
Blues for J.B.-2	-	
The image of love	-	

GENE AMMONS/JAMES MOODY-CHICAGO CONCERT:
Gene Ammons,James Moody(ts)Jodie Christian(p)Cleveland Eaton(b)Marshall
Thompson(dm).

North Park Hotel,Chicago,November 21,1971

Just in time	PR10065
Work song	-
Have you met Miss Jones?	-
Jim jam Jug	-
I'll close my eyes	-
C jam blues	-

SONNY STITT-GOIN' DOWN SLOW:
Sonny Stitt(ts)Hank Jones(p)George Duvivier(b)Idris Muhammad(dm).

NYC,February 15,1972

Where is love	PR10048
Goin' down slow	

Thad Jones(tp)Sonny Stitt(as)Hank Jones(p)Billy Butler,Wally Richardson
(g)George Duvivier(b)Idris Muhammad(dm)Buddy Caldwell(conga,bells)&
strings,Billy Ver Planck(arr,cond). Same date.

Miss Ann,Lisa,Sune & Sadie	PR10048
Living without you	-
Acid funk reprise-1	-

-1:Thad Jones out.

LEON SPENCER Jr.:
Virgil Jones(tp)Sonny Fortune(as)Dave Hubbard(ts)Leon Spencer(org,vo)
Melvin Sparks(g)Idris Muhammad(dm)Buddy Caldwell(conga).

NYC,February 22,1972

Down on Dowling Street-1	PR10042
Hip shaker-2	-
Bad walking woman	
Where I'm coming from-3	PR10063

-1:Leon Spencer,Sparks & Muhammad only;-2:Hubbard,Spencer,Sparks &
Muhammad only;-3:Hubert Laws(fl)added.

GENE AMMONS-FREE AGAIN:
Cat Anderson,John Audino,Reunald Jones,Gene Coe(tp)Jimmy Cleveland,
Benny Powell,Britt Woodman,Mike Wemberley(tb)David Duke,Henry
Sigismonti(frh)John Johnson(tu)Jerome Richardson,Ernie Watts,Herman
Riley,Jack Nimitz(reeds)Gene Ammons,Red Holloway(ts)Joe Sample(p)Dennis
Budimir(g)Bob Saravia(b)Candy Finch(dm)Bob Norris(conga)Bobby Bryant
(arr,cond).

			LA,	1972

      Free again   PR10040
      What are you doing the rest of
                       your life   -
      Jackson   -

Cat Anderson,John Audino,Reunald Jones,Gene Coe,Buddy Childers,Al
Aarons(tp)Jimmy Cleveland,Benny Powell,Britt Woodman,Mike Wemberley,
Grover Mitchell(tb)David Duke,Henry Sigismonti(frh)John Johnson(tu)
Jerome Richardson,Ernie Watts,Herman Riley,Jack Nimitz(reeds)Gene
Ammons,Pete Christlieb(ts)Dwight Dickerson(p)Dennis Budimir(g)Arthur
Adams(g)Bob Saravia(b)Chuck Rainey(el b)Paul Humphrey(dm)Bobby Bryant
(arr,cond).

			LA,	1972

      Crazy Mary   PR10040
      Fru fru   -
      Juggin'   -

CHARLES EARLAND-INTENSITY:
Lee Morgan,Virgil Jones,Victor Paz,Jon Faddis(tp)Dick Griffin,Clifford
Adams-1(tb)Jack Jeffers(bass tb)Hubert Laws(fl)Charles Earland(org)
John Fourie,Greg Millar(g)Billy Cobham(dm)Sonny Morgan(conga).
                                                  1972

      Happy 'cause I'm goin' home   PR10041
      Will you still love me tomorrow -
      Cause I love her-1   -

Lee Morgan(tp)Virgil Jones,Victor Paz,Jon Faddis(tp,flh)Hubert Laws-1
(picc)Billy Harper(ts)William Thorpe-1(bs)Charles Earland(org,p-2)
Maynard Parker(g)Billy Cobham(dm)Sonny Morgan-1(conga).
                                                  1972

      Morgan-1   PR10041
      Speedball-2   PR10061

LEON SPENCER:
Hubert Laws(fl)Buzz Brauer(fl,English horn,oboe)Leon Spencer(org)Joe
Beck(g)Idris Muhammad(dm)Buddy Caldwell-1(perc) & strings-2.
                                                  1972

      When my love has gone-1   PR10042
      If you were me and I were you-1 -
      In search of love-2   -
      When dreams start to fade-2   -

FUNK,Inc.-CHICKEN LICKIN':
Gene Barr(ts)Bobby Watley(org,vo)Steve Weakley(g)Jimmy Munford(dm,vo)
Cecil Hunt(conga).

                                                  1972

      Chicken lickin'   PR10043
      Running away   -
      They trying to get me   -
      The better half   -
      Let's make peace and stop the war -
      Jung bungo   -

HOUSTON PERSON-BROKEN WINDOWS,EMPTY HALLWAYS:
Joe Wilder,Victor Paz(tp)Jim Buffington(frh)Hubert Laws(fl)Houston
Person(ts)Buzz Brauer(ts,bs,English horn,oboe,picc,fl,cl)Ronnie
Jannelli(fl,cl,bs)Cedar Walton(p)Ernie Hayes(org)Grady Tate(dm)Billy
Ver Planck(arr,cond).
                                    NYC,   1972
        I think it's going to rain today PR10044
        Don't mess with Bill   -
        Everything's alright   -
        Mr.Bojangles-2   -
        Moan Er-Uh Lisa   -
        Imagine   -
        Let's call this   -
        Bleeker Street-1   -

-1:Jimmy Watson(org)replaces Hayes
-2:Bunny Briggs(tap dance)added.

BAYETE-WORLDS AROUND THE SUN:
Fred "Mulobo" Berry,Oscar Brashear(tp,flh)Wayne Wallace(tb)Dave Johnson
(Mganda)(ss)Hadley Caliman(fl,ts)Bobby Hutcherson(vb)Todd Cochran
(Bayete)(p,el p,clavinet)James Leary III(b,el b)Thabo Vincar(dm).
                                                    1972

        It ain't   PR10045
        Free Angela   -
        Njeri   -
        I'm on it   -
        Bayete   -
        Eurus   -

HAMPTON HAWES-UNIVERSE:
Oscar Brashear(tp)Harold Land(ts)Hampton Hawes(p,el p,org,synth)Arthur
Adams(g)Chuck Rainey(el b)Leon Chancler(dm).
                                                    1972

        Little bird   PR10046
        Drums for peace   -
        Love is better   -
        Josie black   -
        Don't pass me by   -
        Universe   -
        J.B.'s mind   -

ART BLAKEY JAZZ MESSENGERS:
Ramon Morris(fl)Buddy Terry(ss)John Hicks(el p)Mickey Bass,Stanley
Clarke(b)Art Blakey(dm)Emanuel Rahim(conga)Nathaniel Bettis,Sonny.
Morgan,Richard "Pablo" Landrum(perc).
                                    NYC,May 23,1972

        Song for a lonely woman   PR10047

CHARLES EARLAND-LIVE AT THE LIGHTHOUSE:
Elmer Coles(tp)Clifford Adams(tb)James Vass(ss,as)Charles Earland(org)
Maynard Parker(g)Darryl Washington(dm)Kenneth Nash(conga).
                    Lighthouse Club,Hermosa Beach,Cal.,   1972
        Smiling   PR10050
        We've only just begun   -
        Black gun   -
        Spinky   -
        Freedom jazz dance   -
        Moontrane   -

                                                    [209]

DEXTER GORDON-CA' PURANGE:
Thad Jones(tp)Dexter Gordon(ts)Hank Jones(p)Stanley Clarke(b)Louis
Hayes(dm).

1972

      Ca' purange   PR10051
      The first time ever I saw your
                        face   -
      Airegin   -
      Oh!Karen O   -

DEXTER GORDON-TANGERINE:
Thad Jones(tp,flh)Dexter Gordon(ts)Hank Jones(p)Stanley Clarke(b)Louis
Hayes(dm)

June 22,1972

      Tangerine   P-10091
      August blues   -
      What is was   -

Dexter Gordon(ts)Cedar Walton(p)Buster Williams(b)Billy Higgins(dm).

June 28,1972

      Days of wine and roses   P-10091

DEXTER GORDON-GENERATION:
Freddie Hubbard(tp,flh)Dexter Gordon(ts)Cedar Walton(p)Buster Williams
(b)Billy Higgins(dm).
Supervision:Ozzie Cadena   NYC,July 22,1972

      Milestones   PR10069
      Scared to be alone   -
      We see   -
      The group   -

ART BLAKEY JAZZ MESSENGERS:
Woody Shaw(tp)Manny Boyd-1(fl)Ramon Morris-2(ts)George Cables(p,el p)
Stanley Clarke(b)Art Blakey(dm)Ray Mantilla-2(conga).

July 28,1972

      C.C.-2   PR10047
      Child's dance-1,2   -
      I can't get started   -

RUSTY BRYANT AND THE CASUAL SOCIETY-FRIDAY NIGHT FUNK FOR SATURDAY NIGHT
BROTHERS:
Rusty Bryant(as,ts)Kenneth Moss(el p,org)Harold Young(g)Eddie
Brookshine(el b)Fred Masey(dm)Norman Jones(conga,perc).

1972

      Friday night funk for Saturday
                 night brothers PR10053
      Down by the Cuyahoga   -
      Have you seen her   -
      Mercy,mercy,mercy   -
      Blues for a brother   -

MAYNARD PARKER-MIDNIGHT RIDER:
Buddy Lucas-1(ts,hca)Ernie Hayes(el p,org)Maynard Parker(g)George
Duvivier(b)Jimmy Johnson(dm).

1972?

      The world is a ghetto-1   PR10054
      Killing me softly with his song -
      Midnight rider   -
      Freedom jazz dance   -

Richard Tee(el p)Maynard Parker,Joe Beck(g)Ron Carter(b)Grady Tate(dm).
                                                 1972?

              Mama told me not to come   PR10054
              Lady sings the blues   -
              One hand   -
              Bad Montana   -

HOUSTON PERSON-SWEET BUNS & BARBEQUE:
Houston Person(ts)Richard Tee(el p,p)Joe Beck-1(g,el g,arr)Hugh
McCracken-2(g)Ron Carter(b)Grady Tate(dm).
Supervision:Ozzie Cadena   NYC,September 11(or Nov.7?),1972

              A song for you-1,2   PR10055
              The trouble with hello is
                          goodbye-1   -
              Scared to be alone-2   -

SONNY STITT-SO DOGGONE GOOD:
Sonny Stitt(as,ts)Hampton Hawes(p)Reggie Johnson(b)Lenny McBrowne(dm).
                             Berkeley,September 13 & 14,1972

              Back door   PR10074
              Your love is so doggone good   -
              Orange ash tray   -
              I don't know yet   -
              The more I see you   -
              Speculation   -

BOOGALOO JOE JONES-SNAKE RHYTHM ROCK:
Rusty Bryant(as,ts)Butch Cornell(org)Ivan "Boogaloo Joe" Jones(g)Jimmy
Lewis(el b)Grady Tate(dm).
Supervision:Ozzie Cadena   NYC,_____1972

              Hoochie coo chickie   PR10056
              Snake rhythm rock   -
              The first time ever I saw
                          your face   -
              He's so fine   -
              Big bad midnight roller   -

BAYETE-SEEKING OTHER BEAUTY:
Fred Berry(tp,flh,vo)Dave Johnson(fl,ss,vo,perc)Todd Cochran(Bayete)(p,
el p,clavinet,vo)Hoza Phillips(el b,vo)Augusta Lee Collins(dm,perc).
                                  September 18,1972
                          &   October 2,1972
              Let it take your mind   PR10062
              The time has come   -
              Think on the people arise/
                 Mulobo/People arise!!!   -
              Don't need nobody   -
              Pruda's shoes:
                 I-Duet/II-Trio/III-Ensemble/ -
                 IV-Finale   -

GARY BARTZ-JUJU STREET SONGS:
Gary Bartz(as,ss,sopranino,el p,perc,voice)Andy Bey(el p,perc,vo)Stafford
James(b,el b,perc,voice)Howard King(dm,perc,voice).
                             Berkeley,October   ,1972

              I wanna be where you are   PR10057
              Black maybe   -
              Bertha Baptist   -
              Africans unite   -
              Teheran   -

GARY BARTZ-FOLLOW THE MEDICINE MAN:
Same.

                                     Berkeley,October   ,1972

Sifa Zote	PR10068
Whasaname	-
Betcha by golly,how	-
Etoile des neiges	-
Sing me a song today	-

GENE AMMONS:
Gene Ammons(ts)Ernie Hayes(org)Hank Jones(el p)Joe Beck(g)Ron Carter(b,
el b)Idris Muhammad(dm).
Supervision:Ozzie Cadena   NYC,October 28,1972

Lady sings the blues-1	PR10058
Play me-1	-
Ben-1	-
Fly me	PR10070
Fuzz	-

-1:Strings overdubbed on,Ed Bogas(arr,cond).Berkeley,   1972

Gene Ammons(ts)Hank Jones(el p)Ernie Hayes(org)Joe Beck(g)Ron Carter(b,
el b)Mickey Roker(dm).
Supervision:Ozzie Cadena   NYC,October 30,1972

Fine and mellow	PR10058
Strange fruit-1	-
Big bad Jug	PR10070

-1:Hayes,Beck & Roker out.

Gene Ammons(ts)Sonny Phillips(el p-1,org)Maynard Parker(g)Ron Carter(b,
el b)Billy Cobham(dm).
Supervision:Ozzie Cadena   NYC,November 1,1972

God bless the child	PR10058
Tin shack out back-1	-
Lady Mama	PR10070
I can't help myself	-
Lucille	-
Papa was a rolling stone	-

HOUSTON PERSON-SWEET BUNS AND BARBEQUE:
Houston Person(ts)Joe Beck(g,el g)George Duvivier(b,el b)Grady Tate(dm)
Buddy Caldwell(conga,perc).
Supervision:Ozzie Cadena   NYC,November 7(or Sept.11?),1972

Sweet buns and barbeque	PR10055
This masquerade-2	-
Down here on the ground-1,3	-
Put it where you want it-1	-
Groove thang-4	-

-1:Victor Paz,Ernie Royal(tp)Frank Wess(ts,bs)Billy Ver Planck(arr)added.
-2:Jimmy Watson(org)added;-3:Caldwell out;-4:Beck out.

FUNK,Inc.-HANGIN' OUT:
Gene Barr(ts)Bobby Watley(org)Steve Weakley(g)Gordon Edwards-1(el b)
Jimmy Munford(dm)Cecil Hunt(conga).

                                     December 1,1972

Smokin' at Tiffany's-1	PR10059	
Give me your love	-	
We can be friends	-	
Dirty red-1	-	P-759
I can see clearly now	-	
I'll be around-1	-	

CHARLES EARLAND-CHARLES III:
Victor Paz,Jon Faddis,Richard Williams,Joe Shepley(tp,flh)Garnett
Brown(tb)Jack Jeffers(tb,tu)Billy Harper(ts,alto fl)Seldon Powell(bs,
alto fl)Charles Earland(org,el p,ss-1,perc)Jack Turner(g,perc)Stuart
Sharf-2(g)Darryl Washington(dm,perc)Larry Killian,Joe Lee Wilson(vo).
                                                    1972?

          Charles III -2 voLK   PR10061
          Girl,you need a change of mind-2
                          voLK   -
          Auburn delight voLK,JLW   -
          My favorite things-1   -

HAMPTON HAWES-BLUES FOR WALLS:
Oscar Brashear(tp,flh)Hadley Caliman(ss,ts)Hampton Hawes(p,el p,synth)
George Walker(g)Henry Franklin(b,el b)Leon Chancler(Ngudu)(dm).
Supervision:Orrin Keepnews   Berkeley,January 16,17 & 18,1973

          Blues for walls   PR10060
          Sun dance   -
          Hamp's collard green blues-1 -
          Brother Brantley   -
          Rain forest   -
          Carmel-1,2   -
          Me-ho   -

-1:Brashear & Caliman out;-2:Walker out.

LEON SPENCER Jr.-WHERE I'M COMING FROM:
Victor Paz,Jon Faddis(tp)Frank Wess(fl,bs,cond)Seldon Powell(fl,ts)Leon
Spencer(org)Ernie Hayes(el p)Joe Beck(g)George Duvivier(b)Grady Tate
(dm)Ed Bogas(arr).
Supervision:Ozzie Cadena   NYC,January 26,1973

          Superstition   PR10063
          Give me your love   -
          Keeper of the castle   -
          Trouble man   -

Leon Spencer(org)Joe Beck(g)Grady Tate(dm)Same date.

          The price a po' man's got to pay PR10063

ART BLAKEY JAZZ MESSENGERS-BUHAINA:
Woody Shaw(tp)Carter Jefferson(ss,ts)Cedar Walton(p,el p)Mickey Bass(b)
Art Blakey(dm)Tony Waters(conga)Jon Hendricks(vo).
                                  Berkeley,March   1973

          Moanin' voJH   PR10067
          A chant for Bu   -
          One for Trane-1   -
          Mission eternal-1   -
          Along came Betty-1 voJH -
          Gertrude's bounce   -

-1:Michael Howell(g)added.

RUSTY BRYANT-FOR THE GOOD TIMES:
Rusty Bryant(as,ts)Hank Jones(el p)Joe Beck,Hugh McCracken(g)Tony Levin
(b,el b)Steve Gadd(dm).
Supervision:Ozzie Cadena   NYC,March 9,1973

          For the good times   PR10073
          Killing me softly   -
          The last one out   -
          Appalachian Green   -
          A night in Tunisia   -
          Looking through the eyes of love -
          Theme from Deep Throat

                                                    [213]

ART BLAKEY-ANTHENAGIN:
Woody Shaw(tp)Steve Turre -1(tb)Carter Jefferson(ts)Cedar Walton(p,el
p)Michael Howell-2(g)Mickey Bass(b)Art Blakey(dm)Tony Waters (conga).
                                         Berkeley,March   ,1973

    I'm not so sure   P-10076
    Love:for the one you can't have-1 -
    Fantasy in D -1   -
    Anthenagin   -
    Without a song   -
    Along came Betty-1,2   -

GARY BARTZ:
Gary Bartz(ss,as,sop.voice,el p,perc)Hubert Eaves(p)Hector Centeno(g)
Stafford James(b,el b,voice,perc)Howard King(voice,perc).
                                         NYC,June   ,1973

    Dr.Follow's dance   PR10068
    Standin' on the corner   -

GARY BARTZ NTU TROOP-I'VE KNOWN RIVERS AND OTHER BODIES:
Gary Bartz(as,ss,vo)Hubert Eaves(p,el p)Stafford James(b,el b)Howard
King(dm).
                     Jazz Festival,Montreux(Switzerland),July 7,1973

    Nommo-The Majick song   P-66001
    Sifa Zote   -
    Jujuman   -
    Bertha baptist   -
    Don't fight that feeling   -
    Mama's soul   -
    I've known rivers   -
    The warrior(s song   -
    Uhuru Sassa   -
    Dr.Follow's dance   -
    Peace and love   -

HAMPTON HAWES-PLAYIN' IN THE YARD:
Hampton Hawes(p,el p)Bob Cranshaw(b)Kenny Clarke(dm).
                     Jazz Festival,Montreux(Switzerland),July 7,1973

    Playin' in the yard   P-10077
    Double trouble   -
    Pink peaches   -
    De de   -
    Stella by starlight   -

DEXTER GORDON-BLUES A LA SUISSE:
Dexter Gordon(ts)Hampton Hawes(p,el p)Bob Cranshaw(b)Kenny Clarke(dm).
                     Jazz Festival,Montreux(Switzerland),July 7,1973

    Gingerbread boy   P-10079
    Blues a la Suisse   -
    Some other Spring   -
    Secret love   -

GENE AMMONS AND FRIENDS AT MONTREUX:
Gene Ammons(ts)Hampton Hawes(el p)Bob Cranshaw(el b)Kenny Clarke(dm).
                     Jazz Festival,Montreux(Switzerland),July 7,1973

    Yardbird suite   P-10078
    Since I fell for you   -
    New Sonny's blues   -
    Sophisticated lady   -

Nat Adderley(c)Julian "Cannonball" Adderley(as)Dexter Gordon(ts)added.
                                         Same date.

    Treux bleu   P-10078

FUNK,Inc.-SUPERFUNK:
Gene Barr(ts,vo)Bobby Watley(org,vo)Steve Weakley(g)Jimmy Munford(dm,vo)
Cecil Hunt(conga)with Ollie Mitchell,Allen De Rienzo(tp)George Bohanon
(tb)Jackie Kelso(ts,bs)Don Peake(g)Johnny "Guitar" Watson(el b).
July ,1973

Message from the meters	PR10071
Goodbye so long	-
The hill where the Lord hides	-
Honey,I love you	-
Just don't mean a thing	-
I'm gonna love you just a	
little more baby	-

BOOGALOO JOE JONES-BLACK WHIP:
Dave Hubbard(ss,ts,perc)Bobby Knowles(org)Sonny Phillips(el p)Ivan
"Boogaloo Joe" Jones(g)Ron Carter(b,el b)Bud Kelly(dm,perc)Jimmy Johnson
(perc).
Supervision:Ozzie Cadena   NYC,July 25,1973

Black whip	PR10072
My love	-
Freak off	-
Daniel	-
The ballad of mad dogs and	
Englishmen	-
Crank me up	-

ICE:
Ronnie James(tp,vo)Arthur Young(tp,fl,vo)Frank Abel(p,org,vo)Larry Jones
(g,vo)Lafayette Hudson(b)Donny Donable(dm)Keno Speller(perc,conga).
Supervision:Berjot   1973

Too little room	P-10075
Suicide	-
One chance	-
Love can	-
There's time to change	-
Put an X on the spot(in the sky)	-
Losin'	-
Dgunji	-

GENE AMMONS-BRASSWIND:
Gene Ammons(ts)George Duke(keyb)Michael Howell,Don Peake(g)Carol Kaye
(el b)Johnny Guerin(dm)Kenneth Nash(perc).
Supervision:Orrin Keepnews   Berkeley,October 30,1973

Cantaro-2	P-10080
Cariba-2	-
Once I loved-2	-
Brasswind-3	-
Rozzie-1,3	-

-1:Overdubbed on:Gene Ammons(ts).Berkeley,October 31,1973
-2:Overdubbed on:Snooky Young,Allen De Rienzo(tp)George Bohanon(tb)Bill
Green,Jay Migliori(fl,alto fl,as)Jim Horn(fl,alto fl,bs)David Axelrod
(arr,cond).April 25,1974
-3:Overdubbed on:Same as on -2.April 26,1974

GARY BARTZ-SINGERELLA/A GHETTO FAIRY TALE:
Gary Bartz(cl,ss,as,mouth harp,synth,perc,vo)Hubert Eaves(p,el p,clavinet
Maynard Parker,Hector Centeno(g)James Benjamin(el b)Howard King(dm)Ken-
neth Nash-1(perc).
November ,1973

I don't care	P-10083
Nation time-1	-

CHARLES EARLAND-THE DYNAMITE BROTHERS(Soundtrack):
Collective personnel:Eddie Henderson,Jon Faddis,Victor Paz or Danny
Moore(tp,flh)Wayne Andre(tb)Dave Hubbard(alto fl,ss,ts)Charles Earland
(org,el p,synth,ss-1)Patrick Gleeson(synth)Mark Elf,Cornell Dupree or
Keith Loving(g)Melvin Bronson(el b)Darryl Washington(dm,tympani)Billy
Hart(dm)Larry Killian(perc).
Supervision:Duke Pearson   NYC,November   ,1973

PR-1995 Betty's theme   P-10082
PR-1996 Never ending melody   -
PR-1997 Grasshopper   -
PR-1998 Shanty blues   -
PR-1999 Weedhopper   -
PR-2000 Razor J   -
PR-2001 Snake-1   -
PR-2002 Kungfusion   -
PR-2003 Incense of essence   -

GENE AMMONS/SONNY STITT-TOGETHER AGAIN FOR THE LAST TIME:
Gene Ammons(ts)Junior Mance(p)Sam Jones(b)Mickey Roker(dm).
Supervision:Duke Pearson   NYC,November 20,1973

        I'll close my eyes   P-10100

Gene Ammons-1,Sonny Stitt(ts)Junior Mance(p)Sam Jones(b)Mickey Roker(dm).
Supervision:Duke Pearson   NYC,November 21,1973

        Jeannine-1   unissued
        For all we know   P-10100
        One for Amos-1   -

Gene Ammons,Sonny Stitt-1(ts)Junior Mance(p,el p-2)Sam Jones(b)Ajaramu
J.Shelton(dm)Warren Smith-1(perc).
Supervision:Duke Pearson   NYC,December 10,1973

        The more I see you   P-10100
        Saxification-1   -
        The window pain-1,2   -
        Miss Lulu-1   unissued

CHARLES EARLAND-LEAVING THIS PLANET:
Collective personnel:Eddie Henderson(tp)Freddie Hubbard(tp,flh)Joe
Henderson(ts)Dave Hubbard(ss,ts,fl)Charles Earland(org,synth)Patrick
Gleeson(synth)Mark Elf,Eddie Arkin,Greg Crockett(g)Brian Brake,Harvey
Mason(dm)Larry Killian(perc)Rudy Copeland(vo).
                                        December 11,12 & 13,1973

        Leaving this planet   P-66002
        Red Clay   -
        Warp factor   -
        Brown eyes   -
        Asteroid   -
        Mason's galaxy   -
        No me esqueca(Don't forget me) -
        Tyner   -
        Van Jay   -
        Never ending melody   -

GENE AMMONS-BRASSWIND:
Gene Ammons(ts)George Duke(el p)Michael Howell(g)Walter Booker(b)Roy
McCurdy(dm).   Berkeley,February 13,1974
Overdubbed on:Snooky Young,Allen De Rienzo(tp)George Bohanon(tb)Bill
Green,Jay Migliori(fl,alto fl,as)Jim Horn(fl,alto fl,bs)David Axelrod(arr
cond).   April 26,1974
Supervision:Orrin Keepnews.

      Solitario   P-10080
      'Round midnight   -

GARY BARTZ-SINGERELLA/A GHETTO FAIRY TALE:
Gary Bartz(cl,ss,as,mouth harp,synth,perc,vo)Hubert Eaves(p,el p,clavinet,
Maynard Parker(g)James Benjamin(el b)Howard King(dm)Kenneth Nash-1(perc).
                                          February   ,1974

      St.Felix Street   P-10083
      Dozens(The sounding song)   -
      Blind man-1   -
      Singerella-A ghetto fairy tale   -
      Lady love   -
      Mellow yellow   -

JACK DE JOHNETTE-SORCERY:
Benny Maupin(bass cl,voice)Michael Fellerman(metaphone-1)John Abercrombie
Mick Goodrick(el g,voice)Dave Holland(b,voice)Jack De Johnette(dm,voice).
                                          March   ,1974

      Sorcery No.1   P-10081
      The right time   -
      The rock thing   -

GENE AMMONS-GOODBYE:
Gene Ammons(ts)Nat Adderley(c)Gary Bartz(as)Kenny Drew(p)Sam Jones(b)
Louis Hayes(dm)Ray Barretto(conga).
Supervision:Orrin Keepnews   NYC,March 18,1974

      Jeannine   P-10093
      Alone again(Naturally)   -
      Out in the sticks   -
Same.   NYC,March 19,1974

      Geru's blues   P-10093
      It don't mean a thing   -
Ray Barretto out.   NYC,March 20,1974

      Goodbye   P-10093
JACK DE JOHNETTE-SORCERY:
Michael Fellerman(metaphone,tb)Dave Holland(b)Jack De Johnette(C melody
sax,keyb,dm).
                                          May   ,1974

      The Reverend King suite: P-10081
        Reverend King/   -
        Obstructions/   -
        The fatal shot/   -
        Mourning/   -
        Unrest/   -
        New Spirits on the horizon   -
      Four levels of joy   -
      Epilogue   -

AZAR LAWRENCE-BRIDGE INTO THE NEW AGE:
Black Arthur(as)Azar Lawrence(ss,ts)Julian Priester(tb-1)Hadley Caliman
-1(fl)Joe Bonner(p)John Heard(b)Leon Chancler(Ngudu)(dm)Mtume(conga,perc)
Kenneth Nash-2(perc).

May ,1974

```
        Warriors of peace-2        P-10086
        Forces of nature-1         -
        Fatisha-3                  -
```

-3:Azar Lawrence(ss,ts)Joe Bonner(p)Kenneth Nash(perc)only.

CHARLES EARLAND-KHARMA:
Jon Faddis(tp)Clifford Adams(tb)Dave Hubbard(fl,ss,ts)Charles Earland
(org,el p,synth)Aurell Ray(g)Ron Carter-1(el b)George Johnson(dm).
Supervision:Orrin Keepnews
Jazz Festival,Montreux(Switzerland),July 6,1974

```
        Joe Brown                  P-10095
        Suite for Martin Luther King:
          Pt.1:Offering            -
          Pt.2:Mode for Martin-1   -
        Kharma-1                   -
```

HAMPTON HAWES-NORTHERN WINDOWS:
Allen De Rienzo,Snooky Young(tp)George Bohanon(tb)Jackie Kelso,Bill
Green,Jay Migliori(saxes,fl)Hampton Hawes(p,el p)Carol Kaye(el b)Spider
Webb(dm).

July 18 & 19,1974

```
        Sierra Morena              P-10088
        Go down Moses              -
        Bach                       -
        Web                        -
        Tune Axle grease           -
        C & H sugar                -
```

RUSTY BRYANT-UNTIL IT'S TIME FOR YOU TO GO:
Rusty Bryant(as,ts)Horace Ott(p,clavinet,el p,arr,cond)Ernie Hayes(org)
George Devens(vb,perc)Hugh McCracken,David Spinozza(g)Wilbur Bascomb
(el b)Bernard Purdie(dm).
Supervision:Bob Porter   NYC,August 1,1974

```
        The hump bump-1            P-10085
        Until it's time for you to go-1  -
        Troubles                   -
        Draggin' the line-1        -
```

-1:Overdubbed on:Joe Shepley,Jon Faddis(tp)Garnett Brown(tb)Seldon Powell
(fl,ts)Heywood Henry(fl,bs).   NYC,August 5,1974

Joe Shepley,Jon Faddis(tp)Billy Campbell(tb)Seldon Powell(fl,ts)Rusty
Bryant(ts)Babe Clarke(bs)Horace Ott(p,clavinet,el p,arr,cond)Ernie Hayes
(org)George Devens(vb,perc)Hugh McCracken,David Spinozza(g)Wilbur
Bascomb(el b)Bernard Purdie(dm).
Supervision:Bob Porter   NYC,August 2,1974

```
        Sundown                    rejected
        Ge gang gang goong         P-10085
        Red eye special-1          -
```

-1:McCracken out.

FUNK,Inc.-PRICED TO SELL:
Gene Barr(ts)Bobby Watley(keyb)Rudy Turner(g)William Simmons(b)Michael
Hughes(dm)Cecil Hunt(conga)with Allen De Rienzo,Snooky Young(tp)Jay
Migliori,Bill Green,Jackie Kelso(reeds)Billy Fender(g)Earl Palmer(dm)
Billie Barnum,Gregory Matta,Julia Tillman,Edna Wright,August Johnson,
James Gilstrap(vo)David Axelrod(arr,cond).
Supervision:David Axelrod   Berkeley,July,August & Sept.1974

(session continued on next page)

```
It ain't the spotlight        P-10087
Priced to sell                   -
God only knows                   -
Where are we young               -
Gimme some lovin'                -
Somewhere in my mind             -
The girl of my dreams            -
```

AZAR LAWRENCE-BRIDGE INTO THE NEW AGE:
Woody Shaw(tp)Azar Lawrence(ss,ts)Woody Murray(b)Clint Houston(b)Billy
Hart(dm)Guilherme Franco(perc)Jean Carn(vo).
                                            September   ,1974

```
Bridge into the new age       P-10086
```
Ray Straughter(wood fl)Kenneth Nash(perc)added:

```
The beautiful and omnipresent love
                              P-10086
```

PATRICE RUSHEN-PRELUSION:
Oscar Brashear(tp,flh)George Bohanon(tb)Hadley Caliman(fl,alto fl,ss)
Joe Henderson(ts)Patrice Rushen(p,el p,clavinet,synth)Tony Dumas(b,
"blitz" b)Leon Chancler(Ngudu)(dm)Kenneth Nash(perc).
                                            Berkeley,   1974

```
Shortie's portion             P-10089
7/73                             -
Haw right now                    -
Traverse                         -
Puttered bopcorn                 -
```

NAT ADDERLEY-DOUBLE EXPOSURE:
Nat Adderley(c,vo)Julian "Cannonball" Adderley-1(as)George Duke(keyb)
Ray Copeland-2(synth)Hal Galper-3(p)Billy Fender(g)Don Peake-4(rhythm g)
Johnny "Guitar" Watson(g-5,el b-6)Walter Booker(b)Roy McCurdy(dm).
                                                            1974

```
Watermelon man-2,4,5,7        P-10090
Quit it                          -
59 go and pass                   -
Contant 19 -1,3,8                -
Traffic-1,6                      -
In a silent way-9                -
Song of the Valdez Diamond       -
```

-7:Allen De Rienzo,Snooky Young,Oscar Brashear(tp)George Bohanon,Dick
Hyde(tb)William Green,Jackie Kelso,Jay Migliori(reeds)added.
-8:Phil Upchurch(g)replaces Fender.
-9:Jack Shulman,Gareth Nuttycombe,Alexander Neiman,Henry Roth,William
Hymanson,Jerome Reisler,Nathan Gershman,Walter Rower(strings)added.

GARY BARTZ-THE SHADOW DO:
Gary Bartz(as,ss,synth,vo)Hubert Eaves(p,clavinet,synth)Larry Mizell
(synth,backgr.vo-1)Reggie Lucas(b)Michael Henderson(b,backgr.vo-1)Howard
King(dm,synth)Mtume(conga,perc)Fonce Mizell-1(backgr.vo)James Carter-2
(whistling).
                                                            1975

```
Winding roads                 P-10092
Mother nature                    -
Love tones                       -
Gentle smiles(Saxy)              -
Make me feel better-1            -
Sea Gypsy-2                      -
For my baby                      -
Incident                         -
```

JACK DE JOHNETTE-COSMIC CHICKEN:
Alex Foster(as,ts)John Abercrombie(g)Peter Warren(b)Jack De Johnette
(dm,keyb).
                                        April 24 & 26,1975
        Cosmic chicken   P-10094
        One for devadip and the
                        professor   -
        Memories-1   -
        Stratocruiser   -
        Shades of the phantom   -
        Eiderdown   -
        Sweet and pungent   -
        Last chance stomp   -

-1:Jack De Johnette(p solo).

AZAR LAWRENCE-SUMMER SOLSTICE:
Raul De Souza(tb)Azar Lawrence(ss,ts,perc)Gerald Hayes(fl)Albert
Dailey(p)Amaury Tristao(g)Ron Carter(b)Billy Hart(dm).
                                        April 29,1975
        From the point of love   P-10097
        From the point of light   -
        Summer solstice   -

Raul De Souza(tb)Azar Lawrence(ss,ts,perc)Gerald Hayes(fl)Dom
Salvador(p)Amaury Tristao(g)Ron Carter(b)Guilherme Franco(dm).
                                        May 1,1975
        Novo Ano   P-10097
        Highway   -

ICE-IMPORT EXPORT:
Arthur Grayson(tp,fl,synth,clavinet,vo)Ronnie James Buttacavoli(tp,
synth,b,vo)Frank Abel(p,synth,clavinet,vo)Larry Jones(g)Lafayette
Hudson(b)Ernest Donable(dm,conga)Keno Speller(conga,bongos,bells,
African dm,perc,vo).
Supervision:Berjot   Paris(France)   1975
        Hi fi woman   P-10096
        Don't wonder why   -
        Funky lovin'   -
        Quick   -
        Hey angel girl   -
        The gap   -
        Passing dreams   -
        What cha gonna do about loving
                                me   -
        I need love   -
        Funky bunch   -

PATRICE RUSHEN-BEFORE THE DAWN:
Oscar Brashear(tp)George Bohanon(tb)Hubert Laws(fl)Hadley Caliman
(reeds)Patrice Rushen(keyb)Lee Ritenour(g)Charles Meeks(b)Tony Dumas,
Leon Chancler(Ngudu),Harvey Mason,Kenneth Nash(dm,perc)Nate Alfred,
Josie James(vo).
                                        Berkeley,August   ,1975
        Kickin' back   P-10098
        What's the story   -
        Jubilation   -
        Before the dawn   -
        Razzia   -

AZAR LAWRENCE-PEOPLE MOVING:
Azar Lawrence(ss,as,ts)Patrice Rushen,Michael Stanton,Jerry Peters,
Skip Scarborough(keyb,synth,arr)John Rowin,Lee Ritenour(g)Paul Jackson
(el b)Harvey Mason(dm)Mtume(perc)Dick Ricardo(perc)with Oscar Brashear,
Chuck Findley(tp)George Bohanon(tb)Ernie Watts(as)Buddy Collette(ts)
Cheryl Barnes,Josie James,Patrice Rushen,Michael Wright(voices).
Berkeley,March   ,1976

Theme for a new day	P-10099	
The awakening	-	
Can't hide love	-	
Kickin' back	-	
Canticle for the universe	-	
People moving	-	
Gratitude-1	-	

PATRICE RUSHEN-SHOUT IT OUT:
Patrice Rushen(synth,el p,p,clavinet,el b,vo)Al McKay(g)Charles Meeks
(b)James Gadson(dm)Bill Summers(perc).
Berkeley,   1976

The hump	P-10101	
Shout it out	-	
Stepping stones	-	
Let your heart be free voPR	-	P-766
Roll with the punches	-	
Let there be funk	-	
Yolon	-	
Sojourn	-	P-766

BILL SUMMERS-FEEL THE HEAT:
Fred Berry(tp)Julian Priester(tb)Myron Mu(frh)Roger Glenn(fl)Jose
Hernandez(as)Hadley Caliman(ts)Mark Soskin(el p)Slip Scarborough(synth,
p-1)Ray Obiedo(g,el g)Paul Jackson(el b)Charles Meeks(el b-2,vo-1)
Alphonse Mouzon(dm)Bill Summers(conga,bongos,perc)C.K.Ladzekpo(perc,
vo-3)Zak Diouf(perc,vo-3)Jose Lorenzo(whistle,perc)Baba Duru,Maddy
Perry(perc)Mikki Morris,Deborah Thomas,Diane Reeves,Sigidi,Pete
Escovedo,Sheila Escovedo(vo).
Berkeley,October   ,1976

Just a matter of time	P-10102	
Come into my life-1	-	P-765
People know-2	-	-
No one-1	-	
Brazilian skies	-	
Check it out	-	
Que sabroso	-	
Drum suite-3	-	

DAVID FATHEAD NEWMAN-KEEP THE DREAM ALIVE:
David Newman(fl,as,ts)George Cables,Hilton Ruiz(keyb)George Davis
Lee Ritenour(g)Wilbur Bascomb(tp?)Idris Muhammad(dm)Bill Summers(perc,
conga)with horns & voices,William Fisher(arr).
Berkeley,May   ,1977

Keep the dream alive	P-10106
Destiny	-
Silver morning	-
Freaky beat	-
I am singing	-
Clouds	-
As good as you are	-

BILL SUMMERS AND SUMMERS HEAT-CAYENNE:
George Spencer(tp,flh,backgr.vo)Zane Woodworth,Fred Berry(tp,flh)Julian
Priester(tb,bass tb)Curtis Shaw(tb)Bob Ferreira,Mel Martin(reeds)Hadley
Caliman(ts,fl)Rodney Franklin(keyb)Dawilli Gonga(synth)Jack Perry(synth,
backgr.vo-1)Ray Obiedo(g,backgr.vo)Fred Washington(b)James Levi(dm,
bongos)Munyungo Darryl Jackson(timbales,perc,backgr.vo)Bill Summers
(conga,perc,vo)Leo Miller,Carla Vaughn(lead vo,backgr.vo)Marilyn Anna
Greer,Eva E.Jeffrey,Willette Wells Hutcherson(backgr.vo).

Berkeley,September 1977

What's this mess	P-10103
Magic	-
Latican space mambo-1	-
Don't fade away-1	-
House party-1	-
Try a little tenderness	-
I've been around	-
Djembe de Fanta	-
Flying	-

DAVID FATHEAD NEWMAN-CONCRETE JUNGLE:
David Newman(fl,ss,as,ts)Pat Rebillot(keyb)Jay Graydon(el g)Abraham
Laboriel(el b)Idris Muhammad(dm)Bill Summers(perc,conga)with Jimmy
Owens,Milt Ward(tp)Earl McIntyre(tb)Kenneth Harris(fl)Babe Clarke(ts)
Clarence Thomas(bs)Gene Orloff,Harry Lookofsky,Sanford Allen,Regis
Iandiorio,Kathryn Kienke,Yoko Matsuo,Stan Pollock,Anthony Posk(v)
Alfred Brown,Linda Lawrence(viola)Kermit Moore(cello)William Fisher
(arr).

Berkeley,November   1977
& NYC,November   ,1977

Knocks me off my feet	P-10104
Save your love for me	-
Blues for ball	-
Dance of the honey bee and the funky fly	-
Concrete jungle	-
Sun seeds	-
Distant lover	-

BILL SUMMERS AND SUMMERS HEAT-STRAIGHT TO THE BANK:
Ray Obiedo(g)Fred Washington(b)Bill Summers,Leon Chancler(Ngudu),
Darryl "Munyungo" Jackson(perc)Leo Miller,Virginia Ayers(vo)with
Oscar Brashear(tp)John Barnes,Ernie Watts,horns,strings & voices.

LA & Berkeley,early   1978

Woo me baby,your love	P-10105
Love,not my life	-
Olodo	-
Straight to the bank	-
Creepy crawlers	-
It's on my mind	-
El barrio	-
All I want	-

NOTES

N O T E S

ADDITIONAL PRESTIGE SESSIONS

    Recording dates and complete details are not known for
following sessions issued by Prestige:

SILVER TRUMPETS:
Silver Trumpets(vocal quartet)with unknown g.

J-5   What manner of man is this?   Pr.913
J-8   Master Jesus   -
Rev.FELIX JOHNSON:
Rev.Felix Johnson(preaching)and congregation(singing).

J-9   The 23rd psalm   Pr.910
J-10   When a man dies   -
Note:These sessions were originally issued on the JET label.Matrix
numbers belong to JET series.
BOBBY HARRIS:
Bobby Harris(vo)with unknown p,g,b,dm,band vocal-1.
                                  NYC,   1952

1310   Heavyweight Mama-1   Par 1304
1311   Total stranger   -
BOB KENT BAND:
King Curtis,another(ts)unknown p,b,dm,Bob Kent(vo).

1320   Korea,Korea   Par 1303
1321   Oh!Baby   -
PINEY BROWN:
Piney Brown(vo)with unknown(ts)Ed Swanston(p)unknown g,b,dm.

1330   My heart is achin' baby   Par 1305
1331   Ooh,I want my baby   -
        The stuff is here   Par 1307
        So afraid of losing you   -
Note:Matrix numbers on above sessions belong to Par series.
RUDY FERGUSON:
Details unknown.

        Cool competition   Pr.859
        Ooh baby   -
TONY LUIS TRIO:
Tony Luis(p)Ron Andrews(b)Hank Nanni(dm).
                                  NYC,circa 1954-1955
        You're blaze   NJEP1703
        Unrocco Frisco   -
        Lullaby of the leaves   -
        Between the devil & the deep
                        blue sea   -

SANFORD GOLD-PIANO D'OR:
Sanford Gold(p).

NYC,c.Summer? 1955

Out of nowhere	PRLP7019
In a sentimental mood	-
I'll remember April	-
Penthouse serenade	-
Wait till you see her	-
Autumn in New York	-
The ladies	-
Maxine	-
Pretty bird	-
One minute of music	-
Number 13	-
Midtown	-

MOONDOG-CARIBEA:
Louis Thomas Hardin(various reeds,p,rhythm instruments)Sam Ulano
Japanese,Ray Malone(dm) & tap dancing.

NYC,   1956

Caribea	PRLP7042
Lullaby	-
Tree tail	-
Death,when you come to me	-
Big cat	-
Frog boy	-
To a sea horse	-
Dance rehearsal	-
Surf session	-
Trees against the sky	-
Tap dance	-
Drum suite	-
Street scene	-

MORE MOONDOG:
Louis Thomas Hardin(various perc,p-3)Ray Malone-2(tap dancing).
-1:Unknown(frh)Louis Thomas Hardin(reed).

NYC,   1956

A duet-Queen Elizabeth whistle and bamboo pipe	PRLP7069
Conversation and music at 51st St.and 6th Ave.	-
Hardshoe(7/4) -2	
Tugboat toccata	
Autumn-1	
Seven beat suite (3 parts)	
Oo solo(6/4)	-
Rehearsal of Violetta's "Barefoot dance" and portrait of Ninon a cocker spaniel	-
Oo solo again	-
Ostrich feathers played on drums	-
Oboe round	
Chant	-
All is loneliness	-
Sextet	-
Fiesta piano solo-3	-
Moondog monologue	-

THE STORY OF MOONDOG:
Louis Thomas Hardin(misc.strings & perc)Sam Ulano-1(dm).
                                    NYC,   1956-57
        Up Broadway-1   PRLP7099
        Perpetual motion   -
        Gloving it   -
        Improvisation   -
        Ray Malone softshoe   -
        Two quotations in dialogue   -
        5/8 in two shades   -
        Moondog's theme   -
        In a doorway   -
        Duet-1   -
        Trimbas in quarters   -
        Wildwood   -
        Trimbas in eights   -
        Organ rounds   ;   -

TAMPA RED-DON'T TAMPA WITH THE BLUES:
Tampa Red(vo,g,kazoo-1).
                                    Chicago,   1960
        I'm a stranger here-1   BVLP1030
        Let me play with your poodle   -   BV1055
        Goodbye baby-1   -
        Things about coming my way-1   -
        Kansas City blues   -
        You better do it right-1   -
        Louise blues   -
        It's tight like that-1   -
        You got to love her with a
                          feeling -
        Boogie woogie woman   -

TAMPA RED-DON'T JIVE ME:
Tampa Red(vo,g).

        How long   BVLP1043
        Gin headed woman   -
        You better let my gal alone   -
        Don't jive me   -
        Dark and stormy night   -
        Don't you lie to me   -
        Georgia,Georgia   -
        Jelly whippin' blues   -   BV1055
        Chicago moan blues   -
        Don't dog your woman   -
        Drinkin' my blues away   -

BABS GONZALES:
Babs Gonzales(vo)with unknown ts,p,b,dm.

                                    NYC,June or July 1961
        We ain't got integration   Pr.45-204
        Lonely one   -

Snooks Eaglin(vo,g)Lucius Bridge(vo,g,wbd)Percy Randolph(vo,hca).
NO,   1961

That's all right	BVLP1046
Bottle up and go	-
Malaguena	unissued
Who can your good man be	-
I must see Jesus	-
Give me the good old box car	-
Mama don't you tear my clothes	BVLP1046
She's a black rat	unissued
Who's been fooling you	-
Don't you lie to me	BVLP1046
Blue shadows blues	unissued
The walkin' blues	BVLP1046
Mean old world	unissued
Every day	-
(Well)I had my fun	BVLP1046
Fly right (back) baby	-
Mailman passed and he didn't leave no news	-
Brown skinned woman	-
One more drink	-
I've got a woman	-
I'm a country boy	-
Alberta	-

All titles from BVLP1046 have been reissued on Fantasy F-24716.

K.C.DOUGLAS-K.C.'S BLUES:
K.C.Douglas(vo,g).

Oakland, mid-1961

Broken heart	BVLP1023
Hen house blues	-
Wake up,workin' woman	-
Rootin' ground hog	-
Meanest woman	-
Born in the country	-
Love me all night long	-
Tell me	-
Cryin'	-
K.C.Doctor's blues	-
You got a good thing now	-
Watch dog blues	-

K.C.DOUGLAS-BIG ROAD BLUES:
K.C.Douglas(vo,g).

Oakland, mid-1961

Big road blues	BVLP1050
Howling blues	-
Move to Kansas City	-
Buck dance	-
Tore your playhouse down	-
Bottle up and go	-
Whiskey headed woman	-
Catfish blues	-
Canned heat	-
K.C.Blues	-
Key to the highway	-

```
PINK ANDERSON-MEDICINE SHOW MAN:
Pink Anderson(vo,g).
                                    NYC,                1961

        I got mine                  BVLP1051
        Greasy greens                  -
        I got a woman 'way cross town  -
        Travelin' man                  -
        Ain't nobody home but me       -
        That's no way to do            -
        In the jailhouse now           -
        South forest boogie            -
        Chicken                        -
        Walk through the streets of
                          the city     -

Rev.GARY DAVIS-SAY NO TO THE DEVIL:
Rev.Gary Davis(vo,g,hca-1).
                                    NYC,                1961

        Say no to the devil         BVLP1049
        Time is drawing near           -
        Hold to God's unchanging hand  -
        Bad company brought me here    -
        I decided to go down           -
        Lord I looked down the road    -
        Little bitty baby              -
        No one can do me like Jesus-1  -
        Lost boy in the wilderness     -
        Trying to get to heaven in due
                            time       -

MEMPHIS SLIM-ALL KINDS OF BLUES:
Memphis Slim(vo,p).
                                                       1961

        Blues is troubles           BVLP1053
        Grinder man blues              -
        Three-in-one boogie            -
        Letter home                    -
        Churnin' man blues             -
        Two of a kind                  -
        The blacks                     -
        If you see Kay                 -     BV1055
        Frankie and Johnny boogie      -
        Mother Earth                   -

MEMPHIS SLIM-STEADY ROLLIN' BLUES:
Memphis Slim(vo,p,org-1).

        Steady rollin' blues        BV1075,BV1055
        Sweet root man                 -      -
        Mean mistreatin' Mama          -
        Soon one morning-1             -
        Cella's boogie-1               -
        Big legged woman               -
        Rock me Mama                   -
        Goin' down slow-1              -
        Mr.Freddie boogie              -
        Three women blues              -
```

SONNY TERRY-SONNY IS KING:
Sonny Terry(vo,hca)Brownie McGhee(g).

                                                    1961?

        Sonny's coming   BVLP1059;PR7802
        Ida Mae   -   -
        Callin' Mama   -   -
        Bad luck   -   -
        Blues for the bottom   -   -

SMOKEY BABE-HOTTEST BRAND GOING:
Smokey Babe(vo,g)Clyde Causey(vo,hca-1)Henry Thomas-2(hca).
                                Baton Rouge,La.,   1961

        Now your man done gone   BVLP1063
        Hottest brand goin'   -
        Something's wrong with my
                        machine-2 -
        Insect blues   -
        Long way from home   -
        I'm going back to Mississippi -
        Melvanie blues   -
        Locomotive blues-1 (hca solo) -
        Ocean blues   -
        Boogy woogy rag   -
        Cool hunt-1   -
        Cold cold snow   -

J.T.ADAMS-INDIANA AVE.BLUES:
J.T.Adams,Shirley Griffith(vo,g).

                                Indianapolis,   1961

        Walkin' blues voSG   BV1077
        Match box blues voJTA   -
        Indiana Avenue blues   -
        In the evening   -
        'A' jump   -
        O Mama how I love you voSG -
        Kansas City voJTA   -
        Bright Street jump   -
        Done changed the lock on my
                        door voSG -
        Blind Lemon's blues voJTA -
        Naptown boogie   -

SHIRLEY GRIFFITH-BLUES OF SHIRLEY GRIFFITH:
Shirley Griffith(vo,g).

                                Indianapolis,   1961

        Meet me in the bottom   BV1087
        River line blues   -
        Shirley's jump   -
        Take me back to Mama   -
        Saturday blues   -
        Left alone blues   -
        Big road blues   -
        Bye bye blues   -
        Hard pill to swallow   -
        Maggie Campbell blues   -
        My baby's gone   -

THE NEW GOSPEL KEYS:
Clarence Clay(vo,accordion)William Scott(vo).

                                                            1962?

        Wait till I put on my robe   BV1066
        Every knee must bow   -
        Wake up in glory   -
        Trouble don't last always   -
        Jesus met the woman at the well   -
        In that great gettin' up morning -
        Oh what a beautiful city   -
        Marching to Zion   -
        I'm on my way to the Kingdom land -
        The Lord will make a way somehow -
        Walk all over God's Heaven   -
        All my sins are taken away   -

BROOKS BERRY/SCRAPPER BLACKWELL-MY HEART STRUCK SORROW:
Brooks Berry(vo)Scrapper Blackwell(p-1,g).

                                    Indianapolis,   1962

        Cold blooded murder   BV1074
        My man is studyin' evil   -
        Blues and trouble-1   -
        Sweetest apple   -
        Sun burst all my cotton   -
        'bama bound   -
        Can't sleep   -
        Life ain't worth living   -
        Blues is a feeling-1   -
        I've had my fun   -
        How long   -

ALEC SEWARD-CREEPIN' BLUES:
Alec Seward(vo,g)Larry Johnson(hca).

                                    NYC,
        Big hip Mama   BV1076
        Evil woman blues   -
        Goin' down slow-1   -
        Sweet woman   -
        Some people say   -
        Creepin' blues   -
        I made a mistake in life   -
        Piney Woods-1   -
        Late one Saturday evening   -
        Let a good thing go   -

-1:Johnson out.

JACK McDUFF:
Harold Vick(ts)Jack McDuff(org)Eddie Diehl(g)Joe Dukes(dm).
                                                        1964-65
        You'd be so easy to love   PR7567

JACK McDUFF:
Red Holloway(ts)Jack McDuff(org)George Benson(g)Larry Gales-1(b)Joe
Dukes(dm)Montego Joe(conga).

                                    NYC,   1965

        What's shakin'   PR7404
        The morning song   -
        12" wide   PR7642
        Silk and soul-1   Pr.45-377,PR7404

JACK McDUFF QUARTET:
Red Holloway(ts)Jack McDuff(org)Pat Martino(g)Joe Dukes(dm).
NYC,late 1965 or early 1966

    Around the corner   PR7476
    There is no greater love   -
    Almost like being in love   PR7492
    Spoonin'   PR7642

JIMMY WITHERSPOON-BLUES FOR EASY LIVERS:
Jimmy Witherspoon(vo)with Bill Watrous(tb)Pepper Adams(bs)Roger
Kellaway(p,arr)Richard Davis(b)Mel Lewis(dm).
Russell George(b)Dave Bailey(dm)replace Davis & Lewis on some titles.
NYC,   1965-66

    Lotus blossom   PR7475
    Gee baby,ain't I good to you   -
    Travelin' light   -
    P.S.I love you   -
    I'll always be in love with you -
    Don't worry 'bout me   -
    Easy living   -
    Embraceable you   -
    Blues in the night   -
    Trouble in mind
    How long will it take for me
        to become a man?   -
    I got it bad and that ain't good -

BENNY GREEN:
Benny Green(tb)with small band,Jimmy Mundy(arr).
NYC,c.Spring 1967

    Extra special delight   Pr.45-453
    Oh me,oh my   -
    I loved you   unissued
    I've never ever loved before   -

Part 2
Leased and Purchased Sessions

DUKE ELLINGTON'S ORCHESTRA:
Cootie Williams,Freddie Jenkins,Arthur Whetsol(tp)Lawrence Brown,Joe
"Tricky Sam" Nanton,Juan Tizol(tb)Barney Bigard(cl,ts)Johnny Hodges
(as,ss)Otto Hardwick(as,cl)Harry Carney(bs,cl)Duke Ellington(p)Fred
Guy(g)Wellman Braud(b)Sonny Greer(dm)Ivie Anderson(vo).
(from Columbia)   NYC,February 15,1933

265049-3 Merry-go-round   PR7645
265050-2 Sophisticated lady   -
265051-2 I've got the world on a string
                             voIA   -

Same.
                                           NYC,February 16,1933

265052-3 Down a Carolina lane   PR7645

BENNY CARTER AND HIS ORCHESTRA:
Shad Collins,Leonard Davis,Bill Dillard(tp)George Washington,Wilbur
De Paris(tb)Benny Carter(as,cl,vo)Howard Johnson(as)Chu Berry(ts)
Nicholas Rodriguez(p)Lawrence Lucie(g)Ernest "Bass" Hill(b)Sidney
Catlett(dm).
(from Columbia)   NYC,March 14,1933

265090-2 Swing it voBC   PR7643
265091-3 Synthetic love   -
265092-2 Six bells stampede   -
265093-2 Love,you're not the one for me
                             voBC   -

FLETCHER HENDERSON AND HIS ORCHESTRA:
Russell Smith,Bobby Stark,Henry Allen(tp)Claude Jones,Dicky Wells(tb)
Russell Procope(as,cl)Hilton Jefferson(as)Coleman Hawkins(ts)Horace
Henderson(p)Bernard Addison(g)John Kirby(b)Walter Johnson(dm).
(from Columbia)   Chicago,September 22,1933

265135-2 Queer notions   PR7645
265136-3 It's the talk of the town   -
265137-2 Night life   -
265138-2 Nagasaki voHAllen   -

JOE SULLIVAN:
Joe Sullivan(p solo).
(from Columbia)   NYC,September 26,1933

265139-2 Honeysuckle rose   PR7646
265140-2 Gin mill blues   -
265141-2 Little Rock getaway   -
265142-2 Onyx bring down   -

COLEMAN HAWKINS AND HIS ORCHESTRA:
Henry Allen(tp)J.C.Higginbotham(tb)Hilton Jefferson(as)Coleman Hawkins
(ts)Horace Henderson(p)Bernard Addison(g)John Kirby(b)Walter Johnson
(dm).
(from Columbia)   NYC,September 29,1933

265143-2 The day you came along   PR7647
265144-2 Jamaica shout   -
265145-2 Heart break blues   -

JOE VENUTI AND HIS BLUE SIX:
Joe Venuti(v)Benny Goodman(cl)Bud Freeman(ts)Adrian Rollini(bass sax)
Joe Sullivan(p)Dick McDonough(g)Neil Marshall(dm).
(from Columbia)   NYC,October 2,1933

265146-2 Sweet Lorraine   PR7644
265147-2 Doin' the uptown lowdown   -
265148-2 Jazz me blues   -
265149-2 In De Ruff   -

HORACE HENDERSON AND HIS ORCHESTRA:
Russell Smith,Bobby Stark,Henry Allen(tp)Claude Jones,Dicky Wells(tb)
Russell Procope(cl,as)Hilton Jefferson(as)Coleman Hawkins(ts)Horace
Henderson(p)Bernard Addison(g)John Kirby(b)Walter Johnson(dm).
(from Columbia)   Chicago,October 3,1933

265150-2 Happy feet   PR7645
265151-1 I'm rhythm crazy now   -
265152-1 Old man river voHA   -
265153-2 Minnie the moocher's wedding day -
265154-1 Ain't cha glad   -
265155-1 I've got to sing a torch song -

THE CHOCOLATE DANDIES:
Max Kaminsky(tp)Floyd O'Brien(tb)Benny Carter(as,tp-1)Chu Berry(ts)
Teddy Wilson(p)Lawrence Lucie(g)Ernest "Bass" Hill(b)Sidney Catlett,
Milton "Mezz" Mezzrow-2(dm).
(from Columbia)   NYC,October 10,1933

265156-2 Blue interlude   PR7643
265157-1 I never knew-1   -
265158-1 Once upon a time-1   -
265159-2 Krazy kapers-2   -

BENNY CARTER AND HIS ORCHESTRA:
Eddie Mallory,Bill Dillard,Dick Clark(tp)J.C.Higginbotham,Fred Robinson,
Keg Johnson(tb)Benny Carter(as,cl)Wayman Carver(as,fl)Glyn Pacque(as)
Johnny Russell(ts)Teddy Wilson(p)Lawrence Lucie(g)Ernest "Bass" Hill(b)
Sidney Catlett(dm).
(from Columbia)   NYC,October 16,1933

265160-1 Devil's holiday   PR7643
265161-1 Lonesome nights   -
265162-2 Symphony in riffs   -
265163-2 Blue Lou   -

BENNY GOODMAN AND HIS ORCHESTRA:
Manny Klein,Charlie Teagarden(tp)Jack Teagarden(tb,vo)Benny Goodman(cl)
Art Karle(ts)Joe Sullivan(p)Dick McDonough(g)Artie Bernstein(b)Gene
Krupa(dm).
(from Columbia)   NYC,October 18,1933

265164-2 I gotta right to sing the blues PR7644
265165-2 Ain't cha glad   -

Frank Froeba(p)replaces Sullivan.
(from Columbia)   NYC,October 27,1933

265166-2 Dr.Heckle and Mr.Jibe voDMcD,CT,JT PR7644
265167-2 Texas tea party   -

COLEMAN HAWKINS:
Coleman Hawkins(ts)Buck Washington(p).
(from Columbia)   NYC,March 8,1934

265173-2 I ain't got nobody   PR7647
265174-2 It sends me   -
265175-1 On the sunny side of the street -

COLEMAN HAWKINS:
Coleman Hawkins(ts)with Stanley Black(p)Albert Harris-1(g)Tiny Winters
-1(b).
(from Parlophone)   London,November 18,1934

E6739-1 Lullaby-1   PR7647
E6740-1 Lady be good-1   -
E6741-1 Lost in a frog   -
E6742-1 Honeysuckle rose   -

QUINTET OF THE HOT CLUB DE FRANCE:
Stephane Grappelli(v)Django Reinhardt,Joseph Reinhardt,Roger Chaput(g)
Louis Vola(b).
(from Ultraphone)   Paris,December   ,1934

77161   Dinah   PR7614
77162   Tiger rag   -
77163   Lady be good   -

COLEMAN HAWKINS(ts)acc.by MICHEL WARLOP'S ORCHESTRA:
Arthur Briggs,Noel Chiboust,Pierre Allier(tp)Guy Paquinet(tb)André
Ekyan,Charles Lisee(as)Alix Combelle(ts)Stephane Grappelli(p)Django
Reinhardt(g)Eugène d'Hellemmes(b)Maurice Chaillou(dm).
(from Gramophone)   Paris,March 2,1935

OLA346-1 Blue moon   PR7633
OLA347-1 Avalon   -
OLA348-1 What a difference a day made   -
Coleman Hawkins(ts)Stephane Grappelli(p)Django Reinhardt(g)Eugène
d'Hellemmes(b)Maurice Chaillou(dm).Same session.

OLA349-1 Stardust   PR7633

QUINTET OF THE HOT CLUB DE FRANCE:
Stephane Grappelli(v)Django Reinhardt,Joseph Reinhardt,Roger Chaput(g)
Louis Vola(b).
(from Ultraphone)   Paris,March   ,1935

77242   Confessin'   PR7614

Same.
(from Ultraphone)   Paris,May   ,1935

77351   Blue drag   PR7614
77352   Swanee river   -
77353   The sunshine of your smile   -
77354   Ultra fox   -

Arthur Briggs,Pierre Allier,Alphonse Cox(tp)Eugène d'Hellemmes(tb)
Stephane Grappelli(v)Django Reinhardt,Joseph Reinhardt,Pierre Ferret
(g)Louis Vola(b).
(from Ultraphone)   Paris,July   ,1935

77434   Avalon   PR7614
77435   Smoke rings   -

Alix Combelle(ts)Stephane Grappelli(p)Django Reinhardt,Joseph Reinhardt
(g)Louis Vola(b).
(from Ultraphone)   Paris,September 1,1935

77523   The Sheik of Araby   PR7614

Stephane Grappelli(v)Django Reinhardt,Joseph Reinhardt,Pierre Ferret
(g)Louis Vola(b).
(from Ultraphone)   Paris,September   ,1935

77538   I've had my moments   PR7614

BUD FREEMAN AND HIS WINDY CITY FIVE:
Bunny Berigan(tp)Bud Freeman(cl,ts)Claude Thornhill(p)Eddie Condon(g)
Grachan Moncur(b)Cozy Cole(dm).
(from Decca)   NYC,November 2,1935
60190A What is there to say?   PR7646
60191B The buzzard   -
60192B Tillie's downtown now   -
60193A Keep smilin' at trouble   -

JESSE STACY:
Jesse Stacy(p)Israel Crosby(b)Gene Krupa(dm).
(from Decca)   Chicago,November 16,1935
90445A In the dark/Flashes (p solo)   PR7646
90446A Barrelhouse   -
90447A The world is waiting for the
                           sunrise   -

GENE KRUPA AND HIS CHICAGOANS:
Nate Kazebier(tp)Joe Harris(tb)Benny Goodman(cl)Dick Clark(ts)Jesse
Stacy(p)Allan Reuss(g)Israel Crosby(b)Gene Krupa(dm).
(from Decca)   Chicago,November 19,1935
90460A The last round up   PR7644
90461A Jazz me blues   -
90462A Three little words   -
90463B Blues of Israel   -

GARNET CLARK AND HIS ORCHESTRA:
Bill Coleman(tp,vo)George Johnson(cl)Garnet Clark(p)Django Reinhardt
(g)June Cole(b).
(from Gramophone)   Paris,November 25 1935
OLA730-1 Rosetta   PR7633
OLA731-1 Stardust   -
OLA732-1 The object of my affection voBC -

BUNNY BERIGAN AND HIS BLUE BOYS:
Bunny Berigan(tp)Eddie Miller(cl,ts)Edgar Sampson(cl-1,as)Cliff
Jackson(p)Grachan Moncur(b)Ray Bauduc(dm).
(from Decca)   NYC,December 13,1935
60229   You took advantage of me   PR7646
60230   Chicken and waffles-1   -
60231   I'm coming Virginia   -
60232   Blues   -

MARY LOU WILLIAMS:
Mary Lou Williams(p)Booker Collins(b)Ben Thigpen(dm).
(from Decca)   NYC,March 7,1936
60877A Corny rhythm   PR7647
60878A Overhand(New froggy bottom)   -
60879A Isabelle   -

Same.
(from Decca)   NYC,March 11,1936
60894 Swingin' for joy   PR7647
60895 Clean pickin'   -

Mary Lou Williams(p,celeste)Ted Robinson(g)Booker Collins(b)Ben
Thigpen(dm).
(from Decca)   NYC,April 9,1936
61023A Mary's special   PR7647

COLEMAN HAWKINS AND HIS ALL STAR JAM BAND:
Benny Carter(as,tp-1)André Ekyan(as)Coleman Hawkins(ts)Alix Combelle
(ts,cl-2)Stephane Grappelli(p)Django Reinhardt(g)Eugène d'Hellemmes
(b)Tommy Benford(dm).
(from Gramophone)   Paris,April 28,1937

OLA1742-1 Crazy rhythm   PR7633
OLA1743-1 Honeysuckle rose   -
OLA1744-1 Out of nowhere-1,2   -
OLA1745-1 Sweet Georgia Brown-1,2   -

DICKY WELLS IN PARIS,1937:
Bill Coleman(tp,vo)Bill Dillard,Lester "Shad" Collins(tp-1)Dicky Wells
(tb)Django Reinhardt(g)Richard Fullbright(b)Bill Beason(dm).
(from Gramophone)   Paris,July 7,1937

OLA1884-1 Bugle call rag-1   PR7593
OLA1885-1 Between the devil & the
            deep blue sea-1   -
OLA1886-1 I got rhythm-1   -
OLA1887-1 Sweet sue   -
OLA1888-1 Hangin' around Boudon voBC   -
OLA1889-1 Japanese sandman   -

Bill Dillard-1,Lester "Shad" Collins-2(tp)Dicky Wells(tb)Howard
Johnson-1(as)Sam Allen(p)Roger Chaput(g)Bill Beason(dm).
(from Gramophone)   Paris,July 12,1937

OLA1894-1 I've found a new baby-1,2   PR7593
OLA1895-1 Dinah-1,2   -
OLA1896-1 Nobody's blues but my own-1,2   -
OLA1897-1 Hot Club blues-1   -
OLA1898-1 Lady be good   -
OLA1899-1 Dicky Wells blues   -

BENNY CARTER AND HIS ORCHESTRA:
Benny Carter(tp-1,as)Fletcher Allen(as)Alix Combelle(ts)Bertie King
(cl-1,ts)Raymond De Sota(p)Django Reinhardt(g)Len Harrison(b)Robert
Montmarché(dm).
(from Swing)   Paris,January 24,1938

OSW4-1   I'm coming Virginia   PR7633
OSW5-1   Farewell blues   -
OSW6-1   Blue light blues-1   -

DUKE ELLINGTON CARNEGIE HALL CONCERT-JANUARY 1943:
Harold Baker,Wallace Jones,Ray Nance,Rex Stewart(tp)Lawrence Brown,
Joe "Tricky Sam" Nanton,Juan Tizol(tb)Johnny Hodges,Otto Hardwick(as)
Chauncey Haughton(cl,ts)Ben Webster(ts)Harry Carney(bs)Duke Ellington
(p)Fred Guy(g)Junior Raglin(b)Sonny Greer(dm)Betty Roche(vo).
(from Jerry Valburn)   Carnegie Hall,NYC,January 23,1943

           Black and tan fantasy   Prestige P-34004
           Rockin' in rhythm   -
           Moon mist   -
           Jumpin' punkins   -
           A portrait of Bert Williams   -
           Bojangles   -
           Black beauty-1   -
           Ko-ko   -
           Dirge   -
           Stomp(Johnny come lately)   -
           Are you stickin'?   -
(continued on next page)

```
         Black,brown and beige-1        Prestige P-34004
         Bakiff                                -
         Jack the bear                         -
         Blue belles of Harlem                 -
         Cotton tail                           -
         Day dream                             -
         Boy meets horn                        -
         Rose of the Rio Grande                -
         Don't get around much anymore         -
         Goin' up                              -
         Mood indigo                           -
```

-1:These are spliced versions,first part of these titles coming from
Symphony Hall,Boston,January 27,1943 concert by same band.

WALTER "FOOTS" THOMAS ALL STARS:
Emmett Berry(tp)Walter "Foots" Thomas(as,ts)Ben Webster(ts)Budd Johnson
(ts,bs)Clyde Hart(p)Oscar Pettiford(b)Cozy Cole(dm).
(from Joe Davis)   NYC,April 1,1944

```
         Broke but happy            PR7584
         Blues on the delta            -
         Jumpin' with Judy             -
         Blues on the bayou            -
```

Jonah Jones(tp)Eddie Barefield(cl,ts)Hilton Jefferson(as)Walter "Foots"
Thomas,Coleman Hawkins(ts)Clyde Hart(p)Milt Hinton(b)Cozy Cole(dm).
(from Joe Davis)   NYC,October 11,1944

```
         In the hush of thenight    PR7584
         Out to lunch                  -
         Every man for himself         -
         Look out Jack                 -
```

COLEMAN HAWKINS:
Coleman Hawkins(ts)Thelonious Monk(p)Edward "Bass" Robinson(b)Denzil
Best(dm).
(from Joe Davis)   NYC,October 19,1944

```
         On the Bean                PR7824
         Recollections                 -
         Flyin' Hawk                   -
         Drifting on a reed            -
```

WINGY MANONE:
Wingy Manone(tp,vo)Frank Orchard(tb)Joe Marsala(cl)Conrad Lanoue(p)
Chuck Wayne(g)Irving Lang(b)George Wettling(dm).
(from Joe Davis)   NYC,December 15,1944

```
         O sole mio                 PR7812
         Shake the blues away          -
```

DUKE ELLINGTON CARNEGIE HALL CONCERT-DECEMBER 1944:
Cat Anderson,Shelton Hemphill,Taft Jordan,Ray Nance(tp)Lawrence Brown,
Joe "Tricky Sam" Nanton,Claude Jones(tb)Johnny Hodges,Otto Hardwick(as)
Jimmy Hamilton(ts,cl)Al Sears(ts)Harry Carney(bs)Duke Ellington(p)
Fred Guy(g)Junior Raglin(b)Hillard Brown(dm)Kay Davis,Marie Ellington,
Al Hibbler(vo).
(from Jerry Valburn)   Carnegie Hall,NYC,December 19,1944

```
         Bluetopia                  P-24073
         Midriff                       -
         Creole love call voKD         -
         Suddenly it jumped            -
         Pitter panther patter         -
```
(continued on next page)

[240]
```
```

```
It don't mean a thing          P-24073
Perfume suite                    -
Black,brown and beige            -
Things ain't what they
          used to be             -
The mood to be wooed             -
Blue cellophane                  -
Blue skies                       -

Frankie and Johnny               -
```

ART TATUM:
Joe Thomas(tp)Barney Bigard(cl)Joe Thomas(ts)Art Tatum(p)Billy Taylor
(b)Stan Levey(dm).
(from Black & White)   NYC,January 5,1945

```
BW64     Please don't talk about me
              when I'm gone      P-24052
```

ERROLL GARNER:
Erroll Garner(p)Eddie Brown(b)Harold "Doc" West(dm).
(from Black & White)   NYC,January 10,1945

```
BW67      White rose bounce      P-24052
```

DIZZY GILLESPIE SEXTET:
Dizzy Gillespie(tp)Dexter Gordon(ts)Frank Paparelli(p)Chuck Wayne(g)
Murray Shipinski(b)Irv Kluger(dm).
(from Guild/Musicraft)   NYC,February 9,1945

```
555      Blue 'n 'boogie        PR24030
```

Dizzy Gillespie(tp)Charlie Parker(as)Clyde Hart(p)Remo Palmieri(g)
Slam Stewart(b)Cozy Cole(dm).
(from Guild/Musicraft)   NYC,February 28,1945

```
554      Groovin' high          PR24030
556      All the things you are   -
557      Dizzy atmosphere         -
```

WALTER "FOOTS" THOMAS ALL STARS:
Charlie Shavers(tp)Milt Yaner(cl,as)Walter "Foots" Thomas(as,ts)Ben
Webster(ts)Ernie Caceres(bs)Billy Taylor(p)Slam Stewart(b)Cozy Cole(dm).
(from Joe Davis)   NYC,March 8,1945

```
         The bottle's empty     PR7584
         Save it pretty Mama      -
         For lovers only          -
         Peach tree Street blues  -
```

DIZZY GILLESPIE QUINTET:
Dizzy Gillespie(tp,vo)Charlie Parker(as)Al Haig(p)Curley Russell(b)
Sidney Catlett(dm)Sarah Vaughan(vo).
(from Guild/Musicraft)   NYC,May 11,1945

```
565      Salt peanuts voDG      PR24030
566      Shaw 'nuff               -
567      Lover man voSV           -
568      Hot house                -
```

WALTER "FOOTS" THOMAS ALL STARS:
Doc Cheatham(tp)Eddie Barefield,Hilton Jefferson(cl,as)Walter "Foots"
Thomas,Ted McRae(ts)Buddy Safer(bs)Billy Taylor(p)Milt Hinton(b)Specs
Powell(dm).
(from Joe Davis)   NYC,June 27,1945

```
         Dee tees               PR7584
         Black Maria's blues      -
         Back talk                -
         Bird train               -
```

WINGY MANONE:
Wingy Manone(tp,vo)Ward Silloway(tb)Hank D'Amico(cl)Nick Caiazza(ts)
Dave Bowman(p)Bob Haggart(b)George Wettling(dm).
(from Joe Davis)   NYC,July 3,1945

    That glory day   PR7812
    Bread and gravy   -
    That's a gasser   -
    Georgia girl   -
    Mr.Boogie man   -
    Where can I find a cherry   -

REX STEWART:
Rex Stewart(c)Tyree Glenn(tb)Earl Bostic(as)Cecil Scott(bs)Dave
Rivera(p)Brick Fleagle(g)Alvin "Junior" Raglin(b)J.C.Heard(dm).
                                    NYC,July 30,1945

    Pawnee   PR7812
    Three-horn parley   -
    Dreamer's blues   -
    Shady side of the street   -

DUKE ELLINGTON CARNEGIE HALL CONCERT-JANUARY 1946:
Cat Anderson,Shelton Hemphill,Taft Jordan,Francis Williams(tp)Lawrence
Brown,Wilbur De Paris,Claude Jones(tb)Johnny Hodges,Otto Hardwick(as)
Al Sears(ts)Jimmy Hamilton(ts,cl)Harry Carney(bs)Duke Ellington(p)
Fred Guy(b)Oscar Pettiford,Al Lucas(b)Sonny Greer(dm)Kay Davis,Joya
Sherrill,Al Hibbler(vo).
(from Jerry Valburn)   Carnegie Hall,NYC,January 4,1946

    Caravan   P-24074
    In a mellotone   -
    Solid old man   -
    Black,brown and beige   -
    Rugged Romeo   -
    Sono   -
    Air conditioned jungle   -
    Pitter panther patter   -
    Take the A train   -
    Tone group   -
    Magenta haze   -
    Diminuendo in blue/   -
    Transblucency   -
    Suburbanite   -
    I'm just a lucky so and so   -
    Riffin' drill   -

DIZZY GILLESPIE SEXTET:
Dizzy Gillespie(tp,vo)Sonny Stitt(as)Milt Jackson(vb)Al Haig(p)Ray
Brown(b)Kenny Clarke(dm)Gil Fuller,Alice Roberts(vo).
(from Musicraft)   NYC,May 15,1946

5497 One bass hit   PR24030
5498 Oop bop sh' bam voDG,GF   -
5499 A handfulla gimme voAR   -
5500 That's Earl brother   -

DIZZY GILLESPIE AND HIS ORCHESTRA:
Dizzy Gillespie,Dave Burns,Raymond Orr,Talib Daawud,John Lynch(tp)Al
Moore,Charles Greenlee(tb)John Brown,Howard Johnson(as)Ray Abrams,
Warren Luckey(ts)Pee Wee Moore(bs)Milt Jackson(p)Ray Brown(b)Kenny
Clarke(dm)Alice Roberts(vo).
(from Musicraft)   NYC,June 10,1946

5550 Our delight   PR24030
5551 Good dues blues voAR   -

DIZZY GILLESPIE AND HIS ORCHESTRA:
Dizzy Gillespie,Dave Burns,Talib Daawud,Kenny Dorham,John Lynch,Elmon
Wright(tp)Leon Comegeys,Gordon Thomas,Alton "Slim "Moore(tb)Howard
Johnson,Sonny Stitt(as)Ray Abrams,Warren Luckey(ts)Leo Parker(bs)
Milt Jackson(vb)John Lewis(p)Ray Brown(b)Kenny Clarke(dm)Alice Roberts
(vo).
(from Musicraft)   NYC,July 9,1946
5609   One bass hit No.2   PR24030
5610   Ray's idea   -
5611   Things to come   -
5612   He beeped when he should
              have bopped voAR   -

SWING 1946:
Buck Clayton(tp)Al Grey(tb)Benny Carter(cl,as)Ike Quebec(ts)Sonny
White(p)John Simmons(b)Sidney Catlett(dm).
(from Swing)   NYC,August 23,1946
D6VB2694   Sweet Georgia Brown   PR7604
D6VB2695   Out of my way   -
D6VB2696   What'll it be   -
D6VB2697   Cadillac Slim   -

Jonah Jones(tp)Tyree Glenn(tb)Rudy Powell(cl,as)Ike Quebec(ts)Dave
Rivera(p)Milt Hinton(b)Kansas Fields(dm).
(from Swing)   NYC,September 4,1946
D6VB2788   I can't give you anything
                       but love PR7604
D6VB2789   I'm headin' for Paris   -
D6VB2790   Jonah's wail   -
D6VB2791   That's the lick   -

Lincoln Mills(tp)Gene Sedric(cl,ts,vo)Freddie Jefferson(p)Al Casey(g)
Danny Settle(b)Slick Jones(dm).
(from Swing)   NYC,September 6,1946
D6VB2796   Honeysuckle rose   PR7604
D6VB2797   These foolish things   -
D6VB2798   The session jumped   -
D6VB2799   Clarinet blues   -

DON BYAS IN PARIS:
Peanuts Holland(tp)Tyree Glenn(tb)Hubert Rostaing(cl)Don Byas(ts)Billy
Taylor(p)Ted Sturgis(b)Buford Oliver(dm).
(from Swing)   Paris,October 18,1946
OSW437-1   Working eyes   PR7598
OSW438-1   Gloria-1   -
OSW439-1   Peanut butter blues   -
OSW440-1   Mohawk special   -
-1:Byas & rhythm only.

DUKE ELLINGTON AND HIS ORCHESTRA:
Shelton Hemphill,Francis Williams,Taft Jordan(tp)Ray Nance(tp,v)
Lawrence Brown,Wilbur De Paris,Claude Jones(tb)Jimmy Hamilton(cl,ts)
Russell Procope,Johnny Hodges(as)Al Sears(ts)Harry Carney(bs)Duke
Ellington(p)Fred Guy(g)Oscar Pettiford(b)Sonny Greer(dm).
(from Musicraft)   NYC,October 23,1946
5765   Diminuendo in blue   PR24029
5766   Magenta Haze   -

[243]

DIZZY GILLESPIE AND HIS ORCHESTRA:
Dizzy Gillespie,Dave Burns,Elmon Wright,Matthew McKay,John Lynch(tp)
Alton "Slim" Moore,Taswell Baird,Gordon Thomas(tb)John Brown,Scoops
Carey(as)James Moody,Bill Frazier(ts)Pee Wee Moore(bs)John Lewis(p)
Ray Brown(b)Joe Harris(dm)Milt Jackson(vb)Kenny Hagood(vo).
(from Musicraft)   NYC,November 12,1946

5788   I waited for you voKH   PR24030
5789   Emanon   -

DUKE ELLINGTON AND HIS ORCHESTRA:
Harold Baker,Cat Anderson,Francis Williams,Taft Jordan(tp)Ray Nance
(tp,v)Claude Jones,Wilbur De Paris,Lawrence Brown(tb)Russell Procope
(cl,as)Johnny Hodges(as)Jimmy Hamilton(cl,ts)Al Sears(ts)Harry Carney
(bs,cl,bass cl)Duke Ellington(p)Fred Guy(g)Oscar Pettiford(b)Sonny
Greer(dm).
(from Musicraft)   NYC,November 25,1946

5813   Sultry sunset   PR24029
5814   Happy-go-lucky local,pt.2   -
5815   Blue skies(Trumpet no end)   -
5816   Happy-go-lucky local,pt.1   -
5817   The beautiful Indians:Hiawatha -
5818   Flippant flurry   -

DON BYAS IN PARIS:
Don Byas(ts)Billy Taylor(p)Jean Bouchety(b)Buford Oliver(dm).
(from Swing)   Paris,December 4,1946

OSW444-1   I'm beginning to see the light PR7598
OSW445-2   Rosetta   -
OSW446-1   Ain't misbehavin'   -
OSW447-1   Body and soul   -
OSW448-2   Blue and sentimental   -

DUKE ELLINGTON AND HIS ORCHESTRA:
Harold Baker,Cat Anderson,Francis Williams,Taft Jordan(tp)Ray Nance
(tp,v)Claude Jones,Wilbur De Paris,Lawrence Brown(tb)Russell Procope
(cl,as)Johnny Hodges(as)Jimmy Hamilton(cl,ts)Al Sears(ts)Harry Carney
(bs,cl,bass cl)Duke Ellington(p)Fred Guy(g)Oscar Pettiford(b)Sonny
Greer(dm)Kay Davis(vo).
(from Musicraft)   NYC,December 5,1946

5823   Golden feather   PR24029
5824   The beautiful Indians:
                    Minnehaha voKD   -

Same,with Al Hibbler,Ray Nance(vo).
(from Musicraft)   NYC,December 11,1946

5841   Tulip or turnip voRN   PR24029
5842   It shouldn't happen to
                    a dream voAH   -

Same band.
(from Musicraft)   NYC,December 18,1946

5845   Overture to a jam session,pt.1 PR24029
5846   Overture to a jam session,pt.2 -
5847   Jam-a-ditty   -

COLEMAN HAWKINS:
Fats Navarro(tp)Jay Jay Johnson(tb)Porter Kilbert(as)Coleman Hawkins
(ts)Milt Jackson(vb)Hank Jones(p)Curley Russell(b)Max Roach(dm).
(from Sonora)   NYC,December ,1946

SR1857	I mean you-1	PR7824
SR1858-1	Bean and the boys	-
SR1858-2	Bean and the boys	-
SR1859	You go to my head-2	-
SR1860	Cocktails for two-2	-

-1:Jackson out;-2:Navarro,Johnson & Kilbert out.

CHUBBY JACKSON AND HIS ORCHESTRA:
Conte Candoli(tp)Emmett Carls(ts)Tony Aless(p)Billy Bauer(g)Chubby
Jackson(b,vo)Mel Zelnick(dm).
(from MGM)   NYC,May 22,1947

178A	The happy monster	PR7641
178B	Follow the leader voCJ	-
179A	L'Ana -1	-
179B	'Mom' Jackson voCJ	-

-1:Vocal by The Three Nundicks(Candoli,Carls,Jackson)

DUKE ELLINGTON CARNEGIE HALL CONCERT-DECEMBER 1947:
Harold Baker,Shelton Hemphill,Francis Williams,Ray Nance,Al Killian(tp)
Lawrence Brown,Tyree Glenn,Claude Jones(tb)Johnny Hodges,Russell
Procope(as)Al Sears(ts)Jimmy Hamilton(cl,ts)Harry Carney(bs)Duke
Ellington(p)Fred Guy(g)Oscar Pettiford,Junior Raglin(b)Sonny Greer(dm)
Kay Davis,Al Hibbler(vo).
(from Jerry Valburn)   Carnegie Hall,NYC,December 27,1947

Snibor	P-24075
Blue Serge	-
Triple play	-
Harlem airshaft	-
Wanderlust/	-
Junior hop/	-
Jeep's blues/	-
The jeep is jumpin'	-
Squatty roo/	-
The mood to be wooed	-
Mella brava	-
Kickapoo joy juice	-
Turquoise cloud	-
Bakiff	-
Liberian suite	-
Cotton tail	-
East St.Louis toodle-oo/	-
Echoes of Harlem/	-
Black and tan fantasy/	-
Things ain't what they used to be	-
Basso profundo	-
New York City blues	-
Clothed woman	-
Trumpets no end(Blue skies)	-

DIZZY GILLESPIE BIG BAND-PARIS 1948:
Dizzy Gillespie(tp,vo)Benny Bailey,Dave Burns,Lamar Wright,Elmon
Wright(tp)Ted Kelly,Bill Shepherd(tb)Howard Johnson,John Brown(as)
Joe Gales,George 'Big Nick' Nicholas(ts)Cecil Payne(bs)John Lewis(p)
Al McKibbon(b)Kenny Clarke(dm)Chano Pozo(conga)Kenny Hagood(vo).
(from Vogue)   Salle Pleyel,Paris,February 28,1948

          Oop pop a da   PR7818
          'Round midnight   -
          Algo bueno(Woody'n you) -
          I can't get started   -
          Two bass hit   -
          Good bait   -
          Afro Cuban suite   -
          Ool ya koo   -
          Things to come   -

KENNY CLARKE:
Benny Bailey(tp)John Brown(as)Cecil Payne(bs)Ralph Schecroun(p)Al
McKibbon(b)Kenny Clarke(dm).
(from Swing)   Paris,March 2,1948

OSW496-1 Confirmation   PR7605
OSW497-1 Cheryl(A la Colette)   -
OSW498   Listen here(Jumpin' there) -
OSW499-1 Jay Mac   -

CHARLIE PARKER ALL STARS:
Miles Davis(tp)Charlie Parker(as)Duke Jordan(p)Tommy Potter(b)Max
Roach(dm).
(from Debut/Fantasy)   Onyx Club,NYC,c.Spring 1948

          52nd Street theme I   PR24009
          Shaw 'nuff   -
          Out of nowhere I   -
          Hot house   -
          This time the dream's on me I   -
          Night in Tunisia   -
          My old flame   -
          52nd Street theme   -
          The way you look tonight   -
          Out of nowhere II   -
          Chasin' the Bird   -
          This time the dream's on me II -
          Dizzy atmosphere   -
          How high the moon   -
          52nd Street theme II   -

THE ALL STAR SEXTET:
Reg Arnold(tp)Aubrey Frank(ts)Tommy Pollard(vb)Ralph Sharon(p)Jack
Fallon(b)Norman Burns(dm)Alan Dean(vo).
(from Esquire)   London,April 29,1948

31   First gear voAD   NJ801
32   Confirmation   -

KENNY CLARKE:
Howard McGhee(tp)Jimmy Heath,Hubert Fol-1(as)Jesse Powell(ts)John
Lewis(p)John Collins(g)Percy Heath(b)Kenny Clarke(dm).
(from Swing)   Paris,May 14,1948

OSW531-1 Sweet and lovely   PR7605
OSW532-1 Annel-1(Maggie's draw*)   -*
OSW533   Out of nowhere   -
OSW534-1 I'm in the mood for love-2 -

-2:McGhee & Heath out.

[246]

HOWARD McGHEE BOPTET:
Howard McGhee(tp)Jimmy Heath(as)Jesse Powell(ts)Vernon Biddle(p)Percy
Heath(b)Specs Wright(dm).
(from Blue Star)   Paris,May 15,1948

ST2294   Crossroads   NJ815
ST2297   Dimitar   -

EARL COLEMAN:
Earl Coleman(vo)with Fats Navarro(tp)Don Lanphere(ts)Linton Garner(p)
Al Casey(g)Jim Johnson(b)Max Roach(dm).
(from Dial)   NYC,November 29,1948

D1162A   Guilty   Pr.905
D1165A   As time goes by   -

DON BYAS IN PARIS:
Bill Coleman(tp)Don Byas(ts)Bernard Peiffer(p)Jean Bouchety(b)Roger
Paraboschi(dm).
(from Swing)   Paris,January 5,1949

OSW562-1 What is this thing called love PR7598
OSW563-2 Yesterdays-1   -
OSW564-1 St.Louis blues   -
OSW565-1 Lover man   -
OSW566-1 Liza   -
OSW567-1 Blues at noon   -

-1:Coleman out.

OSCAR PETTIFORD:
Red Rodney(tp)Earl Swope(tb)Al Cohn(ts)Serge Chaloff(bs)Barbara
Carroll(p)Oscar Pettiford(b)Denzil Best(dm)Terry Gibbs(vb)Shorty
Rogers(arr).
(from Futurama)   NYC,March 10,1949

MS704   Chickasaw   PR7813
MS705   Bop scotch   -
MS706   The most   -
MS707   Chasin' the bass   -

Note:This session was previously issued as by Serge Chaloff.

JIMMY McPARTLAND:
Jimmy McPartland(c)Harry Lepp(tb)Jack O'Connel(cl,as)Marian McPartland
(p)Ben Carlton(b)Mousie Alexander(dm).
(from Unison)   Chicago,March   ,1949

UR8815   Royal garden blues   Pr.302
UR8816   Daughter of Sister Kate   Pr.301
UR8817   Singin' the blues   -
UR8818   In a mist   Pr.302

JAMES MOODY QUARTET:
James Moody(ts)Art Simmons(p)Buddy Banks(b)Clarence Terry(dm).
(from Vogue)   Lausanne,April 30,1949

V3005   Stardust   Pr.841,LP157
V3009   Moody and soul   -   -

MAX ROACH QUINTET:
Kenny Dorham(tp)James Moody(ts)Al Haig(p)Tommy Potter(b)Max Roach(dm).
(from Vogue)   Paris,May 15,1949

ST3010   Prince Albert   PR7841
ST3011   Maxology   Pr.702,LP113,PR7841
ST3012   Yesterdays(Tomorrow)   PR7841
ST3013   Maximum   -

Note:Pr.702 issued as by James Moody Quintet;PR7841 issued as by Al
Haig Quintet;ST3011 issued on LP113 as "Baby Sis" by Kenny Dorham.

AL HAIG SEXTET:
Kai Winding(tb)Stan Getz(ts)Al Haig(p)Jimmy Raney(g,vo)Tommy Potter(b)
Roy Haynes(dm)Blossom Dearie(vo).
(from Harry Lim)   NYC,July 28,1949

HLO-1   Pinch bottle   PR7516
HLO-2   Earless engineering   -
HLO-3   Be still TV voJR & band   -
HLO-4   Short P not LP voJR & band   -

ARNE DOMNERUS CLARINET SOLOS:
Arne Domnerus(cl,as)Gösta Theselius(p)Lennart Sundewall(b)Jack Noren
(dm).
(from Metronome)   Stockholm,August 20,1949

MR10   Body and soul   NJ821;PRLP134

Ulf Linde(vb)added.
(from Metronome)   Stockholm,September 19,1949

MR9   I've got my love to keep me warm NJ821;PRLP134

Arne Domnerus(cl)Ulf Linde(vb)Gösta Theselius(p)Yngve Akerberg(b)
Andrew Burman(dm).
(from Metronome)   Stockholm,October 6,1949

MR23   Night and day   PRLP134
MR24   I surrender dear   -

JAMES MOODY:
Leppe   Sundewall(tp)Arne Domnerus(as)James Moody(ts)Per Arne Croona
(bs)Gösta Theselius(p)Yngve Akerberg(b)Andrew Burman(dm).
(from Metronome)   Stockholm,October 7,1949

MR25A   Out of nowhere   Pr.701,EP1340,LP110,PR7431
MR26   These foolish things   Pr.774   -   -

JAMES MOODY QUINTET:
Leppe   Sundewall(tp)James Moody(ts)Thore Swanerud(p)Yngve Akerberg(b)
Jack Noren(dm).
(from Metronome)   Stockholm,October 12,1949

MR29A   I'm in the mood for love   Pr.774*,LP110**,PR7431*
         (I'm in the mood for groovin'*)
         (I'm in the mood for bop**)

James Moody(ts)Gösta Theselius(p)Yngve Akerberg(b)Jack Noren(dm).
(from Metronome)   Same date.

MR30A   The flight of the bopple bee   Pr.703,EP1340,LP110,PR7431

Leppe Sundewall(tp)Arne Domnerus(as)James Moody(as-1,ts-2)Gösta
Theselius-1(ts)Per Arne Croona(bs)Thore Swanerud(p)Yngve Akerberg(b)
Andrew Burman(dm).
(from Metronome)   Same date.

MR31A   Body and soul-1   Pr.730,LP110,PR7431
MR32   I'm in the mood for love-1   Pr.703,45-418,EP1340,LP110,
                                         PR7431,PR24015
MR33   Lester leaps in-2   Pr.701,EP1340,LP110,PR7431

James Moody(ts)Ulf Linde(vb)Thore Swanerud(p)Rolf Berg(g)Yngve Aker-
berg(b)Andrew Burman(dm).
(from Metronome)   Same date.

MR34   Indiana   PRLP110,PR7431
MR35A   Good bait   Pr.716,LP146,PR7431
MR36   Dexterious   -   -   -

JAMES MOODY AND HIS COOL CATS:
James Moody(ts)Thore Swanerud(p)Yngve A kerberg(b)Sven Bollhem(dm).
(from Metronome)   Stockholm,October 18,1949

MR37A   Over the rainbow   PRLP125,PR7431
MR38A   Blue and Moody   Pr.730,45-418,LP146,PR7431

COLEMAN HAWKINS:
Nat Peck(tb)Hubert Fol(as)Coleman Hawkins(ts)Jean-Paul Mengeon(p)
Pierre Michelot(b)Kenny Clarke(dm).
(from Vogue)   Paris,December 21,1949

V3041   Sih-Sah   PR7824
V3042   It's only a paper moon   -
V3043   Bean's talking again   -
V3044   Bay-u-bah   -
V3045   I surrender dear   -
V3046   Sophisticated lady   -

JAMES MOODY:
Nat Peck(tb)James Moody(ts)Jacques Diéval(p)Emmanuel Soudieux(b)Richie
Frost(dm).
(from Pacific)   Paris,February 10,1950

REO44   Bebop tune No.1   PRLP157
REO45   Michele by accident   -

REINHOLD SVENSSON'S QUINTET:
Ulf Linde(vb)Reinhold Svensson(p)Rolf Berg(g)Gunnar Almstedt(b)Andrew
Burman(dm).
(from Metronome)   Stockholm,February 16,1950

MR64   Dinah   NJ824;PRLP106
MR65   Once in a while   -   -
MR66   Sweet and lovely   NJ826   -
MR67   My blue heaven-1   -   -

-1:Reinhold Svensson(org)solo.

CHARLIE PARKER:
Red Rodney(tp)Charlie Parker(as)Al Haig(p)Tommy Potter(b)Roy Haynes(dm).
(from Jazz Workshop/Fantasy)
                   St.Nicholas Arena,NYC,February 18,1950

           52nd Street theme I   PR24009
           Ornithology   -
           I didn't know what time it was -
           Embraceable you   -
           Scrapple from the apple   -
           Hot house   -
           Now's the time   -
           Visa   -
           Star eyes   -
           Confirmation   -
           Out of nowhere   -
           What's new?   -
           Smoke gets in your eyes   -
           I cover the waterfront   -
           52nd Street theme II   -

Note:All these titles are edited as in original recording.

ARNE DOMNERUS CLARINET SOLOS:
Arne Domnerus(cl)Ulf Linde(vb)Gösta Theselius(p)Thore Jederby(b)Andrew
Burman(dm).
(from Metronome)   Stockholm,February 22,1950

MR68   Love walked in   PRLP134
MR69   Don't be that way   -
MR72   All the things you are   -
MR73   Blue mood(Larry's blues)   -

JAMES MOODY:
Nat Peck(tb)James Moody(ts)Jacques Diéval(p)Emmanuel Soudieux(b)
Richie Frost(dm)Annie Ross(vo).
(from Pacific)   Paris,February 22,1950

REO58   Le vent vert voAR   PRLP157
REO59   Emef   -
REO60   Headlight   -
REO61   Big chief Peckham   -

ARNE DOMNERUS SEXTET:
Lennart Sundewall(tp)Arne Domnerus(as)Ulf Linde(vb)Bengt Hallberg(p)
Gunnar Almstedt(b)Andrew Burman(dm).
(from Metronome)   Stockholm,March 15,1950

MR74   Chloe(Cool boy*)(Song of the swamp) NJ831*;PRLP133*
MR75   Stuffy   -   -
MR76   The way you look tonight   Pr.863   -
MR77   I can't get started-1(Sensual*)   -*   -

-1:tp out.

ZOOT SIMS QUARTET:
Zoot Sims(ts)Jimmy Woode(p)Simon Brehm(b)Jack Noren(dm).
(from Gazell)   Stockholm,April 23,1950

18   All the things you are-1   PR7817
21   You go to my head   Pr.719,PR7817
22   Tickle toe(The scene is clean*) -*   -

-1:Toots Thielemans(hca)added.

ZOOT SIMS AND HIS BROTHERS:
Sixten Eriksson-1(tp)Zoot Sims(ts)Lars Gullin-1(bs)Dick Hyman(p)
Charlie Short(b)Ed Shaughnessy(dm).
(from Metronome)   Stockholm,April 24,1950

MR88   Yellow duck-1   NJ837;Pr.837,PR7817
MR89   The way you look tonight   -*   -**   -
          (Americans in Sweden**)(Which way*)

BENGT HALLBERG TRIO:
Bengt Hallberg(p)Gunnar Almstedt(b)Andrew Burman(dm).
(from Metronome)   Stockholm,May 16,1950

MR80   Indiana   PRLP121
MR81   Lover man   -

REINHOLD SVENSSON'S QUINTET:
Ulf Linde(vb)Reinhold Svensson(p)Rolf Berg(g)Gunnar Almstedt(b)Andrew
Burman(dm).
(from Metronome)   Stockholm,May 19,1950

MR102   On the Alamo   NJ833;Pr.833
MR103   Always   -   -

ZOOT SIMS:
Zoot Sims(ts)Gerald Wiggins(p)Pierre Michelot(b)Kenny Clarke(dm).
(from Vogue)   Paris,June 16,1950

V4021-1	Night and day	PR7817
V4021-2	Night and day	-
V4022-1	Slingin' hash	-
V4022-2	Slingin' hash	-
V4023	Tenorly	-
V4024	I understand	-
V4025	Don't worry about me	-
V4026	Crystals	-

DUKE ELLINGTON:
Duke Ellington(p)Billy Strayhorn(celeste)Oscar Pettiford(cello)Lloyd
Trotman(b)Jo Jones(dm).
(from Mercer/Riverside)   NYC,September 13,1950

M4005	Perdido	PR24029
M4006	Take the A train	-
M4007	Oscalypso	-
M4008	Blues for Blanton	-

Duke Ellington,Billy Strayhorn(p)Wendell Marshall(b).
(from Mercer/Riverside)   NYC,October 3,1950

5710	Cotton tail	PR24029,P-24052
5711	C jam blues	-
5712	Flamingo	-
5713	Bang up blues	-

KENNY CLARKE:
James Moody(ts)Raph Schecroun(p)Pierre Michelot(b)Kenny Clarke(dm).
(from Swing)   Paris,October 9,1950

OSW704-1	Nath	PR7605
OSW704-2	Nath	-
OSW705	I can't get started	-
OSW706	Riffin' and Raffin'	-
OSW707	St.Louis blues	-
OSW708	In a rush	-
OSW709	Embraceable you	-

REINHOLD SVENSSON'S QUINTET:
Ulf Linde(vb)Reinhold Svensson(p)Rolf Berg(g)Gunnar Almstedt(b)Andrew
Burman(dm).
(from Metronome)   Stockholm,October 13,1950

MR142	Blue skies	PRLP106		
MR143	9.20 Special	-		
MR144	Dearly beloved	NJ840;Pr.783,LP106		
MR145	That old feeling	-	-	-

Same.
(from Metronome)   Stockholm,November 14,1950

| MR146 | Nevertheless | NJ835;Pr.835 | |
| MR147 | I guess I'll have to dream-1 | - | - |

-1:Jack Noren(dm)replaces Burman.

DUKE ELLINGTON:
Duke Ellington,Billy Strayhorn(p)Joe Shulman(b).
(from Mercer/Riverside)   NYC,November   ,1950

M2479	Tonk	PR24029
M2480	Johnny come lately	-
M2481	In a blue Summer garden	-
M2482	Great times	-

BENGT HALLBERG TRIO:
Bengt Hallberg(p)Gunnar Almstedt(b)Andrew Burman(dm).
(from Metronome)   Stockholm,December 30,1950

MR168	Cool kid	PRLP121
MR169	These foolish things	-

ROY ELDRIDGE:
Roy Eldridge(tp,vo)Lennart Sundewall(bass tp)Carl-Henrik Norin(ts)
Charles Norman(p)Thore Jederby(b)Andrew Burman(dm).
(from Metronome)   Stockholm,January 20,1951

MR184	Echoes of Harlem-1	Pr.737,LP114
MR185	School days voRE	- -
MR186	Saturday fish fry,pt.1 voRE	-
MR187	Saturday fish fry,pt.2 voRE	-
MR188	The heat's on	-

-1:Sundewall & Norin out.

Same.
(from Metronome)   Stockholm,January 22,1951

MR189	No rolling blues voRE	PRLP114
MR190	They raided the joint voRE	-
MR191	Estrad swing'Roy's got rhythm)	-

JAMES MOODY:
Lennart Sundewall(bass tp)Arne Domnerus,James Moody(as)Carl-Henrik
Norin(ts)Lars Gullin(bs)Rolf Larsson(p)Gunnar Almstedt(b)Andrew Burman
(dm).
(from Metronome)   Stockholm,January 23,1951

MR192	The man I love	Pr. LP146,PR7441
MR193	Again	Pr.738,LP125 -
MR194	Embraceable you	Pr.744 -
MR195A	How deep is the ocean	Pr.854,LP146 -

Same.
(from Metronome)   Stockholm,January 24,1951

MR196	Am I blue	Pr.854,LP125,PR7441
MR197	I'll get by	Pr.768,LP146 -

Sixten Eriksson(tp)James Moody(ts)Lars Gullin(bs)Rolf Larsson(p)Gunnar
Almstedt(b)Jack Noren(dm).
(from Metronome)   Stockholm,January 24,1951

MR198A	Love walked in(Good deal)	PRLP146,PR7441
MR199A	Moody's got rhythm	Pr.738,LP125,PR7441
	(Andrew got married)	

James Moody(ts)Lars Gullin(bs)Rolf Larsson(p)Gunnar Almstedt(b)Andrew
Burman(dm).
(from Metronome)   Same date.

MR200	Hey!Jim(Moody's blues)	Pr.768,LP125,PR7441
MR201A	Two feathers(Two fathers*)	Pr.744* - -

JAMES MOODY:
James Moody(ts)Rolf Larsson(p)Gunnar Almstedt(b)Andrew Burman(dm)with
strings & harp.
(from Metronome)   Stockholm,January 25,1951

MR210A   Cherokee   Pr.756,LP125,PR7441
MR211A   Pennies from Heaven   -   -   -

ROY ELDRIDGE:
Roy Eldridge(tp)Ove Lind(cl)Charles Norman(harpsichord)Gunnar Almstedt
(b)Andrew Burman(dm).
(from Metronome)   Stockholm,January 29,1951

MR212   Noppin' John   Pr.747
MR213   Scottie   -

KENNY GRAHAM:
Jo Hunter(tp)Kenny Graham(ts)Jack Honeyborne(p)Roy Plummer(g)Cliff
Ball(b)Dikkie Devere(dm)Leonade(maracas)Bob Caxton(conga)Ginger Johnson
(bongo).
(from Esquire)   London,February 10,1951

130   Mango walk   NJ839;Pr.782
131   Pina colada   -   -   LP135

LARS GULLIN QUARTET:
Lars Gullin(bs)Bengt Hallberg(p)Gunnar Almstedt(b)Jack Noren(dm).
(from Metronome)   Stockholm,February 21,1951

MR218   That's it   NJ841;Pr.784,LP121
MR219   Gull in a Gulsch   Pr.793   -
MR220   All yours   NJ841;Pr.784   -
MR221   Coolin' on S.S.Cool(Deep purple)   Pr.793   -

NEW SOUNDS FROM SWEDEN: (Supervision Leonard Feather)
Putte Wickman(cl)Reinhold Svensson(p)Rolf Berg(g)Simon Brehm(b)Jack
Noren(dm).
(from Cupol)   Stockholm,June 28,1951

2144   Rain on the roof   Pr.749,LP119
2145A   Moonlight saving time   -   -

Rolf Ericson(tp)Arne Domnerus(as)Lars Gullin(bs)Reinhold Svensson(p)
Simon Brehm(b)Jack Noren(dm).   Same date.

2146   The daring young Swedes   PRLP119
2147   A handful of stars   Pr.750
Rolf Ericson(tp)Ake Persson-1(tb)Arne Domnerus(as)Carl Henrik Norin-2
(ts)Lars Gullin-3(bs)Bengt Hallberg(p)Simon Brehm(b)Jack Noren(dm).
(from Cupol)   Stockholm,July 4,1951

2150   The Swedish music of this side
                of heaven-2,5   PRLP119
2151   Swedish butterfly-2,3   -
2152   September serenade-1,3   Pr.750,LP119
2153   Honeysuckle Rosenberg-4   -
2154   Honeysuckle Rosenberg-4   -

-4:Toots Thielemans(mouth harp)added.
-5:Domnerus out.

Svend Asmussen(v)Bengt Hallberg(p)Simon Brehm(b)Jack Noren(dm).
                                      Same date

2155F   A pretty girl is like a melody PRLP119

RALPH WILLIS:
Ralph Willis(vo,g)Brownie McGhee(g)Dumas Ransom(b).
(from Signature)   NYC,   1951

MU1006A   Church bell blues   Pr.907
MU1006B   Tell me pretty baby   -
MU1007A   Goodbye blues   Pr.906
MU1007B   Lazy woman blues   -

REINHOLD SVENSSON QUINTET:
Bo Kallström(vb)Reinhold Svensson(p)Rolf Berg(g)Gunnar Almstedt(b)
Andrew Burman(dm).
(from Metronome)   Stockholm,November 22,1951

MR281   The song is ended   Pr.804,LP129
MR282   Jeepers creepers   -
MR283   Flying home   Pr.789   -
MR284   I wished on the moon   -   -

Same.
(from Metronome)   Stockholm,November 29,1951

MR292   Stars fell on Alabama   Pr.   LP129
MR293   Just a gigolo   -
MR294   Undecided   -
MR295   Beat the clock   Pr.804   -

FOUR TENOR BROTHERS:
Rolf Blomqvist,Arne Domnerus,Lars Gullin,Gösta Theselius(ts)Ingemar
Westberg(p)Bengt Wittstrom(b)Sture Kallin(dm).
(from Metronome)   Stockholm,January 11,1952

MR297   Let's cool one   Pr.792,LP133
MR298   Anytime for you   -   -

LARS GULLIN QUARTET:
Lars Gullin(bs)Ingemar Westberg(p)Bengt Wittstrom(b)Andrew Burman(dm).
(from Metronome)   Same date.

MR299   To Jeru(All the things you are) PRLP133
MR300   Flippant(Mean to me)   -

GERRY MULLIGAN QUARTET:
Chet Baker(tp)Gerry Mulligan(bs)Carson Smith(b)Chico Hamilton(dm).
(from Fantasy)   SF,September 2,1952

9258   Line for Lyons   PR24016
9261   Carioca   -
9266   My funny Valentine   -
9271   Bark for Barksdale   -

REINHOLD SVENSSON SEXTET:
Putte Wickman-1(cl)Bo Kallström(vb)Reinhold Svensson(p)Rolf Berg(g)
Gunnar Almstedt(b)Andrew Burman(dm).
(from Metronome)   Stockholm,September 10,1952

MR385   Because of George-1   Pr.865,LP155
MR386   Tasty pastry   -   -

BENGT HALLBERG QUARTET:
Arne Domnerus(cl)Bengt Hallberg(p)Yngve Akerberg(b)Jack Noren(dm).
(from Metronome)   Stockholm,October 27,1952

MR403   Coast to coast   Pr.   LP145
MR404   Flying saucer   Pr.864   -
MR405   Zig zag-1   -   -
MR406   Cynthia's in love   -

-1:Domnerus out.

LARS GULLIN BAND:
Weine Renliden(tp)Ake Persson(tb)Ake Bjorkman(frh)Arne Domnerus(as)
Lars Gullin(bs)Gunnar Svensson(p)Yngve Akerberg(b)Jack Noren(dm).
(from Metronome)   Stockholm,October 28,1952

MR407   Smooth breeze   PRLP144
MR408   Smart Alec   -

Arnold Johansson(tp)replaces Renliden.
(from Metronome)   Stockholm,December 12,1952

MR417   Apostrophe   PRLP144
MR418   Merlin   -

Ake Persson(tb)Rolf Blomqvist(ts)Lars Gullin(bs)Gunnar Svensson(p)
Yngve Akerberg(b)Jack Noren(dm).   Same date.

MR419   Colon   PRLP144
MR420   Comma   -

Weine Renliden-1(tp)Ake Persson(tb)Ake Bjorkman-1(frh)Arne Domnerus-1
(as)Lars Gullin(bs)Gunnar Svensson(p)Yngve Akerberg(b)Jack Noren(dm).
(from Metronome)   Stockholm,December 15,1952

MR421   Silhouette-1   PRLP144
MR422   Disc major   -

BENGT HALLBERG TRIO/QUARTET:
Arne Domnerus-1(cl)Bengt Hallberg(p)Gunnar Johnson(b)Kenneth Fagerlund
(dm).
(from Metronome)   Stockholm,December 15,1952

MR423   Portrait-1   PRLP145
MR424   Duffer box-1   -
MR425   The things we did last Summer -
MR426   For fishers only   -

GERRY MULLIGAN QUARTET:
Chet Baker(tp)Gerry Mulligan(bs)Carson Smith(b)Chico Hamilton(dm).
(from Fantasy)   SF,January 3,1953

1315   Limelight   PR24016
1316   The lady is a tramp   -
1326   Turnstile   -
1327   Moonlight in Vermont   -

LARS GULLIN QUARTET:
Ake Persson(tb)Lars Gullin(bs)Simon Brehm(b)Jack Noren(dm).
(from Metronome)   Stockholm,February 12,1953

MR451A   Holiday for piano   PRLP151
MR452A   She's funny that way   -
MR453A   Night and day   -
MR454A   Sounds like it   -

Same.
(from Metronome)   Stockholm,February 18,1953

MR455A   Brazil   Pr.862,LP151
MR456A   Four and no one more   -   -
MR457A   Sad Sally   -
MR458A   You blew out the flame   -

ROLF BLOMQVIST SEXTET:
Ake Persson(tb)Arnold Johansson(vtb)Rolf Blomqvist(ts)Gunnar Svensson
(p)Yngve Akerberg(b)Jack Noren(dm).
(from Metronome)   Stockholm,February 19,1953

MR459   Jumping with Queen Anne   PRLP173
MR460   Pops   -

REINHOLD SVENSSON SEXTET:
Putte Wickman(cl)Bo Kallström(vb)Reinhold Svensson(p)Rolf Berg(g)
Gunnar Almstedt(b)Andrew Burman(dm).
(from Metronome)   Stockholm,April 1,1953

    Blue Lou   PRLP155
    Top o' the mornin'   -
    Stealin' apples   -
    Queen of Saba   -
    Bury your worries   -
    Pin up   -

THE GREATEST JAZZ CONCERT EVER:
Dizzy Gillespie(tp,vo)Charlie Parker(as,vo)Bud Powell(p)Charlie Mingus
(b)Max Roach(dm).
(from Debut/Fantasy)   Massey Hall,Toronto(Canada),May 15,1953

    Perdido   PR24024
    Salt peanuts voDG,CP   -
    Wee   -
    Hot house-1   -
    Night in Tunisia-1   -
    All the things you are/52nd
              Street theme-1   -

-1:Charlie Mingus(b)overdubbed on.NYC,c.Summer 1953

Bud Powell Trio:Bud Powell(p)Charlie Mingus(b)Max Roach(dm).
(from Debut/Fantasy)   Same concert.

    Embraceable you   PR24024
    Sure thing   -
    Cherokee   -
    Jubilee   -   P-24052
    Lullaby of Birdland   -
    I've got you under my skin   -

MARY LOU WILLIAMS QUARTET:
Mary Lou Williams(p)Ray Dempsey(g)Rupert Nurse(b)Tony Kinsey(dm).
(from Esquire)   London,June 26,1953

395   Melody maker   PRLP175
396   Musical express   -
397   Sometimes I'm happy   -
398   Mink's tune   -

BILLY TAYLOR TRIO:
Billy Taylor(p)Charlie Mingus(b)Art Taylor(dm).
(from Debut/Fantasy)   NYC,c.Summer 1953

    Bass-ically speaking   PR24024

Note:This title has been issued as by Bud Powell trio.

ZOOT SIMS:
Conte Candoli(tp)Frank Rosolino(tb)Lee Konitz(as)Zoot Sims(ts)Lars
Gullin(bs,arr)Don Bagley(b)Stan Levey(dm).
(from Metronome)   Stockholm,August 25,1953

MR504 Dedicated to Lee   PREP1341,PR7817
MR505 Late date   -   -

Note:PREP1341 issued as by AMERICANS IN SWEDEN (as original issue)

BUD POWELL TRIO:
Bud Powell(p)George Duvivier(b)Art Taylor(dm).
(from Fantasy)   NYC,September   ,1953.

    My devotion   PR24024
    Polka dots and moonbeams   -
    My heart stood still   -
    I want to be happy   -

ANNIE ROSS:
Annie Ross(vo)with Jimmy Cleveland(tb)Anthony Ortega(as)Clifford
Solomon(ts)Lars Gullin(bs)Quincy Jones(p)Simon Brehm(b)Alan Dawson(dm).
(from Metronome)   Stockholm,September 14,1953

MR517   Jackie   Pr.879
MR518   The song is you   -

GEORGE WALLINGTON with THE SWEDISH ALL STARS:
Ake Persson(tb)Arne Domnerus(as)Lars Gullin(bs)George Wallington(p)
Simon Brehm(b)Jack Noren(dm).
(from Metronome)   Stockholm,September 14,1953

    Round about midnight   PREP1347
    Blue Bird   -

AKE PERSSON AND HIS COMBO:
Ake Persson(tb)Arne Domnerus(as)Bengt Hallberg(p)Gunnar Johnson(b)
Jack Noren(dm).
(from Metronome)   Stockholm,September 14,1953

    Hershey bar   PRLP173
    Softly as in a morning sunrise   -
    It might as well be Spring   -
    My blue heaven   -

CLIFFORD BROWN-ART FARMER:
Clifford Brown,Art Farmer(tp)Ake Persson(tb)Arne Domnerus(cl,as)Lars
Gullin(bs)Bengt Hallberg(p)Gunnar Johnson(b)Jack Noren(dm)Quincy Jones
(arr,dir).
(from Metronome)   Stockholm,September 15,1953

MR524   Stockholm sweetnin'   PREP1345,LP167,LP7055
MR525   'Cuse these bloos   -   -   -
MR526   Falling in love with love   -   -
MR527   Lover come back to me   -   -

All titles also issued on NJ8301,PR16008,PR7662.

LEE KONITZ-EZZ-THETIC:
Lee Konitz(as)Henri Renaud(p)Jimmy Gourley(g)Don Bagley(b)Stan Levey(dm)
(from Vogue)   Paris,September 18,1953

(take 1)All the things you are   PR7827
(take 2)All the things you are   -
(take 1)I'll remember April   -
(take 2)I'll remember April   -
(take 3)I'll remember April   -
(take 1)These foolish things   -
(take 2)These foolish things   -
    You'd be so nice to come home to -

CLIFFORD BROWN BIG BAND IN PARIS:
Clifford Brown,Art Farmer,Quincy Jones,Walter Williams,Fernand
Verstraete,Fred Gerard(tp)James Cleveland,Bill Tamper,Al Hayse(tb)Gigi
Gryce,Anthony Ortega(as)Clifford Solomon,Henri Bernard(ts)Henri Jouot
(bs)Henri Renaud(p)Pierre Michelot(b)Alan Dawson(dm).Q.Jones(arr).
(from Vogue)   Paris,September 28,1953

V4655-1 Brown skins   PR7840
V4655-2 Brown skins   -
V4658-1 Keeping up with Jonesy   -
V4658-2 Keeping up with Jonesy   -

THE CLIFFORD BROWN SEXTET IN PARIS:
Clifford Brown(tp)Gigi Gryce(as)Henri Renaud(p)Jimmy Gourley(g)Pierre
Michelot(b)Jean-Louis Viale(dm).
(from Vogue)   Paris,September 29,1953

V4659-1 Conception(Blue concept*)   PR7794*
V4659-2 Conception(Blue concept*)   -
V4660-1 All the things you are   -
V4660-2 All the things you are   -
V4661-1 I cover the waterfront   -
V4662-1 Goofin' with me   -

Same.
(from Vogue)   Paris,October 8,1953

(take 1)Minority   PR7794
(take 2)Minority   -
(take 1)Salute to the bandbox   -
(take 2)Salute to the bandbox   -
(take 1)Strictly romantic-1   -
(take 1)Baby-1   -

-1:Gourley out.

CLIFFORD BROWN BIG BAND IN PARIS:
Clifford Brown,Art Farmer,Quincy Jones,Walter Williams(tp)James
Cleveland,Al Hayse,Benny Vasseur(tb)Gigi Gryce,Anthony Ortega(as)
Clifford Solomon,André Dabonneville(ts)William Boucaya(bs)Henri Renaud
(p)Pierre Michelot(b)Jean-Louis Viale(dm). Quincy Jones(arr).
(from Vogue)   Paris,October 9,1953

        Bum's rush   PR7840

Clifford Brown(tp)James Cleveland(tb)Gigi Gryce(as)Clifford Solomon(ts)
Henri Renaud(p)Jimmy Gourley(g)Pierre Michelot(b)Jean-Louis Viale(dm).
(from Vogue)   Paris,October 10,1953

        No start no end   PR7840
        Chez moi

Clifford Brown(tp)James Cleveland(tb)Gigi Gryce,Anthony Ortega(as)
Clifford Solomon(ts)William Boucaya(bs)Quincy Jones(p)Marcel Dutrieux
(b)Jean-Louis Viale(dm).
(from Vogue)   Paris,October 11,1953

(take 1)All weird   PR7840
(take 2)All weird   -

BENGT HALLBERG TRIO:
Bengt Hallberg(p)Gunnar Johnson(b)Robert Edman(dm).
(from Metronome)   Stockholm,October 12,1953

        Opus one   PRLP174
        Tre birre   -
        Honeysuckle rose   -
        Stars fell on Alabama   -

THE CLIFFORD BROWN QUARTET IN PARIS:
Clifford Brown(tp)Henri Renaud(p)Pierre Michelot(b)Benny Bennett(dm).
(from Vogue)   Paris,October 15,1953

V4718-1 Blue and Brown   PR7761
V4719-1 I can't dream,can't I?   -
V4719-2 I can't dream,can't I?   -
V4719-3 I can't dream,can't I?   -
V4720-1 The song is you   -
V4720-2 The song is you   -
V4721-1 Come rain or come shine   -
V4721-2 Come rain or come shine   -
V4722-1 It might as well be Spring   -
V4723-1 You're a lucky guy   -
V4723-2 You're a lucky guy   -
V4723-3 You're a lucky guy   -

ROLF BLOMQVIST AND HIS BAND:
Ernie Englund(tp)Ake Persson(tb)Rolf Blomqvist,Carl Henrik Norin(ts)
Gunnar Svensson(p)Yngve Akerberg(b)Alan Dawson(dm).
(from Metronome)   Stockholm,November 6,1953

        Walking feet   PRLP173
        Subway   -

BENGT HALLBERG AND HIS SWEDISH ALL STARS:
Ake Persson(tb)Arne Domnerus(cl,as)Lars Gullin(bs)Bengt Hallberg(p)
Simon Brehm(b)William Schiopffe(dm).
(from Metronome)   Stockholm,November 9,1953

        Whiskey sour   PRLP176
        Side car   -
        Limehouse blues   -
        Pink lady   -

QUINCY JONES AND HIS SWEDISH ALL STARS:
Art Farmer(tp)Ake Persson,Jimmy Cleveland(tb)Arne Domnerus(cl,as)Lars
Gullin(bs)Bengt Hallberg(p)Simon Brehm(b)Alan Dawson(dm)Quincy Jones
(arr,dir).
(from Metronome)   Stockholm,November 10,1953

MR560   Pogo stick   PRLP172
MR561   Liza   -
MR562   Jones bones   -
MR563   Sometimes I'm happy   -

REINHOLD SVENSSON TRIO:
Reinhold Svensson(p)Hasse Burman(b)Sture Kallin(dm).
(from Metronome)   Stockholm,November 18,1953

        I got it bad   PRLP174
        My heart belongs to Daddy   -
        The pink elephant   -
        Time on my hands   -

SWINGIN' IN SWEDEN:
Putte Wickman(cl)Bengt Hallberg(p)Jimmy Raney(g)Red Mitchell(b)Elaine
Leighton(dm).Supervision:Leonard Feather
(from Metronome)   Stockholm,January 13,1954

        Darn that dream   PRLP179
        Indian Summer   PREP1341,LP179

Gösta Theselius(ts)Sonny Clark(p)Jimmy Raney(g)Red Mitchell-1 or Simon
Brehm-2(b)Elaine Leighton(dm).   Same date.

        Invention-1   PRLP179
        Jumpin' for Jane-2   PREP1341,LP179

[259]

DUKE JORDAN-JORDU:
Duke Jordan(p)Gene Ramey(b)Lee Abrams(dm).
(from Vogue)   NYC,January 28,1954

    Jordu(Minor encamp)   PR7849
    Scotch blues   -
    Wait and see   -
    Confirmation   -
    Darn that dream   -
    Just one of those things   -
    They can't take that away from me-
    Embraceable you   -

THE OSCAR PETTIFORD MEMORIAL ALBUM:
Kai Winding(tb)Al Cohn(ts)Henri Renaud(p)Tal Farlow(g)Oscar Pettiford
(b,cello)Max Roach(dm).
(from Vogue)   NYC,March 13,1954

    Burt's pad   PR7813
    Marcel the furrier   -
    Ondine   -
    Stardust   -
    E lag   -
    Rhumblues   -

AL HAIG TRIO:
Al Haig(p)Bill Crow(b)Lee Abrams(dm).
(from Vogue)   NYC,March 13,1954

    Yardbird suite   PR7841
    The moon is yellow   -
    'S wonderful   -
    Taboo   -
    Just one of those things   -
    Mighty like a rose   -
    'Round midnight   -
    Just you,just me   -

AL COHN-BROADWAY 1954:
Hal Stein(as)Al Cohn(ts)Harvey Leonard(p)Red Mitchell(b)Chris Febbo(dm)
(from Progressive)   NYC,July 29,1954

    Broadway   PR7819
    Broadway(alt.take)   -
    Red Mitchell's blues   -
    Suddenly it's Spring   -
    Suddenly it's Spring(alt.take) -
    These foolish things   -
    Everything happens to me   -
    Sweet Lorraine   -
    Sleepy time down South   -

MILES DAVIS QUINTET:
Miles Davis(tp)Britt Woodman(tb)Teddy Charles(vb)Charlie Mingus(b)
Elvin Jones(dm).
(from Debut/Fantasy)   NYC,July 9,1955

    Nature boy   PR24022
    There's no you   -
    Easy living   -
    Alone together   -

GEORGE WALLINGTON LIVE!AT THE CAFE BOHEMIA:
Donald Byrd(tp)Jackie McLean(as)George Wallington(p)Paul Chambers(b)
Art Taylor(dm).
(from Progressive)   Cafe Bohemia,NYC,September 9,1955

    Bohemia after dark   PR7820
    Jay Mac's grib   -
    Johnny one note   -
    Minor march   -
    Snakes   -
    Sweet blanche   -
    The peak   -

TAL FARLOW:
Red Norvo(vb)Tal Farlow(g)Red Mitchell(b).
(from Fantasy)   LA,October   ,1955

    Who cares?   PR24042
    Let's fall in love   -
    Old devil moon   -
    Cabin in the sky   -
    How am I to know?   -
    That old black magic   -
    What is this thing called love -
    I brung you finjans for your zarf -
    My funny Valentine   -
    Lullaby of Birdland   -

Note:This session was issued on Fantasy as by The Red Norvo Trio.

CHARLIE MINGUS:
Eddie Bert(tb)George Barrow(ts)Mal Waldron(p)CharlieMingus(b)Willie
Jones(dm).
(from Debut/Fantasy)   Cafe Bohemia,NYC,December 23,1955

    Jump Monk   PR24010
    Serenade in blue   -
    Work song   -
    All the things you are in C
                    sharp minor   -
    Septemberly-1   -
    A foggy day   -
    Lady Bird   -
    Haitian fight song   -
    Love chant   -

-1:Combination of'September in the rain'& 'Tenderly'

Max Roach(dm)replaces Jones.Same session.

    Drums(Work song)   PR24010
    I'll remember April   -
    Percussion discussion-1   -

-1:Charlie Mingus(b)Max Roach(dm) only.Charlie Mingus(cello)overdubbed
on later on.

EARL HINES:
Earl Hines(p)Eddie Duran(g)Dean Reilly(b)Earl Watkins(dm).
(from Fantasy) Marines Memorial Theatre,SF,late 1955 & January   ,1956

    Jitterbug waltz   PR24043
    Darktown strutter's ball   -
    Black and blue   -
    Blue turning grey over you   -
    Honeysuckle rose   -
    Squeeze me   -
(continued on next page)

```
            Ain't misbehavin'                 PR24043
            Keepin' out of mischief now        -
            I can't give you anything but
                                      love     -
            I'm gonna sit right down &
               write myself a letter           -
            Lulu's back in town                -
            Two sleepy people                  -
HERBIE MANN-MANN IN THE MORNING:
Ake Persson(tb)Herbie Mann(fl,ts)Knud Jorgensen(p)Georg Riedel(b)Joe
Harris(dm).
(from Metronome)                      Stockholm,October 10,1956
            Hurry hurry                 Pr.         LP7136,PR7659
            Adam's theme                             -        -
            Early morning blues         Pr.45-318    -        -
            Serenada                                 -        -
            Polka dots and moonbeams                 -        -
                                     /ts)
Bengt Arne Wallin(tp)Herbie Mann(fl,Arne Domnerus(as)Rolf Blomqvist(ts)
Lennart Johnson(bs)Gunnar Svensson(p)Georg Riedel(b)Egil Johansen(dm).
(from Metronome)                      Stockholm,October 12,1956
            Cherry point                Pr.45-318,LP7136,PR7659
            I can't believe that you're in love   -        -
            Song for Ruth                          -        -

Bengt Arne Wallin(tp)Herbie Mann(fl)Rune Ofverman(p)Georg Riedel(b)
Egil Johansen(dm).
(from Metronome)                      Stockholm,October 16,1956
            Ow!                         PRLP7136,PR7659
            Nature boy                              -      -

EARL HINES:
Earl Hines(p)solo.
(from Fantasy)                        SF,December    ,1956
            Deep forest                 PR24043
            Everything depends on you    -
            Am I too late                -
            Blues for Tatum              -
            In San Francisco             -
            Ann                          -
            You can depend on me         -
            When I dream of you          -
            R.R.Blues                    -
            Straight to love             -
            Piano man                    -
            My Monday date               -        P-24052

GEORGE SHEARING:
Emil Richards(vb)George Shearing(p)Toots Thielemans(g)Al McKibbon(b)
Percy Brice(dm)Armando Perazza(conga)& Jud Conlon Singers(vo).
(from Capitol)                        LA,February   ,1957
16531  Darn that dream                 P-24052

TOMMY FLANAGAN TRIO:
Tommy Flanagan(p)Wilbur Little(b)Elvin Jones(dm).
(from Metronome)                      Stockholm,August 15,1957
            Verdandi                    PRLP7134,PR7632
            Dalarna                                  -      -
            Willow weep for me                       -      -
            Chelsea bridge                           -      -
            Relaxin' at Camarillo                    -      -
            Eclypso                                  -      -
            Beat's up                                -      -
            Skal brothers                            -      -
            Little rock                              -      -
```

STAN GETZ/CAL TJADER SEXTET:
Stan Getz(ts)Cal Tjader(vb)Vince Guaraldi(p)Eddie Duran(g)Scott La
Faro(b)Billy Higgins(dm).
(from Fantasy)   SF,February 8,1958
        Ginza samba   PR24019
        I've grown accustomed to her face -
        For all we know   -
        Crow's nest   -
        Liz Anne   -
        Big bear   -
        My buddy   -

PHIL WOODS QUINTET:
Howard McGhee(tp)Phil Woods(as)Dick Hyman(p)Teddy Kotick(b)Roy Haynes
(dm).
                                     NYC,March 3,1959

        Consternation   PR7673
        Lemon drop   -
        The little bandmaster   -
        Pee Wee's dream   -

CAL TJADER-MONTEREY CONCERTS:
Paul Horn(fl)Cal Tjader(vb)Lonnie Hewitt(p)Al McKibbon(b)Willie Bobo
(dm,timbales)Mongo Santamaria(bongos,perc).
(from Fantasy)
                Concert,Sunset Auditorium,Carmel(Calif.),April 20,1959
        Doxy   PR24026
        Afro blue   -
        Laura   -
        Walkin' with Wally   -
        We'll be together again   -
        'Round about midnight   -
        A night in Tunisia   -
        Bess,you is my woman   -
        Lover come back to me   -
        Tumbao   -
        Love me or leave me   -
        Tu cress que   -
        S.S.Groove   -

BILL EVANS:
Bill Evans(p)Scott La Faro(b)Paul Motian(dm).
(from Riverside)   NYC,December 28,1959
        Come rain or come shine   P-24052

BOBBY TIMMONS:
Bobby Timmons(p)Sam Jones(b)Jimmy Cobb(dm).
(from Riverside)   NYC,January 13 or 14,1960
        Moanin'   P-24052

KING PLEASURE:
King Pleasure(vo)with Matthew Gee(tb)Teddy Edwards,Harold Land(ts)
Gerald Wiggins(p)Wilfred Middlebrooks(b)Earl Palmer(dm).
(from Hi Fi Jazz)   LA,April 14,1960
        I'm in the mood for love   PR24017
        The new Symphony Sid   -
        Don't worry 'bout me   -
        Little boy don't get scared   -
        Parker's mood   -
        Golden days   -
        Tomorrow is another day   -
        No,not much   -
        All of me   -

[263]

DUKE PEARSON-DEDICATION!:
Freddie Hubbard(tp)Willie Wilson(tb)Pepper Adams(bs)Duke Pearson(p)
Thomas Howard(b)Lex Humphries(dm).
(from Jazzline)   NYC,August 2,1961

      Minor mishap   PR7729
      Miss Bertha D.Blues   -
      The nearness of you   -
      Apothegm   -
      Lex   -
      Blues for Alvina   -
      Time after time   -

GENE AMMONS/SONNY STITT-WE'LL BE TOGETHER AGAIN:
Sonny Stitt(as,ts)Gene Ammons(ts)John Houston(p)Charles Williams(b)
George Brown(dm).
(from Chess/Argo)   Chicago,August 26,1961

11183 A mess   PR7606
11184 New blues up and down   -
11185 Time on my hands   -
11186 We'll be together again   -
11187 My foolish heart   -
11188 Red sails in the sunset   -
11189 Water Jug(Headin' West on Argo)   -
11190 A pair of red pants   -
11191 Autumn leaves   -
11192 But not for me   -

GENE AMMONS-LIVE IN CHICAGO:
Gene Ammons(ts)Eddie Buster(org)Gerald Donovan(dm).
(from Chess/Argo)   D.J.Lounge,Chicago,August 29,1961

11200 Foot tappin'   PR7495
11201 It could happen to you   -
11202 Sweet Georgia Brown   -
11203 Falling in love with love   -
11204 Please send me someone in love   -
11205 Scrapple from the apple   -
11206 Jug's blue blues(A.M.-P.M.)   -
11207 Fast track   -
      I can't get started   unissued
      C jam blues   -
      Just you,just me   -
      M.J.Blues   -
      But not for me   -

ERIC DOLPHY IN EUROPE:
Eric Dolphy(as-1,bass cl-2,fl-3)Bent Axen(p)Erik Moseholm(b)Jorn
Elniff(dm).
(from Debut)   Berlingske Has,Copenhagen,September 6,1961

(take 1)Don't blame me-3   PR7350,P-24070
(take 2)Don't blame me-3   PR7382   -
      When lights are low-2   PR7366,PR24027
(take 1)Miss Ann   unissued
(take 2)Miss Ann   -

Note:Title mentioned as "Miss Ann" on Prestige issues actually is "Les"
from next session(see on page 265)

Same.
Studenterforeningen Foredragssal,Copenhagen,September 8,1961

Glad to be unhappy-3	PRLP7304,	PR24027
Hi-fly-4	-	-
God bless the child-2	-	-
Oleo-2	-	-
The way you look tonight-1	PRLP7350,	P-24070
Laura-1	-	-
Woody'n you-1	PR7366	PR24027
(take 1)In the blues-1	-	-
(take 2)In the blues-1(not complete)	-	-
(take 3)In the blues-1	-	-
(take 4)In the blues-1	-	-
Les-1,5	PRLP7350,	PR24070

-4:Eric Dolphy(fl)Chuck Israels(b).
-5:issued as "Miss Ann" on Prestige issues.

WALTER BISHOP Jr.:
Walter Bishop(p)Butch Warren(b)Granville T.Hogan(dm).
(from Opus)   NYC,c.Spring   1962

The Bishop moves	PR7730
Easy walkin'	-
Take one of my pills	-
Theme on a legend	-

Note:These titles were mentioned in Prestige files as from July 23,
1965,which could be date of tape purchase.

GENE AMMONS-PREACHIN':
Gene Ammons(ts)Clarence "Sleepy" Anderson(org)Sylvester Hickman(b)
Dorral Anderson(dm).
(from Chess/Argo)   Chicago,May 3,1962

Sweet hour	PR7270
Yield not	-
Abide with me	-
Blessed assurance	-
The prayer	-
You'll never walk alone	-
Precious memories	-
What a friend	-
Holy,holy,holy	-
The light	-

GENE AMMONS:
Gene Ammons(ts)Don Patterson(org)Paul Weeden(g)Billy James(dm).
(from Chess/Argo)   Chicago,May?   1962

11704	I can't stop loving you	PR7791
11705	My babe	-

GENE AMMONS/DODO MARMAROSA:
Gene Ammons-1(ts)Dodo Marmarosa(p)Sam Jones(b)Marshall Thompson(dm).
(from Chess/Argo)   Chicago,May   ,1962

Georgia-1	PR24021
For you-1	-
You're driving me crazy-1	-
(take 1)Yardbird suite	-
(take 2)Yardbird suite	-
I remember you	-
Bluzarumba-1	-

(continued on next page)

```
              Where or when-1                PR24021
              The song is you                -
              Just friends                   -
              The moody blues                -
(take 1)Falling in love with love-1          -
(take 2)Falling in love with love-1          -
              The very thought of you        -
MILT JACKSON:
Kenny Dorham(tp)Jimmy Heath(ts)Milt Jackson(vb)Tommy Flanagan(p)Ron
Carter(b)Connie Kay(dm).
(from Riverside)                     NYC,August 30/October 31,1962
              The sealer                     PR24048
              Ruby my dear                   -
              None shall wonder              -
              Ruby                           -
              Invitation                     -
              Stella by starlight-1          -
-1:Dorham out.


Virgil Jones,Kenny Dorham(tp)Milt Jackson(vb)Tommy Flanagan(p)Ron
Carter(b)Connie Kay(dm).
(from Riverside)                     NYC,November 7,1962
              Too close for comfort          PR24048
              Poom-a-loom                    -
WALTER BISHOP Jr.:
Walter Bishop(p)Butch Warren(b)Jimmy Cobb(dm).
(from Cotillion)                     NYC,October   ,1963
              Tell it the way it is          PR7730
              I thought about you            -
              Things ain't what they used to be  -
              Falling in love with love      -
              Dottie's theme                 -
              Dinkum                         -
              Getting off the ground         -
              Summertime                     -
              Easy to love                   -
              33rd off 3rd                   -
              Love for sale                  -
              Our romance is over            -
Note:These titles were mentioned in Prestige files as from July 23,
1965,which could be date of tape purchase.
OSCAR PETERSON-EASY WALKER:
Oscar Peterson(p)Ray Brown(b)Ed Thigpen(dm).
(from Saba/MPS)                      Villingen(Germany),      c.1964
              At long last love              PR7690
              Easy walker                    -
              Tin tin deo                    -
              I've got a crush on you        -
              A foggy day                    -
              Like someone in love           -
```

THE GREAT CONCERT OF CHARLES MINGUS:
Johnny Coles(tp)Eric Dolphy(as-1,fl-2,bass cl-3)Clifford Jordan(ts)
Jaki Byard(p)Charles Mingus(b)Danny Richmond(dm).
(from America)   Salle Wagram,Paris,April 17,1964

      Introduction & presentation(by Mingus)
                          PRST34001
    So long Eric-1   -

-1:issued as "Good bye pork pie hat,pt.1".

Coles out.
      Théâtre des Champs-Elysées,Paris,April 19,1964

    So long Eric-1,4   PRST34001
    Orange was the colour of her
      dress,then blue silk-3   -
    Parkeriana(Ow/I love you/
      If I should lose you)-1   -
    Meditation for integration-2,3   -
    Fable of Faubus-3 voDR   -

Jaki Byard(p)Charles Mingus(b).Same concert.

    Sophisticated lady   PRST34001

-4:issued as "Good bye pork pie hat,pt.2".

OSCAR PETERSON:
Oscar Peterson(p)Ray Brown(b)Louis Hayes(dm).
(from Saba/MPS)   Villingen(Germany),May   ,1965

    Robbin's nest   PR7649

CARMELL JONES IN EUROPE:
Carmell Jones(tp)Nathan Davis(fl,ss,ts)Francy Boland(p)Jimmy Woode(b)
Kenny Clarke(dm).
(from Saba/MPS)   Villingen,September 1,1965

    The hip walk   PR7669
    That Kay Cee thing   -
    B's blues   -
    Carmell's Black Forest waltz   -

OSCAR PETERSON:
Oscar Peterson(p)Sam Jones(b)Louis Hayes(dm).
(from Saba/MPS)   Villingen,November   ,1965

    I'm in the mood for love   PR7649

CARMELL JONES IN EUROPE:
Carmell Jones(tp)Pony Poindexter(ss,as,vo)Leo Wright(fl,as)Fritz Pauer
(p)André Condouant(g)Jimmy Woode(b)Joe Nay(dm)Annie Ross(vo).
(from Saba/MPS)
      10th German Jazz Festival, Frankfurt(Germany),May 1,1966

    Jumpin' at the Woodside   PR7669
    Twisted   -

THE VIOLIN SUMMIT:
Stuff Smith-1,Stephane Grappelli-2,Svend Asmussen-3,Jean-Luc Ponty-4(v)
Kenny Drew(p)Niels-Henning Orsted Pedersen(b)Alex Riel(dm).
(from Saba/MPS)   Concert,Basel(Switzerland),Sept.30,1966

    Summit soul-2,3,4   PR7631
    Pentup house-2,4   -
    Timmie's blues-1,3   -
    It don't mean a thing-1,2,3,4 -
    Pennies from heaven-2   -
    Only time will tell-1   -
    Hot Toddy-2,3,4   -

MILT BUCKNER IN EUROPE:
Milt Buckner(p)Jimmy Woode(b)Jo Jones(dm).
(from Saba/MPS)   Villingen,November 16,1966

    Feelin' sorta Villingen   PR7668
    Chitlins a la carte   -
    Cute   -
    Alec lovejoy   -
    I only have eyes for you   -
    Pick yourself up   -
    Robbin's nest   -
    Hamp's boogie woogie   -
    Saba house party   -
    Yours is my heart alone   -

THE STUFF SMITH MEMORIAL ALBUM:
Heribert Thusek-1(ts)Stuff Smith(v)Otto Weiss(p)Peter Witte(b)Charlie
Antolini(dm).
(from Saba/MPS)   Villingen,April   ,1967

    Ain't she sweet   PR7691
    April in Paris   -
    Sweet Lorraine   -
    One o'clock jump-1   -
    Cherokee   -
    Yesterdays   -
    What is this thing called love-1 -

JEAN-LUC PONTY-CRITIC'S CHOICE:
Jean-Luc Ponty(v)Wolfgang Dauner(p)Niels-Henning Orsted Pedersen(b)
Daniel Humair(dm).
(from Saba/MPS)   Villingen,June   ,1967

    Sunday walk   PR7676
    Carole's garden   -
    Cat coach   -
    You've changed   -
    Suite for Claudia   -

KENNY CLARKE/FRANCY BOLAND BAND-FIRE,SOUL,HEAT & GUTS:
Benny Bailey,Shake Keane,Idriss Sulieman,Jimmy Deuchar(tp)Ake Persson,
Nat Peck,Eric Van Lier(tb)Derek Humble(as)Karl Drevo,Johnny Griffin,
Eddie "Lockjaw" Davis,Ronnie Scott(ts)Sahib Shihab(bs)Francy Boland
(p,arr)Jimmy Woode(b)Kenny Clarke(dm)Fats Sadi(bongos).
(from Saba/MPS)   Cologne,June 18,1967

    New box   PR7634
    Sax no end   -
    Griff's groove   -
    Lockjaw blues   -
    The Turk-1   -
    Milkshake   -
    Peter's waltz-1   -
    Griff' n'Jaws   -

-1:Davis out.

WYNTON KELLY:
Wynton Kelly(p)Ron McClure(b)Jimmy Cobb(dm).
(from Milestone)   NYC,   1967

    I want a little girl   P-24052

HAMPTON HAWES IN EUROPE:
Hampton Hawes(p)Eberhard Weber(b)Klaus Weiss-1(dm).
(from Saba/MPS)   Villingen,November 8,1967

    Villingen blues   PR7695
    Rhythm-1   -
    Black Forest blues   -
    Autumn leaves-1   -
    What is this thing called love   -
    Sonora-1   -
    I'm all smiles-1   -
    My foolish heart   -

OSCAR PETERSON:
Oscar Peterson(p)Sam Jones(b)Bobby Durham(dm).
(from Saba/MPS)   Villingen,November   ,1967

    On a clear day   Pr.45-727,PR7649
    Girl talk   -   -

MAYNARD FERGUSON BIG BAND:
Maynard Ferguson,Rolf Schneebiegl(tp,flh)Klaus Mitschele,Kurt Sauter,
Siegfried Achhammer(tp)Gerhard Lachmann,Heinz Hermannsdorfer,Georg
Hohne(tb)Werner Betz(bass tb)Bernd Fischer,Werner Baumgart(cl,as)Bert
Husemann(ts,fl)Rudi Flierl(ts,bass cl)Johnny Feigel(bass cl)Dieter
Reith(p)Jurgen Franke(g)Werner Schulze(b)Herman Mutschler(dm)Rolf
Hans Muller(dir).
(from Saba/MPS)   Baden-Baden,December   ,1967

    It's almost like being in love PR7636
    Knarf   -
    Ole   -
    Dancing nitely   -
    Tenderly   -
    Whisper not   -
    Got the spirit   -

DUKE ELLINGTON SECOND SACRED CONCERT:
Coll.personnel:Cat Anderson,Cootie Williams,Herb Jones,Mercer Ellington
or Money Johnson(tp)Lawrence Brown,Buster Cooper,Benny Green(tb)Chuck
Connors(bass tb)Russell Procope(as,cl)Johnny Hodges(as)Jimmy Hamilton
(cl,ts)Paul Gonsalves(ts)Harry Carney(bs)Duke Ellington(p,el p-1)Jeff
Castleman(b)Sam Woodyard,Steve Little(dm)Alice Babs,Tony Watkins,
Devonne Gardner,Trish Turner,Roscoe Gill(vo)The Frank Parker Singers &:
A.M.E.Mother Zion Church Choir,Solomon Herriott(dir)
Choirs of St.Hilda's and St.Hugh's School,William Toole(dir)
Central Connecticut State College Singers,Dr.Robert Soule(dir)
(from Fantasy)   NYC,January & February 1968
        & St.Marks,Canaan(Connecticut),January 20 & 22,1968

    Praise God   PR24045
    Supreme being   -
    Heaven voAB   -
    Something about believing-1   -
    Almighty God voAB   -
    The shepherd(who watches over
            the night flock)   -
    It's freedom-1   -
    Meditation   -
    The biggest and busiest intersection
                                               -
    T.G.T.T.(Too good to title)-1 voAB -
    Don't get down on your knees to
     pray until you have forgiven
               everyone   -
    Father forgive voTW   -
    Praise God and dance-1 voAB   -

DON BYAS MEETS BEN WEBSTER:
Ben Webster,Don Byas(ts)Tete Montoliu(p)Peter Trunk(b)Albert Heath(dm).
(from Saba/MPS)   Villingen,February 1 & 2,1968
                Blues for Dottie Mae   PR7692
                Lullaby to Dottie Mae(Webster out)-
                Sundae   -
                Perdido   -
                When Ash meets Henry(Byas out)   -
                Caravan   -

OSCAR PETERSON-SOUL-O!:
Oscar Peterson(solo p).
(from Saba/MPS)   Villingen,April   ,1968
                Someone to watch over me   PR7595
                Perdido   -
                Body and soul   -
                Who can I turn to   -
                Bye bye blackbird   -
                I should care   -
                Lulu's back in town   -
                Little girl blue   -
                Take the A train   -

THE GREAT OSCAR PETERSON ON PRESTIGE:
Oscar Peterson(p)Sam Jones(b)Bobby Durham(dm).
(from Saba/MPS)   Villingen,April   ,1968
                Waltzing is hip   Pr.   PR7620
                Satin doll   -
                Love is here to stay
                Sandy's blues   Pr.45-711   -
                Alice in Wonderland   -
                Noreen's nocturne   -

OSCAR PETERSON:
Oscar Peterson(p)Ray Brown(b)Louis Hayes(dm).
(from Saba/MPS)   Villingen,April   ,1968
                Medley:I concentrate on you/
                        Moon river   PR7649

KENNY CLARKE/FRANCY BOLAND BIG BAND-LET'S FACE THE MUSIC:
Benny Bailey,Idriss Sulieman,Jimmy Deuchar,Sonny Grey(tp)Ake Persson,
Nat Peck,Erik Van Lier(tb)Derek Humble(as)Johnny Griffin,Ronnie Scott,
Tony Coe(ts)Sahib Shihab(bs)Francy Boland(p,arr)Dave Pike(vb)Jimmy
Woode(b)Kenny Clare,Kenny Clarke(dm).
(from Saba/MPS)   Cologne,May 13 & 14,1968
                Let's face the music and dance PR7699
                I'm all smiles   -
                You stepped out of a dream   -
                I'm glad there is you   -
                Get out of town   -
                By Strauss   -
                When your lover has gone   -
                Gloria   -
                Sweet and lovely   -
                High school cadets   -

ALTO SUMMIT:
Lee Konitz,Pony Poindexter,Phil Woods,Leo Wright(as)Steve Kuhn(p)Palle
Danielson(b)Jon Christensen(dm)..
(from Saba/MPS)   Villingen,June 2 & 3,1968
        Native land   PR7684
        Medley:Skylark/   -
               Blue and sentimental/   -
               Gee baby ain't I good to
                             you/   -
               Body and soul   -
        Prompt   -
        The perils of Poda   -
        Good Booty   -
        Lee-O's blues   -
        Lee's tribute to Bach and Bird -

STEVE KUHN IN EUROPE:
Steve Kuhn(p)Palle Danielson(b)Jon Christensen(dm).
(from Saba/MPS)   Villingen,June 4,1968
        Watch what happens   PR7694
        Silver   -
        Lament   -
        Once we loved   -
        Tom Jones   -
        Windows of the world   -
        Here I am   -
        I fall in love too easily   -
        Ad infinitum   -

THE KENNY CLARKE/FRANCY BOLAND BIG BAND-LATIN KALEIDOSCOPE:
Benny Bailey,Jimmy Deuchar,Idriss Sulieman,Dusko Gojkovic,Milo Pavlovic
(tp)Ake Persson,Nat Peck,Erik Van Lier(tb)Derek Humble,Phil Woods(as)
Johnny Griffin,Tony Coe,Ronnie Scott(ts)Sahib Shihab(fl,bs)Francy Boland
(p)   Jimmy Woode,Jean Warland(b)Kenny Clarke(dm)Kenny Clare,Shake Keane,
Albert "Tootie" Heath,Tony Inzalaco,Sabu Martinez(perc)Manny Albam(arr).
(from Saba/MPS)   Cologne,August 28 & 29,1968
        Latin kaleidoscope: PR7760
          Un graso de areia/   -
          Duas rosas/A rosa negra/   -
          Uma fita de tres cores/   -
          Ollios negros/Ramo de flores -
        Cuban fever:Fiebre Cuban/   -
          Mambo de las brujas/   -
          Strano sueno/Cara bruja/   -
          Crepusculo y aurora   -

THE TEDDY WILSON TRIO IN EUROPE:
Teddy Wilson(p)Niels-Henning Orsted Pedersen(b)Bjarne Rostvold(dm).
(from Saba/MPS)   Copenhagen,November   ,1968
        My silent love   PR7696
        You brought a new kind of love -
        Paradise   -
        My heart stood still   -
        Serenata   -
        Indiana   -
        April in Paris   -
        'Deed I do   -
        Autumn in New York   -
        Ain't misbehavin'   -
        Serenade in blue   -
        It's all right with me   -

ELLA FITZGERALD-SUNSHINE OF YOUR LOVE:
Ella Fitzgerald(vo)with Tommy Flanagan(p)Frank De La Rosa(b)Ed Thigpen
(dm).
(from MPS)   Fairmont Hotel,SF,February or March 1969
            Useless landscape   PR7685
            Old devil moon   -
            Don' cha go 'way mad   -
            A house is not a home   -
            Trouble is a man   -
            Love you madly   -

Same,with orchestra incl.Allen Smith(tp)Ernie Heckscher(dir).Marty
Paich-1,Tee Carson-2,Frank De Vol-3,Bill Holman-4(arr).
                                    Same date.
            Sunshine of your love-1   Pr.45-715,PR7685
            Hey Jude-1   -   -
            Alright,okay,you win-1   -
            Watch what happens-2   -
            This girl's in love with you-3   -
            Give me the simple life-4   -

DEXTER GORDON-A DAY IN COPENHAGEN:
Dizzy Reece(tp)Slide Hampton(tb)Dexter Gordon(ts)Kenny Drew(p)Niels-
Henning Orsted Pedersen(b)Art Taylor(dm).
(from MPS)   Copenhagen,March 10,1969
            My blues   PR7763
            You don't know what love is -
            A new thing   -
            What's new?   -
            The shadow of your smile   -
            A day in Vienna   -

BILLY TAYLOR TODAY!:
Billy Taylor(p)Ben Tucker(b)Grady Tate(dm).
(from MPS)   NYC,April   ,1969
            La petite mambo   PR7762
            Theodora   -
            Paraphrase   -
            Bye y'all   -
            Don't go down South   -
            Brother where are you?   -
            There will never be another you -
            A sleeping bee   -

BEN WEBSTER:
Ben Webster(ts)Cees Slinger(p)Jacques Schols(b)John Engels(dm).
(from Imperial)   Heemstede(Holland),May 26,1969
            I got it bad and that ain't good PR24031
            Drop me off at Harlem   -
            One for the gov' nor   -
            Prelude to a kiss   -
            In a sentimental mood   -
            Rockin' in rhythm   -

HERBIE HANCOCK:
Joe Henderson(ts)Herbie Hancock(p)Ron Carter(b)Jack De Johnette(dm).
(from Milestone)   NYC,May 29,1969
            Black Narcissus   P-24052

THE GREAT CONCERT OF CECIL TAYLOR:
Jimmy Lyons(as)Sam Rivers(ss,ts)Cecil Taylor(p,vo)Andrew Cyrille(dm).
(from Shandar)   St.Paul de Vence(France),July 29,1969
          Second Act of A,pts.1 to 6   P-34003

BEN WEBSTER:
Ben Webster(ts)Kenny Drew(p)Frans Wieringa(p)Niels Henning Orsted
Pedersen(b)Donald McKyre(dm).
(from Catfish)   Copenhagen,October 29,1969
          John Brown's body   PR24031
          Worksong   -
          The preacher   -
          Straight no chaser   -

ARCHIE SHEPP-BLACK GYPSY:
Clifford Thornton(tp)Archie Shepp(ss)Noah Howard(as)Julio Finn(hca)
Dave Burrell(p)Leroy Jenkins(viola)Earl Freeman(b)Sunny Murray(dm)
Chicago Beau(vo).
(from America)   Paris,November 9,1969
          Black Gypsy   PR10034
          Epitaph of a small winner: -
            Rio De Janeiro/   -
            Casablanca/Chicago   -

AHMAD JAMAL:
Ahmad Jamal(p)Jamil Nasser(b)Frank Gant(dm).
(from Impulse)   NYC,February 2 or 3,1970
          Wave   P-24052

ART ENSEMBLE OF CHICAGO-PHASE I:
Lester Bowie(tp,flh,horn,dm)Chicago Beau,Joseph Jarman(saxes)Julio
Finn(hca)Malachi Favors(b)William A.Howell(dm)Don Moye(dm,perc).
(from America)   Paris,May or June,1970
          Ohnedaruth   PR10064
          Lebert Aaly   -

ART ENSEMBLE OF CHICAGO with FONTELLA BASS:
Fontella Bass(vo)added.
(from America)   Paris,May or June,1970
          How strange   PR10049
          Ole Jed voFB   -
          Horn Web   -

ARCHIE SHEPP-CORAL ROCK:
Alan Shorter(flh)Joseph Jarman(tp)Clifford Thornton(vtb)Archie Shepp
(ts,p)Bobby Few(p)Bob Reid(b)Mohammed Ali(dm)Djibrill(conga)Ostaine
Blue Warner(perc).
(from America)   Paris,July 23,1970
          Coral rock   PR10066
          I should care   -

JOE ZAWINUL:
Woody Shaw(tp)George Davis(fl)Earl Turbinton(ss)Joe Zawinul,Herbie
Hancock(el p)Miroslav Vitous,Walter Booker(b)Billy Hart,David Lee(perc)
(from Atlantic)   NYC,August 6,1970
19819 In a silent way   P-24052

CHARLIE MINGUS-REINCARNATION OF A LOVE BIRD:
Eddie Preston(tp)Charles McPherson(as)Bobby Jones(ts)Jaki Byard(p)
Charles Mingus(b)Danny Richmond(dm).
(from America)   Paris,October 31,1970

    Reincarnation of a love bird   PR24028
    I left my heart in San Francisco   -
    Blue Bird   -
    Pithycanthropus erectus   -
    Peggy's blue skylight   -
    Love is a dangerous necessity   -

McCOY TYNER:
McCoy Tyner(solo p).
(from Milestone)   NYC,November 27,1972

    Silent tear   P-24052

OSCAR PETERSON & STEPHANE GRAPPELLI:
Stephane Grappelli(v)Oscar Peterson(p)Niels-Henning Orsted Pedersen(b)
Kenny Clarke(dm).   -1:b,dm out.
(from America)   Paris,February 22 & 23,1973

    Them there eyes   PR24041
    Flamingo   -
    Makin' whoopee   -
    Looking at you   -
    Walking my baby back home   -   P-24052
    My one and only love   -
    Thou swell   -
    I won't dance   -
    The folks who live on the hill-1   -
    Autumn leaves   -
    My heart stood still   -
    Blues for Musidisc   -
    If I had you   -

DIZZY GILLESPIE-THE GIANT:
Dizzy Gillespie(tp)Johnny Griffin-1(ts)Kenny Drew(p)Niels Henning
Orsted Pedersen(b)Kenny Clarke(dm)Humberto Canto(conga).
(from America)   Paris,April 13,1973

    Stella by starlight   PR24047
    I waited for you   -
    Girl of my dreams   -
    Fiesta mo-jo -1   -
    Serenity   -
    Manteca-1   -
    Alone together-1   -
    Brother K -1   -
    Wheatleigh hall-1   -

KEITH JARRETT:
Dewey Redman(ts)Keith Jarrett(p)Charlie Haden(b)Paul Motian(dm)
Guilherme Franco,Danny Johnson(perc).
(from Impulse)   NYC,February 27 or 28,1974

    Intro & Yaqui Indian folk song   P-24052

Part 3
Single Numerical Listings

*:also issued on 45 rpm.

Record No.	Artist	Title	Matrix No.	Page
PRESTIGE label				
301 JIMMY McPARTLAND		Daughter of Sister Kate	UR8816	247
		Singin' the blues	UR8817	247
302 JIMMY McPARTLAND		Royal garden blues	UR8815	247
		In a mist	UR8818	247
303 JIMMY McPARTLAND		Come back sweet Papa	MCP602	8
		Manhattan	MCP603	8
304 JIMMY McPARTLAND		Use your imagination	MCP600	8
		Davenport blues	MCP605	8
701 JAMES MOODY		Lester leaps in	MR33	248
		Out of nowhere	MR25	248
702 JAMES MOODY QUINTET		Maxology,pt.1	ST3011A	247
		Maxology,pt.2	ST3011B	247
703*JAMES MOODY		I'm in the mood for love	MR32	248
		The flight of the bopple bee	MR30	248
704 SONNY STITT		Ain't misbehavin'	JRC1010	5
		Later	JRC1009	5
705 SONNY STITT		All God's chillun got rh.	JRC1000A	4
		Sunset	JRC1003A	4
706 SONNY STITT		Fine and dandy	JRC1007A	5
		Bud's blues	JRC1002B	4
707 WARDELL GRAY		Twisted	JRC46D	4
		Easy living	JRC48B	4
708 STAN GETZ		There's a small hotel	BL1202C	4
		I've got you under my skin	BL1204B	4
709 GENE AMMONS & SONNY STITT		Blues up and down	BL1222-2	5
		You can depend on me	BL1223-1	5
710 STAN GETZ		Long Island Sound	JRC25E	2
		Mar-cia	JRC26D	2
711 WARDELL GRAY		Southside	JRC47E	4
		Sweet Lorraine	JRC49A	4
712 STAN GETZ		My old flame	JRC76B	6
		The lady in red	JRC77B	6
713 GENE AMMONS		Bye bye	BL1220	5
		Let it be	BL1221	5
714 WARDELL GRAY		Blue Gray	JRC80B	6
		Treadin' with Treadwell	JRC82C	6
715 TEDDY WILLIAMS		Touch of the blues	BL1224	6
		Dumb woman blues	BL1225	6
716 JAMES MOODY		Good bait	MR35	248
		Dexterious	MR36	248

741*GENE AMMONS	Blue and sentimental	127	9
	Chabootie	85	7
742 MILES DAVIS	Down	129	9
	Whispering	131	9
743 LEE KONITZ	Ezz-thetic	141	10
	Hi-Beck	142	10
744 JAMES MOODY	Embraceable you	MR194	252
	Two feathers	MR201	252
745 GERRY MULLIGAN	So what	JRC1111	6
CHUBBY JACKSON	Hot dog	JRC1108	6
746 SONNY STITT	'S wonderful	115	8
	The thrill of your kiss	138	9
747 ROY ELDRIDGE	Noppin' John	MR212	253
	Scottie	MR213	253
748*GENE AMMONS &	Stringin' the Jug,pt.1	116	8
SONNY STITT	Stringin' the Jug,pt.2	117	8
749*REINHOLD SVENSSON	Rain on the roof	2144	253
	Moonlight saving time	2145	253
750 ARNE DOMNERUS	September serenade	2152	253
LARS GULLIN	A handful of stars	2147	253
751 ZOOT SIMS	Trotting	164	11
	Swingin' the blues	166	11
752 SONNY STITT	Down with it	156	10
	Mean to me	JRC1011	5
753 LEE KONITZ	Indian Summer	144	10
	Odjenar	140	10
754 GENE AMMONS	Hot stuff	160	10
	When the Saints go march.	162	10
755 LEE KONITZ	Duet for saxophone & g.	145	10
	Yesterdays	143	10
756 JAMES MOODY	Cherokee	MR210	253
	Pennies from heaven	MR211	253
757 SONNY STITT	P.S.I love you	146	9
	Liza	133	9
758 SONNY STITT	I want to be happy	JRC1005B	5
	Strike up the band	JRC1004D	5
759 WARDELL GRAY	Kiddo,pts.1 & 2	1233	7
760 WARDELL GRAY	Kiddo,pts.3 & 4	1234	7
761*GERRY MULLIGAN	Ide's side	172	11
	Roundhouse	171	11
762*GERRY MULLIGAN	Bweebida Bobbida	173	11
	Kaper	174	11
763*GERRY MULLIGAN	Funhouse	175A	11
	Mullenium	176	11
764			
765 RED RODNEY	Smoke gets in your eyes	200	12
	Coogan's bluff	202	12
766 MILES DAVIS	My old flame,pts.1 & 2	233	12

[280]

818	STAN GETZ	Battleground	JRC16E	1
		Prezervation	JRC60	2
819	FATS NAVARRO	Wailing wall	JRC35D	3
		Infatuation	JRC37B	3
820	SONNY STITT	Teapot	JRC602B	3
		Afternoon in Paris	JRC600C	3
821*	KING PLEASURE	Red top	394	19
		Jumpin' with Symphony Sid	395	19
822*	BILLY TAYLOR	The man with a horn	388	19
		Let's get away from it all	389	19
823	AL HAIG	Stairway to the stars	JRC1102C	5
		Opus caprice	JRC1103A	5
824	SONNY STITT	Stairway to the stars	JRC1012	5
		Sonny sounds	336	16
825	CHUBBY JACKSON	Flying the Coop	JRC1104	6
		I may be wrong	JRC1105	6
826	SONNY STITT	Nevertheless	120	8
		Jeepers creepers	121	8
827	LEE KONITZ	You go to my head	JRC72C	6
		Palo Alto	JRC74B	6
828	MODERN JAZZ QUARTET	All the things you are	403	19
		La ronde	404	19
829	JOE CARROLL	I was in the mood	411	20
		Got a penny,Benny	413	20
830	CHUBBY JACKSON ZOOT SIMS	Sex appeal	JRC1107	6
		Leavin' town	JRC1110	6
831	SONNY STITT	This can't be love	147	9
		For the fat man	157	10
832	LENNIE TRISTANO	Progression	JRC3A	1
		Retrospection	JRC4A	1
833	REINHOLD SVENSSON	On the Alamo	MR102	250
		Always	MR103	250
834	LEE KONITZ	Rebecca	JRC71	6
		Ice cream Konitz	JRC73	6
835	REINHOLD SVENSSON	Nevertheless	MR146	251
		I guess I'll have to dream	MR147	251
836	CHUBBY JACKSON	New York	JRC1106	6
		Why not?	JRC1109	6
837	ZOOT SIMS	Yellow duck	88	250
		Americans in Sweden	89	250
838	THELONIOUS MONK	Trinkle tinkle	399	19
		These foolish things	400	19
839*	ANNIE ROSS	Farmer's market	364	17
		The time was right	365	17
840*	WARDELL GRAY	April skies	312	15
		Bright boy	313	15
841*	JAMES MOODY	Stardust	V3005	247
		Moody and soul	V3009	247
842	ZOOT SIMS	So what	JRC1111	6

843	SONNY STITT	'S wonderful	115	8
844	GENE AMMONS	La vie en rose	102	7
		Jug	125	9
845	GENE AMMONS	Bye bye	BL1220	5
		I can't give you anything..	91	7
846	MILES DAVIS	Bluing,pts.1 & 2	231	12
847	BENNIE GREEN	Stardust	345	17
		Embraceable you	344	17
848	JOE HOLIDAY	Hello to you	259	13
		Like someone in love	266	13
849	BILLY TAYLOR	Lover,pts.1 & 2	390	19
850	THELONIOUS MONK	Little rootie tootie	367	18
		Monk's dream	370	18
851	MODERN JAZZ QUARTET	Vendome	405	18
		Rose of the Rio Grande	406	18
852	ZOOT SIMS	There I've said it again	431	20
		Jaguar	432	20
853	WARDELL GRAY	Sweet and lovely	316	15
		Jackie	314	15
854	JAMES MOODY	How deep is the ocean	195	252
		Am I blue	196	252
855	CHARLIE FERGUSON	When day is done	391	19
		Stop talkin' start walkin'	392	19
856	THE MELLO MOODS	I'm lost	385	18
		When I woke up this morning	386	18
857	PAULA GRIMES	It's your own darn fault	375	18
		Makin' a fool of myself	378	18
858*	EDDIE JEFFERSON	Stop talkin',start walkin'	429	21
		Strictly instrumental	427	21
859	RUDY FERGUSON	Cool competition		225
		Ooh baby		225
860*	KING PLEASURE	This is always	514	24
		Sometimes I'm happy	513	24
861	JOE CARROLL	Pennies from heaven	412	20
		Make it right	414	20
862	LARS GULLIN	Brazil	MR455	255
		Four and one more	MR456	255
863	ARNE DOMNERUS	The way you look tonight	MR76	250
		Sensual	MR77	250
864	BENGT HALLBERG	Flying saucer	MR404	254
		Zig zag	MR405	254
865	REINHOLD SVENSSON	Because of George	MR385	254
		Tasty pastry	MR386	254
866	EDDIE DAVIS	Sweet and lovely	BL1207	5
		Squattin'	BL1209	5
867	STAN GETZ	Intoit	BL1210	4
		You stepped out of a dream	JRC75C	6

NEW JAZZ label

				Page
800	TERRY GIBBS	T and S	JRC13B	1
		Terry's tune	JRC14C	1
801	THE ALL STAR SEXTET	First gear	31	246
		Confirmation	32	246
802	STAN GETZ	Four and one Moore	JRC18D	1
	(yellow label)	Five brothers	JRC17E	1
802	STAN GETZ	Four and one Moore	JRC17E	1
	(red label)	Five brothers	JRC18C	1
803	TERRY GIBBS	Cuddles	JRC15D	1
	JAY JAY JOHNSON	Elysees	JRC20B	2
804	TERRY GIBBS	Michelle,pts.1 & 2	JRC12A	1
805	STAN GETZ	Long Island sound	JRC25E	2
		Mar-cia	JRC26D	2
806	JAY JAY JOHNSON	Opus V	JRC21C	2
		Hi Lo	JRC22C	2
807	LEE KONITZ	Marshmallow	JRC29	2
		Fishin' around	JRC30	2
808	LENNIE TRISTANO	Subconscious Lee	JRC8J	1
		Judy	JRC11B	1
809	KAI WINDING	Sid's bounce	JRC34	2
		A night on bop mountain	JRC37B	2
810	JAY JAY JOHNSON	Elysees	JRC20B	2
	DON LANPHERE	Spider's Webb	JRC32	2
811	STAN GETZ	Speedway	JRC15D	1
		Crazy chords	JRC27C	2
812	FATS NAVARRO	Stop	JRC38B	3
		Go	JRC36C	3
813	LEE KONITZ	Tautology	JRC39	3
		Sound Lee	JRC40	3
814	JAY JAY JOHNSON	Elora	JRC601B	3
		Blue mode	JRC603C	3
815	HOWARD McGHEE	Crossroads	ST2294	247
		Dimitar	ST2297	247
816	KAI WINDING	Broadway	JRC904	2
		Waterworks	JRC905	2
817	WARDELL GRAY	Twisted	JRC46D	4
		Easy living	JRC48B	4
818	STAN GETZ	Battleground	JRC16E	1
		Prezervation	JRC60	2
819	FATS NAVARRO	Wailing wall	JRC35D	3
		Infatuation	JRC37B	3
820	JAY JAY JOHNSON	Afternoon in Paris	JRC600C	3
		Teapot	JRC602B	3
821	ARNE DOMNERUS	Body and soul	MR10	248
		I've got my love to keep..	MR9	248
822	AL HAIG	Liza	JRC100C	5
		Stars fell on Alabama	JRC1101C	5
823	AL HAIG	Stairway to the stars	JRC1102C	5
		Opus caprice	JRC1103A	5

				Page
824	REINHOLD SVENSSON	Dinah	MR64	249
		Once in a while	MR65	249
825	CHUBBY JACKSON	Flying the Coop	JRC1104	6
		I may be wrong	JRC1105	6
826	REINHOLD SVENSSON	Sweet and lovely	MR66	249
		My blue heaven	MR67	249
827	LEE KONITZ	You go to my head	JRC72C	6
		Palo Alto	JRC74B	6
828	WARDELL GRAY	Sweet Lorraine	JRC49A	4
		Southside	JRC47E	4
829	STAN GETZ	My old flame	JRC76B	6
		The lady in red	JRC77B	6
830	CHUBBY JACKSON	Sax appeal	JRC1107	6
		Leavin' town	JRC1110	6
831	ARNE DOMNERUS	Cool boy	MR74	250
		Stuffy	MR75	250
832	LENNIE TRISTANO	Progression	JRC3A	1
		Retrospection	JRC4A	1
833	REINHOLD SVENSSON	On the Alamo	MR102	250
		Always	MR103	250
834	LEE KONITZ	Rebecca	JRC71	6
		Ice cream Konitz	JRC73	6
835	REINHOLD SVENSSON	Nevertheless	MR146	251
		I guess I'll have to dream	MR147	251
836	CHUBBY JACKSON	New York	JRC1106	6
		Why not?	JRC1109	6
837	ZOOT SIMS	Yellow duck	MR88	250
		Which way	MR89	250
838	TEDDY CHARLES	I'll remember April	252	13
		The lady is a tramp	253	13
839	KENNY GRAHAM	Mango walk	130	253
		Pina colada	131	253
840	REINHOLD SVENSSON	Dearly beloved	MR144	251
		That old feeling	MR145	251
841	LARS GULLIN	That's it	MR218	253
		All yours	MR220	253
842	CHARLIE MARIANO	The wizard	300	15
		Autumn in New York	304	15
843	LEE KONITZ	Ezz-thetic	141	10
		Hi-beck	142	10
844				
845				
846				
847				
848				
849				

PRESTIGE label

				Page
901	GENE AMMONS	Ammons boogie	148	10
		Echo chamber blues	149	10
902	THE CABINEERS	My,my,my	153	10
		Baby where'd you go	155	10
903	GENE AMMONS	Sirocco	150	10
		Fine and dandy	151	10
904	THE CABINEERS	Each time	152	10
		Lost	154	10
905	EARL COLEMAN	Guilty	D1162	247
		As time goes by	D1165	247
906	RALPH WILLIS	Goodbye blues		254
		Lazy woman blues		254
907	RALPH WILLIS	Church bell blues		254
		Tell me pretty baby		254
908	BENNIE GREEN	Whirl-a-licks	223	12
		Pennies from heaven	224	12
909	JOHNNY GREEN	Pepsi bounce	178	11
(PAR label)		Low boat	179	11
910	Rev.FELIX JOHNSON	The 23rd psalm	J-9	225
		When a man dies	J-10	225
911	LEM DAVIS	The glory of love	215	13
		Sin	216	13
912	LEM DAVIS	Problem child	219	13
		She's a wine-O	220	13
913	SILVER TRUMPETS	What manner of man He is	J-5	225
		Master Jesus	J-8	225
914	GENE SMITH	Make believe	183	11
		Late hour boogie	196	11
915	LEM DAVIS	This is always	217	13
		Knock hop	218	13
916	GENE AMMONS	Undecided	255	13
		Charmaine	258	13
917	THE CABINEERS	What's the matter..	287	14
		Baby mine	288	14
918	H-BOMB FERGUSON	Feel like I do	276	14
		My love	278	14
919	RALPH WILLIS	Old home blues	208	12
		Salty dog	210	12
920	BENNIE GREEN	Tenor sax shuffle	226	12
		Sugar syrup	227	12
921	GENE AMMONS	Until the real thing..	256	13
		Because of rain	257	13
922	JOHN BENNINGS	Goofin' the roofin'	289	14
		Come on home	290	14
923	BROWNIE McGHEE	Cold chills	308	15
		Amen	310	15
924	KING PLEASURE	Moody's mood for love	330	16
		Exclamation blues	332	16

(45 rpm)

[292]

```
45-                                                                    Page
203   JOHN WRIGHT          You do it                    2649           93
                           Yes I know                   2650           93

204   BABS GONZALES        We ain't got integration                   227
                           Lonely one                                 227

205   ETTA JONES           Unchained melody             3175           111
                           Hurry home                   3174           111

206   GENE AMMONS          The breeze and I             3233           116
                           Up tight                     3243           116

207   WILLIS JACKSON       Cookin' sherry,pts.1 & 2     2403           86
208   JIMMY FORREST        Annie Laurie,pts.1 & 2       3254           116

209   JOHNNY "HAMMOND"     Swanee river,pts. 1 & 2      2609           91
         SMITH

210   SHIRLEY SCOTT        Hip twist,pts.1 & 2          3280           117

211   JACK McDUFF          Sanctified waltz             3141           109
                           Goodnight it's time to go    3142           109

212   JOHN WRIGHT          Makin' out,pts. 1 & 2        3109           107

213   OLIVER NELSON        Emancipation blues,pts.1&2   3232           115

214    GENE AMMONS         Twistin' the Jug,pts.1&2     3290           118

215   ETTA JONES           You came a long way..        3380           121
                           Just friends                 3375           121

216   LARRY YOUNG          Groove Street,pts. 1 & 2     3422           123

217   FRANK WESS           Southern comfort,pts. 1 & 2  3441           123

218   JOHN WRIGHT          Blue prelude                 3475           125
                           Strut                        3477           125

219   JACK McDUFF          Mellow gravy,pts. 1 & 2      3361           120

220   EDDIE DAVIS          Please send me someone..     3507           127
                           Goin' to the meetin'         3509           127

221   WILLIS JACKSON       Jambalaya                    3308           119
                           Thunderbird                  3456           124

222

223   JIMMY FORREST        Soft Summer breeze           3527           129
                           Experiments in terror        3529           129

224   FAYE ADAMS           Goodnight my love            3545           130
                           You can trust in me          3546           130

225   JIMMY GRISSOM        I've got you on my mind      3549           130
                           Lover's reverie              3550           130

226   GENE AMMONS          I sold my heart..            3241           116
                           Moonglow                     3235           116

227   GENE AMMONS          Pagan love song              3614           133
                           Anna                         3615           133

228   DAVE PIKE            Mel Valita,pts. 1 & 2        3612           132

229   GENE AMMONS          Ca' purange,pts. 1 & 2       3616           133

230   SHIRLEY SCOTT        Sister Sadie,pts. 1 & 2      3273           117

231   RED GARLAND          Sonny boy                    3639           133
                           Baby won't you please come..3637           133

232   JACK McDUFF          He's a real gone guy,pts.1&23641           134
```

				Page
287	RED HOLLOWAY	Monkey sho can talk	3978	143
		Crib theme	3979	143
288	DAVE VAN RONK	If I had it to do..	not included	
		Ace in the hole	"	"
289	TOM RUSH	Diamond Joe	"	"
		Every day in the week	"	"
290	THE TRUE ENDEAVOR	Blues,just blues..	"	"
	JUG BAND	Jug band blues	"	"
291	JIMMY WITHERSPOON	You made me love you		143
		Goin' to Chicago		143
292	SHIRLEY SCOTT	Satin doll	2906	99
		C jam blues	2907	99
293	WILLIS JACKSON	Gra-a-vy	3920	140
		Brother Elijah	3812	140
294	GENE AMMONS	Love,I've found you	3084	106
		Tubby	3404	122
295	MOSE ALLISON	The seventh son	1563	62
		Parchman farm	1391	56
296	EDDIE DAVIS	Misty	1943	73
		In the kitchen	1526	61
297	DAVE VAN RONK	St.Louis tickle	not included	
		Cake walkin' babies..	"	"
298	JIMMY WITHERSPOON	I had a dream		143
		S.K.Blues		143
299	JACK McDUFF	Dink's blues		142
		Grease monkey		142
300	RED HOLLOWAY	Denise		145
		Wives and lovers		145
301	THE NOMOS	Redwood City		146
		Step out and get it		146
302	EDDIE CHAMBLEE	The honeydripper		146
		You never walk alone		146
303	WILLIS JACKSON	Troubled times	3918	140
		As long as she needs me	3916	140
304	SONNY STITT	Soul shack	3971	142
		Shangri-La		147
305	SHIRLEY SCOTT	Out of it	3793	140
		The second time around	3792	140
306	not used			
307	JIMMY WITHERSPOON	Evening blues		142
		Money's getting cheaper		142
308	KENNY BURRELL	Don't cry baby	1077	46
		Drum boogie	1073	46
309	JACK McDUFF	The carpetbaggers		148
		The pink panther		148
310	LONNIE JOHNSON	Jelly roll baker	2140	78
		I'll get along somehow	2150	78
311	ROLAND KIRK	Three for Dizzy,pts. 1 & 2	3134	108
312	MANFRED MANN	5-4-3-2-1	not included	
		Without you	"	"

[303]

(Series discontinued,and resumed at 45-701 - see on page 306)

[305]

NEW JAZZ label

45-				Page
501	JOHNNY HAMMOND SMITH	Sweet cookies	1850	70
		Secret love	1852	70
502	JOHNNY HAMMOND SMITH	All soul	1848	70
		The masquerade is over	1846	70
503	BENNY GOLSON	Yesterdays	1836	70
		Drum boogie	1837	70
504	LEM WINCHESTER	Down fuzz	1865	70
		If I were a bell	1866	70
505	RAY BRYANT	Joy	1692	65
		Stocking feet	1694	65
506	YUSEF LATEEF	Dopolous	1887	70
		Yesterdays	1888	70
507	OLIVER NELSON	Trane wh stle,pts.1 & 2	2093	77
508	OLIVER NELSON	Screamin' the blues,pts.1&2	2276	82
509	JOHNNY HAMMOND SMITH	I'll remember April	1906	72
		That good feeling	1909	72
510	KING CURTIS	Soul meeting	2473	89
		All the way	2476	89
511				
512	AHMED ABDUL-MALIK	The Hustlers	3045	105
		La Ibkey	3044	105

MOODSVILLE label

45-				
601	SAM TAYLOR	The bad and the beautiful	3415	122

PRESTIGE label

45-				
701	ILLINOIS JACQUET	Bottoms up		185
		Port of Rico		185
702	PUCHO & THE LATIN SOUL BROS.	Georgia on my mind		186
		Heat		186
703	SONNY CRISS	Eleanor Rigby		188
		Rockin' in rhythm		188
704	ERIC KLOSS	Get the money bluze		182
		Comin' home baby		178
705	TRUDY PITTS	Trudy' n'blue,pts.1 & 2		187
706	DUKE EDWARDS & THE YOUNG ONES	Is it too late,pts. 1 & 2		186
707	GENE AMMONS	Jungle soul,pts.1 & 2		133

[306]

45-

737 GENE AMMONS	Jungle strut			197
	Madame queen			196
738 RUSTY BRYANT	Soul liberation			200
739 MELVIN SPARKS	Thank you			201
740 HOUSTON PERSON	The son of my man			202
	Close to you			202
741 CHARLES EARLAND	Westbound No.9,pt.1			201
	Westbound No.9,pt.2			201
742 GENE AMMONS	Jug eyes			202
	He's a real gone guy			197
743 IDRIS MUHAMMAD	Express yourself			202
	Super bad			202
744 KING PLEASURE	I'm in the mood for love	330		16
	Red top	394		19
745 GENE AMMONS	The black cat	F-2895		202
	Something	F-2896		202
746 CHARLES EARLAND	I was made to love her	F-2924		205
	One for Scotty	F-2925		205
747 HOUSTON PERSON	Just my imagination	A-2926		204
	The Houston express	B-2927		204
748 JOHNNY "HAMMOND" SMITH	I'll be there	A-2928		205
	Smokin' Kool	B-2929		205
749 MELVIN SPARKS	Who's gonna take the weight	A-2930		204
	Alone together	A-2931		204
750 RUSTY BRYANT	Fire eater	A-2932		204
	The Hooker	B-2933		204
751 BOOGALOO JOE JONES	I feel the earth move	F-2968		206
	Inside Job	F-2969		206
752 FUNK,Inc.	Whipper,pt.1	F-2970		205
	Whipper,pt.2	F-2971		205
753 GENE AMMONS	My way	F-2972		206
	Chicago breakdown	F-2973		206
754 FUNK,Inc.	The thrill is gone	P-6013		205
	Bowlegs	P-6014		205
755 CHARLES EARLAND	Will you still love me tomorrow	P-6015		208
	'Cause I love her	P-6016		208
756 IDRIS MUHAMMAD	I'm a believer			206
	Rhythm			206
757 GENE AMMONS	Play me			212
	Lady sings the blues			212

758:not used

759 FUNK,Inc.	Dirty red,pt.1			212
	Dirty red,pt.2			212
760 GARY BARTZ NTU TROOP	Standin' on the corner			214
	Dr.Follow's dance			214

[308]

BLUESVILLE label

[310]

Part 4
Album Numerical Listings

Numbers in brackets refer to pages where sessions involved are
described.

45 EPs

PRESTIGE label

PREP
1301   ANNIE ROSS SINGS(17)
1302   JOE HOLIDAY LATIN MOODS(probably 17)
1303   MILT JACKSON MODERN JAZZ QUARTET(19)
1304   BENNIE GREEN WITH STRINGS(17)
1305   JOE HOLIDAY AND HIS BAND(21)
1306   ZOOT SIMS(20)
1307   TEDDY CHARLES WITH WARDELL GRAY(21)
1308   LENNIE TRISTANO WITH LEE KONITZ(1)
1309   STAN GETZ AND HIS FOUR BROTHERS(1)
1310   STAN GETZ QUARTET,Vol.1(2)
1311   STAN GETZ QUARTET,Vol.2(4)
1312   STAN GETZ AND TERRY GIBBS(1)
1313   STAN GETZ QUARTET,Vol.3(6)
1314   LEE KONITZ WITH WARNE MARSH(2,3)
1315   LEE KONITZ WITH BILLY BAUER(6)
1316   SONNY STITT WITH GENE AMMONS(5,8)
1317   GERRY MULLIGAN,Vol.1(11)
1318   GERRY MULLIGAN,Vol.2(6,11)
1319   LEE KONITZ WITH MILES DAVIS(10)
1320   MILES DAVIS SEXTET(9)
1321   FATS NAVARRO(3)
1322   SAM MOST SEXTET(20)
1323   CHUBBY JACKSON BIG BAND(6)
1324   JAMES MOODY AND HIS BAND(25)
1325   MILT JACKSON MODERN JAZZ QUARTET,Vol.2(23)
1326   MILES DAVIS QUARTET(22)
1327   BILLY TAYLOR MAMBOS(22)
1328   AL HAIG TRIO(5)
1329   THELONIOUS MONK TRIO(18)
1330   JAY JAY JOHNSON WITH SONNY ROLLINS(2)
1331   KAI WINDING WITH GERRY MULLIGAN(2)
1332   JAY JAY JOHNSON WITH SONNY STITT(3)
1333   BILLY TAYLOR TRIO,Vol.1(24)
1334   BILLY TAYLOR TRIO,Vol.2(25)
1335   BILLY TAYLOR TRIO,Vol.3(24)
1336   BILLY TAYLOR TRIO,Vol.4(19,24)
1337   SONNY ROLLINS WITH MILT JACKSON(24)
1338   KING PLEASURE SINGS(19.24)
1339   MILES DAVIS WITH SONNY ROLLINS(12)
1340   JAMES MOODYVol.1 IN SWEDEN(248)
1341   AMERICANS IN SWEDEN(256,259)
1342   STAN GETZ AND LEE KONITZ(2,4,   )
1343   BENNIE GREEN SEPTET(12)
1344   BILLY TAYLOR TRIO,Vol.5(28)
1345   CLIFFORD BROWN WITH ART FARMER(257)
1346   SONNY STITT ALTO SAX(8,9)
1347   GEORGE WALLINGTON AND THE SWEDISH ALL STARS(257)
1348   ZOOT SIMS WITH AL COHN(17)
1349   MILES DAVIS WITH SONNY ROLLINS,Vol.2(12)
1350   TEDDY CHARLES NEW DIRECTIONS WITH JIMMY RANEY(19)

```
PREP
1351   BILLY TAYLOR(25)
1352   THELONIOUS MONK QUINTET(24)
1353   CLIFFORD BROWN WITH TADD DAMERON'S BAND(23)
1354   ART FARMER SEPTET(23)
1355   MILES DAVIS(12)
1356   MILT JACKSON QUINTET(27)
1357   MILES DAVIS(26)
1358   MILES DAVIS(26)
1359
1360   MILES DAVIS QUARTET(25)
1361   MILES DAVIS SEXTET(12)
1362   JAY AND KAI(29)
1363   JAMES MOODY(28,31)
1364   PHIL WOODS(29)
1365   MILT JACKSON QUINTET(27)
1366
1367
1368   JAY AND KAI(29)
1369   JAMES MOODY(26)
1370   MODERN JAZZ QUARTET(30)
1371
1372
1373   TONY LUIS TRIO(32)
1374   TERRY MOREL(32)
```

NEW JAZZ label

```
NJEP
1701   JIMMY RANEY QUARTET(26)
1702   JIMMY RANEY QUARTET(26)
1703   TONY LUIS TRIO(225)
```

10 in. LPs

PRESTIGE label

PRLP
101 LENNIE TRISTANO AND LEE KONITZ(1,2,3)
102 STAN GETZ,Volume One(1,2,6)
103 SONNY STITT AND BUD POWELL(4,5)
104 STAN GETZ,Volume Two(1,4)
105 CHUBBY JACKSON ALL STAR BIG BAND(6)
106 REINHOLD SVENSSON PIANO,Volume One(249,251)
107 BATTLE OF THE SAXES-AMMONS Vs.STITT(5,7,8)
108 THE NEW SOUNDS-STAN GETZ/LEE KONITZ:Stan Getz(2,6)/Lee Konitz(6)
109 MODERN JAZZ TROMBONES-KAI WINDING/JAY JAY JOHNSON(2)
110 JAMES MOODY FAVORITES No.1(248)
111 Mr.SAXOPHONE-SONNY STITT(5,8,9)
112 GENE AMMONS TENOR SAX,Volume One(5,7,8)
113 MODERN JAZZ TRUMPETS:Fats Navarro(3)/Dizzy Gillespie(8)/Miles
       Davis(9)/Kenny Dorham(247)
114 ROY ELDRIDGE IN SWEDEN(252)
115 WARDELL GRAY TENOR SAX(4,6)
116 LEE KONITZ-THE NEW SOUNDS(10)
117 SWINGIN' WITH ZOOT SIMS(11)
118 ZOOT SIMS TENOR SAX FAVORITES(8,11)
119 NEW SOUNDS FROM SWEDEN,Volume One(253)
120 GERRY MULLIGAN(11)
121 NEW SOUNDS FROM SWEDEN,Volume Two:Bengt Hallberg(250,252)/Lars
       Gullin(253)
122 RED RODNEY-THE NEW SOUNDS(12)
123 MODERN JAZZ TROMBONES,Volume Two:J.J.Johnson(3)/Bennie Green(12)
124 MILES DAVIS-THE NEW SOUNDS(12)
125 JAMES MOODY FAVORITES No.2(249,252,253)
126 SONNY STITT FAVORITES,Volume Two(5,7,8)
127 GENE AMMONS FAVORITES,Volume Two(9,10)
128 JAZZ CONCERT-WARDELL GRAY(7)
129 REINHOLD SVENSSON FAVORITES,Volume Two(254)
130 CHARLIE MARIANO(15)
131 JOE HOLIDAY(13)
132 TEDDY CHARLES VIBE SOLOS(13)
133 NEW SOUNDS FROM SWEDEN,Volume Three:Arne Domnerus(250)/Lars Gullin
       (254)
134 NEW SOUNDS FROM SWEDEN,Volume Four-ARNE DOMNERUS CLARINET SOLOS
       (248,250)
135 MAMBO JAZZ:Sonny Rollins(14)/Sonny Stitt(16)/Joe Holiday(17)/
       Kenny Graham(253)
136 GEORGE WALLINGTON TRIO(17)
137 SONNY ROLLINS QUARTET(9,14)
138 ZOOT SIMS ALL STARS-KAI WINDING-AL COHN(17)
139 BILLY TAYLOR TRIO(18,19)
140 MILES DAVIS BLUE PERIOD(9,12)
141 GERRY MULLIGAN BLOWS(11)
142 THELONIOUS MONK TRIO(18,19)
143 TEDDY CHARLES NEW DIRECTIONS,Volume 1(19)
144 NEW SOUNDS FROM SWEDEN,Volume Five-LARS GULLIN(255)
145 NEW SOUNDS FROM SWEDEN,Volume Six-Bengt Hallberg/Arne Domnerus
       (254,255)
146 JAMES MOODY,Volume Three(248,249,252)
147 WARDELL GRAY LOS ANGELES STARS(15)
148 SONNY STITT TENOR SAX,Volume Two(8,10)
149 GENE AMMONS FAVORITES,Volume 3(10,13)
150 TEDDY CHARLES/HALL OVERTON-NEW DIRECTIONS,Volume Two(20)
151 NEW SOUNDS FROM SWEDEN,Volume Seven-LARS GULLIN(255)

```
PRLP
152  AL VEGA PIANO SOLOS WITH BONGOS(20)
153  CHARLIE MARIANO BOSTON ALL STARS(20)
154  MILES DAVIS PLAYS AL COHN COMPOSITIONS(21)
155  NEW SOUNDS FROM SWEDEN,Volume 8-REINHOLD SVENSSON SEXTET(254,256)
156  JIMMY RANEY PLAYS(22)
157  NEW SOUNDS FROM FRANCE WITH JAMES MOODY(247,249,250)
158  GEORGE WALLINGTON TRIO,Volume 2(22)
159  A STUDY IN DAMERONIA WITH TADD DAMERON/CLIFFORD BROWN(23)
160  THE MODERN JAZZ QUARTET(19,23)
161  MILES DAVIS(22,25)
162  WORK OF ART WITH ART FARMER(23)
163  NEW SOUNDS FROM ROCHESTER WITH THE CONTEMPORARY JAZZ ENSEMBLE(23)
164  TEDDY CHARLES-NEW DIRECTIONS,Volume Three(23)
165  BILLY TAYLOR TRIO,Volume Two(19,24)
166  THELONIOUS MONK QUINTET(24)
167  CLIFFORD BROWN AND ART FARMER WITH THE SWEDISH ALL STARS(257)
168  BILLY TAYLOR TRIO,Volume Three(24,25)
169  TEDDY CHARLES NEW DIRECTIONS,Volume Four(24)
170  MODERN JAZZ QUARTET,Volume Two(30,31)
171  MAMBO JAZZ: OE HOLIDAY/BILLY TAYLOR(24,28)
172  QUINCY JONES SWEDISH AMERICAN ALL STARS(259)
173  AKE PERSSON SWEDISH ALL STARS(256,257,259)
174  PIANO MODERNS:Bengt Hallberg(258)/Reinhold Svensson(259)
175  PIANO MODERNS:Al Haig(5)/Mary Lou Williams(255)
176  BENGT HALLBERG SWEDISH ALL STARS(259)
177  ART FARMER(25)
178  TEDDY CHARLES/BOB BROOKMEYER(25)
179  SWINGIN' IN SWEDEN(259)
180  THELONIOUS MONK QUINTET(26)
181  ART FARMER QUINTET(26)
182  MILES DAVIS(26)
183  MILT JACKSON QUINTET(27)
184  BILLY TAYLOR TRIO(27)
185  MILES DAVIS QUINTET(26)
186  SONNY ROLLINS QUINTET(28)
187  MILES DAVIS QUINTET(27)
188  BILLY TAYLOR TRIO(28)
189  THELONIOUS MONK TRIO(28)
190  SONNY ROLLINS(29)
191  PHIL WOODS(31)
192  JAMES MOODY(25,26)
193  ART FARMER QUARTET(29)
194  BILLY TAYLOR AT TOWN HALL(30)
195  JAY AND KAI(29)
196  MILES DAVIS ALL STARS(30)
197  FREDDIE REDD TRIO(32)
198  JAMES MOODY(28,31)
199  JIMMY RANEY QUINTET(31)
200  MILES DAVIS ALL STARS(30)
201  JIMMY RANEY QUARTET(reissue of NJLP1101)(26)
202  ZOOT SIMS QUINTET(reissue of NJLP1102)(27)
203  JIMMY RANEY QUINTET(reissue of NJLP1103)(28)
204  PHIL WOODS QUINTET(reissue of NJLP1104)(29)
205  JON EARDLEY QUARTET(reissue of NJLP1105)(30)
206  TEDDY CHARLES QUARTET(reissue of NJLP1106)(31)
207  JON EARDLEY QUINTET(32)
208  KING PLEASURE(19,24,25,30)
209  ART FARMER QUINTET(33)
210  BENNIE GREEN SEXTET(33)
211  GENE AMMONS ALL STARS(33)
212  HAMPTON HAWES QUARTET(18)
213  JIM CHAPIN SEXTET(34)
214  BOB BROOKMEYER QUARTET(33)
```

NEW JAZZ label
NJLP1101 to NJLP1106:reissued on PRLP201 to PRLP206(see previous page)

----

12 in. LPs

MOODSVILLE label

MVLP
1   RED GARLAND TRIO PLUS EDDIE "LOCKJAW" DAVIS(73)
2   MODERN MOODS:Sonny Stitt(8)/Miles Davis(33)/Modern Jazz Quartet(34)/
    Art Farmer(41)/John Coltrane(53)
3   RED GARLAND-RED ALONE(78)
4   EDDIE "LOCKJAW" DAVIS WITH SHIRLEY SCOTT(75)
5   SHIRLEY SCOTT TRIO(64,79)
6   THE RED GARLAND TRIO(65)
7   AT EASE WITH COLEMAN HAWKINS(74)
8   FRANK WESS QUARTET(81)
9   THE TOMMY FLANAGAN TRIO(82)
10 RED GARLAND-ALONE WITH THE BLUES(78)
11 LEM WINCHESTER-WITH FEELING(91)
12 AL CASEY QUARTET(93)
13 OLIVER NELSON-NOCTURNE(87)
14 ARNETT COBB-BALLADS BY COBB(92)
15 COLEMAN HAWKINS-THE HAWK RELAXES(99)
16 BILLY TAYLOR-INTERLUDE(96)
17 WILLIS JACKSON-IN MY SOLITUDE(97,102)
18 GENE AMMONS-NICE AND COOL(97)
19 SHIRLEY SCOTT-LIKE COZY(90)
20 CLARK TERRY-EVERYTHING'S MELLOW(110)
21 TAFT JORDAN PLAYS DUKE ELLINGTON-MOOD INDIGO(108)
22 YUSEF LATEEF-EASTERN SOUNDS(114)
23 COLEMAN HAWKINS-GOOD OLD BROADWAY(119)
24 SAM "THE MAN" TAYLOR-THE BAD AND THE BEAUTIFUL(122)
25 COLEMAN HAWKINS-THE JAZZ VERSION OF NO STRINGS(124)
26 CLARK TERRY-THE NIGHT LIFE(127,128)
27 THE SOLID TRUMPET OF COOTIE WILLIAMS(125)
28 THE SOULFUL MOODS OF GENE AMMONS(126)
29 KENNY BURRELL WITH COLEMAN HAWKINS-BLUESY BURRELL(133)
30 EDDIE "LOCKJAW" DAVIS WITH SHIRLEY SCOTT-MISTY(73,79)
31 COLEMAN HAWKINS-MAKE SOMEONE HAPPY(131)
32 MILES DAVIS AND JOHN COLTRANE PLAY RICHARD RODGERS:Miles Davis(9,
    38,43)/John Coltrane(61)
33 AMERICA'S GREATEST JAZZMEN PLAY GEORGE GERSHWIN:Billy Taylor(25)/
    J.J.Johnson(29)/Modern Jazz Quartet(34)/Sonny Rollins(42)/Red
    Garland(41)/Eddie "Lockjaw" Davis(75)/Gene Ammons(97)/Jaki Byard
    (100)
34 AMERICA'S GREATEST JAZZMEN PLAY COLE PORTER:Stan Getz(4)/Billy
    Taylor(29)/Modern Jazz Quartet(34)/Red Garland(41)/Gil Evans(55)
    Frank Wess(63)/Shirley Scott(90)/Coleman Hawkins(119)/Gene
    Ammons(133)
35 AMERICA'S GREATEST JAZZMEN PLAY RICHARD RODGERS:Stan Getz(4)/Sonny
    Rollins(14)/Billy Taylor(19)/James Moody(28)/Red Garland(78)/
    Shirley Scott(79)/Lem Winchester(91)/Gene Ammons(97)/Coleman
    Hawkins(124)/Eddie "Lockjaw" Davis(127)
36 DAVE PIKE PLAYS THE JAZZ VERSION OF OLIVER!(136)
37 LUSTY MOODS:Wardell Gray(4)/Miles Davis(38)/Yusef Lateef(55)/Frank
    Wess(59)/Johnny "Hammond" Smith(79)/Shirley Scott(90)/Willis
    Jackson(102)/Sam "The Man" Taylor(122)/Gene Ammons(133)
38 AMERICA'S GREATEST JAZZMEN-THE BROADWAY SCENE:Gene Ammons(97)/
    Tommy Flanagan(124)/Coleman Hawkins(131)Willis Jackson(134)/

```
         Dave Pike(136)/Ted Curson(135)/Frank Wess(136)
39  LUCKY THOMPSON PLAYS JEROME KERN AND NO MORE(138)

BLUESVILLE label

BVLP
1001  AL SMITH-HEAR MY BLUES(70)
1002  BROWNIE McGHEE & SONNY TERRY-DOWN HOME BLUES(86)
1003  WILLIE DIXON-WILLIE'S BLUES(72)
1004  MILDRED ANDERSON-PERSON TO PERSON(74)
1005  BROWNIE McGHEE & SONNY TERRY-BLUES AND FOLK(87)
1006  THE RETURN OF ROOSEVELT SYKES(75,76)
1007  LONNIE JOHNSON-BLUES BY LONNIE(76)
1008  SHAKEY JAKE-GOOD TIMES(81)
1009  SOUL JAZZ,Volume I:All Day Long(45)/Red Garland(56)/Jackie
        McLean(37)
1010  SOUL JAZZ,Volume 2:Gene Ammons(57)/Eddie Davis(65)/Willis Jackson
        (68)/Bill Jennings(69)
1011  LONNIE JOHNSON-BLUES AND BALLADS(78)
1012  LITTLE BROTHER MONTGOMERY-TASTY BLUES(84)
1013  AL SMITH-MIDNIGHT SPECIAL(85)
1014  ROOSEVELT SYKES-THE HONEYDRIPPER(88)
1015  BLIND GARY DAVIS-HARLEM STREET SINGER(87,88)
1016  SUNNYLAND SLIM-SLIM'S SHOUT(89)
1017  MILDRED ANDERSON-NO MORE IN LIFE(90)
1018  MEMPHIS SLIM-JUST BLUES(80,94)
1019  LIGHTNIN' HOPKINS-LIGHTNIN'(93)
1020  BROWNIE McGHEE & SONNY TERRY-BLUES ALL AROUND MY HEAD(86)
1021  ARBEE STIDHAM-TIRED OF WANDERING(92)
1022  CURTIS JONES-TROUBLE BLUES(93)
1023  K.C.DOUGLAS-K.C.'S BLUES(228)
1024  LONNIE JOHNSON-LOSING GAME(96)
1025  SONNY TERRY-SONNY'S STORY(91)
1026  ROBERT PETE WILLIAMS-FREE AGAIN(93)
1027  SHAKEY JAKE-MOUTH HARP BLUES(94)
1028  ST.LOUIS JIMMY-GOIN' DOWN BLUES(94)
1029  LIGHTNIN' HOPKINS-LAST NIGHT BLUES(92)
1030  TAMPA RED-DON'T TAMPA WITH THE BLUES(227)
1031  MEMPHIS SLIM-NO STRAIN(80,94)
1032  REV.GARY DAVIS-HAVE A LITTLE FAITH(111)
1033  BROWNIE McGHEE & SONNY TERRY-BLUES IN MY SOUL(87)
1034  MEMPHIS WILLIE B.-INTRODUCING MEMPHIS WILLIE B.(112)
1035  SIDNEY MAIDEN-TROUBLE AN' BLUES(102)
1036  FURRY LEWIS-BACK ON MY FEET AGAIN(101)
1037  FURRY LEWIS-DONE CHANGED MY MIND(101)
1038  PINK ANDERSON-CAROLINA BLUES MAN(102)
1039  MERCY DEE WALTON-PITY AND A SHAME(103)
1040  BLIND WILLIE McTELL-LAST SESSION (42)
1041  HENRY TOWNSEND-TIRED BEIN' MISTREATED(105)
1042  BROWNIE McGHEE-BROWNIE'S BLUES(90)
1043  TAMPA RED-DON'T JIVE ME(227)
1044  LONNIE JOHNSON WITH VICTORIA SPIVEY-IDLE HOURS(109)
1045  LIGHTNIN' HOPKINS-BLUES IN MY BOTTLE(111)
1046  SNOOKS EAGLIN-THAT'S ALL RIGHT(228)
1047  SCRAPPER BLACKWELL-Mr.SCRAPPER'S BLUES(109)
1048  MEMPHIS WILLIE B.-HARD WORKING MAN BLUES(112)
1049  REV.GARY DAVIS-SAY NO TO THE DEVIL(229)
1050  K.C.DOUGLAS-BIG ROAD BLUES(228)
1051  PINK ANDERSON-MEDICINE SHOW MAN(229)
1052  BLUES WE TAUGHT YOUR MOTHER(113)
1053  MEMPHIS SLIM-ALL KINDS OF BLUES(229)
1054  VICTORIA SPIVEY with LONNIE JOHNSON-WOMAN BLUES(114,115)
```

```
BVLP
1055   BAWDY BLUES:Blind Willie McTell(42)/Lonnie Johnson(78)/Pink
       Anderson(102)/Memphis Willie B.(112)/Victoria Spivey(114,115)/
       Tampa Red(227)/Memphis Slim(229)
1056   BIG JOE WILLIAMS-BLUES FOR 9 STRINGS(115)
1057   LIGHTNIN' HOPKINS-WALKIN' THIS STREET(108,122)
1058   BROWNIE McGHEE & SONNY TERRY AT THE SECOND FRET(127)
1059   SONNY TERRY-SONNY IS KING(91,230)
1060   WADE WALTON-SHAKE 'EM ON DOWN(131)
1061   LIGHTNIN' HOPKINS-LIGHTNIN' AND CO.(122)
1062   LONNIE JOHNSON-ANOTHER NIGHT TO CRY(125)
1063   SMOKEY BABE-HOTTEST BRAND GOING(230)
1064   ROBERT CURTIS SMITH-CLARKSDALE BLUES(131)
1065   DOUG QUATTLEBAUM-SOFTEE MAN BLUES(117,118)
1066   THE NEW GOSPEL KEYS(231)
1067   BIG JOE WILLIAMS AT FOLK CITY(123)
1068   PETE FRANKLIN-GUITAR PETE'S BLUES(109)
1069   BLUES SHOUT(reissue of BVLP1001)(70)
1070   LIGHTNIN' HOPKINS-SMOKES LIKE LIGHTNIN'(120,122)
1071   PINK ANDERSON-BALLAD AND FOLK SINGER,Volume 3(112)
1072   BABY TATE-SEE WHAT YOU DONE(112)
1073   LIGHTNIN' HOPKINS-GOIN' AWAY(140)
1074   BROOKS BERRY & SCRAPPER BLACKWELL-MY HEART STRUCK SORROW(231)
1075   MEMPHIS SLIM-STEADY ROLLIN' BLUES(229)
1076   ALEC SEWARD-CREEPIN' BLUES(231)
1077   J.T.ADAMS-INDIANA AVE.BLUES(230)
1078   RAVI SHANKAR & ALI AKBAR KHAN-THE MASTERS MUSICIANS OF INDIA(not
       included)
1079   ALI AKBAR KHAN-CLASSICAL MUSIC OF INDIA(not included)
1080   not used
1081   LIGHTNIN' HOPKINS-GOTTA MOVE YOUR BABY(reissue of BVLP1029)(92)
1082   not used
1083   BIG JOE WILLIAMS-STUDIO BLUES(116)
1084   LIGHTNIN' HOPKINS-GREATEST HITS(92,93,122,140)
1085   not used
1086   LIGHTNIN' HOPKINS-DOWN HOME  BLUES(149)
1087   BLUES OF SHIRLEY GRIFFITH(230)
1088   not used
1089   OUDI HRANT-TURKISH DELIGHTS(not included)

SWINGVILLE label

SVLP
2001   COLEMAN HAWKINS PLUS THE RED GARLAND TRIO(69)
2002   TINY GRIMES-TINY IN SWINGVILLE(69)
2003   BUDDY TATE-TATE'S DATE(73)
2004   TINY GRIMES-CALLIN' THE BLUES(reissue of PRLP7144)(61)
2005   COLEMAN HAWKINS ALL STARS(74)
2006   REX STEWART-THE HAPPY JAZZ(77)
2007   AL CASEY-BUCK JUMPIN'(76)
2008   PEE WEE RUSSELL-SWINGIN' WITH PEE WEE(77)
2009   CLAUDE HOPKINS-YES INDEED!(77)
2010   THE SWINGVILLE ALL STARS(77)
2011   JOE NEWMAN-JIVE AT FIVE(80)
2012   BUD FREEMAN ALL STARS(81)
2013   PRESTIGE BLUES SWINGERS-STASCH(66)
2014   BUDDY TATE-TATE A TATE(91)
2015   BUDD JOHNSON-LET'S SWING(95)
2016   COLEMAN HAWKINS/EDDIE DAVIS-NIGHT HAWK(96)
2017   BUCK CLAYTON-BUCK  AND BUDDY(95)
2018   AL SEARS-SWING THE THING(94)
2019   JOE NEWMAN-GOOD' N' GROOVY(100)
2020   CLAUDE HOPKINS-LET'S JAM(98)
```

```
SVLP
2021   SHORTY BAKER & DOC CHEATHAM-SHORTY & DOC(97)
2022   JIMMY HAMILTON-IT'S ABOUT TIME(100)
2023   HAL SINGER-BLUE STOMPIN'(reissue of PRLP7153)(66)
2024   COLEMAN HAWKINS-THINGS AIN'T WHAT THEY USED TO BE(102,105)
2025   COLEMAN HAWKINS-YEARS AGO(102,105)
2026   DICK WELLSTOOD & CLIFF JACKSON-UPTOWN AND LOWDOWN(110,111)
2027   JOE NEWMAN-JOE'S HAP'NIN'S(104)
2028   JIMMY HAMILTON-CAN'T HELP SWINGIN'(101)
2029   BUDDY TATE-GROOVIN' WITH TATE(98)
2030   BUCK CLAYTON-BUCK AND BUDDY BLOW THE BLUES(114)
2031   LEONARD GASKIN-AT THE JAZZ BAND BALL(118)
2032   BENNY CARTER WITH BEN WEBSTER & BARNEY BIGARD-B.B.B. AND CO.(126)
2033   LEONARD GASKIN-AT THE DARKTOWN STRUTTER'S BALL(132)
2034   HENRY RED ALLEN-Mr.ALLEN(129)
2035   COLEMAN HAWKINS-BLUES GROOVE(reissue of PRLP7138)(59)
2036   PAUL QUINICHETTE-FOR BASIE(reissue of PRLP7127)(56)
2037   BUCK CLAYTON AND PAUL QUINICHETTE(reissue of PRLP7147)(62)
2038   COLEMAN HAWKINS-SOUL(reissue of PRLP7149)(64)
2039   COLEMAN HAWKINS-HAWK EYES(reissue of PRLP7156)(67)
2040   DIXIELAND HITS(132)
2041   CLAUDE HOPKINS-SWING TIME(139)

PRESTIGE label

PRLP
7001   BILLY TAYLOR-A TOUCH OF TAYLOR(32)
7002   STAN GETZ QUARTET(2,4,6)
7003   MILT JACKSON QUARTET(33)
7004   LEE KONITZ-SUBCONSCIOUS LEE(1,2,3,6)
7005   MODERN JAZZ QUARTET-CONCORDE(34)
7006   GERRY MULLUGAN-MULLIGAN PLAYS MULLIGAN(11)
7007   MILES DAVIS-THE MUSINGS OF MILES(33)
7008   WARDELL GRAY MEMORIAL,Volume 1(4,6,21)
7009   WARDELL GRAY MEMORIAL,Volume 2(7,15)
7010   ELMO HOPE TRIO-MEDITATIONS(34)
7011   JAMES MOODY-HI FI PARTY(35)
7012   MILES DAVIS-DIG(12)
7013   CONCEPTION:Stan Getz(2,4)/Chubby Jackson(6)/Lee Konitz(10)/Miles
           Davis(12)
7014   MILES DAVIS QUINTET-MILES(36)
7015   BILLY TAYLOR TRIO,Volume 1(18,19,24)
7016   BILLY TAYLOR TRIO,Volume 2(24,25)
7017   ART FARMER-EVENING IN CASABLANCA(35)
7018   PHIL WOODS-WOODLORE(36)
7019   SANFORD GOLD TRIO-PIANO D'OR(226)
7020   SONNY ROLLINS-WORK TIME(36)
7021   ELMO HOPE/FRANK FOSTER-WAIL,FRANK,WAIL(35)
7022   THE BROTHERS:Stan Getz Brothers(1)/Zoot Sims(17)
7023   TROMBONE BY THREE:J.J.Johnson(2)/Kai Winding(2)/Bennie Green(12)
7024   SONNY STITT WITH BUD POWELL & JAY JAY JOHNSON(3,4,5)
7025   MILES DAVIS-MILES AND HORNS(9,21)
7026   ZOOT SIMS(8,11)
7027   THELONIOUS MONK TRIO(18,19,28)
7028   TEDDY CHARLES-COLLABORATION(23,24)
7029   SONNY ROLLINS  WITH THE MODERN JAZZ QUARTET(9,14,24)
7030   JAY JAY JOHNSON/KAI WINDING/BENNIE GREEN:Bennie Green(17)/Jay
           and Kai(29,30)
7031   ART FARMER SEPTET(23,27)
7032   GEORGE WALLINGTON QUINTET-JAZZ FOR THE CARRIAGE TRADE(37)
7033   JON EARDLEY SEVEN(36)
7034   MILT & MILES(34)
```

```
PRLP
7035   JACKIE McLEAN-LIGHTS OUT(37)
7036   JAMES MOODY-WAIL,MOODY,WAIL(36)
7037   TADD DAMERON-FONTAINEBLEAU(37)
7038   SONNY ROLLINS PLUS FOUR(37)
7039   GENE AMMONS-THE HAPPY BLUES(38)
7040   GIL MELLE QUARTET(38,39)
7041   BENNIE GREEN & ART FARMER(38)
7042   MOONDOG-CARIBEA(226)
7043   ELMO HOPE-INFORMAL JAZZ(38)
7044   MILES DAVIS-COLLECTOR'S ITEMS(21,37)
7045   EARL COLEMAN RETURNS(37,39)
7046   PHIL WOODS SEPTET-PAIRING OFF(39)
7047   SONNY ROLLINS-TENOR MADNESS(39)
7048   JACKIE McLEAN 4,5 AND 6(40)
7049   BENNIE GREEN-WALKING DOWN(40)
7050   GENE AMMONS-WOOFIN' AND TWEETIN'(5,8,9,33)
7051   BILLY TAYLOR TRIO WITH CANDIDO(28)
7052   BENNIE GREEN BLOWS HIS HORN(33,35)
7053   THELONIOUS MONK-MONK(24,26)
7054   MILES DAVIS-BLUE HAZE(22,25,26)
7055   CLIFFORD BROWN MEMORIAL(23,257)
7056   JAMES MOODY-MOODY'S MOODS(28,31,36)
7057   THE MODERN JAZZ QUARTET-DJANGO(23,30,31)
7058   SONNY ROLLINS-MOVIN' OUT(28,29)
7059   MODERN JAZZ QUARTET-MJQ(19,27)
7060   GENE AMMONS-JAMMIN' WITH GENE(40)
7061   HANK MOBLEY-MOBLEY'S MESSAGE(40)
7062   TWO TRUMPETS-ART FARMER & DONALD BYRD(41)
7063   GIL MELLE-GIL'S GUESTS(41)
7064   RED GARLAND-A GARLAND OF RED(41)
7065   BARBARA LEA(43)
7066   THE DUAL ROLE OF BOB BROOKMEYER(25,33)
7067   FREDDIE REDD/HAMPTON HAWES-PIANO:EAST/WEST:Hampton Hawes(18)/
          Freddie Redd(32)
7068   JACKIE McLEAN-JACKIE'S PAL(42)
7069   MOONDOG-MORE MOONDOG(226)
7070   TADD DAMERON-MATING CALL(44)
7071   BILLY TAYLOR-CROSS SECTION(22,27)
7072   JAMES MOODY-MOODY(25,26,28)
7073   ALL NIGHT LONG(45)
7074   TENOR CONCLAVE(42)
7075   SONNY ROLLINS/THELONIOUS MONK:Th.Monk(24,28)/Sonny Rollins(29)
7076   MILES DAVIS-WALKIN'(26)
7077   SONNY STITT-KALEIDOSCOPE(5,8,9,16)
7078   TEDDY CHARLES-EVOLUTION(24,31)
7079   SONNY ROLLINS-SAXOPHONE COLOSSUS(39)
7080   THE YOUNG BLOODS(43)
7081   ALL DAY LONG(45)
7082   HANK MOBLEY-MOBLEY'S MESSAGE No.2(41)
7083   GENE AMMONS-FUNKY(45)
7084   OLIO(46)
7085   ART FARMER-WHEN FARMER MET GRYCE(26,33)
7086   RED GARLAND'S PIANO(44,48)
7087   JACKIE McLEAN & CO.(46)
7088   KENNY BURRELL-BLUE MOODS(46)
7089   JIMMY RANEY-A(31,31)
7090   MAL WALDRON-MAL 1(44)
7091   MOSE ALLISON-BACK COUNTRY SUITE(47)
7092   THREE TRUMPETS(45)
7093   BILLY TAYLOR TRIO AT TOWN HALL(30)
7094   COOKIN' WITH THE MILES DAVIS QUINTET(43)
7095   SONNY ROLLINS PLAYS FOR BIRD(42,43)
```

```
PRLP
7096  RAY DRAPER QUINTET-TUBA SOUNDS(48)
7097  GIL MELLE-QUADRAMA(50)
7098  RAY BRYANT TRIO-DJANGO(49)
7099  THE STORY OF MOONDOG(227)
7100  BARBARA LEA-LEA IN LOVE(50,51)
7101  HERBIE MANN-FLUTE SOUFFLE(48)
7102  EARTHY(45)
7103  PAUL QUINICHETTE'S NEW STARS(51)
7104  TEO MACERO & THE PRESTIGE JAZZ QUARTET(51)
7105  JOHN COLTRANE-COLTRANE(53)
7106  WEBSTER YOUNG-FOR LADY(53)
7107  CURTIS FULLER-NEW TROMBONE(51)
7108  PRESTIGE JAZZ QUARTET(53)
7109  MILES DAVIS-BAGS' GROOVE(27,30)
7110  GENE AMMONS-JAMMIN' IN HI FI WITH GENE AMMONS(49)
7111  MAL WALDRON-MAL 2(50,52)
7112  INTERPLAY FOR TWO TRUMPETS AND TWO TENORS(48)
7113  RED GARLAND-GROOVY(44,52,54)
7114  JACKIE McLEAN & JOHN JENKINS-ALTO MADNESS(51)
7115  PHIL AND QUILL(49)
7116  FOUR ALTOS(46)
7117  ART TAYLOR-TAYLOR'S WAILERS(47,48)
7118  AFTER HOURS(53)
7119  TWO GUITARS(47)
7120  GIL EVANS PLUS TEN(55)
7121  MOSE ALLISON-LOCAL COLOR(56)
7122  YUSEF LATEEF-THE SOUNDS OF YUSEF(55)
7123  JOHN COLTRANE-TRANE-ING IN(54)
7124  HERBIE MANN-FLUTE FLIGHT(48)
7125  STEVE LACY-SOPRANO TODAY(56)
7126  SONNY ROLLINS-TOUR DE FORCE(44)
7127  PAUL QUINICHETTE-FOR BASIE(56)
7128  KING PLEASURE AND ANNIE ROSS SING:Annie Ross(17)/King Pleasure
         (19,24,25,30)
7129  RELAXIN' WITH THE MILES DAVIS QUINTET(38,43)
7130  RED GARLAND QUINTET-ALL MORNIN' LONG(56)
7131  JOHN COLTRANE/PAUL QUINICHETTE-WHEELIN' AND DEALIN'(55)
7132  GENE AMMONS-THE BIG SOUND(57)
7133  SONNY STITT-STITT'S BITS(5,7,8)
7134  TOMMY FLANAGAN TRIO(262)
7135  HAL McKUSICK-TRIPLE EXPOSURE(57)
7136  HERBIE MANN-MANN IN THE MORNING(262)
7137  MOSE ALLISON-YOUNG MAN MOSE(58)
7138  TINY GRIMES-BLUES GROOVE(59)
7139  RED GARLAND-MANTECA(60)
7140  DOROTHY ASHBY-HIP HARP(59)
7141  THE EDDIE LOCKJAW DAVIS COOKBOOK,Volume 1(61)
7142  JOHN COLTRANE-SOULTRANE(58)
7143  SHIRLEY SCOTT-GREAT SCOTT!(60)
7144  TINY GRIMES-CALLIN' THE BLUES(61)
7145  PRESTIGE BLUES SWINGERS-OUTSKIRTS OF TOWN(62)
7146  GENE AMMONS-BLUE GENE(60)
7147  PAUL QUINICHETTE-BASIE REUNION(62)
7148  RED GARLAND-ALL KINDS OF WEATHER(65)
7149  COLEMAN HAWKINS-SOUL(64)
7150  MILES DAVIS & THE MODERN JAZZ GIANTS(30,43)
7151  ARNETT COBB-BLOW,ARNETT,BLOW(66)
7152  MOSE ALLISON-CREEK BANK(62)
7153  HAL SINGER-BLUE STOMPIN'(66)
7154  EDDIE LOCKJAW DAVIS-JAWS(63)
7155  SHIRLEY SCOTT-SCOTTIE(64)
```

```
PRLP
7156   COLEMAN HAWKINS-HAWK EYES(67)
7157   RED GARLAND-RED IN BLUESVILLE(67)
7158   CATTIN' WITH COLTRANE & QUINICHETTE(52)
7159   THELONIOUS MONK-MONK'S MOODS(reissue of PRLP7027)(18,19)
7160   BENNIE GREEN BLOWS HIS HORN(reissue of PRLP7052)(33,35)
7161   THE EDDIE LOCKJAW DAVIS COOKBOOK,Volume 2(65)
7162   WILLIS JACKSON-PLEASE Mr.JACKSON(68)
7163   SHIRLEY SCOTT-SCOTTIE PLAYS THE DUKE(67)
7164   BILL JENNINGS-ENOUGH SAID(69)
7165   ARNETT COBB-PARTY TIME(68)
7166   WORKIN' WITH THE MILES DAVIS QUINTET(38,43)
7167   VERY SAXY(67)
7168   MILES DAVIS-EARLY MILES(reissue of PRLP7025)(9,21)
7169   THELONIOUS MONK-WORK(reissue of PRLP7075)(24,28,29)
7170   RED GARLAND AT THE PRELUDE(71)
7171   EDDIE LOCKJAW DAVIS-JAWS IN ORBIT(68)
7172   WILLIS JACKSON-COOL GATOR(68,72)
7173   SHIRLEY SCOTT-SOUL SEARCHING(73)
7174   JACK McDUFF-BROTHER JACK(74)
7175   ARNETT COBB-MORE PARTY TIME(75)
7176   GENE AMMONS-THE TWISTER(reissue of PRLP7110)(49)
7177   BILL JENNINGS-GLIDE ON(74)
7178   EDDIE LOCKJAW DAVIS-BACALAO(73)
7179   JAMES MOODY-MOODY'S WORKSHOP(25,26,28,31)
7180   GENE AMMONS-BOSS TENOR(83)
7181   RED GARLAND QUINTET WITH COLTRANE-SOUL JUNCTION(56)
7182   SHIRLEY SCOTT-MUCHO,MUCHO(84)
7183   WILLIS JACKSON-BLUE GATOR(68,72,75,86)
7184   ARNETT COBB-SMOOTH SAILING(66)
7185   JACK McDUFF-TOUGH DUFF(85)
7186   ETTA JONES-DON'T GO TO STRANGERS(83)
7187   BETTY ROCHE-SINGIN' AND SWINGIN'(82)
7188   JOHN COLTRANE-LUSH LIFE(53,54,58)
7189   MOSE ALLISON-AUTUMN SONG(66)
7190   JOHN WRIGHT-SOUTH SIDE SOUL(88)
7191   EDDIE DAVIS/JOHNNY GRIFFIN-THE TENOR SCENE(96)
7192   GENE AMMONS-JUG(98)
7193   RED GARLAND-ROJO(62)
7194   ETTA JONES-SOMETHING NICE(89,101)
7195   SHIRLEY SCOTT-SHIRLEY'S SOUNDS(60)
7196   WILLIS JACKSON-REALLY GROOVIN'(97,102)
7197   JOHN WRIGHT-NICE ' N' TASTY(92)
7198   BETTY ROCHE-LIGHTLY AND POLITELY(97)
7199   JACK McDUFF-THE HONEYDRIPPER(98)
7200   STEAMIN' WITH THE MILES DAVIS QUINTET(38,43)
7201   GENE AMMONS-GROOVE BLUES(57)
7202   JIMMY FORREST-OUT OF THE FORREST(103)
7203   JOHNNY "HAMMOND" SMITH-STIMULATION(98,104)
7204   ETTA JONES AND STRINGS-SO WARM(106,110,111)
7205   SHIRLEY SCOTT-HIP SOUL(106)
7206   EDDIE LOCKJAW DAVIS BIG BAND-TRANE WHISTLE(89)
7207   SONNY ROLLINS-SONNY BOY(42,44)
7208   GENE AMMONS-UP TIGHT(116)
7209   RED GARLAND QUINTET-HIGH PRESSURE(56,57)
7210   ROLAND KIRK-KIRK'S WORKS(108)
7211   WILLIS JACKSON-COOKIN' SHERRY(72,75,86)
7212   JOHN WRIGHT-MAKIN' OUT(107)
7213   JOHN COLTRANE-SETTIN' THE PACE(59)
7214   ETTA JONES-FROM THE HEART(121)
7215   MOSE ALLISON-RAMBLIN' WITH MOSE(60)
7216   ARNETT COBB-MOVIN' RIGHT ALONG(75)
7217   JOHNNY "HAMMOND" SMITH-GETTIN' THE MESSAGE(91)
7218   JIMMY FORREST-MOST MUCH(116)
```

```
PRLP
7219   EDDIE LOCKJAW DAVIS COOKBOOK,Volume 3(63,65)
7220   JACK McDUFF-GOODNIGHT,IT'S TIME TO GO(109)
7221   MILES DAVIS-THE BEGINNING(reissue of PRLP7007)(33)
7222   KING CURTIS-SOUL MEETING(89)
7223   SOUL BATTLE(88)
7224   MILT JACKSON WITH HORACE SILVER-SOUL PIONEERS(reissue of
         PRLP7003)(33)
7225   OLIVER NELSON-AFRO-AMERICAN SKETCHES(115,117)
7226   SHIRLEY SCOTT-HIP TWIST(117)
7227   ARNETT COBB-SIZZLIN'(92)
7228   JACK McDUFF WITH GENE AMMONS-MELLOW GRAVY(120)
         (BROTHER JACK MEETS THE BOSS)
7229   RED GARLAND WITH JOHN COLTRANE-DIG IT(48,57,58)
7230   HONI GORDON SINGS-HONI(124)
7231   FRANK WESS-SOUTHERN COMFORT(123)
7232   WILLIS JACKSON-THUNDERBIRD(124)
7233   JOHN WRIGHT-Mr.SOUL(125)
7234   GENE AMMONS/SONNY STITT/JACK McDUFF-SOUL SUMMIT(122)
7235   JIMMY FORREST-SIT DOWN AND RELAX(113)
7236   OLIVER NELSON-MAIN STEM(113)
7237   LARRY YOUNG-GROOVE STREET(123)
7238   GENE AMMONS-TWISTIN' THE JUG(118)
7239   JOHNNY "HAMMOND" SMITH COOKS WITH GATOR TAIL(130)
7240   SHIRLEY SCOTT PLAYS HORACE SILVER(117)
7241   ETTA JONES-LONELY AND BLUE(125,127)
7242   EDDIE LOCKJAW DAVIS-GOING TO THE MEETING(127)
7243   JOHN COLTRANE-STANDARD COLTRANE(61)
7244   STITT MEETS BROTHER JACK(121)
7245   THELONIOUS MONK-WE SEE(reissue of PRLP7053)(24,26)
7246   SONNY ROLLINS-WORK TIME(reissue of PRLP7020)(36)
7247   JOHN COLTRANE WITH TADD DAMERON-MATING CALL(reissue of PRLP7070)
         (44)
7248   SONNY STITT/BUD POWELL-ALL GOD'S CHILLUN GOT RHYTHM(reissue of
         PRLP7024)(3,4,5)
7249   JOHN COLTRANE-TENOR CONCLAVE(reissue of PRLP7074)(42)
7250   LEE KONITZ-SUBCONSCIOUS LEE(reissue of PRLP7004)(1,2,3,6)
7251   GERRY MULLIGAN-HISTORICALLY SPEAKING(reissue of PRLP7006)(11)
7252   STAN GETZ-THE BROTHERS(reissue of PRLP7022)(1,17)
7253   JAY JAY JOHNSON-LOOKING BACK(2,29,30)
7254   MILES DAVIS-THE ORIGINAL QUINTET(reissue of PRLP7014)(36)
7255   STAN GETZ-EARLY STAN(1,22)
7256   STAN GETZ QUARTET-GREATEST HITS(reissue of PRLP7002(2,4,6)
7257   GENE AMMONS-JUNGLE SOUL(BAD!BOSSA NOVA)(133)
7258   RED GARLAND-WHEN THERE ARE GREY SKIES(133)
7259   JACK McDUFF-SCREAMIN'(134)
7260   WILLIS JACKSON-SHUCKIN'(134)
7261   EDDIE LOCKJAW DAVIS-I ONLY HAVE EYES FOR YOU(134)
7262   SHIRLEY SCOTT-HAPPY TALK(135)
7263   TED CURSON-FIRE DOWN BELOW(135)
7264   WILLIS JACKSON-NEAPOLITAN NIGHTS(135)
7265   JACK McDUFF-SOMETHING SLICK(136)
7266   FRANK WESS-YO HO(136)
7267   SHIRLEY SCOTT-THE SOUL IS WILLING(136)
7268   JOHN COLTRANE-STARDUST(61,65)
7269   SONNY ROLLINS-SONNY AND THE STARS(reissue of PRLP7029)(9,14,24)
7270   GENE AMMONS-PREACHIN'(265)
7271   EDDIE LOCKJAW DAVIS-TRACKIN'(134)
7272   ETTA JONES-LOVE SHOUT(134,137)
7273   WILLIS JACKSON-LOOSE(138)
7274   JACK McDUFF-LIVE!(140)
7275   GENE AMMONS-SOUL SUMMIT,Volume 2(106,120,126)/Jack McDuff(118)
```

```
PRLP
7276  RED GARLAND-CAN'T SEE FOR LOOKIN'(61)
7277  KENNY BURRELL-ALL DAY LONG(reissue of PRLP7081)(45)
7278  FRANK WESS/KENNY BURRELL-STEAMIN'(reissue of PRLP7118)
7279  MOSE ALLISON SINGS-THE SEVENTH SON(47,56,58,60,62,66)
7280  JOHN COLTRANE-DAKAR(50)
7281  MILES DAVIS-DIGGIN'(reissue of PRLP7012)(12)
7282  EDDIE LOCKJAW DAVIS-BATTLE STATIONS(88)
7283  SHIRLEY SCOTT-SATIN DOLL(99)
7284  ETTA JONES-HOLLAR(89,101,134)
7285  WILLIS JACKSON-GREASE AND GRAVY(140)
7286  JACK McDUFF-LIVE!AT THE JAZZ WORKSHOP(142)
7287  GENE AMMONS-LATE HOUR SPECIAL(106,126)
7288  RED GARLAND-HALLELLO-Y'ALL(85)
7289  ALL NIGHT LONG-KENNY BURRELL(reissue of PRLP7073)(45)
7290  JIMMY WITHERSPOON-BABY,BABY,BABY(138,141)
7291  SONNY ROLLINS & CLIFFORD BROWN-THREE GIANTS(reissue of PRLP7038)
7292  JOHN COLTRANE-THE BELIEVER(58,65)
7293  BOOKER ERVIN-EXULTATION(141)
7294  ERIC DOLPHY-LIVE!AT THE FIVE SPOT,Volume 2(110)
7295  BOOKER ERVIN-THE FREEDOM BOOK(144)
7296  WILLIS JACKSON-THE GOOD LIFE(140)
7297  SONNY STITT WITH JACK McDUFF-SOUL SHACK(142)
7298  PRESTIGE GROOVY GOODIES,Volume 1:Miles Davis(12)/John Coltrane(61)/
      Mose Allison(62)/Kenny Burrell(45)/Gene Ammons(98)/Shirley
      Scott(99)/Jimmy Witherspoon(138)/Jack McDuff(140)/Willis
      Jackson(140)/Booker Ervin(141)/Sonny Stitt(142)/Red Holloway(143)
7299  RED HOLLOWAY-THE BURNER(142,143)
7300  JIMMY WITHERSPOON-EVENIN' BLUES(142)
7301  EDDIE LOCKJAW DAVIS/SHIRLEY SCOTT-SMOKIN'(63)
7302  SONNY STITT-PRIMITIVO SOUL!(145)
7303  RONNIE MATHEWS-DOIN' THE THANG(144)
7304  ERIC DOLPHY IN EUROPE,Volume 1(265)
7305  SHIRLEY SCOTT-DRAG 'EM OUT(140)
7306  GENE AMMONS-BIGGEST SOUL HITS(40,49,57,60,83,98)
7307  RED GARLAND-SOUL BURNIN'(85,100)
7308  KENNY BURRELL-BLUE MOODS(reissue of PRLP7088)(46)
7309  EDDIE LOCKJAW DAVIS-LIVE!THE FIRST SET(96)
7310  GEORGE BENSON-NEW BOSS GUITAR(148)
7311  ERIC DOLPHY-OUTWARD BOUND(reissue of NJLP8236)(78)
7312  SHIRLEY SCOTT-SOUL SHOUTING(143)
7313  PRESTIGE GROOVY GOODIES,Volume 2:Kenny Burrell(45)/John Coltrane
      (50)/Mose Allison(56)/Eddie Lockjaw Davis(63)/Gene Ammons(106)/
      Sonny Stitt(121)/Etta Jones(126)/Shirley Scott(136)/Willis
      Jackson(140)/Jack McDuff(142)/Jimmy Witherspoon(143)/Red
      Holloway(143)
7314  JIMMY WITHERSPOON-BLUES AROUND THE CLOCK(143)
7315  KENNY BURRELL-SOUL CALL(148)
7316  JOHN COLTRANE-BLACK PEARLS(60)
7317  WILLIS JACKSON-MORE GRAVY(143)
7318  BOOKER ERVIN-THE SONG BOOK(146)
7319  YUSEF LATEEF-EASTERN SOUNDS(reissue of MVLP22)(114)
7320  GENE AMMONS-VELVET SOUL(83,106,132)
7321  EDDIE CHAMBLEE-ROCKIN' TENOR SAX(146)
7322  MILES DAVIS & JOHN COLTRANE PLAY RODGERS & HART(reissue of MVLP32)
      (9,38,43,61)
7323  JACK McDUFF BIG BAND-DYNAMIC!(145,148)
7324  JOE DUKES WITH JACK McDUFF QUARTET-THE SOULFUL DRUMS(149)
7325  RED HOLLOWAY WITH JACK McDUFF QUARTET-COOKIN' TOGETHER(145)
7326  SONNY ROLLINS-SAXOPHONE COLOSSUS(reissue of PRLP7079)(39)
7327  JIMMY WITHERSPOON-BLUE SPOON(146)
7328  SHIRLEY SCOTT & KENNY BURRELL-TRAVELIN' LIGHT(146)
```

PR
```
7329  WILLIS JACKSON-BOSS SHOUTIN'(145)
7330  EDDIE LOCKJAW DAVIS-LIVE!THE MIDNIGHT SHOW(97)
7331  THE EXCITING NEW ORGAN OF DON PATTERSON(149)
7332  SONNY STITT & DON PATTERSON-SHANGRI-LA(147)
7333  BROTHER JACK McDUFF BIG BAND-PRELUDE(144)
7334  ERIC DOLPHY MEMORIAL ALBUM(110)
7335  BOBBY TIMMONS-LITTLE BAREFOOT SOUL(150)
7336  MONTEGO JOE-ARRIBA CON MONTEGO JOE(150)
7337  STAN GETZ GREATEST HITS(reissue of PRLP7002)(2,4,6)
7338  SHIRLEY SCOTT & STANLEY TURRENTINE-BLUE FLAMES(148)
7339  THE SOULFUL PIANO OF GILDO MAHONES(2LP set)(137,141,142,150)
7340  BOOKER ERVIN-THE BLUES BOOK(151)
7341  JAZZ INTERPLAY(2LP set)(reissue of PRLP7111 & PRLP7112)(48,50,52)
7342  HARD COOKIN'(2LP set)(reissue of PRLP7117 & NJLP8219)(47,48,68)
7343  WARDELL GRAY MEMORIAL ALBUM(2LP set)(reissue of PRLP7008 & PRLP
         7009)(4,6,7,15,21)
7344  DONALD BYRD & ART FARMER-TRUMPETS ALL OUT(2LP set)(reissue of
         PRLP7062 & PRLP7092)(41,45)
7345  THE MORRIS NANTON TRIO-PREFACE(153,154)
7346  ANDY AND THE BEY SISTERS-NOW!HEAR(153)
7347  KENNY BURRELL WITH JACK McDUFF-CRASH(137)
7348  WILLIS JACKSON-LIVE!JACKSON'S ACTION(147)
7349  DON PATTERSON WITH BOOKER ERVIN-HIP CAKE WALK(149,151)
7350  ERIC DOLPHY IN EUROPE,Volume 2(264,265)
7351  BOBBY TIMMONS-CHUNGKING(153)
7352  MILES DAVIS PLAYS FOR LOVERS(22,25,26,33,36,38)
7353  JOHN COLTRANE-BAHIA(61,65)
7354  EDDIE BONNEMERE-JAZZ ORIENT-ED(154)
7355  LEN AND JUDY-FOLK SONGS SWEET BITTER SWEET(not included)
7356  JIMMY WITHERSPOON-SOME OF MY BEST FRIENDS ARE THE BLUES(152)
7357  EDDIE LOCKJAW DAVIS-LIVE!THE LATE SHOW(97)
7358  CAROL VENTURA-CAROL(152)
7359  CHARLES McPHERSON & CARMELL JONES-BE BOP REVISITED(155)
7360  SHIRLEY SCOTT-SWEET SOUL(reissue of PRLP7262)(135)
7361  BENNY GOLSON INTERNATIONAL JAZZ ORCHESTRA-STOCKHOLM SOJOURN(151)
7362  JACK McDUFF QUARTET-THE CONCERT McDUFF(152)
7363  THELONIOUS MONK-THE GOLDEN MONK(reissue of PRLP7053)(24,26)
7364  WILLIS JACKSON WITH JACK McDUFF-TOGETHER AGAIN(68,72,75,86)
7365  LUCKY THOMPSON-LUCKY STRIKES(154)
7366  ERIC DOLPHY IN EUROPE,Volume 3(264,265)
7367  CHUCK WAYNE-MORNING MIST(157)
7368  JESSE FULLER FAVORITES(139)
7369  GENE AMMONS-ANGEL EYES(83,132)
7370  LIGHTNIN' HOPKINS-MY LIFE WITH THE BLUES(2LP set)(156,157)
7371  THE FOLK STRINGERS(not included)
7372  SONNY STITT WITH DON PATTERSON-SOUL PEOPLE(154)
7373  MILES DAVIS-JAZZ CLASSICS(38,43)
7374  TOM RUSH-FOLK SONGS AND BLUES(not included)
7375  PETE/PEGGY/MIKE SEEGERS(2LP set)(not included)
7376  SHIRLEY SCOTT-BLUE SEVEN(113)
7377  LIGHTNIN' HOPKINS-SOUL BLUES(149)
7378  JOHN COLTRANE-THE LAST TRANE(54,58,59)
7379  A.K.SALIM-AFRO SOUL DRUM ORGY(155)
7380  WILLIS JACKSON-LIVE ACTION(147)
7381  DON PATTERSON WITH SONNY STITT-PATTERSON'S PEOPLE(147,149,151)
7382  ERIC DOLPHY-HERE AND THERE(78,110,264)
7383  TERRY CALLIER-THE NEW FOLK SOUND(not included)
7384  ERIC VON SCHMIDT-ERIC SINGS VON SCHMIDT(not included)
7385  PAT BOWIE-OUT OF SIGHT(155)
7386  BOOKER ERVIN-THE SPACE BOOK(154)
7387  BOBBY TIMMONS WITH JOHNNY LYTLE-WORKIN' OUT(150,155)
```

```
PR
7388  HOMESICK JAMES-BLUES ON THE SOUTH SIDE(145)
7389  BILLY BOY ARNOLD-MORE BLUES ON THE SOUTHSIDE(144)
7390  RED HOLLOWAY-SAX,STRINGS AND SOUL(153)
7391  OTIS SPANN-THE BLUES WILL NEVER DIE(156)
7392  SHIRLEY SCOTT-SOUL SISTER(84)
7393  TRACY NELSON-DEEP ARE THE ROOTS(not included)
7394  LUCKY THOMPSON-HAPPY DAYS ARE HERE AGAIN(158)
7395  FREDDIE McCOY-LONELY AVENUE(157)
7396  WILLIS JACKSON-SOUL NIGHT-LIVE!(147)
7397  JAKI BYARD-OUT FRONT(150)
7398  YUSEF LATEEF-THE SOUNDS OF YUSEF(reissue of PRLP7122)(55)
7399  THE ROGER KELLAWAY TRIO(159)
7400  GENE AMMONS-SOCK(29,35,126,132)
7401  CARMELL JONES-JAY HAWK TALK(159)
7402  ALI AKBAR KHAN-TRADITIONAL INDIAN MUSIC(not included)
7403  ALI AKBAR KHAN-THE SOUL OF INDIAN MUSIC(not included)
7404  BROTHER JACK McDUFF-SILK AND SOUL(152,151,231)
7405  CAROL VENTURA-I LOVE TO SING(160)
7406  THE TALISMEN-FOLK SWINGERS EXTRAORDINAIRE(not included)
7407  EDDIE LOCKJAW DAVIS-LIVE!THE BREAKFAST SHOW(reissue of PRLP7191)(96)
7408  JOHNNY "HAMMOND" SMITH-THE STINGER(159)
7409  MORRIS NANTON-SOMETHING WE'VE GOT(159,160)
7410  THE HOLY MODAL ROUNDERS No.2(not included)
7411  ANDY BEY AND THE BEY SISTERS-ROUND ABOUT MIDNIGHT(158,160)
7412  WILLIS JACKSON-TELL IT(148)
7413  MONTEGO JOE-WILD AND WARM(160)
7414  BOBBY TIMMONS-HOLIDAY SOUL(156)
7415  DON PATTERSON-HOLIDAY SOUL(156)
7416  BENJY AARONOFF-FOLK SONGS(not included)
7417  BOOKER ERVIN-GROOVIN' HIGH(144,151,154)
7418  JIMMY WITHERSPOON-SPOON IN LONDON(161)
7419  JAKI BYARD QUARTET-LIVE AT LENNIE'S,Volume 1(158)
7420  JOHNNY "HAMMOND" SMITH-OPUS DE FUNK(98,104)
7421  THE MODERN JAZZ QUARTET PLAYS FOR LOVERS(19,23,34)
7422  BROTHER JACK McDUFF-HOT BARBECUE(163)
7423  MOSE ALLISON-DOWN HOME PIANO(56,60,62,66)
7424  SHIRLEY SCOTT-WORKIN'(60,79,100)
7425  THE MODERN JAZZ QUARTET PLAYS JAZZ CLASSICS(19,23,30,31,34)
7426  JOHN COLTRANE PLAYS FOR LOVERS(44,53,54,65)
7427  CHARLES McPHERSON-CON ALMA!(161)
7428  WILLIS JACKSON & JACK McDUFF-TOGETHER AGAIN,AGAIN(68,72,75,119)
7429  BOBBY TIMMONS-CHICKEN AND DUMPLIN'S(161)
7430  DON PATTERSON-SATISFACTION(161)
7431  JAMES MOODY'S GREATEST HITS(248,249)
7432  THE BEST OF HERBIE MANN(48)
7433  SONNY ROLLINS-JAZZ CLASSICS(reissue of PRLP7058)(28,29)
7434  STAN GETZ JAZZ CLASSICS(reissue of PRLP7255)(1,22)
7435  RICHARD "GROOVE" HOLMES-SOUL MESSAGE(161)
7436  SONNY STITT WITH DON PATTERSON-NIGHT CRAWLER(163)
7437  PAT BOWIE-FEELIN' GOOD(163)
7438  MITCH GREENHILL-SHEPHERD OF THE HIGHWAY(not included)
7439  SYMVIA SYMS-SYLVIA IS(161,162)
7440  SHIRLEY SCOTT-NOW'S THE TIME(60,64,84,113,148)
7441  JAMES MOODY'S GREATEST HITS,Volume 2(252,253)
7442  INTRODUCING ERIC KLOSS(162)
7443  ETTA JONES' GREATEST HITS(83,89,101,106,121,125,126,127,137)
7444  FREDDIE McCOY-SPIDER MAN(163)
7445  GENE AMMONS-BOSS SOUL(116)
7446  MOSE ALLISON PLAYS FOR LOVERS(47,58,60,62,66)
7447  YUSEF LATEEF PLAYS FOR LOVERS(55,71,114,119)
```

PR
7448 THE BEST OF KENNY BURRELL(45,51)
7449 SMOKIN' WITH THE CHET BAKER QUINTET(162)
7450 ROLAND KIRK WITH JACK McDUFF-FUNK UNDERNEATH(reissue of PRLP7210)
     (108)
7451 THE HOLY MODAL ROUNDERS,Volume 1(not included)
7452 SONNY STITT WITH JACK McDUFF-NUTHER FU'THER(reissue of PRLP7244)
     (121)
7453 RAMBLIN' JACK ELLIOTT SINGS WOODY GUTHRIE(not included)
7454 SOUL SUMMIT(reissue of PRLP7234)(122)
7455 BOOKER ERVIN WITH DEXTER GORDON-SETTIN' THE PACE(164)
7456 SHIRLEY SCOTT-STOMPIN'(79,100)
7457 MILES DAVIS' GREATEST HITS(12,22,26,30,43)
7458 STAN HUNTER & SONNY FORTUNE-TRIP ON THE STRIP(164)
7459 SONNY STITT-POW!(163)
7460 GROOVIN' WITH THE CHET BAKER QUINTET(162)
7461 FEARLESS FRANK FOSTER(164)
7462 BOOKER ERVIN-THE TRANCE(164)
7463 JAKI BYARD-FREEDOM TOGETHER(165)
7464 JOHNNY "HAMMOND" SMITH-THE STINGER MEETS THE GOLDEN THRUSH(165)
7465 BOBBY TIMMONS-SOUL MAN
7466 DON PATTERSON WITH SONNY STITT-THE BOSS MEN(165)
7467 MORRIS NANTON-SOUL FINGERS(172)
7468 RICHARD "GROOVE" HOLMES-LIVING SOUL(167)
7469 ERIC KLOSS-LOVE AND ALL THAT JAZZ(167)
7470 FREDDIE McCOY-FUNK DROPS(168)
7471 PUCHO AND THE LATIN SOUL BROTHERS-TOUGH(166)
7472 LARRY & HANK-THE BLUES:A NEW GENERATION(164)
7473 RED HOLLOWAY-RED SOUL(164,165)
7474 GEORGE BRAITH-LAUGHING SOUL(166)
7475 JIMMY WITHERSPOON-BLUES FOR EASY LIVERS(232)
7476 BROTHER JACK McDUFF-WALK ON BY(166,232)
7477 JAKI BYARD-LIVE AT LENNIE'S,Volume 2(158)
7478 COMIN' ON WITH THE CHET BAKER QUINTET(162)
7479 FRANK FOSTER-SOUL OUTING(168,169)
7480 CHARLES McPHERSON-THE QUINTET-LIVE!
7481 BROTHER JACK McDUFF'S GREATEST HITS(74,85,98,109,134,136,140,142)
7482 JOHNNY "HAMMOND" SMITH-LOVE POTION No.9(170)
7483 BOBBY TIMMONS-SOUL FOOD(170,171)
7484 DON PATTERSON-SOUL HAPPENING(169)
7485 RICHARD "GROOVE" HOLMES-MISTY(161,170)
7486 ERIC KLOSS-GRITS AND GRAVY(173)
7487 FREDDIE McCOY-PEAS ' N' RICE(163,175,177)
7488 DON FRIEDMAN-METAMORPHOSIS(166)
7489 SYLVIA SYMS-FOR ONCE IN MY LIFE(175)
7490 FREDDIE ROACH-THE SOUL BOOK(168)
7491 HOUSTON PERSON-UNDERGROUND SOUL(168)
7492 BROTHER JACK McDUFF-HALLELUJAH TIME(140,151,166,232)
7493 RICHARD "GROOVE" HOLMES-SPICY(172)
7494 JOHNNY "HAMMOND" SMITH-EBB TIDE(174)
7495 GENE AMMONS-LIVE IN CHICAGO(264)
7496 CHET BAKER-COOL BURNIN'(162)
7497 RICHARD "GROOVE" HOLMES-SUPER SOUL(176)
7498 BARRY HARRIS-LUMINESCENCE!(176)
7499 BOOKER ERVIN-HEAVY!(170)
7500 JACKIE McLEAN-STRANGE BLUES(46,53,54)
7501 BILLY HAWKS-NEW GENIUS OF THE BLUES(172)
7502 PUCHO AND THE LATIN SOUL BROTHERS-SAFFRON AND SOUL(171)
7503 BY DIE GREEN-THE GOLDEN THRUSH STRIKES AT MIDNIGHT(169)
7504 SHINICHI YUIZE-THE ARTISTRY OF JAPAN(not included)
7505 SHINICHI YUIZE-THE ROMANCE OF JAPAN(not included)
7506 EDDIE DANIELS-FIRST PRIZE!(170)

```
PR
7507  FREDDIE ROACH-MOCHA MOTION(173)
7508  THELONIOUS MONK-THE HIGH PRIEST(reissue of PRLP7027)(18,19)
7509  BYRDIE GREEN-I GOT IT BAD(176)
7510  DON PATTERSON WITH DAVID NEWMAN-MELLOW SOUL(177)
7511  SONNY CRISS-THIS IS CRISS(171)
7512  CHET BAKER-BOPPIN'(162)
7513  PAT MARTINO-EL HOMBRE(176)
7514  RICHARD "GROOVE" HOLMES-GET UP AND GET IT(177)
7515  GEORGE BRAITH-MUSART(172,173)
7516  STAN GETZ with AL HAIG-PREZERVATION:Stan Getz(2,4,248)/Al Haig(5)
7517  HOUSTON PERSON-CHOCOMOTIVE(177)
7518  TEDDY EDWARDS-NOTHIN' BUT THE TRUTH(173)
7519  CEDAR WALTON-CEDAR!(178)
7520  ERIC KLOSS-FIRST CLASS KLOSS(178)
7521  FREDDIE ROACH-MY PEOPLE(SOUL PEOPLE)(178)
7522  TEDDY EDWARDS-IT'S ALRIGHT(177)
7523  INTRODUCING TRUDY PITTS(174)
7524  JAKI BYARD-ON THE SPOT(158,174)
7525  BUDDY TERRY-ELECTRIC SOUL(174)
7526  SONNY CRISS-PORTRAIT OF SONNY CRISS(175)
7527  DAVE VAN RONK-FOLK SINGER(not included)
7528  PUCHO AND THE LATIN SOUL BROTHERS-SHUCKIN' AND JIVIN'(178)
7529  BROTHER McDUFF-THE MIDNIGHT SUN(140,151,166)
7530  SONNY CRISS-UP,UP AND AWAY(179)
7531  JOHN COLTRANE-SOULTRANE(reissue of PRLP7142)(58)
7532  KENNY BURRELL QUINTET WITH JOHN COLTRANE(reissue of NJLP8276)(59)
7533  DON PATTERSON-FOUR DIMENSIONS(179)
7534  GENE AMMONS-BOSS TENOR(reissue of PRLP7180)(83)
7535  ERIC KLOSS-LIFE FORCE(179)
7536  TOM RUSH-GOT A MIND TO RAMBLE(not included)
7537  RAVI SHANKAR AND ALI AKBAR KHAN-THE MASTER MUSICIANS OF INDIA
         (reissue of PR1078)(not included)
7538  TRUDY PITTS-THESE BLUES ARE MINE(179)
7539  PSYCHEDELIC HITS-TAKE A TRIP WITH ME(not included)
7540  MILES DAVIS-ODYSSEY(reissue of PRLP7034)(34)
7541  BUDDY TERRY-NATURAL SOUL(181)
7542  FREDDIE McCOY-BEANS AND GREENS(180)
7543  RICHARD "GROOVE" HOLMES-SOUL POWER(182)
7544  ALI AKBAR KHAN-CLASSICAL MUSIC OF INDIA(reissue of PR1079)(not
         included)
7545  ALI AKBAR KHAN-TRADITIONAL MUSIC OF INDIA(reissue of PR7402)(not
         included)
7546  ALI AKBAR KHAN-THE SOUL OF INDIAN MUSIC(reissue of PR7403)(not
         included)
7547  PAT MARTINO-STRINGS!(180)
7548  HOUSTON PERSON_TRUST IN ME(180)
7549  JOHNNY "HAMMOND" SMITH-SOUL FLOWERS(179)
7550  JAKI BYARD WITH ELVIN JONES-THE SUNSHINE OF MY SOUL(181)
7551  WILLIS JACKSON-SOUL GRABBER(180,181)
7552  GENE AMMONS-JUNGLE SOUL(reissue of PRLP7257)
7553  SONNY ROLLINS PLAYS FOR BIRD(reissue of PRLP7095)(42,43)
7554  JAMES MOODY'S MOODS(reissue of PRLP7056)(28,31,36)
7555  PUCHO AND THE LATIN SOUL BROTHERS-BIG STICK(181)
7556  BILLY HAWKS-MORE HEAVY SOUL(182)
7557  JOE JONES-PSYCHEDELIC SOUL JAZZ(175,182)
7558  SONNY CRISS-THE BEAT GOES ON(183)
7559  CHARLES McPHERSON-FROM THIS MOMENT ON(183)
7560  TRUDY PITTS-BUCKETFUL OF SOUL(182,184)
7561  FREDDIE McCOY-SOUL YOGI(183,184)
7562  PAT MARTINO-EAST(183)
7563  DON PATTERSON-BOPPIN' & BURNIN'(184)
```

PR
7564   JOHNNY "HAMMOND" SMITH-DIRTY GRAPE(183)
7565   ERIC KLOSS-WE'RE GOIN' UP(182)
7566   HOUSTON PERSON-BLUE ODYSSEY(185)
7567   BROTHER JACK McDUFF-SOUL CIRCLE(151,166,232)
7568   HAROLD MABERN-A FEW MILES FROM MEMPHIS(185)
7569   WALLY RICHARDSON-SOUL GURU(184)
7570   RICHARD "GROOVE" HOLMES-THE GROOVER(184)
7571   WILLIS JACKSON-STAR BAG(185)
7572   PUCHO AND THE LATIN SOUL BROTHERS-HEAT!(186)
7573   JAKI BYARD WITH STRINGS!(186)
7574   BYRDIE GREEN-SISTER BYRDIE(185,186)
7575   ILLINOIS JACQUET ON PRESTIGE!BOTTOMS UP(185)
7576   SONNY CRISS ORCHESTRA-SONNY'S DREAM(186)
7577   DON PATTERSON-OPUS DE DON(187)
7578   KENNY BURRELL-OUT OF THIS WORLD(reissue of MV29)(133)
7579   ERIC DOLPHY AND BOOKER ERVIN WITH MAL WALDRON-THE QUEST(reissue
         of NJLP8269)(107)
7580   MILES DAVIS WITH JOHN COLTRANE-STEAMIN'(reissue of PRLP7200)(38,43)
7581   JOHN COLTRANE-LUSH LIFE(reissue of PRLP7188)(53,54,58)
7582   FREDDIE McCOY-LISTEN HERE!(187)
7583   THE EXCITEMENT OF TRUDY PITTS(187)
7584   WALTER "FOOTS" THOMAS ALL STARS(240,241)
7585   SONNY STITT-STITT'S BITS,Volume 1(5,7,8,9)
7586   KING PLEASURE-ORIGINAL MOODY'S MOOD(16,19,24,25,30)
7587   GEORGE WALLINGTON TRIOS(17,22)
7588   JOHNNY "HAMMOND" SMITH-NASTY(188)
7589   PAT MARTINO-BAIYINA(THE CLEAR EVIDENCE)(188)
7590   DUKE EDWARDS AND THE YOUNG ONES-IS IT TOO LATE?(186)
7591   CEDAR WALTON-SPECTRUM(187)
7592   LIGHTNIN' HOPKINS-GREATEST HITS(reissue of PR1084)(92,93,122,140)
7593   DICKY WELLS IN PARIS-1937(239)
7594   ERIC KLOSS-SKY SHADOWS(188)
7595   OSCAR PETERSON-SOUL-O!(270)
7596   BROTHER JACK McDUFF PLAYS FOR BEAUTIFUL PEOPLE(74,85,98,134,136,
         137)
7597   ILLINOIS JACQUET-THE KING!(188)
7598   DON BYAS IN PARIS(243,244,247)
7599   CHARLES KYNARD-PROFESSOR SOUL(188)
7600   BARRY HARRIS-BULL'S EYE(187)
7601   RICHARD "GROOVE" HOLMES-THAT HEALIN' FEELIN'(189)
7602   WILLIS JACKSON-SWIVEL HIPS(189)
7603   CHARLES McPHERSON-HORIZONS(189)
7604   SWING 1946(Benny Carter/Jonah Jones/Gene Sedric)(243)
7605   KENNY CLARKE -PARIS BEBOP SESSIONS(1948-50)(246,251)
7606   GENE AMMONS AND SONNY STITT-WE'LL BE TOGETHER AGAIN(264)
7607   DON ELLIS-NEW IDEAS(reissue of NJLP8257)(104)
7608   MILES DAVIS-WALKIN'(reissue of PRLP7076)(26)
7609   JOHN COLTRANE-THE FIRST TRANE(reissue of PRLP7105)(53)
7610   SONNY CRISS-ROCKIN' IN RHYTHM(188)
7611   ERIC DOLPHY-LIVE!AT THE FIVE SPOT,Volume 1(reissue of NJLP8260)
         (110)
7612   SONNY STITT-STITT'S BITS,Volume 2(8,9,10,16)
7613   DON PATTERSON-FUNK YOU(190)
7614   QUINTET OF THE HOT CLUB DE FRANCE-FIRST RECORDINGS(237)
7615   THE JAKI BYARD EXPERIENCE(189)
7616   PUCHO & THE LATIN SOUL BROTHERS-DATELINE(192)
7617   JOE JONES-MY FIRE(190)
7618   CEDAR WALTON-THE ELECTRIC BOOGALOO SONG(191)
7619   EDDIE JEFFERSON-BODY AND SOUL(190)
7620   THE GREAT OSCAR PETERSON ON PRESTIGE!(270)
7621   HOUSTON PERSON-SOUL DANCE(190)
7622   THIS IS BILLY BUTLER!(191)

```
PR
7623   DEXTER GORDON-THE TOWER OF POWER(193)
7624   HAROLD MABERN-RAKIN' AND SCRAPIN'(191)
7625   JAMES MOODY-DON'T LOOK AWAY NOW!(192)
7626   RUSTY BRYANT RETURNS(192)
7627   ERIC KLOSS IN THE LAND OF THE GIANTS(191)
7628   SONNY CRISS-I'LL CATCH THE SUN(192)
7629   ILLINOIS JACQUET BIG BAND-THE SOUL EXPLOSION(193)
7630   CHARLES KYNARD-THE SOUL BROTHERHOOD(192)
7631   THE VIOLIN SUMMIS(267)
7632   THE TOMMY FLANAGAN TRIO-OVERSEAS(reissue of PRLP7134)(262)
7633   DJANGO REINHARDT & AMERICA JAZZ GIANTS:Coleman Hawkins(237,239)/
           Garnet Clark(238)/Benny Carter(239)
7634   KENNY CLARKE/FRANCY BOLAND BAND-FIRE,SOUL,HEAT & GUTS(268)
7635   SONNY STITT-SOUL ELECTRICITY(189)
7636   MAYNARD FERGUSON BIG BAND-MAYNARD FERGUSON 1969(269)
7637   YUSEF LATEEF-INTO SOMETHING(reissue of NJLP8272)(119)
7638   THE BEST OF DOROTHY ASHBY(reissue of PRLP7140)(59)
7639   DOROTHY PLAYS FOR BEAUTIFUL PEOPLE(reissue of NJLP8209)(63)
7640   DON PATTERSON-OH HAPPY DAY!(193)
7641   CHUBBY JACKSON SEXTET & BIG BAND(6,245)
7642   BROTHER JACK McDUFF-I GOT A WOMAN(151,157,166,231,232)
7643   BENNY CARTER-1933(235,236)
7644   BENNY GOODMAN & THE GIANTS OF SWING:Joe Venuti(236)/Benny Goodman
           (236)/Gene Krupa(238)
7645   THE BIG BANDS-1933:Duke Ellington(235)/Fletcher Henderson(235)/
           Horace Henderson(236)
7646   SWING CLASSICS-1935:Joe Sullivan(235)/Bud Freeman(238)/Jess
           Stacy(238)/Bunny Berigan(238)
7647   JAZZ PIONEERS(1933-36):Coleman Hawkins(235,236,237)/Mary Lou
           Williams(238)
7648   WILLIS JACKSON-GATOR'S GROOVE(190)
7649   OSCAR PETERSON PLAYS FOR LOVERS(267,269,270)
7650   MILES DAVIS & THE MODERN JAZZ GIANTS(30)
7651   JOHN COLTRANE-TRANEING IN(1957)(reissue of PRLP7123)(54)
7652   ERIC DOLPHY-OUT THERE(reissue of NJLP8252)(86)
7653   YUSEF LATEEF-EXPRESSIONS(reissue of NJLP8218)(55)
7654   GENE AMMONS JAM SESSIONS,Volume 1:THE HAPPY BLUES(reissue of
           PRLP7039)(38)
7655   THE COMPLETE MILT JACKSON(27,33)
7656   THE GENIUS OF THELONIOUS MONK(reissue of PRLP7075)(24,28,29)
7657   SONNY ROLLINS-TENOR MADNESS(reissue of PRLP7047)(39)
7658   RED GARLAND REVISITED(52)
7659   HERBIE MANN IN SWEDEN(reissue of PRLP7136)(262)
7660   EDDIE LOCKJAW DAVIS COOKBOOK,Volume 1-IN THE KITCHEN(reissue of
           PRLP7141)(61)
7661   HANK MOBLEY'S MESSAGE(reissue of PRLP7061)(40)
7662   THE CLIFFORD BROWN MEMORIAL ALBUM(reissue of PRLP7055)(23,257)
7663   JAMES MOODY,Volume 1-WORKSHOP(25,26,28,31)
7664   BILLY TAYLOR TRIO-A TOUCH OF TAYLOR(reissue of PRLP7001)(32)
7665   ART FARMER-EARLY ART(reissue of NJLP8258)(25,29)
7666   BROTHER JACK McDUFF-STEPPIN' OUT(109,136,137,151,157,166)
7667   HANK MOBLEY'S SECOND MESSAGE(reissue of PRLP7082)(41)
7668   MILT BUCKNER IN EUROPE(268)
7669   CARMELL JONES IN EUROPE(267)
7670   JOHN COLTRANE-TWO TENORS(reissue of PRLP7043)(38)
7671   COLEMAN HAWKINS-NIGHT HAWK(reissue of SVLP2016)(96)
7672   THE PEE WEE RUSSELL MEMORIAL ALBUM(reissue of SVLP2008)(77)
7673   PHIL WOODS-EARLY QUINTETS(28,263)
7674   MILES DAVIS-EARLY MILES(9,21)
7675   THE ELMO HOPE MEMORIAL ALBUM(reissue of PRLP7010)(34)
7676   JEAN-LUC PONTY-CRITIC'S CHOICE(268)
```

```
PR
7677   PEPPER ADAMS/ZOOT SIMS-ENCOUNTER!(191)
7678   HOUSTON PERSON-GOODNESS!(195)
7679   THE BEST OF PUCHO & THE LATIN SOUL BROTHERS(178,181,186)
7680   DEXTER GORDON-MORE POWER(193)
7681   JOHNNY "HAMMOND" SMITH-SOUL TALK(193)
7682   NORMAN MAILER READS NORMAN MAILER(not included)
7683   PHILLIP ROTH'S EPSTEIN READ BY LARRY STORCH(not included)
7684   ALTO SUMMIT(266)
7685   ELLA FITZGERALD-SUNSHINE OF YOUR LOVE(272)
7686   JAKI BYARD SOLO PIANO(194)
7687   HAROLD MABERN-WORKIN' & WAILIN'(194)
7688   CHARLES KYNARD-REELIN' WITH THE FEELIN'(194)
7689   ERIC KLOSS-TO HEAR IS TO SEE(194)
7690   OSCAR PETERSON-EASY WALKER(266)
7691   THE STUFF SMITH MEMORIAL ALBUM(268)
7692   DON BYAS MEETS BEN WEBSTER(270)
7693   CEDAR WALTON-SOUL CYCLE(193)
7694   STEVE KUHN IN EUROPE(271)
7695   HAMPTON HAWES IN EUROPE(271)
7696   THE TEDDY WILSON TRIO IN EUROPE(271)
7697   JOE JONES-BOOGALOO JOE(194)
7698   EDDIE JEFFERSON-COME ALONG WITH ME(195)
7699   KENNY CLARKE/FRANCY BOLAND BIG BAND-LET'S FACE THE MUSIC(270)
7700   THE BEST OF RICHARD "GROOVE" HOLMES(161,167,169,172,176,177,182)
7701   THE BEST OF SONNY STITT WITH BROTHER JACK McDUFF(121,142)
7702   THE BEST OF WILLIS JACKSON WITH BROTHER JACK McDUFF(68,75,86)
7703   THE BEST OF BROTHER JACK McDUFF-LIVE!(140,142,152)
7704   THE BEST OF DON PATTERSON(147,149,151,161,165,169,177,179)
7705   THE BEST OF JOHNNY "HAMMOND" SMITH(104,130,159,165,170,174,179,183)
7706   THE BEST OF FREDDIE McCOY(157,163,177,180,184,187)
7707   THE BEST OF SHIRLEY SCOTT & STANLEY TURRENTINE(106,117,136,143,148)
7708   THE BEST OF GENE AMMONS FOR BEAUTIFUL PEOPLE(83,98,116,118,132)
7709   THE BEST OF KING CURTIS(108,114,115,120,121)
7710   THE BEST OF LOCKJAW DAVIS & SHIRLEY SCOTT(63,65,67,68)
7711   THE BEST OF ARNETT COBB(66,68,75,92)
7712   THE BEST OF JIMMY FORREST(88,103,113,116,129)
7713   THE BEST OF JIMMY WITHERSPOON(138,142,143,146)
7714   THE BEST OF LIGHTNIN' HOPKINS & HIS TEXAS BLUES BAND(122)
7715   THE BEST OF SONNY TERRY & BROWNIE McGHEE(86,87,90,127)
7716   INSIDE DAVE VAN RONK(reissue of PR14025)(not included)
7717   THE FOLK BLUES OF ERIC VON SCHMIDT(reissue of PR14005)(not included)
7718   JESSE FULLER-SAN FRANCISCO BAY BLUES(reissue of PR14006)(139)
7719   OTIS SPANN-THE BLUES WILL NEVER DIE(reissue of PR7391)(156)
7720   THE HOLY MODAL ROUNDERS,Volume 1(reissue of PR7451)(not included)
7721   RAMBLIN' JACK ELLIOTT(reissue of PR14014)(not included)
7722   THE BLUES OF ROOSEVELT SYKES(reissue of BVLP1014)(88)
7723   THE BLUES OF SUNNYLAND SLIM(reissue of BVLP1016)(89)
7724   THE BLUES OF LONNIE JOHNSON(reissue of BVLP1024)(96)
7725   THE BLUES GUITAR & BANJO OF REV.GARY DAVIS(reissue of PR7393)(147)
7726   TRACY NELSON-DEEP ARE THE ROOTS(reissue of PR7393)(not included)
7727   GEOFF MULDAUR-SLEEPY MAN BLUES(reissue of PR14004)(not included)
7728   REX STEWART MEMORIAL ALBUM(reissue of SVLP2006)(77)
7729   DUKE PEARSON-DEDICATION(264)
7730   WALTER BISHOP Jr.TRIO-1965(265,266)
7731   ILLINOIS JACQUET-THE BLUES:THAT'S ME(195)
7732   TAL FARLOW RETURNS-1969(196)
7733   BARRY HARRIS TRIO-MAGNIFICENT(197)
7734   BILLY BUTLER-GUITAR SOUL(195)
7735   RUSTY BRYANT-NIGHT TRAIN NOW!(196)
7736   JOHNNY "HAMMOND" SMITH-BLACK FEELING(197)
7737   SONNY PHILLIPS-SURE 'NUFF(196)
7738   DON PATTERSON-BROTHERS-4(195)
```

PR
7739 GENE AMMONS-THE BOSS IS BACK(196,197)
7740 JAMES MOODY-HI FI PARTY No.2(35)
7741 RICHARD "GROOVE" HOLMES-SOUL MIST(167,169)
7742 SONNY CRISS-THE BEST OF CRISS/HITS OF 1960's(175,179,183,188)
7743 CHARLES McPHERSON-McPHERSON'S MOOD(197)
7744 MILES DAVIS-CONCEPTION(12)
7745 TADD DAMERON/JOHN COLTRANE(1956)(reissue of PRLP7070)(44)
7746 JOHN COLTRANE-TRANE'S REIGN(reissue of PRLP7213)(59)
7747 ERIC DOLPHY-FAR CRY(reissue of NJLP8270)(95)
7748 YUSEF LATEEF-CRY-TENDER!(reissue of NJLP8234)(71)
7749 THE MODERN JAZZ QUARTET-FIRST RECORDINGS!(19,23,30,31)
7750 SONNY ROLLINS-WORKTIME(reissue of PRLP7020)(36)
7751 THELONIOUS MONK-REFLECTIONS,Vol.1(18,19,24)
7752 THE RED GARLAND TRIO-THE P.C.BLUES(38,48,54)
7753 COLEMAN HAWKINS-BLUES GROOVE(59)
7754 KENNY DORHAM(72)
7755 THE HENRY "RED" ALLEN MEMORIAL ALBUM(reissue of SVLP2034)(129)
7756 GIL EVANS-BIG STUFF(reissue of PRLP7120)(55)
7757 JACKIE McLEAN-LIGHTS OUT(reissue of PRLP7035)(37)
7758 CHARLIE EARLAND-BLACK TALK(197)
7759 SONNY STITT-NIGHT LETTER(196)
7760 KENNY CLARKE/FRANCY BOLAND BIG BAND-LATIN KALEIDOSCOPE(271)
7761 THE CLIFFORD BROWN QUARTET IN PARIS(259)
7762 BILLY TAYLOR TODAY!(272)
7763 DEXTER GORDON-A DAY IN COPENHAGEN(272)
7764 HAROLD MABERN-GREASY KID STUFF(198)
7765 PUCHO & THE LATIN SOUL BROTHERS-JUNGLE FIRE(198)
7766 BOOGALOO JOE JONES-RIGHT ON BROTHER(198)
7767 HOUSTON PERSON-TRUTH(199)
7768 THE BEST OF RICHARD "GROOVE" HOLMES FOR LOVERS(169,170,176,182,
      184,189)
7769 THE BEST OF SONNY STITT(with JACK McDUFF)FOR LOVERS(121,142)
7770 THE BEST OF WILLIS JACKSON-SOUL STOMPIN'(97,124,134,135)
7771 THE BEST OF BROTHER JACK McDUFF & THE BIG SOUL BAND(152,157,166)
7772 THE BEST OF DON PATTERSON & THE JAZZ GIANTS(147,177,184,187,190,
      193)
7773 THE BEST OF SHIRLEY SCOTT & STANLEY TURRENTINE(106,117,136,143,148)
7774 THE BEST OF GENE AMMONS with BROTHER JACK McDUFF(118,120,122)
7775 THE BEST OF KING CURTIS-ONE MORE TIME(108,114,115,120,121)
7776 THE BEST OF BENNY GREEN(33,35,38,40)
7777 THE BEST OF JOHNNY "HAMMOND" SMITH FOR LOVERS(70,72,79,104,159,165)
7778 THE BEST OF RED HOLLOWAY & THE SOUL ORGAN GIANTS(143,145,164)
7779 THE BEST OF HOUSTON PERSON(168,177,180,185,190,195)
7780 THE BEST OF BOBBY TIMMONS & HIS SOUL PIANO(150,153,155,161,170,171)
7781 GENE AMMONS JAM SESSIONS,Vol.2-JAMMIN' WITH GENE(reissue of
      PRLP7060)(40)
7782 EDDIE LOCKJAW DAVIS COOKBOOK,Vol.2-THE REV(reissue of PRLP7161)(65)
7783 WILLIS JACKSON-PLEASE Mr.JACKSON(reissue of PRLP7162)(68)
7784 ETTA JONES-LOVE IS THE THING(reissue of PRLP7194)(89,101)
7785 BROTHER JACK McDUFF-BROTHER JACK-reissue of PRLP7174)(74)
7786 JOHNNY "HAMMOND" SMITH-STIMULATION(reissue of PRLP7203)(98,104)
7787 THE PRESTIGE BLUES SWINGERS-OUTSKIRTS OF TOWN(reissue of PRLP7145)
      (62)
7788 BILL JENNINGS WITH BROTHER JACK McDUFF-ENOUGH SAID(reissue of
      PRLP7164)(69)
7789 KING CURTIS-KING SOUL(reissue of NJLP8237)(79)
7790 VERY SAXY(reissue of PRLP7167)(67)
7791 THE SOUL JAZZ GIANTS:Eddie "Lockjaw" Davis(63)/Jack McDuff(136)/
      The Nomos(146)/Willis Jackson(151)/Richard "Groove" Holmes(167)/
      Willis Jackson(181)/Gene Ammons(265)
7792 GENE AMMONS-BROTHER JUG!(196,197)

```
PR
7793   ERIC KLOSS-CONSCIOUSNESS!(198)
7794   THE CLIFFORD BROWN SEXTET IN PARIS,Vol.2(258)
7795   PAT MARTINO-DESPERADO(199)
7796   CHARLES KYNARD-AFRO-DISIAC(199)
7797   BILLY BUTLER-YESTERDAY,TODAY & TOMORROW(199,200)
7798   RUSTY BRYANT-SOUL LIBERATION(200)
7799   SONNY PHILLIPS-BLACK MAGIC(199)
7800   DAVE VAN RONK-IN THE TRADITION(reissue of PR14001)(not included)
7801   BONNIE DOBSON-DEAR COMPANION(reissue of PR14007)(not included)
7802   SONNY TERRY-SONNY IS KING(reissue of BVLP1059)(91,230)
7803   SONNY TERRY & BROWNIE McGHEE-LIVE!AT THE SECOND FRET(reissue of
          BVLP1058)(127)
7804   JACK ELLIOTT-COUNTRY STYLE(reissue of PR14029)(not included)
7805   GARY DAVIS-PURE RELIGION(reissue of PR14028)(87)
7806   LIGHTNIN' HOPKINS-HOOTIN' THE BLUES(reissue of PR14021)(128)
7807   LITTLE BROTHER MONTGOMERY-TASTY BLUES(reissue of BVLP1012)(84)
7808   ROBERT PETE WILLIAMS-FREE AGAIN(reissue of BVLP1026)(93)
7809   BLIND WILLIE McTELL-LAST SESSION(reissue of BVLP1040)(42)
7810   FURRY LEWIS-BACK ON MY FEET AGAIN(reissue of BVLP1036)(101)
7811   THE BLUES OF LIGHTNIN' HOPKINS(reissue of BVLP1019)(93)
7812   REX STEWART/WINGY MANONE-TRUMPET JIVE!:W.Manone(240,242)/Rex
          Stewart(242)
7813   THE OSCAR PETTIFORD MEMORIAL ALBUM(247,260)
7814   BROTHER JACK McDUFF-TOUGH DUFF(reissue of PRLP7185)(85)
7815   CHARLIE EARLAND-BLACK DROPS(200)
7816   DON PATTERSON-DONNYBROOK(195)
7817   ZOOT SIMS-FIRST RECORDINGS!(250,251,256)
7818   DIZZY GILLESPIE BIG BAND-PARIS 1948(246)
7819   AL COHN-BROADWAY 1954(260)
7820   GEORGE WALLINGTON LIVE!AT THE CAFE BOHEMIA(261)
7821   SONNY ROLLINS-THREE GIANTS(reissue of PRLP7038)(37)
7822   MILES DAVIS-MILES AHEAD(21,22,25)
7823   GENE AMMONS-BLUES UP AND DOWN,Vol.1(5,6,7)
7824   COLEMAN HAWKINS-BEAN AND THE BOYS(240,245,249)
7825   JOHN COLTRANE-THE MASTER(reissue of PRLP7243)(61)
7826   ERIC DOLPHY-LIVE AT THE FIVE SPOT,Vol.2(reissue of PRLP7294)(110)
7827   LEE KONITZ-EZZ-THETIC(10,257)
7828   THE BE-BOP SINGERS:Annie Ross(17)/Joe Carroll(20)/Eddie Jefferson
          (21)
7829   DEXTER GORDON-THE PANTHER!(200)
7830   WILLIS JACKSON-KEEP ON BLOWIN'(reissue of PRLP7172)(68,72)
7831   LIGHTNIN' HOPKINS-GOTTA MOVE YOUR BABY(reissue of BVLP1029)(92)
7832   YUSEF LATEEF-IMAGINATION(reissue of NJLP8238)(81)
7833   KING CURTIS-SOUL MEETING(reissue of PRLP7222)(89)
7834   EDDIE "LOCKJAW" DAVIS BIG BAND-STOLEN MOMENTS(reissue of PRLP7206)
          (89)
7835   ARNETT COBB/EDDIE "LOCKJAW" DAVIS-GO POWER(reissue of PRLP7151)
          (66)
7836   BILL JENNINGS-GLIDE ON(reissue of PRLP7177)(74)
7837   RAY BRYANT-ALONE WITH THE BLUES(reissue of NJLP8213)(65)
7838   RED GARLAND TRIO-IT'S A BLUE WORLD(58)
7839   SONNY STITT-BUD'S BLUES(3,4,5)
7840   CLIFFORD BROWN BIG BAND IN PARIS(258)
7841   AL HAIG TRIO & QUINTET(247,260)
7842   THE TADD DAMERON MEMORIAL ALBUM(reissue of PRLP7037)(37)
7843   ERIC DOLPHY-WHERE?(reissue of NJLP8265)(107)
7844   BOOKER ERVIN-EXULTATION(141)
7845   SHIRLEY SCOTT-THE SOUL IS WILLING(reissue of PRLP7267)(136)
7846   JOHNNY "HAMMOND" SMITH-GOOD 'NUFF(reissue of PRLP7239)(130)
7847   MILES DAVIS-OLEO(27,37)
7848   THELONIOUS MONK-BLUE MONK,Vol.2(26,28)
7849   DUKE JORDAN-JOR-DU(2,260)
```

PR
7850   WILLIS JACKSON-BLUE GAT R(reissue of PRLP7183)(68,72,75,86)
7851   BROTHER JACK McDUFF-ON WITH IT(118)
7852   DON PATTERSON-TUNE UP(151,154,193,195)
7853   JAMES MOODY-WAIL MOODY WAIL,Vol.3(36)
7854   BILLY BUTLER-NIGHT LIFE(203)
7855   JIMMY WITHERSPOON-MEAN OLD FRISCO(reissue of PRLP7290)(138,141)
7856   SONNY ROLLINS-FIRST RECORDINGS!(reissue of PRLP7029)(9,14,24)
7857   COLEMAN HAWKINS-HAWK EYES(reissue of PRLP7156)(67)

Note:Further reissue albums in this series were planned,but never
issued,the series being discontinued when Prestige was bought by
Fantasy.

NEW JAZZ label

NJLP
8201   MAL WALDRON-MAL 3/SOUNDS(58)
8202   ROOTS(56,57)
8203   ART FARMER-FARMER'S MARKET(44)
8204   BIRD FEATHERS:Phil Woods(49)/Jackie McLean(51)/Hal McKusick(57)
8205   JEROME RICHARDSON SEXTET(63)
8206   STEVE LACY PLAYS THE MUSIC OF THELONIOUS MONK(64)
8207   GEORGE WALLINGTON QUINTET-THE NEW YORK SCENE(47)
8208   MAL WALDRON TRIO-MAL 4(63)
8209   DOROTHY ASHBY-IN A MINOR GROOVE(63)
8210   ROY HAYNES WITH PHINEAS NEWBORN-WE THREE(64)
8211   HERBIE MANN-JUST WAILIN'(59)
8212   JACKIE McLEAN-McLEAN'S SCENE(44,46)
8213   RAY BRYANT-ALONE WITH THE BLUES(65)
8214   STAN GETZ-LONG ISLAND SOUND(reissue of PRLP7002)(2,4,6)
8215   GIL EVANS-BIG STUFF(reissue of PRLP7120)(55)
8216   COOLIN' (49)
8217   THE CATS(49)
8218   YUSEF LATEEF-OTHER SOUNDS(55)
8219   ART TAYLOR-TAYLOR'S TENORS(68)
8220   BENNY GOLSON-GROOVIN' WITH GOLSON(70)
8221   JOHNNY "HAMMOND" SMITH-ALL SOUL(70)
8222   MODERN JAZZ DISCIPLES(70)
8223   LEM WINCHESTER-WINCHESTER SPECIAL(70)
8224   OLIVER NELSON-MEET OLIVER NELSON(71)
8225   KENNY DORHAM-QUIET KENNY(72)
8226   JEROME RICHARDSON-ROAMIN'(71)
8227   RAY BRYANT TRIO(reissue of PRLP7098)(49)
8228   RAY DRAPER WITH JOHN COLTRANE(57)
8229   JOHNNY "HAMMOND" SMITH-THAT GOOD FEELING(72)
8230   GIGI GRYCE-SAYIN' SOMETHIN'(76)
8231   JACKIE McLEAN-MAKIN' THE CHANGES(46,54)
8232   JENKINS,JORDAN & TIMMONS(54)
8233   OLIVER NELSON-TAKIN' CARE OF BUSINESS(77)
8234   YUSEF LATEEF-CRY!TENDER(71)
8235   BENNY GOLSON-GONE WITH GOLSON(69)
8236   ERIC DOLPHY-OUTWARD BOUND(78)
8237   THE NEW SCENE OF KING CURTIS(79)
8238   DOUG WATKINS-SOULNIK(81)
8239   LEM WINCHESTER-LEM'S BEAT(79)
8240   THE MODERN JAZZ DISCIPLES-RIGHT DOWN FRONT(70,82)
8241   JOHNNY "HAMMOND" SMITH-TALK THAT TALK(79)
8242   MAL WALDRON TRIO-IMPRESSIONS(67)
8243   OLIVER NELSON-SCREAMIN' THE BLUES(82)
8244   LEM WINCHESTER-ANOTHER OPUS(83)
8245   ROY HAYNES-JUST US(84)
8246   GIGI GRYCE-THE HAP' NIN'S (80)

```
NJLP
8247   KEN McINTYRE & ERIC DOLPHY-LOOKING AHEAD(84)
8248   BENNY GOLSON-GETTIN' WITH IT(73)
8249   LARRY YOUNG-TESTIFYING(85)
8250   JIMMY FORREST-FORREST FIRE(85)
8251   THE LATIN JAZZ QUINTET WITH ERIC DOLPHY-CARIBE(86)
8252   ERIC DOLPHY-OUT THERE(86)
8253   JACKIE McLEAN-A LONG DRINK OF THE BLUES(46,54)
8254   THIS IS WALT DICKERSON(99)
8255   OLIVER NELSON WITH ERIC DOLPHY-STRAIGHT AHEAD(99)
8256   JAKI BYARD-HERE'S JAKI(100)
8257   DON ELLIS-NEW IDEAS(104)
8258   ART FARMER-EARLY ART(25,29)
8259   KEN McINTYRE-STONE BLUES(82)
8260   ERIC DOLPHY AT THE FIVE SPOT,Vol.1(110)
8261   YUSEF LATEEF-THE SOUNDS OF YUSEF(reissue of PRLP7122)(55)
8262   GIGI GRYCE-THE RAT RACE BLUES(83)
8263   JACKIE McLEAN-LIGHTS OUT(reissue of PRLP7035)
8264   LARRY YOUNG-YOUNG BLUES(90)
8265   RON CARTER WITH ERIC DOLPHY-WHERE?(107)
8266   THE MUSIC OF AHMED ABDUL-MALIK(105)
8267   ROLAND ALEXANDER-PLEASURE BENT(106)
8268   WALT DICKERSON-A SENSE OF DIRECTION(104)
8269   MAL WALDRON WITH ERIC DOLPHY-THE QUEST(107)
8270   ERIC DOLPHY-FAR CRY(95)
8271   STEVE LACY WITH DON CHERRY-EVIDENCE!(117)
8272   YUSEF LATEEF-INTO SOMETHING(119)
8273   JAKI BYARD-HI FLY(121)
8274   DIZZY REECE-ASIA MINOR(123)
8275   WALT DICKERSON-RELATIVITY(120)
8276   KENNY BURRELL WITH JOHN COLTRANE(59)
8277   CURTIS FULLER WITH RED GARLAND(52)
8278   ART FARMER-WORK OF ART(reissue of PRLP7031)(23,27)
8279   JACKIE McLEAN 4,5 AND 6(reissue of PRLP7048)
8280   ZOOT SIMS-GOOD OLD ZOOT(6,27)
8281   DAVE PIKE-BOSSA NOVA CARNIVAL(132)
8282   AHMED ABDUL-MALIK-SOUNDS OF AFRICA(105,131)
8283   WALT DICKERSON-TO MY QUEEN(133)
8284   DAVE PIKE-LIMBO CARNIVAL(135)
8285   PONY POINDEXTER PLAYS THE BIG ONES(137)
8286   ROY HAYNES WITH BOOKER ERVIN-CRACKLIN'(138)
8287   ROY HAYNES-CYMBALISM(142)
8288   JOHNNY "HAMMOND" SMITH-LOOK OUT(120)
8289   ART FARMER-CASABLANCA(reissue of PRLP7017)(35)
8290   JACKIE McLEAN-STEEPLECHASE(reissue of PRLP7068)(42)
8291   PHIL WOODS-POT PIE(29,31)
8292   JAZZ SOUL OF CLEOPATRA:John Coltrane(53)/Yusef Lateef(55)/Ahmed
         Abdul-Malik(105)/Dizzy Reece(123)/Oudi Hrant(not included)
8293   JIMMY FORREST-SOUL STREET(88,113,116,129)
8294   BOB BROOKMEYER-REVELATION(reissue of PRLP7066)(25,33)
8295   EZZ-THETIC:Lee Konitz & Miles Davis(10)/Lee Konitz(10)/Teddy
         Charles & Jimmy Raney(19)
8296   TRUMPET GIANTS:Fats Navarro(3)/Dizzy Gillespie(8)/Miles Davis(12)
8297   PONY POINDEXTER-GUMBO(unissued)(see PR16001)
8298   AHMED ABDUL-MALIK-EASTERN MOODS(unissued)(see PR16003)
8299   GILDO MAHONES-SHOOTING HIGH(unissued)(see PR16004)
8300   TADD DAMERON-DAMERONIA(unissued)(see PR16007)
8301   CLIFFORD BROWN(unissued)(see PR16008)
8302   ZOOT SIMS-TROTTING(unissued)(see PR16009)
8303   AHMED ABDUL-MALIK-SPELLBOUND(147)

Note:Some albums of this series have been issued on Status label as
ST8...(same number).
```

```
ST
8304  RED GARLAND WITH PHIL WOODS-SUGAN(54)
8305  CURTIS FULLER & HAMPTON HAWES & FRENCH HORNS(52)
8306  BROADWAY:Gerry Mulligan-Kai Winding(2)/Red Rodney(12)
8307  HAMP HAWES/FREDDIE REDD-MOVIN'(reissue of PRLP7067)(18,32)
8308  WYNTON KELLY WITH STEVE LACY(reissue of PRLP7125)(56)
8309  ZOOT SIMS WITH PHIL WOODS-KOO KOO(reissue of PRLP7033)(36)
8310  FRANK WESS WITH THAD JONES-TOUCHE(reissue of PRLP7084)(46)
8311  52nd STREET THEME(reissue of PRLP7061)(40)
8312  JACKIE McLEAN-ALTO MADNESS(reissue of PRLP7114)(57)
8313  BILLY TAYLOR LIVE!AT TOWN HALL(reissue of PRLP7093)(30)
8314  RED GARLAND-LITTLE DARLIN'(71)
8315  MY FAIR LADY:Sonny Rollins(42)/Etta Jones(83)/Shirley Scott(84)/
          Coleman Hawkins(131)/Ted Curson(135)/Bobby Timmons(153)
8316  THE DEALERS:Mal Waldron(50)/John Coltrane(55)
8317  DONALD BYRD,HANK MOBLEY & KENNY BURRELL(45,51,52)
8318  GUITAR SOUL:Kenny Burrell-Barry Galbraith(51)/Tiny Grimes(61)/
          Bill Jennings(69)
8319  LUSTY MOODS(reissue of MV37)(4,38,55,59,79,90,102,122,133)
8320  CLEA BRADFORD WITH CLARK TERRY(reissue of TRU15005)(107)
8321  THE LATIN JAZZ QUINTET-LATIN SOUL(95,105)
8322  JOHN WRIGHT-THE LAST AMEN(119)
8323  JACKIE McLEAN AND COMPANY(reissue of PRLP7087)(46)
8324  OLIVER NELSON & ERIC DOLPHY-SCREAMIN' THE BLUES(reissue of
8325  RED GARLAND/JOHN COLTRANE-HIGH PRESSURE(reissue of PRLP7209)(56,
          57)
8326  RED GARLAND-LIVE(71)
8327  JOHN COLTRANE/FRANK WESS-WHEELIN' AND DEALIN'(55)


PRESTIGE label

PR
10001 MELVIN SPARKS-SPARKS!(201)
10002 JOHNNY "HAMMOND" SMITH-HERE IT IS(202)
10003 HOUSTON PERSON-PERSON TO PERSON(202)
10004 BOOGALOO JOE JONES-NO WAY!(202)
10005 IDRIS MUHAMMAD-BLACK RHYTHM REVOLUTION(202)
10006 GENE AMMONS-THE BLACK CAT(202)
10007 SONNY PHILLIPS-BLACK ON BLACK(201)
10008 CHARLES KYNARD-WA TU WA ZUI(203)
10009 CHARLIE EARLAND-LIVING BLACK!(201)
10010 GENE AMMONS/DEXTER GORDON-THE CHASE(200)
10011 LEON SPENCER Jr.-SNEAK PREVIEW(203)
10012 SONNY STITT-TURN IT ON!(203)
10013 BERNARD PURDIE-PURDIE GOOD(203)
10014 RUSTY BRYANT-FIRE EATER(204)
10015 JOHNNY "HAMMOND" SMITH-WHAT'S GOIN' ON?(205)
10016 MELVIN SPARKS-SPARKPLUG(204)
10017 HOUSTON PERSON-HOUSTON EXPRESS(204)
10018 CHARLES EARLAND-SOUL STORY(205)
10019 GENE AMMONS/SONNY STITT-YOU TALK THAT TALK!(204)
10020 DEXTER GORDON-THE JUMPIN' BLUES(201)
10021 GENE AMMONS-BROTHER JUG(reissue of PR7792)(196,197)
10022 GENE AMMONS-MY WAY(206)
10023 GENE AMMONS-THE BOSS IS BACK(reissue of PR7739)(196,197)
10024 CHARLES EARLAND-BLACK TALK(reissue of PR7758)(197)
10025 BOOGALOO JOE JONES-RIGHT ON BROTHER(reissue of PR7766)(198)
10026 HOUSTON PERSON-THE TRUTH!(reissue of PR7767)(199)
10027 HOUSTON PERSON-GOODNESS!(reissue of PR7678)(195)
10028 RUSTY BRYANT-SOUL LIBERATION(reissue of PR7798)(200)
10029 CHARLES EARLAND-BLACK DROPS(reissue of PR7815)(200)
10030 DEXTER GORDON-THE PANTHER(reissue of PR7829)(200)
```

```
PR
10031   FUNK,Inc.(205)
10032   SONNY STITT-BLACK VIBRATIONS(205,206)
10033   LEON SPENCER Jr.-LOUISIANA SLIM(205)
10034   ARCHIE SHEPP-BLACK GYPSY(273)
10035   BOOGALOO JOE JONES-WHAT IT IS(206)
10036   IDRIS MUHAMMAD-PEACE AND RHYTHM(206)
10037   RUSTY BRYANT-WILD FIRE(207)
10038   BERNARD PURDIE-SHAFT(207)
10039   MELVIN SPARKS-AKILAH!(207)
10040   GENE AMMONS-FREE AGAIN(208)
10041   CHARLES EARLAND-INTENSITY(208)
10042   LEON SPENCER Jr.-BAD WALKING WOMAN(207,208)
10043   FUNK,Inc.-CHICKEN LICKIN'(208)
10044   HOUSTON PERSON-BROKEN WINDOWS,EMPTY HALLWAYS(209)
10045   BAYETE-WORLD AROUND THE SUN(209)
10046   HAMPTON HAWES-UNIVERSE(209)
10047   ART BLAKEY JAZZ MESSENGERS-BUHAINA(209,210)
10048   SONNY STITT-GOIN' DOWN SLOW(207)
10049   ART ENSEMBLE OF CHICAGO WITH FONTELLA BASS(273)
10050   CHARLES EARLAND-LIVE AT THE LIGHTHOUSE(209)
10051   DEXTER GORDON-CA' PURANGE(210)
10052   MOSE ALLISON-THE SEVENTH SON(47,56,58,60,62,66)
10053   RUSTY BRYANT-FRIDAY NIGHT FUNK FOR SATURDAY NIGHT BROTHERS(210)
10054   MAYNARD PARKER-MIDNIGHT RIDER(210,211)
10055   HOUSTON PERSON-SWEET BUNS & BARBEQUE(211,212)
10056   BOOGALOO JOE JONES-SNAKE RHYTHM ROCK(211)
10057   GARY BARTZ-JUJU ST.SONGS(211)
10058   GENE AMMONS-GET MY OWN(212)
10059   FUNK,Inc.-HANGIN' OUT(212)
10060   HAMPTON HAWES-BLUES FOR WALLS(213)
10061   CHARLES EARLAND-CHARLES III(208,213)
10062   BAYETE-SEEKING OTHER BEAUTY(211)
10063   LEON SPENCER Jr.-WHERE I'M COMING FROM(207,213)
10064   ART ENSEMBLE OF CHICAGO-PHASE I(273)
10065   GENE AMMONS/JAMES MOODY-CHICAGO CONCERT(207)
10066   ARCHIE SHEPP-CORAL ROCK(273)
10067   ART BLAKEY'S JAZZ MESSENGERS-BUHAINA(213)
10068   GARY BARTZ-FOLLOW THE MEDICINE MAN(212,214)
10069   DEXTER GORDON-GENERATION(210)
10070   GENE AMMONS-BIG BAND JUG(212)
10071   FUNK,Inc.-SUPERFUNK(215)
10072   BOOGALOO JOE JONES-BLACK WHIP(215)
10073   RUSTY BRYANT-FOR THE GOOD TIMES(213)
10074   SONNY STITT-SO DOGGONE GOOD(211)
10075   ICE(215)
10076   ART BLAKEY-ANTHENAGIN(214)
10077   HAMPTON HAWES-PLAYIN' IN THE YARD(214)
10078   GENE AMMONS AND FRIENDS AT MONTREUX(214)
10079   DEXTER GORDON-BLUES A LA SUISSE(214)
10080   GENE AMMONS-BRASSWIND(215,217)
10081   JACK DE JOHNETTE-SORCERY(217)
10082   CHARLES EARLAND-THE DYNAMITE BROTHERS(216)
10083   GARY BARTZ-SINGERELLA/A GHETTO FAIRY TALE(215,217)
10084   GENE AMMONS GREATEST HITS(83,98,133,197,206)
10085   RUSTY BRYANT-UNTIL IT'S TIME FOR YOU TO GO(218)
10086   AZAR LAWRENCE-BRIDGE INTO NEW AGE(218,219)
10087   FUNK,Inc.-PRICED TO SELL(218)
10088   HAMPTON HAWES-NORTHERN WINDOWS(218)
10089   PATRICE RUSHEN-PRELUSION(219)
10090   NAT ADDERLEY-DOUBLE EXPOSURE(219)
10091   DEXTER GORDON-TANGERINE(210)
10092   GARY BARTZ-THE SHADOW DO(219)
10093   GENE AMMONS-GOODBYE(217)
```

```
P-
10094  JACK DE JOHNETTE-COSMIC CHICKEN(220)
10095  CHARLES EARLAND-KHARMA(218)
10096  ICE-IMPORT EXPORT(220)
10097  AZAR LAWRENCE-SUMMER SOLSTICE(220)
10098  PATRICE RUSHEN-BEFORE THE DAWN(220)
10099  AZAR LAWRENCE-PEOPLE MOVING(221)
10100  GENE AMMONS/SONNY STITT-TOGETHER AGAIN FOR THE LAST TIME(216)
10101  PATRICE RUSHEN-SHOUT IT OUT(221)
10102  BILL SUMMERS-FEEL THE HEAT(221)
10103  BILL SUMMERS AND SUMMERS HEAT-CAYENNE(222)
10104  DAVID "FATHEAD" NEWMAN-CONCRETE JUNGLE(222)
10105  BILL SUMMERS AND SUMMERS HEAT-STRAIGHT TO THE BANK(222)
10106  DAVID "FATHEAD" NEWMAN-KEEP THE DREAM ALIVE(221)
```

PRESTIGE INTERNATIONAL label

Albums from this series are not described in this book,except for some
titles on PR13072.

```
PR
13001  GOLDEN SONGS OF GREECE
13002  THE BEST OF ED McCURDY
13003  THE BEST OF JEAN RITCHIE
13004  THE BEST OF EWAN MacCOLL
13005  THE BEST OF PEGGY SEEGER
13006  JEANNIE ROBERTSON-SCOTTISH BALLADS AND FOLK SONGS
13007  DOMINGO ALVARADO/ROGELIO REUGERA-FLAMENCO
13008  PICK TEMPLE-THE PICK OF THE CROP
13009  OBRAY RAMSEY-JIMMIE RODGERS FAVORITES
13010  THE BEST OF CYNTHIA GOODING
13011  JOHN GREENWAY-"THE CAT CAME BACK" AND OTHER FUN SONGS
13012  FRANK WARNER AND SONS-SONGS OF THE CIVIL WAR
13013  THE BEST OF GUY CARAWAY
13014  ROGELIO REGUERA-GUITARRA CLASICA Y FLAMENCA
13015  POLA CHAPELLE-ITALIAN FOLK SONGS
13016  JACK ELLIOTT-THE SONGS OF WOODY GUTHRIE
13017  THE BEST OF ROBIN ROBERTS
13018  THE McPEAKE FAMILY OF BELFAST
13019  RUTH RUBIN-YIDDISH FOLK SONGS
13020  OBRAY RAMSEY-FOLK SONGS FROM THE THREE LAURELS
13021  BPNNIE DOBSON-SHE'S LIKE A SWALLOW
13022  MOLLY SCOTT-WAITIN' ON YOU
13023  J.BARRE TOELKEN-A GARLAND OF AMERICAN FOLK SONGS
13024  THEODORE ALEVIZOS-GREEK FOLK SONGS
13025  ROSALIE SORRELS-ROSALIE'S SONGBAG(AMERICAN FOLK SONGS)
13026  TOMMY HUNTER'S CAROLINA STRING BAND-MOUNTAIN MUSIC
13027  TOSSI AARON-TOSSI SINGS FOLK SONGS & BALLADS
13028  ROBERT H.BEERS-THE ART OF THE PSALTERY
13029  PEGGY SEEGER-THE THREE SISTERS
13030  OBRAY RAMSEY-GREAT SMOKIES SONGS
13031  BONNIE DOBSON-DEAR COMPANION
13032  GARDNERS-INTERNATIONAL FOLK SONGS
13033  RAMBLIN' JACK ELLIOTT
```

```
PR
13034    ROGER ABRAHAMS-MAKE ME A PALLET ON THE FLOOR
13035    LOUISIANA HONEYDRIPPERS-BLUEGRASS
13036    TONY SALETAN-I'M A STRANGER HERE
13037    CHARLOTTE DANIELS AND PAT WEBB
13038    JEAN WEST-ROAMIN' THE BLUE RIDGE
13039    RAY CONRAD-THE COTTON PICKIN' LIFT TOWER AND OTHER SKIING SONGS
13040    U.UTAH PHILLIPS-NO ONE KNOWS ME
13041    JEAN REDPATH-WALK BAREFOOT THROUGH THE HEATHER(SCOTCH)
13042    THE BEST OF ISLA CAMERON
13043    EWAN MacCOLL/A.L.LLOYD-A SAILOR'S GARLAND
13044    ED McCURDY-LYRICA EROTICA,Vol.1
13045
13046    RON ELIRAN-TWILIGHT SONGS OF ISRAEL
13047    ROBERT FIDDLER BEERS-PSALTY PSONGS WITH PSALTERY AND PFIDDLE
13048    ARTHUR ARGO-LYRICA EROTICA
13049    JEAN WEST-COUNTRY BLUEGRASS
13050    ED McCURDY-LYRICA EROTICA,Vol.3
13051    THE KUBIKS-CZECHOSLOVAKIAN FOLK SONGS
13052    LOS MORENOS-THE SOUND OF FLAMENCO
13053    EVELYN BEERS-THE GENTLE ART
13054    RON ELIRAN-NEW SOUNDS OF ISRAEL
13055    TOSSI AARON SINGS JEWISH SONGS
13056
13057
13058    PEGGY SEEGER-A SONG FOR YOU AND ME
13059    ISLA CAMERON AND LOU KILLEN-THE WATERS OF TYNE
13060    ALF EDWARDS-ART OF THE CONCERTINA
13061    PEGGY SEEGER AND EWAN MacCOLL-A LOVER'S GARLAND
13062    GARDNERS-FOLK SONGS FAR & NEAR
13063    RON ELIRAN-LADINO(Jewish Songs)
13064    BONNIE DOBSON-MERRY GO-ROUND OF CHILDREN'S SONGS
13065
13066    THE BEST OF A.L.LLOYD
13067    YAFFA YARKONI-INTERNATIONAL SONGS
13068    DUKE OF IRON-LIMBO,LIMBO,LIMBO
13069    RON ELIRAN-GOLDEN SONGS OF ISRAEL
13070    RUTH BEN ZVI-ISRAELI PERCUSSION
13071
13072    includes titles by Rev.Gary Davis(133)
13073    FOLK SONGS FOR CHILDREN(Jack Elliott/Peggy Seeger/Tossi Aaron/
            Bonnie Dobson/Rosalie Sorels/Tony Saletan/Ed McCurdy/Jean
            Rirchie/John Greenway/Frank Warner/Pick Temple)
13074
13075    JEANNE ROBERTSON-SCOTCH FOLK SONGS
13076    CHIEF THUNDERCLOUD-A CHILD'S INTRODUCTION TO THE AMERICAN INDIAN
13077    FERNANDO SIRVENT-FLAMENCO FANTASTICO
13078
13079    EAST OF ATHENS
13080    ARTISTRY OF GREECE


PRESTIGE FOLKLORE label

PR
14001    DAVE VAN RONK-IN THE TRADITION
14002    KEITH & ROONEY-LIVING ON THE MOUNTAIN(Bluegrass)
14003    TOM RUSH-GOT A MIND TO RAMBLE
14004    GEOFF MULDAUR-SLEEPY MAN BLUES
14005    ERIC VON SCHMIDT-FOLK BLUES
14006    JESSE FULLER-SAN FRANCISCO BAY BLUES(139)
14007    BONNIE DOBSON-DEAR COMPANION(same as PR13031)
14008    HAMPER MacBEE-CUMBERLAND MOONSHINER
```

```
PR
14009   THE BEST OF JEAN RITCHIE(same as PR13003)
14010   LILLY BROTHERS-BLUEGRASS BREAKDOWN
14011   RAMBLIN' JACK ELLIOTT SINGS THE SONGS OF WOODY GUTHRIE(=PR13016)
14012   DAVE VAN RONK-FOLK SINGER
14013   BROWNIE McGHEE & SONNY TERRY-DOWN HOME BLUES(reissue of BVLP1002)
          (86)
14014   JACK ELLIOTT-RAMBLIN'(same as PR13033)
14015   BONNIE DOBSON-SHE'S LIKE A SWALLOW(same as PR13021)
14016   THE BEST OF PEGGY SEEGER(same as PR13005)
14017   CHARLES RIVER VALLEY BOYS-BLUEGRASS AND OLD TIMEY MUSIC
14018   HOOTENANNY WITH BONNIE DOBSON
14019   HOOTENANNY WITH JACK ELLIOTT
14020   HOOTENANNY WITH PETE SEEGER/MIKE SEEGER/BONNIE DOBSON/JACK
          ELLIOTT/KEITH AND ROONEY
14021   LIGHTNIN' HOPKINS-HOOTIN' THE BLUES(128)
14022   TRUE ENDEAVOR JUG BAND-THE ART OF THE JUG BAND
14023   FOLKLORE JAMBOREE:Keith & Rooney/Tom Rush/Bonnie Dobson-Eric
          Van Ronk/Jack Elliott/Jesse Fuller(139)/Dave Van Ronk/Bonnie
          Dobson/Brownie McGhee & Sonny Terry(86)/Dave Van Ronk/Jack
          Elliott/Peggy Seeger/Geoff Muldaur/Charles River Valley Boys
14024   CHARLES RIVER VALLEY BOYS with TEX LOGAN-BLUEGRASS GET TOGETHER
14025   INSIDE DAVE VAN RONK
14026   MITCH GREENHILL-PICKIN' THE CITY BLUES
14027   MEET THE NEW STRANGERS
14028   Rev.GARY DAVIS-PURE RELIGION(reissue of BVLP1015)(87,88)
14029   RAMBLIN' JACK ELLIOTT-COUNTRY STYLE
14030   OLD TIME FIDDLING AT UNION GROVE,NORTH CAROLINA:Je Mainer/Thomas
          Holland/Morris Herbert/Charles Hawks/L.W.Lambert Jr./Bert
          Edwards/Esker Hutchins/Norman Edwards/Ray Childress/Kenneth
          Edwards/James Lindsay/Franklin Bailey/Larry Campbell
14031   HOLY MODAL ROUNDERS
14032   MAXINE SELLERS-FOLK SONGS
14033   Rev.GARY DAVIS-GUITAR AND BANJO(147)
14034
14035   THE LILLY BROTHERS-COUNTRY SONGS


TRU-SOUND label

TRU
15001   KING CURTIS-TROUBLE IN MIND(103)
15002   THE JIMMY NEELEY TRIO-MISIRLOU(95)
15003   THE LATIN JAZZ QUINTET-HOT SAUCE(95,105)
15004   ERNESTINE ALLEN-LET IT ROLL(106)
15005   CLEA BRADFORD-THESE DUES(107)
15006   KING CURTIS-OLD GOLD(114,115)
15007   JESSE POWELL-IT'S PARTY TIME(114,116,119)
15008   KING CURTIS-IT'S PARTY TIME(108,120)
15009   KING CURTIS-DOIN' THE DIXIE TWIST(121)
15010   EDDIE "BLUESMAN" KIRKLAND-THAT'S THE BLUES MAN(118,123)
15011   BUDDY LUCAS-DOWN HOME TURN AROUND(124,126)
15012   THE LATIN JAZZ QUINTET-THE CHANT(126)
15013   RHODA SCOTT-HEY,HEY,HEY(130,134)
15014   RHODA SCOTT-LIVE!AT THE KEY CLUB(138)
```

PRESTIGE label

PR
16001   PONY POINDEXTER-GUMBO(141)
16002   TRUMPET GIANTS(same as NJLP8296)(3,8,12)
16003   AHMED ABDUL-MALIK-EASTERN MOODS(141)
16004   GILDO MAHONES-SHOOTING HIGH(137,141,142)
16005   JOHNNY "HAMMOND" SMITH-LOOK OUT(same as NJLP8288)(never issued)
16006   JIMMY FORREST-SOUL STREET(same as NJLP8293)(never issued)
16007   TADD DAMERON-DAMERONIA(reissue of PRLP7037)(37)
16008   CLIFFORD BROWN MEMORIAL(reissue of PRLP7055)(23,257)
16009   ZOOT SIMS-TROTTING(reissue of PRLP7026)(8,11)
16010
16011   LEE KONITZ-EZZ-THETIC(reissue of NJLP8295)(10,19)

PRESTIGE INTERNATIONAL label

These albums are not described in this book

PR
25001   GEORGIA SEA ISLANDS,Vol.1
25002   GEORGIA SEA ISLANDS,Vol.2
25003   BALLADS AND BREAK DOWNS FROM THE SOUTHERN MOUNTAINS
25004   BANJO SONGS,BALLADS AND REELS FROM THE SOUTHERN MOUNTAINS
25005   DEEP SOUTH...SACRED AND SINFUL
25006   FOLK SONGS FROM THE OZARKS
25007   ALL DAY SINGING FROM "THE SACRED HARP"
25008   THE EASTERN SHORES
25009   BAD MAN BALLADS
25010   YAZOO DELTA BLUES AND SPIRITUALS
25011   SOUTHERN WHITE SPIRITUALS
25012   BELLEVILLE A CAPELLA CHOIR-HONOR THE LAMB
25013   MUSIC OF NEW GUINEA
25014   TRADITIONAL SONGS OF ONTARIO
25015
25016   BERRY FIELDS OF BLAIR

LIVELY ARTS label

30001   BILLY DEE WILLIAMS-LET'S MISBEHAVE
30002   A TASTE OF HERMOINE BADDELEY
30003   RODDY McDOWALL READS THE HORROR STORIES OF H.P.LOVECRAFT
30004   BURGESS MEREDITH READS RAY BRADBURY
30005   LARRY STORCH READS PHILIP ROTH'S EPSTEIN
30006   JAMES MASON READS THE IMP OF THE PERVERSE AND OTHER STORIES BY
        EDGAR ALLEN POE
30007   JAMES MASON READS HERMAN MELVILLE'S BARTLEBY,THE SCRIVENER
30008   MORRIS CARNOVSKY READS DOSTOEVSKY'S NOTES FROM UNDERGROUND
30009   NORMAN MAILER READS NORMAN MAILER

IRISH label

35001   MARGARET BARRY AND MICHAEL GORMAN-THE BLARNEY STONE
35002
35003   MICKEY AND MARY CARTON-THE IMMIGRANT IRISH BOY

NEAR EAST label

45001   SPERO SPYROS-GOLDEN SONGS OF GREECE(same as PR13001)
45002   SPERO SPYROS-MORE GOLDEN SONGS OF GREECE
45003   SPERO SPYROS-ANATOLIAN INTRODUCTION
45004   SPERO SPYROS-ANATOLIAN FEAST

TRU-SOUND label(Gospel Series)

TRU
60001   THE CLEFS OF CALVARY-BAPTIZED(128)
60002   GATE CITY SINGERS-PEACE IN THE VALLEY(125,129) ·
60003   CAPITOL CITY STARS-WE'VE COME THIS FAR BY FAITH(127,130)
60004   THE BACK HOME CHOIR-COME OUT OF THE WILDERNESS(128)
60005   PENTECOSTAL CHOIR-SAVED(129)
60006   PSALMS OF GRACE-TIME IS WINDING UP(129)
60007   THE CLEFS OF CALVARY-GOD'S LIGHT(143)

TRU-SOUND label(Latin American Series)

80001   ALFREDITO VALDES-SABRINA!(PACHANGA)
80002   ANDRES HERNANDEZ SEXTET CARIBE-"RECUERDOS"

2-LP SETS

SV4001   THE SWINGVILLE ALL STARS-THINGS AIN'T WHAT THEY USED TO BE
         (same as SVLP2024 + SVLP2025)(102,105)

PRESTIGE label

PR
24001   MILES DAVIS(same as PRLP7094 + PRLP7129)(38,43)
24002   MOSE ALLISON(reissue of PRLP7091 + PRLP7121)(47,56)
24003   JOHN COLTRANE(reissue of PRLP7123 + PRLP7142)(54,58)
24004   SONNY ROLLINS(14,24,28,29,36,37,39)
24005   MODERN JAZZ QUARTET(19,23,30,31,34)
24006   THELONIOUS MONK(18,19,24,26,28)
24007   YUSEF LATEEF(55,71,119)
24008   ERIC DOLPHY(reissue of NJLP8236 + NJLP8252)(78,86)
24009   CHARLIE PARKER(246,249)
24010   CHARLIE MINGUS(261)
24011   OSCAR PETERSON(not issued)
24012   MILES DAVIS-TALLEST TREES(22,25,27,30,43)
24013   JACK McDUFF-ROCK CANDY(74,85,98,120,134,137,140,142,206)
24014   JOHN COLTRANE-MORE LASTING THAN BRONZE(reissue of PRLP7105 +
         PRLP7188)(53,54,58)
24015   JAMES MOODY(25,26,28,31,35,36,192)
24016   GERRY MULLIGAN/CHET BAKER(11,162,254,255)
24017   KING PLEASURE-THE SOURCE(16,19,24,25,30,263)
24018   MONGO SANTAMARIA-AFRO ROOTS(not included)
24019   STAN GETZ-FIVE BROTHERS(1,2,4,6,263)
24020   CLIFFORD BROWN IN PARIS(258,259?)
24021   GENE AMMONS/DODO MARMAROSA-JUG & DODO(265,266)
24022   MILES DAVIS-COLLECTOR'S ITEMS(12,21,37,260)
24023   RED GARLAND-JAZZ JUNCTION(reissue of PRLP7130 + PRLP7181)(56)
24024   THE GREATEST JAZZ CONCERT EVER(256,257)
24025   KENNY BURRELL-ALL DAY LONG & ALL NIGHT LONG(reissue of PRLP7073
         + PRLP7081)(45)
24026   CAL TJADER-MONTEREY CONCERTS(263)
24027   ERIC DOLPHY-COPENHAGEN CONCERT(reissue of PR7304 + PR7366)(264,
         265)
24028   CHARLIE MINGUS-REINCARNATION OF A LOVE BIRD(274)
24029   DUKE ELLINGTON-THE GOLDEN DUKE(243,244,251,252)
24030   DIZZY GILLESPIE-IN THE BEGINNING(241,242,243,244)
24031   BEN WEBSTER AT WORK IN EUROPE(272,273)
24032   ART FARMER-FARMER'S MARKET(23,25,26,27,29,35,44)
24033   KING CURTIS-I REMEMBER KING CURTIS(reissue of NJLP8237 + PRLP7222
         (79,89)
24034   MILES DAVIS-WORKIN' & STEAMIN'(reissue of PRLP7166 + PRLP7200)
         (38,43)
24035   YUSEF LATEEF-BLUES FOR THE ORIENT(reissue of MVLP22 + PRLP7122)
         (55,114)
24036   GENE AMMONS-JUGANTHOLOGY(33,38,40,45,49)
24037   JOHN COLTRANE-BLACK PEARLS(reissue of PR7316 + PR7292)(58,60,65)
24038   RAY BRYANT-ME AND THE BLUES(reissue of PRLP7098 + NJLP8213)(49,
         65)
24039   EDDIE "LOCKJAW" DAVIS-THE COOKBOOK(reissue of PRLP7141 + PRLP
         7161)(61,65)
24040   BUCK CLAYTON/BUDDY TATE-KANSAS CITY NIGHTS(reissue of SVLP2017
         + SVLP2030)(95,114)
24041   OSCAR PETERSON & STEPHANE GRAPPELLI(274)
24042   TAL FARLOW-GUITAR PLAYER(196,261)
24043   EARL HINES-ANOTHER MONDAY DATE(261,262)

```
P-
24044  SONNY STITT-GENESIS(3,4,5,7,8,9,10)
24045  DUKE ELLINGTON SECOND SACRED CONCERT(269)
24046  25 YEARS OF PRESTIGE:Lennie Tristano(1)/Stan Getz(1)/Kai Winding
       (2)/Fats Navarro(3)/Wardell Gray(4)/Leo Parker(7)/Miles Davis(9)
       Joe Holiday(13)/Thelonious Monk(24)/King Pleasure(25)/Earl
       Coleman(44)/John Coltrane(50)/Red Garland(60)/Benny Golson(69)/·
       Eddie "Lockjaw" Davis(73)/Eric Dolphy(95)/Kenny Burrell(148)/
       Gene Ammons(198)/Dexter Gordon(201)
24047  DIZZY GILLESPIE-THE GIANT(274)
24048  MILT JACKSON-OPUS DE FUNK(27,33,266)
24049  GIL EVANS/TADD DAMERON-THE ARRANGER'S TOUCH:Gil Evans(55)/Tadd
       Dameron(23,37)
24050  SONNY ROLLINS-SAXOPHONE COLOSSUS AND MORE(37,39,42)
24051  JAM SESSION IN SWINGVILLE(102,105)
24052  PIANO GIANTS:Duke Ellington(251)/Earl Hines(262)/Art Tatum(241)/
       Erroll Garner(241)/Thelonious Monk(18)/Bud Powell(256)/Lennie
       Tristano(1)/Al Haig(5)/George Shearing(262)/John Lewis(34)/
       Horace Silver(25)/Hampton Hawes(18)/Bobby Timmons(263)/Oscar
       Peterson(274)/Phineas Newborn(64)/Ahmad Jamal(273)/Red Garland
       (52)Bill Evans(263)/Wynton Kelly(268)/Herbie Hancock(272)/Joe
       Zawinul(273)/Keith Jarrett(274)/McCoy Tyner(274)
24053  ERIC DOLPHY/RON CARTER-MAGIC(reissue of NJLP8265 + NJLP8270)(95,
       107)
24054  MILES DAVIS-DIG(9,12,21)
24055  MOSE ALLISON-CREEK BANK(reissue of PRLP7137 + PRLP7152)(58,62)
24056  JOHN COLTRANE-THE STARDUST SESSION(61)
24057  ILLINOIS JACQUET-HOW HIGH THE MOON(185,188,193,195)
24058  THE GENE AMMONS STORY-THE 78 ERA(5,7,8,9,10,13,29,31,35)
24059  JOHN COLTRANE/KENNY BURRELL(reissue of NJLP8217 + NJLP8276)(49,
       59)
24060  OLIVER NELSON-IMAGES(reissue of NJLP8243 + NJLP8255)(82,99)
24061  ZOOT SIMS-ZOOT CASE(8,11,17,27)
24062  WARDELL GRAY-CENTRAL AVENUE(4,6,7,15,21)
24063  HANK MOBLEY-MESSAGES(reissue of PRLP7061 + PRLP7082)(40,41)
24064  MILES DAVIS-GREEN HAZE(reissue of PRLP7007 + PRLP7014)(33,36)
24065  PHIL WOODS-ALTOLOGY(39,49)
24066  DONALD BYRD-HOUSE OF BYRD(reissue of PRLP7062 + PRLP7080)(41,43)
24067  EARLY BONES:J.J.Johnson(2)/Kai Winding(2)/Bennie Green(12)/Jay
       and Kai(29)/Bennie Green(33)
24068  MAL WALDRON-ONE & TWO(reissue of PRLP7090 + PRLP7111)(44,50,52)
24069  JOHN COLTRANE-WHEELIN'(50,55)
24070  ERIC DOLPHY-STATUS(reissue of PRLP7350 + PRLP7382)(78,110,264,
       265)
24071  THE GENE AMMONS STORY-ORGAN COMBOS(83,118)
24072  GEORGE BENSON/JACK McDUFF(148,163)
24073  DUKE ELLINGTON CARNEGIE HALL CONCERT DECEMBER 1944(240)
24074  DUKE ELLINGTON CARNEGIE HALL CONCERT JANUARY 1946(242)
24075  DUKE ELLINGTON CARNEGIE HALL CONCERT DECEMBER 1947(244)
24076  JACKIE McLEAN-CONTOUR(reissue of PRLP7035 + PRLP7048)(37,40)
24077  MILES DAVIS-TUNE UP(22,25,26,30)
24078  RED GARLAND-REDISCOVERED MASTERS(61,69,100)
24079  THE GENE AMMONS STORY-GENTLE JUG(reissue of MV18 + MV28)(97,126)
24080  ROLAND KIRK-PRE-RAHSAAN(reissue of PRLP7210 + PR7615)(108,189)
24081  FIRST SESSIONS 1949-50:Lennie Tristano(1)/Lee Konitz(2,3)/Don
       Lanphere(2)/Kai Winding(2)/Fats Navarro(3)/J.J.Johnson(3)/
       Wardell Gray(4)/Sonny Stitt(5)/Eddie "Lockjaw" Davis(5)/Al Haig
       (5)/Leo Parker(7)
24082  SONNY ROLLINS-TAKIN' CARE OF BUSINESS(36,39,44)
24083  COLEMAN HAWKINS-THE REAL THING(64,69,74)
24084  JOHN COLTRANE-ON A MISTY NIGHT(42,44)
```

P-
24085   ERIC DOLPHY-FIRE WALTZ(84,107)(reissue of NJLP 8247 + NJLP8269)
24086   JAKI BYARD-GIANT STEPS(100,121)(incl.NJLP8256 + NJLP8273)
24087   DEXTER GORDON-POWER!(193)(reissue of PR7623 + PR7680)

<u>PRESTIGE label</u>

P-
66001   GARY BARTZ NTU TROOP-I'VE KNOWN RIVERS AND OTHER BODIES(214)
66002   CHARLES EARLAND-LEAVING THIS PLANET(216)

PRESTIGE label

P-
34001   THE GREAT CONCERT OF CHARLES MINGUS(267)
34002   THE GREAT CONCERT OF ERIC DOLPHY(110)
34003   THE GREAT CONCERT OF CECIL TAYLOR(273)
34004   THE DUKE ELLINGTON CARNEGIE HALL CONCERT-JANUARY 1943(239)

16 2/3 rpm Albums

PRESTIGE label

LP16-
1   MILT JACKSON(same as PRLP7003 + PRLP7005)(33,34)
2   BILLY TAYLOR(same as PRLP7015 + PRLP7016)(18,19,24,25)
3   MILES DAVIS(same as PRLP7109 + PRLP7150)(27,30,43)
4   TROMBONES(same as PRLP7023 + PRLP7030):J.J.Johnson(2)/Kai Winding
     (2)/Bennie Green(12,17)/Jay and Kai(29,30)
5   GEORGE WALLINGTON/PHIL WOODS(same as NJLP8207 + NJLP8304)(47,54)
6   same as PRLP7280 + NJLP8305(50,52)

Table of Equivalent
Foreign Issues

(12in. LPs)

<u>Labels:</u>

English issues(E)   Esquire 32-000 series
Fontana 688200 series(mono)
        888200 series(stereo)
Stateside SL10000 series
Xtra 5000 series

French issues(F)   Barclay 84000 series   Vogue(LDM/SLDP/CLDPseries
Bel Air 331000 series   (SLVLXP series
Fantasy 5900/6000 series
Prestige CPRX240000 series/HTX series
Voix de son Maitre FELP10000 series

German issues(G)   Bellaphon BJS40000 series
              BLST6500 series

Japanese issues(J)   Prestige SMJ6500 series

US issue	US reissue	(E)	(F)	(G)	(J)
MV2		688200ZL			
MV22	7319	688202ZL			
		888202ZY			
MV26		5047			
MV27		5045			
MV29		5048			
MV32	7322	688204ZL			
		SL10111			
1002	14013		6027		
1005/1020			5973		
1006)	F-24717		6017		
1012)					
1014	7722		LDM30173		
1015	14028				
	7805				
1015)	F-24704		5986		
1032)					
1016	7723		SLVLXP512		
1022			LDM30202		
1025		5025			
1029	1081	5044			
	7831				
1033/1002	F-24708		6027		
1045		5036	SLDP829		
1046		5051			
1053		5060			
1065			CLDP830		
1067		5059			
1075			CPRX240619		
1086		SL10155			
2017			FELP15001		
2032			FELP15002		

US issue	US reissue	(E)	(F)	(G)	(J)
7001	7664	32-010			
7002	7256	32-011	84027		
	7337	SL10161			
	8214				
7003	7224	32-009/5016	84016		
7004	7250	32-027	84062		SMJ6522
			FELP10013		
7005		32-024	84028		
			FELP10017		
7006	7251	32-014	84044		
		5009			
7007	7221	32-012	84029		SMJ6518
			FELP10012		
7008		32-016	84045		
		SL10144			
7009		32-023			
		SL10145			
7010	7675			BJS40150	
7012	7281	32-062	FELP10003		SMJ6525
7013		32-052			
7014	7254	32-021	CPRX240757		SMJ6531
7017	8289	32-037	FELP10015		
7018		32-020			SMJ6515
7020	7246/7750	32-038			
		5026			
7021		32-033			
7022	7252	5002	84061		
7023		32-036	84054		
7024	7248	32-049	84055		SMJ6508
		5015	FELP10008		
7025	7168	32-118			SMJ6523
		5018			
7026	16009	5001			
7027	7159	32-119	84058		
	7508				
7029	7269	32-035	84057		BJS4057
	7856				
7030		32-145	FELP10010		
7031	8278	32-042	84049		
7032		32-032			SMJ6517
7033	8309	32-040			
7034	7540	32-028	84050	BJS40118	SMJ6530
7035	8263	32-041			
	7757				
7037	16007	32-034			
	7842				
7038	7291	32-025	84051		
	7821		FELP10006		
7039	7654	32-047			
7043	7670	32-039		BJS40145	SMJ6536
7044		32-030	84052		SMJ6526
7046		32-026	84053		
7047	7657	32-058	84060	BJS40149	SMJ6521
7053	7245	SL10152	84082		
	7363				
7054		32-088	2C054-10134		SMJ6527
7055	7662/8301	SL10122			
	16008				

US issue	US reissue	(E)	(F)	(G)	(J)
7057		32-124	FELP10026 CPRX240576		SMJ6502
7058	7433	32-155	84059	BJS40117	
7059		32-134	HTX40406		
7060	7781	32-097			
7061	8311/7661	32-029	84056		
7062		32-072 5010			
7064		32-046			
7065		32-043			
7066	8294	5022			
7068	8290	32-111			
7070	7247/7745			BJS40154	SMJ6538
7073	7289	32-140		BJS40102	
7074	7249	32-059			SMJ6539
7075	7169/7656	32-115	84080	BJS40144	
7076	7608	32-098		BJS40134	SMJ6528
7077		32-112			
7079	7326	32-045 SL10164	84084 CPRX240857	BJS40104	
7080		32-060			
7081	7277	32-107			
7083		32-077			
7084	8310	32-065			
7088	7308		CPRX240689		
7090					SMJ6509
7091		32-051			
7092		32-093 5010			
7094		32-048	84077 CPRX240530		SMJ6534
7095	7553	32-075		BJS40133	
7098	8227	32-068	84079		
7100		32-063			
7101		32-054			
7102		32-120			
7103		32-057			
7104		32-113			
7105	7609	32-079		BJS40126	SMJ6547
7106		32-084			
7109		32-090	FELP10021 CPRX240802		SMJ6520
7111					SMJ6510 LPR88055
7113		32-056			SMJ6504
7115		32-050			
7116		32-074			
7118	7278	32-080			
7120	8215/7756	32-070 5034			
7121		32-071			
7122	8261/7398	32-069			
7123	7651	32-091		BJS40148	
7125	8308	32-143			
7126		32-085			
7127	2036	32-067			
7129		32-068	84074		SMJ6532
7130		32-099			LPJ70030 SMJ6551
7131					SMJ6549
7133		32-078			
7134	7632			BJS40135	
7135		32-073			

US issue	US reissue	(E)	(F)	(G)	(J)
7137		32-083			
7138	2035	32-082	HTX40341		
7139		32-096			
7141	7660	32-104			
7142	7531	32-089	84078	BJS4063	SMJ6559
7143		32-086			
7144	2004	32-092	FELP10023		
7145	7787	32-110			
7146		32-147			
7147	2037	32-087			
7149	2038	32-095			
7150		32-100	FELP15003 CPRX240745		SMJ6529
7151	7835	32-114			
7152		32-094			
7153	2023	32-122	CPRX240583 331008		
7156	2039 7857	32-102 5029			
7157		32-116			
7158		32-101			SMJ6542
7161	7782		331002		
7165		32-154			
7166		32-108	84083 CPRX240383		SMJ6503
7167	7790	32-117	331005		
7170		32-126			
7171		32-128			
7175		32-184			
7181		32-136			SMJ6552
7186		32-127			
7187		32-167			
7188	7581	32-129	84086		SMJ6505
7189		32-131			
7191	7407	32-144	331007		
7193		32-146			
7200	7580	32-138	84087	BJS4054	SMJ6533 SMJ6555
7201					
7206	7834	32-174/5019			
7207		32-175			
7209	8325	32-166			SMJ6553
7210	7450	32-164	FELP10025	BJS4062	
7213	7746			BJS40155	SMJ6560
7215		32-171			
7223		32-189			
7225				BJS40100	
7226		32-186			
7229					SMJ6550
7232		32-182			
7235		32-192			
7236		32-188			
7240			FELP10007	BJS40101	
7242		32-194			
7243	7825	32-179		BJS40163	SMJ6562
7255	7434			BJS40111	
7257	7552	32-178			
7258			FELP10020		
7259		32-196			
7268			FELP10004		SMJ6564
7274		SL10060			
7279		SL10106			
7280					SMJ6541
7282			FELP10005		

US issue	US reissue	(E)	(F)	(G)	(J)
7292			FELP10016		SMJ6558
7294					SMJ6573
7300		SL10088	FELP10009		
7301			FELP10018		
7303		5027			
7304		SL10104	PRX40441		
7309		SL10102			
7314		SL10105			
7316		SL10124			SMJ6561
7323		SL10101			
7327		SL10139			
7331			FELP10024		
7333		SL10142			
7334		SL10160	HTX40343 CPRX240343		SMJ6574
7336		SL10159			
7338				BJS40116	
7347		SL10163			
7349				BJS40105	
7352		SL10168			
7353		SL10162			SMJ6563
7356		SL10114			
7358		SL10146			
7359		SL10151			
7361		SL10150			
7362		SL10165			
7364			HTX40403		
7368		SL10154			
7363		SL10152	HTX40416		
7373				BJS40106	
7378					SMJ6557
7386			CPRX240533		
7388				BJS40107	
7389				BJS40108	
7391	7719	SL10169			
7401				BJS40109	
7405		SL10180			
7419			CPRX240584		
7421			CPRX240755		
7424				BJS40131	
7425				BJS40110	
7430			HTX40422		
7468				BJS40112	
7485			CPRX240756		
7550				BJS40115	
7584				BJS40122	
7587				BJS40123	
7593				BJS40152	
7615				BJS40128	
7623				BJS40129	
7628				BJS40130	
7641				BJS40137	
7650				BJS40147	
7655				BJS40143	
7673				BJS4056	
7674				BJS40161	
7677				BJS40151	
7709				BJS4055	
7744				BJS40153	
7749				BJS40157	
7761				BJS40158	
7794				BJS40162	
7812				BJS40159	

US issue	US reissue	(E)	(F)	(G)	(J)
7847				BJS40167	
7853				BJS4058	
8201					SMJ6511
8203		32-137			
8207		32-132			
8208					SMJ6512
8210		32-103			
8211		5007			
8212		32-141			
		5035			
8213	7837	32-106	84085	BJS40165	
8217		32-156			SMJ6540
8219		32-149			
8220		32-105	331004		
8221			331001		
8223		32-142			
8225					SMJ6513
8228					SMJ6554
8230		32-151			
8234	7748	32-139			
		5040			
8235		32-125			
8236	7311	32-123	FELP10019	BJS40103	SMJ6514
			331006		
8237	7789	32-161			
8239		32-152			
8242		32-176			
8243	8324	32-148			SMJ6565
		5039			
8244		32-172			
8245		32-163			
8247		32-133			SMJ7560/6566
8248		32-165			
8251					SMJ6568
8252	7652	32-153		BJS40142	SMJ6567
		5054			
8253		5030			SMJ6507
8255		32-168			SMJ6506
8257	7607			BJS40125	
8258	7665	32-187			VIP5019
8260	7611	32-173	2C054-10135		SMJ6572
8262		32-181			
8265	7843			BJS40166	SMJ6570
8269	7579	5006			SMJ6571
8270	7747	32-193		BJS40156	SMJ6569
8274		32-185			
8276	7532				LPR8856/SMJ
					6556
8280		5046			
8281		32-180			
8295					SMJ6524
8296	16002	SL10103	FELP10011		
14006	7718	SL10166			
14011		SL10167			
14021	7806	SL10110			
14025	7716	SL10153			
14029	7804	SL10143			
24001				BLST6511	
24002				BLST6512	
24003				BLST6513	
24004				BLST6514	
24005				BLST6515	
24006				BLST6516	

US issue	(G)
24007	BLST6517
24008	BLST6518
24009	BLST6519
24010	BLST6520
24012	BLST6524
24013	BLST6525
24014	BLST6527
24016	BLST6528
24019	BLST6531
24021	BLST6532
7295+7386	BLST6547
7455+7462	BLST6541

NOTES

Index of Artists

This index includes all artists mentioned in parts 1 and 2,with
numbers of pages where they appear as leaders or sidemen(numbers in
parentheses).The index includes also album titles for all star albums
issued without leader.

BOND,Jimmy(b)(141)
BONNEMERE,Eddie(p) 154
BONNER,Joe(p)(218)
BOOKER,Walter(b)(189 217 219 273)
BOOZIER,Henry(tp)(27)
BOSTIC,Earl(as)(242)
BOSTON,Charles(org)(168)
BOUCAYA,William(bs)(258)
BOUCHETY,Jean(b)(244 247)
BOWIE,Lester(tp)(273)
BOWIE,Pat(vo) 155 163
BOWMAN,Dave(p)(242)
BOWN,Patti(p)(107 116 125 126 127)
BOYD,Jimmy(p)(26 28 31 35 36)
BOYD,Manny(fl)(210)
BOYD,Nelson(b)(3 155)
BOYKINS,Ronnie(b)(148 173)
BRACKEEN,JoAnne(p,org)(168 175 177
   180 183 184 187)
BRADLEY,Bill(dm)(37)
BRADFORD,Clea(vo) 107
BRAITH,George(ts) 166 172 173 180
BRAITHWAITE,Gilbert(perc)(173)
BRAKE,Bryan(dm)(216)
BRANNON,Teddy(p)(12)
BRASHEAR,Oscar(tp)(209 213 219 220
   221 222)
BRAUD,Wellman(b)(235)
BRAUER,Buzz(fl,oboe,ts,bs)(208 209)
BREHM,Simon(b)(250 253 255 257 259)
BRESLIN,Paul(b)(165)
BRICE,Percy(dm)(30 32 262)
BRIDGE,Lucius(vo,g,wbd)(228)
BRIDGES,Willie(ts)(207)
BRIDGEWATER,Cecil(tp)(204)
BRIGGS,Arthur(tp)(237)
BRIGGS,Freddie(perc)(173)
BROBERG,Bo(tp)(151 152)
BRONSON,Melvin(el b)(216)
BROOKMEYER,Bob(vtb,p) 25 33
BROOKS,Gene(dm)(113)
BROOKS,Roy(dm)(98 106 107 135 140
   162 163 197 201)
BROOSHINE,Eddie(b)(210)
BROWN,Billy(p)(70 79 82)
BROWN,Buster "Harpie"(hca)(94)
BROWN,Carl(b)(117)
BROWN,Charlie(ts)(203 207)
BROWN,Clifford(tp)(23 37)257 258
   259
BROWN,Eddie(b)(241)
BROWN,Everett(dm)(186)
BROWN,Garnett(tb)(170 177 204 206
   213 218)
BROWN,George(dm)(29 31 154 264)
BROWN,Hillard(dm)(240)
BROWN,John(as)(242 244 246)
BROWN,Julian(org)(186)
BROWN,Lawrence(tb)(235 239 240 242
   243 244 245 269)
BROWN,Phil(dm)(12)
BROWN,Piney(vo)(225)

BROWN,Ray(b)(242 243 244 266 267
   270)
BROWN,Sonny(dm)(150)
BROWN,Tyrone(b)(183 199)
BRUNO,Sam(b)(134 175)
BRYANT,Bob(tp,arr)(89,141,208)
BRYANT,Ray(p)(34 36 47)49(59 61 62
   64)65(66 67 68 69 70 71 155)
BRYANT,Rusty(as,ts)(189)192(193
   194)196(197 198)200(201 203)204
   206 210(211)213 218
BRYANT,Tom(b)(69)
BUCKNER,Milt(p,org)(188 193)268
BUDIMIR,Dennis(g)(208)
BUDWIG,Monty(b)(192)
BUFFINGTON,Jim(frh)(115 209)
BUNKER,Larry(vb,dm)(18 30)
BUNN,Jimmy(p)(7)
BURGESS,Lucille(vo)(185 186)
BURKE,Vinnie(b)(41 45)
BURMAN,Andrew(dm)(248 249 250 251
   252 253 254 256)
BURMAN,Hasse(b)(258)
BURNS,Dave(tp)(25 26 28 31 35 36
   190 242 243 244 246)
BURNS,Norman(dm)(246)
BURRELL,Dave(p)(273)
BURRELL,Kenny(g)(45)46 47(48 49)
   51(52 53 59)59(63 64 99 108 132
   133)133(134 136 137)137(138 141
   146)148(153 154 155 158 161 162)
BURRIS,J.C.(dm)(91)
BUSHELL,Garvin(bassoon)(50)
BUSHNELL,Bob(b)(114 115 121 124 126
   180 181 191 192 193 195 196 197
   199 203)
BUSTER,Eddie(org)(264)
BUTCHER,George(org)(142)
BUTLER,Billy(g)(108 114 115 118 120
   121 123 168 169 173 188 189)191
   (195)195(197 198 199)199 200 203
   (204 206)207
BUTTACAVOLI:see Ronnie JAMES
BUTTERFIELD,Don(tu)(41 115 117)
BYARD,Jaki(p)(78 95)100(104)121
   (124 144)158 159(164)165(170 173)
   174 181 186(188)189(191)194(267
   274)
BYAS,Don(ts) 243 244 247 270
BYERS,Billy(tb)(34 57 117 144)
BYRD,Donald(tp)(37 38 39 40)41(43
   45 47 56 57 58 60 261)
BYRD,Jerry(g)(161)

CABINEERS,The(vo) 10 14
CABLES,George(p)(210 221)
CACERES,Ernie(bs)(50 241)
CADAVIEJO,Juan(conga)(155)
CAIAZZA,Nick(ts)(242)
CALDWELL,Buddy(conga)(195 197 199
   201 202 203 204 205 206 207 208
   212)
CALHOUN,Eddie(b)(134)

CALIMAN,Hadley(fl,ts)(209 213 218 219 220 221 222)
CALLENDER,Red(b)(23)
CAMERO,Candido(conga)(28 33 38 151 196)
CAMPBELL,Billy(tb)(218)
CAMPBELL,Wilbur(dm)(200)
CANDIDO,See CAMERO
CANDOLI,Conte(tp)(186 245 256)
CANTO,Humberto (conga)(274)
CAPERS,Bobby(as)(95 105 226)
CAPITOL CITY STARS(vo) 127 130
CAREY,Scoops(as)(244)
CARISI,Johnny(tp)(55)
CARLS,Emmett(ts)(245)
CARLTON,Ben(b)(247)
CARN,Jean(vo)(219)
CARNEY,Bill(dm)(174 179 182 184 187)
CARNEY,Harry(bs)(235 239 240 242 243 244 245 269)
CARROLL,Barbara(p)(247)
CARROLL,Joe(vo) 20
CARSON,Tee(arr)(272)
CARTER,Benny(as) 126 235(236)236 (239)243
CARTER,Betty(vo)(19)
CARTER,James(whistling)(219)
CARTER,Jay(g)(172)
CARTER,Jimmy(org)(196)
CARTER,Ron(b,cello)(86 95 96 99 100 104)107(107 121 123 165 174 182 186 191 197 202 206 211 212 215 218 220 266 272)
CARVER,Wayman(as)(236)
CARY,Dick(alto horn,p)(43 50 51)
CASAMENTI,Al(g)(43 50)
CASEY,Al(g)(5)76 93(103 106 243 247)
CASEY,Floyd(wbd,kazoo)(110)
CASEY,Gene(p)(84 86 88)103 108
CASTLEMAN,Jeff(b)(269)
CATLETT,Buddy(b)(127 136)
CATLETT,Sidney(dm)(235 236 241 243)
CATS,The 49
CAUSEY,Clyde(vo,hca)(230)
CAXTON,Bob(conga)(253)
CENTENO,Hector(g)(214 215)
CENTRAL CONN.STATE COLLEGE SINGERS (vo)(269)
CERA,Pete:see Pete JOLLY
CHAILLOU,Maurice(dm)(237)
CHALOFF,Serge(bs)(247)
CHAMBERS,Henderson(tb)(29 31)
CHAMBERS,Joe(dm)(166)
CHAMBERS,Paul(b)(30 33 35 36 37 38 39 41 42 43 44 48 49 52 53 54 55 57 58 59 60 61 64 65 70 72 79 171 173 174 175 177 180 187 261)
CHAMBLEE,Eddie(ts) 146
CHANDLER,Gary(tp)(201 205)
CHANDLER,Leon(Ngudu)(dm)(209 213 218 219 220 222)

CHANDLER,Taft(ts)(131)
CHAPIN,Jim(dm) 34
CHAPUT,Roger(g)(237 239)
CHARLES,Dennis(dm)(56)
CHARLES,Teddy(vb,p) 13 19 20 21 23 24 25 31(46 49 51)53(173 260)
CHASE,Jiggs(org)(181)
CHEATHAM,Doc(tp)(97 118 241)
CHERRY,Don(tp)(117)
CHERRY,Otis(dm)(103)
CHIBOUST,Noel(tp)(237)
CHIEF Bay(African dm)(131)
CHILDERS,Buddy(tp)(208)
CHILDS,Alvin A.(preach) 14
CHOCOLATE DANDIES,The 236
CHOIRS of ST.HILDA & ST.HUGH'S SCHOOL(vo)(269)
CHRISTENSEN,Jon(dm)(27)
CHRISTIAN,Jodie(p)(200 207)
CHRISTIANSSON,Bengt(fl)(151 152)
CHRISTLIEB,Pete(ts,bs)(186 208)
CINDERELLA,Joe(g)(38 39 41 45 50)
CLARE,Kenny(dm)(270 271)
CLARK,Dick(tp,ts)(236 238)
CLARK,Garnet(p) 238
CLARK,James(g)(202 205)
CLARK,Jim(ts)(15)
CLARK,Sonny(p)(21 259)
CLARKE,Arthur "Babe"(reeds)(110 111 204 218 222)
CLARKE,Buck(conga)(75)
CLARKE,Kenny(dm)(19 21 23 24 25 26 27 30 31 33 214 242 243 246)246 (249 251)251(267)268 270 271(274)
CLARKE,Stanley(b)(209 210)
CLAY,Clarence(vo,accordion)(231)
CLAY,Omar(perc)(206)
CLAYTON,Buck(tp)(62 77)95 114 243
CLEFS OF CALVARY(vo) 128 143
CLEVELAND,Jimmy(tb)(23 27 55 56 63 89 129 208 257 258 259)
COBB,Arnett(ts) 66(67)68 75 92
COBB,Jimmy(dm)(59 61 165 263 266 268)
COBHAM,Billy(dm)(208 212)
COCHRAN,Todd:see BAYETE
COE,Gene(tp)(208)
COE,Tony(ts)(270 271)
COGGINS,Gil(p)(54 57)
COHEN,Teddy:see Teddy CHARLES
COHN,Al(ts)(1 17 21 42 247 260)260
COLE,Cozy(dm)(238 240 241)
COLE,June(b)(238)
COLEMAN,Bill(tp)(238 239 247)
COLEMAN,Earl(vo)(31 35)37 39(44 79) 247
COLEMAN,George(ts)(162 185 191 193 194 207)
COLEMAN,Willie(vb)(95 105)
COLES,Elmer(tp)(209)
COLES,Johnny(tp)(155 267)
COLLETTE,Buddy(ts)(221)

COLLIER,Robert(conga)(15)
COLLINS,Augusta Lee(dm)(211)
COLLINS,Booker(b)(238)
COLLINS,Burt(tb)(144)
COLLINS,John(g)(246)
COLLINS,Lester "Shad"(tp)(56 62
   235 239)
COLLINS,Rudy(dm)(131 132 191 198)
COLLOWAY,Jimmy(timbales)(154)
COLTRANE,John(ts)(36 38 42 43 44 48
   49 50 52)52 53 54(55 56 57)58 59
   60 61 65
COMBELLE,Alix(ts)(237 239)
COMEGEYS,Leon(tb)(243)
CONDON,Eddie(g)(238)
CONDOUANT,André(g)(267)
CONLON,Frank(bongo)(29)
CONLON SINGERS,The Jud(vo)(262)
CONNORS,Chuck(bass tb)(269)
CONTEMPORARY JAZZ ENSEMBLE 23
COOK,Junior(ts)(178 187)
COOKIES,The(vo)(103)
COOKS,Donald(b)(122)
COOLIN' 49
COOPER,George "Buster"(tb)(62 66
   136 269)
COPELAND,Ray(synth)(219)
COPELAND,Ray(tp)(26 54)
COPELAND,Rudy(vo)(216)
COREA,Chick(p)(150 194 198)
CORNELL,Butch(org)(202 206 211)
CORRAO,Vinnie(g)(167 168 169 173)
CORREA,William(Willie BOBO)(dm,
   timbales)(127 135 155 263)
COSTA,Eddie(p,vb)(57 127 128)
COTTON,James(vo,hca)(156)
COUNCE,Curtis(b)(23 24)
COURTNEY,Neil(b)(23)
COX,Alphonse(tp)(237)
COX,Kenny(p)(137)
CRAIG,Ann(vo)(185 186)
CRANSHAW,Bob(b)(148 150 176 177 179
   182 183 185 188 191 192 214)
CREQUE,Neal(p)(178 181 186 192 198
   207)
CRISS,Sonny(as)(7)171 175 179 183
   186 188 192
CROCKETT,Greg(g)(216)
CROONA,Per Arne(bs)(248)
CROSBY,Harper(b)(15)
CROSBY,Israel(b)(238)
CROW,Bill(b)(28 260)
CROWDER,Robert(perc)(150)
CROWE,Austin(p)(99 104 120)
CUNNINGHAM,Bob(b,dm)(164 168 169)
CURSON,Ted(tp) 135
CURTIS,King(ts) 79(85 88 89)89(92)
   103(106)108 114 115 118 120 121
   123(225)
CURTIS,William(b)(114)
CURTIS,William(dm)(171)
CUTSHALL,Cutty(tb)(118)
CYRILLE,Andrew(dm)(99 105 120 133
   273)

D'AMICO,Hank(cl)(242)
D'HELLEMMES,Eugène(b,tb)(237 239)
DAAWUD,Talib(tp)(242 243)
DABNEY,Eli(tb)(10 13)
DABONNEVILLE,André(ts)(258)
DAILEY,Albert(p)(164 220)
DAMERON,Tadd(p,arr) 23 37 44
DANIELS,Eddie(ts,cl) 170
DANIELS,Lynn(vo)(185 186)
DANIELS,Warren(ts)(203)
DANIELSON,Palle(b)(271)
DARR,Jerome(g)(77)
DAUNER,Wolfgang(p)(268)
DAVERN,Kenny(cl)(132)
DAVIS,Art(b)(115 116 117 122 127
   128)
DAVIS,Carl(o)(5)
DAVIS,Charles(bs)(136 144)
DAVIS,Eddie "Lockjaw"(ts)5(12)61
   (61)63 65(66 67)68(70)73(74)75
   79 88 89(96)96 127 134(268)
DAVIS,Rev"Blind"Gary(vo,g) 87
   88 111 133 147 229
DAVIS,George(fl)(273)
DAVIS,George(g)(221)
DAVIS,Kay(vo)(240 242 244 245)
DAVIS,Lem(as) 13(14)14(16)
DAVIS,Leonard(tp)(235)
DAVIS,Lloyd(g)(180 181 207)
DAVIS,Miles(tp) 9(10)12 21 22 25
   26 27 30 33 34 36 37 38 43(246)
   260
DAVIS,Nathan(fl,ss,ts)(267)
DAVIS,Richard(b)(110 129 144 146
   151 153 154 165 166 168 169 170
   173 184 186 187 188 189 191 232
DAVIS,Steve(b)(163 190)
DAVIS,Victor(el b,org)(172)
DAVIS,Walter(p)(68 171 173 175)
DAVIS,Wild Bill(org)(66)
DAVIS,Will(p)(148)
DAVISON,Joseph(vo)(125)
DAWSON,Alan(dm) (144 146 151 154
   158 159 161 164 165 168 169?
   170 171 173 175 177 178 179
   182 183 185 186 188 189 191 192
   196 200 257 258 259)
DE BREST,Spanky(b)(48 57)
DE HAAS,Eddie(b)(84)
DE JOHNETTE,Jack(dm)(187 188 194
   198)217 220(272)
DE LA ROSA,Frank(b)(272)
DE PARIS,Sidney(tp)(113 132)
DE PARIS,Wilbur(tb)(235 242 243
   244)
DE RIENZO,Allen(tp)(215 217 218
   219)
DE SOTA,Raymond(p)(239)
DE SOUZA,Raul(tb)(220)
DE VOL,Frank(arr)(272)
DEAN,Alan(vo)(246)
DEARIE,Blossom(vo)(16 248)
DEMPSEY,Ray(g)(256)
DENGLER,John(bass sax,wbd)(77)

[359]

DENNIS,Kenny(dm)(63)
DEUCHAR,Jimmy(tp)(268 270 271)
DEVENS,George(vb,perc)(218)
DEVERE,Dikkie(dm)(253)
DIAZ,Phil(bongos)(84)
DICKENSON,Vic(tb)(8 74 105 118 139)
DICKERSON,Dwight(p)(208)
DICKERSON,Walt(vb) 99 104 120 133
DIEHL,Eddie(g)(118 120 121 136 166
   169 170 173 231)
DIEVAL,Jack(p)(249 250)
DILLARD,Bill(tp)(235 236 239)
DIMITRIADES,Peter(v)(184)
DIOUF,Zak(perc)(221)
DIXIEAIRES,The(vo) 15
DIXON,Ben(dm)(48 98 166 172 182
   199)
DIXON,Eric(ts)(40 58 105 110 111
   117 136)
DIXON,Willie(b)(72 115 116)
DJIBRILL(conga)(273)
DODGION,Jerry(as,fl)(115 121)
DODSON,Harold(b)(125)
DOLPHY,Eric(as,fl,bass cl) 78(82)
   (84)86(89)95(99 107)110 264 265
   267
DOMNERUS,Arne(as,cl)(151)248(248)
   250 252 253(254 255 257 259 262)
DONABLE,Ernest "Donny"(dm)(215 220)
DONALDSON,Bobby(dm)(48 51 76 81 85
   90 134 135 184 185)
DONALDSON,Lou(as)(33)
DONOVAN,Gerald(dm)(264)
DORHAM,Kenny(tp)(2 28 39 41 42 71)
   72(178 187 243 247 266)
DORSEY,Ralph(conga)(173 180 189)
DOTSON,Hobart(tp)(106 142)
DOUGLAS,Bill(dm)(23)
DOUGLAS,K.C.(g)(102)228
DRAPER,Ray(tu)(46)48 53 57(186)
DREARES,Al(dm)(187)
DRERNAK,John(b)(29)
DREVO,Karl(ts)(268)
DREW,Kenny(p)(5 14 27 44 217 267
   272 273 274)
DUKE,David(frh)(208)
DUKE,George(el p,org)(215 217)
DUKES,Joe(dm)(109 118 120 134 136
   137 140 142 144 145 146 148)149
   (151 152 157 163 166 231 232)
DUMAS,Tony(b,perc)(219 220)
DUNBAR,Ted(g)(203 205 206)
DUPREE,Cornell(g)(216)
DURAN,Eddie(g)(261 263)
DURHAM,Bobby(dm)(142 269,270)
DURU,Baba(perc)(221)
DUTRIEUX,Marcel(b)(258)
DUVIVIER,George(b)(50 60 61 63 64
   65 66 67 68 73 74 75 81 82 83 84
   86 87 88 89 90 91 95 99 106 107
   110 111 113 116 123 124 125 126
   134 135 198 207 210 212 213 257)

DYLAG,Roman(b)(151 152)

EAGER,Allen(ts)(1 11)
EAGLIN,Snooks(vo,g) 228
EARDLEY,Jon(tp)(29)30(31)32 36
EARLAND,Charles(org) 197(198)200
   (200)201 205 208 209 213 216 218
EARLY,Sally(vo)(10)
EARTHY 45
EASTON,Gene(bs)(29 31)
EATON,Cleveland(b)(200 207)
EAVES,Hubert(p)(214 215 217 219)
EDGE,Norman(b)(133 153 154 159 160
   169 172)
EDGEHILL,Arthur(dm)(44 60 61 63 64
   65 66 67 68 70 73 74 75 79 84 90)
EDMAN,Robert(dm)(258)
EDWARDS,Duke(vo,perc) 186
EDWARDS,Earl(ts)(159 179 183)
EDWARDS,Gene(g)(161 167 169 170 172)
EDWARDS,Gordon(el b)(203 207 212)
EDWARDS,Teddy(ts) 173 177(177 186
   263)
EKYAN,André(as)(237 239)
ELDRIDGE,Roy(tp) 252 253
ELF,Mark(g)(216)
ELLINGTON,Bill(b)(84 86 95 105 108
   126)
ELLINGTON,Duke(p,orch) 235 239 240
   242 243 244 245 251 252 269
ELLINGTON,Marie(vo)(240)
ELLINGTON,Mercer(tp,dm)(10 269)
ELLIOT,Bill(dm)(85 86 130 134 138)
ELLIOTT,Don(vb)(29)
ELLIS,Don(tp) 104
ELNIFF,Jorn(dm)(264 265)
ENGELS,John(dm)(272)
ENGLISH,Bill(dm)(40 100 102 104 106
   107 148 190 195)
ENGLUND,Ernie(tp)(259)
ERICSON,Rolf(tp)(253)
ERIKSSON,Rune(euph)(151 152)
ERIKSSON,Sixten(tp)(250 252)
ERRISON,King(conga)(168)
ERSKINE,Bill(dm)(91)
ERVIN,Booker(ts)(107 137 138)141(141)
   144 146(149 150)151(151 154)154
   164 170 191
ERWIN,Pee Wee(tp)(132)
ESCOVEDO,Pete(vo)(221)
ESCOVEDO,Sheila(vo)(221)
ESTELLE,Oscar(bs)(23)
EUELL,Julian(b)(44 50 52 80 83 84)
EVANS,Belton(dm)(76 88 89 91 92 93
   103 106 116)
EVANS,Bill(p)(57 263)
EVANS,Gil(p,arr)55
EVANS,Lawrence(el b)(183 184)
EVANS,Richard(dir)(176)
EVERETT,Ferdinand(dm)(139)

FADDIS,Jon(tp)(208 213 216 218)

HUSEMANN,Bert(ts,fl)(269)
HUTCHERSON,Bobby(vb)(209)
HUTCHERSON,Willette Wells(vo)(222)
HYDE,Dick(tb)(219)
HYMAN,Dick(org,p)(20 130 250 263)

ICE 215 220
INGALLS,Frank(g)(75 76)
INTERPLAY 48
INZALACO,Tony(perc)(271)
ISAACS,Ike(b)(49)
ISOLA,Frank(dm)(22 47)
ISRAELS,Chuck(b)(265)
IVORY,Jackie(p)(189 190)
IZENZON,David(b)(181)

JACKSON,Armand "Jump"(dm)(75 76 92)
JACKSON,Billy(dm)(184)
JACKSON,Cecil(conga)(178 181 186)
JACKSON,Chubby(b) 6 245
JACKSON,Cliff(p)(105 109)110 113
    (238)
JACKSON,Darryl "Munyungo"(perc)
    (222)
JACKSON,Milt(p,vb) (8 19 23 24)27
    (30 31)33(34 242 243 244 245)265
JACKSON,Oliver(dm)(55 79 80 133
    137 153 154 195)
JACKSON,Paul(el b)(221)
JACKSON,Quentin(tb)(187)
JACKSON,Wilbur "Slim"(dm)(82)
JACQUET,Illinois(ts) 185 188 193
    195
JACQUET,Russell(tp)(193)
JAKE,Shakey(vo,hca) 81 94
JAMAL,Ahmad(p) 273
JAMES,Billy(dm) (134 147 149 151
    154 156 161 162 163 165 167 169
    177 179 184 187 189 190 195 265)
JAMES,Clifton(dm)(145)
JAMES,Josie(vo)(220 221)
JAMES,Prince(ts)(196)
JAMES,Ronnie(tp)(185 215)
JAMES,Stafford(b)(211 212 214)
JANNELLI,Ronnie(fl,cl,bs)(209)
JARMAN,Joseph(tp,saxes)(273)
JARRETT,Keith(p) 274
JASPAR,Bobby(ts,fl) 48(48)
JEDERBY,Thore(b)(250 252)
JEFFERS,Jack(tb)(204 208 213)
JEFFERSON,Carter(ss,ts)(213 214)
JEFFERSON,Eddie(vo) 21(25 30 31 35)
    190(192)195
JEFFERSON,Freddie(p)(243)
JEFFERSON,Hilton(as)(77 102 235
    236 240 241)
JEFFERSON,Ron(dm)(32)
JEFFREY,Eva(vo)(222)
JEMMOTT,Gerry(el b)(204)
JENKINS,Arthur(Artie)(p)(105 160
    205)
JENKINS,Freddie(tp)(235)
JENKINS,John(as)(49 51)54

JENKINS,Leroy(viola)(273)
JENKINS Les(dm)(117)
JENKINS,Pat(tp)(73)
JENNINGS,Al(vb,g)(74)
JENNINGS,Bill(g)(68)69(72)74(74)
    (75 81 82 86 119 124 185 189
    190)
JOBIM,Antonio Carlos(p,g)(153)
JOHANSEN,Egil(dm)(151 152 262)
JOHANSSON,Arnold(tp,tb)(255)
JOHANSSON,Jan(p)(152)
JOHANSSON,Jörgen(tb)(151 152)
JOHNSON,Abdu(perc)(176)
JOHNSON,Alvin(dm)(68 69 72 74 75)
JOHNSON,August(vo)(218)
JOHNSON,Bobby(tp)(139)
JOHNSON,Budd(ts) 95(127 128 240)
JOHNSON,Clarence(b)(13 17)
JOHNSON,Clarence(dm)(28 31 35 36)
JOHNSON,Clayton(dm)(186)
JOHNSON,Danny(perc)(274)
JOHNSON,Dave(ss)(209 211)
JOHNSON,Rev.Felix(preach) 225
JOHNSON,Garnell(conga)(174)
JOHNSON,George(cl)(238)
JOHNSON,George(dm)(218)
JOHNSON,Ginger(bongo)(253)
JOHNSON,Gunnar(b)(255 257 258)
JOHNSON,Gus(dm)(72 77 83 96 97 114)
JOHNSON,Harold "Money"(tp)(204 269)
JOHNSON,Howard(as)(235 239 242 243
    246)
JOHNSON,Jay Jay(tb) 2 3(6 26)29(30)
    (245)
JOHNSON,Jim(b)(247)
JOHNSON,Jimmy(dm,perc)(199 200 203
    210 215)
JOHNSON,John(tu)(208)
JOHNSON,Keg(tb)(95 236)
JOHNSON,Larry(vo,g,hca)(115 116)
    164(231)
JOHNSON,Lennart(bs)(262)
JOHNSON,Lonnie(vo,g) 76 78 96 109
    114 115 125
JOHNSON,Osie(dm)(17 33 35 43 50 61
    62 64 66 67 73 74 77 123 153 155
    158 160 161 162 163)
JOHNSON,Reggie(b)(211)
JOHNSON,Sonny(dm)(23)
JOHNSON,Walter(dm)(235 236)
JOHNSTON,Clarence(dm)(103 113 116)
JOLLY,Pete(p)(30)
JONES,Al(dm)(20)
JONES,Bill(g)(138)
JONES,Bobby(ts)(274)
JONES,Carmell(tp)(151 155)159 267
JONES,Clarence(b)(18 142)
JONES,Claude(tb)(235 236 240 242
    243 244 245)
JONES,Curtis(vo,p) 93
JONES,Eddie(b)(62 80 81 83 100)
JONES,Elvin(dm)(44 46 5658 64 119
    181 191 260 262)

MARTINO,Pat(g)(140 143 145 147 156
162 166 174)176(177 179)180 183
(184 187)188(188 189 190 196 198)
199(232)
MASEY,Fred(dm)(210)
MASON,Bill(org)(204 206)
MASON,Harvey(dm)(216 220 221)
MASON,Orville(elb)(184)
MASSEY,Bill(tp)(5 7 8 9 10 13 16)
MATHEWS,Ronnie(p)(106 138 142)144
(145)
MATHIAS,Eddie(b)(194 196)
MATTA,Gregory(vo)(218)
MAUPIN,Benny(bass cl)(217)
MAY,Earl(b)(10 18 19 22 24 25 27
28 30 32 53 54 135 143)
MAYERS,Lloyd(p)(40 121 122)
McBROWNE,Lenny(dm)(176 177 179 180
183 211)
McCALL,Steve(dm)(200)
McCANTS,Walter(dm)(88 119)
McCLURE,Ron(b)(268)
McCOY,Freddie(vb)(98 104)157'163
168 175 177 180 183 184 187
McCRACKEN,Charles(cello)(115)
McCRACKEN,Hugh(g)(211 213 218)
McCURDY,Roy(dm)(70 217 219)
McDONOUGH,Dick(g)(236)
McDUFF,Jack(org)(68 69 72 74)74
(75 81 82)85(86)98(108)109(114 115
118)118 119 120 121(122)134 136
137 140 142 144 145(146)148 149
151 152 157 163 166 231 232
McELROY,Max(bs)(11)
McEWAN,Vincent(tp)(166 171 178)
McFADDEN,Eddie(g)(91 98 104 130 165)
McFARLAND,Gary(vb,vo) 153
McGHEE,Brownie(vo,g) 15 86 87 90
127(230 254)
McGHEE,Howard(tp)(6 184 246)247(263)
McGHEE,Sticks(g)(91)
McINTOSH,Tom(tb)(144)
McINTYRE,Earl(tb)(222)
McINTYRE,Ken(fl,as) 82 84(124)
McKAY,Al(g)(221)
McKAY,Matthew(tp)(244)
McKIBBON,Al(b)(186 246 262 263)
McKINNEY,Earl(dm)(157)
McKINNEY,Raymond(Ray)(b)(171 187)
McKUSICK,Hal(as,fl)(41)57
McKYRE,Donald(dm)(273)
McLEAN,Jackie(as)(12 34)37(38 40)
40(41)42 44(45)46(47 48 49 50 51)
53 54(261)
McLEOD,Dorothy(vo) 16
McPARTLAND,Jimmy(c) 8 247
McPARTLAND,Marian(p)(8 247)
McPHERSON,Charles(as) 155 161(163)
171 183(184 187)189(190 195)197
(274)
McRAE,Ted(ts)(241)
McTELL,Blind Willie(vo,g) 42
MEEKS,Charles(b)(220 221)

MELADY,Jack(harp)(158)
MELLE,Gil(as,bs) 38 39 41 45 50
MELLO MOODS,The(vo) 18
MEMPHIS MANGO(g)(131)
MEMPHIS SLIM(p,vo) 72 80 94 229
MEMPHIS WILLIE B.(g,vo) 112
MENGEON,Jean-Paul(p)(249)
METTOME,Doug(tp)(20)
MEYERS,George(bs)(15)
MEYERS,John(p)(53)
MEZZROW,Milton(Mezz)(dm)(236)
MICHELOT,Pierre(b)(249 251 258 259)
MIDDLEBROOKS,Wilfred(b)(145 263)
MIGLIORI,Jay(fl,as)(215 217 218
219)
MILAS,Benjamin(b)(125)
MILLER,Greg(g)(208)
MILLER,Jimmy(dm)(141)
MILLER,Leo(vo)(222)
MILLS,Jackie(dm)(168)
MILLS,Lincoln(tp)(243)
MINGUS,Charles(b)(31 256 260)261
267 274
MITCHELL,Austin(org)(66)
MITCHELL,Blue(tp)(136 169 187 191
192)
MITCHELL,Grover(tb)(208)
MITCHELL,Herman(g)(141)
MITCHELL,Ollie(tp)(215)
MITCHELL,Red(b)(22 30 259 260 261)
MITSCHELE,Klaus(tp)(269)
MIZELL,Fonce(vo)(219)
MIZELL,Larry(synth)(219)
MOBLEY,Hank(ts)(38 40)40 41 42(44
45)
MODERN JAZZ DISCIPLES 70 82
MODERN JAZZ QUARTET 19 23 24 30 31
34
MOFFETT,Jack(dm)(20)
MONCEL(conga,bongos)(154)
MONCUR,Grachan(b)(238)
MONCUR III,Grachan(tb)(151)
MONK,Thelonious(p) 18 19 24 26 28
(29 30 240)
MONTEGO JOE(conga,bongo)(131 134
135 148)150 160(173 184 187 188
231)
MONTEROSE,J.R.(ts)(31 32)
MONTGOMERY,Bill(b)(23)
MONTGOMERY,Little Brother(p,vo) 84
MONTMARCHE,Robert(dm)(239)
MONTOLIU,Tete(p)(270)
MOODY,James(as,ts) 25 26 28 31 35
36(190)192 193(193)207(244 247)
248 249 250(251)252 253
MOONDOG 226 227
MOORE,Alton "Slim"(tb)(242 243 244)
MOORE,Bernard(ts,ss,fl)(186)
MOORE,Brew(ts)(1 2)
MOORE,Danny(tp)(207 216)
MOORE,Edwin(tb)(35)
MOORE,Kermit(cello)(222)
MOORE,Numa "Pee Wee"(bs)(25 26 28

PAICH,Marty(arr)(272)
PALMER,Earl(dm)(218 263)
PALMER,Thomas(b)(142)
PALMIERI,Remo(g)(241)
PAPARELLI,Frank(p)(241)
PARABOSCHI,Roger(dm)(247)
PARKER,Charlie(as,ts)(21 241)246
  249(256)
PARKER,Jack "The Bear"(dm)(7 14)
PARKER,Junior(vo) 4(165)
PARKER,Leo(as,bs) 7(243)
PARKER,Maynard(g)(182 200 201 205
  209)210 211(212 215 217)
PARKER SINGERS,The Frank(vo)(269)
PARLAN,Horace(p)(127 141)
PASS,Joe(g)(194)
PATRICK,Laurdine(bs)(168)
PATRICK,Pat(fl,as,bs)(155)
PATTERSON,Don(org)(134 147)149 151
  (154)156 161(162)163 165(167)169
  177 179 184 187(189)190 193 195
  206(265)
PATTON,Bernard(vo)(125)
PATTON,John(org)(143 166)
PAUER,Fritz(p)(267)
PAULO,Jose(perc)(132 134)
PAVLOVIC,Milo(tp)(271)
PAYNE,Cecil(bs)(16 21 35 46 50 56
  123 151 193 246)
PAYNE,Don(g,el b)(153 180)
PAZ,Victor(tp)(208 209 212 213 216)
PAZANT,Al(tp)(186 192 198)
PAZANT,Eddie(ts,bs,fl)(186 192 198
  199)
PEAGLER,Curtis(as,ts)(70 79 82)
PEAKE,Don(g)(215 219)
PEARSON,Duke(p) 264
PECK,Nat(tb)(249 250 268 270 271)
PEDERSEN,Niels-Henning Orsted(b)
  (267 268 271 273 274)
PEEPLES,Bill(dm)(125)
PEER,Beverly(b)(50 51)
PEIFFER,Barnard(p)(247)
PENA,Ralph(b)(27)
PENTECOSTAL CHOIR OF DETROIT(vo)
  129
PERAZZA,Armando(conga)(262)
PEREZ,Luis(conga)(73)
PERKINS,Walter(dm)(118 125 126 136
  141 147 150 156 158 180 185)
PERRY,Charlie(dm)(1)
PERRY,Clarence(ts)(75 76)
PERRY,Jack(synth)(222)
PERRY,Maddy(perc)(221)
PERSIP,Charlie(dm)(43 57 62 63 71
  95 100 104 107 108 110 111 113
  122 123 133 188)
PERSON,Houston(ts)(159 165)168(174
  176)177 179(179)180(183)185(188)
  190(191 193)195(196 197)199(199)
  (200 202)202(203)204(205 207)209
  211 212

PERSSON,Ake(tb)(151 253 255 257)257
  (259 262 268 270 271)
PETERS,Jerry(keyb)(221)
PETERSON,Oscar(p) 266 267 269 270
  274
PETTIFORD,Oscar(b,cello)(7 17 33 37
  240 242 243 244 245 247 251)260
PHILLIPS,Hoza(el b,vo)(211)
PHILLIPS,James(Jimmy)(b)(171 178 186)
PHILLIPS,Sonny(org,arr)(192 194 195)
  196(197 198 199)201(202 212 215
PHILLIPS,Tubby(b)(2)
PHIPPS,Arthur(b)(46)
PHIPPS,Bill(b)(38 39)
PICKENS,Buster(p)(122)
PIERCE,Mae(g)(103)
PIERCE,Nat(p)(56 62)
PIKE,Dave(vb) 132 135 136(270)
PITTS,Trudy(org) 174(176)179 182 184
  (185)187
PIZZARELLI,John "Bucky"(g)(133 134
  135 162 175)
PLEASURE,King(vo) 16 19 24 25 30 263
PLUMMER,Roy(g)(253)
POINDEXTER,Pony(ss,as) 137 141(267
  271)
POLLARD,Tommy(vb)(246)
POMEROY,Herb(tp)(20)
PONDER,Jimmy(g)(206)
PONTY,Jean-Luc(v)(267)268
PORCINO,Al(tp)(6)
PORTER,Bill(dm)(23)
PORTER,Robbie(bs)(181)
POTTER,Jerry(dm)(129 189 190)
POWELL,Benny(tb)(208)
POWELL,Bud(p)(4 5 256)256 257
POWELL,Jesse(ts) 114 116 119(203 246
  247)
POWELL,Richie(p)(37)
POWELL,Rudy(cl,as)(76 110 243)
POWELL,Seldon(ts,fl)(21 22 120 129
  147 155 195 213 218)
POWELL,Specs(dm)(241)
POZO,Chano(conga)(246)
PRADO,Robert(tp)(206)
PRATT,Jimmy(dm)(27)
PRESTIGE BLUES SWINGERS 62 66
PRESTIGE JAZZ QUARTET 51 53
PRESTON,Eddie(tp)(274)
PRIDE,Norman(conga)(203 207)
PRIESTER,Julian(tb)(218 221 222)
PROCOPE,Russell(as,cl)(235 236 243
  244 245 269)
PRUDEN,Clayton(tb)(200)
PRUE,Wayne(g)(186)
PSALMS OF GRACE(vo) 129
PUCHO(Henry BROWN)(timbales) 166 171
  (172)178 181 186 192 198(198)
PULLIAM,Steve(tb)(68)
PUMA,Joe(g)(48 53)
PURDIE,Bernard(dm)(168 187 193 194
  196 197 198 199 201 202)203(204
  206)207(218)

PYLES,Billy(g)(114 116 119)

QUATTLEBAUM,Doug(vo,g) 117
QUEBEC,Ike(ts)(243)
QUEENER,Charlie(p)(132)
QUILL,Gene(as)(39 46)49
QUINICHETTE,Paul(ts) 51 52(53 55)
    56 57(62)
QUINTET OF THE H.C.F. 237

RAESINGER,Clyde(tp)(117)
RAGLIN,Junior(b)(239 240 242 245)
RAHIM,Emanuel(conga)(209)
RAINEY,Charles(Chuck)(b)(164 199
    206 208 209)
RAMEY,Gene(b)(1 2 95 114 260)
RAMIREZ,Ram(org)(17)
RAMOS,Manny(timbales)(84 86 126)
RANDALL,George(dm)(167 169 170 172)
RANDOLPH,Percy(vo,hca)(228)
RANEY,Jimmy(g)(19 22 26)28 31 32
    (33 47 50 51 135 136 248 259)
RANSOM,Dumas(b)(254)
RAY,Aurell(g)(218)
REBILLOT,Pat(p)(168 169 222)
RECTOR,Milt(el b)(156)
RED,Sonny(as)(51 52)
REDD,Freddie(p) 32(33)
REDD,Vi(vo)(200)
REDMAN,Dewey(ts)(274)
REECE,Dizzy(tp) 123 272
REED,Ernest(g)(206)
REEVES,Diane(vo)(221)
REHAK,Frank(tb)(57)
REID,Bob(b)(273)
REID,Rufus(b)(200)
REILLY,Dean(b)(261)
REINHARDT,Django(g)(237 239)
REINHARDT,Joseph(g)(237 238)
REITH,Dieter(p)(269)
RENAUD,Henri(p)(257 258 259 260)
RENLIDEN,Weine(tp)(255)
REUSS,Allan(g)(238)
RICCI,Jose(p)(95)
RICARDO,Dick(perc)(221)
RICHARDS,Emil(vb)(262)
RICHARDS,Red(p)(132)
RICHARDSON,Ben(cl,as,bs)(73)
RICHARDSON,Doug(ts)(186)
RICHARDSON,Jerome(ts,fl)(45 57 61
    62)63(65 66 69)71(89 110 111 134
    153 175 199)
RICHARDSON,John(b)(6)
RICHARDSON,Wally(g)(72 94 97 98
    100 101 120 121 122 124 125 126
    151 157 175 179 180 181 182 183)
    184(185 186 187 193 197 207 208)
RICHMOND,Dannie(dm)(54 267 274)
RIDLEY,Larry(b)(138 142 200)
RIEDEL,Georg(b)(262)
RIEL,Alex(dm)(267)
RILEY,Ben(dm)(88 96)
RILEY,Herman(reeds)(208)

RITCHIE,Larry(dm)(53 57)
RITENOUR,Lee(g)(220 221)
RITTER,Loretta(vo)(206)
RIVERA,Dave(p)(242 243)
RIVERA,Martin(b)(148 157)
RIVERS,Sam(ss,ts)(273)
ROACH,Freddie(org)(124)168 173 178
ROACH,Max(dm)(2 3 4 5 7 10 17 19
    21 22 36 37 39 42 44 245 246 247)
    247(256 260 261)
ROBERTS,Alice(vo)(242 243)
ROBERTS,Don(g)(13)
ROBERTS,Wendell(b)(88)
ROBERTSON,Wayne(dm)(142)
ROBINSON,Edward "Bass"(b)(240)
ROBINSON,Eli(tb)(73)
ROBINSON,Frank(tp)(138 140 143 145
    147)
ROBINSON,Fred(tb)(236)
ROBINSON,James(tp)(168)
ROBINSON,Lester(tb)(127 128)
ROBINSON,Ted(g)(238)
ROCHE,Betty(vo) 82 97(239)
RODNEY,Red(tp) 12(247 249)
RODRIGUEZ,Nicholas(p)(235)
RODRIGUEZ,Willie(conga,bongo)(114
    115 144 153 162)
ROGERS,Alvin(dm)(158)
ROGERS,Barry(tb)(192)
ROGERS,Shorty(tp,arr)(1 23 24 247)
ROKER,Granville "Mickey"(dm)(76 80
    83 102 103 191 192 212 216)
ROLLINI,Adrian(bass sax)(236)
ROLLINS,Sonny(ts) 9 14 24 28 29 36
    37 39 42 44(2 9 12 21 24 25 27
    37)
ROMERO,Hector(p)(29)
ROOTS 56 57
ROSE,Bobby(g)(188)
ROSENDAHL,Claes(cl,saxes)(151 152)
ROSENGARDEN,Bobby(dm)(175)
ROSOLINO,Frank(tb)(256)
ROSS,Annie(vo) 17 250 257(265)
ROSTAING,Hubert(cl)(243)
ROSTVOLD,Bjarne(dm)(271)
ROUSE,Charlie(ts)(27 33 35 47 59 68)
ROWIN,John(g)(221)
ROWLES,Jimmy(p)(126)
ROWSER,Jimmy(b)(71)
ROYAL,Ernie(tp)(115 117 129 193 204
    206 207 212)
ROYAL,John(dm)(164)
RUFF,Willie(frh)(55)
RUIZ,Hilton(p)(221)
RUSHEN,Patrice(p,keyb) 219 220(221)
    221
RUSSELL,Curley(b)(1 2 4 5 8 22 26
    241 245)
RUSSELL,Johnny(ts)(236)
RUSSELL,Pee Wee(cl) 77(105)

THOMAS,Gerry(tp)(207)
THOMAS,Gordon(tb)(243 244)
THOMAS,Henry(hca)(230)
THOMAS,James(org)(157)
THOMAS,Jerry(dm)(137)
THOMAS,Joe(tp)(74 98 241)
THOMAS,Joe(ts)(130 134 138 181)
THOMAS,Lafayette(g)(80 84)
THOMAS,Marcellus(vo)(103)
THOMAS,Walter "Foots"(ts) 240 241
THOMPSON,Sir Charles(p)(95 114)
THOMPSON,Chuck(dm)(7)
THOMPSON,Ed(b)(160)
THOMPSON,Lucky(ts,ss,as)(26 30)
 138 154 158
THOMPSON,Marshall(dm)(207 265)
THORNHILL,Claude(p)(238)
THORNTON,Clifford(tp.vtb)(273)
THREE RIFFS,The(vo)(30)
THREE TRUMPETS 45
THUSEK,Heribert(ts)(268)
TILLMAN,Julia(vo)(218)
TIMMONS,Bobby(p)54(75)150 153 155
 156 161 165 170 171 263
TIRADO,Juan(timbales) 29
TIZOL,Juan(tb)(235 239)
TJADER,Cal(vb) 263
TORRES,Chico(perc)(173)
TOWNSEND,Henry(vo,p,g) 105
TOWNSEND,Larry (vo)(8 9)
TRAVIS,Nick(tp)(11)
TRISTANO,Lennie(p) 1
TRISTAO,Amaury(g)(220)
TROTMAN,Lloyd(b)(251)
TRUITT,Sonny(p,tb)(15 21 34)
TRUNK,Peter(b)(270)
TUCKER,Ben(b)(177 179 180 183 185
 189 272)
TUCKER,George(b)(70 71 72 77 78 79
 92 98 99 103 117 133 135 136 137
 138 141 142 145 150 151 158 159
 161)
TUCKER,Lee(b)(70 82)
TURBINTON,Earl(ss)(273)
TURNER,Augustus(b)(168)
TURNER,Danny(as,fl)(136 176)
TURNER,Jack(g)(213)
TURNER,Jimmy(dm)(200)
TURNER,Rudy(g)(218)
TURNER,Trish(vo)(269)
TURRE,Steve(tb)(214)
TURRENTINE,Stanley(ts)(106 117 136
 143 148)
TURRENTINE,Tommy(tp)(105)
TWARDZICK,Dick(p)(15 20)
TWO GUITARS 47
TWO TRUMPETS 41
TYLER,Alvin "Red"(bs)(146)
TYNER,McCoy(p) 274

ULANO,Sam(dm)(226 227)
UNDERWOOD,Ronnie(g) 158
UPCHURCH,Phil(g)(219)

VALENTINE,Billy(vo,p) 21
VALENTINE,Jerry(arr)(62 66)
VAN LIER,Erik(tb)(268 270 271)
VARNEY,Bob(dm)(8)
VARSALONA,Bart(tb)(55)
VASS,Jimmy(fl,as,ss)(205 209)
VASSEUR,Benny(tb)(258)
VAUGHAN,Sarah(vo)(241)
VAUGHN,Carla(vo)(222)
VEGA,Al(p) 13 20
VENTURA,Carol(vo) 152 160
VENUTI,Joe(v) 236
VER PLANCK,Billy(arr)(207 209 212)
VERNON,Georg(tb)(151 152)
VERSTRAETE,Fernand(tp)(258)
VERY SAXY 67
VIALE,Jean-Louis(dm)(258)
VICK,Harold(ts)(109 118 120 136
 137 142 169 204 231)
VINCAR,Thabo(dm)(209)
VINNEGAR,Leroy(b)(126 178)
VIOLIN SUMMIT 267
VITOUS,Miroslav(b)(273)
VOLA,Louis(b)(237)

WADE,Iona(vo)(26)
WAITS,Freddie(dm)(167 174)
WALDRON,Elaine(vo)(58)
WALDRON,Mal(p)(40 42)44(45 46 47
 48 49 50)50(51 52)52(53 55 57)58
 (59 60)63(64)67(106 107)107(110
 132 261)
WALKER,Gene(as,ts)(169 170 187)
WALKER,George(g)(213)
WALKER,Hugh(dm)(191)
WALKER,Johnny "Moose John"(g)(93)
WALKER,T-Bone(g)(142)
WALLIN,Bengt-Arne(tp)(151 152 262)
WALLINGTON,George(p)(1 2 11 17)17
 22 37 47 257 261
WALTON,Cedar(p)(177)178(178)179
 (180 183 185)187(189)191 193 209
 210 213 214
WALTON,Mercy Dee(vo,p) 103
WALTON,Wade(vo,hca,g) 131
WARD,Bobby(dm)(82)
WARD,Milt(tp)(222)
WARE,James "Deacon"(vo) 23
WARE,Wilbur(b)(54)
WARLAND,Jean(b)(271)
WARLOP,Michel(orch)(237)
WARREN,Butch(b)(141 156 265 266)
WARREN,Earl(as)(21)
WARREN,Peter(b)(220)
WARNER,Ostaine Blue(perc)(273)
WARWICK,Dee Dee(vo)(126)
WARWICK,Dionne(vo)(126)
WASHINGTON,Buck(p)(236)
WASHINGTON,Darryl(dm)(209 213 216)
WASHINGTON,Fred(b)(222)
WASHINGTON,George(tb)(235)
WASHINGTON Jr.Grover(ts)(201 202
 203 204 205 206)
WASHINGTON,Jack(bs)(62)

WATERS,Tony(conga)(213 214)
WATKINS,Doug(b)(37 39 40 41 45 46
47 48 49 50 51 55 56 57 60 69 73)
81(83 96 97 98)
WATKINS,Earl(dm)(261)
WATKINS,Julius(frh)(24 41 52 115)
WATKINS,Tony(vo)(269)
WATLEY,Bobby(org,vo)(205 208 212
215 218)
WATROUS,Bill(tb)(232)
WATTS,Ernie(reeds)(208 221 222)
WAYNE,Chuck(g)(20)156 157(240 241)
WAYNE,Max(b)(8)
WEATLEY,Steve(g)(205 208 212 215)
WEBB,Spider(dm)(218)
WEBER,Eberhard(b)(269)
WEBSTER,Ben(ts) 126(239 240 241)
270 272 273
WEEDEN,Paul(g)(134 265)
WEISS,Klaus(dm)(269)
WEISS,Otto(p)(268)
WELLESLEY,Charles(b)(175)
WELLESLEY,Sonny(b)(40)
WELLS,Clement(vb)(120)
WELLS,Dicky(tb)(132 235 236)239
WELLSTOOD,Dick(p) 111(118)
WEMBERLEY,Mike(tb)(208)
WENNBERG,Torsten(cl,saxes)(151 152)
WESS,Frank(ts,fl)(46 53 55 59 63
80)81(83)123 136(212 213)
WEST,Harold "Doc"(dm)(241)
WESTBERG,Ingemar(p)(254)
WESTBROOK,Lord "Chauncey"(g)(20
22 90 143)
WESTBROOK,Seborn(b)(198)
WETTLING,George(dm)(240 242)
WHARBY,Niels(fl)(151 152)
WHEATLEY,Lawrence(p)(35)
WHEELER,Harold(el p)(203)
WHEELIN' AND DEALIN' 55
WHETSOL,Arthur(tp)(235)
WHITE,Chris(b)(132)
WHITE,Henry(flh)(178)
WHITE,Sonny(p)(243)
WICKMAN,Putte(cl)(253 254 256 259)
WIERINGA,Franz(p)(273)
WIGGINS,Gerry(p)(23 251 263)
WILDER,Joe(tp)(115 121 209)
WILKINS,Ernie(arr)(89)
WILKINS,Ezell(p)(143)
WILLIAMS,Alfred(Al)(p,org)(124 168
173)
WILLIAMS,Big Joe(vo,g) 115 116 123
WILLIAMS,Buster(b)(193 194 195 196
197 198 210)
WILLIAMS,Charles(b)(264)
WILLIAMS,Cootie(tp) 125(235 269)
WILLIAMS,Earl(dm)(101)
WILLIAMS,Edward David(tp,vo)-175
180 187 190)
WILLIAMS,Eddie(ts)(107)
WILLIAMS,Francis(tp)(242 243 244
245)

WILLIAMS,Joe(b)(156 157)
WILLIAMS,John(p)(36)
WILLIAMS,Juanita(vo) 173)
WILLIAMS,Leroy(dm)(197)
WILLIAMS,Mary Lou(p) 238 256
WILLIAMS,Richard(tp)(76 80 82 83
89 100 131 150 213)
WILLIAMS,Robert Pete(vo,g) 93
WILLIAMS,Rudy(bs)(10 12)
WILLIAMS,Teddy(vo) 6
WILLIAMS,Walter(tp)(258)
WILLIAMSON,Homesick James(vo,g) 145
WILLIAMSON,Stu(tp,vtb)(27)
WILLIS,Ralph(vo,g) 12(15) 254
WILSON,Carl(org)(138 140 143 145
147 180 181)
WILSON,Charlie L.(org)(163)
WILSON,Joe Lee(vo)(213)
WILSON,John(tp)(28 31 32)
WILSON,Ollie(tb)(11)
WILSON,Shadow(dm)(1 16 37 50)
WILSON,Teddy(p)(236) 271
WILSON,Willie(tb)(264)
WILTSHIRE,Teacho(p,arr)(13 14 16
17 18)
WINCHESTER,Lem(vb) 70(77)79 83(84
85 87 89)91(91)
WINDHURST,Johnny(tp)(43 50 51)
WINDING,Kai(tb)2(6 17)29(30 248
260)
WINSTON,Albert(org,el b)(114 168)
WINTERS,Tiny(g)(237)
WISE,Arnie(dm)(153)
WISNER,Jimmy(dm)(20)
WITHERSPOON,Alexander(el b)(175)
WITHERSPOON,Jimmy(vo) 138 141 142
143 146 152 160 232
WITTE,Peter(b)(268)
WITTSTROM,Bengt(b)(254)
WOLFE,Linda(vo)(206)
WOLFE,Steve(g,sitar)(182 183)
WOODE,Jimmy(b)(267 268 270 271)
WOODE,Jimmy(p)(250)
WOODMAN,Britt(tb)(100 115 121 208
260)
WOODS,Chris(p)(129)
WOODS,Phil(as)(28)29 31(34 36)36
(37)39(43 45 46 47)49 54 263(271)
WOODSON,Richard(tb)(186)
WOODWORTH,Zane(tp)(222)
WOODYARD,Nat(tp)(35)
WOODYARD,Sam(dm)(17 269)
WORKMAN,Reggie(b)(76 164 193)
WORMACK,Earl(b)(59)
WORMACK,Lawrence(b)(157)
WRIGHT,Arthur(hca)(141)
WRIGHT,Charles "Specs"(dm)(49 69
71 247)
WRIGHT,Eddie(g)(178)
WRIGHT,Edna(vo)(218)
WRIGHT,Elmon(tp)(243 244 246)
WRIGHT,Gene(b)(7 8 9 59 63)

WRIGHT,Herman(b)(71 81 119 162
  163)
WRIGHT,John(p) 88(92)92 107 119
  125
WRIGHT,Lamar(tp)(246)
WRIGHT,Lawrence(dm)(180 181)
WRIGHT,Leo(as,fl)(134 135 138 141
  267 271)
WRIGHT,Michael(vo)(221)
WYANDS,Richard(p)(71 76 80 82 83
  84 87 89 91 97 98 99 102 106 108)

YANER,Milt(cl,as)(241)
YOUNG,Arthur(tp,fl,vo)(215)

YOUNG,Harold(g)(210)
YOUNG,John(p)(200)
YOUNG,Larry(org) 85(85)90 123(137)
  137(181)
YOUNG,Mighty Joe(g)(144)
YOUNG,Snooky(tp)(215 217 218 219)
YOUNG,Webster(tp)(48)53(53 54)
YOUNG BLOODS 43

ZACHAROFF,Zane(bass cl)(184)
ZAWADI,Kiane(tb)(178 192)
ZAWINUL,Joe(p)(103)273
ZELNICK,Mel(dm)(245)
ZITANO,Jimmy(dm,bongo)(20)
ZOLLER,Attila(g)(166)

P.16-KING PLEASURE:Master 330 also issued on Pr.45-744 as "I'm in the mood for love".
P.19-KING PLEASURE:Master 394(Red top)also issued on Pr.45-744.
P.126-GENE AMMONS:Correct title for 3496 is "Three little words".
P.197-GENE AMMONS:"He's a real gone guy" also issued on Pr.45-742.
P.201-CHARLES EARLAND:"Westbound No.9" also issued on Pr.45-744.
P.202-IDRIS MUHAMMAD:"Super bad" and "Express yourself" also issued on Pr.45-743.
    GENE AMMONS:"Jug eyes" also issued on Pr.45-742."Something" and "The black cat" also issued on Pr.745.
P.204-RUSTY BRYANT:"The Hooker" and "Fireeater" also issued on Pr.750.
    MELVIN SPARKS:"Who's goin' to take the weight" and "Alone together" also issued on Pr.749.
    HOUSTON PERSON:"The Houston express" and "Just my imagination" also issued on Pr.747.
P.205-JOHNNY "HAMMOND" SMITH:"Smokin' Kool" and "I'll be there" also issued on Pr.748.
    CHARLES EARLAND:"One for Scotty" and "I was made to love her" also issued on Pr.746.
    FUNK,Inc.:recording date is June 28,1971."The whipper" also issued on Pr.752."Bowlegs" and "The thrill is gone" also issued on Pr.754
P.206-GENE AMMONS:first session recorded on June 21 & 22,1971."Chicago breakdown" and "My way" also issued on Pr.753.
    BOOGALOO JOE JONES:"I feel the earth move" and "Inside Job" also issued on Pr.751.
    IDRIS MUHAMMAD:"I'm a believer" and "Rhythm" also issued on Pr.756
P.207-BERNARD PURDIE session recorded on October 11,1971.
    MELVIN SPARKS session recorded on February 14 and 21,1972.
P.208-GENE AMMONS sessions recorded on March 20,1972.
    CHARLES EARLAND sessions recorded on February 16 and 17,1972(order not known)."Will you still love me tomorrow" and "'Cause I love her" also issued on Pr.755.
    FUNK,Inc.:session recorded on March 18,1972.
P.209-HOUSTON PERSON session recorded on May 1,1972.
    BAYETE session recorded on June 26,1972.
    HAMPTON HAWES session recorded c.June 1972.
    CHARLES EARLAND session recorded on October 9,1972.
P.210-RUSTY BRYANT session recorded on July 17,1972.
    MAYNARD PARKER session recorded on November 7,1972.
P.211-BOOGALOO JOE JONES session recorded on November 24,1972.
P.212-GENE AMMONS:"Lady sings the blues" and "Play me" also issued on Pr.757.
P.213-CHARLES EARLAND titles recorded on February 14 and March 23,1973. "Charles III" and "Girl you need a change of mind" also issued on Pr.761.
P.214-GARY BARTZ(June 1973 session):"Dr.Follow's dance" and "Standin' on the corner" also issued on Pr.760.
P.215-FUNK,Inc.:"Goodbye so long" and "Just don't mean a thing" also issued on Pr.762.
P.216-CHARLES EARLAND:"Leaving this planet" and "Brown eyes" also issued on Pr.763.
P.219-PATRICE RUSHEN album recorded on August 8 and 9,1974.
    GARY BARTZ album recorded c.April 1975.
P.220-PATRICE RUSHAN:"Kickin' back" and "What's the story" also issued on Pr.764.
P.221-DAVID NEWMAN album(P-10106)recorded on May 23 and c.July 1978.
P.222-BILL SUMMERS:album P-10103 recorded c.September and c.November 1977.Album P-10105 recorded c.April and c.June 1978.
P.258-CLIFFORD BROWN:"I cover the waterfront","Goofin' with me","Strictly romantic","Baby","Bum's rush","Chez moi" and one take of "Brown skins","Keepin' up with Jonesy","Blue concept","All the things you are","Minority","Salute to the bandbox","All weird"

also issued on PR24020.
P.259-CLIFFORD BROWN:V4718-1,V4719-2,V4720-2,V4721-1,V4722-1 and
V4723-3 also issued on PR24020.
P.342-PR24020 definitely contained in pages 258 and 259.

(all above details thanks to Jamie DePaoli of Universal Music Service
Corp.).

About the Compiler—

Michel Ruppli has compiled *The Savoy Label: A Discography* (Greenwood Press, 1980) and *Atlantic Records* (Greenwood Press, 1979), in addition to individual discographies of such jazz artists as Miles Davis, Ornette Coleman, and Charles Mingus, published in *Jazz-Hot* magazine.

R0141555365